World History

World History

A Concise Thematic Analysis
VOLUME TWO

Steven Wallech
Long Beach City College
Craig Hendricks
Long Beach City College
Touraj Daryaee
California State University–Fullerton
Anne Lynne Negus
Fullerton College
Peter Wan
Fullerton College
Gordon Morris Bakken
California State University–Fullerton

Brenda Farrington, Developmental Editor
Chapman University

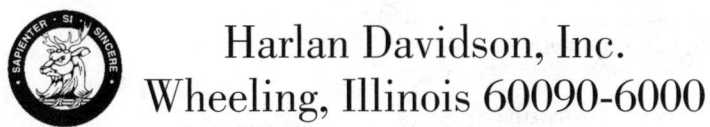
Harlan Davidson, Inc.
Wheeling, Illinois 60090-6000

Library of Congress Cataloging-in-Publication Data

Wallech, Steven.
  World history : a concise thematic analysis / Steven Wallech, principal author and editor ; Gordon Morris Bakken, project founder and coordinator [and] U.S. specialist ; Peter Wan, Chinese and Japanese specialist ; Craig Hendricks, Latin and Native American specialist ; Anne Lynne Negus, African specialist ; Touraj Daryaee, Persian, Greek, and Roman specialist ; Brenda Farrington, developmental editor.
      p. cm.
  Includes bibliographical references and index.
  ISBN-13: 978-0-88295-252-9 (alk. paper)
  1. World history. 2. Civilization—History. I. Bakken, Gordon Morris. II. Farrington, Brenda. III. Title.
  D20.W355 2007
  909—dc22

                        2006030630

Cover photograph: "Machu Picchu," flourished around 1500 CE. Photograph by Mike Lopez, www.vagabum.com.
Cover design: Chris Calvetti, c2itgraphics.

Manufactured in the United States of America
09 08 07 06 1 2 3 4 VP

TABLE OF CONTENTS

Reference Contents for VOLUME ONE

Themes, Unit One: The Ancient World
Chapter I
BIOLOGY AND WORLD HISTORY:
Civilization and Nomads
Local Circumstances and the
  Domestication of Plants
The Domestication of Animals
The Biological and Cultural
Consequences of Domestication
The Nomads
Disease History
Suggested Reading

Chapter II
MESOPOTAMIA:
The Land between the Rivers
A Temple Economy
The Causes of Trade
Kings, War, and Ecocide
The Art of Writing and Hammurabi's
  Code
The General Matrix of Civilization
The Dawn of Religion: Creation Myths
Iron and Mesopotamia
The Hebrews
The Emergence of Monotheism
Suggested Reading

Chapter III
EGYPT: The Gift of the Nile
The Pyramid Age: The Old Kingdom
  (2700–2200 BCE)
A Time of Chaos: The First Intermed-
  iate Period (2200–2000 BCE) and the
  Middle Kingdom (2000–1786 BCE)
The Hyksos and Second Intermediate
  Period (ca. 1786–1575 BCE) and
  The New Kingdom 1575–1050 BCE)

INTRODUCTION

Teaching a course in World History at the college-level presents an instructor with an especially difficult challenge. Unlike most historians who conduct courses in the study of a particular culture, nation, or region, those who teach World History ostensibly must have familiarity with the history of all the earth's peoples. As daunting as such a proposition is, the matter is even more complicated. Because imparting the history of humanity within the confines of a college-level course is, of course, impossible, world historians must convey to their students an appreciation of the short- and long-term effects of human practices on local and regional environments, the interdependencies of humans, animals, plants, and pathogens, and the diffusion of ideas, technologies, and disease through trade, migration, war, empire building, and human resistance—phenomena that create crosscultural, transnational, and transregional patterns over time.

To make things even more difficult, much of the historical literature on world history emphasizes the differences between regional cultures and local histories, leaving the instructor scrambling to find the similarities that might produce a lucid global narrative. In particular, the current generation of world history textbooks fails to succeed in conveying a unified, coherent account. Indeed, linear surveys lack a central storyline, with any potential core narrative submerged under a sea of details that simply overwhelms the student reader.

What probably explains this bleak state of affairs is the fact that as a distinct discipline, World History is only about six decades old. Begun in the 1960s as part of a slow shift from Western Civilization, World History gradually became a subdiscipline as increasing numbers of historians recognized the usefulness of a global perspective to understand humanity's past. Developing steadily despite the vast amount of material that had to be digested and the necessary development of new mental habits of synthesis, World History finally achieved recognition as a discipline in 1982 with the establishment of the World History Association. Since then, the WHA has grown to 1,500 members,

World History has become a standard general education requirement at the college level, and several major universities now offer advanced degrees in the field. Nonetheless, no one, until now, has written an accessible, concise world history textbook.

With decades of combined experience teaching World History—in community colleges and four-year institutions—we have witnessed firsthand the frustration instructors and students of world history experience with current survey textbooks. Deeming a new approach necessary, even overdue, we spent the last several years conceiving of and writing *World History: A Concise Thematic Analysis*.

It will be immediately apparent to anyone familiar with the full-length or even so-called concise world history surveys currently on the market that this book stands alone: its interesting and recurrent themes—conceptual bridges that span the many centuries—give it a unique voice. Its format helps the reader see the larger picture, to conceptualize patterns over time by importing concepts from one unit to another. And while this book might not offer flashy four-color maps and illustrations, its length and price speak for themselves. Too often students are required to pay a great deal of money for books they have no hope of finishing, let alone comprehending or remembering long after they turn in the last exam.

To achieve the brief but coherent account of global events, *World History: A Concise Thematic Analysis* comprises four complete units: the first is long (ten chapters); the second, short (six chapters); the third, long (again, ten chapters); and the fourth and last is short (seven chapters).

Unit One covers the ancient world, using two scientific themes: symbiosis to explain agriculture, and parasitism to account for eras of sudden death. Coupled with these two biological themes are several geographic concepts that facilitate an understanding of the movement of plants, animals, tools, ideas, and germs from one of the world's major cultural hearths to another. Equally important is the condition of geographic isolation, which denied such movement. Finally, this unit introduces the concept of culture, explaining how it organized human creativity in response to the circumstances of life in the ancient world.

Unit Two, the middle years of world history, develops further the concept of culture, elevating it to the central theme that governs the six chapters that consider the years 500 to 1000 [1500] CE. Culture serves to explain how the dominant human communities of the globe expanded to their limits, while only one of them developed the potential to change world events. Hence, a broad analysis of each major civilization reveals why most of them preferred stability to change, even as one of them broke the mold of tradition to set in motion a whirlwind of change that laid the foundation for globalism and the modern era.

Unit Three addresses the modern era, 1492 to 1914. Its major themes are modernization, the differential of power, and globalization. Focusing on European culture as the one [that] proactively transformed the world, this analysis of modernization considers the key institutional changes that created the nation-state in the West. Using a comparative cultural analysis of political, economic, and military institutions to demonstrate the growing material might of Europe in contrast with the waning power of non-European societies, Unit Three outlines the material advantages that Western peoples and cultures enjoyed as they expanded outward—and were themselves transformed by the peoples, ideas, and resources they encountered in the Western Hemisphere, Africa, and Asia. Next, the theme of globalization helps explain how other cultures of the world imported many of the Western institutions, adapting them in an effort to survive, but ultimately sought to expel Europeans from their territories through the long and difficult process known as decolonization.

Unit Four considers the postmodern world, 1914 to 2006. It begins by showing how global warfare, a harvest of violence set in motion by the empire building of Unit Three, destroyed Europe's hold over its colonies, protectorates, and spheres of influence and shifted dramatically the global differential of power. At the same time, we approached Unit Four in a unique way. Given that 1914 to 2006 constitutes slightly less than one hundred years of world history, we strived to maintain an appropriate balance between its content and the remainder of the text. In other words, the last 93 years established the contemporary world but deserve no more space then any other period of global history. Accordingly, the content of Unit Four is as concise as possible, even as we show that its tumultuous events and the state of the world today are the product of, and the conclusion to, the preceding three units.

The advantage of this long-, short-, long-, short-unit presentation is that it allows for a logical division of the text for use in either the semester or the quarter system. For those on the semester system, the completion of Units One and Two bring the reader to the modern age (1500 CE), the classic stopping point for the first half of world history. Units Three and Four complete the story in the second semester. For those on the quarter system, Unit One covers the ancient world, the standard stopping point in a ten-week class. Unit Two and the first half of Unit Three link the middle years to the early modern era (1000–1750 CE) and bring the narrative up to the formation of nation-states, the standard stopping point for the second ten-week period of study. Finally, the second half of Unit Three and all of Unit Four cover modernization and the postmodern age.

As mentioned, each unit features a dominant set of themes. Not only do these themes make up the thesis for the unit under consideration, but they also reappear throughout the text, providing cohesiveness and unity where none otherwise exists and making World History accessible and meaningful to student readers. On the other side of the desk, both experienced and inexperienced instructors, eager to find footholds as an otherwise unwieldy narrative unfolds, will find the use of overriding themes helpful. In short, the introduction of themes in a world history text eliminates the problem of presenting an isolated and seemingly endless list of facts, figures, and dates: the "one darn thing after another" phenomenon that gives World History a bad name.

Themes also help build a comparative analysis of regional histories. Such comparisons help students grasp how human creativity produces a unique stamp on the development of distinct cultures, even as people everywhere struggle with a common set of problems. Finally, themes highlight contrasts between cultural hearths, making the text relevant to an increasingly diverse student population, as well as useful in the new comparative World History courses.

Whether you are new to the field of World History or have taught the subject for years, it is our hope that you will give our approach a chance-and that you will agree that a thematic analysis goes a long way toward making a complicated compendium of human numbers, economies, and cultures meaningful to student readers.

Steven Wallech
Craig Hendricks
Touraj Daryaee
Anne Lynne Negus

The Modern World

The creative energy of culture from Unit Two and the biological and geographical concepts of Unit One underlie the themes of Unit Three, which include modernization, globalization, and a new idea called *the differential of power*. The theme of culture helps explain the spontaneous process of change that transformed traditional European peoples into powerful, new, and proactive societies capable of imposing their will on the world. And, the concept of *culture* itself emerged from the intellectual changes occurring in Europe that spawned a new way for human beings to see the world. Finally, once the idea of culture became entrenched, Europeans came to believe they could measure the "superiority" of their society in contrast with the "backward" cultures of Asian, African, and American peoples. This kind of thinking convinced Europeans that they not only could but *should* change the world.

The biological and geographical concepts of Unit One mesh with the themes of Unit Three by returning to the consequences of the material advantages enjoyed by some cultures, especially in Europe, when compared to the rest of the world. Europe was the beneficiary of the vast biological resources of the Ancient Near East: the numerous domesticated plants and animals, and the associated agricultural tools drawn by beasts of burden that developed as a result, plus a long disease history that bestowed upon Europeans substantial resistance to the world's infections when they began to explore it in the fifteenth century. Furthermore, those less fortunate peoples living in places like the Americas and Africa, which had long histories of geographic isolation, did not have the time or resources to develop military institutions to match those found in Eurasian societies. Africa did enjoy a disease barrier that excluded foreign entry into its interior until the nineteenth century, but Africans did not have a plow or wheel to help generate the food surpluses needed to feed a growing population. In addition, African states had become dependent on foreign trade to build their political institutions; this made sub-Saharan cultures vulnerable to foreign influences. The Americas suffered a geographic quarantine that excluded its peoples from the wealth of ideas, goods, and tools that had developed in Europe, Asia, and Africa and also made Native Americans vulnerable to a biological disaster once Christopher Columbus breached their geographic isolation in 1492.

In this unit we will see how the new themes of modernization, globalization, and the differential of power fit within the existing cultural, biological, and geographical context. Modernization refers to that extraordinary series of events that pulled Europe out of the bounds of tradition and pushed it onto a new cultural level where change was both tolerated and encouraged. What is so amazing about this process is that Europeans were unaware of what was happening to them even as the momentum of change transformed their cultural landscape.

In contrast to modernization, tradition generates a set of complementary practices that require people to repeat their behavior without question; they believe that their way of life is sacred and therefore holds intrinsic value that should not be changed. Despite the power of tradition, however, a process of change began in Europe that undermined this commitment to repeated behavior and inspired an opposing set of values that encouraged change by labeling it as *progress*. These changes took place simultaneously in Europe's intellectual, economic, social, and political institutions: the Renaissance (1300–1600); the Commercial Revolution (1492–1763); the Rise of Territorial States (1494–1648); the Reformation (1517–1648), and the Scientific Revolution (1543–1687). Each of these overlapping upheavals occurred in the entrenched institutions of European culture. Once the first cycle of modernization was complete, Europe had become aware of the changes taking place, so that Europeans now sought to accelerate the process. They did so through the Enlightenment (1690–1789), the French Revolution (1789–1815), and the Industrial Revolution (1750–1850). This second cycle of parallel events created both the nation-state and an awareness of the concept of culture itself.

Given the complexity of the European story, and its spontaneous break with tradition, a significant amount of space in this text is dedicated to the explanation of this process of change. Once one understands how this process unfolded, then it is easy to see how modernization was exported to the rest of the world, thereby spawning globalization. Globalization involves the use of Europeans' growing hostility to tradition as their self-awareness of modernization took root. And if Europeans came to condemn their own traditional patterns of life, then they came to have even less patience with foreign beliefs and practices. Hence, as the people of Europe set up outposts in alien cultures, Europeans justified the imposition of their institutions on the "backward, pagan, or savage" communities of foreign lands that still suffered the "superstitions" that plagued their traditional societies.

To accomplish the process of globalization, Europeans first had to capture the differential of power. This ratio contrasts the military and political potential of one European culture with that of the rest the world. Military power determined which culture held the means to attack, penetrate, and defeat a foreign foe. Political power defined the resources needed by the victorious society to consolidate its hold on captured lands. Together, military and political power delineated the tools needed to invade, occupy, and change foreign cultures.

Europe captured the differential of power in the modern era, and modernization bestowed on Europe a newly integrated political entity called the "nation-state." Building on the wealth generated by the Age of Discovery and the Commercial Revolution, Europe enjoyed the financial resources needed to fuel changes at home through empires built abroad. Using this newly won wealth to sustain the rise of the Royal Army (1494–1648), as kings fought the religious wars (1556–1648) that settled the issues raised by the Reformation (1517–1648), Territorial States (1648–1789) emerged with either a monarch or a parliament functioning as sovereign. Then, once the Scientific Revolution (1543–1687) questioned a religious explanation of the universe, and reinforced these inquiries with questions raised by the Enlightenment (1690–1789), public opinion emerged in the eighteenth century as a new force in politics.

Combining public opinion with a growing hostility toward tradition within Europe, the French Revolution (1789–1815) and the British Industrial Revolution (1750–1850) reintegrated the geographic unity of the state to create the nation. The French Revolution created the national army, a professional bureaucracy, a national tax system, and a positive political consensus, as well as the concept of citizenship. The British industrial revolution caused a demographic shift in which people moved from the countryside to the city, producing an *urban hierarchy* (a realignment of a nation's cities through a national market system) and causing these migrants to learn *urban skills* (literacy, calculation, and critical thinking). The combination of both the French and industrial revolutions integrated the political, economic, and social space in Britain and France with public opinion to create a new *internal coherence* (a modern geographer's term for the national unity of people capable of mobilizing their entire strength). This new internal coherence became the nation-state and gave Europeans an extraordinary concentration of power: they now had the ability to muster the people and resources of an entire nation, mass-produce weapons, and combine military might with a national will to take new territories and create new markets, regionally and around the globe.

Just as the nation-state grew strong in Europe, most of the other major Eurasian and African civilizations reached the nadir of their existence. While the Americas and sub-Saharan Africa had fallen under European influence during the Commercial Revolution (see Chapter Seventeen of this Unit), the Dynastic Cycle, discussed in Chapters Five, Ten, and Thirteen, robbed China of its strength (see Chapter Twenty-five). Japan's self-imposed isolation denied the Japanese access to military and political changes occurring in Europe, despite Japan's own version of modernization (see Chapter Twenty-two). The Mogul Empire experienced internal decay as the Muslim rulers in India commanded some of the poorest military units in world history (see Chapter Twenty-five). The Middle East produced several powerful gunpowder empires, but once they had reached the limits of their expansion under Jihad, the age-old problem of stagnation and religious rivalry between Sunni and Shiites began sapping the Islamic states of their military might (see Chapter Twenty-six). Finally, the disease barrier that had long protected sub-Saharan Africa from foreign intrusion collapsed thanks to the development of germ theory and modern medicine, which opened the entire continent to potential European exploration (see Chapter Twenty-six).

Naturally, the differential of power accelerated the process of globalization, which increased Europe's capacity to capture foreign lands and transform the world. As a result, modern imperialism, fuelled by the illusions of progress (see modern philosophical teleology in Chapter Twenty-two), linked Europe's capacity for mass transportation to a global economic system of change. Old empires, like those established by Western Europe during the Commercial Revolution, expanded to embrace all corners of the world. Central European nations, such as Germany and Italy, tried to imitate their neighbors to the west, yearning to compensate for years without access to the new trade routes developed after 1492. These Central European states planned to build empires in all the places of the world that Western Europeans had not ventured. In addition, new non-European nations like the United States and Japan, after a quick development of power, considered the consequences of not joining in this scramble for global markets and set aside their scruples to build comparable empires.

Meanwhile, non-European cultures around the world had to re-evaluate the effectiveness of their ancient ways as they failed to help people resist the modern onslaught. These traditional, non-European cultures had to consider whether they should join the United States and Japan in forming nations of their own in order to preserve their social, ethnic, and political integrity. The result was the globalization of the modernization process. Modern changes occurred under Europe's initiative, or because of lessons learned from contact with Europeans, or as a result of a combination of both. The traditional, non-European peoples began to contemplate how quickly and how completely they should take on a modern face.

The modern (imperial) age ended with the onset of World War I (1914–18). Not only did the Great War dramatically change the differential of power globally, it also drew into question things Europeans had been taking for granted since 1492: that they were "superior" in might, intellect, and energy as compared to the rest of the peoples of the world. For more than four hundred years, Europeans had used this sense of superiority to justify taking action against tradition everywhere in an effort to reshape the world. And, once Europeans transmitted the same notions of progress to several non-European nations such as the United States and Japan, they joined in, also hoping to "civilize" the rest of the world by modernizing "backward" peoples for the benefit of everyone.

Meanwhile, the rest of the world had learned enough from Europe during the modern age to begin to employ the means to resist during the post-modern era (1914–91). Hence, by 1914, the forces analyzed in this unit had thoroughly changed the face of the world because of the reintegration of European institutions through modernization, the role of the differential of power, and the impact of globalization. All three themes laid the foundation for the twentieth century and the postmodern world covered in Unit Four.

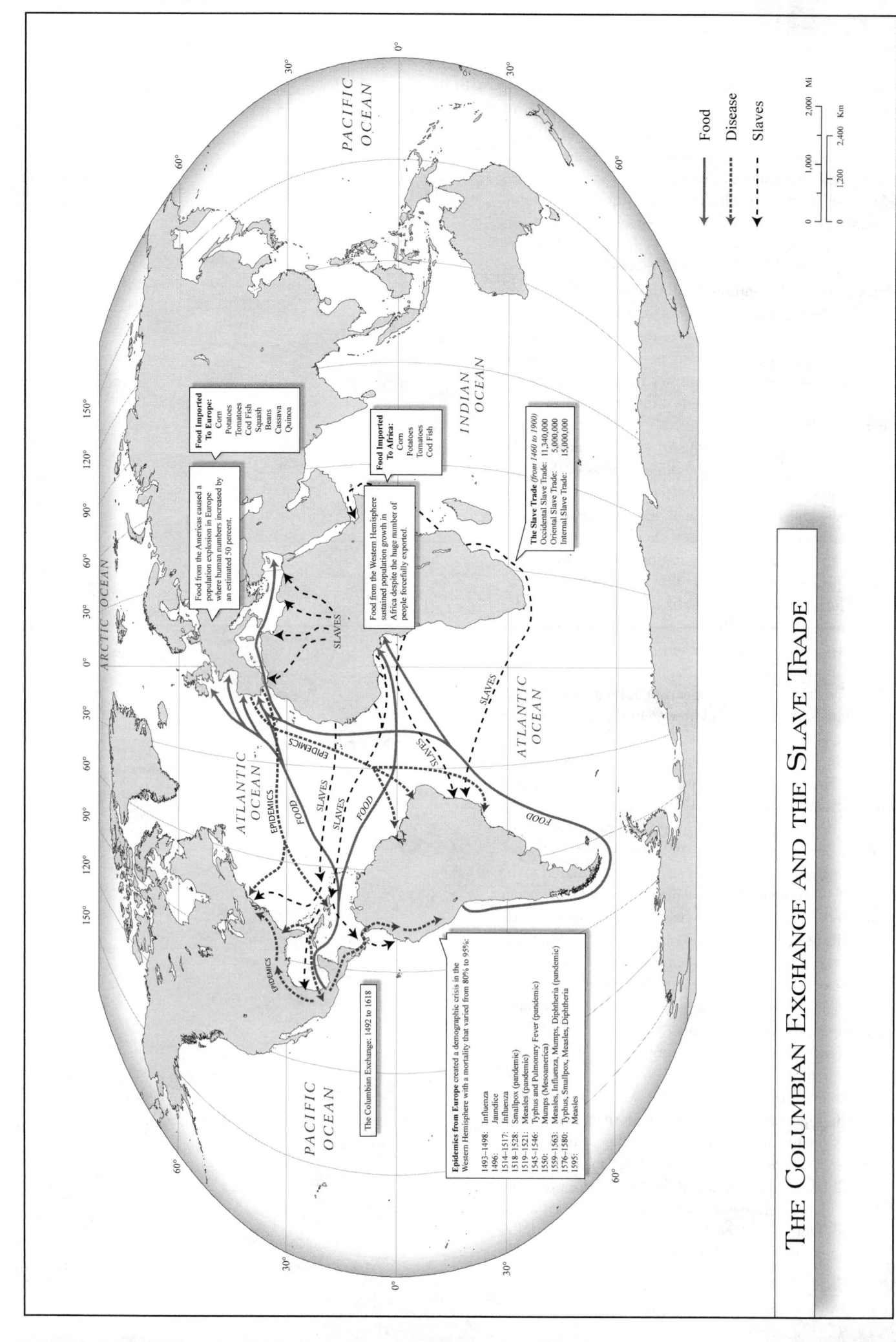

THE COLUMBIAN EXCHANGE AND THE SLAVE TRADE

Food Imported To Europe:
Corn
Potatoes
Tomatoes
Cod Fish
Squash
Beans
Cassava
Quinoa

Food Imported To Africa:
Corn
Potatoes
Tomatoes
Cod Fish

Food from the Americas caused a population explosion in Europe where human numbers increased by an estimated 50 percent.

Food from the Western Hemisphere sustained population growth in Africa despite the huge number of people forcefully exported.

The Slave Trade *(from 1460 to 1900)*
Occidental Slave Trade: 11,340,000
Oriental Slave Trade: 5,000,000
Internal Slave Trade: 15,000,000

The Columbian Exchange: 1492 to 1618

Epidemics from Europe created a demographic crisis in the Western Hemisphere with a mortality that varied from 80% to 95%:

1493–1498:   Influenza
1496:   Jaundice
1514–1517:   Influenza
1518–1528:   Smallpox (pandemic)
1519–1521:   Measles (pandemic)
1545–1546:   Typhus and Pulmonary Fever (pandemic)
1550:   Mumps (Mesoamerica)
1559–1563:   Measles, Influenza, Mumps, Diphtheria (pandemic)
1576–1580:   Typhus, Smallpox, Measles, Diphtheria
1595:   Measles

Food
Disease
Slaves

XVII

THE COMMERCIAL REVOLUTION

Europeans called the process that launched the first modern global trade system the Commercial Revolution, a phenomenon sparked by the trans-Atlantic voyages of Christopher Columbus who discovered the Americas and Vasco da Gama who opened the route to India in the so-called Age of Discovery. The term Age of Discovery, exhibits the shock to Europeans caused by their having found the Western Hemisphere, to their minds truly a "New World." The Commercial Revolution ultimately triggered modernization, which, in turn, transformed the world.

The new, ocean-based trade routes generated a new commercial system that emerged after 1492. These routes breached the near absolute isolation experienced by Native American cultures for thirty millennia. At the same time, the new routes opened access to sub-Saharan markets, giving African monarchs an alternative to conducting trade via caravan trails across the Sahara Desert. Finally, the new routes gave Europeans direct access to Indian and Chinese markets and opened the possibility of trade without having to go through the Middle East or Central Asia. As a result, the volume of goods and people that could be transported by sea between the Americas, Africa, Asia, and Europe redefined the cost, profits, and consequences of global commerce. The lower cost, higher volume, and the new level of demand fueled by Europe's Commercial Revolution, irreversibly changed the world's economy.

Contact with heretofore isolated peoples and extended trade penetrated well-established cultural biospheres: the biological relationships developed between ancient and medieval cultures, their domesticated plants and animals, and their parasites, all moved along these new commercial pathways. For the Western Hemisphere, this cultural and commercial penetration generated a biological shock that devastated Native Americans as well as their plant and animal populations. For sub-Saharan Africans, local pathogens functioned as a biological barrier to European penetration to reinforce native resistance. Yet this barrier did not stop the realignment of global trade as Africans below the Sahara responded to the new demand for slaves along their Atlantic coast. Native Americans succumbed to a biological as well as military invasion, and Asians set limits to commerce. All three histories are connected, yet their impact on Europe really defined the Commercial Revolution (1492–1763).

One can appreciate the power of geographic isolation by considering the consequences of its sudden removal in the case of the Americas and sub-Saharan Africa. The economic and military successes Europeans enjoyed during the Early Modern Era (1492–1763) derived in part from the biological effects generated by breaching an ancient condition of isolation. These accidental effects created a whole new set of population dynamics worldwide that in turn generated profound political and economic changes.

The complex biological conditions generated five distinct stories: first, a story of the rising human numbers in Europe that responded to commercial capitalism and the new domesticated plants imported from the Western Hemisphere; second, the dramatic death rate among Native Americans that resulted from epidemics caused by European and African parasites; third, the European migrations and high reproductive rates that filled the population vacuum created by the shock of disease in the Western Hemisphere; fourth, the transport of plants and animals from Europe to the Americas that created a new zone of economic productivity there; and, fifth, the creation of a slave trade along the Atlantic coast of Africa that stimulated an increased sale of slaves to Muslims and created an internal African market for human beings that caused people to move back and forth across the continent.

Each of these histories developed along parallel lines, but they generated profoundly different cultural experiences for the peoples involved. From the European perspective what followed was an "adventure" of discovery and conquest as they tried to deal with some 16 million square miles of previously unknown land that they had stumbled on in an effort to find a more direct sea route to Asia. From the European point of view, this adventure transformed the material conditions of their culture and fueled the financial engines of modernization.

Yet from the perspective of the peoples of North and South America, the European adventure began a devastating and massive die-off that weakened any potential opposition to the invaders. From the African point of view, this adventure entailed the exportation of millions of healthy people who went to the Western Hemisphere under duress as slave laborers. Finally, from a global perspective, this adventure required specific cultural circumstances in Europe, the Americas, and Africa.

In retrospect, when Europe was ready for global exploration and the commercial exploitation of the new trade routes, Native Americans offered a level of cultural vulnerability that allowed Europeans to penetrate local societies and transmit the pathogens that caused epidemics. The Africans were already active partners in a slave trade and helped the Europeans sell millions of people into slavery in the Western Hemisphere. All three of these histories intertwined to produce biological, military, and economic changes on a global scale.

The Biological Shock Suffered by Native Americans

At the end of the last Ice Age 75,000 to 10,000 years ago, the Western Hemisphere became essentially an enormous island. Surrounded by the Atlantic and Pacific oceans, the Americas had been connected to Eurasia only by an ice-covered land bridge that spanned the Bering Straits. Once the ice melted, the Americas became isolated. Thus, those human societies that developed in the Western Hemisphere enjoyed the protection of a general condition of isolation that secured the existing gene pools of native plants, animals, and people for millennia.

Isolation to this degree quarantines populations. The evolutionary conditions that shape the local gene pools over time depend on this isolation as part of *speciation*, the local conditions that allow new species to separate from an original parent gene pool. Isolation identifies and separates populations within a species to allow variation and natural selection to do their work. The 30,000 years of isolation after the last Ice Age that separated human populations in the Western Hemisphere from their parent gene pools was not sufficient time for speciation to occur. Yet 30,000 years was long enough for *microevolution* to take place. Microevolution represents the differences in biospheres that separated the American biological environment from those found in Europe, Asia, and Africa.

Therefore humans living in the Americas had long remained isolated from the contacts that Eurasians and Africans had shared throughout their histories. Native Americans never experienced the disease diffusion that helped to destroy the ancient world in Eurasia. Nor did they experience the epidemics spread during the middle years of world history. Thus, Native Americans never developed any degree of immunity to the diseases that had greatly reduced human numbers in the rest of the world during the middle years.

As mentioned in Chapter One, initial contact with pathogens kills nonresistant humans while reshaping the gene pool of the parasite. Those humans who survive a disease epidemic develop a resistance to it, which they pass on to their offspring. At the same time, those pathogens that did not kill their host also survive and pass a less-virulent version of themselves onto their offspring. Such contact between parasites and humans converts epidemics into endemic childhood diseases so that these humans become the hosts who can carry their pathogens wherever they go.

Parallel to the absence of Eurasian and African diseases among Native Americans is the story of how so many pathogens took up residence with Europeans as a host population. The conditions that generated so many European diseases reflected the long periods of contact between Europe, Asia, and Africa from ancient to modern times. These contacts included two key factors: first, Europeans, Asians, and Africans had domesticated an impressive number of animals that led to some 276 known diseases that frequently infected their owners; and second, Africa was the home of the original human gene pool that first became host to parasites.

Immigration out of Africa millions of years ago had distributed humanity's ancestors throughout the world. Departure from Africa, however, also meant that European, Asian, and American humanoid populations lost contact with African parasites. Over time, this separation resulted in the loss of immunities to African diseases. In addition, the domestication of plants and animals that sustained human civilization outside Africa then generated different biospheres wherever new cultural hearths emerged. The result was five major cultural biospheres: the sub-Saharan African, European, North African–Middle Eastern, Indian, and Chinese. Each produced a regional ecology based on a local balance between symbiosis and parasitism, as discussed in Chapter One.

Over the course of ancient and medieval history contact through trade made each of the four Eurasian cultural zones a collecting point for many of the parasites that accompanied local civilizations. The pool of pathogens that came to live in Europe thus represented a long and complex history of disease exchange. This accumulation generated a disease-rich—but resistant—host population who traveled out into the world during the Age of Discovery. These same European travelers broke down the conditions of isolation enjoyed by Native Americans.

In the Americas, the absence of domesticated mammals, save for the dog, turkey, llama, and alpaca, reduced the possibility of disease transmission through an animal-human pathogen vector. In addition since the large mammals, the llama and alpaca, lived at such high altitudes and in conditions of relative isolation, South Americans did not develop a close and intimate relationship with their domesticated animals, as did Europeans, Asians, and Africans. The only other large mammal domesticated on a significant scale in the Americas, the dog, lived in scattered bands with their owners, which reduced the contact necessary for widespread epidemics.

One can see the vulnerability of American populations in a number of ways. One that scholars tend to overlook is the impact of plant migration that followed in the wake of first contact with Europeans. Once in the Americas, Europeans planted their domesticated crops intentionally but inadvertently also planted their weeds. Many species of these weeds that had evolved in Europe also had developed the capacity to resist the efforts of farmers to eliminate their seedling offspring. The success of these weeds depended on how many seeds they produced and how well the wind dispersed them.

Some varieties of European weeds generated as many as 13,000 to 15,000 seeds per individual plant, as in the case of mayweed. Seeds in such numbers made this plant part of an invasion force every bit as powerful as the humans who brought them. Other weeds, such as shepherd's purse, produce fewer seeds but start several generations of plants each year. Mayweed, shepherd's purse, wormwood, bloodwort, black henbane, blue grass, dandelions, clover, daisies, and even peach trees came to dominate the landscape in which they took root. Even this short list of plants illustrates how several hundred European weed-species simply joined the humans that migrated to the Western Hemisphere.

A second biological story parallels weeds and tells of the weakness of American pathogens when compared to those of European or African origin. Skeletal remains of Native Americans indicate that some diseases had always existed in their gene pools. But the absence of any major epidemic traveling back to Europe after first contact speaks to the relative weakness of the Native American parasites. They simply could not compete

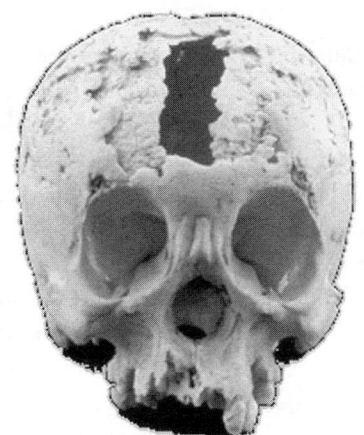

Syphilis can cause severe destruction to the skeleton in the late stages of the disease, as shown in this skull from a young man. The large holes in the bone and the shape of the nasal bones are typical of the changes resulting from the disease. Courtesy of the National Museum of Health and Medicine, Armed Forces Institute of Pathology, Washington, D.C. (AFIP-563).

with the resistance developed among Europeans after their long disease history.

Only syphilis had a major impact on Europe, yet its origin is still under debate by scholars. Syphilis, however, took years to incubate, so while numerous people became infected with the disease, they did not die of it immediately. Furthermore, syphilis goes dormant for long periods of time during which no symptoms are displayed. This "latent" or dormant phase could last from three to ten years, or indefinitely, depending on the resistance of the infected person. Accordingly, syphilis does not fall into that class of epidemics like smallpox, measles, cholera, or bubonic plague, which traveled from human victim to human victim who merely breathed the same air or drank the same water and took millions of lives in a very short period. Hence, Europe absorbed syphilis with relative ease and added it to the list of pathogens European host populations took elsewhere.

A third biological story revealed evidence that the Native Americans had reached the productive limits of their agricultural systems as their human numbers peaked around 1492. The symbiosis between Native Americans and their plants had generated such a large human population that local cultures suffered severe ecological strain by 1500. In both Mexico and the Andean highlands, soil erosion and salt accumulation constituted significant signs that humans had overused the land for too long. Indeed, ecological failure is one of the explanations developed to account for the mysterious decay of previous civilizations. Generating and feeding as many humans as they did without a metal technology, the plow, or the wheel indicates how well Native American cultures succeeded. At the same time, this success carried an ecological price tag: some Native American communities had simply exhausted their land.

These signs of agricultural strain would have reduced the number of calories consumed by Native Americans by 1500. Low caloric intake, the relative absence of large domesticated mammals—the meat of which is a source of amino acids to build immunities—and the absence of a food bank in the form of soil potential, or draft animals, suggests that Native Americans were extremely vulnerable to infections; Native American susceptibility to disease probably exceeded all other cultures in the world at that time.

The cycle of diseases that helped to bring down the Roman Empire and the Han Dynasty in China could not compare to the impact of those epidemics that hit the Western Hemisphere. The ancient Eurasian cycle of epidemics would have to have been combined with the medieval cycle to equal the shock experienced by Native Americans. Hence, by 1492, when Columbus arrived in the Western Hemisphere, he opened the most severe avenue of infection in world history.

Spain and America: First Contact

In the same year of Columbus's first trans-Atlantic voyage, 1492, Spain had inflicted a final defeat on the Moors with the fall of Granada. The Reconquista ended in January with a Spanish Catholic victory after seven centuries of struggle. Released from the trials of war on the Iberian Peninsula were thousands of soldiers and priests looking for some new adventure. Using these men in other enterprises became a possibility that both King Ferdinand V (1452–1516) of Aragon and Queen Isabella I (1451–1504) of Castile sought with enthusiasm. Their marriage in 1469 had united Catholic Spain, made victory in the Reconquista possible, and financed Columbus's voyages of discovery.

Isabella's general ignorance of the difficulties of ocean travel, Spain's awareness of Portugal's feats along the African coast, and the insistence by Columbus that it was possible to reach Asia directly by sailing west created a perfect combination of events to launch a voyage of discovery. Born in Genoa, and hired by Spain, Cristoforo Colombo, whom we know as Columbus, exploited Isabella's lack of knowledge about the dangers of voyages of discovery and persuaded her to finance his famous trip. Hence, when Columbus returned with the news of landfall to the west, the Spanish monarchy found a use for its surplus soldiers and priests.

These local cultural circumstances link the story of Spain's readiness with the biological accidents that followed. Columbus's voyage began with three ships, the *Santa María*, *Pinta*, and *Niña*, that sailed to the Canary Islands owned by Castile since 1344. From there he let the "slingshot" effect of the currents and wind patterns called the "westerlies" carry him swiftly across the Atlantic to the Caribbean Sea. Just above the Equator, this combination of wind and current is a powerful

and stable one. Thus, Columbus crossed the Atlantic in only 36 days; any longer and his men might have mutinied; he arrived in San Salvador (the Bahamas) on October 12, 1492. He then explored the Caribbean—sighting Cuba on October 27 and discovering Hispaniola on December 5. He lost the *Santa María* off the coast of Hispaniola on December 25 and had to race back to Spain on the *Niña* to prevent the captain of the *Pinta* from claiming Columbus's successes.

Columbus was completely wrong about where he ended up. He thought the world was about half its actual size. When he sighted land, he expressed his error by calling the natives "Indians." He thought he had landed on islands off the coast of India. He never really accepted the idea that he had actually found an unknown western hemisphere. Laboring under this misconception partly explains why he was such a failure at administering the discovery he had made.

For forty years after his first voyage to America, Columbus followed up with three more, and the Spanish continued to outfit ships and send them west. No fabled riches had returned along the new routes opened up, and each adventure required a heavy investment by the Spanish monarchy. The crown continued to support these voyages because of their stubborn belief in the potential wealth that lay ahead, while, they reasoned, millions of souls awaited saving. Yet the fact that Spain stuck with this enterprise until it paid off is amazing in itself. The payoff finally came when Hernán Cortés stumbled across the Aztecs in 1519. This contact opened the door to a full-scale commitment by Europe to exploring the Americas.

Spanish Conquest of the Americas

Explorers such as Amerigo Vespucci charted the coast of South America first in the service of Spain (1499) and then in the service of Portugal (1501). His description of the lands he had discovered convinced him that he had explored a continent; the impact of this knowledge led the German geographer Martin Waldseemuller to put Amerigo's name (America) on an early map of the "New World" in 1508. Working for Spain, Vasco Nuñez de Balboa cross the Panama Isthmus in 1513 to discover the Pacific, and Juan Ponce de Léon explored Florida in 1513–14 and attempted a colony in 1521 that cost him his life. Many others followed, encountering and eventually exploring the coasts of Venezuela, Central America, and Brazil. The epic of European exploration and conquest would continue unabated over the next two centuries. The Spanish soon colonized the Caribbean islands of Cuba and Hispaniola, thereafter launching expeditions to the south, east and west, always in search of new sources of wealth. The Spanish governor of Cuba, Diego Velazquez ordered Spaniards to chart the Mexican coast in 1517 and 1518. Both expeditions returned with tangible amounts of gold, encouraging him in 1519 to authorize a much larger mission headed by Hernán Cortés.

Cortés, a successful landowner and soldier in Cuba, mounted an expedition of 600 men, dozens of cannon, and a few Spanish warhorses. Suspicious of Cortés's ambitions to establish an independent colony in Mexico, Velazquez ordered Cortés removed from command. Warned of the order, Cortés sailed his small fleet of eleven ships westward, knowing that he must succeed or face the governor's wrath.

As the small fleet explored the coastal areas of Mexico, Cortés's luck ran high. First, he rescued a shipwrecked Spanish sailor who had lived among the Mayas and spoke their language. Then, after a fierce battle initiated by a tribe called the Totonacs, Cortés defeated these Native Americans due to their fear of horses, which they had never seen before. Celebrating his victory, the Totonac leaders pledged loyalty to Cortés, presenting him with several young women as guides and translators. One known as Malinche in Mexican history, proved an invaluable source of information about Aztec society, history, and culture, as she spoke the Aztec language, Nahuatl, fluently. Also, she soon learned to speak Spanish and acted as Cortés's interpreter. Now, Cortés had a critical advantage in dealing with the Aztecs and other Amerindians in Mexico. Malinche (or Doña Marina, as the Spanish baptized her) and other allies eventually told Cortés of the wealth and power of the Aztec empire, centered at the great city of Tenochtitlán, as well as the religious history of the Toltec king/god Toplitzin-Quetzalcoatl and One Reed, an important marker on the calendars developed in central Mexico. One Reed would signal to the Aztecs that the cycle of history had turned once again, and the elaborate social and political hierarchy they constructed in the great valley was in mortal danger.

The arrival of Cortés just happened to coincide with One Reed. One Reed was not only Toplitzin-Quetzalcoatl's birthday, but also the fabled day of his return to reclaim the Toltec throne (mentioned in Chapter Sixteen). Although some recent scholarship casts doubt on this version of the conquest, the Spanish made effective use of this redeemer mythology, and postconquest documents such as the Florentine Codex, recorded by Bernardino

Sahagun in the sixteenth century, acknowledged the critical role that such ideas played in the destruction of the Aztecs. Thus, Moctezuma II (reigned 1502–20) believed Cortés might be Toplitzin-Quetzalcoatl and faced the chilling prospect of an angry god determined to reclaim what was rightfully his.

Although Moctezuma commanded impressive military resources of 30,000 to 40,000 soldiers and a well-organized and highly trained command structure, glaring weaknesses remained. At the time of Cortés's arrival, the soldiers were dispersed across Mexico, guarding friends and watching for any threat from unconquered rival states, such as the Tarascans. Crops and trade routes, vital to the survival of Tenochtitlán, lay vulnerable to attack. Additionally, the fragile alliance system, patched together over the last seven decades in the great valley by the Aztecs, could disintegrate under pressure.

Cortés meanwhile formulated a daring plan. Armed with the knowledge of the Toplitzin-Quetzalcoatl myth, thanks to Malinche, and using his experience in Cuba where he learned that attacking the heart of the empire and capturing its leader could lead to a quick victory,

Bernhardino de Sahagún, a Spanish missionary, created the Codex Florentino, a rich source of Aztec/Mexica imagery. Natives wrote the work under the supervision of Sahagún in the 1500s. This illustration depicts individuals infected by the smallpox epidemic which emerged with the arrival of Cortéz and the Spaniards, killing an estimated 3 million Native Americans. From B. de Sahagún, *Historia de las cosas de Nueva Espana* (1569–75), pub. by F. del Paso y Troncoso, Book 12, Codex Florentino, Florence 1926/27, table 114. Photo: akg-images, London.

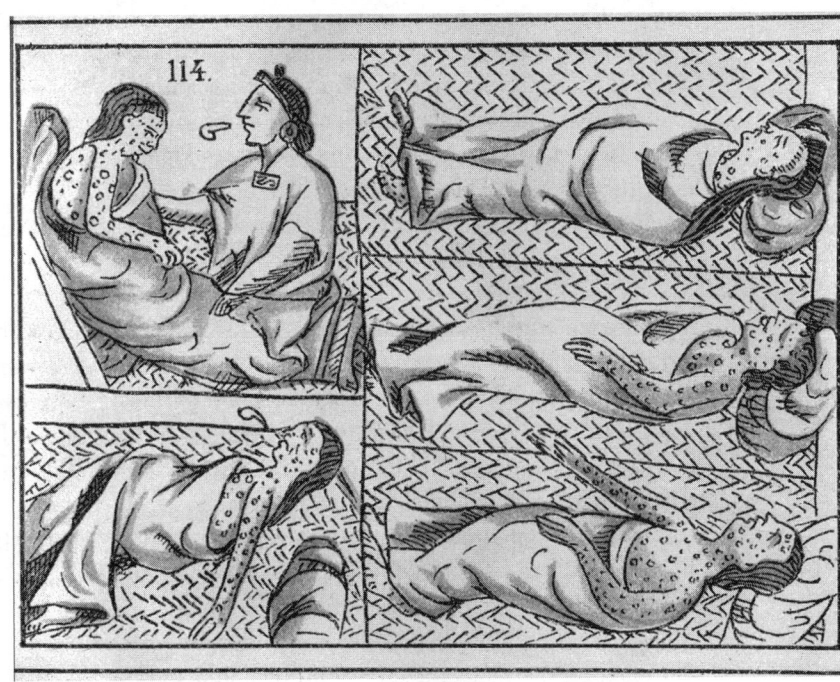

New Spain

Cortés's conquest of the Aztecs forced the young king of Spain and the Holy Roman Emperor, Charles V, to contemplate how best to run his growing empire in the "New World." Three years after Cortés's victory, in 1524, Charles launched what became a massive Spanish bureaucratic system. Starting with the Council of the Indies, chartered in that year as a way of both extracting wealth from the conquered territories and exerting as much royal control as possible, royal officers such as viceroys, judges, tax officials, captains-general, and governors all drew their authority to act in the Western Hemisphere from the crown. By 1535, the first viceroy of New Spain, Antonio de Mendoza, took office and commanded all lands acquired in North America. Although New Spain originally embraced Central America, in 1549 this area came to be known as the Kingdom of Guatemala, which received its own governor stationed in Panama. Technically, all of North America fell under Spanish rule through viceroyalty of New Spain and the Kingdom of Guatemala, but eventually, in 1670, the Spanish had to acknowledge the presence of other Euro-pean powers such as France and England that had colonized or claimed the Eastern Seaboard, Canada, and the vast Louisiana territories. By 1670, the Savannah River in Georgia had become the official boundary between England and Spanish Florida.

By the early 1700s, two great viceroyalties, New Spain (Mexico, territories to the north, and parts of Central America) and Peru (Spanish colonies south of the Isthmus of Panama) administered the crown's holdings, sending back to Spain tons of gold and silver, along with a growing list of agricultural products. The viceroy of New Spain resided in Mexico City and oversaw the work of governors in smaller jurisdictions, such Panama, as well as new conquests by captains-general to the north (Texas and later California). The viceroy of Peru operated from his capital in Lima and monitored the rich trade in silver, hides, and dried beef that passed through the Caribbean from Rio de la Plata to Chile. The viceroys were not all-powerful, as they shared legal, religious, and military duties with many other Spanish officials. Also, as regions grew in population and economic importance, they were elevated to the status of viceroyalty. Thus, in 1739, New Granada (present-day Ecuador, Colombia, and Venezuela) began operating as an independent viceroyalty.

Benjamin Keen and Keith Haynes, *A History of Latin America*, Seventh Edition (Boston: Houghton, Mifflin, p. 69–80).

Cortés assumed the mantel of the Toltec god. With conquest in mind, he divided his small force, leaving some men behind in the first Spanish settlement in Mexico, Vera Cruz, then marching into the great valley with the rest of them, determined to strike at the Aztec heartland. As Cortés and company slowly wound their way to the lakes of the central valley and Tenochtitlán, Cortés formed alliances with angry subject peoples to whom he demonstrated the superiority and killing power of Spanish cannon and steel swords. Warned of an ambush planned by the leaders of Cholula, an Aztec ally, Cortés struck first, an attack in which the Spaniards slaughtered thousands of Cholulan warriors. This action clearly demonstrated Spanish power to Cortés's new allies.

When the Spanish army arrived at Tenochtitlán, they camped near the great lake-city and demanded an audience with Moctezuma. Although his generals and aides implored him to remain in the city, the emperor felt compelled to respond. The meeting of these two central figures sealed the fate of the Aztecs. Cortés demanded access to Tenochtitlán and the emperor now agreed, treating the Spanish as honored guests, giving Cortés and his men accommodations and free run of the city. Although some Aztec leaders were outraged by this turn of events, Moctezuma's will held.

The beauty of the capitol astonished the Spaniards. The bustling markets, graceful buildings, and indus-trious people awed the conquistadores, who compared Tenochtitlán favorably with major European cities. Moctezuma showered the Spanish with gifts and praise, hoping that they would be grateful and depart peacefully. Cortés responded by seizing the emperor and making him a hostage in his own capitol. Aztec commanders wondered at their emperor's timidity and confusion.

After months of uncertainty, unexpected events brought a bloody conclusion. The governor in Cuba had dispatched another expedition to find and arrest Cortés. More than 1,000 Spanish soldiers now waited at Vera Cruz to end Cortés's command. Facing defeat and perhaps execution, Cortés left more than half of his force at Tenochtitlán and marched with the rest to the coast. His small force surprised the sleeping garrison at Vera Cruz and disarmed them after a fierce struggle. Demonstrating his genius, Cortés persuaded most of the men sent to arrest him to join the Spanish force in Tenochtitlán. He promised the men gold and glory, as well as the protection of Spanish officials pleased by success against the Aztecs.

When Cortés returned to the capitol, all was in chaos. Pedro de Alvarado, left in command by Cortés and unnerved by growing Aztec hostility, decided to attack one of the temples in the city, kill as many Aztec nobles as possible, and flee. Now, Alvarado and his men were trapped, fighting for their lives as Cortés entered the city. Assessing the situation, Cortés decided to fight his way out. The Aztecs, thoroughly angered and now aware that the Spanish and their horses were mortal, killed hundreds of Spanish soldiers as they tried to flee. Moctezuma, now despised by his people, died in the fighting; each side claimed the other killed the hapless emperor. Although the losses of *Noche Triste* (the sad night), as the Spanish called this disaster, were great, Cortés and remnants of his army escaped to the safety of his allied Amerindians at Tlaxcala.

Unfortunately, the dying was far from over; some of the Spanish soldiers captured for sacrifice by the Aztecs were carrying smallpox. The disease spread quickly in the city, killing at least one-half of the population in the next year, the year that Cortés needed to rebuild his army at Tlaxcala and prepare another attack. It came in the spring of 1521, as more than 1,000 Spaniards and thousands of Indian allies swarmed the city. The Aztecs fought street to street and house to house, but by August the great city lay in ruins, with most of the population either dead or captured by Cortés. In the months that followed, the Spanish destroyed Tenochtitlán and built Mexico City upon the smoking ruins. Cortés vowed to obliterate every trace of Aztec civilization.

Over the next few decades, Spanish soldiers drove north into the highlands and eventually into Texas and New Mexico, extending their control over all of Mexico. Other military commanders pushed south into the Yucatan Peninsula and Guatemala, bringing down the surviving Mayan sites. They encountered resistance well into the 1580s along both frontiers, but by the start of the seventeenth century Spanish viceroys in Mexico City could report high revenues from silver mines, hacienda production, and Indian tribute throughout the former Aztec and Maya empires.

The Incas

Not long after the smashing success of Cortés, which drew thousands more Spanish adventurers to New Spain, the Spanish governor of Panama grew eager to investigate the rumors of a great Indian empire to the south, along the Pacific coast of South America. Earlier Spanish expeditions to the area in the 1520s had skirted the northern end of the Inca Empire, but none of the parties engaged in serious military activity. The Spanish left an unwitting calling card, however. Smallpox had spread south from Mexico through what is now modern Ecuador as part of a pandemic infection that swept through all the Americas in the mid-1520s. The great Inca, Huayna Capac (reigned 1493–1527) died

suddenly while investigating reports of strange visitors to the empire. His principal heir also died, setting off a dynastic struggle over succession (mentioned in Chapter Sixteen) that flamed into a deadly civil war lasting until 1531 and claimed the lives of tens of thousands of Incan soldiers. Atahualpa, victorious, imprisoned his rival and half-brother, Huascar, and then rested in the highlands as he recuperated from serious war wounds.

It was at this point that the governor of Panama dispatched an expeditionary force led by Francisco Pizzaro, a tough veteran of more than a decade of exploration and conquest in the Caribbean. Pizzaro, along with his four brothers and about two hundred soldiers, arrived in the Inca land just as their civil war was winding down. Pizzaro was able to establish a headquarters, find allies, and gather information about the empire; the Incas observed his movements but did little to impede his small force. In 1532 Pizzaro moved decisively. He asked for a meeting with the great Inca at Cajamarca. Atahualpa, assured by his advisors that the Spanish represented no real threat, agreed. The meeting took place at night, as the Incas believed that the Spanish derived their powers from the sun. At this dramatic meeting, a Spanish priest approached the emperor and demanded that he accept Christianity and swear allegiance to the king of Spain. Atahualpa was mystified, then angered by these demands and tossed aside a proffered Bible. At this, Spanish mounted knights swarmed from their hiding places, slaughtered Atahualpa's small force of guards and captured him. Thus Pizzaro neatly duplicated Cortés's feat of capturing the head of a great empire. The next step would be to extend Spanish control over the remainder of the Great Inca's empire and tribute system. This would prove more difficult.

The Spanish attempted to rule through Atahualpa, who at first played along. He even supplied a huge ransom of gold and silver to his captors, filling his jail cell with thousands of pounds of precious metals. Yet when Pizzaro determined that the emperor's usefulness had ended, Atahualpa was tied to a stake and strangled in a public plaza. Unfortunately for the Inca Empire, no leader emerged to unite the Incas against Pizzaro and the growing number of Spanish invaders. Atahualpa, still focusing on Huascar as the main threat to his rule, ordered his imprisoned half-brother killed in Cuzco. Thus, although Incan generals could harass and endanger Spanish supply lines and garrisons, they could not dislodge the conquerors from Peru, Ecuador, or Chile—all major areas of the old empire. The Spanish finally broke Inca power in the 1570s when they captured and executed the last acknowledged emperor, Tupac Amaru. Although Pizzaro and his brothers soon found themselves involved in deadly quarrels with both old allies and newly arriving Spanish officials, the fate of the Incan Empire was sealed. Pizzaro himself was assassinated in 1541, yet Spanish conquistadors explored and conquered what is now modern Colombia and Chile by the 1560s. By the early 1600s, most of western and northern South America, including the Caribbean, lay under Spanish control.

How did a relatively small number of Spanish soldiers accomplish such a huge enterprise so successfully? Historians such as Benjamin Keen and Jonathan C. Brown pinpoint three or four major reasons that led to the rapid demise of complex Amerindian civilizations. Firearms, cannon, horses, terrifying war dogs, and steel swords devastated Aztec and Inca battle formations. Less useful against the evade-and-ambush tactics practiced in southern Chile or northern Mexico by smaller groups, such weapons and animals nonetheless filled native opponents with awe. Epidemic diseases, unwittingly introduced everywhere in the Americas by Europeans, killed off millions of native peoples from Canada to Argentina. Scholars refer to this as the "demographic crisis" of the sixteenth century, for as much as 95 percent of local populations perished before the surviving populations developed some immunity to smallpox, cholera, and influenza. Finally, Indian communities and alliances were often weak and prone to division, even in the face of imminent danger of conquest. Indeed, the fear and hatred of subject peoples towards the Aztecs gave Cortés powerful allies during the assault on Tenochtitlán.

Brazil

Parallel to the story of Spain's conquests elsewhere in the Americas, was that of Portugal's establishment of colonies in present-day Brazil. Portugal's entry in the Western Hemisphere began when the Pope, Spain, and Portugal signed the Treaty of Tordesillas in 1494. This treaty divided the world in half, giving Spain everything west of a line that ran north and south some 370 miles west of the Cape Verdes Islands in the Atlantic, while Portugal received anything to the east. The treaty acknowledged all the exploration undertaken by the Portuguese and the Spanish during the fifteenth century and went far enough west to give Brazil to Portugal. The Portuguese, however, were slow to investigate or explore the new territory in the west, since their trading empires in Africa and South Asia drew their attention and their best administrators. Pedro Alvares Cabral, a friend of Vasco da Gama and Portuguese navigator, however, reached the eastern coast of South America in 1500, allegedly driven off-course on a trip to India by a storm.

His report to the king indicated a broad, well-watered coastal plain with good soil and covered with an immense hardwood forest. Cabral uncovered little else of immediate commercial value to the Portuguese. The main interest, therefore, lay in tree bark, which could be stripped and then crushed into a fine powder that produced a beautiful red dye. For the next few decades, the Portuguese focused on lumber camps to exploit this resource, known as brazilwood, but put little thought or resources into developing a true colony. The native communities of Tupi and Guarani Indians, living in small villages along the coast and interior rivers, tolerated the strangers because they became a source of new technologies such as fishhooks, copper pots, and cloth, given in exchange for the red bark. Only when the Portuguese grew more numerous and began to enslave natives did the Tupi react to protect themselves. But by that time disease had already begun to destroy native communities, and the Portuguese officials worried about other challenges to their control.

Faced with growing French interest in his claim to coastal South America, King João III of Portugal divided the Brazilian coast into colonies he doled out to Portuguese nobles or captains willing to settle the land, establish towns and plantations, and populate the region. Of the fifteen captaincies given to Court favorites, only three or four prospered. In the northeast, local landowners in Pernambuco and Salvador began to plant sugarcane and force local Tupi villagers to till their fields. This proved a failure as the Indian people, exposed to European diseases and a brutal labor regime, died by the thousands. Many Indians retreated to the vast Amazonian watershed, shielded by the rainforest's immensity. Others began to attack and harass Portuguese settlements, making some coastal areas dangerous places for *fazendas* (sugar plantations) for the next two centuries. With a growing labor problem, the Portuguese began importing slaves from the west coast of Africa into Brazil in the 1550s. Under the careful administration of governors Tome de Souza (1549–53) and Mem de Sa (1557–72), Brazilian sugar dominated the growth of what became the most valuable crop in the commercial revolution (see below: the sugar and slave trade).

The native population of Brazil, variously estimated by scholars at between 2 and 4 million, melted away to less than 10 percent of its precontact size. Only the protests of Portuguese Jesuit priests, such as Manoel da Nobrega, and later Antonio Viera, denounced the decline and enslavement of Indian people. By 1600, sugar plantations had guaranteed the success of Portuguese colonization, as thousands of new settlers rushed to cash in on the growing world demand for processed sugar. Brazil would soon contain the largest African slave population in the New World. By the first decades of the seventeenth century, the Spanish and the Portuguese had firmly imprinted European culture throughout the Americas. Only the northeastern coasts of North America lacked successful Iberian colonies. From Florida to New Mexico, from Mexico south through the Caribbean to Brazil, Chile, and Argentina, the legacy of Columbus held sway.

Europe's Changing Market Conditions

While the age of discovery and conquest had begun under Spanish and Portuguese leadership, major changes were already underway in Europe. A shifting market system in Europe reflected the effects of these changes. This new market system began with increasing population pressure.

Europe's population grew rapidly after the disastrous period of death that had spanned the Late Middle Ages (1300–1450). A warmer climate, generous crop yields, a redefinition of land use and labor, and new foods from the Americas fed people who had grown accustomed to famine, plague, and warfare. Accordingly, Europe experienced a net gain of some 25 million people as the total number of Europeans reached an estimated 90 million by 1600. This increase in human numbers took place everywhere in Europe between 1500 and 1610, fueling a new demand for necessities in Western culture. England, France, Holland, the Holy Roman Empire, Spain, Portugal, and Russia all saw their populations grow.

Simultaneously, new political capitals began to emerge to reflect the will of those sovereigns who acquired their power as a product of the Reformation (1517–1648). Such cities as London, Versailles-Paris, Amsterdam, Lisbon, and Madrid redefined their relationship to their local markets because of the political and religious events associated with permanent seats of government (see the discussion of London below). Soon, a new urban-rural integration of supply and demand began to take place when kings and parliaments took up fixed residence in these principal centerplace cities. Each new royal capital also helped to sustain the links developing between royal politics and commercial exchanges. Hence, as territorial states grew stronger and their political power came more clearly into focus, so did the economic changes that supported and accelerated the growth in newly formed local, regional, territorial, and global market systems.

Adding to the growth in political power, new sources of gold and silver introduced into Europe through direct contact with Africa and the Americas provided a rich supply of freshly minted coins that created a general condition of inflation. Called the "price revolu-

tion," this inflation hit Europe with a force that thoroughly disrupted traditional medieval markets. No one anticipated the steady rise in prices that began after 1500 because everyone had grown accustomed to very stable market conditions.

In the Middle Ages (500–1500), local towns and their adjacent rural districts formed a basic economic unit. Licensed craftsmen who had organized local guilds received permission from their feudal lords to produce goods for consumption. Rural raw materials were exchanged for urban manufactured products in a stable system of supply and demand that remained basically the same for centuries. Manufacturing took place within a craftsman's home, in which a guild master housed his laborers, provided all the tools needed to make goods, and purchased the necessary materials. Workers drew salaries that included food, clothing, and shelter, as well as a modest disposable income that could be saved for some future day when marriage, or a new household, could occur within the guild. A financial state of affairs called "known demand" defined the conditions of production because the number of master households depended on the available supply of customers whose tastes and expectations were already well established. Profits were small, risks were few, and there was little demand for innovation.

Yet inflation caused these conditions to change. Since inflation can only occur when demand exceeds supply, a price revolution destroyed the medieval concept of "known demand." Thus, the slow and steady increase in prices set in motion by inflation so disrupted the medieval guild system that the focus of production had to shift from "known demand" to the "supply side" of manufacturing. Producers now found themselves compelled by their rising costs to create new, more efficient, and less expensive methods of producing goods to meet the expanding demand offered by powerful new sovereigns, a growing population, and a new supply of coins based on gold and silver from the Americas and Africa. Thus, successful manufacturers were those willing to take risks, invent new techniques, and introduce a new supply of goods into an "unknown" market in order to meet their new costs of doing business. All this took place despite a lull in inflation that hit during the Thirty Years War (1618–48) that marked the end of the Reformation's religious conflicts.

The Cost of Food

Parallel to the story of inflation is a specific account of the rising cost of food. Considering the expense of feeding a growing population alone, agricultural prices rose an estimated 500 percent between 1500 and 1625. Such an increase in demand for food stimulated a redefinition of agricultural production and traditional land use. New practices such as growing crops for profit in Western Europe joined with a revival of serfdom in Eastern Europe to increase the food supply.

Since inflation eroded the earnings of any aristocrat who tried to live on a fixed feudal income, more land in Western Europe came under cultivation. Marginal acreage once considered wasteland began to appear on the market for farmers willing to try new methods of growing food. These methods included cultivating land once judged untillable, using animal dung as fertilizer, and raising legumes like alfalfa to feed livestock. (Legumes, as mentioned, take nitrogen from the atmosphere and deposit it in the soil, increasing its fertility.) Occurring first in Italy but later elsewhere, the buying and leasing of any obtainable property introduced Western Europeans to a new type of commercial farmer: someone who raised crops and animals for profit rather than personal consumption.

Like his counterpart in manufacturing, the new farmer responded to growing demand and began to produce a new supply of food for an expanding market. Under their management, these risk-taking cultivators transformed Western European agriculture from subsistence to commercial farming. Keeping only a small portion of their harvest for personal use, these new farmers simply sold the rest and reinvested their profits in their new enterprise.

Since demand exceeded supply during these years of inflation (1500–1610), any farmer who used these new commercial techniques enjoyed a handsome income, while his more traditional neighbors failed. Simultaneously, any farm that failed made land available for use in this new commercial system of cultivation. The result was a general trend of change that saw successful mercantile farms replace unsuccessful traditional methods of land cultivation. Furthermore, the more affluent a commercial farmer became, the more money he had available to expand his holdings. Accordingly, larger farms proved more prosperous than smaller ones wherever Western European cultivators decoded this basic secret to success: that growing food for sale during a time of rising prices led to personal prosperity.

In contrast, in Eastern Europe land use retreated into neo-feudalism in response to the possibility of landlords making a profit during this era of inflation. While a general increase in state power, expansion in city size, and growth in human numbers stimulated a rising demand for food in all of Europe, wheat cultivation in Prussia, Poland, Lithuania, Austria, Hungary, Transylvania, Russia, and the Ukraine responded. Large estates in Eastern Europe began producing grain for export, brought marginal land into use, and forced landlords to redefine agricultural labor. On these Eastern

European estates, the prince or the local landlord imposed a new style of serfdom on his peasants that ensured the supply of labor he needed to produce food for profitable sale. Thus, lands situated east of the Elbe River saw a trend of development that ran contrary to the changes occurring in the west. Rather than the personal freedom, individual choice, and inventive risk-taking found in Western Europe's new commercial farming, a revived form of agricultural bondage trapped Eastern European peasants on the land.

The "Junkers" of Prussia created the prototype for this neo-feudal style of cultivation. A Junker, or Prussian knight, shifted his focus from being a professional soldier to an aristocratic landlord. As new military technology made knights obsolete on the battlefield during the Reformation, these Junkers replaced their primary commitment to military service with a desire to focus on cultivation as their chief business. Using their political power to trap peasant labor on their estates, the Junkers demonstrated that if an Eastern European landlord could supply the draft animals, seed, and tools that their new serfs (those trapped peasant laborers) needed, the landlords could produce a new supply of food for sale. Such a system of cultivation could make the bonded agricultural laborer into a type of sharecropper who generated the harvests needed by the landlord to fund his new commercial enterprise. Refined in Prussia, this new system of serfdom became the hallmark of agricultural labor in Eastern Europe and played a central role in the "Russian Paradox" mentioned below in Chapter Twenty-Four. Accordingly, while the East tended to return to feudal practices, Western Europe chose the path of modern innovation.

Meanwhile, as both Eastern and Western European agricultural techniques changed food production, so rising food prices stimulated the introduction of new plants from abroad into the European diet. Maize (American corn), potatoes, sweet potatoes, sugar, squash, beans, peanuts, tomatoes, cassava, and codfish, to name a few, caused changes in traditional European eating habits. Such changes in part reflected the demand that population pressure and inflation had on breaking down century-old dietary practices. Simultaneously, people who previously would have starved to death due to the rising cost of living now had new food sources.

Although cod was not entirely new to the European diet, the lavish new supplies brought in from the Grand Banks off the coast of Newfoundland (breeding grounds for cod) had a profound effect on Europe's caloric intake. Exploited for centuries by Basque whalers, these incredibly abundant fisheries remained a secret until they were discovered by Jacques Cartier, a French navigator sailing for Francis I, who led a voyage in 1534. An enormously prolific fish, the cod that spawned in the waters off Newfoundland generated 100,000 eggs per female. Therefore, this fishery went a long way to easing the tensions of inflation as dried and pickled forms of cod made the voyage across the Atlantic and became part of the expanding European population's diet.

In the meantime, the poorest people in Europe found that they had to experiment with new foods to keep from starvation as the cost of living rose. The introduction of maize, potatoes, and tomatoes to Europe illustrated this point. Maize arrived via a circuitous route from the Americas to Europe. Rather than traveling directly from Mexico to Spain to Europe, maize went from Spain to north Italy, most likely Venice, and from there to the Middle East, taking root in Syria, the Lebanese coast, and Egypt. From the Middle East, maize then reentered Europe through the Balkans and spread throughout Central Europe, where serfs cultivated the plant to supplement their diet. Since maize was new to the area, the plant went untaxed until the eighteenth century. Accordingly, peasants had access to a food that they could eat during even the worst years of the rising cost of living.

Also important, but less influential than corn due to its local nature, the potato and tomato made a strong impression on the Irish and the Italians. The Irish began cultivating the potato as the principal staple of their diet several centuries before the rest of Europe; their precocious approach to this plant kept their people alive even as their role in the growing English Empire worsened in the sixteenth century. The rest of Europe, however, had to wait until the late eighteenth century before the potato overcame its association with the botanical family called *Solanaceae*, a family containing some poisonous plants, and the fear that eating potatoes might cause disease. In contrast, the tomato entered Italy in the sixteenth century via Naples, where southern Italians, who could not afford to put cream in their sauces, substituted what they called *pomodoro* (golden apple) to provide a key new ingredient in their cooking. Hence, tomatoes, like potatoes, sustained life in a specific location where starvation would have otherwise reduced human numbers.

Proto-Industry

The rising cost of food, which put so much pressure on the peasant-farmer, also helped to change the price of labor, especially in Western Europe. There, peasants caught in the financial double bind of competing with expanding commercial farms and facing the higher cost of living turned to manufacturing to supplement their income. These peasants found themselves drawn into a new type of production that had already begun to transform the way Western Europeans generated their goods. Joining those risk-taking manufacturers mentioned above, hungry peasants served as the labor pool needed to change production from "known demand" to a growing supply. Hence, agricultural laborers soon became part of the expanding new Western European market system.

Any agricultural family living in the countryside, trapped with a fixed income during a time of inflation and faced with rival commercial production, felt mounting pressures. Happy to work for anyone who might ease the pain of rising prices and a falling purchasing power, this pool of potential rural laborers became part of a new system of urban employment. These new entrepreneurs, and this rural labor pool, or cottagers, joined in the development of a pre-industrial revolution. Both groups were willing to try anything new to meet the rising demand made available by inflation. The entrepreneurs supplied the jobs, tools, and materials needed in the manufacturing process, and the cottagers provided the work. The combination of both created what was called "the putting out system."

Entrepreneurs took their name from two French terms: *entre* and *prendre*. *Entre* literally means "between," and *prendre* means "to take." Hence, an entrepreneur was a "between taker." Less literal in translation, such a person was a "middle-man," an "undertaker," or a "go-between." Starting in the 1500s but becoming more prevalent thereafter, the entrepreneur left the city, where guilds had begun to fail due to inflation, and ventured into the countryside to redefine the conditions of production. No longer housing laborers with himself in a licensed establishment, the entrepreneur took his "capital" to rural districts and placed his tools and raw materials inside the cottages of desperate and hungry peasants. Distributing his stock along a path that constituted the steps needed in the manufacturing of specific items, the entrepreneur created a "horizontal" division of labor that also separated the worker from his employer. The result was a completely new relationship between labor and management, a completely new method of manufacturing, and a completely new means of reintegrating the rural and urban districts of a territorial state into an expanding market. All of this took place under the steady influence of inflation.

Taking each of these factors in order, the new relationship between management and labor released the employer from having to provide for all the needs of his workers. Instead, the worker now found himself with the responsibility of providing his own food, clothing, and shelter. This new arrangement compelled agricultural laborers to accept a wage-dependency that made them subject to market conditions, just like the manufacturer or merchant. As the demand of a product rose or fell, so did the demand for labor. And if a new method of production made an old technique obsolete, the laborers had to adjust their patterns of employment. Hence, as an increasing number of peasants in Western Europe found themselves drawn into cottage industry, the rural labor pool within a territorial state became subject to the same market conditions. This situation created what eventually became known as a "national economy."

At the same time, the entrepreneur who managed the whole productive affair found himself no longer responsible for the well-being of his employees. Consequently, he was free to calculate the potential profits of whatever enterprise he wished to set in motion. Using woolen textiles as an example, the entrepreneur estimated the tools, materials, and labor needed to manufacture clothing. Distributing his tools and materials into the cottages of his workforce, the entrepreneur created a logical pattern to production. One group of peasant laborers received spinning wheels and spun raw wool into yarn. Then the entrepreneur transported this yarn to another group, whom he supplied with looms. This second cohort of laborers produced cloth. Next, a third group of workers received this woven cloth, vats, and dyes and produced colored fabric. Finally, this prepared fabric ended up in the hands of a fourth group of cottagers who used needles, thread, and labor to produce finished clothing. Throughout the entire process, the entrepreneur owned the raw materials, the tools, and the finished product.

Meanwhile, peasant laborers eagerly accepted employment from the entrepreneur. Not knowing the value of their labor, because they never saw their products sold, these cottagers settled into a growing dependency on the entrepreneur and this new manufacturing technique. In areas where the "putting out system" became general, an increasing number of peasant laborers joined the entrepreneurial workforce. For example, by 1739 as many as 4.25 million English cottagers supplied the labor used to manufacture goods made available for sale in this island realm. This figure included men, women, and children and comprised 50 percent of the entire English population. In addition, the same type of manufacturing became popular in France and Holland; northwestern Europe seemed to be the economic zone where most of this entrepreneurial activity took place, but entrepreneurs also did business in Central Europe.

Larger entrepreneurial enterprises spread back into towns and absorbed the failing guilds located there. Prosperous entrepreneurs who needed the urban skills of a guild household turned to master weavers and cobblers and converted them into subcontractors. Great "clothiers" or "drapers" remade the guilds into associations of subordinate employees who no longer could control the circumstances that determined how the finished product would be made or sold. Such powerful entrepreneurs became the richest manufacturers in Europe.

All the productive forces mentioned above combined to create what economic historians have called the "profit-inflation spiral." The profit-inflation spiral linked all the elements of inflation (population pressures, rising state demand, and the increased supply of coins) with productive innovations (those found in agriculture and manufacturing) to generate extraordinary profits. Any employer who invested in the new techniques of production during this era of inflation found himself in an expanding market because *inflation* means "demand exceeds supply." At the same time, this risk-taking producer hired laborers who were eager to work for any wage that would pay for their rising cost of food, clothing, and shelter. Since the exceptional demand caused by inflation ensured a steady supply of new customers willing to absorb the growing number of goods produced, the manufacturer found himself in an expanding market.

Economic Crisis, 1625–1700

Finally, while the profit-inflation spiral maintained a high level of financial returns on new investments during the Commercial Revolution, an intense economic crisis between 1625 and 1700 accelerated change. During this period, Europe experienced its first modern recession. The causes of this slump included several integrated factors that had their greatest impact on the European continent.

The first of these factors was the devastation caused by the Thirty Years War (1618–48); death and destruction had swept though the Holy Roman Empire killing an estimated 25 percent of the people. Second, a decline in the amount of imported silver from the Americas reduced the supply of metals that could be used to coin new currency; this decline occurred because European epidemics had devastated the Native American populations that were used to mine this precious ore in the Western Hemisphere. Third, the rising cost of food in Europe had outstripped parallel increases in wages and reduced much of the continent's peasant population to the brink of famine. Fourth, the rising demand by European kings to field larger and larger armies during the Reformation (1517–1648) had occurred at a time when the consequences of religious warfare had also severely damaged many territorial economies. Fifth, shrinking productivity in both manufacturing and agriculture reflected the consequences of excessive royal taxation, while inflation slowed due to a high death rate caused by famine, disease, warfare, and the declining supplies of Spanish silver used to make new coins. Sixth, the reappearance of disease and famine swept through Central Europe, where the last spasms of religious warfare had attracted nearly all the great powers of Europe, except for England, to resolve their religious differences. Finally, a cooling trend in the climate reintroduced the West to a mini-Ice Age that caused severe winters and extensive crop damage during the harvest season due to hail and sleet storms. All these factors combined to undercut economic expansion in Europe in the midst of the Commercial Revolution.

Ironically, however, this recession did not affect all of Europe the same way; in fact, the economic crisis of the seventeenth century actually accelerated many of the key changes associated with the Commercial Revolution. For example, this crisis brought to an end the financial dominance enjoyed by the Mediterranean region over the European economy since ancient times; after 1700, the center of commerce shifted to the northwest Atlantic coast. At the same time, the general increase in population experienced by most European kingdoms up to 1600 first slowed and then stopped because of the devastation caused by religious warfare, which had also brought plague and famine in its wake. Yet states like England and the Dutch Republic continued to enjoy expanding human numbers because both territorial states had introduced the most significant collection of agricultural innovations into European food production between 1500 and 1650. Furthermore, England, the Dutch Republic, and France had successfully broken Spain's and Portugal's hold on the Atlantic trade routes and begun to develop their own mercantile systems. Finally, this relocation of the economy from the Mediterranean to the northwestern Atlantic coast had redefined the financial center of gravity for Europe's commercial and industrial future.

Even as the focus of Europe's economy shifted away from the Mediterranean, the differences in Eastern and Western European agricultural practices were consolidated during the economic recession. Because labor shortages continued to dominate production in England, Holland, and France, as each vied for commercial leadership, peasants in all three territorial states could earn sufficient wages to maintain their independence. Accordingly, Western European peasant laborers had greater opportunities in these three realms than did their

Central and Eastern European counterparts; in fact, peasants living east of the Elbe River suffered increased bondage.

As mentioned above, Eastern European nobles working in conjunction with local rulers had already ensnared their peasants in an expanding system of serfdom. During the recession, however, these same nobles exploited the desperation of their serfs to exert even more control over them. Prussian Junkers, the Polish, Lithuanian, and Ukrainian nobility, and the Russian czar and his aristocracy increased their power over agricultural labor to ensure continued grain production during hard times. When the recession began after 1625, peasants grew even more dependent on their landlords to secure the support needed to survive cycles of famine and disease. Consequently, Eastern European peasants found themselves increasingly tied to the land (for the details concerning Russian serfdom see Chapter Twenty-four).

The Special Case of England

The commercial system that England (and later Great Britain) assembled between 1550 and 1763 required significant changes at home. Central to these changes was the aforementioned rise in Europe's population. In England's case, however, the population increased some 120 percent between the years 1500 and 1700—the fastest growth rate prior to the Industrial Revolution. By 1770, England had added more than 3 million people to its original 2.5 million, but the way these people distributed themselves contrasted sharply with the traditional urban-rural ratios of the Middle Ages.

Using London as an example, this city reflected the basic changes that took place in England between 1500 and 1700. In 1500 the ratio of urban dwellers to farmers represented the standard one-to-nine distribution common to most traditional societies throughout world history. In 1700, England's ratio had shifted to an unprecedented one urban dweller for every three farmers. This extraordinary urban-rural ratio represented the impact of the economic changes that occurred in England during the Commercial Revolution. At the heart of this new urban distribution was London; the city grew from 50,000 in 1500 to 500,000 in 1700. This growth pattern meant that London alone held 9 percent of the total English population. Thus, by itself, London nearly housed the traditional one urban dweller for every nine farmers found throughout world history.

The growth of London, however, still denoted certain traditional limits. Migration from England's rural districts, and not birthrate, generated the rise in London's population. The average rural migrant lived only 11 months in this massive city if he or she did not find an occupation there. Such a short life span reflected the high incidence of disease, the lack of adequate shelter, the cold, and the threadbare clothing worn by the poor. Despite the fact that London had the best poor-relief system in England, those rural migrants who did not find a place of employment quickly, or did not have good family connections, simply did not last long.

Between 1600 and 1700, 900,000 people moved to London. Despite this sudden influx, the city's population had only grown by 300,000. This meant that for every three people who moved to London, one died, one found a place to stay, and one had to leave England altogether in order to survive. Hence, London became a permanent home for only one-third of its migrants, while it also served as a staging ground for the export of people abroad.

Of those who came to London but then ventured out into the world in order to survive, most went to England's mainland North American colonies after 1607. In a pattern of step-stage migration that became typical of Europeans after the Industrial Revolution, people left rural England due to inflation and changes in land use, ventured to the city to find new jobs, and then found themselves expelled from England entirely because of financial, political, or religious circumstances. Between 1600 and 1670 more than 250,000 people left England for the colonies in what was called the Great Migration. Made during an era of political and religious upheaval, when England's population peaked, the English Civil War and the Interregnum (see Chapter Twenty) pushed people out of Europe. These 250,000 immigrants felt the pull of the colonies and composed that portion of the English population that occupied the growing empire. In the colonies, these people then generated the new babies that secured Great Britain's hold on North America, the West Indies, and India after 1705.

London's growth reflected the fact that this city had finally become the permanent capital of England between 1500 and 1700. The king and parliament had begun to stay in London rather than moving the court from town to town, as was the habit of medieval monarchs. And as the crown and parliament struggled to strike a balance of sovereignty between themselves, the elite of England moved to London to participate in politics.

Simultaneously, the concentration of the elite in the capital drew merchants, artisans, and shopkeepers into the city. These people supplied the goods and services consumed by the elite. Other forms of labor required to supply these merchants, artisans, and shopkeepers with

their necessities further increased the number of people living in London. Finally, the vast number of poor who migrated into the city found the best poor-relief program in England, for London merchants used charity to control riots. Yet a good poor-relief program eventually attracted more people in need of charity than the system could handle. Thus, this rapid influx of poor partly explains why such a high death rate occurred within the city, and why a step-stage migratory process accompanied the rapid growth of London.

Altogether, the growth of London represented major changes in English agriculture. These changes included enclosures of once open-access grazing lands for everyone on an estate, new strategies to increase the size of farms, the development of crop rotation, new methods of raising livestock, and experimentation in selective breeding. Each change, in turn, placed England ahead of all other European states in the development of commercial food production. Eventually, the combination of these innovations resulted in what was called an "agricultural revolution." These changes explain why the English could support such an unusually high urban-rural ratio of one to three.

Enclosures became famous in England wherever landlords fenced off "commons" and denied their peasants access to the untilled acres used for grazing draft animals. Commons received its name from the medieval practice of allowing everyone on a feudal estate to use a specific section of wasteland in common to feed their livestock. Commons had been a traditional property right passed down from one generation to the next and had allowed peasants to keep alive those animals they needed to grow the food they gave to their landlord as part of their feudal services. Later, when these services were converted into moneyed rents, peasants sold this food to raise the funds they needed to pay their masters for the right to use the soil. While the commons was considered wasteland, inflation had increased the value of all acreage and caused English landlords to reconsider how their estates should be farmed.

Based on the medieval method of cultivation called the "three-field system," commons existed apart from the acreage tilled each year. At the same time, the three-field system took its name from the practice of plowing only two sections of an aristocrat's estate, while leaving the third fallow. By rotating these fields each growing season, English peasants had learned that when they allowed this third section of land to rest, the unused acreage recovered much of its fertility. While this system worked well during the Middle Ages, it left unplanted 33 percent of all the land that might have been cultivated at any one time. Enclosures, however, changed these agricultural practices and allowed English landlords to bring all their land into use.

Enclosures denied peasants their grazing rights and forced those with small holdings to eat their draft animals and abandon their strips of land. Driven from the estate, these small landholders released acreage that the landlord could consolidate into larger farms. Collecting these strips of land into new and more efficient agricultural units, these enterprising landowners now had access to acreage that they could use to increase food production or raise sheep. At the same time, the expelled peasants made up a growing population of vagabonds (see below) who migrated to cities like London. As this process accelerated, and the number of sheep in England began to compete with the number of people for food, landlords began to look at their fallow fields.

Accordingly, English landlords found that to create a new supply of fodder for their expanding herds, or to feed people, the third fallow field had to be brought under cultivation. Unintentionally planting legumes among the many foods that they grew to feed their animals, some of these English landlords introduced Europe to the modern process of "crop rotation." Since a legume draws nitrogen from the air into the soil, crops like clover or alfalfa accelerated the process of fertilizing exhausted soil. At the same time, by putting this third field into use, all the land on an aristocrat's estate came under cultivation.

Simultaneously, by increasing the supply of animals living within an enclosed area, other English landlords had generated a new supply of manure that they could use to increase soil fertility. Thus, those landlords who chose hay, turnips, or oats to feed their livestock, instead of legumes, soon found themselves also able to restore the fertility of their land by spreading animal waste in their fields. Consequently, all the landlords who enclosed their fields had also gradually discovered the secrets of how to increase the total number of acres under tillage, how to renew soil fertility to maintain the productivity of their farms, and how to in avoid leaving any of their land fallow.

Furthermore, by fencing off specific animal populations within an enclosed area, some of these inventive landlords had begun to experiment with selective breeding. These experiments in animal husbandry included choosing the most valuable animals for reproduction, which increased the quality and quantity of meat, wool, and hides available for sale. In time, not only could English landlords grow more food for both people and livestock, but they also could produce a greater supply of high quality animal byproducts for sale.

Discovered by accident early in the process of enclosure, this new style of total land use became more methodical after 1688. By that year, the landlords of England had won their struggle with the crown over the issue of sovereignty and had secured parliament's role as England's sole legislature. In the process of elevating parliament, landowners had also come to dominate English politics and used this power to establish their absolute control over the land. Working in alliance with the great merchants in England's corporate towns, this landowning aristocracy took charge of their estates and self-consciously applied everything they had learned about raising animals and increasing food production.

In retrospect, two centuries of enclosures, shifting cultivation practices, and fluctuations in the prices of wool and food stocks had to take place before English farmers began to understand the revolutionary changes set in motion by the Commercial Revolution. By 1700, however, a sufficient number of innovations had occurred that English cultivators could grasp the significance of the events taking place around them. Using this knowledge during the eighteenth century, English landowners changed food production enough that they were able to feed the labor pool that would migrate to cities during the Industrial Revolution.

Thus, a new set of agricultural practices began spontaneously in England that brought an increasing amount of land into cultivation over the next three hundred years (1500–1800). This combination of new cultivation techniques, land use, and accelerated meat, wool, and vegetable production added enough new calories to the food supply to feed a rapidly growing population. At the same time, new foods from the Americas helped to feed the desperate during a time of profound economic changes.

Meanwhile, in England, the Reformation, inflation, and agricultural innovations combined to set the price of labor at subsistence for several centuries. The Reformation began in England when Henry VIII (reigned 1509–47) tried to divorce his wife, Catherine of Aragon, in 1529. Henry's quest for this divorce derived from his desire to have a legitimate male heir. By 1529, Catherine had become infertile, and she had borne Henry only one living child, their daughter Mary (reigned as Queen of England from 1553 to 1558). Catherine's inability to provide Henry with the desired son had forced him to contrive a reason to annul his marriage, for he feared that if he did not produce a male heir, the Tudor claim to the English throne would collapse after his death. This fear was based on the fact that Henry's father was one of the few survivors of the War of the Roses (1455–85), a conflict that had pitted numerous claim-

King Henry VIII (1491–1547). This portrait of Henry VIII, circa 1536, was produced during the height of his reign (1509–47). Oil on copper, after Hans Holbein the Younger. National Portrait Gallery, London.

ants to England's crown against one another with only one survivor, Henry's father, Henry VII (reigned 1485–1509). Henry VII had trained his son to do everything within his power to ensure against a return to the civil strife that had raised the Tudors to the throne. Accordingly, while Henry sought a divorce, he, at the same time, indirectly launched the Reformation in England and caused a redefinition of the price of labor in England that would help secure Britain's success in the Commercial Revolution.

Ironically, Henry's quest for a divorce failed because circumstances had worked against him. By 1529, the European Reformation was already twelve years old. The pope, Clement VII, had refused to grant Henry an annulment because such a request would have raised questions about papal infallibility—a power the pope claimed against attacks leveled by Martin Luther (see Chapter Eighteen). Previously, Pope Julius II had granted Henry and Catherine a dispensation to marry to overcome her original match to Arthur, Henry VII's first born son, heir, and Henry VIII's older brother. Arthur's death in 1503 had elevated Henry VIII to the throne, but his failure to father a legitimate son with Catherine raised doubts twenty-five years later. Now Henry argued that God had punished the English king for marrying his brother's wife, a sin according to Leviticus (18:16). Henry hoped to reverse Julius II's original decision as an error, but such a reversal would have forced Clement VII to accept Biblical authority

over the judgment of a sitting pope—a claim Martin Luther never grew tired of asserting. A declaration of this nature by Clement VII would have been unthinkable because Martin Luther's challenge to papal infallibility had already ruptured the unity of Christendom during Luther's numerous disputes with the Roman Catholic Church between 1517 and 1521.

At the same time, Clement VII had just survived a major invasion of Italy by Charles V, Catherine's nephew. Clement VII had joined with Francis I of France to expel Charles V from the Italian Peninsula, but had failed due to Charles's superior forces (Charles was also the king of Spain, ruler of the Austrian Netherlands, and the Holy Roman emperor). Having witnessed Charles's power, and the fury of his soldiers during the sacking of Rome in 1527, Clement VII did not want to do anything to provoke Catherine's nephew. When the pope failed to grant Henry his divorce, Henry broke with the Roman Catholic Church and became the head of the newly created Church of England.

As the ultimate religious authority in England, Henry VIII then took possession of all church land. Allowing the parishes to remain open, Henry, however, confiscated the monasteries and convents, turned out all the monks and nuns, and sold a generous number of these reclaimed acres at very low prices to his supporters in parliament. This began a vast redistribution of land that not only won Henry the votes he needed to secure his divorce, but had also allowed well-connected and enterprising farmers during the reigns of Henry VIII, Edward VI, and Elizabeth I (1529–1603) to rise to the prestige of landowner. Even Mary Tudor's short reign began with a reconciliation with the new landowners that secured their newly acquired estates from monasteries and convents despite the queen's intention of restoring Catholicism.

Meanwhile, by closing the monasteries and convents of England, Henry had unintentionally brought the church's role in charity to an end; thus, he destroyed an important social net used to support the poor during hard times. Like their counterparts in other European kingdoms, England's monasteries and convents had provided the poor with economic relief when they could not find employment or when they had been displaced from their homes. Given the forces of inflation and enclosures during Henry's reign, many desperate peasants began to roam the countryside in search of their next meal. Called "healthy beggars" by contemporaries, this mobile population represented a potential social danger because of England's history of rural rebellions during bad times. To deal with this growing crisis, England's elite joined with the crown to produce a series of Poor Laws designed to control the movement of these people. The Poor Laws later developed into a parish-relief program throughout England.

The Poor Laws created the Poor House, or Workhouse, for vagrants who could not find employment elsewhere. Controlled by the justice of the peace, the Poor House confined healthy beggars to the parish of their birth, where they were required to work for their subsistence. At the same time, the justice of the peace who administered the Poor House was also the local landlord; that is, he was the aristocrat who was responsible for enclosures, or had acquired the land that once belonged to monasteries and convents.

As both the justice of the peace and the local landlord, this aristocrat was the person most responsible for the plight of these vagrants. Accordingly, he had in fact placed these healthy beggars in a financial double bind. As the landlord, he was the principal employer in the parish. As the justice of the peace, he restricted the movement of healthy beggars, defined vagrancy, and confined the unemployed to the Poor House. Hence, he determined the primary conditions of labor as the chief private employer, while, at the same time, serving as the public administrator of the Workhouse. He was therefore in a position to set the price of labor at subsistence, and hold it there until the Industrial Revolution changed the Poor Laws. Simultaneously, he made those living within his parish eager to work for any entrepreneur who would venture out from a local town to offer a supplemental income to England's vast rural labor force.

Given the low cost of labor in England, and the process of enclosures, the conditions for entrepreneurial investments on the British Isles were ideal. Since enclosures accidentally stimulated a significant number of agricultural innovations in England after 1500, the British Isles eventually became the leader in what historians now refer to as the "agricultural revolution." At the same time, creating a generous supply of food during an era of commercial development allowed the English to support their unprecedented urban-rural ratio of one to three. And combined with the Poor Laws and the end of church-sponsored charity during the Reformation, enclosures placed extraordinary pressures on English peasants to find a supplemental income. This, in turn, encouraged cottage industry laborers to develop in England at a rate that surpassed everyone else in Europe. Under these circumstances, an unusually large number of entrepreneurs exploited the opportunities offered by this growing rural labor pool.

Simultaneously, the profit-inflation spiral stimulated exceptional profits for English entrepreneurs. The profits, in turn, were reinvested in an expanding proto-industrial system that continued to grow even after the era of inflation itself came to an end (see below). Eventually, the spread of proto-industry caused these English entrepreneurs to enlist the aid of 50 percent of the rural population by 1739. Thus, the profit-inflation spiral and the development of proto-industry in England, laid a foundation for a national economy that, in turn, generated the preconditions needed for the Industrial Revolution.

Mercantilism

The new transoceanic trade routes required major political backing in order to succeed. Shipbuilding was so expensive, and required such costly materials as cannons, timber, muskets, canvas sails, and rope, that state participation was essential. Thus, the appearance of new monarchies at the end of the Middle Ages provided a necessary and fundamental element to the Commercial Revolution.

More thoroughly discussed in Chapter Twenty, modern state formation played a key role in the development of commercial capitalism. Began during the late Middle Ages (1300–1450) and accelerated during the Reformation (1517–1648), state formation refined the modern concept of sovereignty through a process that centralized political authority in the hands of one primary institution. As royal armies and navies bestowed a monopoly on coercion to either a king or parliament, so political rivals like the papacy and Europe's great feudal lords had to retreat.

By 1648, when the Reformation had ended with the signing of the Treaty of Westphalia, both Protestant and Catholic monarchs alike agreed that princes and kings should determine the religion of their realms. This general agreement eliminated the papacy as a political competitor and allowed only one ultimate authority to emerge within each state. At the same time, the development of royal armies using well-organized military units based on cannon, the pike, and the musket had also eliminated the chances of any great lord rising up and challenging a monarch's ability to rule his domain. Consequently, royal absolutism on the European continent, and parliamentary sovereignty in England replaced the feudal system by 1690.

Power concentrated in the hands of kings, or maintained by England's parliament, provided the political support needed to establish colonies around the world. Unlike any other culture active in global trade during the early modern era (1492–1763), the Europeans alone built commercial empires capable of sustaining their expanding global system of trade. Even England's form of sovereignty, the partnership between parliament and the crown that emerged after the Glorious Revolution (1688–89), saw the value of politically supporting colonial ventures.

Yet only those colonial systems with strong diplomatic, political, and military resources survived, while all others failed. No free city, small principality, or commercial league could compete with a determined king or parliament. Thus, the more completely centralized states of Western Europe had a significant material advantage over their Central European neighbors. This allowed France, Holland, England, Sweden, Spain, and Portugal to initiate, expand, and maintain global commercial outposts, while the great cities of the Holy Roman Empire and Italy began to lose economic ground.

What role the sovereigns of Europe played in stimulating trade depended on the answers to several key questions. When did colonization begin? What theory of value, or definition of wealth, did a European monarch use? How restrictive was royal authority when applied to the process of controlling economic development abroad? And what scale of military support did a king offer his subjects in terms of protection against rival monarchs seeking to eliminate competition?

Although Portugal introduced Europe to the idea of exploring the Atlantic and capturing foreign sources of pagan wealth, the Spanish were the first to begin the process of colonization on a large scale. The Spanish discovered the Western Hemisphere and opened the way for Europeans to contemplate the possibility of conquering and assimilating the 16 million square miles of land that lay across the Atlantic. Called the New World, a phrase that reflects how Europeans ethnocentrically viewed the Western Hemisphere, as a place virtually empty of native peoples, the Spanish were the first to set about occupying this vast supply of land. Hence, Spain played the key role in initiating the process of planting European colonies on foreign soil.

But while the Spanish may have set the pattern for conquest and colonization, their early start was actually a disadvantage, for the Spanish had begun the process of colonizing the New World with the least sophisticated concept of value. Still very much bound by medieval traditions, the Spanish launched the Commercial Revolution in the opening days of modernization when no one could have foreseen the monumental changes about to take place. Hence, the Spanish introduced Europe to one of the key forces of economic change, inflation, without being aware of the power of this financial agency. Accordingly, when Spain gained

access to the immense amount of gold and silver that they took from Native Americans, they also encouraged other kings in Europe to debase their coins. This released the price revolution.

Furthermore, the Habsburg rulers of Spain chose to use their gold and silver to finance the wars of the Catholic Counter-Reformation (1556–1648) by which they squandered an enormous pool of capital on unproductive enterprises. The Habsburgs had acquired control of Spain when Ferdinand and Isabella's daughter, Joanna, married Philip I of Austria. Their son, Charles V, united Spain, the Austrian Netherlands, and the Holy Roman Empire under one crown and linked Spain's political destiny to Charles V's determination to resist Protestantism. Thus, the kings of Spain did not expand their productive base during a time when demand exceeded supply and instead watched their neighbors become the chief beneficiaries of the profit-inflation spiral. In addition, Spain's Habsburg kings followed a traditional theory of value called "bullionism" to define their royal policy in the New World.

Bullionism stated that all value was located in gold and silver. Believing this simple idea, the Spanish crown sought to extract as much gold and silver as possible from the Americas and stockpile it in Europe. Such a policy concentrated gold and silver in Spain, accelerated inflation there, and removed potential capital from the Western Hemisphere. Combined with squandering money on religious wars and not investing in production at home, Spanish kings instituted the worst possible fiscal program. First, they removed capital from their American colonies that could have been used there to generate goods. Second, they concentrated precious metals in one place, which accelerated inflation in Spain to a point where it exceeded that of all other states in Europe. Third, they wasted this potential capital on warfare, which impoverished their kingdom and caused multiple dynastic bankruptcies. Fourth, their failure to encourage production at home denied the possibility of bringing supply back in line with demand so that they could defeat the inflation that raged throughout their realm. Finally, Spanish kings began a policy of importation from their neighbors because the cost of living in Spain made the price of labor there more expensive than any other state in Europe.

In contrast, England started later than Spain, had a better grasp of the changes taking place during the Commercial Revolution, and developed a more coherent state policy concerning fiscal affairs. The English followed the "Dutch theory of value," which stated that gold and silver functioned as a lubricant to trade, while trade itself was the true source of all wealth. Like the

Dutch, the English believed that global commerce re-distributed the world's total supply of riches from one location to another. To acquire the greatest amount of this limited supply of wealth, a state had to encourage trade through investing gold and silver in the machinery of exchange. Unaware of the concept of production, the English, like the Spanish, did not really understand where value actually originated. Like the Spanish, the English would have to wait until the *Physiocrats* (French intellectuals who developed the first complete theory of production) and early economists like Adam Smith decoded the secrets of production in the 1760s and 1770s (see Chapter Nineteen). Meanwhile, the English had stumbled onto a theory of value that actually stimulated generating new goods despite the fact they did not yet have the conceptual framework to understand what they were doing.

Unlike the Spanish, the English did not discover vast supplies of gold and silver in their colonial holding. This seemingly unfortunate state of affairs proved, however, to be a boon to the English economy. The absence of immediate profits like those enjoyed by the Spanish forced the English to develop complex new corporations, and caused their colonial settlers to seek out local products for export. The result was a very productive and highly profitable system of transatlantic trade.

Between 1550 and 1630, the English slowly developed the means to become the world's greatest commercial empire. Central to this process were the first great transoceanic corporations called "joint-stock companies." These early modern companies developed new and sophisticated ways of recruiting anonymous partners by separating ownership from control. Those who acquired stock did not participate in formulating the company's policies; instead, an elected board of directors made the decisions. The investors merely served as silent partners who reaped the rewards of a successful venture.

Some of these joint-stock companies were assembled for a single foreign adventure, while others became ongoing business concerns. If investors did not like the policies of the corporation, all they had to do was sell their shares; this did not disrupt the organization of the company. Most joint-stock enterprises were designed with the expectation that several years would pass before the stockholders saw any profits. During this time, the joint-stock companies built up their capital base in order to develop the means needed to establish, protect, and maintain outposts abroad.

Raising money for economic activities outside Europe, these corporations did not engage in domestic manufacturing or intra-European trade. In Europe, the capital held by an entrepreneur proved sufficient for local, regional, or territorial exchanges. Joint-stock companies, however, provided the funds needed for expensive, long-range, and highly risky foreign enterprises. A round trip to Asia, for example, took an average of three years. If a company planned to establish a colony, then even more time would have to pass before anyone could expect to see any profits. Often these companies included within their charter a final date of liquidation that could be set as much as twenty years in the future. When this date finally arrived, and their "ship had come in," the investors were assured that they would receive the rewards appropriate to the uncertainty of their investment. Thus, the English joint-stock companies provided an effective mechanism for distributing the cost and risk of a foreign venture over a broad base of silent partners.

In the eighty years between 1550 and 1630, the English established their first colonies along the North American coast. At the same time, they launched the great East India Company in Asia. Furthermore, numerous joint-stock companies assembled to engage in trade with Russia, Africa, and the Middle East. Silent partners invested an estimated £13 million in joint-stock enterprises that sought profits from aboard. Yet, nearly one-third of this money went into privateering ventures: these were government-licensed and regulated forms of piracy. The most common targets of this legitimate form of global theft were the Spanish treasure ships.

Thus, the biggest and most important portion of these initial foreign investments, privateering, also proved to be the most profitable. Between 1550 and 1630, stock purchased in privateering ventures returned an estimated 60 percent on each share, while the East India Company paid only 20 percent, and the Virginia Company never showed a profit for the Jamestown colony. Furthermore, government-licensed piracy appealed far more to the aristocrat or gentile investor than did the mundane enterprise of trade; both felt a common disdain for commerce. Accordingly, the glory accrued by the most successful of these pirates, Francis Drake, led to a knighthood, partnership with Queen Elizabeth I (reigned 1558–1603), and the status of a popular hero.

Given the nature of early modern European commerce, privateering made perfect financial sense. Virtually all the European overseas exchanges were in luxury goods: spices, gold, silver, furs, high-quality textiles, and later slaves and sugar (see below); one could sell such cargoes in any English port for an immediate and enormous profit. Furthermore, every kingdom in equal partners, the crown and parliament, and created a new political concept called the commonwealth. By 1690, this commonwealth had produced an image of England as being more than merely a state; rather, it was an estate shared by the wealthy of the realm whose private interests were inseparable from public prosperity. Hence, the English were the first to see the explicit link between public and private affairs.

At the same time, the kingdom of England had gone to war successfully with its commercial rivals and had bested them at every turn. Accordingly, the Portuguese, Spanish, Dutch, and French could not compete with the methods of raising money and financing military campaigns that the English launched. The joint-stock companies had trained the English in the uses of capital and had instituted a credit system that turned war itself into an enterprise. Called the "fund," the English during the seventeenth and eighteenth centuries attracted investors into government-sponsored military adventures that gave England command of the sea. Thus, the English proved to be the most successful risk-takers of the Commercial Revolution.

By 1705, Scotland, Wales, and Ireland had joined England to create the "United Kingdom." Dominated by the English, this new political union, also called "Great Britain," mustered the military resources of all four realms. Together, they ensured the safety of Britain's numerous commercial outposts and made possible a complex system of global trade. Seen as a single "mercantile" system, all these outposts took advantage of "geographic differentiation." Geographic differentiation merely means that each outpost in the British Empire produced its own unique supply of goods, all of which might be exchanged in a vast global network of trade.

Exporting tobacco from Virginia, codfish, ship stores, and timber from Massachusetts, rice from South Carolina, wheat and corn from the middle colonies of North America, sugar from the West Indies, slaves from Africa, cotton and spices from India, and tea from China, the English stimulated a highly profitable system of global exchange. Based on the principle of buy low (at the point of supply), and sell high (at the point of demand), the diversity of these various goods made every port of call in the British commercial empire a potential zone of profit. As ships traveled from one port to another, they distributed goods throughout this transatlantic commercial network.

For example, by the eighteenth century, the joint-stock company turned colony, Massachusetts Bay, produced timber, ships, ship stores, and fish; all of these goods were in high demand in Great Britain. Thus, this New English colony could launch a very profitable pattern of trade. Using one of the ships built in Boston, a merchant could load his vessel with a cargo of fish or

"The Merchant," by Jost Amman. From *Symbols, Signs & Signets,* by Ernst Lehner.

Europe viewed the ships of its rival states as legitimate targets—especially during the Reformation, when a general state of war existed between Catholic and Protestant realms for nearly every one of the ninety-two years between 1556 and 1648. Thus, commercial warfare merely became part of the risks joint-stock companies had to be prepared to take.

Such long-term ventures as the East India Company developed a permanent life because this was the only way a corporation could deal with the violence of European trade. Licensed to make war on the Portuguese, the East India Company served as a commercial privateering enterprise that built its own fortifications, raised its own military units, and used its own armed merchant fleet. West India Companies, and corporations located on the North American coast, faced Spanish and Portuguese rivals in much the same way. Violence was merely a part of the adventure, and since the glory and profits were so good, in the long run, these capital-intense commercial firms successfully planted English outposts all over the world.

After 1630, the English refined their constitution, defined sovereignty as a joint enterprise between two timber and sail to England, sell it for a profit and buy a cargo of luxury goods there. Sailing next to Jamaica (an island attacked twice by the English in 1596 and 1643, captured in 1655, and acquired legally at the Treaty of Madrid in 1670), this same Boston merchant could sell the luxury goods purchased in England for another profit and purchase a cargo of sugar. Returning to his home port, the merchant could use the sugar to make rum, sell the liquor for a third profit, and then outfit his ship for the next voyage.

Using these accumulated profits, this Boston merchant could then take his rum back to England, sell it for a fourth profit, collect another cargo of luxury goods, and sail to Virginia. Since both Virginia and Jamaica used a plantation system to produce commercial crops for export, and neither had a diversified economy capable of manufacturing high-quality goods, the luxury items from Britain always sold well. While in Virginia, a Boston merchant could acquire a cargo of tobacco, then arrange a voyage back to England. There, he could exchange the tobacco for manufactured goods and plan a voyage to Pennsylvania. Once there, he could exchange the manufactured goods for corn or wheat and prepare his trip back home to Boston. The only exceptions to this style of commerce within the British Empire was the occasional trip to Spain during times of peace, when goods could be exchanged for precious metals, the influx of gold and silver serving to lubricate this commercial system.

This multiport trade pattern allowed Great Britain to stimulate agriculture and manufacturing everywhere within the empire even though no one as yet understood the concept of "production" itself. Demand in Great Britain drew raw materials from the Americas, the West Indies, and Asia, as well as labor from Africa, in exchange for finished products provided by the "mother country." Each port within the empire served as a potential market, bought goods, and exported local products. The overall demand caused by the Atlantic trade system sustained entrepreneurial production in Great Britain even after inflation subsided in the seventeenth century (see above). Accordingly, as all these ports matured, the empire became a web of trade that supported anyone who participated.

By 1650, the English realized the value of what they could create. Thus, every effort at capturing global commerce became a principal goal of English politics. A series of wars with the Netherlands, combined with the Navigation Acts of 1651, 1660, 1662, 1663, 1670, and 1673, laid the groundwork for success in global trade. Called the Dutch Wars (1652–54, 1665–67, and 1672–74), these conflicts with the Netherlands allowed England, in conjunction with France, to break Holland's control over Europe's carrying trade. At the same time, the Navigation Acts forbade English goods from being carried on foreign ships. Continued through the close of the seventeenth and into the eighteenth century, British commercial warfare next sought to drive the French from their key colonial outposts around the world. The combined results of all these legal and military efforts bore fruit in the Seven Years' War (1756–63) when the British effectively disposed of France as a commercial rival by expelling the French from Canada and India. With no one left to challenge British supremacy in global trade, Great Britain added the last key factor essential for the Industrial Revolution: a world marketplace.

The Slave Trade

As the demand for labor grew in the Western Hemisphere, the slave trade accelerated, drawing Africans into the new Atlantic commercial network. As mentioned, Africans had sold slaves to other Africans and outsiders for centuries before 1492. Part of a list of goods available to foreign customers, African slaves went on the market during the ancient era, continued in high demand during the Middle Ages, and reached a zenith in sales during the modern age. After 1492, European labor requirements in the Western Hemisphere transformed Africa's role in world trade by making slaves one of the principal exports sold from that continent.

Throughout the Western Hemisphere, wherever Europeans created new jobs that they themselves could, or would not do, they employed African slaves to do them. Thus, this new European demand for human labor partly realigned Africa's slave trade away from the caravan trails across the Sahara to the Middle East and shifted them to Africa's Atlantic Coast. Such a commercial realignment allowed Europeans to replace the Muslims as Africa's primary customers.

At the same time, the possibility of a new Atlantic slave trade required a willingness on the part of one African society to sell members of another to outsiders. This willingness was not unique to Africa. Throughout world history, on nearly every continent, countless numbers of people have been bought or sold as slaves, both within a culture, or to foreigners. In each case, the person who became a victim of the slave trade had to exist in some way as an outsider within the social fabric of a civilization. In African history, such an outcast status was essential to the sale of slaves.

The possibility of a slave trade developing in Africa required that various African cultures view other African societies as somehow being filled with "legitimate commodities" for sale. In other words, to see another human being as a potential slave, an African had to assign him or her some kind of nonhuman status. Such a status befell those in an African community who could not pay their debts, committed crimes, or were taken as prisoners of war. Hence, anyone sold in the African slave trade had somehow "lost" his or her humanity.

Thus, from 1500 to 1800 several European countries became directly involved in the African slave trade—first Portugal and the Netherlands, then England after 1700, with its private merchants being the dominant slavers, and then France. Yet none entered the trade earlier, or proved more rapacious, than Portugal.

By the mid-1500s, plantation owners in the Western Hemisphere had exhausted Native American labor due to epidemics and brutal working conditions, but the planters had realized that the few Africans arriving in the New World were hardier and more resistant to European diseases than were Native Americans—who also could run away successfully and rejoin their tribes. Consequently, the demand for labor on sugar and coffee plantations, especially in the West Indies and Brazil, fueled the hunt for more African slaves.

Like the Muslims, Europeans were in Africa as intermediaries from the outset. The African disease barrier gave a European only a 50 percent probability of living if he ventured into the interior. Accordingly, in both state trade and numerous private merchant enterprises, partnership with Africans was required. Furthermore, it was the Africans who set the rules of the game. After all, natives of a region understood the territory and customs of their neighbors better than non-Africans. Also, since European states as well as African communities were in competition with each other, alliances shifted constantly. To operate successfully then, Europeans had to make treaties with local rulers who allowed Western commercial interests to maintain trading posts and harbor forts in Africa.

Yet the slave trade proved even more complex when one considers that while most enslaved persons were sold to Europeans, demand for slaves in the Middle East and in the interior of Africa itself continued. Hence, three slave trades competed with one another: the "occidental slave trade" (European), the "oriental slave trade" (Muslim) and the "interior slave trade" (African). While mostly men caught by slavers crossed the Atlantic to satisfy European demand, women proved most attractive in the harems of the Middle East. Yet, Africans coveted slaves as well, as a status symbol, as subordinate members of a lineage, or for later exchange for goods such as alcohol, tobacco, iron, copper, beads, cloth, and above all, firearms, gunpowder, and horses. In all three slave systems, $1/3$ of the slaves were prisoners of war, $1/10$ were adulterers, and others were common criminals, orphans, widows, the idle, feebleminded, or debtors sold for repayment.

The African elite and new merchants frequently monopolized the slave trade. The coastal state of Dahomey made the export of slaves its policy and became a major player in the occidental slave trade, leading raids against neighboring villages or remote groups. Sometimes, as in the case of seventeenth-century Kongo, captured humans amongst their own people became victims of this trade. Some slaves were taken within the African community to fill military positions. Dahomey was famous for its slave musketeers and "Amazons," women who originally served as palace bodyguards. Dahomey also was notorious for its brutal treatment of slaves. This harshly primitive military state, with its ritualized and luxurious royal cult, and with women in important positions through matrilineal authority, such as the politically significant office of Queen Mother, exchanged gold and ivory for guns and slaves.

The heartlessness of the slavers was recognized and feared everywhere. From the point of capture to the marketplace, one-third to one-half of the slaves perished through disease or suicide, or managed to escape. The whole experience was so horrendous that West Africans were told that European customers ate black flesh and drank African blood in wine cups. One account describes a Niger River convoy of twenty to thirty canoes packed with hog-tied slaves. These miserable victims cowered in the bottom of the leaky boats, half covered with water and chained and roped during their overland journey hundreds of miles to the coast. There they were imprisoned in cattle corrals or forts before being shipped overseas. From such coastal departure points as "the Door of No Return" in the slave house on Goree Island, for example, the Middle Atlantic passage began. Then, on a slave ship, the slaves were shackled and made to sleep in "kennels." Typically, a tenth to a quarter of the 200 or 300 Africans on each ship died en route.

Slave rebellions against captors were commonplace. The Liberian Kru and Guinea Baga tribes proved so fearless against European commercial interests, often murdering their oppressors or committing suicide, that both became unprofitable to enslave. Sharks usually followed slave ships for the guaranteed meals they offered when the dead, and even the living sometimes, were thrown overboard. In the Americas, in 1791, Haiti was the site of the only major slave rebellion that successfully expelled its masters.

With all this cruelty, it is nevertheless important to note that intra-African slavery varied tremendously. Some slaves could own property, accumulate wealth, and rise to power in government. Some slavers were compassionate, after a fashion. Around 1700, however,

The Middle Passage: The Transport of Slaves on the Trans-Atlantic Trip

The common image of the Middle Passage, slave ships crammed with Africans, packed in without room to breath, chained to each other, exposed to the brutality of their capturers, and dying from disease and thirst, belies the complexity of the complete trip these people actually made. To grasp the deadly nature of their voyage to the "New World," one should begin by considering the condition of these slaves when they reached the African coast. Their weakened state from their trek from the interior yoked to one another by their African masters, as well as their exposure to the psychological terror of being shipped on vessels across an ocean by a pale people they had never seen before, created a state of extreme melancholy that raised their death rate during the voyage. Hence, one should not view the Middle Passage as a separate event disconnected from the whole experience of being captured, transported from the interior, placed in pens like cattle, and being loaded onto vessels for a voyage across a seemingly endless body of water to an unknown destination.

Slaves were people taken in warfare, such as raids, kidnappings, and wars of conquest, (34 percent), those who had been found guilty of a crime (11 percent), those resold as slaves from an African to a European master (30 percent), those who could not pay their debts (7 percent), and those classified as helpless: orphans, widows, poor relations, and vagrants (18 percent). All of these people were a "perishable com-modity" in the sense that they could die or escape. Selling them as soon as possible therefore guaranteed a profit. Some were sold numerous times as they moved toward the coast, frequently being branded by each person who had made such a purchase. Once the slave reached the coast—usually after several hundred miles of travel—the African slave merchant, or royal agent, began to haggle with Europeans interested in loading their ships. Penned up in fortified areas, young, heal-thy males brought the highest prices; they fetched sev-eral firearms, or numerous glass beads, mirrors, and semiprecious gems, or raw iron and copper, alcohol, and tobacco. Of all these items, firearms proved to be the most highly prized because they offered Africans the power to continue their quest for future victims.

Meanwhile, the trip to the coast had seriously weakened many of the people captured for export. Once there, these fettered humans now faced the terror of being sold to a white master (a complete stranger) who had them manacled, imprisoned, and confined on a ship that was about to sail on a vast body of water of unknown dimensions. The psychological impact of these circumstances, plus the weakness of the depleted victims, often set a mood of doom that was fueled by the confusion caused by the different languages of the victims collected together on the ship. Where they were going, under the watchful eye of "white demons," whose appetite for human flesh might mean that the slave was about to become a meal, was a common misunder-standing of their fate. European came from the sea and disappeared into it; maybe they made their home on the water and had nothing else to eat but their purchased cargo.

Olauduh Equiano (in Interesting Narrative of the Life of Olauduh Equian, or Gustavus Vasa, the African, *written by himself, 1789, edited by Paul Edwards, 1967), from southern Nigeria, recalls the experience vividly:*

The first object which saluted my eyes when I arrived on the coast was the sea, and a slave ship which was then riding at anchor and wait-ing for its cargo. These filled me with astonish-ment, which was soon converted into terror when I was carried on board. I was immed-iately handled and tossed up to see if I were sound by some of the crew, and I was now per-suaded that I had gotten into a world of bad spirits and that they were going to kill me. Their complexions too differing so much from ours, their long hair and the language they spoke (which I had [n]ever heard), united to confirm me in this belief. Indeed such were the horrors of my views and fears at the moment that, if ten thousand worlds had been my own, I would freely have parted with them all to have ex-changed my condition with that of the meanest slave in my own country. When I looked round the ship too and saw a large furnace or copper boiling, a multitude of black people of every description chained together, every one of their countenances expressing dejection and sorrow, I no longer doubted my fate; and quite over-powered with horror and anguish, I fell motion-less on the deck and fainted.

Given the weakened state of a slave, the terror of the voyage, the depression of captivity, and the un-known that they faced, these conditions took the lives of thousands who simply gave up the struggle to survive. Diseases, such as dysentery, measles, small-pox, and scurvy, claimed thousands more. Violence, such as brutal treatment, mutinies, and slave rebellions, added to the death rate. Confinement on a vessel of an average length of 65 feet, and an average width of 20 feet, left slaves with only a space of about 18 inches by 5 feet. Sailing for two to three months with only the food and water taken aboard for the trip restricted the calories and liquids ingested. Despite the horrors of these conditions, recent scholarship has estimated the num-bers of slaves that died proved relatively minor to be from 4.1 to 10.4 percent with 23.4 percent being considered a disaster. In contrast, more slaves died on the way to the coast then on the Atlantic voyage due to the difficulty, dangers, and vigilant brutality of their capturers (who could kidnap replacements) when compared to merchant captains (whose supply of slaves depended on a limited cargo) eager to get their commodity to market. Nonetheless, to discuss the selling humans in these terms (i.e., the number of people who reached the slave market) is to forget that each victim was an individual who had been thoroughly depersonalized by the entire process.

James A. Rawley, *The Trans-Atlantic Slave Trade* **(New York: W. W. Norton & Company, 1981), p. 278–306.**

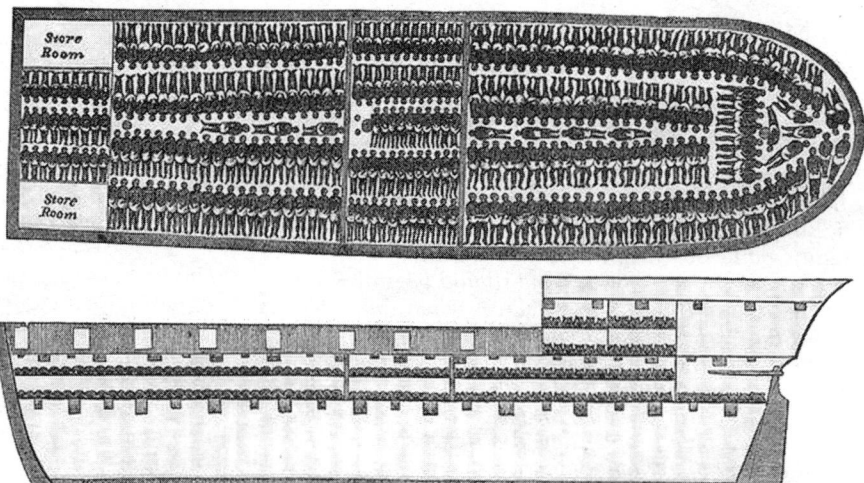

Decks of a Slave Ship. Manuscripts, Archives and Rare Books Division, Schomburg Center for Research in Black Culture, The New York Public Library, Astor, Lenox and Tilden Foundations.

a groundswell of moral revulsion against slavery and the opportunistic and compromised behaviors of rulers prompted Muslim merchants and imams to join with mainly Fulani pastoral nomads against slaving. They formed a community based on a purer form of Islam. The immediate consequences, ironically, were war and increased slaving. Outside Africa, the British slaver John Newton could stand the trade no longer, and in 1752 he became a minister and composed his great prayer of forgiveness, "Amazing Grace."

The Sale of Slaves

The North, East, South, and Central portions of Africa had participated in the world slave trade long before the arrival of the Europeans. While these regions continued as part of the slave system, now West Africa fueled the slave trade of the Atlantic world, Africa, Europe, North and South America, and the Caribbean. In North Africa, Moroccan traders were busy with ventures into the Songhai Empire, but were opposed by Tuareg Saharan nomads. Sultan Mulay Ismail of the Ottoman Empire (1672–1727) stands out as a cosmopolitan ruler respected and involved within the European firearms trade. His prosperity rested on agriculture and commerce and a huge army staffed in part with Sudanese slaves. In the Chad Kanem–Borno area, Idris Aloma (1542–1619) similarly relied on military and slave troops and welcomed European firearms in exchange for humans.

Westerners still could not penetrate the interior of Africa, where the culture remained tribal and animistic, either pastoral or agricultural. There, fewer people made each person more valuable as a potential commodity. Hence, intra-African slavery proved profitable.

In West Africa after 1460, the Portuguese initially sought to dominate the gold exchange in Africa and ultimately all the gold sources. Soon, however, human cargo joined gold exports. As a result, the West African coast bore two new names: the Gold Coast and the Slave Coast. Thirty-seven percent of all the humans sold in the occidental slave trade between 1460 and 1871 ended up in the hands of Portuguese slavers.

In East Africa, the Portuguese began a quest for gold as well. Yet whenever diplomacy and alliances failed to produce the results they required, the Portuguese took to attacking settlements all along the East African seaboard, anchoring their power in military forts and a navy that constantly prowled the Red Sea. They then sold the prisoners they had taken in these ventures as property. For two centuries after 1500, the Portuguese manipulated African slavery politics to their advantage, eventually taking over huge tracts of land along the Zambezi River on which to base their native raiders and slave armies who hunted other human victims as well as elephants for ivory. Despite the destruction, a vividly dynamic Swahili culture managed to survive.

The Portuguese made their presence known in South Africa as well, but were far less interested in the native hunter-gatherers of the San culture, or the pastoral peoples of the Khoikhoi, Nguni, or Sotho. Doubtless the absence of known gold sources in the area contributed to their disinterest. Some trading went on at Table Bay to replenish ship galleys with fresh food in return for the usual tobacco, beads, and metals, yet humans were not sold in significant numbers.

Just before 1600, Dutch sailors and soldiers decided to set up small farms using hired and slave labor in South Africa. Enterprising Dutch merchants soon followed. By 1800, around Capetown 21,000 English, Dutch, and Portuguese were engaged in business and small manufacturing, overseeing some 25,000 slaves. At the same time, Boer (Dutch colonists who became farmers and ranchers) homesteads began to encroach on San and Khoikhoi lands. Inevitably, conflicts broke out. Well-armed and defiant, the Boers usually triumphed, absorbing conquered Africans into a slave class called "the Cape coloureds." By 1800 the British also had gently insinuated themselves into the Cape as wine and wool merchants, often siding with the native Africans against the Dutch Boer cattle ranchers.

The British parliament abolished the slave trade for Britain in 1807. The Enlightenment (1690–1789), with its new values of individual rights and compassion and self-determination, played a role in this process. So did the Industrial Revolution (1750–1850), which valued a free and mobile labor market as well as the ability to exchange British manufactured goods for raw materials in places like Africa. Finally, a decline in plantation economies in the Western Hemisphere and the rising cost of slave labor made extracting humans from Africa increasingly unattractive. The British ban did not suddenly curtail slavery but managed to change its nature. Many slaves, especially women, were allowed to stay where they currently were and remained de facto dependents. From 1810 to 1820, the number of child slaves increased to as much as 50 percent per shipload; they ended up in Brazil or Cuba despite the unitlateral British effort to block the trade using naval patrols off the slave coasts and the seizure of hundreds of ships at sea. Over 160,000 freed slaves found new homes in Sierra Leone and Liberia. The British created Sierra Leone in 1787 as a sanctuary for escaped slaves from North America, Africans freed by the British navy, and the black poor of London; Liberia emerged in 1822 as a colony for freed blacks from the United States.

In time, the African market turned from slaves to agricultural exports needed in response to Europe's industrial boom. Following Britain's example, the rest of Europe finally concluded that labor left in Africa produced desired raw materials and made good customers. Hence, trade with African commercial farms developed for such commodities as palm oil for soap, candles, rubber, wax, coffee, and ivory. In the end, good business reasoning combined with humanitarian sentiments as the power of the new political weapon, public opinion, turned against the slave trade.

Consequences of the Atlantic Slave System

Overall, trans-Atlantic slavery had a profound but widely varying effect on African societies. Certainly the occidental slave trade gave a new impetus to the exceptionally brutal exploitation of the weak, while the capture of numerous humans disturbed regional demographic patterns and their associated social and economic development. The occidental slave trade profited the modernizing European states, but it crippled West Africa in particular through the Commercial Revolution. The pattern of exchange that developed began when slaves were sent to the Americas and Caribbean to work plantations that produced the bulk of raw commodities such as sugar, bananas, molasses, tobacco, and coffee. These were then shipped to Europe's urban centers for consumption and exchanged for finished products. At the same time, an abundance of firearms traveled to Africa to sell to kingdoms like Dahomey to be used in the capture of more slaves to feed the demand for labor in the Western Hemisphere. All this stimulated European commercial capitalism at the expense of African potential productivity.

Another result of the Atlantic System was the loss of an estimated 15–21 million men and women, 12–13 million of whom reached the Western Hemisphere with between 4–8 million perishing en route. Simultaneously, as slaves traveled across the Atlantic, the demand for humans in the oriental and internal slave trade increased as well: an estimated 20 million persons disappeared into these two markets. Thus, the human productive potential of Africa seems to have been greatly reduced, and the family systems turned upside down. At the same time, however, the introduction of new high-calorie foods like potatoes and corn, as well as ideas imported from overseas, were extending the life spans and raising fertility rates among Africans who escaped the slave trade. Hence, human numbers actually increased in Africa as people sold into slavery left the continent. Thus, while the net effect in loss of humans may have been less than originally calculated, the relative loss remains a question.

The growth of population in Africa mentioned above hides the fact that a relative study of human numbers would reveal a loss of people when compared to the rest of the world. Everywhere in the world, populations grew. Even in the Americas, the number of people increased yearly thanks to migrations, very high reproductive rates, and the gradual development of native resistance to foreign diseases. Yet Africa's position relative to other regional studies of population reveals that Africans lost significant ground because of the slave trade.

In 1600, the number of Africans approached approximately three for every seven people living in Europe, the Middle East, and the Americas. Yet by 1900, this ratio had fallen to a little more than one African for every nine people found in Europe, the Middle East, and the Americas. Keeping in mind that these figures are only estimates, Africa lost relative position in terms of human numbers in the world. Therefore, not only did Africa lose an enormous number of people, but this vast continent also lost relative human productive potential.

How could the number of people in Africa increase during the slave trade? When considered as an absolute number, the impact of the slave trade on Africa's population is masked by the fact that despite this loss of human beings, the number of people in Africa grew between 1600 and 1900: in 1600 approximately 50 million lived in Africa; in 1900, 70 million. This growth rate can be explained in a number of ways. First, the number of slaves exported annually from the most active region in the occidental slave trade, Dahomey, ranged from as high as 3.77 percent to as low as .01 percent of the total local population. Second, European demand selected men as slaves in far greater numbers than women. Third, marriage practices changed in Africa wherever females outnumbered males, so that men with more than one wife could maintain birth rates despite the loss of people. Finally, new foods imported from the Americas supported the lives of infants born into these new polygamous families found in Africa.

If one were to analyze the impact of selling humans from Dahomey, for example, one would see how the occidental slave trade operated. Dahomey comprised five lineages (Africa's way of organizing kinship): the Aja, Yoruba, Voltaic, Nupe, and Hausa. Each exported slaves throughout the 229 years between 1640 and 1869. Together these five lineages sold 20 percent of all the slaves exported in the occidental slave trade. Figures for these exports show numbers that range from as high as 70,000 to 150,000 per decade between 1690 and 1850. This steady stream of people leaving Africa totaled nearly 2 million, or one-fifth the total volume of slaves sent to the Western Hemisphere during this 160-year period. Yet since exports varied from 3.77 percent to .01 percent per year, and the average birth rate fell between 2.5 and 3.5 percent, during many of the decades between 1640 and 1869, human numbers increased. Hence Africa's total population grew.

Beyond the horrors of slavery, however, the impact of the slave trade represented lost human potential. Africans taken to the Americas as a source of labor came to equal half the number of Europeans who lived in the Western Hemisphere by 1820: 6 million Africans to 12 million Europeans. Yet only 2 million Europeans had migrated to the New World where their natural fecundity in a friendly, temperate environment generated a population six times larger. In contrast, 12 million enslaved African arrivals produced a population of only 6 million in the same time. Hence, death had destroyed far more Africans than their human fertility could replace.

Since for every two Africans transported to the Western Hemisphere, only one new person was added to the population by 1820, this figure indicates that the conditions of labor were destructive to human potential. This observation is especially true when compared to European fertility. For every single European transported to the New World, six new people joined American communities. The fact that European numbers increased so dramatically suggests the degree of difference in the standards of living for both populations. Finally, the survival of so many European offspring also reveals the absence of any major American epidemic to claim young babies—the most vulnerable population in a new environment.

Of the entire number of slaves who arrived in the Western Hemisphere, 4.19 million, or 37 percent landed in Brazil. This means that the Portuguese purchased the greatest number of slaves and had the worst record among Europeans in their treatment of Africans. The best record belongs to the British Americans in Virginia and the Carolinas. Concentrated in these southern colonies, slaves represented 12 percent of the number of Africans sent to Brazil, or .5 million. Yet these slaves became one of the only populations in world history that reproduced more people than their British masters added by importation.

Reasons given for the different reproductive rates of slaves in Virginia, the Carolinas, and Brazil reflect the different purchasing power of these two colonial systems, as well as the gender of the Africans sold. Brazil and the Caribbean Islands exported sugar and imported the largest number of slaves. They preferred to buy young, strong males and generated a population profile with too few females to sustain families or reproduce offspring. British America exported tobacco and rice, could not afford to buy the more expensive slaves sent to the sugar plantations, and, instead, imported a more balanced ratio of males to females. Thus, Virginia and the Carolinas accidentally created a population profile that could form families and reproduce.

The role that the African American family played in sustaining the will for slaves to survive in sometimes horrendous conditions is incalculable. One can only say that slaves in Virginia and the Carolinas were among the few bonded populations in the story of slavery that increased their numbers through natural reproduction. Thus, the presence of family life must have eased the pain of slavery in British America, while its absence in Brazil demoralized the Africans sent there.

The value of slaves to the Commercial Revolution cannot be accurately measured because of the destructive nature of this form of labor. Perhaps more potential was lost than wealth produced. Yet without slave labor, the vast profits of the Western Hemisphere could not have been added to the rewards gained from early modern commercial capitalism. When compared to the meager number of Europeans who migrated to the Western Hemisphere, the value of the work done by 12 million African bondservants is incalculable. If slaves had not replaced the mere 225,000 indentured servants sent from British America between 1650 and 1780, then the great commercial system that fueled England's economic successes could never have developed.

Confounding further the value of African labor is the role that these slaves played in the sugar trade. Sugar exported from Jamaica, Barbados, and St. Kitts generated more profits for Great Britain between 1700 and 1800 than the combined trade of India and China, £162 million in profits as compared to £104 million. The extra £58 million produced by three small islands in the Caribbean reveals the value of sugar when contrasted with the vast wealth one should have expected to see from an area the size of Asia. Yet the extra money introduced into Britain's commercial system by Caribbean plantations explains why sugar was king between 1700 and 1810. At the same time, one has to keep in mind that since Great Britain became the leading economic power during the Commercial Revolution, and since industrialization began on the British Isles, the role that sugar played in financing both revolutions suggests the value of African labor.

When calculating the value of slave labor in the Western Hemisphere, one must also consider the consequences of extracting so many people from Africa. Not only did the population of that continent fall from 30 percent to 10 percent of Europe, the Middle East, and the Americas between 1600 and 1900, but also Africans became dependent on European trade. Keeping in mind that commerce itself traditionally defined African politics, the economic links forged between European merchants and African middlemen rewarded those native kings willing to sell human beings for the muskets they needed to increase their power. At the same time, any African culture that did not become involved in the slave trade usually became its victim. Hence, the market conditions that developed between Europe and Africa ultimately eroded economic and social potential south of the Sahara. Thus, as many African economies grew dependent on European goods, the native monarchs who gained political power from the slave trade paid for their successes by exporting potential labor.

Such political, economic, and social dependency meant that European demand would ultimately dictate Africa's financial future. European demand, therefore, would shape the way African societies organized the labor that remained after the slave trade. This organization would cater to Africa's principal customers in such a way as to restructure the numerous civilizations located there. Thus, Africa would become open to financial encroachment as effectively as if Europeans had invaded the continent. Hence, Africa must join the Americas as one of three continents profoundly changed by the Commercial Revolution.

Therefore the Commercial Revolution reshaped more than one continent before the start of the Industrial Revolution. Thus, when these years of economic change had passed, Europe's human numbers were growing relatively faster than that of any other part of the world. At the same time, Europeans developed the greatest economic potential for the future when compared to other non-European cultures. As a step in this process, 50 to 90 percent of the Native American people living in the Western Hemisphere before 1492 died because of contact with European diseases. At the same time, the population of Africa had fallen from 30 percent to 10 percent of that of Europe, the Middle East, and the Americas combined. Hence, a new global market generated enough wealth to forecast the future: Europe was on the rise.

Meanwhile, each society found in Europe, the Americas, and Africa that had met one another between 1492 and 1763, had joined a process that defined human relations during the early modern era. Europe's prosperity and economic growth suggested to the Europeans themselves that they were "superior" to those with whom they did business. Reinforced by their Christian, and later scientific perceptions, of the world, Europeans had defined all other cultures besides their own as "inferior." Thus, Europeans developed a set of terms to describe the people they met on their voyages of discovery, including "pagan," "heathen," "savage," "black," "red," "yellow," and "primitive" to name a few. Europeans' sense of superiority did not bode well for the future. What occurred in general was that as European states waxed in power, so did their determination to reshape the global economy.

Taken together, Europe, the Americas, and Africa participated in a complex process called the "Commercial Revolution." This name, however, describes the rewards won by Europe, while ignoring the devastation experienced by other cultures. The disproportionate consequences of economic change occurring between 1400 and 1750 reveals the complexity of economic events when seen from more than one perspective.

Suggested Reading

Bethel, Leslie, ed., *The Cambridge History of Latin America,* Vol. II (Cambridge: Cambridge University Press, 1984).

Burns, E.B., *Latin America,* 7th ed. (Upper Saddle River, N.J.: Prentice-Hall, 2002).

Calloway, Colin G., *First Peoples: A Documentary Survey of American Indian History* (Boston: Bedford-St. Martin's Press, 2004).

Chambers, J. D., and G. E. Mingay, *The Agricultural Revolution* (London: Batsford, 1966).

Clarkson, L. A., *Proto-Industrialization: The First Phase of Industrialization?* (London: Macmillan, 1985).

Cook, Noble David, *Born to Die: Disease and the New World Conquest, 1492–1650* (New York: Cambridge University Press, 1999).

Crosby, Alfred W., *Ecological Imperialism: The Biological Expansion of Europe, 900–1900* (Cambridge: Cambridge University Press, 1986).

———, *The Columbian Exchange: Biological and Cultural Consequences of 1492* (Westport, Conn.: Greenwood Publishing Group, Inc., 1987).

Curtin, Philip D., *The Atlantic Slave Trade* (Madison: University of Wisconsin Press, 1969).

Diamond, Jared, *Guns, Germs, and Steel: The Fate of Human Societies* (New York: Norton, 1999).

Gauci, Perry, *The Overseas Merchant in State and Society, 1660–1720* (Oxford: Oxford University Press, 2001).

Hassig, Ross, *Mexico and the Spanish Conquest* (London: Longman, 1994).

Iliffe, John, *Africans: The History of a Continent* (New York: Cambridge University Press, 1995).

Inikori, Joseph and Engerman, Stanley, eds., *The Atlantic Slave Trade* (Durham, N.C.: Duke University Press, 1992).

Leon-Portillo, Miguel, *The Broken Spears* (Boston: Beacon Press, 1972).

Lovejoy, Paul, *Transformation of Slavery: A History of Slavery in Africa* (New York: Cambridge University Press, 1983).

Manning, Patrick, *Slavery and African Life: Occidental, Oriental, and African Slave Trades, African Studies,* No. 67 (New York: Cambridge University Press, 1990).

Manning, Patrick, *Slavery, Colonization, and Economic Growth in Dahomey, 1640–1960, African Studies* No. 30 (New York: Cambridge University Press, 1990).

McCusker, John J, *Essays in the Economic History of the Atlantic World* (London and New York: Routledge, 1997).

McNeill, William H., *Plagues and People* (New York: Anchor Press, 1976).

Phillips, William D., Jr., *Slavery from Roman Times to the early Transatlantic Trade* (Minneapolis: University of Minnesota Press, 1985).

Plumb, J. H., *England in the Eighteenth Century, 1714–1815* (Baltimore: Penguin Books, 1965).

Pomeranz, Kenneth and Steven Topik, *The World that Trade Created: Society, Culture, and the World Economy, 1400 to the Present* (Armonk, N.Y.: M. E. Sharpe, 1999).

Rawley, James A., *The Trans-Atlantic Slave Trade* (New York: W. W. Norton, 1981).

Restall, Matthew, *Seven Myths of the Spanish Conquest* (New York: Oxford University Press).

Ringrose, David R., *Expansion and Global Interaction, 1200–1700* (New York: Longman, 2001).

Thorton, John, *Africa and the Africans in the Making of the Atlantic World, 1400–1680,* Second Edition (New York: Cambridge University Press, 1998).

Toussaint-Samat, Maguelonne, *The History of Food* (Oxford, England: The Blackwell Publishers, Inc., 2000).

Tracy, James D., *The Rise of the Merchant Empires: Long Distance Trade in the Early Modern World, 1350–1750* (Cambridge: Cambridge University Press, 1993).

Wrigley, E. A., *Continuity, Chance, and Change* (Cambridge: Cambridge University Press, 1988)).

XVIII

THE MAKING
OF THE MODERN INTELLECT,
PART ONE:
The Renaissance and Reformation

Europe entered the modern age as the result of a momentous process of change, as several key institutions of this integrated culture mutated simultaneously and released medieval Europeans from their traditional past. Consequently, economic, social, intellectual, political, and diplomatic events merged in a new set of human practices that no longer relied on ancient or medieval standards of conduct.

At the heart of this change lay four intellectual movements: the Renaissance (1300–1600) and the Reformation (1517–1648), discussed in this chapter, and the Scientific Revolution (1543–1687) and the Enlightenment (1690–1789), discussed in the next chapter. Each movement embraced a range of conceptual possibilities that compelled European thinkers to first question, and then reject, their immediate past in order to find new solutions to the specific problems facing their world. Ironically, the condition of change, as embedded in the various conclusions offered by the Renaissance, Reformation, Scientific Revolution, and Enlightenment, became a desirable state in itself. As encountered in European thought, the condition of change itself became the hallmark of the new age.

The Renaissance began the process of change when fourteenth-, fifteenth-, and sixteenth-century European thinkers rejected the Christian norms of their era and reached back into a pagan past for solutions to contemporary problems. The standards of thought they recovered through their resurrection of a Greco-Roman worldview set in motion a critique of the Roman Catholic Church that fuelled an independent assault on the papacy called the Reformation. Next, the shattering of the Catholic orthodoxy opened up the intellectual space needed for Europe's scientists to contemplate a universe ruled by laws independent of a knowable God. Then again, the substitution of natural laws in place of the Divine Will during the Scientific Revolution undercut the body of texts that constituted the basis of knowledge itself and set in motion a complete redefinition of philosophy through a movement called the Enlightenment. Each step in this process followed a path

of change that slowly but surely substituted the human mind for the Divine Will.

This modern worldview came into its own during the Enlightenment, the movement that released Europeans from their traditional past by substituting the human capacity to create an ideal, rational society as an independent act of will separate from that of a knowable God. This occurred with the creation of the concept of culture, the capacity for humanity to create its own world as an expression of art. In addition, the idea of culture released Europeans to construct a new image of society based on the idea of justified, rational behavior supported by public opinion. Finally, culture liberated Europeans to presume that they were the masters of their own destiny, eager to embrace an unknown future, and willing to ask the questions that would lead to an ever better lifestyle. Hence, the Enlightenment represents the last step in the process that made change tolerable, even desirable, to Europeans in general.

The Renaissance

As mentioned in Chapter Fourteen, the Renaissance began in Italy as an expression of an urban culture based on incorporeal property, wealth without "legal body," or legitimate existence. A product of the fourteenth and fifteenth centuries, the Renaissance reflected the antifeudal standards of conduct that pitted money and goods as incorporeal property against Real Estate and caused the network cities of Italy to oppose the legalized "state and status" that land bestowed on its owners. Living in a city in medieval Europe placed a person outside the boundaries of traditional behavior because the unsanctioned existence of money and goods forced people to create new ways of making a living. Hence, cities everywhere, but especially in Italy (due to their fabulous wealth based on their command of the medieval trade routes), developed methods of defending themselves against the legitimate power of men of estate that included such extremes as importing weapons from abroad. New weapons like the crossbow and gunpowder from China gave Italian cities political independence, while other European urban centers used the legal strategy of forming corporations under the protection of kings to ensure against assaults by feudal lords on incorporeal property.

Thus, success in a city created a thirst for invention that made people wealthy, elevated their status, and placed them in a new patrician class that lived outside medieval tradition. And along with illegitimate income came an appetite for refinement that represented the merits of each person's accomplishments, symbols of their climb to the top of an urban society and reflections of their personal attributes. Accordingly, as individuals distinguished themselves in business, so they became patrons of the arts in order to show off their status and leave their personal mark on local urban history. Hence, the most successful risk-takers in commercial and manufacturing enterprises set aside a portion of their wealth to pay for intellectual inquiries, the development of aesthetic tastes, and the adornment of their cities. As a result, Italian cities in particular became centerplaces for cultural refinement in a manner that went well beyond the limits of medieval tradition.

Italian cities became the focal point for Renaissance energy because local merchants and manufacturers earned the greatest amount of incorporeal wealth, cherished regional memories of Italy's role in the Roman Empire, and cultivated the strongest sense of civic pride in feudal Europe. As the entrepôts of the medieval trade routes, the merchants of these Italian cities perfected networks of commerce that had allowed theirs to become the wealthiest towns in medieval Europe. In fact, as mentioned above, their income grew to the point where they could achieve political independence from the Holy Roman Empire on the strength of their role in global trade and the military power that their wealth purchased for them. As a result, Italian city-states developed a sense of community that set them apart, not only from one another but from the rest of medieval Europe.

The people of Venice, Genoa, Florence, Pisa, and even Papal Rome remembered well the glories of the Roman Empire. Now these cities were independent of one another, and each one launched its own personal history based on the same urban skills that made ancient Rome so powerful. Thus, each Italian city-state understood that by developing the ability to use all the personal talents praised by Greek and Roman philosophers, they could exploit the means needed to succeed in business and survive in medieval politics.

Finally, the role of civic pride in the Italian Renaissance complemented each city's fascination with ancient learning because all the independent urban centers on the peninsula had developed a very strong sense of self that set them apart from the medieval world. Fuelling this sense of self were the skills and knowledge that ancient Greek and Roman texts had to offer. These skills and knowledge mixed with the daily problems that every independent city faced in order to survive in a culture that excluded urban wealth from traditional legitimacy. Hence, independent Italian city-states combined their sense of civic pride with their memory of the ancient past and recently unearthed Greek and Roman texts to create a volatile mix, one that launched a new age of inquiry.

Perhaps the most prolific Italian city-state was Florence, which long had thrived on the trade routes between Rome and the rich commercial cities to the north. Unlike Venice and Genoa who boasted the wealthiest maritime economies in Europe, or Rome, which had a collection of classical monuments that no one else could match, Florence manufactured woolen goods for export and lent money to the kings and popes of Europe. Strategically located, Florence represented a valuable asset to any local lord eager to expand his holdings. One such family, the Visconti of Milan, coveted Florence and wished to add it to their powerful Duchy. In opposition to attempted takeovers, Florentine citizens developed a sharp sense of self-preservation that made them particularly curious about ancient Greek and Roman texts. In these books, they came across political, historical, and philosophical materials that brought into focus the answer to the question: how does a city-state survive when surrounded by enemies? Accordingly, writers and artists flocked to Florence to provide instruction in these texts so that Florentines could best address this question. Hence, Florence became the most productive intellectual center during the Italian Renaissance.

Based on the work initiated by Francisco Petrarch (1304–74), Florentine intellectuals dominated the Italian Renaissance. Raised in Florence, but also educated in France, Petrarch himself started out to be a lawyer. At first he sought employment from the papacy in Avignon, but ultimately became a writer, creating a career for himself as a literary figure. In fact, his work became so popular that he could actually make a living based on the reputation he had earned from his writings. These included biographies, imagined correspondence with ancient heroes, love sonnets, epic poems, and a revival of Latin that breathed new life into this dead language. In the process, he generated a new image of time, changed the value of how people saw the past, and became famous enough to attract several patrons and live where he pleased.

According to Petrarch, the medieval era was a "Dark Age" brought on by the conquest of civilization as the result of barbarian invasions. What had been lost was an "Age of Light" to which Petrarch now devoted his life to resurrecting. The consequence of his efforts was the creation of a new set of standards by which people could judge the quality of literature. If a text matched the depth of thought and elegance found in ancient works, it was worthy of the highest respect; if on the other hand, a work represented the recent labors of medieval scholars, it was only worthy of contempt. Accordingly, Petrarch defined the new standards of literature for others to imitate.

Petrarch's friend, literary associate, and pupil, Giovanni Boccaccio (1313–75), followed his lead. Born in Paris but raised on a farm outside Florence and living as a traveler much of his life, Boccaccio is most famous for a secular work entitled the *Decameron*, which comprises a series of bawdy stories. Combining tales from classical, medieval, and Arabic sources, these stories focus solely on human foibles rather than serving as a moral commentary on how people should act. At the same time, the personalities represented in these tales came from all walks of life, high and low, religious and secular, in which anyone could be a sinner or a villain. Indeed, in this book, pillars of the church who should have been regarded as moral guides for the laity appeared no better than the worst of the secular scoundrels.

Both Petrarch and Boccaccio represented the first generation of Renaissance scholarship. The next generation, from 1375 to 1450, shifted the focus of classical inquiry from literature to civic and political issues. This generation combined the works of two Florentine scholars, Coluccio Salutati (1331–1406) and Leonardo Bruni (1361–1444), who asserted that learning was a tool that could be used to improve the conditions of life within the city. These two men argued that such urban skills as literacy, rhetoric, and critical thinking served a common civic end, and that the study of history, philosophy, and politics could elevate the quality of life for everyone. In order to produce the best results, the leaders of a great city merely had to apply the lessons of the classical past to the present. Hence, the classical past offered a boundless collection of tools that could be used to resurrect the *vita activa*, the philosophical, historical, and active life, instead of wasting energy on the medieval pursuit of the *vita contemplativa*, the monastic or contemplative life.

In the third generation of the Italian Renaissance, the rapid recovery of Greek manuscripts and contact with Greek scholars from the Byzantine world elevated the study of the work of Plato to a status equal to that of

Renaissance Florence. Giovanni Boccaccio (1313–75), Italian poet and Humanist lectures on Dante in the church of Santo Stefano in Florence. Painting by Stefano Ussi (1822–1901). Florence, University, Istituto di Storia della letteratura italiana. Photo: akg-images / Rabatti - Domingie.

Aristotle. While Aristotle had dominated intellectual thought in the High Middle Ages, Plato came into his own during the Renaissance in Florence. Human studies based on Plato's work brought the spiritual and material world into very sharp focus. The result of this new interest was the creation of a Platonic Academy in Florence patronized by the Medici family.

Leading the study of Plato, Marsilio Ficino (1433–99) and Pico della Mirandola (1463–94) translated and interpreted all the works of Aristotle's teacher. Ficino began the process by making every Platonic dialogue available in Latin. Once he accomplished this task, Ficino then turned his attention to integrating his new understanding of Plato with the works of Plotinus and St. Augustine. Here he hoped to link Neo-Platonism with Christian theology and German mysticism to create a master synthesis of all Christian knowledge. In the end, he hoped to use Plato as a guide to find the one truth that united all aspects of knowledge about humanity, creation, and God.

This search for a conceptual unity between the new Platonic studies in Florence and the intellectual pillars of the Christian Church inspired Pico della Mirandola to discover all the links he could between the individual's religious yearnings and God. Convinced that there was an all-embracing unity between medieval scholasticism, Hebrew speculations on the nature of God, and Plato's insights into the world of form and matter, Pico consulted every ancient and medieval manuscript he could find. Adding Hebrew to his study of religion, Pico expanded Europe's understanding of the original written material on God by including a religious community that had gone largely ignored throughout the Middle Ages: the Jews. Pico's extensive study of the *Talmud* and cabalistic writings added a whole new dimension to the Renaissance image of God.

The result of Pico's labors concerning humanity's yearning to understand God helped bring into focus the concept of the individual. The individual represented a unique personality whose character comprised all the elemental forces found in the universe. These elemental forces included the power of the angels, the perfection of the Platonic forms, and the corruption of matter. Hence, all these elemental forces taken together made the individual a microcosm of everything around him. Accordingly, the individual was a composite of all the cosmic conditions. The individual also needed to fit him or herself firmly within the hierarchy of nature as dictated by Plato's Great Chain of Being (i.e., the scale of substances that stretched from pure transcendental form found in Heaven to finite and corrupt material existence located on Earth). Furthermore, given free will at birth, every individual had the capacity to strive to achieve moral perfection because within each person's makeup were all the resources that he or she needed to choose between good or evil. Finally, over the course of any one person's life, an individual could ascend into Heaven or descend into Hell. Hence, Pico had armed every Christian in Europe with the means to purify themselves and their church as independent agents endowed with a unique will and intellect, or become an agent of evil.

The fourth and final generation of Florentine Renaissance thinkers included two outstanding intellectuals: Niccoló Machiavelli (1469–1527) and Francesco Guicciardini (1483–1540). Machiavelli began his intellectual career when the failure of the republican form of government in Florence in 1512 inspired him to develop the political theories that made him famous. The circumstances that had led to the failure of the Republic of Florence, and Machiavelli's political speculations, emerged from Italian politics in the year 1494, when Charles VIII had led a French army into Italy to make good on his claim to the throne of Naples and Sicily and to dominate the political affairs of the peninsula. Piero de' Medici, who ruled Florence, had tried to save the city from French occupation by granting Charles territorial concessions. The Florentine people, however,

rose up in rebellion and expelled the Medici family; then the citizens of Florence restored a republican form of government from 1494 to 1512.

During these eighteen years, Florence careened from the religious passion of Girolamo Savonarola (1452–98), a Dominican monk, religious reformer, and spiritual ruler of Florence until his death as a heretic, to the unstable rule of the Council of Ten, Florentine politicians who tried to provide executive rule to the republic. In the midst of this republican experiment, Machiavelli served as a secretary and a diplomat to the council, traveling throughout Europe on city business. His career, however, came to a sudden end when the Medici family overthrew the Council of Ten and recaptured power. The result was that Machiavelli lost his job working for the city, suffered a brief period of torture and imprisonment, and then was exiled to a family estate. There he began his study of raw power and created political essays that spoke to the collapse of hope in the ethical ideals espoused by Marsilio Ficino and Pico della Mirandola. In their place, Machiavelli substituted a study of politics to explain how the uses of power, both moral and amoral, could realize a ruler's political goals.

Dedicating his work to his political enemy, Lorenzo de' Medici, Machiavelli had offered the family that had exiled him from Florence an explanation of how princes should rule their states. Making this dedication in the hopes of inspiring a powerful man to step forward and save Italy from foreign rule, Machiavelli had developed a complete study of princely conduct in order to instruct his reader in how to unify the peninsula. In the process of writing this study, however, Machiavelli had also created a new discipline called political science. This he did by explaining how a political innovator, a "new prince," captured, expanded, and managed power.

Written in 1513, and published posthumously in 1532, Machiavelli's *The Prince* described the world as it is. A short work of twenty-six chapters, a mere 15,000 words, *The Prince* has buried within its text two voices: one that spoke with the dispassion of science, and another that made an ardent appeal for action. The action to which Machiavelli appealed was for a hero to step forward and unify all the Italian principalities into a single state as powerful as France or England.

Read carefully, one notices that this ardent appeal was the central message of the book. Where Machiavelli called for action, the calm, single-minded use of cunning stripped politics of any moral content. Machiavelli argued that such a use of the rational mind produced the best political consequences regardless of the means employed.

Machiavelli used *Lo Stato* (the state) to mean *estate* in the medieval sense because he saw the prince as the only active political agent in the creation of a state. The state was an estate that belonged to him alone. The state itself was an object without will, a thing that was won or lost depending on the skills, courage, and cunning of the prince. Yet Machiavelli recommended a citizen army as an essential military tool to create and hold the state. A citizen army comprised active political personalities—citizens—who willingly fought for their own political destiny, as did the people in the city-states of ancient Greece and the republic of Rome.

To have a state filled with citizen-soldiers, and to use that state as a passive object in a prince's political career, required that this monarch trick his followers into accepting a submissive role as his subjects. The prince, however, had to be careful in his use of this trickery so that he did not lose the vitality of citizenship as the motivating force in his army. Such political manipulation justified the new amoral standards that made *The Prince* famous. A prince had to appear to be moral while never allowing ethics to restrict his political choices. In short any means that achieved a political end was legitimate.

The tension between the citizen army and the prince reflected the transitional state of politics in which Europe found itself on the eve of the modern era. Princes and kings appeared to be Christian, to follow tradition, and to justify their position by time-honored practices. Yet they were, in fact, agents of change. Machiavelli had accurately described the political scene of his day. He argued that the sole function of a prince was to make war, and that when the prince was not fighting a war he must use all his energy in preparation for the next conflict. In addition, Machiavelli had correctly assessed the pope's political future. Machiavelli had called the pope a political absurdity because he was an unarmed prince. A prince without an army was a monarch who soon lost his "estate," the state.

Like Machiavelli, Francesco Guicciardini reacted sharply to the French invasion of 1494, having witnessed firsthand the agony felt by Italians who opposed foreign rule when the Valois of France and the Habsburgs of the Holy Roman Empire, the Austrian Netherlands, and Spain used Italy as a battlefield between 1494 and 1559. Like Machiavelli, Guicciardini found himself compelled to abandon civic humanism in favor of developing a new phase of Renaissance historiography that depicted politics as an exercise of raw power. And like Machiavelli, Guicciardini helped to pioneer a new view of history that developed political rules from lessons extracted from the past.

Guicciardini's premier example of Renaissance history, the *History of Italy*, examined Florence in relation to the rest of Europe. The theme of this long work asked the question: can peace be restored to Florence and the other Italian city-states after the French Invasion? Guicciardini's answer derived from his analysis of the statesmen, states, and politics of Italy and Europe.

Fortuna (fortune) functioned in Guicciardini's history the same way as it did in *The Prince*. Human conduct was a balance between reasoned action and chance, with fortuna favoring the bold. Guicciardini argued that political leaders always had to be prepared to face fortune, not a goddess but an independent, unknowable, and powerful agency that gave shape to events. Therefore a politician had to face accidents in political and military affairs with courage, determination, and reason.

Since humanity could not foresee the consequences of fortuna, historical events would be different every time. History, therefore, did not "repeat itself" and could not be a "formal" model for events in the future. Consequently, the value of studying history had to be something other than a Platonic, spiritual, or religious guide. Instead, history had to serve as a rational explanation for why human decisions and actions gave shape to the events that they did. Hence, the historian was someone who linked cause and effect to the psychological strengths and weaknesses of policymakers; in other words, the historian was more concerned with the question of "why" something happened rather than "what" took place. In this way, Guicciardini added an amoral feature to the view of history that functioned in a similar fashion to the decision-making process of the "new prince" in Machiavelli's work.

Outside of Florence, the most outstanding Italian intellectual was Lorenzo Valla (1405–57). Valla's contribution to the Renaissance was his skill at textual analysis and his historical sense of language. Using Petrarch's model of time, in which the Middle Ages was an era of darkness and the classical epoch was one of light, Valla knew that the fall of Rome had both ended one historical period and started another. Since the medieval model of time used St. Augustine's *City of God* to assign darkness to the age that preceded Christ and light to anything that followed, authors of the Middle Ages did not see the fall of Rome as a shift in the historical epoch. Thus, medieval art and literature lumped together the events of Rome after Christ with the Middle Ages as if both belonged to the same era. Understanding this well, Valla was far more sensitive to historical and linguistic evidence than those who had come before him.

Turning his attention to the papal document, *Constitutum Constantini (The Donation of Constantine)*, Valla discovered a significant anachronism. The authors of *The Donation of Constantine*, an eighth-century church document, had used St. Augustine's "era of light" to see Emperor Constantine as a man of their own historical period. Hence, when the emperor supposedly invested the pope with vast temporal powers, Constantine had given the papacy a fief. Since Romans could not have known this later, feudal term, *The Donation of Constantine* had to have been written after the fall of the Western Roman Empire. Consequently, Valla concluded that *The Donation of Constantine* was a forgery created to invest the pope with powers that the bishop of Rome wanted to claim during the Early Middle Ages. Such sensitivity to the history of language proved very important not only because of the damage it did the papal office, but also in teaching others how to engage in accurate textual analysis.

Such historical and linguistic criticism served those less loyal than Valla to the church by teaching them how to review all religious documents and texts with a new sense of temporal accuracy. These men lived to the north of Italy and comprised a new branch of the Renaissance that shifted attention from secular issues to church reform. These men focused on Christian and classical documents to restore purity to the original message of Christ. Despite their individual differences, all of these northern European scholars believed that they could change society, and restore unity to the church, by applying the new learning to the sources of Christianity itself. Hence, they formed schools, studied ancient documents, and returned to the Bible to provide the most accurate text.

Chief among these northern intellectuals were Erasmus of Rotterdam (the Netherlands) and Sir Thomas More of England. Desiderius Erasmus (1466?–1536) was a cosmopolitan intellectual who optimistically devoted most of his life to restoring unity to Christendom. Erasmus exercised the greatest influence among the Christian Humanists working outside of Italy. While the Italians spoke to people's political souls, Erasmus appealed to the Christian spirit in humanity. Together, both voices released Europeans to think the unthinkable: that change was more desirable than repeating traditional behavior without question.

Interested in the past as a source for philosophical insights, Erasmus began his literary career compiling ancient quotations useful for educating the young. Published in 1500 in a work called *Adages*, these quotes won Erasmus instant fame and gave him a reputation as a scholar. Shortly thereafter, in 1501 Erasmus published an edition of Cicero's *De officiis (On Duty)* and began to study Greek. By 1506, Erasmus's translations of Euripides and Lucian appeared in print, as well as his first effort at enlightening the religious spirit, *The Handbook of the Christian Knight*. This latter work offered a brief manual on Christian ethics that showed how a gentleman might participate in the affairs of the world without losing his devotion to Christ.

While developing his Christian philosophy, Erasmus ran across a copy of Lorenzo Valla's *Notes on the New Testament* in the abbey library at Louvain; this discovery inspired his interest in the art of linguistic analysis. Publishing Valla's work in 1505, Erasmus turned his attention to translating the Bible based on the original Greek and Latin manuscripts that he had found in England. With the use of still more ancient texts sent to him from Switzerland, Erasmus completed a Greek edition of the New Testament in 1516, and a Latin version in 1519. Motivated by a belief that an unadulterated Bible would lead to a purification of Christian life, Erasmus unintentionally revealed weaknesses in St. Jerome's Vulgate. In his Greek and Latin versions of St. Jerome's work, Erasmus demonstrated that the official Roman Catholic biblical text had misplaced the Trinity in the Gospel according to John (I John V, 7–8). And since the Trinity had generated so much theological controversy in the third century, it could not have been part of a first-century Gospel because such a scriptural location would have eliminated these disputes. The implied criticism of the Vulgate through Erasmus's "improvements" on the text inspired many people eager for church reform to welcome his new Bible with praise. Indeed, after the Protestant rebellion, the Catholic Church placed Erasmus's Bible on its Index of Forbidden Books, for Martin Luther had used Erasmus's work to create his German version of the New Testament.

While in England, during which time he lived with Sir Thomas More, Erasmus completed the book that became his most widely read Renaissance text: *The*

Erasmus of Rotterdam exercised the greatest influence among the Christian Humanists working outside of Italy. While the Italians spoke to people's political souls, Erasmus appealed to the Christian spirit in humanity.

Praise of Folly, which focused on the ills of the day by revealing that human foibles were the source of all the problems facing Christendom. Representing Folly as a sweet-tempered woman with a rich sense of humor, Erasmus ironically demonstrated that human weaknesses should be praised rather than condemned because they motivated people to do the things that made society possible. Without folly, procreation would not occur. Without folly, governments and their supporting institutions would fall. Without folly, literature and art would not be produced. And without folly, the church would lose its following. Hence, in this work Erasmus used satire to force Europeans to face the truth about themselves: they had used the formal ceremonies of Christianity to appear to be Christian while, in fact, their hearts were truly invested in the vanities.

Like Erasmus, Sir Thomas More (1477–1535) had won fame before the Reformation, but also had suffered at the hands of the religious passions that the Renaissance had released. Erasmus could not keep up with the changes launched by the Reformation, which caused Catholics and Protestants alike to condemn him, and More fell from favor with his king. A lawyer by profession, More entered royal service in 1517 and became lord chancellor to Henry VIII in 1529. Trapped in the break between Henry and the papacy over the divorce of Catherine of Aragon, More could not swear loyalty to the Act of Supremacy that would officially make Henry the head of the Anglican Church. More was beheaded as a traitor in 1535.

More's greatest contribution to the northern Renaissance was his work *Utopia*, published in 1516, before the Reformation. Best seen in contrast with Machiavelli's *The Prince*, More's *Utopia* revealed just how far from their Christian anchor Europeans had drifted. Nearly developed in the same year as *The Prince*, More's *Utopia* also represented a significant break with the past. Yet while Machiavelli described royal conduct as it existed in 1513, More's work proposed a purely ethical approach to politics in 1516. Thus, *Utopia* complemented *The Prince* by speaking with the opposite voice on issues of morality and creating a dynamic tension between what is and what ought to be.

Following Plato's lead, in *Utopia* More described an ideal state where all citizens worked to meet their material needs, turned their surplus wealth over to the community, and generated so much abundance that poverty was unknown in the realm. The citizens of *Utopia* generated all this creative energy as an expression of an ethical commitment to share responsibilities because they were all members of the same society. Once every material need had been met, the citizens of *Utopia* used their leisure time to study the "good."

Living by standards far more Christian than those in any real European state, yet still pagan, *Utopia* stood as a model of how a state should function if it sincerely followed Christ's tenets. Such excellence of virtue signaled to Europeans everywhere that a need for reform existed. More proposed that Europeans reach back into their past to find the classical virtues that had previously guided their earlier Christian lives. Once they had rediscovered them, More suggested that Europeans could use these virtues as they had been intended and restore the concept of a "common" sense of justice found in the idea of the "community" itself. He also recommended that those who called themselves Christians reconstitute their covenant with God and live up to the code of conduct their name implied.

The stark contrast between the work of Machiavelli and More combined to show the direction in which the European imagination was headed. Both voices spoke of an institutional reality and the need for change. Machiavelli offered the means to power for anyone cunning enough to know the limits of his political reach, while More spoke to the need for reform to recover the justice buried within the heart of Christianity. Both signaled that the world of politics and religious faith were about to undergo profound change—and ultimately separate from one another. Thus, the world of politics would come to represent the world as it was, while Catholics and Protestants would begin a fight over the world as it ought to be.

The Reformation

The human studies of the Renaissance and the religious passion of the Reformation belonged to two entirely different intellectual impulses, but they linked through several common interests. The Renaissance writers prepared the way for the Reformation through their development of new linguistic and historical techniques, their interest in the Church Fathers and their study of Biblical texts. Furthermore, many Renaissance thinkers wanted to restore primitive Christianity in order to contrast their view of Christ's original church with the ornate institution of their day, and to condemn the secular impulses of the contemporary clergy. Finally, they demanded reforms for the current, highly organized ecclesiastical hierarchy and urged the church to return to the simplicity of the gospels by promoting a uniform morality and peace.

Although the vast majority of Renaissance thinkers believed in the elite authority of the clergy when compared to the laity, they also sought to narrow the gulf that separated the priest from his flock. Attracted to the beauty of Christ's Sermon on the Mount, these thinkers preferred the simple ethics of the Stoics to the elaborate ceremonies of the papacy. Their criticism of a corrupt priesthood filled with material desires rather than concern for human souls sent Renaissance intellectuals reaching into the classical past for ancient models of conduct to replace medieval standards. Their emphasis on the inwardness of faith rather than on the complex collection of sacred images, music, festivals, and sacraments that had grown into Europe's everyday religious life threw doubt on the power of the church. Hence, their simple view of Christianity laid a foundation for Martin Luther's and John Calvin's assaults on the sacraments and their common stress on faith.

Yet the Renaissance was predominately an intellectual movement that spoke to an elite group of thinkers rather than a mass religious campaign. As an intellectual movement, the Renaissance appealed to the mind and not the soul. Hence, it built upon a Christian philosophical tradition that made individual thinkers far more conservative than their Protestant contemporaries. Accordingly, most Renaissance intellectuals tried to remain aloof from the religious struggle that unfolded after 1517 because they preferred the life of ideas to the passionate creeds exposed by contending Christian communities. Finally, most of the Renaissance thinkers had no common formula for how to fix the Roman Catholic Church. Thus, they could not unite to create a positive consensus that might have restored Christ's simple message to Christendom. Consequently, the Reformation differed from the Renaissance because reform-minded Christians spoke with the voice of the inner spirit as it emerged from the religious impulses of Europe's mystics rather than appealing to the intellect in an effort to critique the church.

Christian mysticism developed out of the desire for salvation in the midst of death during the Late Middle Ages. As the Bubonic Plague, famine, and warfare filled Europeans with fear, Christian mysticism sought to bypass the complex ceremonies of a church deeply mired in the need for reform. Simultaneously, late medieval Christian mystics also wanted to replace the complex rituals of the Church with a life of piety that brought them closer to God and filled them with a sense of His Divine presence. As frustrated as were the Renaissance intellectuals with contemporary scholasticism and the ornate hierarchy of the church, these Christian mystics preferred a simple, practical, and intuitive faith instead of elaborate ceremonies or classical inquiries of the mind.

In Germany, Meister Johannes Eckhart (1260–1327) developed a speculative theology concerning God as the one true Being that permeated all life. Because

God was everywhere, Eckhart argued that His nearness to humanity could not be denied. Eckhart, therefore, preached that each Christian had to be humble and seek out the Divine spark in every human being. Eckhart's evangelical activities reached from the top of society to the bottom, and his various sermons and tracts soon raised suspicion in the church. Thus, when Eckhart won election as the Provincial of the Dominican Order in Germany, the pope did not confirm his new title. Finally accused of heresy near the end of his life, Eckhart traveled to Rome to appeal his case, but he died in 1327. After his death, pope John XXII upheld the charge of heresy and condemned several of Eckhart's doctrines. His disciples tried in vain to have the decree of heresy overturned. But Eckhart's theology continued to thrive in Germany despite the papal bull condemning it.

Several Dominican leaders, notably Johannes Tauler (1300–61) and Heinrich Suso (1295–1366) were pupils of Eckhart. Both developed a less abstract, more practical interpretation of Eckhart's doctrines. The result was the creation of a vision of God that Martin Luther later published, calling it *A German Theology* (1516). Their vision of Eckhart's message was for every Christian to abandon themselves completely to the Will of God until the soul became one with the Divine in Christ. Such an approach anticipated Luther's vision of faith as the means by which each individual Christian experienced God's grace.

In the Low Countries (present-day Holland and Belgium), Christian mysticism took a new form called "the modern devotion." Inspired by a Carthusian deacon named Gerard Groote (1340–84), the modern devotion condemned the clergy and laity alike for their abandonment of a truly religious life. In 1383, however, Groote's clerical enemies managed to impose a papal ban against his preaching, but before he was silenced he had established the Brothers of the Common Life, a semimonastic order of preachers who had not taken any irrevocable vocational vows that set them apart from the laity. Instead they were pious individuals who opened schools to teach the ethic found in the Sermon on the Mount. Cultivating the "inner life" of an individual in close touch with Jesus, members of this order gave care to the poor and instruction to the young. Some of their more famous students included both Thomas à Kempis and Desiderius Erasmus.

Thomas à Kempis (1380–1471) spent his entire adult life as a priest in the convent of St. Agnes near Zwolle, Holland. There, Kempis developed his masterwork, *The Imitation of Christ*. Thoroughly medieval in outlook, Kempis's *The Imitation of Christ* accepted traditional Roman Catholic dogma with complete devotion. Urging the use of the sacraments, stressing the importance of monastic orders, and advocating the quest for salvation through imitating Christ while still alive, Kempis stressed an individual's commitment to the Sermon on the Mount. What was original in Kempis's work was his insistence on personalizing religion. Thomas à Kempis minimized the importance of the formal aspects of worship and substituted a quest for peace within the soul, purity of thought, and simplicity of life. His faith was one of an "inward light" that became so important to Martin Luther later.

The groundwork laid by Christian mysticism for the development of an "inward light" was all-important to the eventual Protestant break with the papacy. The inner spirituality that was central to Meister Eckhart, Johannes Tauler, Heinrich Suso, Gerard Groote, and Thomas à Kempis also became critical to Martin Luther. This same inner spirituality that inspired men like Erasmus to write his satires on human folly and to condemn the scholastic approach to theology also undermined the church's emphasis on the formal aspects of contemporary Catholicism. Finally, the same inner spirituality that had proven to be the critical point of departure for Christian mystics, also became the central thesis for the Protestant rejection of good works (the sacraments) as the sole method of winning salvation for Roman Catholics. Hence, the development of Christian mysticism joined the intellectual assaults of the Renaissance on the medieval church as both prepared the way for Luther's Protestant Revolution.

Luther's rebellion against the Catholic doctrine of good works emerged from the fact that he was a troubled man who believed that he was unworthy of Divine grace so long as he tried to earn God's favor. Consequently, his efforts at good works left him with no sense of well-being. Furthermore, this feeling of worthlessness arose from the fact that anyone as sinful as Luther felt himself to be made him incapable of earning the merits needed to win salvation; this was true because every effort he made was unworthy of God's mercy. Hence, salvation based on the formal ceremonies of the church left Luther feeling he could never achieve righteousness.

The crux of Luther's misery was his conception of sin as measured against the purity of God. Despite his faithful use of the sacrament of penance, Luther felt that his own natural tendency to sin was so great that he could never achieve the appropriate state of submission needed to express his love for God. Hence, Luther's intense emotions, his impetuous temper, his strong will, and his powerful intellect set him so far apart from God that he could never overcome the wick-

Martin Luther (1483–1546), the controversial church reformer, initiated the Reformation and influenced many subsequent Protestant Reformers through his writings. Painting of Luther with Biretta, 1528, studio of Lucas Cranach the Elder (1472–1553). Oil on wood, from the Lutherhalle Collection. Photo: akg-images, London.

edness of pride and anger that riddled his soul. Thus, he came to fear that the harder he tried to earn his salvation, the less likely he would be to succeed.

Luther's confidence in humanity's ability to acquire the merit needed for salvation was profoundly weakened when he visited Rome in 1510. In the autumn of that year, he traveled to the Vatican from Erfurt in north central Germany on a mission to lead the opposition to the union of a group of monks called the "Observantines" with another group called the "Conventuals." Although this mission failed, the significance of the trip for Luther was that he witnessed firsthand just how secularized the papal curia had become. Rome at the time held a population of 40,000, was one of the centers of the Italian Renaissance, and obeyed the authority of the "warrior pope," Julius II. Such a large city, where religion had become a major economic enterprise, filled Luther with despair, for while Rome was the center of his religion, it had also become corrupt.

Meanwhile, when Luther returned to Erfurt in the spring of 1511, he found himself so much at odds with the majority of monks in his order over the union between the Observantines and Conventuals that he was happily transferred to the Augustinian monastery at Wittenburg. Once in Wittenburg, Luther became a subprior who preached to the monks while studying for his doctorate of theology at the university. This he earned in 1512, which allowed him to teach theology. At the same time, Luther began to preach in the City Church in 1514. Together, his studies and preaching allowed Luther to refine his doctrine of faith.

Luther's study of the New Testament in preparation for his lectures and sermons led him to St. Paul. In St. Paul's Romans, Luther discovered that he did not have to work to earn salvation. He also developed the belief that the doctrine of good works itself was "wrong." In his review of St. Paul's message, Luther had stumbled upon the passage called "The True Gates of Paradise," (Romans 1:17) which stated, "Man is justified by faith alone." Trained as a lawyer prior to becoming a monk, Luther interpreted the verb "justified" to mean "judged." Hence, Luther concluded that God judged humanity solely by the quality of each person's faith in Jesus.

Since Luther's own salvation was central to his being, this discovery created for him a mystical awakening. He experienced a form of rapture as he realized that humanity did not have to earn salvation. Rather, God granted entrance into Heaven through his infinite love for those who surrendered completely to His Will. Such surrender required absolute faith in God's infinite mercy.

Romans 1:17 cleansed Luther of his sense of worthlessness. This discovery released him from his awesome burden of sin and energized him to spread the word. Yet to discover salvation in faith alone meant that all humans were equally competent to achieve a state of grace without the direct intervention of a priest. Implicitly, therefore, Luther had challenged the entire structure of the Roman Catholic Church by undermining the sacrament of Holy Orders: the ceremony that granted a priest the sacred skills needed to administer the consecrated services of the church (the sacraments).

Luther's explicit challenge to Catholicism and the papacy began with his *Ninety-five Theses*, a tract that he nailed to the church door in Wittenburg on October 31, 1517. These *Ninety-five Theses* listed a series of arguments against the sale of indulgences. Indulgences were a device developed by the papacy to raise money. The pope and his subordinates sold the spiritual merits of the saints and Christ through indulgences to release sinners from the time that they presumably would have to spend in Purgatory prior to their entry into Heaven. Since most humans performed the sacraments out of fear of God, rather than the love they should have felt for His infinite generosity, whatever penance they performed never completely cleansed them of sin. Hence, few people could expect to enter Heaven directly upon death; instead most had to spend an extended amount of time in Purgatory. Accordingly, an indulgence could allow one to forego this wait in Purgatory by purchasing the surplus merits that the saints and Jesus Christ accumulated during their holy lives.

The *Ninety-five Theses* listed Luther's theological reasons for rejecting the sale of indulgences and would serve, he hoped, as a means to open a debate. Yet soon thereafter, Luther's challenge mushroomed into a general theological assault on the church doctrine of good works and its relationship to salvation. The implicit challenges in Luther's vision became explicit in the disputes that followed between 1517 and 1521. During these four years, Luther's theology matured into a major religious confrontation with the church that expanded the doctrine of faith to include questions about papal authority and the legitimacy of the sacraments. Simultaneously, Luther opened the door to reform so wide that even he could not control the pattern of changes that followed.

In 1519, at Leipzig in eastern Germany, Luther debated Johannes Eck and approached the position that papal declarations of infallibility were false. During the debates, Luther began to realize that there was an unbridgeable gap between himself and the Roman Catholic Church. Luther was better informed about Biblical matters, while Eck was a master of scholastic theology, canon law, and the church councils. Neither side could find common ground.

In 1520, Luther wrote three treatises that outlined his new theology. His first treatise, *The Address to the Christian Nobility of the German Nation*, appealed to the Holy Roman emperor, the German princes, the knights, and the imperial cities to cast off papal authority. Developing the idea of a "German Church," Luther declared that when the spiritual arm of an established government refused to reform itself, then the temporal arm had to intervene and find a remedy for the problem. This declaration freed the "German Church" from three papal claims. First, Luther rejected the papal assertion that the pope held supreme authority over all temporal governments. Then, Luther declared that the sole location of any religious "truth" was to be found in scripture. Finally, Luther denied the pope's claim that he held the exclusive right to summon a general church council.

In his second treatise, *On the Babylonian Captivity of the Church*, Luther rejected four of the Roman Catholic sacraments. He retained baptism, the Eucharist, and penance, but he abandoned the idea that good works transformed the spiritual makeup of the individual. Thus, Luther denied the Mass and transubstantiation (i.e., the physical union of the blood and flesh of Christ with the worshipper), reasserted the supremacy of scripture, and declared the independence of every individual's conscience. As a result, Luther held everyone responsible for his or her own sins as well as their quest for the faith that might lead to their salvation. Meanwhile, by rejecting the spiritual transformation that occurred during confirmation, marriage, extreme unction, and Holy Orders, he reduced these four sacraments to simple ceremonies. Consequently, Luther eliminated the sacramental passages of a Christian's life and the social and religious distinctions of the priesthood when he set forth his theory that every individual was his or her own minister. This "universal priesthood of humanity" empowered every Christian to take responsibility for their own salvation, which undermined the power of the papacy as well as the entire hierarchy of the Catholic Church.

The final treatise, *The Liberty of the Christian Man*, explained Luther's doctrine of faith. Ironically dedicated to pope Leo X, Luther insisted that humanity did not have the capacity to achieve salvation as a direct consequence of doing good works. Instead, a Christian was, in reality, a being as powerless as a worm trapped in the corruption of original sin. As a worm, each Christian was incapable of doing a sufficient number of good works to achieve salvation. Consequently, to believe in earning salvation through good works was to increase the distance between a Christian and salvation. Accordingly, only through faith in God's infinite mercy and Christ's supreme sacrifice on humanity's behalf could a Christian experience grace. Grace, in turn, transformed the soul and freed the individual Christian from the carnal knowledge and will that had stained everyone since Adam and Eve. Thus, faith alone, and the gift of grace it created, liberated the soul and made salvation possible.

While Luther wrote the last two treatises, Pope Leo X issued a bull, *Exsurge domine*, commanding Luther to recant or suffer excommunication. Instead of retracting his theological claims, Luther burned copies of *Exsurge domine* as well as canon law, denying the pope the power to judge him. The pope responded by issuing the bull of formal excommunication, *Decet Romanum ponticiem*, in January 1521. Finally, in April 1521, the Holy Roman Emperor Charles V ordered Luther to appear at the imperial Diet of Worms in southwestern Germany for a hearing to address the potential heresy of Luther's beliefs. Traveling under a safe conduct from Saxony, where Luther enjoyed the protection of Prince Frederick the Wise, one of seven electors in the Holy Roman Empire, Luther took the risk of experiencing the same betrayal that had taken the life of John Hus at the Council of Constance. While Luther was condemned for his beliefs at the Diet of Worms, Emperor Charles V still chose to honor the safe conduct that allowed Luther to leave alive. Fleeing to Saxony, Luther went into hiding among the many castles that Frederick the Wise owned. Now Luther's break with the Catholic Church was complete.

Luther's break with Rome, and his emphasis on faith over the sacraments, produced a collateral impact on language that reflected the new Protestant theology. Since faith occurred within the individual, and empowered everyone to take responsibility for his or her own salvation according to the principle of "the universal priesthood of humanity," then Latin no longer had the power to serve as the universal or sacred tongue of Christendom. Accordingly, part of Luther's reform movement was his development of a standardized German that served as a "national" vehicle to convey the new beliefs. Consequently, Luther began a lifelong project of systematizing the German of Saxony so that it could serve as the standard language of his faith. He translated Erasmus's Bible, wrote religious hymns, and developed a common German vocabulary to give the Protestant faith a means to communicate. As a result, Latin began a long slow death encouraged by events that took place in science and politics (see the sections on language below).

In the meantime, during the first decade of the Lutheran movement (1521–31), Protestant reform remained virtually confined to the Germanys and Switzerland. Outside the German principalities and the Swiss Cantons, the royal governments of France, Spain, Portugal, and England suppressed any expression of the new beliefs. But by 1534, a French clergyman named John Calvin (1509–64) launched the second generation of theological inquiry when he resigned his church offices in France and fled to the Swiss city of Basel. Basel had opened its doors to reform and also had supplied the pikemen, infantry armed with knight-killing spears, needed to defend those who sought refuge. Since the Swiss provided the best pikemen in Europe, Calvin was safe in Basel.

Calvin's arrival there placed him in an environment in which he could refine his *The Institutes of the Christian Religion*. Revised numerous times, this book generated such an orderly vision of the Protestant movement that Calvin's leadership in reform overshadowed that of Luther. Luther had the passion but lacked the systematic mind of Calvin; and Luther had pinned the future of his reform on the German princes. When he rejected any other pattern of social change by writing against the German peasants who rebelled in

1524–25, his religious movement became linked to the political success of the German princes in their struggle against the pope and the Holy Roman Emperor Charles V. Luther's stand on reform thus became associated with German issues and remained in the Germanys.

But in Switzerland Calvin had an opportunity to create a Christian utopia. In Geneva, where Calvin took up residence in 1536, he accepted the assignment to compose a public confession of the reformed faith, to generate a catechism and rules of liturgical worship, and to function as the city's chief minister (in 1537). Interrupted by opposition, his stay in Geneva ended in 1538, but his return in 1541 permitted him to complete his socioreligious experiment.

As a spiritual leader, Calvin's ecclesiastical ordinances became a model used throughout Europe and North America. Wherever his faith spread, local churches took on his formal design: ministers, teachers, elders, and deacons. Ministers preached the Word of God and administered the sacraments: Baptism and the Eucharist. Teachers instructed children and new converts to the "true faith" that governed the community they planned to join. Elders supervised and censored the congregation to ensure Christian purity. Finally, deacons cared for the poor and the sick. While Luther's gift for reform sprang from the charismatic passion of his mysticism, Calvin's orderly mind produced a solid church organization that diffused the new faith widely.

The new faith itself drew its perception of God from a synthesis Calvin created based on St. Augustine's *City of God* and *The Confessions*, certain scholastic theologians, the Christian Humanists, and Martin Luther. Developing a vision of God as the Absolute Sovereign of the Universe whose Will was completely inscrutable, Calvin concluded that humanity was worthless in the eyes of such majesty. Therefore, humanity could only be saved by the grace of God through the redemption made possible by Jesus's sacrifice on the cross. Divine law had been given to humanity as a means to reveal the utter helplessness of each individual because of original sin. Thus, Divine law served as a warning to all sinners that a life of absolute submission and complete discipline to God's Will served as the sole means of acquiring the grace needed for salvation. Good works as an expression of free will were meaningless in the presence of an all-powerful, sovereign Deity. Hence, grace, however, came as a gift from God, one that could not be earned no matter how hard the sinner might try.

Faith alone in God's infinite mercy served as the signal that perhaps the Supreme Lord of the universe had selected an individual for salvation. Belief in the Holy Spirit through the Word of God as found only in scripture meant that a person had to discover the hope that perhaps God may have selected him or her for the paradise of Heaven. This hope, and not the sacraments, served as the initial sign that God dwelled within a particular individual's heart. As this hope matured into faith, the "true" sacraments, Baptism and the Eucharist, served as an exercise that indicated a person's willingness to obey God's law. Thus, the Lord was present in Baptism and the Eucharist, but only in the spiritual rather than the physical sense. Consequently, like Luther, Calvin believed that transubstantiation did not occur.

Because of this emphasis on faith, Calvin completely rejected the sacramental character of confirmation, marriage, extreme unction, penance, and Holy Orders. Arguing that the belief in these "false" sacraments placed a sinful barrier between the worshipper and God, Calvin felt that those who attempted to use these practices to achieve salvation would suffer from the illusion that they could persuade God to choose them. Instead, humanity had to realize that it had no such power, that one's entrance into heaven was predestined.

Completed in 1535, when Calvin was only twenty-six years old, his new theology cited above was not fully refined until 1559, when he published the final edition of *The Institutes of the Christian Religion*. In that year, Calvin presented the doctrine of predestination that became the hallmark of his religious system. Virtually every other Protestant reformer had emphasized the majesty and power of God over the doctrine of free will, but none of them had actually taken an unwavering stand on the principle of God's Absolute Power.

For Calvin, predestination derived from the logical consequences of God's absolute authority over everyone and everything. As the eternal lawgiver who judged every event in the universe, God towered over human sin. Since humanity was completely worthless when compared to the purity of God, no one had the capacity to sway the Divine judgment that had already been made concerning an individual's destiny. Therefore, the "true" Christian could only be saved by the direct intervention of God. This occurred only if a person knew God, knew the nature of original sin, and knew the utter helplessness with which everyone must approach the Divine. Such complete knowledge could only come from an understanding of scripture.

Calvin maintained that human will and knowledge were the sources of all sin. Human will and knowledge were carnal since both derived from Adam's and Eve's violation of God's law. Human will and knowledge were alien to faith and salvation. Thus, like Luther, Calvin helped to drive a wedge between what humans could know and what they should believe. This wedge separated the impulses of the Reformation from the inquiries launched by the Renaissance. Simultaneously, the success of the Reformation broke the hold the pope had long held on orthodoxy and opened the intellectual space needed by those who did not agree with Calvin and Luther, that is that people were all powerless in God's eyes. Hence, the Reformation played a key role in liberating other Europeans to continue in the vein of thought initiated by the Renaissance.

This wedge driven between faith and knowledge became a central feature of the modern imagination. As Luther and Calvin's theologies subordinated human will and knowledge to faith and separated one from the other as a means to win salvation, those Europeans who accepted the tenets of the Renaissance sustained a life of the mind that opened up new avenues of inquiry. One of these avenues, science, further accelerated changes in the modern imagination because it followed an aloof intellectual path fuelled by its own discoveries. Unlike the reformed theologians, and very much like Machiavelli, Guicciardini, Erasmus, and More, the European scientists of the sixteenth and seventeenth centuries developed a vision of knowledge that they discovered in Renaissance literature and refined in Nominalism (see the beginning of Chapter Nineteen). Thus, the nature of human knowledge as advanced by the Renaissance had continued to follow a powerful intellectual impulse to perfect the human condition, while Calvin's vision of faith had declared humanity's helplessness before God. Ironically, as both faith and knowledge separated from one another during the Reformation and the Scientific Revolution, both also continued to serve as the means to liberate the individual from the authority of the pope. Hence, even as they began to separate, faith and knowledge reinforced one another and replaced an absolute orthodoxy controlled by the papacy, the former with individual acts of faith, and the latter with individual inquiries into the nature of reality.

Suggested Reading

The Renaissance

Burke, P., *Culture and Society in Renaissance Italy* (Princeton, N.J.: Princeton University Press, 1999).

Foucault, Michel, *The Order of Things: An Archaeology of the Human Sciences* (New York: Vantage Books, 1970).

Gilbert, F., *Machiavelli and Guicciardini* (1984).

Grendler, Paul, ed., *Encyclopedia of the Renaissance* (New York: Scribners, 1999).

Hay, Denys, *The Italian Renaissance* (Cambridge, England: Cambridge University Press, 1977).

Hexter, J. H., *Utopia: The Biography of an Idea* (Westport, Conn.: Greenwood Press, 1972).

Perry, Marvin, *An Intellectual History of Modern Europe* (Boston: Houghton Mifflin, 1993).

Pocock, J. B. A., *The Machiavellian Moment in Florentine Political Thought and the Atlantic Republican Tradition* (Princeton, N.J.: Princeton University Press, 1975).

Skinner, Quentin, *The Foundations of Modern Political Thought, Volume I, The Renaissance* (Cambridge, England: Cambridge University Press, 1978).

Strauss, Leo, *Thoughts on Machiavelli* (Seattle: Washington University Press, 1969).

The Reformation

Bainton, Roland, *Erasmus of Christendom* (New York: Charles Scribner's Sons, 1969).

Bousma, William, *John Calvin* (Oxford: Oxford University Press, 1988).

Cameron, Euan, *The European Reformation* (Oxford: Oxford University Press, 1991).

DeMolen, Richard L., *Erasmus* (New York: St. Martin's Press, 1974).

Dillenberger, John, *Martin Luther: Selections from His Writings* (New York: Doubleday, 1961).

———, *John Calvin: Selections from His Writings* (New York: Doubleday, 1971).

Foucault, Michel, *The Order of Things: An Archaeology of the Human Sciences* (New York: Vantage Books, 1970).

Grimm, Harold J., *The Reformation Era, 1500–1650* (New York: Macmillan, 1966).

Marius, Richard, *Thomas More* (New York: Alfred A. Knopf, 1984).

Ozment, Steven, *The Age of Reform, 1250–1550* (New Haven, Conn.: Yale University Press, 1980).

Perry, Marvin, *An Intellectual History of Modern Europe* (Boston: Houghton Mifflin, 1993).

Skinner, Quenton, *The Foundations of Modern Political Thought, Volume II: The Age of Reformation* (Cambridge, England: Cambridge University Press, 1978).

THE MAKING OF THE MODERN INTELLECT, PART TWO:
Science and the Enlightenment

The Scientific Revolution

Modern science slowly began to emerge from its religious entanglements with the Christian God near the end of the Middle Ages, while the Reformation drove a wedge between faith and knowledge. The process of this separation began with the age-old dispute in Western philosophy: which is more real, the thing or the idea? The thing represented individual objects as they appeared in nature. The idea referred to the soul, essence, or name as defined by the Greek term *logos* (see Chapters Seven and Eight) and Plato's forms. The result of this new debate allowed science to function independently of its ancient and medieval links to religion as established by Christian theology.

This liberation of science from religion began at the end of the High Middle Ages as two branches of medieval philosophy took up the question of the thing versus the idea. A Scottish Franciscan metaphysician and college professor named John Duns Scotus (1266–1308) led one branch of the debate; known as the *Realists*, they argued that God was the infinite Being, or the Ultimate Idea, who had revealed Himself to Moses as the Creator by saying, "I am who am" (Exodus 3:14). The Realists represented an Eternal Existence who had manifested Himself as an entity apart from matter by giving all things their form. Such a Being fashioned everything in the universe as an act of love by providing the eternal shape for all creation. Thus, things were merely contingent entities that took their reality from the Creator who existed in them as ultimate, transcendental actuality.

In contrast, the *Nominalists*, led by William of Ockham (1285–1347), took the opposite approach; they turned their attention away from transcendental forms and focused on the material world to begin an inquiry that would eventually liberate science. Unlike Realism, which speculated about the nature of God and Being, Nominalism looked at nature as a source of evidence that became the sole basis of knowledge. For the Nominalists, a reversal of Greco-Christian reality

was underway: while medieval Christian theology had dwelt on St Augustine's Neo-Platonic forms and the soul of humanity as entities distinct from matter and body, the Nominalists focused on the thing as an entity-in-itself. For the Nominalists, the thing had become more real in terms of knowledge than the idea, the form, the soul, or even God's Being. Such a reversal shifted Europe's focus from transcendental forms to nature, the study of which became the first step to acquiring knowledge, to an awareness of objects as things-in-themselves. William of Ockham became the first intellectual to develop this approach systematically.

William of Ockham asserted that only individual things served as the true source of information about reality, void of universals, forms, souls, or essences. To know the truth required clustering individual things into categories of the "same" and the "different," by analyzing their traits, and generating accurate names. Accordingly, the name of a thing was only as accurate as the evidence that supported it. Since Nominalism itself meant "naming" things (as in *nominate* and *nominal*), knowledge derived solely from experience and the formulation of an accurate language about these observations rather than any kind of theological or transcendental speculation.

Contrary to the theology of the High Middle Ages, Nominalism reversed the fundamental strategy behind an inquiry into nature. Theology in the High Middle Ages had taken its lead from St. Thomas Aquinas, its supreme practitioner. Aquinas had combined reason and faith through rational speculation about the nature of God, salvation, universals, and the soul. In contrast, in Nominalism Ockham developed the argument that matters of knowledge differed from matters of faith. To know anything required a mental strategy that studied individual things. Therefore universals were merely signs by which the mind represented reality to itself through linguistic concepts captured in names. Consequently, universals such as the terms *soul* and *God*, could not be experienced, so they were not part of knowledge. Hence, Ockham excluded from what humans knew such ideas as "immortality," "the existence of God," and "the nature of the soul."

Since "immortality," "the existence of God," and the "soul" were names without evidence to substantiate their existence in knowledge, they belonged to a different realm of belief than science. This realm was one of faith—the cornerstone of Luther's and Calvin's theology. No one had ever observed God or the soul, and yet no one could doubt the existence of either; therefore, this realm of faith held as much sway over the Late Medieval imagination as did knowledge. Faith, however, still occupied a different location in the human mind. Hence, during William of Ockham's day, it was unthinkable to conceive of a universe without God or the soul, but knowledge now required data based on experiences that became the sole criteria upon which one could form accurate names. Thus, phenomena that the Realists would have ignored as irrelevant suddenly became critically important to the Nominalists. This led to an accumulation of anomalies within the contemporary sciences that proved vastly destructive to medieval beliefs. One of these flawed theories was the concept of the *geocentric universe.*

The accepted medieval theory, the Ptolemaic model of the geocentric universe, failed because it had several conceptual problems. First, the Ptolemaic model was extremely complex, requiring a major orbit for each planet called "the deferent," and numerous minor orbits called "epicycles" to account for the apparent backward and forward motion of the planets when Ptolemy placed the Earth at the center of the universe. Second, any geocentric model should have had only one center, whereas Ptolemy's model had several: one for the orbit of the sun, one for that of the moon, and more than one for the inferior and superior planets. Third, the geocentric model required circular orbits; Ptolemy's model, however, had to postulate *equant* points, or off-centered centers, to account for the eccentric orbits of the sun, the moon, and the planets. And fourth, not all the parts of Ptolemy's geocentric system worked in harmony with one another, which required constant adjustments to his model; in short, the system never really functioned properly.

Finally, in 1543, Nicholas Copernicus (1473–1543) published an alternative to the Ptolemaic model. Copernicus made his living as a *canon* (a clergyman on staff at a cathedral) in Frauenberg, East Prussia, but he had studied astronomy in Poland and Italy and had rejected Ptolemy's system early in life. It took years, however, for Copernicus to develop an alternative theory (1530), and even longer to build the courage to publish his findings. Copernicus knew a bitter debate would follow so he waited until he was deathly ill in 1543 before he proposed a *heliocentric* (sun-centered) universe that not only abandoned traditional beliefs, but also replaced what at the time seemed common sense. Whereas the geocentric model saw the sun rise and set each day, Copernicus's heliocentric universe saw the Earth rotate. In addition, Copernicus's model forced European scientists to imagine what the universe would look like from a planet that was in motion around the sun. Such an image of the universe was very complex and forced Copernicus's supporters to consider how they could justify their confidence in his new theory. Yet, the heliocentric model eliminated the deferent and epicycles of each planetary orbit and had only one center: the sun.

Meanwhile, when the heliocentric model of the universe challenged the Ptolemaic model, Copernicus included two observational flaws in the old theory: one had to do with the orbit of the planets, and the other raised questions about the size of the cosmos. Ptolemy's model relied on circular, not elliptical, orbits; unfortunately, Copernicus kept this erroneous design. In addition, Ptolemy's model was small and personal, while Copernicus's universe forced scientists to imagine a much larger cosmos to take into account the different positions that the Earth had to occupy as it traveled

The Copernican Universe. Polish astronomer, Nicolaus Copernicus (1473–1543), developed the revolutionary theory that the sun was the center of the universe, and the earth, spinning on its axis, revolved annually around the sun— a heliocentric universe. From *De revolutionibus orbium coelestium (The Revolution of Celestial Spheres)* (Nuremberg, 1543). Image credit: Royal Astronomical Society.

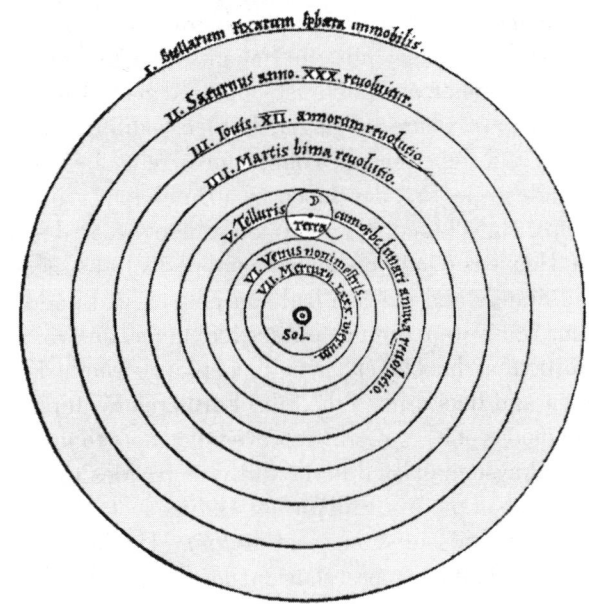

around the sun. Due to these shifts in the Earth's orbit, all the objects in the night sky should have looked very different in relation to one another as observers on the Earth looked up from different positions in their trip around the Sun during the summer and the winter, or during the spring and the fall.

Responding to these flaws, two scientists supported Copernicus's theory while reinforcing his break with tradition. The first of these was Johann Kepler (1571–1630), who changed the shape of planetary orbits. Born in Weil der Stadt, near Stuttgart, Germany, and educated at the University of Turbingen as a mathematician and Lutheran pastor, Kepler had to move to Protestant Prague to avoid Catholic persecution. There he met, worked with, and eventually replaced Tycho Brahe (1546–1601)—the most careful observer of the heavens to date. Inheriting Brahe's priceless data on his death in 1601, Kepler took eight years of careful study to finally redesign planetary motion. In 1609, Kepler proceeded to justify Copernicus's hypothesis by proving mathematically that Mars followed an elliptical path around the sun instead of a circular orbit. And along this path, at different times of the Martian year, the planet increased and decreased in speed because an ellipse had two centers instead of one. Since the Sun occupied one of these two centers, when Mars moved faster, it was on the side of orbit closest to the Sun; when Mars moved slower, it was on the side of the orbit farthest from the Sun. Furthermore, Kepler generalized his theory and applied it to all the planets via establishing an inverse ratio between distance and speed. He proved that the time of any planet's orbit around the Sun squared (t^2) divided by its mean distance from the Sun cubed (d^3) established a common mathematical bond to describe all the relationship of all the planets to one another in their heavenly travels.

The second scientist, an Italian astronomer, natural philosopher, and physicist, educated at the University of Pisa, where he taught, Galileo Galilei (1564–1642) redesigned the idea of the universe itself. Using the telescope, first developed by a Dutch lens grinder named Hans Lippershey in 1608, Galileo revealed that the Heavens (God's realm) were not perfect: the moon had craters and the Sun had sunspots on it. In addition, Venus went through phases like the moon, which proved that this planet had neither epicycles nor a deferent and thus orbited the Sun. Furthermore, Jupiter had moons of its own, which proved that more than one orbital system existed in the universe besides that of the Earth or the sun. Still further, Galileo looked at the stars and discovered the idea of *infinity*. He did so because he found that most stars did not change size when magnified. This meant that they had to be extremely far away. Finally, if the universe was as large as Galileo's telescope suggested, then humans had to be physically insignificant in the grand scheme of things. Yet if humans could imagine how small they were, then their imagination had to be infinite in size and potential. Hence, if one could not find God in this expanding cosmos, the idea of the power of the human mind suggested that perhaps the Divine Plan intended for us to develop our infinite intellect.

Building on concepts firmly established by Kepler and Galileo, Sir Isaac Newton (1642–1727) formulated his theory of gravity in 1687. Born in Woolsthorpe, Lincolnshire, and educated at Cambridge University, where he eventually taught, Newton reasoned that a combination of forces had to be holding the Earth in orbit as it traveled around the Sun. One of these forces tried to throw us out into space based on the speed of our orbital motion. The other force tried to draw us into the Sun. Indeed, Kepler had shown that the speed of the Earth varied according to its distance from the Sun: faster when closer and slower when farther away. The second force was gravity, and it balanced exactly with the centrifugal energy of the motion of the Earth as it orbited the Sun. To prove his theory, Newton created a new mathematical system called calculus that allowed him to describe precisely where the Earth was in its orbit around the Sun at any given time in the year.

What became known as the Scientific Revolution took nearly a century and a half, 1543–1687. It shattered an old and familiar image of the universe. The old view had offered comfort because it was small, intimate, centered on the Earth, and God's creation. The geocentric model had satisfied Westerners for centuries because human beings occupied the central stage of the cosmic drama.

Now the universe comprised infinite space, had no center stage, and made God so distant that His personal attention seemed unlikely. The degree of change that science brought to what European thinkers thought was real had thoroughly destroyed the authority of ancient texts for many of the leading intellectuals of Europe. These books had served as the basis of universal knowledge for more than 2,000 years. In their place, gravity merely described a machine of infinite size running on automatic pilot. And God ceased to be a part of the explanation of why events occurred in nature.

At the same time, to eliminate God from the sciences implied that informed moral decisions, those that defined Divine purposes in all natural processes no longer belonged to the realm of scientific knowledge. Yet since scientific knowledge provided the best information about nature, then the elimination of God from the sciences posed a problem: how, and who, should define the way humans should act? Thus, the problem of applying the sciences to human behavior required a major philosophical revolution that followed in the wake of the Scientific Revolution, one that adjusted the new amoral voice of the sciences to ethics. This philosophical revolution would try to redefine the "good" and the "beautiful" in a new context, while ignoring the fact that maybe such a context no longer existed.

However, since the sciences were no longer related to the moral voice of religion, how were the two to relate to one another? Just as Machiavelli and More had divided the world of "what is" from "what ought to be," and Ockham, Luther, and Calvin had separated knowledge from faith, so the amoral voice of the sciences could no longer address the ethical issues of religion. Furthermore, those who ignored the differences between science and religion, and tried to mix amoral knowledge with the moral voice, converted humans into objects very much like Machiavelli had done in *The Prince*. Indeed, Machiavelli had created political science to allow rulers to manipulate people through the use of power to achieve specific political ends. Hence, buried within scientific knowledge, and its differences with faith, lay new philosophical problems.

Nature had once been a place rich in life and God's moral force. In fact, this was how Martin Luther and John Calvin continued to see the universe as they subordinated human will and intellect to Divine revelation. Rejecting Luther's and Calvin's view, however, the sciences had redefined nature as a cosmos filled with dead matter, located in an imperfect realm called the heavens, and occupying empty, infinite space. Life was the exception and not the rule. Consequently, the universe was a vast and boundless vacuum punctuated with specks of exploding dust called stars in which the occasional system of planets might be found whose mechanical order suggested, but did not prove, a Divine Intelligence. Gravity influenced all things, but punished the wicked and the good with equal efficiency as a blind force that hurled objects through space. The moral purpose of the universe, therefore, seemed to have disappeared into a vast sea of infinite space.

Meanwhile, as the Scientific Revolution removed God from nature, so the Reformation had joined with scientists to destroy Latin as a universal, sacred language. Like all traditional societies, Europe before 1500 had associated the sacred qualities of its communities with a universal symbolic system provided by God. Just as Arabic represented the voice of Allah, and Chinese revealed the will of the ancestors, Latin had served Europeans as the symbolic vehicle to know God's mind.

Protestants and scientists everywhere, however, had destroyed Latin as a sacred medium in favor of the vulgar tongues. These vulgar, or common, languages, in turn, ceased to be vulgar and had become the new vehicles to redefine *community* in Europe. The result of both, the Reformation and Scientific Revolution, was to create a new vision of society. This new vision began to come into focus during the Enlightenment.

The Enlightenment

As stated above, the Scientific Revolution had undercut the authority of ancient texts in Europe by replacing a small, intimate, and God-driven universe with an infinite cosmos governed by mechanical laws and seemingly devoid of any ultimate purpose. Simultaneously, the Reformation had destroyed the power of dogma by successfully undercutting the Roman Catholic Church's monopoly on the "truth." These two sudden shifts in basic beliefs had put the traditional heritage of the West on trial, as modern philosophy began to respond to the new image of reality developed by the Copernican Revolution as well as the freedom of conscience offered by Luther's universal priesthood of humanity. Now Europeans had to rethink everything that they had held to be true because they could no longer trust their old worldview.

Now a new philosophy based on two key strategies for acquiring knowledge, self-evident truth and experience, began to emerge. Both of these key intellectual strategies would create new *epistemologies* (studies of knowledge) that would supercede the failure of ancient texts in explaining reality. These new epistemologies, in turn, would free European thinkers from tradition so that they could begin to develop a fresh, new philosophical perspective. A new generation of intellectuals like René Descartes (1596–1650) and Sir Francis Bacon (1561–1626) sought to develop a modern worldview by declaring doubt to be the first step in exploring humanity's capacity to know the truth.

René Descartes

Educated in the Jesuit school at La Flèche and the University of Poitiers, a soldier by profession who retired to Holland to engage in scientific research and philosophical speculation, René Descartes was a great mathematician who invented Analytical Geometry by creating a coordinate system based on algebra that corresponded to geometric forms. This fascination with math revealed Descartes' passion for self-evident truth. He loved the certainty that came from deduction as a process that extended conclusions derived from truths whose understanding was immediate to the human in-

René Descartes (1596–1650) is considered the father of modern philosophy and the founder of analytic geometry. His groundbreaking work *La Géométrie* explained how certain geometrical problems can be solved by way of algebraic equations, making calculus and many other advances in mathematics possible. "La geometrie," essay from *Discours de la Methode (Discourse on the Method)*, Descarte's first published work.

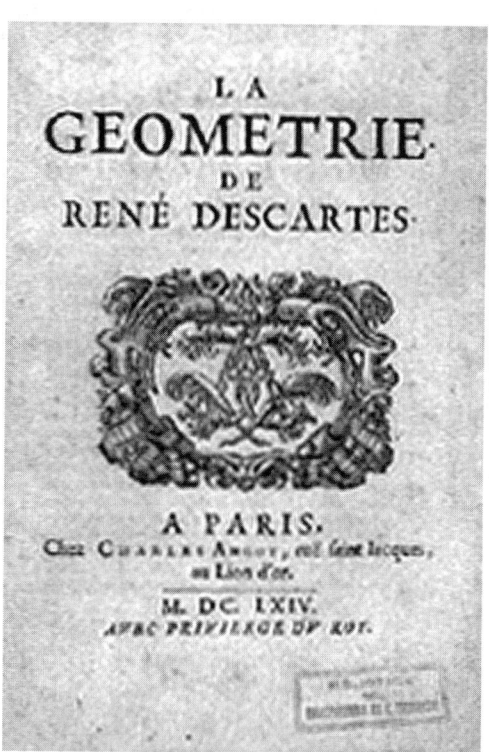

LA
GEOMETRIE.
DE
RENÉ DESCARTES

A PARIS,
Chez Charles Angot, ...

M. DC. LXIV.
AVEC PRIVILEGE DU ROY.

tellect. If this process of thought existed in math, he mused, why not in philosophy?

Since science had demonstrated that the collective authority of ancient texts were in error, how could one begin a new philosophy based on any education received in Europe's universities? Descartes considered this question, and, like Bacon, his English counterpart, concluded that one had to doubt everything in order to rediscover universal truth in philosophy. Yet to doubt everything meant the elimination of any form of belief in which the possibility of error could exist. Thus, Descartes began anew by casting aside the past and seeking a complete recovery of certainty on a foundation of self-evident truth.

In his *Discourses on Method* (1637) and *Meditations* (1641), Descartes eliminated experience as a source of knowledge because it was riddled with opinion and error. Since science had already removed authority, he knew only self-evident truth remained. But what basic truths were self-evident? After long deliberation, Descartes found himself left only with doubt. Yet, doubt itself was thought used with great rigor. Therefore, if doubt occurred, then thought had to exist. And if thought existed, then the thinker who had these thoughts had to exist as well. Hence, Descartes settled on his famous epigram: *I think, therefore, I am.*

This revelation led Descartes to consider what actually existed in thought. This line of inquiry forced him to conclude that existence was thought itself. By thought, he meant that existence took the form of those

ideas that humans hold with absolute certainty. Such ideas came from logic and math and transcended time and space. Since all humans had these ideas, Descartes concluded that they had to come from a common source as powerful and binding as the ideas themselves. Only one source had such power, God. Yet, this Deity was not the God of Christianity; rather, this was a God that functioned as an infinite, universal, and impersonal mind whose intelligence was the cosmic design.

Such a Divine Intelligence placed in human beings the capacity to exist in thought as thinkers whose ideas were innate to our being. Universal concepts like mathematical formulas were known with absolute certainty by any thinker, regardless of where or when he or she lived. Since such thoughts existed before the thinker, all such thoughts combined to represent objectivity, and as such were features of reality as innate ideas. Thus, God as a Universal Intelligence existed to create such ideas, but now this God took the form of a transparent Entity that represented the source of certainty. In other words, God ceased to be an immediate, personal, and all-loving Creator.

Such a God did not intervene in our daily lives as a wrathful but merciful Father as Luther and Calvin had argued in their theologies. Instead, such a God was an impersonal Creator whose transcendental nature was known to us only through the colorless dispassionate forms of thought found in math and logic. Finally, such a God released the universe and humanity to rely on Pure Intellect as a clear and distinct means of dealing with the world.

According to Descartes, looking inside consciousness revealed more about the nature of reality than searching outside the mind in the world of things. In a manner similar to the Realists of the High and Late Middle Ages, Descartes had sought reality through rational speculation based on self-evident truth as the principal source of knowledge. Yet this quest ran contrary to the momentum of science. It also transformed the image of God into an Entity as indifferent to humans as a mind engaged in pure mathematical calculations.

Sir Francis Bacon

In contrast to Descartes' self-evident truth, Sir Francis Bacon looked to experience as his source of knowledge. Educated in Cambridge, Bacon became a Member of Parliament in 1548 and served James I as attorney general (1613), lord keeper (1617), and lord chancellor (1621). Yet his political career ended abruptly when he pled guilty to bribery and found himself forced into retirement. Prior to the end of his political career, however, Bacon had already developed a fascination with philosophy and planned a massive work called

Instauratio Magna, the Great Renewal, that would set philosophy on the correct course after the impact of the Scientific Revolution. Finishing two volumes of this projected work, however, Bacon gave Europe only part of his vision. The first of these volumes, the *Novum Organum*, New Method (1620), used doubt with a similar intent as Descartes, but achieved quite a different result. Bacon sought to eliminate what he called "the idols of the mind" in order to release humanity to discover the truth about nature and reality.

According to Bacon, there were four such idols. First, the idols of the tribe came from the error of people reading their desires and needs into natural phenomena to create false transcendental purposes that humans assigned to reality. Second, the idols of the cave reflected the prejudices and predisposition of individuals who pushed their personal whims and fancies onto beliefs about nature. Third, the idols of the marketplace used the imprecision of common sense to generate a shared, everyday language that, in turn, produced a form of false belief called "conventional wisdom." Fourth and last, the idols of the theater derived from the authority of the past that projected the received errors of the first three idols into the present. Thus, all four idols assigned false, subjective purposes to natural objective processes as guides to human conduct.

Humanity needed to reject these idols. In their place, humanity had to establish a new form of knowledge. This new knowledge, however, did not have to achieve the absolute certainty prescribed by Descartes. Rather, Bacon advanced the maxim that knowledge is power. According to this maxim, Bacon proposed a test that replaced certainty with the command over nature that people gained from what they knew. This test substituted the practical consequences of human knowledge for the clear and distinct ideas found in Cartesian Rationalism. Therefore, in place of Descartes' *deductive* approach, Bacon accepted *induction* as the key mental strategy to deal with reality.

Induction reasoned from the particular to the general and offered only probability as a source of truth. These probabilities relied on conditional sentences derived from experience that took the following form: if these conditions are met, then this event will occur. Such sentences led to useful knowledge that gave us power over our surroundings. Like the Nominalists, Bacon sought to create a functional language based on accurate names that derived from an understanding of individual things.

To approach the problem of knowledge from a supposed universal or general truth, leaves one with no data with which to begin. Thus, Bacon asserted that humans would be reasoning from an empty category.

To use deduction (to reason from the general to the particular) Bacon argued, was to derive knowledge from emptiness: to reason in a vacuum. Hence, Bacon proposed that if humans began anew, they had to set aside all their received ideas and return to nature as the source of data. From immediate experience, humans then had to restructure their taxonomy of nature. With these new and accurate terms, Bacon concluded that people would finally be able to assemble their observations and experiences into a workable system of probable truths.

Bacon felt that such probable truths derived from the understanding of natural laws. These natural laws, he argued, imposed fixed forms on material events that humans could observe and comprehend. One such fixed form, causation, functioned as a universal principle not only to account for daily events, but also to give shape to the cosmic design. To discover causation, Bacon argued that people first had to study change by seeking out all positive instances in which an effect in nature followed a recognizable cause. Then, humans had to determine if the same cause ever failed to produce the same effect. Finally, humans had to try to find cases wherein the change was present to some greater or lesser degree in order to establish what degree of the cause was necessary to create the effect under study.

With his inductive strategy, Bacon sought to empower humanity with a practical knowledge of causation, but he offered no effective moral guide as to its use. Thus, the maxim that knowledge is power served as an intellectual test to discover useful "truths," but it did not reveal how to link the "good" and the "beautiful" with what people had come to know.

The power of Bacon's ideas remained untested while he spent most of his adult life in English politics. Sidetracked though he was by his political career, Bacon completed *The Advancement of Knowledge* in 1605 and later, during his retirement, translated it into Latin in 1623, as *De dignitate et augmentis scientarum*, while the *Novum Organum* appeared in 1620. Then he began *The New Atlantis* in 1627, but he never finished it. Also, *De dignitate et augmentis scientarum* merely reinforced his arguments in the *Novum Organum*, while the *New Atlantis* began a description of a scientific utopia that may have defined new human purposes. Bacon, however, was neither a mathematician nor a scientist, and he did not keep abreast of the developments in the Scientific Revolution. Unlike Descartes, Bacon was not a direct participant. Hence, his ideas remained a powerful influence in England but did not become general in Europe.

Yet England was the nation that had consolidated the Scientific Revolution based on experimentation and mathematics. Sir Isaac Newton demonstrated the power of experience as a source of truth with his theory of gravity. Hence, England championed the idea of experience and experimentation. As a result, a contemporary of Newton, John Locke (1632–1704), had an opportunity to transform Bacon's empiricism into a comprehensive philosophy that rivaled Cartesian Rationalism. John Locke published several new works that surpassed Descartes and launched the Enlightenment.

John Locke

Generating empiricism as a core strategy for epistemology, Locke not only created a groundwork for reason as a human power, but he also provided the intellectual basis for a new discipline later called psychology, and he renewed the foundations of political philosophy. Locke's empiricism built a logical bridge between psychology and political philosophy to propose a protomodern worldview that temporarily satisfied Europe. Furthermore, empiricism, psychology, and political philosophy all served as the new critical study for a modern social and intellectual weapon called "public opinion."

Like the binding consensus that mechanics sought through the theory of gravity, public opinion asked Europeans to question their past, test their institutions with reason, and decide if contemporary conventions provided a wide general agreement that the current social order satisfied the needs of everyone. By meeting these needs, Locke's philosophy hoped to bring into focus the relationships between knowledge, individual personality, social conduct, and good government. Once in focus, Locke sought to place all these features of human existence into a new, modern, and rational context.

John Locke greatly affected the development of political philosophy and the reach of his influence is even apparent in the U.S. Declaration of Independence. This bronze medal was created in memoriam of the renowned English philospher by Jean Dassier. National Portrait Gallery, London.

Beginning with his empiricism, Locke published the *Essay Concerning Human Understanding* (1690) only three years after Newton had produced his *Mathematical Principles of Natural Philosophy* (1687). Locke's *Essay* questioned Descartes' conclusions about thought and reality by asking: if ideas are innate and given by God to humans, why do we have so many different beliefs? Reasoning that since our basic beliefs varied so greatly, there had to be a different design to knowledge besides innate ideas. Thus Locke concluded that a Universal Being could not have directly planted in our minds the concepts we actually live by. Instead, the truths we used in our daily lives must come from some other source. Accepting Bacon's thesis that experience was the means by which we acquired most of our ideas, Locke constructed a vision of how the mind interpreted data. From this mental process, Locke also derived the origins of personality and individual variation.

Locke postulated that at birth humans had the capacity to reason, but their minds were *tabula rasas* (blank slates). Endowed with rational powers, the new infant lies passively and begins to receive data through sensations transmitted by the surrounding world. Like an unformed piece of soft warm wax, the human mind receives *primary* (i.e., measurable) impressions from nature as if reality were an enormous signet ring. This enormous "natural signet ring" then left a common, objective imprint on the human imagination as a result of our daily exposure to external reality.

The primary data transmitted to each infant contained the same information, since only objects in nature produced the stimuli. Called sense data, these bundles of objective information first filled the human mind and then clustered into orderly patterns of impressions that took shape with a machinelike precision as reason processed sensation. Thus, the mind functioned like an efficient receiver whose interpretations reflected the organization of the data generated by reason as both formed into our first concepts.

Called simple ideas, these first concepts allowed humans to grasp traits. The primary or measurable qualities of colors, smells, tastes, sounds, and tactile impressions clustered into ideas that allowed us to recognize the things that were the same as well as to distinguish them from those that were different. The primary qualities of red became different from blue, but both colors had more in common with each other in our experience than the tastes of sweet or bitter. Simultaneously, each of these simple ideas then became the rational building blocks that a young mind could use to expand its interpretation of nature. With enough of these simple ideas, the infant's mind began to cluster

John Locke, the Earl of Shaftesbury, and Contemporary Politics

Considered the cofounder of the Enlightenment with Sir Isaac Newton, John Locke (1632–1704) led a rich and varied life excelling in more than one profession. Educated at Christ Church College, Oxford, he became a lecturer in 1660 in three different disciplines: Greek, rhetoric, and philosophy. Science and medicine fascinated him, and he became a qualified doctor and lawyer before leaving his teaching assignment. In 1667, Locke accepted an appointment as secretary and advisor to the first Earl of Shaftesbury, Lord Anthony Ashley Cooper (1621–83), gave up his teaching responsibilities at Oxford, and developed a lifelong association with one of the most influential and gifted politicians of his age.

The Earl of Shaftesbury had already led a complex political and military career when Locke met him in 1666. Shaftesbury began as a Royal General in Charles I's army and then switched to the parliamentary side during the English Civil War (1640–49—see Chapter Twenty). After the parliamentary forces defeated Charles I, Shaftesbury served as a statesman who supported Oliver Cromwell as Lord Protector of England until his autocratic nature surfaced after he beheaded Charles I (reigned 1625–49) and purged parliament of those voices that opposed Cromwell's Puritan views. Thereafter Shaftesbury became a staunch parliamentarian who sided with General George Monck and helped to engineer the restoration of Charles II (reigned 1660–85) in opposition to Richard Cromwell's rise to power after his father, Oliver's death, on September 3, 1658. While the Earl of Shaftesbury served Charles II in the Privy Council, as the chancellor of the exchequer (1661), as a proprietor of Carolina (1663), and as lord chancellor (1672), John Locke provided his employer with excellent medical and legal advice after 1667.

Yet Shaftesbury fell from power in 1673 due to his strong support of the Test Act (1672) that required all royal officeholders to take communion in the Anglican Church; this began Locke's career as an opponent of absolute monarchy. The Test Act had served to neutralize Charles II's edict, the Declaration of Indulgences (earlier in 1672), which had allowed the crown to appoint Catholics to office without consulting parliament. Catholics were the most loyal supporters of absolute monarchy in Europe, and Charles had hoped to use them in imposing his unfettered royal will on parliament; the Test Act frustrated this goal. Charles II, his brother, James II (reigned 1685–88), and their court were pro-Catholic, but their support of Catholicism had also managed to unite the majority of Protestant England against the crown.

Meanwhile, ill health had forced Locke to travel to France in 1675, while the Earl of Shaftesbury formed the Whig Party in opposition to Charles in England. In France, Locke met most of the continental leaders in science and philosophy, while Shaftesbury found himself imprisoned in the Tower due to his effectiveness in frustrating Charles II's ambitions. Parliament, however, managed to pressure Charles II into releasing the earl who became Lord President of the Privy Council in 1678. Returning to England in 1679, Locke had hoped to retire, but he soon found himself enmeshed in Shaftesbury's politics. Forming several parliaments to oppose Charles, Shaftesbury was once again imprisoned and tried for treason, but acquitted. Pressure to eliminate Shaftesbury's opposition by Charles finally forced the earl to flee England, and Locke accompanied his master to Holland only to see him die in Amsterdam in 1683.

Living in Holland from 1683–89, Locke then completed all the philosophical works that made him famous—most of which enjoyed publication after the Glorious Revolution (see Chapter Twenty) 1688–89. The Glorious Revolution removed the staunch Catholic, James Stuart, then James II, King of England, from the throne and gave it to his sister's husband, the Protestant William III (reigned 1689–1702) from Holland. As king, William III signed the legislation that produced a stable government in England by clearly separating and balancing the powers of the legislature and the crown. Returning to England from Holland in the wake of William III's rise to power, Locke's work then became the justification for this royal-parliamentary agreement that the Glorious Revolution had achieved. Hence, Locke's epistemology, psychology, and political philosophy (see above) explained why a rational society had to rebel against the tyranny of absolute monarchy in favor of creating a constitutional commonwealth.

Aaron, Richard I., *John Locke*, Third Edition. (Oxford: The Clarendon Press, 1971), p. 1–49.

these elemental concepts into categories like color or taste. At this point, the mind was ready for its next epistemological leap to a new level of thought called complex ideas.

A complex idea was a cluster of simple ideas assembled around a common, repeated experience that led to the recognition of an object. These objects fell into categories of the same and different, just like simple ideas, as the mind reviewed their traits and recognized their qualities. Each of these qualities linked categories like color, flavor, shape, and texture to produce a clear mental image of the object in the infant's mind. Then, as the assembly of complex ideas grew, this youth was ready for another epistemological leap. Once again, the orderly features of nature, as well as the powers of reason, prepared this maturing intelligence for the next step.

Once a sufficient number of objects had been assembled from recognizable patterns of the same and different to become a common experience, the human mind then formulated vocalizations that served as words to name these objects. These words represented the highest level of mental development: an abstract idea. This level of thought constituted the first time that the mind functioned in a realm outside the objective information gathered by clustered primary sensations.

An abstract idea represented an interpretation that went beyond the stimuli offered by nature. An abstract idea created a general mental category that captured all data classified as "the same" and fit it within a common category so as to allow the mind to capture, house, and identify future evidence. This general category was a word that functioned as the name for any future object that reason might classify as the same according to past sensations. This word became the basis of a rational language that represented the names of knowledge to the observer. But, since an abstract idea went beyond the data, it was also partly subjective.

Given the flexibility of Locke's abstract ideas, his presentation of how the rational process shaped knowledge and gave rise to language created the most systematic treatment of Nominalism offered to date. With the help of later authors like Voltaire, who simplified and popularized Locke's *Essay* and Newton's *Mathematical Principles*, the quality of this new epistemology made it immediately compelling to an eager audience. Born François-Marie Arouet, Voltaire's acerbic wit and devastating satires carved a hole in traditional beliefs that he filled with plays, poems, essays, stories, and books that popularized Locke and Newton. Voltaire prepared Europeans to receive Locke's explanation of how the rational, or scientific, mind worked. As mentioned above, Nominalism made the Scientific Revolution possible by focusing attention on the primary value of data. Now Locke had explained why Nominalism worked so well in terms of generating knowledge. Locke also had showed where this strategy could err. To these features of reason and language, Locke now added a new ingredient: personality.

Not only could objective information cluster into ideas, but feelings could be assembled with these ideas as well. Hence, something sweet could give rise to a sensation of pleasure at the same time that the human mind experienced a specific flavor. This combination of pleasure and taste would then add a feeling of "goodness" whenever this sensation of flavor occurred. Such events created human preferences or *secondary* traits that explained why opinions of good or bad might come into existence. Then a human being would seek out this type of experience a second time.

Sensations of pleasure and pain as secondary traits were associated with abstract ideas to give shape to personality. The way each individual developed personal preferences distinguished one human character from another according to the different sensations that he or she had experienced. Using these different personal histories, Locke could explain why some people preferred one type of food to another, or why some children grew up to be more agreeable than others. Furthermore, Locke could explain why all humans struggled to survive, and why some people seemed more rational and quick-witted than others. In effect, individuality took shape from the same natural processes that gave humanity its ideas, but personality did so through an internal mechanism that matched emotions with personal experiences.

Now knowledge and individuality became part of the same process that generated a whole host of rational, political, and social concepts. For example, well-trained children nurtured by loving, rational parents developed the best qualities available to humanity. Such children would grow up to behave rationally, feel affection for their parents, develop agreeable characters, and understand their social roles. They would seek to maintain their family and reproduce another generation of humans that could enjoy the same rewards in life. The family, therefore, would become a rational social unit, and from this unit the community could take the form of a rational assembly.

These features of Locke's epistemology and psychology closely blended with his political philosophy. In the realm of politics, his readers saw with clarity his protomodern vision. Offered in his work *Two Treatises on Government*, published anonymously also in 1690, Locke created a political theory that reinforced his vision of reason. Justified by the rule of law that derived from reason, Locke demonstrated why a legislature comprised of rational humans should produce the legal code while a king should only enforce it.

Locke began his *First Treatise* by dismissing the traditional explanation that justified political authority. His careful dissection of a tract on absolute monarchy destroyed Sir Robert Filmer's argument that the origins of royal authority derived from Adam and Eve. Locke revealed that such a claim was impossible to justify by empirical evidence since no one could possibly trace their ancestry back to Adam and Eve without accepting these original parents on faith. Such faith, Locke argued, belonged to ideas that came from a realm of belief called religion that existed apart from knowledge. Since religion generated ideas that existed beyond experience, these ideas could not rationally justify any form of government.

Locke was unwilling to submit blindly to any authority without questioning why humans had been granted a power like reason in the first place. After all, reason shaped the beliefs that directed us as humans every day of our lives. Therefore, government should be rational, should be an extension of the realm of knowledge, and should reflect the rules of reason in the form of laws. In his *Second Treatise*, Locke developed his political alternative to tradition and absolute monarchy.

At the heart of his theory rests the law of reason as the Law of Nature created for humans by God. The existence of God was a matter of faith that Locke did not question; yet God appears in the *Second Treatise* only to mark a beginning to Locke's analysis. Locke started by simply stating that the world comprised three natural ranks: God, humanity, and animals. Since God, however, functioned at a level as mysterious to us as we were to animals, we could no more understand Him than animals could understand us. Therefore, to determine what we were supposed to do as humans, we could not look to God; rather we had to look to ourselves. By this argument Locke meant that we were to use the power of reason presumably given to us by God.

According to Locke, the law of reason dictated certain policies. These policies included the actions needed to maintain an individual's existence. Since everyone began in a *state of nature* (i.e., a condition without government), the law of reason dictated that survival required that people use the labor of their bodies to harvest from the world around them food, clothing, and shelter.

The act of working created the first principle of private property. By giving up the time and energy of labor as represented by a portion of one's life and liberty, humans gained possession of objects found in nature, which now became private property. From this description, a compound definition of property emerged: ownership comprised life, liberty, and the possessions earned by labor.

Locke argued that people could take what they wanted from nature, but they could not take more than they needed. To take more than a person needed was to waste nature's bounty and deny survival to others. Yet the discovery of gold overcame this problem of waste.

Gold preserved the value of nature's wealth in a form that did not spoil. Hence, humans accumulated gold and used it to create cooperative patterns of labor that enhanced the survival of all that participated. These cooperative patterns took place within a household and defined the relationship between the father and his son, and the master and his servants. Accordingly, wealth derived from this household economy supplied each member with greater security and the likelihood of survival.

Since gold stimulated these patterns of cooperative labor, a stockpile of this precious metal served the rational ends of human existence: survival. This positive consequence justified collecting and using gold. Therefore, working to accumulate gold was both good and rational. Yet a treasury of gold generated a state of inequality among humans because no two households necessarily gathered the same amount. This inequality, however, was "just" in the sense that it sustained the power to organize people into cooperative patterns of labor that secured the survival of all members.

Organized labor, "just" inequality, and the increased ability to plan for a family's survival created both a social hierarchy and a standard to measure the level of reason possessed by each participating human. The wealthy came from families where the highest quality of reason existed in abundance because the founder of a rich household had used his ability to plan and accumulate gold as a means to secure the survival of his children, his servants, and their families. In contrast, the poor came from those families whose share of reason proved less plentiful because their ancestors did not have the original foresight needed to see the rational uses of gold that had established wealthy households. In addition, since parents nurtured their children, wealthy families continued to maintain higher levels of reason because they had far greater access to the means needed to cultivate the minds of their offspring, while the poor did not. Hence, the poor suffered from the absence of reason and surrendered to animal impulses due to their weak mental abilities. When they gave into these animal impulses, the poor frequently attacked the rich to capture wealth unjustly. Such assaults led to a state of war in this state of nature that supported the next rational step in the formation of a human society: the formation of government.

Accordingly, the wealthiest and most rational members of a community formed a government for the sole purpose of protecting their property. Property, however, was not merely a collection of possessions, it also included life and liberty as well as all the promises (i.e., contracts) needed to preserve estates. Hence, a government served as a general legal contract to secure a person's life, liberty, and accumulated possessions as well as all the cooperative agreements derived from this body of wealth. All contracts, such as master-servant agreements and marriage and inheritance documents, fell within the boundaries of the legal system needed to preserve property. Thus, taken together, all the features of property and the legal promises of contracts became the sole responsibility of a rational political system. At the same time, such a system constituted the only just form of government that humanity could accept. This political system therefore took the name of a "commonwealth," for it preserved all wealth in common.

Meanwhile, as this commonwealth came into existence, it included at least two separate legal branches: a legislature and an executive. The legislature came first and represented a society's wealthiest and most rational members as they assembled to form their government. To be eligible to vote, or hold office in the legislature, estate owners had to have a sufficient supply of accumulated possessions to demonstrate that they had a substantial commitment to the new commonwealth. Mere life and liberty was not enough for three reasons. First, the poor did not have a vested interest in protecting the existing order of wealth within a realm. Second, the poor did not have a family history that marked their numbers as having exceptional powers of reason. And third, the poor did not have the leisure time needed to receive sufficient training to develop the social character desirable in a lawmaker. Hence, only wealthy families should make the laws that protected property. Yet once these laws were made, the task of the legislature was complete, and the job of enforcing the law now fell to the executive branch.

The executive took the form of a monarchy where the king came from a family that had accepted responsibility to enforce the laws in the past. All a king could do, however, was impose the will of the law; he could not issue new statutes by edict. Since law reflected the collective reason of the community's most rational members as represented by the legislature, when the king stayed within the legal boundaries set by the lawmakers, the commonwealth prospered. Thus, the king had to recognize that his sole purpose was to enforce the law that protected property, and he must use force only against those who would abandon reason to attack the life, liberty, and possessions of others.

Locke's treatment of property, contract, and government created a new standard to justify how a society should be organized. The Law of Nature defined a person's humanity based on reason itself. A person was human to the degree that he or she could be rational. Authority existed in society to control those who demonstrated that they lacked sufficient reason even though they took human form. And since the wealthy had a family history of reason based on the accumulation of their possessions, only they could participate in government. The poor were simply excluded.

At the same time, just as a commonwealth was a collection of wealthy estates, so a government was a collection of the *rational* men of estate (i.e., the rich). Such a thesis implied that every government should be subject to review to discover if it was rational. If reason existed in sufficient supply, then a government had the right to exist. If not, then such a government should be overthrown. Through his thoughts, Locke had created a new political weapon called "public opinion."

The Response to Locke and Public Opinion

Public opinion matured as more and more Europeans accepted Sir Isaac Newton's new view of the universe and John Locke's new justification for human society. Europeans participated in the Enlightenment in ever-greater numbers, as new authors in Western and Central Europe began to follow the lead of Newton and Locke. Early in the eighteenth century, these writers popularized rational thought and science to earn the name *philosophes* (thinkers dedicated to creating a more rational and humane society). As the century unfolded, these philosophes shifted the emphasis of their literature to expose contemporary social and political abuses. Since these efforts lacked any form of organization, the product generated was anything but steady. Nevertheless, a consensus began to emerge that society needed a major overhaul, even if the individual authors could not agree on the proper solutions to attempt.

Opposed only in a haphazard fashion by vested social, economic, and political interests, these philosophes brought into question such public institutions as the nobility, the church, the law, and the principles of government. By the mid-1700s, a variety of attitudes took shape that became the conventions of this movement. Terms like *superstition* and *enthusiasm*, for example, spoke of dangerous irrational tendencies that enlightened thinkers condemned.

Superstition reflected the folly of allowing beliefs and practices to continue without demonstrating their rational value. Enthusiasm referred to a form of human conduct that fixated prematurely on a new concept. This type of fixation launched social or political movements before the quality of the new idea could be thoroughly tested by reason. Both terms became conceptual weapons used against religion.

For the newly enlightened thinkers, religion was a system of beliefs that encouraged humanity to perform acts of superstition or enthusiasm. For example, in Europe, Catholicism became equated with superstition because the philosophes condemned its 1,300-year-old history of "mindless repeated rituals." In contrast, these same philosophes denounced Protestantism for its enthusiasm as this revived form of Christianity started a new, seemingly uncontrollable religious movement based on Martin Luther's and John Calvin's redefinition of faith. Therefore, these enlightened thinkers felt that both Catholics and Protestants had created social chaos during the Reformation, for each had ignored reason in favor of religious passion to define their goals for human behavior. Accordingly, the philosophes argued that the religious wars caused by Catholic superstition and Protestant enthusiasm illustrated the degree of human folly found in both forms of Christianity.

By the second half of the eighteenth century, the philosophes felt sufficiently secure in their critique of Europe's religious traditions to challenge each other through literary debates. They focused their attention on social, economic, and political issues, and began to prescribe specific reforms. Their literature generated a more intense look at the communal fabric, while their debates stimulated new and creative solutions to particular ills. They clustered in key cities. They met in the *salons* (elegant rooms used for after-dinner discussions in fashionable homes) of wealthy families. Finally, they produced the first modern intellectual movement that sustained a collective assault upon Europe's past.

Leading figures emerged who acquired a cosmopolitan reputation that reflected a wide variety of opinions. A short list of such individuals in the French Enlightenment includes five outstanding intellectuals. Persons like Charles Louis de Secondat, Baron de Montesquieu (1689–1755) compared different social solutions to the problem of political organization to reveal how various governmental forms succeeded or failed due to the way humans responded to the natural laws buried in physics and geography. Mentioned, above François Marie Arouet (1694–1778), known as Voltaire, spanned the Enlightenment to produce a mountain of published works that both popularized Newton's science and Locke's philosophy as well as led the attack on tradition. Denis Diderot (1713–84) spent a lifetime compiling the *Encyclopedie* to marshal all the leading opinions of the day in science and philosophy so that Europeans could see the light of reason in one multivolume source. Jean-Jacques Rousseau (1712–78) spoke to the less rational components of the human personality by reflecting on how nature imprinted humanity with noble sentiments that irrational social practices perverted into corrupt passions. A final example included a school of thought called *Physiocracy* that began when a French royal physician named François Quesnay (1694–1774) laid the foundations for economics; he equated the theory of production with physical law to argue for an agricultural policy that ensured against general famine.

This cluster of gifted French writers joined other Europeans to transform God into an impersonal artisan who had created many universes that he had thereafter left alone so that the mechanisms set in motion ran forever. Each of these clock-like cosmic systems could be understood by any rational being who could appreciate the laws of modern science. These same enlightened thinkers also raised issues of tolerance by emphasizing the differences between knowledge and faith and allowing each individual to worship as he or she wished. Furthermore, they spoke to the necessity of redesigning the law so that the punishment inflicted on a criminal matched the crime committed, rather than allowing a monarch to inflict pain on others for his private and selfish ends. Finally, they raised questions about human society so that they could discover the most rational design; they wanted to generate economic and social harmony so that all members of society might develop a sense of attachment to the community as a whole.

Also on the list of enlightened intellectuals, three more stand out: David Hume (1711–76), Adam Smith (1723–90), and Immanuel Kant (1724–1804). Each of these philosophers deserves special attention because each one contributed to the discovery of culture as a human addition to the scientific inquiry that had captured the European imagination. Furthermore, each man helped to link the idea of culture to public opinion as both new social concepts began to mobilize a new political will in Europe. Finally, all three made these contributions without being aware that his philosophy might have such a dramatic impact on its readers.

David Hume

Born and educated in Edinburgh, David Hume (1711–76) spent a lifetime writing in the mainstream of the Enlightenment. As one of the numerous authors of this movement, Hume accepted completely Locke's critique of Descartes. Hume also asked why, if existence derived from God as an infinite, universal source of self-evident truth, did individuals vary so much in their understanding of the world? Furthermore, he pointed out that Descartes' reliance on innate ideas required a separation of thought and extension, mind and body, and reason and experience; then Hume asked how such a separation could satisfy anyone's sense of what was real. Perhaps even more problematic in Descartes' system was that the existence of the self proved to be far more compelling than his argument for the existence of God. If one did not accept Descartes' proof of God's existence, then one was left with no access to the innate ideas that existed behind universal reality. Thus, without Descartes' "God," humanity sank into *solipsism*, the theory that the self can know nothing but its own view of the world.

While critical of Descartes in a manner similar to Locke, Hume was equally dissatisfied with Locke's assumption that all humans were born with the power of reason. For Hume, reason comprised abstract concepts that had to be learned, just like any other ideas, or acquired through experience and the interpretation thereof. Hume concluded that the capacity to reason emerged slowly in each individual as a product of education.

Therefore, a person's understanding of such complex, abstract philosophical categories as resemblance, contiguity, time, space, and causation relied on learning as a disciplined pattern of experiences. These abstract ideas were not simply part of our arsenal of mental powers at birth. Thus, John Locke's formulation of empiricism and psychology rested on as shaky a foundation as did Descartes' conclusions. Nevertheless, Hume believed that Locke's empirical approach had hit upon a more fruitful mental strategy then Rationalism.

Simultaneously, if such ideas as causation were indeed learned, what type or set of experiences made us aware of this all-important concept? If no such experience could be found, then causation itself, the principal idea in physics and astronomy, had to rely solely on the authority of education. Such authority, however, had already fallen victim to the Scientific Revolution. Thus, if one could not discover causation through experience, then empiricism itself had no justification.

Hume provided an explanation for causation but revealed that the knowledge derived from this philosophical category was extremely limited. Stated simply, Hume's argument proposed that one needed to see events repeated numerous times in a very specific relationship before one could identify cause and effect. This relationship required a clear understanding of resemblance, contiguity, time, and space: the cause always had to precede the effect in time; both had to occupy the same space, and both had to be contiguous. Finally, the repetition of these three features of causation had to be recognized by their resemblance (their identical primary traits).

The first time these conditions were met, an observer would not see anything unusual because he or she would be unfamiliar with the sequences of experiences taking place. The second time, if the observer was aware, then the sequence might be recognized through its resemblance with the past. The more times this sequence was repeated, the more cause and effect became firmly rooted in the observer's mind. Yet even the most firmly anchored experiences of causation could lead to error. How, for example, could individuals ever know for certain whether the next meal they ate would nourish or poison them?

Worse, even the thing we knew the best, our knowledge of our self, dissolves in Hume's empiricism. What we know of our self is limited to our experience of this self. Since the future holds events beyond our experience, it is possible that we could do things completely out of character with what we know of our self. Hence, even if we think ourselves to be moral, and that the act of murder is unjust, we do not know for certain that sometime in the future a set of circumstances may arise to make us become murderers.

Hume's assault on Locke, and his rejection of Descartes, eroded both sides of Europe's new philosophies: rationalism and empiricism. Hence, Hume was in danger of retreating into complete skepticism. To avoid such an intellectual collapse, Hume developed a theory of the passions that he related to custom in order to create the possibility of a stable social order.

Hume's theory of the passions linked humanity's subjective pleasures and pains with desirable objects to create the concept of property and the pride of ownership as well as the humility caused by the misery of poverty. Correlated to wealth and pride were the opportunities to form associations such as marriage based on wealth and love while humility and poverty generated a sense of low self-esteem and self-loathing. Also, linked to humility were two dangerous passions, envy and malice, that threatened the social fabric with violence when the poor took pleasure from attacking the rich. To deal with these unstable but powerful feelings, Hume developed a concept of interest.

Interest combined passion with reason to create a form of directed action. A passion generated the motive, while reason created socially accepted methods of achieving one's goals. Private interests led to actions that resulted in such things as profit or successful liaisons with other human beings, while public interests produced governments. To create a public interest, however, Hume had to put together two contradictory ideas: property and justice; yet the tension in the contradiction created a dynamic energy that sustained the government.

Property produced inequality based on an ownership that excluded all others, created the pride of possession while facilitating marriage, and provided the means to organize labor in households as well as the community that fed all its members. This organization of labor generated an abundance of goods through a style of cooperation based on mutually supporting private interests. The interests of the master as employer arranged specialized occupations in a division of labor that maximized human efficiency for profit. The interests of the servant as employee enjoyed a life-sustaining job while generating a surplus of goods for the community to consume. In contrast, justice generated equality by forcing everyone to face the same standards of judgment when violations of the law against person or possessions occurred. Hence the inequality of ownership, and its material and social benefits, joined with the equality of the law to create a common sense of well being.

Hume maintained that a society endured only so long as the vast majority of individuals living within it felt that most of their interests were being met. As a result, the laws created to preserve human society succeeded only when they proved useful. In addition, these laws had to create a positive consensus shared by society's membership; these members had to believe that their mutual association had produced pleasurable results. Thus, this system of association relied heavily on public opinion.

Any order of law that generated a positive consensus among the members of a society, no matter how arbitrary or artificial in design, was just, and any such just design was called custom. Yet, Hume's use of philosophy to question the origins of society, and his requirement of evaluating the justice found within the division of labor based on private property, made his appeal to custom modern. Hume's use of custom was modern in the sense that humanity did not repeat its behavior without question; rather, humanity had to test the usefulness of its social bonds before they could be accepted or become the standard for communal association. This test measured the material rewards derived from the positive tension created by the paired but opposing ideas of property and justice.

Because these communal bonds were artificial, however, society was therefore subjective in the sense that it was the product of human passion, reason, and interests, as all three defined different systems of property and justice created by the various human communities found in the world rather than any natural or objective laws. Consequently, social existence measured success by the accumulation of pleasures enjoyed by the greatest number of people through their common association based on their artificially created customs. Yet such social happiness sustained by public opinion could tolerate the suffering of the few. These few, however, had to be in such small numbers that the positive consensus produced by public opinion continued to exist.

Hume's newly developed sense of social subjectivity, and the necessity of public opinion, laid the foundation for two groundbreaking philosophers: Adam Smith and Immanuel Kant. Both men responded to Hume's critique of Locke by developing an understanding of the way human beings created their own world. Both men also generated a new groundwork upon which to build human order. Smith created a social science called economics, and Kant returned to the mind to establish a rational architecture that governed what we know.

Adam Smith

Educated at Glasgow and Cambridge, a professor of moral philosophy at the University of Glasgow and the tutor of the Duke of Buccleuch, Adam Smith (1723–90) traveled to France, met the Physiocrats in the 1760s, and became thoroughly familiar with their theory of production. Using what he had learned, Smith began his powerful work, *An Inquiry into the Nature and Causes of the Wealth of Nations* (1776), by declaring: "labor is the fund." This declaration created the first fully integrated image of the power of production as a modern economic concept. Production served as the driving energy that generated wealth, value, exchange, and social organization. Production was both process and purpose reunited as the new strategy to understand how humans lived after the Scientific Revolution had separated these two concepts with the law of gravity.

The theory of gravity had merely explained how natural phenomena occurred, but it did not reveal the purpose behind physical events. Thus, when the concept of gravity had removed God from nature as an explanation, Europeans had also lost contact with His ultimate purpose for natural phenomena. Now Smith generated a theory using the rules of science to recover purpose by making it human.

Simultaneously, Smith, like Hume, rejected Locke's claim that people were born with the power of reason. Locke's view of humanity as rational creatures at birth had made everyone passive, rational observers who received all their knowledge from the impressions made on them by nature. Also, Locke had made God the Author of this relationship between humans and nature, but then had immediately removed Him and His Design from the realm of human knowledge. Thus humanity merely obeyed the laws of nature without grasping their purposes.

In contrast, Smith and Hume transformed human beings into active agents who shaped events in nature. For Smith and Hume, people wrote their own law of reason based on their passions and interests. And both Smith and Hume identified the social processes that met the needs of human purposes. Finally, both authors revealed that humans shaped their own future when *they* used their intellect, their will, and their art/culture—to build a functional society.

According to Smith, individual variation created a range of talents that made each person better at one occupation than any other. This particular ability to do a superior job in one line of work when compared to another suggested that specialized forms of labor were far more efficient than having each person try to produce everything for him or herself. Thus, quite naturally, humans tended to distribute themselves into a division of labor that reflected their various skills, talents, and attributes.

Given this tendency for labor to divide, Smith then argued that people quickly lost the ability to survive on their own. Accordingly, as the members of a society focused their productive energies on one particular occupation, they soon learned that everyone needed the products of one another in order to subsist. Quite naturally, then, everyone began to exchange their goods to meet their own personal needs, while the efficiency buried within the division of labor became an unexpected benefit for all. As a result, Smith then argued that the simple act of exchange itself compelled every participating laborer to discover the social concept of "cooperation." Cooperation, in turn, converted individual variation, the division of labor, and exchange into a functional social integration that provided a communal bond between all its working members. Consequently, humans quickly developed a sense of mutual dependency as they enjoyed the fruits of their new, productive union.

Cooperation created the basis for an integrated social experience, but it reflected only the range of individual differences found within the division of labor. Another tendency was for some laborers to use similar talents and abilities to seek the same occupation within a specific community. On such occasions, a new principle developed called "competition," which allowed those claiming these same abilities to test themselves; the results of this test revealed which of these laborers actually possessed the superior talents.

The test was simple, natural, and necessary to the well-being of the new community. Those claiming the same talents produced goods for sale in the marketplace. Then the public selected the best merchandise based on the labor of the person who could produce the greatest quantity without sacrificing quality. The greatest quantity of goods for sale increased the supply and lowered the commodity's price, while the continued quality satisfied the customer. Succeeding in the competition, this laborer captured the market while his skill and efficiency met the demands of the community. Yet competition now functioned as the paired opposite of cooperation; the former described individuals seeking the same job, and the latter reflected the mutual benefits of those who discharged their labor because they filled different occupations in a division of labor.

To cooperation and competition, Smith then added *natural price* and *market price*. Natural price described the income needed by all workers in a division of labor to sustain their lives as well as raise a family. Market price defined the income generated by the sale of a commodity; thus market price reflected the demand for specific goods. Hence, while the natural price described what laborers required to survive, market price defined the actual income paid the laborer to meet his needs. If market price exceeded natural price, the laborer and

his family prospered. If market price barely met natural price, the laborer merely subsisted; if market price fell below natural price, the division of labor collapsed. These three conditions explained how the division of labor changed over time, as market price shifted to reward the most innovative and productive laborers with the highest income.

The potential explanatory power of Smith's theories allowed his readers to study any society to see how its productive processes matched their country's economic purposes. Smith's analysis of Great Britain's current economic policies demonstrated how contemporary trade had failed to allow the full force of cooperation and competition—natural price and market price—to work their productive influences. Thus analyzed, he condemned the contemporary theory and practice called mercantilism for its restrictive commercial policies.

Smith argued that mercantilism denied the benefits of competition because it assigned wealth to the wrong sources, namely gold and trade. This error concerning the origins of wealth, either recommended hoarding gold, or regulating trade through monopolistic commercial policies. Consequently, Smith stated that mercantilism denied the freedom needed to develop new productive techniques as economic forces in the marketplace. Therefore, mercantilism prevented Great Britain from achieving an appropriate balance between competition and cooperation—natural price and market price—to realize the greatest prosperity possible.

Given all that Smith's theory of production explained about production and its relation to society and politics, his audience realized that the *Wealth of Nations* had placed in humanity's hands the power of self-creation. Smith's readers understood that he had followed Hume in reversing Locke's relationship between humans and nature by combining reason and self-interest to create an economic force that could transform the world into a desirable social and political reality. Furthermore, the power of Smith's theory helped his audience to see that just as humanity cultivated the soil for food, so people could cultivate themselves as creative agents. Simultaneously, as the eighteenth century ended, the way Europeans used the word *cultivation* (to mean agri*culture*) evolved into a new social term called culture. Consequently, Smith's economic theory contributed to a new human self-awareness bound up in the creation of the term *culture* by making people the manufacturers of their own social reality.

Smith's contribution to the developing concept of "culture" came through his use of Hume's strategy: paired concepts. To pair two opposing concepts as in Hume's property and justice, and Smith's cooperation and competition, natural price and market price, was to link in dynamic tension a creative new human potential. This integration of opposites became the foundation for society itself. Therefore, Smith's treatment of production pulled together economic, social, and political aspirations to create a clear image of what he called "the wealth of nations." This, in turn, joined with the new term *culture* to make this human phenomenon an integrated and positive experience.

Immanuel Kant

Born in Königsberg, Prussia, and educated and employed by the university there, Immanuel Kant (1724–1804) was as successful as Smith in breaking new intellectual ground. While Smith focused on the power of production in social organization, Kant awakened Europe's awareness of the power of human reason as a creative force. Kant created a field of inquiry as stimulating as economics by challenging Locke's conclusions concerning objectivity. Kant demonstrated that Locke had erred in his belief that sight, sound, smell, taste, and touch generated universally shared bias-free primary data. Thus, Kant's conclusions produced as dramatic an influence on the European imagination as did Smith's labor theory of value.

Kant began his intellectual challenge to Locke by defining the transcendental aesthetic—two observational limitations imposed on human perception he called time and space. Kant disagreed with Locke that sensation generated an immediate and objective impression made by nature on the human mind. He also disagreed with Hume, who had argued that time and space were philosophical categories like causation, resemblance, and contiguity that humans developed through education to process data from nature. Kant argued instead that time and space belonged to our perceptual faculties; that both governed how we received impressions from nature. Kant therefore claimed that time and space intervened during observation to function as mediating factors in our capacity to obtain direct, objective data from nature.

Kant began his attack on empiricism by stating that space imposed a specific point of view on every impression made during observation. This point of view caused all sensations to vary from person to person as well as from place to place. Kant stated that since individual sensations of the same object tended to differ, then observations of nature made from varying locations created an internal cluster of diverging impressions. These diverging impressions took the form of a collection of data that no longer conformed to the objective standards that Locke used to explain the origins of humanity's first ideas. Thus, space created the logical problem of interpreting observation: which of these different clusters of data was the same as the object itself?

Just as space jumbled data for the observer, so did time. Yet, rather than varying from place to place, or person to person, time clustered impressions of the same object into bundles that changed from moment to moment. Thus, time produced the same logistical problem as space when the observer tried to decide which of these different moments was the same as the object observed. Therefore, time reinforced space as both generated complex and subjective impressions of all the objects we observed in nature.

Locke had claimed, for example, that everyone received the same primary impressions of "red" when we formed the simple idea of this color from our exposure to its sense data. In contrast to Locke, Hume had admitted that humanity could not know for certain if the impressions made by "red" came from either the external stimuli caused by this color, or from the creative forces of the mind. Yet, Hume had assumed that given the constant coherence of our perceptions, that they represented nature with sufficient justice as to proceed from them as if they were an accurate and reliable source of data. Kant disagreed with both approaches and demonstrated that sensation was neither primary (i.e., measurable) nor constantly coherent. According to Kant, "red" generated a complex, not a simple, series of impressions given the number of different ways humans perceive this color during different moments in time and from different locations in space. In addition, the complexity of our understanding of "red" changed as individuals struggled with the problem of deciding what this color actually *was* given this stream of shifting evidence. In short, the impact of time and space on our observations made no simple clustering of sensations possible.

Kant therefore argued that the human mind had to intervene to organize actively the data offered by its impressions of nature. The role the mind played in evaluating data changed the meaning of the term *objectivity* from Locke's universal, bias-free primary impressions made by nature to the rules of reason Kant used to deal with sight, sound, smell, touch, and taste. Now a simple observation had so much variation within itself that objectivity could no longer rely on the impressions made by nature. Instead, Kant forced us to consider how the human mind actually worked.

According to Kant, everyone experienced significantly different sensations based on the variations in their points of view and the complexity of their temporal data. One person's impression of "red" differed widely from another. Only the mind could overcome these differences by relying on reason in a manner similar to Descartes' self-evident truths. Hence, Kant used Rationalism to design the inner workings of the mind.

Kant relocated objectivity in human intelligence by building a rational architecture of the mind that served to organize sense data. This mental architecture provided impartial, unbiased intellectual chambers that housed and processed our jumbled sense data. These mental chambers also created a rational interpretation that could be used to assemble ideas through symbolic systems such as math, logic, and language. Hence the objective mental architecture found in every human's mind became the means that defeated the jumble of sense data created by our perceptual apparatus of time and space. Also, the rational powers of the mind converted our immediate intuitions of nature into rational judgments that numbers, symbolic logic, and words could capture and process, which humans could now exchange through a rigorous, enlightened dialogue. Accordingly, Kant's readers could now see that the human power of reason generated a field of knowledge based on the objective architecture of the mind that created a linguistic means to produce a common, functional understanding of the world.

Kant's readers could see how his use of the term objectivity identified how humans applied reason to create theories of reality rather than receiving them directly from observing nature. Objectivity no longer came from nature itself; now it relied on everyone's vigilant use of their internal mental architecture to give shape to their ideas. Thus, Kant's audience recognized that his philosophy had cut humanity off from continuing to perceive nature as an objective entity in and of itself.

Simultaneously, however, Kant's readers also realized that once knowledge conformed to the mind's rational categories, humanity could apply what it knew to nature. Hence, knowledge was a functional construction that gave humans the potential to shape nature as if it were a neutral medium. As such, knowledge became a rational potential residing within human intelligence that now could function like a mental signet ring to reshape nature as if it were hot wax.

Because of Kant's relocation of objectivity within the human mind, Europeans began to see humanity's rational potential as possessing the same creative qualities as Smith's labor theory of value. Cultivating knowledge using Kant's architecture of the mind, like Smith's division of labor, produced an understanding of the world that could transform nature. In Kant's case, the objective qualities of the mind mixed with the subjective features of sense data to create the means to transform the immediate environment. These means change a local geographic setting into a rational, artificial setting that served human needs to the degree that a society had cultivated and applied its knowledge. Again, the image of *cultivation* suggested to Kant's audience the idea of *culture* itself.

Implicit in Smith's and Kant's revolutionary inquiries into human creativity lay the seeds of a new pattern of belief called *ideology*, the integrated theories and aims of a social, economic, and political program. Ideology produced a fresh pattern of beliefs that would become the new intellectual arena for public opinion as Europeans tried to take charge of their future. Ideology mobilized rational arguments to link human processes with human purpose to create the most positive and "progressive" (creative, useful) changes required by society. Consequently, ideology would join with the concept of culture to serve as a new political agenda that licensed Europeans to change the world. It was through ideology that Europeans interpreting Smith's and Kant's contributions to their modern worldview would have the greatest impact: both on how Europeans would see themselves as well as how they would approach a world full of foreign cultures.

The Modern Worldview

Obviously, the Renaissance, the Reformation, the Scientific Revolution, and the Enlightenment had created a significant pattern of changing beliefs that frequently contradicted one another. The Renaissance started these changes by helping to set in motion the Reformation's assault on orthodoxy; yet, the Renaissance also rejected the Protestant emphasis on faith over the power of human knowledge. Simultaneously, while the Reformation was underway, the Scientific Revolution built on the Renaissance's view of knowledge but sharply disagreed with the Protestant demand that humans subordinate their will and intellect to God's Divine Plan. Finally, the Enlightenment drew energy from the Renaissance and the Scientific Revolution, while rejecting the Reformation's argument that the Almighty should be the sole source of reality for the universe.

The evolution of ideas, as they passed through these four major intellectual movements, had transformed Europe's perception of human society from a natural to an artificial system. Simultaneously, while the Renaissance and the Reformation raised no doubt about God's role in nature and the formation of society, the Scientific Revolution had removed God from the realm of knowledge. And the Scientific Revolution and the Enlightenment had set in motion an inquiry into human nature and the formation of government that transformed the way Europeans saw their community. Even before David Hume, Adam Smith, and Immanuel Kant had finished with their analyses of humanity's role in the world, these three intellectuals had contributed significantly to the concept of culture. In the process, all three intellectuals had released the people of Europe to construct their own community based on the idea that society was a product of public opinion and human art.

Consequently, the Renaissance, the Reformation, the Scientific Revolution, and the Enlightenment had liberated the European imagination from its traditional past. They had destroyed a universal and sacred orthodoxy and replaced it with both a secular and religious heterodoxy. Meanwhile, as the Reformation released the individual to redefine his or her relationship with God, the Renaissance, the Scientific Revolution, and the Enlightenment had freed individuals and territorial states to become the masters of their own destiny, the genesis of the modern personality (see Chapter Twenty).

Suggested Reading

Scientific Revolution

Aliotto, Anthony, *A History of Western Science* (Englewood, N.J.: Prentice Hall, 1992).

Cohen, H. F., *The Scientific Revolution* (Chicago: University of Chicago Press, 1996).

Foucault, Michel, *The Order of Things: An Archaeology of the Human Sciences* (New York: Vantage Books, 1970).

Hall, A. Rupert, *The Revolution in Science, 1500–1750* (London: Longman, 1983).

Jacob, Margaret C., *The Cultural Meaning of the Scientific Revolution* (New York: Alfred A. Knopf, 1988).

Kuhn, Thomas S., *The Copernican Revolution: Planetary Astronomy in the Development of Western Thought* (Cambridge, Mass.: Harvard University Press, 1985).

Lindberg, David and Robert Westman, eds., *Reappraisals of the Scientific Revolution* (Cambridge: Cambridge University Press, 1990).

Perry, Marvin, *An Intellectual History of Modern Europe* (Boston: Houghton Mifflin, 1993).

Shapin, Steven, *The Scientific Revolution* (Chicago: University of Chicago Press, 1996).

Smith, Alan G. R., *Science and Society in the Sixteenth and Seventeenth Centuries* (London: Thames and Hudson, Ltd., 1972).

Westfall, Richard, *The Life of Sir Isaac Newton* (Cambridge: Cambridge University Press, 1993).

The Enlightenment

Aaron, Richard I., *John Locke,* Third Edition (Oxford: The Clarenton Press, 1971).

Foucault, Michel, *The Order of Things: An Archaeology of the Human Sciences* (New York: Vantage Books, 1970).

Harris, I., *The Mind of John Locke: A Study of Political Theory in Its Intellectual Setting* (Cambridge: Cambridge University Press, 1994).

Hof, Ulrich Im, *The Enlightenment* (Oxford: Blackwell, 1994).

Krieger, Leonard, *Kings and Philosophers, 1689–1789* (New York: Norton, 1982).

Outram, Dorinda, *The Enlightenment* (Cambridge: Cambridge University Press, 1995).

Perry, Marvin, *An Intellectual History of Modern Europe* (Boston: Houghton Mifflin, 1993).

Williams, Raymond, *Culture and Society, 1780–1950* (New York: Columbia University Press, 1968).

XX

THE RISE OF THE NATION-STATE, PART ONE:
The Territorial State

The nation-state emerged from a tangle of modernizing forces. The combined effects of the Commercial Revolution (1492–1763), the Reformation (1517–1648), and the Enlightenment (1690–1789), produced a new political concept called *popular sovereignty* (rule by the people). The Commercial Revolution contributed a vast new supply of wealth that combined with the rising cost of government to challenge the traditional distribution of power inherited from medieval Europe. The Reformation combined the passions of religious reform with dynastic warfare to spur the refinement of the royal army, a new instrument of political coercion that elevated most European kings to sovereignty. And the Enlightenment mobilized a new political weapon called public opinion that had no legitimate outlet for civil expression but nonetheless transformed the people's understanding of the contemporary state.

As discussed in Chapter Seventeen, the Commercial Revolution not only gave Europe direct access to every major port and coastline on the globe, but the Atlantic trade routes also bestowed on the West the initiative in cultural contacts around the world. Command of the initiative in cultural contacts made Europe the center of global trade for more than four centuries (1492–1914) because, for the first time in world history, Western civilization did not have to consult any other human society to determine when Europeans would arrive on foreign shores. This exceptional power granted the West the ability to test its military and commercial strength against the civilizations of the world to determine if the time was ripe to penetrate an alien society's traditional resistance to a foreign presence. Called the differential of power, this test of relative military and economic power set in motion a process of globalization that made Europe the first modernizing, proactive culture in world history. Together, the differential of power and globalization then became two major cultural themes that combined with Europe's determination to build empires that infused the West with extraordinary political, economic, and military potential (see Chapter Twenty-two).

Meanwhile, the Reformation pitted the Protestant theology of Martin Luther and John Calvin against Catholic resistance, while the political aspirations of Europe's monarchs generated an era of warfare that resulted in the development of sovereignty. After nearly a century of combat (1556–1648), the princes of Europe settled on an agreement that removed the papacy from politics while granting each monarch the power to determine the religion of his or her realm. Reinforced by the refinement of a royal army as the sole instrument of domestic coercion available to European princes, Royal Absolutism emerged in territorial states where the king could rule without consulting his men of estate. At the same time, the rising cost of government associated with the expenses created by the monarchy forced Europe's monarchs to develop new methods of taxation. The principle of "no taxation without representation," however, severely restricted the measures a king could use to raise the funds needed to run his state. The result was an effective avenue of change bestowed upon those who ultimately controlled the power of the purse.

Lastly, the Enlightenment unleashed a powerful new political weapon called public opinion that challenged tradition through a so-called rational critique of existing European institutions that either confirmed or denied the justice of contemporary society. Released from the constraints of the past, a new breed of European intellectuals drew strength from a mounting series of questions that demonstrated how the power of the human mind could command the existing order of human society. Either justifying the current political system so that a positive consensus developed within a territorial state, as in the case of England, or producing a mounting attack on the principal institutions of a given society, as in the case of France, the Enlightenment welded together a new political will that helped produce the nation-state. Forged in the caldron of revolution, the nation-state combined the social and economic changes of England's Industrial Revolution (1750–1850) with the political events of the French

Revolution (1789–1815). The result was a modern civil society that combined geography, language, and national identity into a new community, one whose understanding of itself derived from the consensus generated by public opinion.

The Territorial State

The first step in the formation of the modern nation-state was an intermediate level of cultural development between a feudal past and a modern future that emerged from the religious wars of the Reformation. Called the territorial state because it united the geographic regions of a single nation under the protomodern integration of a common set of political institutions, this new system of government became the norm from 1660 to 1789. Linked to the process of change that removed the pope from politics, the territorial state emerged after the rivalry between Catholics and Protestants had helped the monarchs of Europe develop the royal army. Combined with the corrosive intellectual consequences that emerged from the Renaissance, the Reformation, the Scientific Revolution, and the Enlightenment, the territorial state represented a resting place for Europeans to catch their breath before embarking on the next great era of change.

As a temporary era of calm before another great political storm, the territorial state marked a brief period when Europeans agreed to talk to one another to settle their differences rather than use war. To achieve this level of calm, however, Western civilization had to remove the residue of the feudal system. The steps taken to achieve this transformation of the European political landscape included: the concentration of military and financial power in the hands of kings; the elimination of Latin as the universal language of Christendom; and the integration of political authority within several European countries under one ultimate set of governmental institutions. Fundamental to this process of political change was an integration of commercial capitalism and the political consequences of the Reformation.

While religion dominated politics during the Reformation, the wars that settled the issues of a kingdom's faith allowed local monarchs to take power into their own hands, as Niccoló Machiavelli had recommended they do in *The Prince*. As kings discovered the potential power available to them through religious warfare, those who abandoned issues of faith in favor of the amoral thinking proposed by *The Prince* discovered a new source of political success. These emerging successful kings constituted a new social character called the *politique* personality.

Technically, the term *politique* referred to a faction of French Catholics and Protestants who objected to the political and economic mismanagement of their country during the era of religious civil war from 1562 to 1598. This politique party placed the common good of France above their religious differences and attempted to create a rational solution to their country's problems by shifting back and forth between the Catholic and Protestant leaders. The leading politique thinker, Jean Bodin (1530–96), established the modern concept of sovereignty by arguing that every society needed one ultimate authority capable of imposing law, preferably with the consent of the people, but by force if necessary. Consequently, the term politique defined the modern political thinking of this group, but the term is used in this chapter to depict the reasonable yet amoral practices of a far more important coterie of people: the successful leaders who profited politically from the Reformation.

Accordingly, politique individuals used Machiavelli's principle of "the ends justify the means" to achieve their goals. Simultaneously, politique monarchs followed Machiavelli's advice and wore morality as a mask to cover their actions. The combination of these two strategies allowed politique kings to appear to be moral and justify their conduct while also achieving their political goals by whatever means possible.

At the heart of politique behavior was the use of reason alone to decide political issues. Practitioners of this new political conduct applied themselves to the process of solving problems in a dispassionate manner calculated solely for the purpose of success. Such individuals were the first to discover that religious warfare could not offer either side a decisive victory, and that religious pluralism would become the political reality of Europe. When surviving kings finally came to this realization, they discovered that a careful, rational application of their material resources to the problem of acquiring power served best to achieve their political ends.

Like many of the intellectuals who had begun to appear as a result of the Scientific Revolution, these politique kings concluded that religion itself was suspect as a political instrument. It became clear to them that Europe was no longer going to be dominated by a single, universal faith. Thus, the act of fighting wars to create such conformity was both wasteful financially and entailed unnecessary cruelty and carnage. Hence, after 1648, these politique monarchs had redefined political authority in their realms. Achieving this new level of political reality, however, took time.

The events that drew Europe into religious warfare between 1556 and 1648 involved the momentum of dynastic rivalry that actually proceeded this century of combat. Reaching back to Charles VIII's invasion of Italy (1494–95), the nature of warfare caused matters of faith and royal claims to European estates to overlap. For example, after Charles VIII marched into Italy, the Valois of France fought the Habsburgs over who would rule this peninsula. Using their control of the Holy Roman Empire, the Austrian Netherlands, and Spain, the Habsburgs then proved to be more than a match for the Valois as both dynasties turned Italy into a battlefield. The struggle that followed spanned the years between 1494 and 1559 until the Valois finally admitted military failure and relinquished their claim to both Italy and their estates in the Low Countries. Yet, by 1559 the first phases of religious combat had also erupted, as Catholics and Protestants across Europe squared off to determine what form of Christianity their countries would embrace.

Meanwhile, the Valois' hunger for Italy, and the religious strife that followed on the heels of France's failure to realize its dreams of conquest, combined to transform the role of warfare in European politics. Between 1556 and 1648 any war fought in Europe allowed the combatants to test and refine their arms while consolidating power in the hands of the monarchy. The French, English, Spanish, Portuguese, Italians, Germans, Poles, Czechs, Hungarians, Danes, Swedes, and Swiss all engaged in a pan-European struggle that destroyed obsolete feudal practices and advanced the modern forms of combat. Simultaneously, all types of regional European weapons, tactics, and practices met one another on the battlefield just when dynastic and religious rivalry burned their hottest. The intensity of this military era refined the uses of violence while kings and princes everywhere pressed their political claims. At the same time, continuous armed trials in combat introduced new weapons like artillery and muskets that changed the nature of tactics and strategy. The result was the emergence of a new model of military might that defined the political landscape in the West between 1660 and 1789.

Only when the kings and princes of Europe had resolved their dynastic disputes did the pan-European era of violence officially subside. At that moment, the political developments that unfolded alongside Catholic and Protestant hostility could finally separate secular from religious issues. When this separation occurred, kings and princes everywhere agreed that political conduct could no longer be linked to establishing a universal church. In addition, each monarch was now free to determine the religion of his own realm.

Thus, the religious wars masked an underlying dynastic story that began at the end of Charles V's reign.

Charles V (1500–58), the Holy Roman Emperor, King of Spain (and its rich colonies), and ruler of the Netherlands, set the stage for this era of violence as he tried to maintain the medieval order in Europe during an age of change. Surrounding him were rivals in both religious and political institutions who did everything in their power to challenge his efforts. Exhausted by wars with France over Italy, the appearance of Protestants on his German estates and in the Netherlands, and the invasion of his Austrian lands by the Turks, Charles V died a frustrated man. It was his exhaustion that released the floodgates of warfare between 1556 and 1648.

The full force of religious war, and its dynastic consequences, began after Charles V abdicated his numerous thrones in 1556. Charles retired from the monarchy by bequeathing to his son, Philip II (1527–98), the Kingdom of Spain and the Netherlands, and leaving his brother, Ferdinand I (1503–64), the Holy Roman Empire and the Austrian estates. Sapped by his struggle with both the Protestants and the Turks, Charles V split up his massive political holdings so that his two heirs could focus their attention on local problems. The Turkish threat to the southeast, that of France to the northeast, and the Protestant movement in Germany and elsewhere would occupy the attention of these new monarchs.

For Philip II, suppression of Protestantism became his highest priority. Philip's good fortune as a young king allowed him to focus on this priority because the failure of the Valois to win its wars with Charles V over who would command Italy had weakened France. Ironically, while Charles died an exhausted man, France had reached an even greater degree of fatigue and entered an era of decay that caused the Valois dynasty to spiral into collapse.

Royal weakness dominated the politics of France from 1559 to 1598. The Valois gave up their claims to the Netherlands and Italy that traced back to Louis XI (reigned 1460–83) and Charles VIII (reigned 1483–98). The Low Countries had been part of the French crown until the Duke of Burgundy, Charles the Bold (1433–77), had tried to create a new kingdom. War between Burgundy and France lasted until Louis XI hired the Swiss to dispose of this troublesome duke. The death of Charles the Bold at the Battle of Nancy in 1477 dissolved his potential kingdom, but the Holy Roman emperor, the Habsburg Maximilian I (1459–1519), acquired the Low Countries through his wife, Charles's daughter and heir. Thus the Valois lost valuable estates to their dynastic rivals the Habsburgs.

Simultaneously, Italy had been a battlefield between France and Spain ever since Charles VIII won the battle of Fornovo in 1495. A series of wars began between the Habsburgs and the Valois over who would control the Italian Peninsula. Spain prevailed, as the Habsburgs under Charles V defeated and captured Francis I (1494–1547) of France at the Battle of Pavia in 1525. Yet the Valois continued to press their claims to Italy, and even the Netherlands, until the exhausted dynasty surrendered these efforts in 1559 by signing the Treaty of Cateau-Cambresis.

At the same time, within France itself Calvinist and Catholic forces squared off to launch an era of internal religious strife, with the great nobles rising to dominate local politics in the power vacuum left by the declining Valois. An on-again, off-again civil war occurred between rival religious factions, with the Calvinist Huguenots following the Bourbon family and the Catholics mobilizing under the Guise banner. The last Valois king died in 1589 without an heir, and Henry of Navarre, a Bourbon Calvinist, claimed the throne.

As a Calvinist, Henry led the Protestants to victory by 1594, but he realized that France was overwhelmingly Catholic. Careful thought led him to the conclusion that he would have to convert to Catholicism to rule France. This conclusion reflected Henry IV's willingness to sacrifice religious matters, even though he led the Protestant cause, in the interest of a stable kingdom. This rational attitude toward religion compelled him to give up Calvinism. Thus, he became a Catholic to secure the loyalty of the majority of his subjects so that he could rule France with relative calm.

Abandoning the Protestant cause revealed Henry to be a politique personality. Yet he was not so foolish as to leave his old Protestant followers without providing for their protection. He issued the Edict of Nantes in 1598 that guaranteed tolerance to those great nobles and towns who had become Calvinist. He issued this edict in the same year that Philip II of Spain died. Fortune now smiled on France.

Prior to his death, however, Philip II of Spain was the principal political figure that supported the Catholic Counter-Reformation during his forty-two-year reign (1556–98). Philip II waged war against all opponents of Catholicism that fell within his sphere of operation. He fought the Turks to a standstill in the Mediterranean by defeating them at the battle of Lepanto (1571). He could not, however, break Turkish power on land and recognized their rights to North Africa as far as Algiers by his failure to drive them off these northern shores during the 1580s.

Simultaneously, Philip concentrated his royal energies on cleansing the Austrian Netherlands of Calvinism, just as he had kept Spain pure for Catholicism by using the Inquisition. The Inquisition was a thirteenth-century papal institution designed to weed out heresy; the Spanish revived it at the end of the fifteenth century when it became an instrument of politics to ensure the purity of faith of all the king's subjects. This commitment to orthodoxy, religious homogeneity, and political purity in the Netherlands however, generated a military adventure that Philip could not draw to a successful conclusion. Under the duke of Alba, the Spanish invaded the Netherlands and recovered the portion of the Low Countries later called Belgium. Yet no matter how hard the duke tried to take it, the other portion, later called Holland, remained independent. The Dutch navy managed to outflank every invasion launched overland by the duke of Alba. And aid to the Netherlands from Anglican England only exacerbated Philip's military problems.

While the war in the Netherlands dragged on, Philip involved himself in the affairs of the Scottish, English, and French. Supporting the Catholic League led by the Guise family, Philip tried to defeat Henry of Navarre's claim to the French Throne. Failure there was compounded by his support of Mary, Queen of Scots. Mary's inability to control religious matters in Scotland had forced her to flee to England. There, Queen Elizabeth had imprisoned this Catholic monarch on the grounds that the Catholic Mary held a good claim to the English throne and therefore was a potential focal point for rebellion in England. In prison, Mary did indeed plot against Elizabeth, which eventually forced this English Queen to execute her Scottish captive. In her will, read after her execution, Mary had disinherited her son James in favor of Philip II. Thus, Mary's will gave Philip the pretext he needed to intervene in English politics as an ally of Holland and an enemy of Spain.

Using Mary's execution and her offer of good claims to the English and Scottish crowns as an excuse, Philip raised the mighty Spanish Armada—a fleet of 130 ships. In 1588, he attempted an invasion of England that exceeded the capabilities of his military: a coordinated naval attack from Spain combined with a land assault from Holland. Approaching England from the southwest, the Spanish sailed against a determined English fleet with the winds to their back. Met by smaller, more maneuverable English galleons and fire ships, the Spanish could not anchor in Holland or retreat along the French coast; they had to sail around Scotland to return home. Storms off the Scottish coast, however, destroyed the armada and Philip lost an irreplaceable fleet. The destruction of the armada not only set Spanish sea power back substantially but also launched England's rise to the role of a major naval power. Shortly thereafter, England's development of a

The Elizabethan Era

Queen Elizabeth I (1558–1603) became the third Queen of England to rule in her own right after Lady Jane Gray, who reigned for a mere nine days in 1553, and Mary Tudor, whose five years on the throne have been vilified by English Protestants. In contrast, Elizabeth proved to be such a competent and popular monarch that she gave her name to an entire age.

Coming to the throne at the age of twenty-five, Elizabeth was truly the Reformation's child. Her father, Henry VIII, had divorced his first wife, Catherine of Aragon, to marry Anne Boleyn, his second wife and Elizabeth's mother. This marriage had required Henry to break with the Catholic Church so that all of Anne's children would be legitimate. Anne's failure, however, to produce a living son (after two miscarriages) had left Henry with only another daughter, Elizabeth. Feeling himself cursed with Anne as he had felt with Catherine, Henry allowed his chief minister, Thomas Cromwell, to engineer Anne's execution. Accused of adultery, incest, and plotting to murder the king, Anne, her brother George Boleyn (Lord Rochford), her music teacher, Mark Smeaton, and several others, all felt Henry's wrath and suffered death. Elizabeth now had to cope with the stain of her mother's execution as she grew up in the shadow of her younger half brother, Edward, son of Jane Seymour (Henry's third wife) and her older half sister Mary (Catherine's daughter).

Surviving the anger of Mary's reign (1553–58), when Catholicism enjoyed a resurgence, Elizabeth as Anne Boleyn's daughter spent time in the tower but managed to outlive her half sister. Once in power, then Elizabeth exhibited excellent judgment in the selection of her advisors as well as in politics when it came to guiding her policies through parliament. Her subjects loved her because they could see their ambitions coinciding with hers. And her personal ability to direct the affairs of men, while remaining a glamorous woman, helped her to achieve an unprecedented record of administrative successes in an era fraught with religious, political, and military pitfalls.

Early in her reign, Elizabeth faced religion as a growing domestic and foreign problem. Upon her ascension to the throne, Elizabeth restored the Anglican Church after Mary attempted to turn back the tide of Protestantism. Elizabeth instituted a new Act of Supremacy hoping to restore her father's religious settlement, but the Protestants who had fled to the continent during Mary's reign, returned with a far more radical outlook. They had come in contact with John Calvin's religious ideas and hoped to impose a far more rigorous religious conformity on England through a Protestant Act of Uniformity (1558). Their success, however, was partially neutralized by Elizabeth's acceptance of their legal position while she carefully avoided enforcing the new act. At the same time, Elizabeth's determination to use marriage as a diplomatic tool led her to deliberately delay the selection of a husband. Yet, her remaining single made her cousin Mary, Queen of the Scots, her closest living relative and the heir to the English crown. Mary's devout Catholicism posed a threat to Protestants so long as Elizabeth remained single and childless. This became obvious to all Protestants when Elizabeth contracted smallpox and nearly died. Her survival increased her popularity,

while her reliance on a red wig, her use of heavy white make up, and her ornately bejeweled dresses spoke both to her spirit and to the fact that smallpox survivors were frequently both pockmarked and hairless.

After the religious settlement of the early years of her reign, Elizabeth enjoyed relative calm until 1570. The Anglican religion was the only established Church in the realm so everyone was technically an Anglican (derived from Anglicana, Latin for English). Happily for Elizabeth, Calvinists and Catholics were basically mute for twelve years as both parties lacked a coherent or focused program of opposition. After 1570, however, things changed.

A failed Catholic uprising in the north in 1569, Mary, Queen of the Scots' self-imposed exile and virtual house arrest in England during that same year, and Elizabeth's excommunication by the pope in 1570, convinced the majority of English that "papists" were traitors. Radical Protestantism also began to demand a "purification" of the Anglican church to remove any remaining papist vestiges; this demand for religious purity of faith created the Puritan move-ment. Together, the Catholic threat and Puritan demands forced Elizabeth to walk a political tight rope—something at which she excelled.

The Catholic threat combined a new missionary zeal that involved a steady stream of returning English exiles determined serve the church and convert the uncertain. Joined by young men trained by the Jesuits (see the Catholic Counter-Reformation above), the number of Englishmen willing to confront Elizabeth increased, while making Mary Stuart of Scotland a growing threat. This mounting Catholic pressure forced Elizabeth to request of parliament anti-Catholic legislation in the 1570s and '80s that isolated the Catholic opposition. Simultaneously, the Catholic threat inspired the Puritans to demand an accelerated reform of the Anglican Church that Elizabeth opposed. These Puritans grew in number and power as they developed strongholds in eastern England as well as in parliamentary representation.

In the later years of Elizabeth's reign (1585–1603) a state of war between Spain and England dominated the political scene. Precipitating this war, Elizabeth's execution of her cousin Mary eliminated the possibility of a Catholic heir to the English throne: Elizabeth felt compelled to eliminate Mary after catching her in several plots to end the Tudor reign in England. This execution, however, made Elizabeth a regicide, and gave Philip II of Spain the excuse he needed to invade England with his fabled Spanish Armada (see above). Yet Elizabeth's survival of this war, with a resounding English victory, placed a capstone on her political career. Now, with most of her friends and advisors dead, however, Elizabeth grew less interested in government as she aged. Her passing in 1603, began a new political era in England because James VI of Scotland (Mary Stuart's son), who became James I of England, lacked Elizabeth's good judgment in selecting advisors as well as in managing the religious and political opposition in parliament.

Youngs, Frederick, Jr., Henry L. Snyder, and E. A. Reitan, *The English Heritage, Volume One: to 1714,* Second Edition (Arlington Heights, Illinois: Forum Press, Inc. 1988) p. 109–30.

colonial empire made this island kingdom a major participant in the Commercial Revolution (1492–1763).

Only in matters of heresy did Philip enjoy substantial success. His commitment to the Catholic Counter-Reformation energized the Catholic camp. Led by Pope Paul III (1534–49), the Catholics had undergone rejuvenation during the Council of Trent (1545–63). Responding too late to the Protestant challenge, the papacy under Paul III focused on retaining control of those states that had remained Catholic. Scholars and pious individuals in positions of power within the church took heart at Paul III's leadership. He established the Society of Jesus in the year of his death, he revived the Inquisition in 1542, and launched the Council of Trent to fortify Catholic doctrines.

The first of Paul III's initiatives, the Society of Jesus, or the Jesuits, differed from other religious orders in three key ways. First, its members offered themselves for any sort of service their leaders dictated. Second, the head of the order, Ignatius Loyola, used a military discipline among its members that was as rigorous as the religious passion released by Luther and Calvin. And third, the order became a standing army of intellectuals dedicated to the church and at the disposal of the pope. Using Jesuits as intellectual agents, the Church secured the education of future Catholic monarchs and challenged the religious passions of the Protestants on an equal footing.

In addition, to the Society of Jesus, the Council of Trent also rejuvenated Catholic spirits. The Council of Trent answered the theological questions raised by the Protestants. The Council declared that the Bible was not the only source of Christian beliefs. Rather, the traditions of the church as they descended from the Apostles to the bishops created an unbroken line of religious principles that held as much truth as did the Bible. The Council declared Christianity to be a living religion whose vitality resided in the church. These themes clearly marked the boundaries between Protestantism and Catholicism and guaranteed that no one would ever reunite Europe under one religious authority.

The energy released by the combination of Paul III's theological work and Philip II's military championship of Catholicism, defined the battle lines. Philip II's military failures against England, Scotland, and Holland secured Protestantism in those places. Philip's joint efforts with his relatives in Austria spurred the Catholics of Central and Eastern Europe. Together, the Habsburgs and Jesuits worked to overwhelm Protestantism in Italy, southern Germany, Hungary, and Poland. The zones potentially open to religious change, north Germany and the Scandinavian countries, felt the pressure growing in the south and prepared for war.

Queen Elizabeth I, (1533–1603). Painted for Sir Henry Lee in 1592, this oil on canvas is known as the "Ditchley Portrait" referring to Lee's home near Oxford. Sir Henry Lee had been appointed the Queen's Champion for decades. The Ditchley Portrait, by Marcus Gheeraerts the Younger. National Portrait Gallery, London.

Yet all the energy Philip II invested in the Counter-Reformation injured more than helped his kingdom. During his reign (1556–98), the Spanish consolidated their hold on Mexico and Peru in the Western Hemisphere. The potential wealth available to the Spanish was enormous because of their access to new capital, their occupation of rich territories in the Western Hemisphere, and their initial ability to command the Atlantic trade route. Yet Philip's use of this wealth actually eroded his country's economy.

As Spain expanded its hold on its American colonies, gold and silver poured into Spain, with 20 percent, or "the royal fifth," going directly into the Spanish treasury. This abundance of precious metal released the slow and grinding force of inflation within Philip's kingdom. His habit of spending wealth on religious wars, and his faith in the principle of bullionism (i.e., stockpiling gold and silver as the only source of wealth) meant that he squandered potential capital on destructive, unproductive enterprises even as he accelerated inflation. Thus, as gold and silver poured into Spain, the productive base of Philip's economy not only failed to grow, but actually eroded. Consequently, Spain became a victim of the Commercial Revolution rather than a beneficiary.

Thus, while all this gold and silver should have stimulated the Spanish economy, Spain experienced economic failure. Simultaneously, the extension of Spanish holdings in the Western Hemisphere, combined with its political commitments in Europe, led to a depopulation of Spain during its peak years of power. The flow of people to the colonies and into religious wars reduced Spain's numbers while the other European states enjoyed population growth. Finally, excessive taxation to raise money to fight the Catholic cause, and later the use of loans that added interest to Spain's costs, made Spanish goods even more expensive when compared to foreign commodities. As a result, Spain did not benefit from the Commercial Revolution that it had helped launch in 1492.

While Spain floundered, the preparation for war in the Germanys came into focus in the generation after Philip II's death. Europe's religious division pitted the Protestant kingdoms and principalities in England, Scotland, Holland, Scandinavia, and north Germany against the Austrian branch of the Habsburg family supported by a weakened Spain. In between, the politique kingdom of France under the Bourbons took a neutral stand. War erupted in 1618 as the last great conflict of the Reformation began in an effort to define the religious space of the Germanys.

At first the Habsburgs nearly captured all the Germanys for Catholicism. Between 1618 and 1631, Catholic armies in the Germanys won several stunning victories. In 1618, the Czech nobility in Bohemia, who had become Protestants, feared the revived Counter-Reformation. They attempted to win their independence by expelling their Habsburg officials. The Bohemians then turned to Frederick V, the German elector of the Palatine, and offered to make him their new king. The Habsburg, Ferdinand (1578–1637), later the Holy Roman Emperor, Ferdinand II (1619–37), counterattacked using Count Johannes Tserlaes Tilly (1559–1632) and Maximilian I of Bavaria (1573–1651) as his generals. The combined Habsburg forces defeated the Bohemians at White Mountain near Prague in 1620 and crushed this revolt.

Frederick of Palatine, a German Duchy, lost his hold on Bohemia and suffered an invasion of his home state. The Protestant princes of Germany rallied to Frederick's aid, but Tilly crushed them at the battles of Wimpfen and Hochst (1622). Frederick lost his lands to Maximilian I of Bavaria and Ferdinand II while the war spread. Christian IV of Denmark (1577–1648) now entered the conflict on the Protestant side. At the same time, the Catholics gained the services of Albrecht Wenzel Eusebius von Wallenstein (1538–1634), an imperial general of substantial talents. Wallenstein finished off the resistance of the German princes at Dessau in 1623 and invaded Jutland, Denmark, the same year. Christian IV sued for peace in 1629, but just as the

future looked bleakest for the Protestants, the king of Sweden, Gustavus Adolphus (1594–1632), joined the battle.

The entry of Sweden shifted the fortunes of war to the Protestants. Wishing to capture control of the Baltic Sea, Gustavus Adolphus saw what would become known as the Thirty Years War as an opportunity. Motivated by gain rather than a pure religious passion, Gustavus was another politique personality who emerged from these religious conflicts. His leadership and new model army proved to be the best in the field. He believed the war was a reasonable gamble and plunged in.

He prepared the way by negotiating an understanding with Armand Jean du Plessis, Duc de Richelieu and cardinal of the Catholic Church (1585–1642), a man who revealed himself as yet another politique personality. Gustavus and Richelieu both wanted to limit Habsburg power and used religion as an excuse for war. Richelieu stayed in the background because his was a Catholic cardinal, but he supported Gustavus, who stepped forward on center stage as the Lutheran monarch who championed the Protestant cause.

For the most part, Gustavus had correctly assessed the military opportunities offered by war. He crushed Tilly at Breitenfeld in 1631 and liberated north Germany. Gustavus then turned south and fatally wounded Tilly in another Catholic defeat at Lech in 1632. On the verge of liberating all of Germany for Protestantism, Gustavus attacked Wallenstein at Lutzen in 1632, won another victory, but died in battle. Gustavus's gamble did not pay off, but the Protestant cause had survived.

In the meantime, an anti-imperial prince murdered the Catholics' best general, Wallenstein, in 1634. Yet even the Habsburgs did not mourn Wallenstein's death, for they had begun to see him as a potential enemy. Ferdinand II had begun to suspect that Wallenstein intended to become the new king of a Catholic Germany.

Exhausted by war, the Germans signed the Treaty of Prague with the Habsburgs to get rid of all the foreigners who had moved into their lands. The death of Gustavus Adolphus, Johannes Tilly, and Albrecht von Wallenstein left both sides in confusion. Yet, the struggle was still not over.

The final phase of the war saw Richelieu openly back the Protestant princes, his politique nature coming into full view. Religion had given way to dynastic interest. Now the Habsburgs faced a Bourbon challenge to define the strongest monarchy in Europe.

All of continental Europe was drawn into the fray as the United Provinces of Holland and France opposed Spain in the Low Countries, while Portugal revolted against Spanish rule on the Iberian Peninsula. Also, France fought Spain in Italy, while control of France and Germany became a contest between the French and Spanish armies in both regions. Finally, the Austrians invaded France to aid the Spanish, while the Swedish and German princes defeated the Austrian Habsburgs in the Germanys. These crosscurrents of war revealed to the Europeans that perhaps a redefinition of the relationship between political power and religion was best for all.

The Treaty of Westphalia marked the end of the Thirty Years War and the Reformation in 1648. The general results of the war saw a tremendous loss of life in the Germanys, destruction of property there, and the collapse of the Holy Roman Empire as a meaningful political organization. As a result, the Germanys, the Italian principalities, and Austria filled Central Europe with a fragmented political landscape. Simultaneously, the Habsburgs had lost their primacy as the leading monarchs of Europe.

The history of the Habsburgs during the Reformation stood as an object lesson of what happens to a dynasty that used religion as the basis of political reasoning. In contrast, the Bourbon century was about to begin, the result of the politique management of French affairs by both Henry IV and Richelieu. Now the princes and kings of Europe were free to decide the political and religious destiny of their states, while the pope would no longer participate in politics.

The Politics of Language

Just as papal authority ceased to be political by 1648, so Latin died as a universal language. In addition, since religious warfare had split Europe into two broad Christian camps, one filled with Protestant sects while the other remained Catholic, so the concept of community in Europe could no longer be defined by one common or sacred tongue. Simultaneously, as Protestant princes supported the publication of Bibles to distribute the Word of God, so half of Europe chose to use a local language rather than continue the speech of ancient Rome. Also, since monarchs had acquired a monopoly on violence with the rise of the royal army, and wished to rule everyone within their domain, so the use of a common territorial language proved far more serviceable than retaining the tongue of a defunct universal church. Furthermore, since science had shattered the authority of the past as efficiently as the Reformation had broken the pope's hold on politics, so language had to adjust to its new responsibilities to convey a nonsacred truth to Europe's literate population. Finally, when reason replaced faith as the ultimate source of knowledge, so political authority had to adapt Nominalism as the linguistic strategy to name all things.

European languages had to change to meet the needs of the new, emerging territorial-state. Just as politics and science forced philosophy to adjust to a modern sense of secular reality, so language had to take on modern qualities to explain how reason could capture and convey the impressions made by nature with any accuracy. Accordingly, all symbols of speech had to represent nature by developing two seemingly contradictory qualities: first, words had to be preeminent, and second, language had to be unobtrusive. Words had to be preeminent in the sense that language functioned as the only means to trap Locke's objective sense data and construct images to represent these universal impressions with absolute accuracy. At the same time, language had to be unobtrusive in the sense that words could not be entities-in-themselves that might interfere with meaning. Instead, each term had to form in the human mind like a rational reflection of objects in nature and serve as a system of universal representations. Thus, language became a common vehicle for facilitating rational thought, but existed as a two-dimensional system of mental images that reflected objects in nature as they acted on the human mind.

Because protomodern Europeans believed that language captured thought in this manner, Enlightenment thinkers like Thomas Hobbes (1588–1679), John Locke (1632–1704), Étienne Bonnett de Condillac (1715–80), Denis Diderot, (1713–84), Jean le Rond D'Alembard (1717–83), Jean Jacques Rousseau (1712–78), Adam Smith (1723–90), and Antoine Louis Claude, Comte de Destutt de Tracy (1754–1836) all concluded that words could not interfere with meaning. For example, Hobbes described language in his masterpiece, *The Leviathan* (1651), as a system of notations that individuals used to recall representations of thought as they reflected the impressions made by nature. Locke stated in his *Essay Concerning Human Understanding* (1690) that words were the marks used by humans to represent ideas as the speaker assembled sense data through the use of reason. According to Locke, language reflected reason's power to interpret nature's impressions and express them as new concepts. For both Hobbes and Locke, as well as those that followed, language became the voice of the rational mind, representing through words the logical purity of thought, and serving as an unobtrusive symbolic system of reason.

Yet language was also an instrument of power. Its ability to capture thought made the spoken word a vehicle for Sir Francis Bacon's maxim: knowledge is power. Accordingly, protomodern Europeans believed that language bridged the gap between the world of rational thought and the realm of political action. They felt that with an accurate language, the power found in the new sciences and philosophy could find expression in this world.

Thus, the monarchs of Europe set about standardizing the languages of their realms. Each sovereign sought to create a general grammar that matched the objectivity of logic and math so that communication and reason would become one. Consequently, such a general grammar would recover universal meaning the way Latin had once served a universal church. Now, however, this universal meaning would be anchored in reason and serve the purposes of the state.

As a result, language became an instrument of politics and practical action as well as thought. For example, the Académie Française (founded in 1635) and the Royal Society of England (founded in 1662) set up committees to modify, clarify, purify, and standardize French and English. What had once been the vulgar tongues now became the voice of reason. As more people learned to read in response to Protestantism's call for personal study of the Bible or commerce's demand for the critical thinking skills needed to engage in trade, so literary style adjusted itself to a growing public eagerness for information about the affairs of state. Just as the philosophes appealed to reason as the new human capacity to reflect nature's images, so Europeans in the seventeenth and eighteenth centuries developed a style of speech designed to convey precise facts briefly and plainly.

Setting aside the superstition and folly of the past, the languages of each territorial state would have two things in common. One, competent rulers sought to encourage the refinement of speech through their royal societies so that they could capture reason without obstructing meaning. Two, they believed that language could serve government as an instrument to create a rational order for society rather than suffer the flights of fancy that had tantalized the imagination in the past.

Simultaneously, although each territorial tongue vocalized different sounds, the content of their words had to be identical. Thus, the rulers of Europe encouraged intellectuals to polish local languages so that all territorial voices could cross the frontier without losing meaning. Each language had to be refined to the point that it had the capacity to move from one mind to the next through acts of translation without a loss of sense. Accordingly, Europeans had come to believe that each newly purified territorial language conveyed the same meaning because words and grammar represented objective truth as constituted by reason.

Consequently, as sovereigns imposed their will on their realms, French, English, Spanish, Portuguese, Italian, German, and so on, slowly began to merge with local political identity. Each language gave form to the modern sense of community, as sovereignty became the sole source of political power in the various realms of Europe. Finally, each tongue gave the public a new sense of being, as regional languages converted passive subjects into rational, active agents with efficient minds capable of forming objective opinions.

Sovereignty, Commerce, and Taxation

By 1650, Spain, Portugal, France, the Italys, and the Germanys had developed a political form called Royal Absolutism wherein monarchs and princes tried to govern without consulting the leading figures within their realms. The only limitation on the power of an absolute monarch or prince, which undermined the term *absolute* itself, arose from the problem of paying for the new regime. If the cost of government increased to the point that the absolute ruler could not pay for the instruments of power from his or her own sources of income, that ruler faced a fiscal crisis that could erode absolute authority. This fiscal crisis focused on a central question: who controlled the power of taxation?

The problem facing any absolute ruler when it came to matters of new taxes is that legitimate forms of property within a king's or prince's realm possessed certain rights and privileges he or she had to recognize. Surviving from feudal law, these legitimate forms of property existed as real estate and corporate towns scattered throughout the realm. Each of these forms of legal possessions included specific immunities to royal interference that required a monarch or prince to consult the men of estate before imposing a new tax on them. Thus, Royal Absolutism required sovereigns to limit their impulses to spend money foolishly, or else face the battle cry of those taxed: no taxation without representation.

Thus, financing sovereignty posed a special problem for the monarchy that revealed absolute authority to be an illusion. Given the new expenses caused by the royal army, and taking control of all features of political power, these absolute rulers had to chart a careful course through the financial world of protomodern politics. Either a king or queen created a partnership with real estate and corporate towns that he or she could live with, or they avoided assembling representatives from either of these two sources of legitimate wealth. Of these two options, Royal Absolutism selected the latter; the king or queen ruled without calling an assembly of nobles and corporate towns, which meant this ruler had to live on his or her own income.

The reason for this decision to avoid assemblies rests with issues already mentioned in Chapter Four—

teen. For example, for someone who possessed real estate, land offered economic identity (estate), social position (status), and political authority (state). Hence, an individual who possessed land called himself a man of estate, which meant attached to his property were rights and privileges a monarch could not ignore. Simultaneously, charted towns received acts of royal incorporation that granted them legal identity and protected the rewards of trade for both merchants and kings. Once a king granted corporate existence, the merchants who occupied these towns now fit into the legal fabric of society and could not be taxed without consultation, or changing the terms of their charter. Accordingly, both land and chartered towns forced monarchs to confer with elected representatives if he or she wished to raise taxes. Hence, although the absolute monarch claimed to be above the law as a royal sovereign, he or she could not rule as such unless they could afford to pay for government on their own. A case in point is the monarchy of France.

France

Louis XIV's France was the largest and richest country in Europe during the seventeenth century. He commanded 19 million people, or four times the number that lived in England. France had the most favorable climate and the most fertile soil; it also had the greatest concentration of wealth. Yet despite these advantages, the French lost most of their wars with the new United Kingdom (i.e., the union of England, Scotland, Wales, and Ireland in 1707) which speaks to an underlying weakness in Louis XIV's political system.

Louis was an absolute monarch who transformed France into a protomodern state based on the newly developed concept of sovereignty. Louis dominated French politics as the agent of God, similar to James I of England's definition of royal authority in his *The True Law of Free Monarchy*. As the agent of God, Louis XIV, who hailed himself as the "Sun King," had a free hand to do as he pleased within the limits of his royal resources. Only God could intervene and show displeasure at Louis's conduct by frustrating France in achieving its goals.

To enforce God's will on Earth, Louis had to develop an efficient administration and army. These two arms of government would serve as the basis for exercising royal power. Yet real power itself lay in his soldiers. Here the king concentrated nearly all his efforts to complete the process started by the Valois Dynasty.

The French military had developed out of the Reformation to become a profession of specialists hired by kings for combat. Commanded by colonels, these professional officers raised enough money to outfit a regiment and hire themselves out as mercenaries. The enterprise of war had made the regiment the most responsive unit on the battlefield. Only the best had survived the religious wars of 1556–1648 to create a new standard for military performance.

But this new standard fell short of Louis XIV's goals. Louis wanted to make the army an instrument of the state and not the tool of a mercenary colonel. If a person was to be armed in France, that person had to represent the king. Thus, Louis systematically overhauled the French army. He integrated every branch of the military to be responsive to his will as the general. From this exalted position, he created a direct chain of command through a common system of ranks. His government supervised recruiting and kept a ledger of colonels responsible for all his regiments. These regiments had to be equipped with the proper number of men, weapons, provisions, and housing. A Quartermaster General's office was set up to control supply. The king's color, white, became the standard for all uniforms. Troops were taught to take up their stations by word of command through rigorous discipline imposed by an officer who gave his name to such military order: the Royal Inspector named Jean Martenet. Regular audits of these military units held colonels accountable for failure to meet royal standards.

The army thus became the king's political tool. Mobilized and ready to implement his will, Louis demonstrated to Europe that a monopoly on coercion was the key to absolute power. This example did not escape the British, who feared absolute monarchy and saw to it that their army never grew very large, while their navy became the envy of Europe. Thus, the British realized that as an army secured royal authority, while ships secured commerce and revenue streams.

The foundation of military power, however, rested with the French royal bureaucracy. Here, too, Louis took long strides in modernizing his state. Louis preferred men who had acquired their rank recently. Called, "new men" these individuals were more loyal to the monarch's will than were the hereditary nobility. Thus, Louis made these men into *intendants* (superintendents or government officials) and placed them throughout France in order to run his reorganized territorial state.

These intendants received districts to administer wherein they supervised military recruiting, checked the inventories raised by colonels, kept an eye on the local nobility, dealt with town officials and guilds, and generally secured the obedience of the populace. Social order took definition under the watchful eye of the intendants. It was their responsibility to control hereditary offices, prevent crime, run local markets, watch

Construction of the Hall of Mirrors at Versailles began in 1678, when Versailles became the official residence of Louis XIV and was completed in 1684. It is a tribute to the hall inside the Ancient Persian Kingdom of Persepolis and considered one of the major attractions of the palace. It was here that the German Empire was proclaimed in 1871, after France was defeated in the Franco-Prussian war and also where Germany signed the Treaty of Versailles in 1919, ending World War I. Château de Versailles, Versailles, France.

over the courts, provide famine relief, and serve as an office of appeals in local disputes. As a result, the intendant became an extension of Louis's royal will.

In contrast to the intendant, Louis viewed the ancient noble families of France as the unstable portion of his kingdom. To make sure that these ancient families had nothing to do with po-litics, Louis avoided calling the *Estates General* (i.e., France's parliament). Accordingly, Louis excluded the French nobility from political power, but at the same time made them tax-exempt. Thus, he did not consult his nobility on matters of revenue and ran his government by placing the tax burden on those who had no rights, privileges, or power to resist.

The financial system that Louis created ran smoothly as long as the monarchy stayed within its means. Yet war upset the internal financial balance between taxation and the cost of governing and eventually strained the French state to its limits. Since Louis was not willing to share power with his nobility, war constantly caused his government to run short of funds.

Meanwhile, taxes fell upon the unprivileged people of France, meaning that France's peasants as well as those in the middle of society usually funded the French political system. Together, however, these two groups of people made up the population who could least afford to carry the cost of government. Consequently, tax exemption became the principal weakness of Royal Absolutism as established in France and eventually led to royal bankruptcy in 1789.

When Louis ran short of money, he often resorted to the sale of nobility to raise needed revenues, but this only made fiscal matters worse. Those who pur-chased a noble title also sought tax-exempt status, which decreased the king's tax revenue, even as it increased the tax burden on the peasants. Thus, France became a paradox: it was the richest nation in Europe, but the French king was poor compared to his chief rival, his royal cousin in Great Britain, and while Royal Absolutism claimed unlimited power, the monarchy found itself restricted as to what the king could afford.

Seemingly disregarding the state of his finances, Louis fought a series of ruinous wars during his long seventy-two-year reign (1643–1715). Taken together, these military adventures did not produce sufficient gains to justify Louis's expenses. But his successors did not learn from Louis's mistakes. As a result, Louis XIV, Louis XV, and Louis XVI all ran up massive debts.

At the same time, the French nobility felt no obligation to the state to help bail the French government out of its financial woes. Since the French nobility had been excluded from politics, they took pleasure in their tax-exempt status, happy to let the French poor carry the full burden of taxation. Unlike England's men of estate, whom parliament elevated to the role of equal partner with the king creating a form of civic virtue that bound them in the idea of a commonwealth (see below), France never gained this type of internal unity. Hence, Louis XIV created a smooth system of power but asked too much of it financially.

England

In contrast to Royal Absolutism, England demonstrated how kings and queens had to work in partnership with real estate and corporate towns to create a stable government. The creation of this partnership did not occur without a struggle as the English monarchy flirted with absolute monarchy during the seventeenth century, but had to settle on a political arrangement that recognized the illusions of power invested in the term *absolutism*. Accordingly, the English people generated a political contract that balanced the will of their king with the politically privileged of the realm; this arrangement became the great exception to Royal Absolutism between the years 1660 and 1789.

England was an island kingdom at the edge of the European continent separated from the concentrated military power of absolute monarchy. This geographic circumstance allowed the English to experiment with politics free from direct continental pressures. Because the English enjoyed a water barrier to overland invasion, the people of this island realm ultimately invested more resources in developing a navy rather than an army. Accordingly, the English monarchy had fewer opportunities to justify producing a standing military force and was denied the principal instrument of royal power located on the continent. As a result, the English had only come close to Royal Absolutism when the Tudors reigned (1485–1603), but parliament quickly pulled away from its subordination to the crown after Elizabeth I died in 1603. Under the Stuarts, who succeeded Elizabeth, parliament then asserted itself and claimed the right to set the tax rates for the realm whenever the king asked for more money to pay for the rising costs of the state. This parliamentary claim led to nearly a century of political struggle (1603–89).

Unlike Poland or Germany, where an assembly of landlords, aristocrats, and townspeople had successfully asserted themselves against the crown, in England the rise of parliament did not lead to decentralization. Also, in contrast to the continent, where successful governments meant the rise of Royal Absolutism, in England sovereignty developed on the principle of representation. This unique success reflected the character of parliament.

Parliament was the only representative body for the entire state, while the notable men of Spain, France, the Germanys, and Poland met in local assemblies that often competed with central deliberating councils. In England, however, the parliament concentrated all the power of the great magnates in two houses that united the financial strengths of corporate towns with real estate. These two houses were the House of Commons and the House of Lords.

Commons mixed the political interests of non-titled, landed aristocrats called squires or the gentry with merchants from England's great commercial centers. Both groups of wealthy men had the tendency to elect representatives who shared one general goal: to protect property rights. In the House of Lords, the titled, secular aristocracy outnumbered the bishops 82 to 26 because Henry VIII had confiscated the monasteries and eliminated the abbots. This aspect of the Anglican Church's reform converted Lords into a legislative chamber that tended to agree with Commons on issues of property rights, which required the crown to consult with a proprietor before raising taxes. Therefore, the mood in both houses reflected the secular concerns voiced by men of estate who controlled the growing wealth enjoyed by a country that had responded to the economic opportunities offered by the Commercial Revolution (1492–1763). Both forms of ownership, real estate and corporate towns, possessed rights and privileges linked to their possessions that forced the king to consult with parliament on the matter of raising new taxes. Hence, parliament developed the doctrine of "no taxation without representation" well before this phrase helped inspire the American Revolution of 1776.

In 1603 when Queen Elizabeth I died, parliament was ready to assert its will. In the closing years of Elizabeth's reign, parliament had already hinted at a growing desire to intervene in politics. The old queen's great popularity forestalled any such move, but her death released parliamentarians to voice their political opinions.

The new king, James VI of Scotland (son of Mary, Queen of the Scots, and Elizabeth's heir—see insert above), became James I of England. A Scot, he was viewed by the English as a foreigner. On top of this perception, James wrote *The True Law of Free Monarchy* (1598) which argued that a king had a right to rule without consulting any representative body. Based on the thesis that the crown held absolute power as granted by God, James I tended to lecture parliament on his vision of royal authority rather than attempt to work with these men of estate. Needless to say, James's views on monarchy conflicted directly with the desire of parliament to intervene in government using the power of taxation.

James I would not have had any problems with parliament if he could have ruled so frugally that he did not have to consult this representative body for new taxes. But he was in constant need of money. The struggle with Spain during Elizabeth I's reign had contracted substantial debts. James himself was far from restrained in his tastes for splendor or gifts to his friends. Furthermore, inflation caused the price of running the state to climb, which in turn required more money. Finally, since James drew income from fixed sources as was customary for a feudal inheritance, his purchasing power declined each year. Hence, he needed to work with parliament rather than merely tell Commons and Lords to obey his will.

Throughout James I's reign a mounting hostility between the crown and parliament continued, but no open rupture occurred. James's heir, Charles I, was not so fortunate. Having learned about monarchy from his father, and having witnessed the crown's struggle with parliament, Charles I inherited the throne with the same attitudes as James I. Hence, the struggle continued and intensified during Charles's reign (1625–49).

Only four years into Charles's rule, the crown and parliament became deadlocked over issues of taxation. After 1629, Charles I tried to govern without parliament, but again he had to be frugal. If he had succeeded, Charles would have created a regime very much like the one that developed in France under Louis XIV. Louis ran his state without having to consult the Estates General, the principal French parliament, as he attempted to stay within existing royal sources of income.

Like the eventual financial failure of the French monarchy, however, Charles I simply had too many expenses. The mounting cost of government, and Charles' unwillingness to be a frugal monarch led him to experiment with taxation. He put forth the theory that traditional revenues had to adjust to contemporary times. Using ship money, for example, as a test case, he tried to alter tradition.

Ship money was a source of taxation the crown could collect from coastal cities to build a navy that protected these ports. Charles wanted to extend this principle to the entire kingdom and build an English navy based on the idea that such a modern military institution served to protect the entire state. Yet to tax the interior of the realm without consulting parliament was to create a precedent that could not go unchallenged. One English gentleman, John Hampton, took this challenge in 1637 and refused to pay. His trial focused public opinion on Charles I's efforts.

Coincidentally, 1637 marked the same year that the Scots launched a rebellion against Charles I. Charles had also pressed for religious conformity in both his realms, England and Scotland, by supporting the High Anglican Church and pursuing a policy of hostility to Calvinists. Furthermore, his reforms in Ireland hinted at pro-Catholic sympathies that also antagonized the Calvinists. Finally, this religious policy required strict conformity to Anglican doctrine and had pushed some 25,000 Puritans (see insert on Elizabeth I above—Puritans were radical Calvinist reformers determined to "purify" the Anglican church) out of England to found the Massachusetts Bay Colony as part of the Great Migration.

Like the Puritans, most Scots wanted to preserve the integrity of their churches. As Calvinists, too, the Scots reacted to Charles I's religious policies by rebelling against his rigid intolerance. Needing money to deal with the Scots, Charles called on parliament in 1640 when the members' mood was its darkest because the king had not assembled his men of estate for eleven years (1629–40). As Charles requested new taxes from parliament, the representatives of wealth expressed their own political goals: they wanted a voice in state affairs.

Parliament's leaders, such as John Hampton who had opposed ship money, John Pym, an outspoken leader of parliamentarianism, and a Puritan named Oliver Cromwell, brought the right combination of opposition together to launch the English Civil War (1640–49). Parliament was to sit in various forms for the next twenty years, while Charles lost his fight to rule as an absolute monarch. The outcome of the Civil War produced the first major step in determining England's modern political destiny.

Led by Cromwell, the parliamentary forces won a very difficult struggle. Nine years of fighting and internal strife removed England from the continental politics of the Thirty Years War, which had come to a close one year before the English Civil War in 1648. Charles lost this contest and then found himself a prisoner of the most radical elements of his realm. While other parliamentary generals had either retired or died, Cromwell had continued in command of the army whose composition of ardent Calvinists insisted on greater changes than the majority of England's men of estate sought. Using the army to purge parliament, Cromwell soon found himself the head of a government that wanted to end the monarchy, close the House of Lords,

A member of parliament at the outbreak of the English Civil War, Oliver Cromwell became a formidable military leader, winning the war against Charles I in 1649. As one of the judges at Charles I's trial, Cromwell signed the king's death warrant and later became lord protector. During his rule, he campaigned vigorously for religious liberty for Protestants and Nonconformists. Terracotta bust by Louis-Frantois Roubiliac. © The Trustees of the British Museum.

and punish Charles. After an intense trial, Charles was beheaded on January 30, 1649.

As regicides, however, Cromwell and his followers now faced a bleak political and diplomatic future. In England, Cromwell had to rule a state that sought fewer political changes than he actually implemented. He therefore had to maintain a standing army to enforce his will while functioning in complete isolation from the rest of Europe. His Calvinist ideals, however, made his style of government too harsh for his old parliamentarian allies, while his reputation as a "king-killer" made his regime a pariah to foreign countries. Consequently, he repeatedly had to purge Commons to secure the right mix of opinion that he needed to support his vision for England's future. Simultaneously, he had to rule with an iron fist because he lacked support beyond the minority of Puritans found in England. Ironically, therefore, Cromwell acted like an absolute monarch even if he had not assumed the title of "king."

During the Interregnum (1650–59), meaning the era between the kings, Cromwell governed the English as their sovereign using the title, "lord protector." With the authority granted by a standing army, Cromwell's will became law as he ruled a conquered realm by usurping more authority from parliament than had any Stuart king. Yet soon after Cromwell died on September 3, 1658, parliament returned to a more familiar system of government. First it restored Lords which joined Commons to invite Charles I's son, Charles II, back to England to reestablish a less severe political regime than the one offered by Cromwell's followers. Thus, from 1660 to 1688 the Stuarts again reigned during an era known as The Restoration, but questions concerning sovereignty remained unanswered.

Simultaneously, as part of the price charged by parliament for the return of the Stuart line to the throne, the legislature revised the legal definition of property rights to secure further the concept of "estate" from invasion from the king. Parliament sought to make a proprietor's control over his estate absolute. Accordingly, parliament redefined property by ending knight's service.

Knight's service was the last vestige of feudalism in English Common Law that defined the obligations the possessor of real estate had to the crown. These obligations included feudal dues to the king that symbolized his title to all the land in England. Thus, parliament eliminated the legal principle of *allodial* title. Allodial title assigned ownership of all land within a kingdom to the monarchy as an agent of God; this concept allowed the king to bestow estates on all his retainers so that they held legal rights of possession so long as they performed specific services in the king's army.

Clearly, allodial title was essential for the operation of a feudal monarchy. To eliminate allodial title meant that the king no longer existed in partnership with the possessor of an estate as part owner of the kingdom's land. At the same time, to eliminate allodial title acknowledged that the new nature of contemporary military service had replaced the knight with professional mercenaries who composed a royal army. Thus, by eliminating the knights' service, parliament recognized the reality of those changes that had taken place in warfare while also creating the principle of absolute property, meaning that the landlord now controlled both the title and all rights of possession to his estate; such a combination of elements within proprietorship gave men of estate absolute ownership of their holdings. From this point forward, taxation could only come from the consent of the taxed.

The idea of absolute property converted real estate into a form of wealth more like capital. Landlords began to think of themselves as owners of a type of property that could be used to generate more income and reinforced trends already set in motion by the Commercial Revolution, such as enclosures, crop rotation, and animal husbandry (mentioned in Chapter Seventeen). At the same time, landlords began to change the way they leased acreage. Now they replaced leases that secured land for a number of years with leases of will, that is terms of rent given to tenants for as long as these people pleased the will of the landlord.

Meanwhile, the fact that when consulted parliament proved generous with its kings on issues of taxation meant that English property owners were developing a sense of duty to the state. This sense of duty led them to tax themselves in times of need far more than any other people in Europe. In addition, this sense of duty to the state foreshadowed the modern concept of citizenship as a key ingredient in the nation-state.

In contrast, aristocrats in France across the channel from England developed the opposite sentiment. Since they had no share in government, they did not have to pay taxes. Since their kings avoided consulting with them, they developed the attitude that their status set them apart from the state and the rest of society. Thus, tax exemption came to equal freedom from state responsibilities as a mark of the highest possible status in France. This meant that if anyone wished to demonstrate his or her social position, he or she had to seek this tax-exempt status. As a result, no comparable sense of duty developed in France. Finally, this new sense of duty to the state made England much stronger and richer than its neighbors—especially in the eighteenth century under the leadership of Sir Robert Walpole (1676–1745), chancellor of the exchequer, first lord of the treasury, and, in effect, the first prime minister in English history after the issue of sovereignty had been solved (see below).

Walpole created the Sinking Fund in 1716, which was a fiscal mechanism that assigned certain British taxes to reduce the government's debts each year. This Sinking Fund produced such confidence in Britain's debt that the wealthy came to believe investing in government was a gilt-edged security. This faith in the Fund grew over the course of the century as trade generated by the Commercial Revolution produced unexpected revenues. Hence, the wealthy in Britain invested in government with a growing understanding that they were investing in themselves.

In England, therefore, participation in government drew taxpaying aristocrats closer together with their fellow townspeople in corporate cities to create a sense of ownership in a common endeavor to make Britain powerful and prosperous. Together landlords and merchants created a solid financial basis for investing in government. Linking these interests to one another also led to a government that protected the state's economy.

Expressed by the term commonwealth, first used during the Civil War and Interregnum eras and found in Locke's *Second Treatise on Government*, estate holders saw economic prosperity and politics as belonging to a common unity of property interests. Like commonwealth, a second term, *interest*, as found in Hume's *Treatise of Human Nature*, also matured to define both the economic and political concerns of property owners who participated in government. Now, only the final struggle over sovereignty remained.

The principal issue in need of resolution was the relationship between legislative and prerogative powers. Could a king produce an edict that contradicted parliamentary law? If so, which power took precedence: the king's will or the majority opinion of the commonwealth's elected representatives? Charles II proved to be sufficiently competent to sidestep this issue so that his rule was not interrupted with rebellion. His Catholic brother and heir, James II, however, was not so lucky.

James II became king in 1685 with the accumulated power that Charles had amassed during his reign. James had the support of a friendly parliament led by the Tories, the party of the court. Furthermore, he was backed by the leading figures of the Anglican Church. Finally, his treasury was full. If he had ruled quietly, the crown would have prevailed. Instead, James pressed for Royal Absolutism with a vengeance.

First he violated parliament's expressed will by ignoring the Test Act that required all officeholders to take communion in the Anglican church in order to prove that they were members of the Church of England. He tolerated both Calvinists and Catholics alike

so that he could bring Catholics back into politics. Consequently, he undercut his Anglican support in parliament. Next, he enrolled Irish Catholics as officers in the English army and tried to expand this arm of the military to increase his ability to punish those who would disobey his rule. Finally, he advanced the legal position of James I on royal authority: kings had no one to answer to except God.

When James II's wife gave birth to a son that he had baptized Catholic, thus ensuring another generation of "papist" rule, the great magnates of England shifted their loyalty to his opponents, the Whigs, the party of the country. Completely out of step with his own kingdom, James II continued to press for Royal Absolutism. Eventually, his single-minded efforts prompted his subjects to rebel. Consequently, leading figures of the opposition began to look around for a potentially friendly king who might be willing to replace James II.

The so-called Glorious Revolution (1688–89) resolved the issue of sovereignty by establishing a contract between parliament and one such friendly monarch who accepted the English crown. Seeking an alternative to James II, the Whigs and their new Tory allies approached Mary Stuart, James I's daughter and wife of William of Orange. William of Orange ruled Holland and had spent most of his life fighting French aggression against the Low Countries. Offered a new monarchy as part of his power base in his struggle with Louis XIV, William happily agreed to nearly any terms parliament might impose on his new kingdom. William's only concern was that England might not actually rise up to support him when he made his attempt to overthrow James II.

Landing on English soil in 1688 with every intention of withdrawing if James II resisted, William III waited to see how the English might respond to an alien force on their shores. Yet James so completely distrusted his own people that he failed to react. Marching with increased confidence on London, William discovered that the English in fact wished a change of government. More and more notable Englishmen joined William's camp as the English aristocracy abandoned James II to his political destiny. As a result, James II's support melted away until the outcome became clear. Thus, James abandoned England without a fight as this transition of royal power became a fact.

Louis XIV of France continued to back James as the king of England, but this only strengthened English resolve to support their new monarch. Thus, in 1689 a new political settlement developed into what the English called their *constitution* (i.e., the contract between men of estate and the monarchy that produced the commonwealth). Foremost among the new laws were the Bill of Rights, the Toleration Act, and the Settlement Act.

The Bill of Rights stipulated that the king was bound by the law and could not suspend an act of parliament. Furthermore, a king could not levee taxes or raise an army except by parliamentary consent. Finally, a king could not arrest or detain a subject without due process of law.

Added to the Bill of Rights was the Toleration Act, which allowed Protestant Dissenters or Calvinists to worship as they pleased but excluded them from public office. Like the Test Act before it, the Toleration Act measured an official's loyalty to the commonwealth by his willingness to swear his allegiance to the new government by acknowledging the Anglican church. The Toleration Act also officially recognized that matters of faith and knowledge belonged to two different realms of belief. Thus, the power of science and reason had surfaced in English law to reveal that parliament now comprised politique personalities.

Finally, parliament added the Settlement Act of 1701, which stated no Catholic could rule England. Aimed specifically at James II, his son, and grandson, this Act implicitly excluded all male descendants of the Stuart line. Parliament would no longer align itself with any Catholic members from James II's family.

And to close the door on a possible Stuart invasion from the north through Scotland, parliament worked on a union between the two kingdoms. To overcome Scottish opposition to a merger with England, parliament used the growing commercial network of its Atlantic trade system as bait. The Scots had no rights to commerce within the English empire unless they joined England in a United Kingdom. The Lowland Scots accepted this commercial opportunity and joined with England and Wales to form the United Kingdom, or Great Britain. The Highland Scots, called Jacobites, resisted. Nevertheless, a Parliamentary Union passed between Scotland and England in 1707, while the last Jacobite effort to oppose this union failed after the bloody battle of Culloden Moor in 1746.

Outside the Scottish Highlands, Ireland remained the only trouble spot after the Glorious Revolution of 1688–89. Here James centered his resistance to William III by mobilizing a force supported by Louis XIV. Losing the Battle of the Boyne River (1690) in Ireland to William III, however, officially ended James II's hold on England. All potential support for the ousted king evaporated, but the status of Ireland now lay open to parliament's wrath.

Wishing to punish them for their stubborn support of James II, the English brought the Irish into the United Kingdom as a zone of abject poverty, by imposing on Ireland the Penal Codes. First, parliament banished the Catholic clergy from Ireland. Second, the codes declared that Catholics could not vote for or sit as members of the Irish Parliament. Third, Catholic teachers could not teach, and Catholic parents could not send their children abroad for a Catholic education. Fourth, no Catholic could take a degree from the University of Dublin. Fifth, the Catholic Irish could not purchase land, hold a lease of more than thirty years, inherit property from a Protestant, or own a house worth more than £5. Sixth, a Catholic son who converted to Protestantism inherited the family's wealth despite his order of birth. Seventh, Catholics could not become attorneys, constables, enter trade, or employ more than two apprentices.

Economically, Irish shipping was excluded from the British colonies. In addition, Ireland could not import colonial goods except through England. The Irish could not export goods such as woolens and glass products but could only export agricultural products. Furthermore, the Irish could not impose a tariff on English imports. Primary goods produced on Irish estates, however, belonged to English landlords who had taken up residence in Ireland as a new nobility, which explains why Ireland was allowed to export agricultural products.

The purpose of the Penal Codes and their economic consequences were obvious: England intended to weaken Ireland as a potentially hostile country that could support the return to power of James II or any of his Catholic heirs. These codes also ensured that Ireland could not compete with England in the expanding commercial system generated by Atlantic trade. At the same time, however, the imposition of the Penal Codes ensured hostility between Ireland and England for centuries to come, despite the fact that England relented on some of the more severe features of these codes later.

These codes made Ireland a zone of utter poverty in the new United Kingdom. They also explain why hunger could pressure the Irish to accept a foreign food like the potato as a staple in their diet. Finally, these codes remind the reader that England had only developed a nascent version of such modern concepts as toleration and political representation. The harsh way England treated the Irish indicated a deeply rooted fear of Ireland as a source of political instability.

Viewed as a land willing to rise up in support of a tyrant turned subjugator, the Irish took much of the blame for supporting James II's last efforts to recover his country's crown. Implicitly described by John Locke in his *Second Treatise* as an irrational people willing to support a "conqueror," the Irish received a form of "economic enslavement" as the price paid for following the most "animal-like" of humans. Explicitly depicted as an irrational tribe of people by Charles Davenant, a *political arithmetician* (one of the founders of early statistics) in his *Essay Upon the Probable Method of Making a People Gainers in the Balance of Trade* (1699), Davenant condemned Ireland to its fate as a conquered land. In this explicit attack on the Irish, Davenant was unrestrained in his indictment of these people as he converted Locke's implicit argument into a statement of "fact."

Davenant's wrath fueled a new type of ethnic hostility that foreshadowed the concept of racism. Davenant viewed the Irish as a special type of people whose blind refusal to adhere to reason placed them in a human category all of their own. This category defined the Irish as beasts in human form who lacked the capacity to rule themselves rationally. As a result, they had to feel the heavy hand of a just, paternal, and sagacious foreign monarch. Thus, Ireland joined the United Kingdom as a conquered land filled with people who needed the attention of a political parent imposed on them due to their failure to act like rational human beings. Simply stated, Davenant said that Ireland should be reduced to the status of an English colony.

With the addition of Ireland to the United Kingdom, Great Britain was now complete. As a complex combination of several estates, the United Kingdom represented the great exception to the political design adopted by Europe during the early modern era: Great Britain, save for Ireland, enjoyed the rights and privileges of a constitutional monarchy. In contrast, the standard model used by the remaining kings on the European continent followed the lead of France under Louis XIV (1638–1715), who had developed the most efficient example of Royal Absolutism found in Europe. Furthermore, Louis XIV and his heirs were the dominant political figures in this period of calm between 1660 and 1789.

Between 1660 and 1789, France and England had become the key political models for the rest of Europe. But the contrast between these two governments, and their style of self-justification, had become the focal point of political debate during the Enlightenment. Sharpened by the intellectual consequences of the Scientific Revolution (1543–1687), this political debate grew ever more intense as the people of Europe tried to redefine their purpose after losing sight of God in nature.

After 1690, a stark contrast between France and Britain began to form. John Locke (1632–1704), who had justified the political changes of the Glorious Revolution by making his appeal to reason, became the principal voice used in this contrast. Locke, himself, rejected Royal Absolutism as having no foundation in reason.

Those who followed Locke's lead realized that God's name no longer belonged in a political discussion. God's existence was not questioned, but His Divine purposes could not be decoded. Without God as the agency behind such institutions as the church, the king, and his nobility, what was to become the proper form of government?

As mentioned in Chapter Nineteen, philosophy tried to answer this question by trying to synchronize the standards of knowledge with science to recreate a synthesis as elegant as the one developed in ancient Greece. The philosophy of the Enlightenment sought to reintegrate the criteria of what we can know with what we should believe and how we should act.

The influence of public opinion spawned by the Enlightenment filled the territorial state with a growing number of politically active people who questioned tradition as well as existing institutions. These activists generated a political passion for a positive, rational consensus concerning state affairs; this passion, in turn, eventually called for change. Simultaneously, these activists launched a drive toward creating the nation-state, which is the subject of the next chapter.

Suggested Reading

The Territorial State

Bercé, Yves-Marie, *The Birth of Absolutism* (London: Macmillan, 1996).

Beik, William, *Absolutism and Society in Seventeenth Century France* (Cambridge: Cambridge University Press, 1985).

Campbell, Peter R., *Louis XIV, 1661–1715* (London: Longman, 1993).

Burgess, Glenn, *Absolute Monarchy and the Stuart Constitution* (New Haven, Conn.: Yale University Press, 1996).

Hughes, Ann, *The Causes of the English Civil War* (New York: St. Martin's Press, 1991).

Israel, Jonathan, ed., *The Anglo-Dutch Moment* (Cambridge: Cambridge University Press, 1991).

Kamen, Henry, *Empire: How Spain Became a World Power, 14921763* (New York: Harper Collins, 2003).

Munck, Thomas, *Seventeenth Century Europe, 1598–1700* (New York: St. Martin's Press, 1990).

Parker, Geoffrey, *The Military Revolution* (Cambridge: Cambridge University Press, 1988.

Plumb, J. H., *England in the Eighteenth Century* (Baltimore, Md., 1965).

Speck, W. A., *The Revolution of 1688* (Oxford: Oxford University Press, 1988).

THE RISE OF THE NATION-STATE, PART TWO:
The Ideology of Revolution

Following the Commercial Revolution (1492–1763), the rise of the royal army (1494–1648), the Reformation (1517–1648), and the Scientific Revolution (1543–1687), Europe experienced a second burst of rapid cultural change between 1750 and 1850. During this second phase of modernization, two key consequences of the preceding era asserted themselves. First, public opinion, a product of the Enlightenment (1690–1789) gained momentum, transforming passive subjects into active citizens. Second, the critical economic mass generated by Commercial Capitalism launched a new level of productive energy called the Industrial Revolution (ca. 1750–1850).

Public opinion first appeared after 1690 and sustained the possibility of formulating a positive political consensus within a territorial state. Such a consensus could win the loyalty of an entire people and serve as the popular basis for the nation-state. The Industrial Revolution occurred next, around 1750, took longer, and developed a set of economic and demographic circumstances that redefined political geography. The Industrial Revolution created urbanization and mass communication, both necessary to integrate the physical space of the nation-state. Together, public opinion and industrial-urbanization created a new political reality.

The nation-state first appeared in Western Europe, in the guise of Great Britain and France. The contrast between France's potential and Great Britain's successes led most French philosophes to admire the British system, argue for its rational features, and express a desire to copy their neighbor's aptitude for social, economic, and political harmony. Simultaneously, while the United Kingdom concentrated the economic rewards of the Commercial Revolution within its empire, the British people had accumulated enough resources to launch industrialization. Meanwhile, across the English Channel, the French people harbored such a powerful negative public consensus against the irrational features of their territorial society that their discontent erupted into a major political revolution. Thereaf-

ter, both England and France produced such dramatic modern changes that the British and the French became examples for the rest of Western Civilization to imitate.

Great Britain's Industrial Revolution (ca. 1750–1850) created a new urban environment, an economic and social setting that required literacy, calculation, and innovation to succeed. At the same time, British cities also produced a form of communal self-awareness by linking regional and local markets to a national economy through a system of mass transportation that generated an urban hierarchy. This urban hierarchy, in turn, integrated geographic space by linking farms to villages, villages to towns, towns to cities, cities to provincial urban centers, and provincial urban centers to a centerplace, capital city: London. Consequently, Britain's Industrial Revolution made the nation-state a physical and geographic reality.

In contrast, France produced a complex political revolution that shaped national formation through violence. The French Revolution (1789–1815) went through four phases that produced twenty-six years of legal, fiscal, bureaucratic, and military innovations. Each phase ended in failure. Yet, ironically, all four combined to cause so much political change as to destroy eight centuries of feudal tradition (987–1789).

The result was that France had created a modern political culture, which, in turn, produced a new, intangible loyalty called nationalism. Finally, nationalism joined with Britain's industry to establish the institutional basis for other nation-states.

In contrast to Western Europe in the mid-eighteenth century, Central Europe suffered from political disunity and occupied a geographic site that denied it direct access to the new Atlantic trade routes. As a result, Central European states did not have as many protomodern features as did France and Britain. Accordingly, Central Europeans had not developed united territorial states based on a common language, had not acquired global commercial empires, and had not refined protoindustry on the same scale as their western neighbors. Unified by spoken German and Italian, two great potential nations in Central Europe formed two loosely defined communities, while several other smaller ethnic groups watched changes in Britain and France with envy. All of these ethnic communities knew that if they did not imitate the British and the French, they would fail to keep pace with these emerging nation-states.

Yet while the Germans and Italians hungered to join the ranks of modern nations, their closest neighbor, the Austrian Empire, struggled to disrupt the formation of any such political societies. The Austrians feared the appearance of any new nation-state because Austria ruled a multinational empire. Consequently, the Austrians saw nation-building as a threat to their political existence. Central Europe, therefore, represented a complex cultural zone that differed sharply from Western Europe.

These cultural and political differences led nation formation down two separate paths. Western Europe linked together freedom of expression, public opinion, urbanization, and industry to create the potential for democracy. In contrast, the Germans and the Italians could not freely form a positive political consensus because neither had produced a unified territorial state that enlightened public opinion could critique as in Britain and France. Also both the Germans and Italians lacked an urban hierarchy, the regional, economic, and political integration offered by such a hierarchy, the same number of literate people, or the same ratios of innovators to traditional laborers as found in Western Europe. Furthermore, the Germans and Italians faced a diplomatic problem created by Austria's opposition to nation formation; this required a high level of political and military focus to defeat a powerful, hostile foe.

The absence of a broad, protomodern foundation in Central Europe, when compared to Western Europe, plus steady opposition from a powerful neighbor, combined to create a centralized state wherein powerful leaders who manipulated public opinion directed events. Lacking a comparable exposure to commercial capitalism and individual freedom to take risks and innovate, the Italians and Germans could not rely on spontaneous revolution to achieve their national goals. Instead, they found that they could build nation-states only at the expense of personal freedom.

The leaders in Germany and Italy who directed the formation of nation-states realized that they had to forestall freedom in order to retain their inherited posts in society. Matching the circumstances of power described by Machiavelli in *The Prince*, these traditional leaders understood that somehow they needed to blend the passive obedience of subjects with the active passions of participatory citizenship so that they could transform their territorial societies into nation-states.

Machiavelli had said that the great state builders of the past possessed the correct political virtues essential to accomplish their goals, but that they also had used any means necessary to achieve their political ends. Thus, both Germany and Italy required a different type of leader, an authoritarian one capable of creating a political process quite different from the democratic spontaneity of Western Europe.

Once completed Western and Central European nation-states offered the world two different models of the nation-state: one was spontaneous and democratic, and the other was a product of the autocratic manipulation of a people's nationalistic passions. The dividing line in time, 1850, separated the Western from the Central European experience. Britain and France had formed nation-states before 1850, while Italy and Germany completed their national tasks after 1850. Historically, this division in time marked the moment when Central Europeans discovered that they could not successfully use the spontaneous techniques developed by Britain and France; thus, the mid-nineteenth century marked the era when Germans and Italians chose, instead, the Machiavellian approach to state-building.

As a result, the uses of public opinion, popular consensus, and the role of industry in the nations formed before 1850 differed sharply from the autocratic processes used in the post-1850 states. Yet each model of national formation linked a territory, a people, and their local culture and language together into a political design that achieved what geographers call internal coherence. Internal coherence defined the way a people integrated a national, industrial, and urban economy into a nation-state by tying their vision of the future to a collective sense of self generated through a shared language. The concept of internal coherence also linked the national loyalties of a people with the urban skills of literacy, computation, and critical thinking to create the national awareness needed to create a political culture. Finally, internal coherence measured the degree of actual geographic integration achieved by a nation-state as a regional political society found within a larger European cultural setting.

The Ideology of Revolution

While Kant was one of the great intellectuals of Central Europe, Smith was one of a much larger number of such thinkers in Western Europe. Thus, although Kant contributed as much to the intellectual development of the West as Smith, this German thinker did so in a cultural environment quite different from his Scottish counterpart. Therefore, the impact of both men's inquiries generated a different rate of cultural change in their respective regions.

Both thinkers, however, altered the European worldview. Smith and Kant described human society as a collective body of creative participants. Such creativity suggested that the highest form of human organization could only come from the free association of rational individuals. Such an association created a community that relied on the human mind to shape a rational public opinion and participate in the natural consequences of the division of labor. Both a rational public opinion and the division of labor, in turn, generated the cultural conditions that produced the Industrial Revolution (1750–1850) and the French Revolution (1789–1815).

The philosophes of the Enlightenment (those who used philosophy to shape public opinion) made John Locke and Sir Isaac Newton the twin heroes of the eighteenth century. The philosophes argued that Locke's and Newton's dedication to reason had awakened the European imagination. At the same time, the English generally received good press from such French thinkers as Montesquieu, Voltaire, and the Physiocrats led by Quesnay, while France suffered severe criticism. Thus, a type of negative consensus began to form in France that none of these intellectuals foresaw.

In his *Spirit of the Laws* (1748), Montesquieu praised the English for their balanced form of government. He claimed that the British constitution separated the basic functions of politics into legislative, executive, and judicial branches and pitted each against the rest to ensure that no corruption would follow. Montesquieu also argued that this separation and balance of powers secured a stable popular consensus among the rational members of the British Commonwealth. At the same time, Montesquieu condemned France for drifting in the direction of *despotism*, a term Montesquieu employed to describe an irrational form of government. Based on slavery and fear, despotism, he argued, destroyed the qualities of reason that defined the human species.

Next, Voltaire, in his *Letters Concerning the English* (1732), contrasted England with France and found France wanting. Then, he popularized the works of Newton and Locke to create a general understanding of their achievements. Finally, Voltaire demonstrated with great humor in *Candide* (1759) that the best way for people to live was to cultivate their own personalities, that each life was like a garden one could weed and nurture into rational perfection. Voltaire's career spanned the entire Enlightenment to create a widespread feeling that France stood in urgent need of change.

Lastly, Quesnay, with his *Tableau Economiqué* (1758) inspired a group of followers such as Honore Gabriel Riquetti, Count de Miranbeau, Anne Robert Jacques Turgot, Baron de L'Aulne, Le Mercier de la Riviere, and Pierre Samuel Du Pont de Nemours, all of whom analyzed Great Britain's changing agricultural system. These Physiocrats praised the English for their entrepreneurial inventiveness and condemned France for relying on medieval practices to produce and sell food. They based their critique on the new concept of production, declaring it a physical law that no society could ignore. Their praise of Great Britain revealed how cultivation there had transformed the economic potential of that country. Their criticism of French agriculture blamed tradition as the source of the French people's misery. They strongly advocated changes based on *laissez-faire* (productive and commercial freedom) in order to duplicate Britain's successes.

Each of these philosophes offered a critique of France that agreed on how the French people held vast potential but suffered under a tyranny of the irrational. Yet, each man also disagreed with one another on what solutions would best establish reason in the French system. Montesquieu wanted to reverse France's development of Royal Absolutism. He called for a return to the Salic law, which had governed French feudalism, hoping to use it to create a British-style constitution. Voltaire advocated the opposite. He proposed expanding royal power to create an Enlightened Despotism. He saw the king as France's salvation if the monarchy could rule within the laws of reason. Finally, the Physiocrats proposed abandoning all the *seigniorial* (manorial) rights found in French agriculture to stimulate a free market in food production, with an absolute monarch overseeing the process. In short, the Physiocrats wanted to invest all political power in the hands of an economist-king who believed in the laws of production.

Each of these French philosophes anticipated change; each also expected that this change would be peaceful and rational. Furthermore, each had an optimistic faith in humanity's mental capacity to debate, form a consensus, and reshape its political destiny. Yet, as each thinker contributed to a general negative consensus within France, he also left the French with no common direction to follow.

Meanwhile, intellectuals such as Denis Diderot popularized this enlightened opinion by creating a general source that distributed this negative consensus to as wide an audience as possible. His labor produced the *Encylopedie*, a series of volumes that published the latest critical voices of the Enlightenment. Coupled with

Jean Jacques Rousseau, who condemned all current civilization as a paradox of wealth generated by irrational passion, Diderot's friendliness organized intellectuals in Paris into a protomodern think tank whose members frequented salons to debate with one another.

The product of their thought found its way into a new forum for public information later called newspapers. These newspapers, in turn, found readers in popular meeting places like coffeehouses, where caffeine combined with public readings to inspire heated political discussions.

These discussions created politically charged associations called *sociétés des pensées* (thinking societies), which became the bastions of public opinion prior to the French Revolution. Once started, however, coffeehouses also became the meeting grounds for the first political parties in France that used public opinion to mobilize revolutionary action.

The example of political self-determination set by the American Revolution (1775–83) was something the French could not ignore, for it had compelled British subjects to declare their independence from tyranny and redefine their political destiny. This example of successful political rebellion based on an enlightened document called the *Declaration of Independence* suggested similar political action for France. And the fact that the French monarchy had helped to finance the American Revolution, and had suffered financial collapse from its military support of the rebels, created the precise circumstances needed to launch a revolt in France.

The French Revolution

When the French Revolution began in 1789, the Estates General (the French parliament) had been called to resolve the financial crisis of Royal Absolutism that had been building since Louis XIV instituted this political system. As mentioned in Chapter Twenty, by excluding France's nobility from politics and making them tax exempt, the king had placed too great a financial burden on the remaining French subjects. Also by selling noble titles to raise money to meet the financial shortcomings of the absolute monarchy, the king had narrowed the tax base and increased the tax burden on those least capable of paying. Finally, after financing the American Revolution without achieving any material rewards, and suffering military defeat after the British colonies had accomplished their political ends in 1781, the French monarchy faced a fiscal crisis. This crisis required Louis XVI (reigned 1774–93) to call the Estates General that had not met for 175 years (1614 to 1789).

Once assembled, the Third Estate, which represented lawyers, bankers, businessmen, government creditors, shopkeepers, artisans, workingmen, and peasants (i.e., the French people) refused to meet as an Estate and pit their one vote against the First Estate (the Church) and the Second Estate (the nobility). Accordingly, the Third Estate broke away, were joined by the parish priests from the First Estate, and formed a National Assembly on June 17, 1789. This new assembly, an illegal body, now set about drafting a constitution, while Louis XVI faltered, unable to force these representatives to adhere to French law. Hence, royal weakness coupled with the bold actions of a new assembly launched the French Revolution.

In 1789, however, only a negative consensus existed. As a result, when the French tried to remove eight centuries of tradition dating back to their first medieval monarchs, the Capet Dynasty of 987–1328, they did so without any real agreement on what to do next. All they had was faith in their collective reason. Consequently, as collective reason failed, their struggle for political redefinition resulted in four phases of revolutionary violence. Each phase ran the full gambit of political forms while the French people planted the seeds of national formation.

Beginning in 1789, Phase I of the Revolution (1789–91) attempted to institute a constitutional monarchy in a haphazard manner by copying the British. The new National Assembly declared the Rights of Man that ensured freedom for the French people. Yet this freedom merely released revolutionary passion. Popular riots in Paris became common; one of them had forced the king to leave his Palace of Versailles, return to Paris, and become a virtual hostage. In the countryside peasants stormed manor houses on rural landed estates, destroyed local records, and took possession of the land. Finally, the revolutionary government began a process of redefinition that attempted to redesign the law, taxation, the currency system, the role of the church, and citizenship all at once.

Phase I failed because the revolutionaries could not agree on how much change should occur, or what the appropriate rate should be. The French king, Louis XVI, did not comprehend his new role in a constitutional monarchy. He could not grasp the meaning of his new assignment as a king restricted by a rapidly changing legal system. His growing fear of the revolutionary process prompted him to flee his new residence in Paris, leaving behind a letter repudiating the revolution, but he was captured in Varennes, a town in Lorraine. He soon found himself in prison, later to be tried as a traitor to the revolution. At this point, the debate over the king's fate and France's revolutionary

Execution of Louis XVI, King of France (1754–93) by guillotine on January 21, 1793, on the Place de la Republique (Concorde) in Paris. The head of Louis is shown to the crowd. Photo: akg-images, London.

future set in motion a new burst of change that resulted in Phase II.

Phase II (1792–95) generated a radical rebellion in August of 1792, replaced the National Assembly with a National Convention, and declared the king guilty of treason, executing him in January 1793. Called citizen Louis Capet after the first feudal dynasty of France, Louis XVI's death symbolically severed the revolution's link with the past as efficiently as the guillotine removed the king's head. This execution also set in motion the Reign of Terror as a political tool under the direction of the Committee of Public Safety, a group of twelve members of the Convention reelected every month. Maximilian Robespierre (1758–94) was the Committee's dominant voice.

The Reign of Terror relied on daily executions, the regular use of the guillotine creating sufficient political intimidation to ensure control of the revolutionary process. Dominated by the Committee of Public Safety, the Reign of Terror temporarily stabilized politics so that this radical republic could deal with an internal and external crisis. The internal crisis required disposing of all the domestic enemies of the new revolutionary program found in France. The external crisis focused on the military threat of those monarchs outside France who had organized an invasion to end the revolution.

A general European war began during the transition period between Phase I and Phase II of the revolution. This war required emergency action in France. Since the French had to fight a coalition of monarchs who feared the example of revolution might spread, the Committee of Public Safety had to innovate to save their republic. What they created was the first national army.

Building a massive force from the ranks of their people, the radical republic generated an army of 800,000 soldiers between 1793 and 1794. This force doubled the military strength produced by Louis XIV during his great wars of the seventeenth century. Furthermore, these 800,000 fought as citizens with a passion Machiavelli had described in *The Prince*.

For the next twenty years, France defeated every force sent against its people because this emerging revolutionary state had become a nation-in-arms. During these twenty years, the French national army continued to grow, reaching 1.5 million soldiers and internally partitioned itself into independent commands that had generated the modern military division. Now a French general had at his fingertips divisions of 4,000 men commanded by subordinate generals who had won their promotions on the battlefield. Each division functioned like a separate unit to give the French commander the opportunity to coordinate assaults against any royal army sent against him.

French *élan* (the political passion of their citizens) added to the military force that France could mobilize against its enemies. Élan overwhelmed the robot-like behavior of the professional soldiers found in royal armies. Thus, France won a series of victories. Accordingly, the French Revolution spread abroad and began to change the politics in all of Europe.

This successful response to foreign invasion plus the domestic peace ensured by the Reign of Terror, reduced the level of crisis facing France. The Committee of Public Safety, however, refused to reduce the intensity of its rule. Justified by political emergency, this intensity should have eased as the crisis itself dissipated. Instead, the pattern of public executions continued until 1794, when France began to exhibit signs of popular exhaustion that derived from the fear and radical passions released by Phase II. Hence, a coup d'état against Robespierre's leadership of the Committee of Public Safety on July 27, 1794, generated Phase III of the revolution after an eleven-month transition period.

Led by the Directory (a committee of five), Phase III (1795–99), however, proved to be a corrupt political experiment. Based on a new middle class that formed out of the restructuring of French society during the revolution, Phase III established a new republic that comprised a bicameral legislature with a lower chamber of 500 representatives and an upper one with 250; both elected the executive (the Directory). Designed to represent the wealthy, this new republic relied on a body of voters who met a substantial property requirement, elected an electoral body of well-to-do proprietors, who, in turn, selected the representatives. Since two-thirds of this legislature had to be incumbents, this bicameral system created a very stable representation of the rich. Hence, the interests of wealth replaced the revolutionary passion in civil government, while the glory of radical change belonged to the generals who won victories abroad.

Ensuring stability through a combination of military force and the manipulation of its very complex election process, the Directory lost touch with the French people. Domestic affairs no longer had revolutionary purpose. Instead, the French people shifted their political passion and loyalties to successful generals. One of these generals, Napoleon Bonaparte, had the good sense to stay away from France as his fame grew, so that he did not become a victim of the Directory's envy.

By 1799, however, Napoleon was ready to take charge, engineering a coup that toppled the Directory after he abandoned his army in Egypt; thus began Phase IV (1799–1815). The longest and most stable phase of the French Revolution, Phase IV returned France to a form of power the French recognized: imperial rule.

Bonaparte began Phase IV as first consul, like a Roman magistrate, but his popularity as general allowed him to become Napoleon I, Emperor of France in 1804 through a *plebiscite* (a vote to affirm a political decision), which supported a solid financial and legal foundation for Napoleon's rule. Yet internally, France had been transformed during the preceding three phases.

A new national code of law had been perfected in the years between 1791 and 1799 whereby France had developed a national bureaucracy to tax its people and supply its massive army. The provincial design of the French interior went from a complex pattern of three hundred legal systems to one uniform, efficient administrative structure. All the French people owed loyalty to the French state, for now the state derived ultimate authority from the French people themselves. What Napoleon commanded was a national consensus that would follow him as long as he won victories on the battlefield.

Napoleon's military career became the focus of revolutionary change after 1800. He swept his opponents from the battlefield in a series of victories that gave him control of the continent. He defeated the Austrians at Ulm in 1805, the Austrians and the Russians at Austerlitz also in 1805, the Prussians at Jena in 1806, and the Russians once again at Friedland in 1807. At the same time, however, he lost his combined French and Spanish fleets to the British under Lord Horatio Nelson (1758–1805) at Trafalgar in 1805. Thus, by 1807, Napoleon's alliance with the defeated Russian czar at the Treaty of Tilset recognized his command of the European continent while the British still ruled the seas. This land-versus-sea stalemate led to commercial warfare in which Napoleon tried to close the continent to Great Britain, while the British blockaded the mainland of Europe from international commerce.

Of all the European states, Russia alone remained independent from Napoleon's direct influence. Yet by 1812 the French emperor decided to force Russia into submission as well. Leading an army of 600,000 into Russia, Napoleon overlooked two crucial obstacles: typhus and the harsh Russian winter.

The frequency of typhus in Eastern Europe and Russia far exceeds the rate of contraction of this disease in Central and Western Europe. Transmitted by the feces of lice that infects humans when they scratch irritated bites, typhus kills through several complications: high fever; a rash that covers the body that may become hemorrhagic (bleeding), which can lead to gangrene; hypertension that can cause kidney failure; and a secondary infection that may lead to pneumonia. When the French invaded Russia, typhus broke out

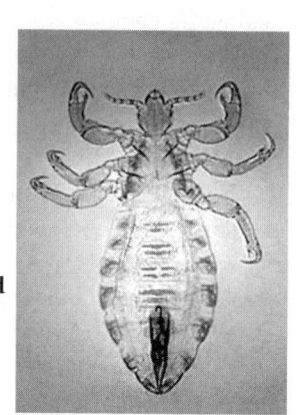

A typhus louse. *Pediculus humanus corporis* are parasitic insects that live on the body, clothing, and bedding of infested humans, feeding on their blood and laying eggs in their hair. This agent of epidemic typhus was photographed during a 1972 study of migrant labor camp disease vectors. Infestation is common and found worldwide. Courtesy of the CDC.

among their soldiers. Weakened by the disease, the French could not catch or deliver a crushing blow to the Russian Army.

Retreating rather than fighting, the Russians drew Napoleon deeper into their territory. Unable to win in a single campaign season despite his victory at Borodino, near Moscow, where the Russian Army managed to escape a decisive blow, Napoleon now found himself trapped in the heart of Russia during winter with a severely weakened military force. Napoleon finally decided to retreat, but it was too late; the extreme cold killed most of his Grand Army before they made it out of Russia. After this disaster in Russia, Napoleon no longer had the military resources needed to rule the European continent.

From 1812 to 1814, Napoleon tried to hold onto his continental empire, but his opponents were fresh and his own people were exhausted. Learning how to fight from the French, the monarchies of Europe had adopted the ideology of a national defense to revive their armies. Now they began to win victories in the same style in which France had. Defeated, Napoleon was driven from power. Trying one last time, in 1815, to recover political authority, Napoleon lost the battle of Waterloo and the French Revolution came to an end.

The victors tried to restore the French monarchy under the Bourbons by placing Louis XVI's younger brother on the French throne. Louis XVIII, however, ruled a France that had completely changed. At the end of this agonizing twenty-six-year revolutionary process, the French had created all the political institutions and national passions that sustained a nation-state.

Political stability now required the consent of the people because political power now came from a population willing to support a professional bureaucracy and national army. United by the idea of a common will, the French had institutionalized public opinion as the central tool to focus national loyalty on political goals. The only thing France lacked was an industrial revolution to completely integrate a national economy (see below). Louis XVIII had to live with this new national will. Thus, even though the French had suffered defeat at the hands of a foreign coalition, the French nation still existed in the popular imagination as the key model of political power for the rest of Europe to imitate.

Great Britain

Complementing the new political institutions developed in France between 1789 and 1815, the Industrial Revolution (1750–1850) transformed Great Britain into a physically integrated state whose internal market structure would become a national economy. Starting with several basic changes in cultivation prior to 1750, the British created modern commercial agriculture to increase the total food supply while introducing new domesticated plants from the Americas into the European diet. As mentioned in Chapter Seventeen, crop rotation, the use of fertilizers, animal husbandry, new property rights, the redefinition of tenant leases, and enclosures all had developed out of the Reformation and the Commercial Revolution. Each of these innovations combined to produce more food, sustain a new urban population, and force some people to migrate to new jobs.

At the same time, the appearance of the entrepreneur and his relationship to the cottager supported the development of a wage-dependent population that paralleled the changes in agriculture. The entrepreneur generated cottage industry in the countryside to offer supplemental income to families still involved in cultivation. The cottager worked from his or her home for the entrepreneur to meet the rising cost of living. Together entrepreneurs and cottagers created a new productive process called protoindustry that laid the foundation for a national economy. As a result, the entrepreneur employed as much as 50 percent of all Britain's subjects by 1739.

Complementing the entrepreneur and cottager, the migration of those leaving the countryside to live in cities foreshadowed the massive urbanization of the Industrial Revolution. Between 1500 and 1750, some of Britain's poorest people left their homes to find employment in large cities like London. Simultaneously, when London could no longer support any more of these people, these same poor then left the United Kingdom for the colonies. Joined by religious dissenters, these poor travelers made up a wave of step-stage migration that fueled a global market system based on commercial capitalism. Commercial capitalism, in turn, joined with entrepreneurial production in Great Britain to create an expanding market economy. Finally, as the people of the United Kingdom grew accustomed to rapid economic change based on this new market system, so they were soon ready for the next burst of innovation.

Then, when new technology began to appear in the eighteenth century, the location of labor shifted from rural cottages to industrial urban centers within Great Britain. Wage-dependent labor had to follow the demand for work, as these new machines collected employees first in mills and then in factory towns. At the same time, new levels of food production generated by commercial agriculture joined with disease-resistant people who had survived infections from the pathogens that concentrated in British cities to sustain population growth throughout the United Kingdom.

As more people left the countryside in response to the changing demand for labor, empty lands increased the opportunity for the expansion of commercial agriculture. Parallel rural-urban economic changes thus integrated local, regional, and national markets. Cities demanded labor and new food sources that stimulated cultivation. Commercial agriculture in turn responded with increased efficiency in production while consuming manufactured goods such as industrially produced farm tools, machines, or spare parts. Thus, an urban-rural link developed that eventually tied all the regions of Great Britain together into a common national market system.

Also, the combined development of industry and modern agriculture sustained a new demographic reality that reversed the ancient and medieval rural-urban ratios. As mentioned numerous times, traditional societies typically placed nine farmers in the countryside to feed one person in a city. Now Great Britain had begun a rural-urban shift that first placed 50 percent of its population in cities by 1850. After this date, Great Britain's cities would continue to grow and hold the vast majority of its people by the twentieth century. In addition, as people left the countryside, farms continued to increase food production and integrate with urban demand. Thus, the more efficient agriculture became, the more people could leave the countryside, migrate to cities to find work, as well as be fed by Britain's modern methods of cultivation.

Meanwhile, Great Britain's cities sprang up in regions empty of people, but rich in fuel. As the first in-

An Early Loom. Artist William Hogarth shows the interior of a weaving workroom located in Spitalfields, the center of London's thriving silk industry. A drawing for his series Industry and Idleness, Hogarth shows us Francis Goodchild applying his skills as a deft weaver, and Tom Idle, asleep having drunk a copious amount of beer. © The Trustees of the British Museum.

dustrial nation, Britain's new technology was extraordinary for its time, but inefficient compared to what followed. This inefficiency made fuel costs more expensive than labor and forced employers to locate their factories near coalfields. Nations that later imitated Britain's industrialization developed factories once more efficient machinery was obtained. For these nations, labor costs exceeded the expense of fuel so that new factories took up residence in established urban areas rather than on the coalfields. Thus, the demographic shift for Great Britain required greater social and political adjustments than those of later industrial states.

Since Great Britain was the first to industrialize, the British had to follow a path of spontaneous economic integration in which most of the participants did not fully understand the changes taking place. Starting in several industries at once, British innovation linked hand tools used in manufacturing textiles with steam power used to pump water out of coalmines. Coal had replaced wood to become Britain's primary fuel source by the seventeenth century, as the remaining forests of the kingdom became dedicated to shipbuilding. Imports of timber and ship products from New England later compensated for dwindling supplies of trees. In the meantime, coal became the general source of fuel for the British people.

Coal seams, however, were porous, and mines soon filled with groundwater as miners extracted this fuel from the earth. Hand pumps could not keep up with the water seeping into mines as miners cut deeper into the coal seams. Eventually Thomas Newcomen (1663–1729) developed a steam engine that could pump water from mines by 1702. Too inefficient for other uses, however, this machine was confined to the coalfields for more than sixty years. Still, the idea of a mechanical implement suggested all kinds of productive possibilities for the future.

In textiles, entrepreneurs sought innovations to replace cottage labor as the demand for their products grew with the success of British commercial capitalism. One invention, the "flying shuttle," developed by James Kay in 1733, allowed one weaver to pull thread through the loom single-handedly to produce cloth that previously required the work of two people. This increased efficiency created a new demand for more thread that in turn inspired James Hargreaves's "spinning jenny" in 1760. The spinning jenny replaced the spinning wheel and increased the production of thread. Hargreaves's simple hand tool later led Richard Arkwright in 1769 to develop the "water-frame" as a water-powered spinning system that ran several spinning jennies from a single power source. Next, Samuel Compton developed a power loom called the "mule" in

"Locomotion Number One." George Stephenson's first steam engine (1825) operated on the opening day of the Stockton and Darlington Railway, the world's first public railway. The original is on display at the North Road Station Museum in Darlington, one of the oldest railway stations in the world. Collection of E.A. Reitan.

Stephenson's more famous "Rocket," would go on to victory at Lancashire's Rainhill Trials in 1829.

1779 to replace the hand-loom weaver who could not keep up with the production of thread. Finally, James Watt refined Thomas Newcomen's steam engine (patented in 1769) to release it from the coal mines so that it could move into the textile industry. Eleven years later, the steam engine joined with Richard Arkwright's water frame to produce the first factory in 1780. Other factories followed by taking up locations close to coalmines; these factories then generated the urbanization that caused Britain's extraordinary rural-urban demographic shift.

Moving to the midlands and northern counties, where most of the coal lay, British labor created new cities in sparsely populated districts and empty shires. These new industrial towns required iron, food, and transportation to sustain life. The construction of roads and canals helped, but a new form of transportation was needed to keep pace with these expanding urban markets. In the United States Robert Fulton combined steam power with shipping to make the first steamboat in 1807, but this vessel still required water as the basis of travel. The key step that made a national economy truly possible came from George Stephenson (1781–1848), who developed the "Rocket," a steam-powered vehicle that ran on rails.

Stephenson experimented with the possibility of steam-powered locomotion in 1814 and had a working model by 1815. It would be another fourteen years, however, before the railroad became a practical means of transportation. By 1829 Stephenson had refined his idea and opened a railroad line that carried goods between Liverpool and Manchester at the rate of twenty miles per hour. Now Britain's global empire, industrial economy, and local farms could be integrated on a national scale.

Stephenson's railroad started a mass communication system that began to generate the first industrial-urban hierarchy. Centered on Britain's principal city, London, the railroad integrated regional capitals into an evolving national market system. London itself functioned as the political, financial, social, intellectual, fashion, and advertising center of Great Britain. Each regional capital, in turn, slowly matured into the center for local production. Supported by local cities, towns, villages, and agricultural hamlets, each regional capital integrated provincial production with the national economy. All levels of this urban hierarchy then linked people, raw materials, food, fuel, and manufacturing through the high-bulk, long-distance, and low-cost transportation offered by Britain's railroads. As a result, the British people joined one another in a common economic destiny that took its shape within the iron frame of rails.

At the heart of this industrial story is the physical integration of national economic space based on urban markets. Pulling all of Britain's regional production into one urban hierarchy focused human awareness on the idea of the *nation*, wherein the well-being of the economy equaled the well-being of the *people*. Simultaneously, the French Revolution suggested that the *people* themselves were the *nation*. Thus, when a national economy emerged in Britain to complement the image of the nation created by France, the idea of such a political unity became firmly etched in the European imagination.

Most of the rural and urban products of Great Britain's new national economy exchanged in an expanding market system that effected the prosperity of the entire country. Growth in population, increased wealth, and the relocation of labor had all become part of daily life. Intellectuals like Robert Thomas Malthus and David Ricardo corrected Adam Smith's landmark work to speak to this new awareness. Hence, the people of Great Britain had awakened to the realization that their mutual dependency united them in a common national cause, even if their individual political ideas might conflict.

This awareness set Britain along a political course of redefinition based on the threat of revolution as suggested by the French experience. What the British achieved by 1832, in the first of their fundamental, political reforms, was to acknowledge the reality of industrial change. The Reform Bill of 1832 recognized the new distribution of wealth caused by the relocation of people in new industrial cities through the reapportionment of the vote from depopulated areas to the new towns and counties in the North and midlands. This bill also created new property requirements to define the right to vote that acknowledged occupations connected with industrial capitalism. Finally, the Reform of 1832 reshaped Britain's conservative opposition to change. British conservatives became the first group of rich and powerful men of estate to acknowledge the reality of social and economic modernization.

Such reform did not come easy or without human cost. This first step in political redefinition was only the beginning of a process that continued to 1928. The Reform Bill of 1867 followed the reforms of 1832 and extended the vote to urban labor. The Reform Bill of 1884 then expanded the franchise to include agricultural workers. Finally, the reforms of 1918 and 1928 broke the gender barrier and embraced British women in universal suffrage. In short, the United Kingdom had demonstrated a viable alternative to revolution: it was called *reform*.

The British pattern of reform met the demands of public opinion without the violent dislocation of revolution. Such political flexibility could not have occurred had not the supporters of tradition, Britain's conservatives, also become partners in the modern political process. Thus, British conservatives became the first traditional leaders in Europe to develop an effective modern political strategy.

As reform shaped politics in Great Britain, industry had integrated the geographic space of this nation-state. France meanwhile had created the structural and legal definitions of a similar new political culture. Now the rest of Europe looked to France's and Britain's successes at nation-building. But few peoples in other portions of Europe had experienced the same level of protomodern development as had the French and British. Thus, the formation of modern political societies elsewhere in Europe would not be as spontaneous as in Britain and France, where the cost had already been very high: twenty-six years of revolution and warfare for the French, and countless riots, strikes, and political posturing for the British.

Language and the Will of the People

While the thinkers of the Enlightenment had studied language as a representational system, unobtrusive in communicating nature's objective impressions, German philologists of the nineteenth century proved this perception of speech incorrect. They argued that language existed as a medium that not only reflected nature's stamp but also included elements of human will in its system of communication. According to these thinkers, the sounds of language had their own history, just like ideas, and existed in a realm of human desires apart from the impartial imprints made by nature. In addition, these sounds revealed how language could focus human will to mobilize a people into a national community.

The three German philologists responsible for this radical revision of Europe's understanding of language were Frederich von Schlegel (1772–1829), Jakob Ludwig Karl Grimm (1785–1863), and Franz Bopp (1791–1867). These men not only restructured the role that language played in shaping the human imagination, but each also clarified Europe's understanding of culture itself. This linguistic component of culture reminded Central Europeans that they too possessed unique national identities that should have defined their political communities.

The German philologists also built a conceptual bridge between language, culture, and ethnicity. If language was the vehicle that united a people through collective consciousness, then the history of the spoken word revealed the achievements of a specific family of humans at a given moment in time. Thus, the evolution of a particular language represented the collective awareness of a tribe of individuals that captured their spirit and knowledge as a distinct community of people. Accordingly, the ideas of community, language, and culture began to blend with the concepts of tribe, ethnicity, and race to link the goals and accomplishments represented by a particular nation of humans with the identity of their ethnic-linguistic heritage. Consequently, pride of self bonded Schlegel's, Grimm's, and Bopp's work with language to the nineteenth century concept of culture to create a passion for national formation in Central Europe.

Central Europeans and Internal Coherence

Central Europeans were well aware that they lacked the same economic, social, military, or political resources as Great Britain or France. The Central Europeans also felt that if they did not keep pace with the events occurring to the west, Germany and Italy would have to accept a second-class status as cultural regions. Thus, the people of Central Europe felt that they had to develop their own national potential to fulfill their cultural, ethnic, and linguistic destiny. During the French Revolution (1789–1815), Germans and Italians alike discovered a very strong urge to form their own nation-states.

The Italians looked back to the glory of Rome, while the Germans had developed a strong sense of their own culture and history based on the philosophy of Kant as well as the philology of Schlegel, Grimm, and Bopp. Both the Italian and German peoples realized they had the potential to form their own nation-states, but both also knew that they would have to challenge tradition to achieve their political goals. Standing directly in their way was a second major obstacle to national formation in Central Europe: Austria.

Austria emerged as a new political creation based on the power of the Habsburg Dynasty after the Thirty Years War (1618–48). As we have seen in previous chapters, during the reign of Charles V (1500–58), the Habsburgs had become the dominant dynasty in Europe by combining the throne of Spain with the Austrian Netherlands and the Holy Roman Empire. In the seventeenth century, however, this combination of realms had collapsed. Holland won its independence during Philip II's reign (1556–98); the Holy Roman Empire existed in name but ceased to be a political reality after the Thirty Years War; and the Bourbons of France gained the throne of Spain in the War of the Spanish Succession (1702–14). Austria now stood alone as one of the German principalities and sought to recover its power by expanding east and south. In the process, the Austrian Empire emerged as a multiethnic realm comprised of Austria, Silesia, Bohemia, Moravia, Galicia, and parts of Croatia and Transylvania; Austria also had ambitions to dominate the Balkans in southeastern Europe. Yet as this multiethnic, multilinguistic empire grew, its cultural complexity increased and made the Austrians the enemy of national formation. Many potential nation-states existed within its borders, and the Austrians resisted any loss of land.

Between 1815 and 1848, the rigid conservative voice of Clemens Wenzel Nepomuk Lothar Furst von Metternich (1773–1853) spoke for Austria. A skilled diplomat, Metternich tried to thwart all revolutions as well as any popular, spontaneous effort to achieve national formation. He did so to protect Austria's political existence as an empire comprising more than ten major language groups in the nineteenth century. Fearing the new emphasis on linking a people's speech with national identity, Metternich knew that creating new nation-states would pull Austria apart. Hence, he marshaled every fiber of his being to prevent the Germans, Italians, Czechs, Slovaks, Poles, Ukrainians, Magyars, Croatians, Slovenes, Serbians, and Rumanians from achieving their national goals.

To block national formation in Central Europe, Metternich created an inflexible form of conservatism called "legitimacy" that stated, "What is, shall remain as it is." Unlike British conservatives, who had an easier task of defending a United Kingdom comprised of four different cultural heritages, Metternich tried to protect a political society composed of a multitude of different ethnicities. While Great Britain's conservatives had outlawed the use of Welsh and Gaelic, so that everyone in the United Kingdom had learned to speak English, Metternich led a divided and polyglot empire filled with numerous peoples seeking their own national destiny.

Metternich had to rule the Germans, Italians, Czechs, Slovaks, Poles, Ukrainians, Magyars, Croatians, Serbians, and Romanians living within his empire while using German as the administrative tongue. Simultaneously, Metternich had to prevent all the subject peoples from achieving their national aspirations for fear of the fragmentation of the Austrian Empire. Hence, Metternich had to work against common national identities and linguistic media to accomplish his diplomatic goals. Only temporarily at his disposal, the Great Powers of Europe (Britain, Prussia, Austria, Russia, and a restored France) were united for a mere thirty-three years in an effort to suppress revolution. They were willing to support Metternich these thirty-three years since most of his goals in Central Europe did not conflict with their interests; also they were exhausted after the twenty-six years of struggle with revolutionary France. As a result, in 1815, they joined Metternich in an alliance called the Congress System to preserve his vision of a legitimate Europe until 1848.

The Congress System was an international organization of states designed to ensure that no new revolution would succeed in Europe. Using this conservative alliance, Metternich manipulated affairs on the continent so that his diplomacy frustrated all spontaneous, liberal, or radical change. Consistently successful in Central Europe, he obstructed all national aspirations there. Less successful in the Americas and the Balkans, Metternich could not prevent Latin America's separation from Spain (1810–26), or the Greek revolt from the Turks (1821–29). In addition, Western Europeans continued to use both revolution and reform to refine their own national identities between 1815 and 1848.

Yet Metternich had managed to defeat revolution after revolution in both the Austrian, German, and Italian territories before 1848. Thus, Austria became the focal point for national rage in Central Europe. Then, the final burst of spontaneous revolutionary passion that swept through Western civilization between 1848 and 1850 drove Metternich from power. His form of rigid conservatism had proven too inflexible. Now, traditional European leaders began to realize that Britain's conservative strategy of becoming part of the modern political dialogue worked best.

Ironically, while the spontaneous revolutions of 1848 drove Metternich from power, they also failed to establish their goals. The German and Italian principalities, Austria, Hungary, Prussia, and Poland had revolted in particular to create national democracies, but all had fallen to conservative counterrevolutions in their separate territories. This failure proved instructive to Central European conservatives who realized that if they joined the process of modernization, they, too, might be able to preserve their positions of power in a national setting. For the people of Germany and Italy in particular, this meant that the liberal model of national formation used by Great Britain and France might be modified into a conservative alternative in Central Europe. In short both Italian and German conservatives realized that nation-building might be the best way to avoid the dangers of too much freedom and spontaneity.

Led by men like Camillo Benso, Count di Cavour (1810–61) and Otto von Bismarck (1815–98), Italian and German conservatives alike created the era of *Realpolitik*, wherein the ends justified the means in the best tradition of politique thinking. Based on a design that mixed conservative goals with nationalistic fervor so that traditional rulers could still retain power, Cavour and Bismarck applied Machiavelli's principles to create a new standard for state-building. Each in his own way gave his respective people the possibility of winning nationhood by sacrificing personal freedom and spontaneity in politics.

Count Camillo Benso di Cavour of Piedmont-Savoy-Sardinia was the first to realize the necessity of abandoning spontaneous revolution. Cavour had begun his career in the army but quickly shifted to politics. He pressed for modernization in the small principality of Piedmont-Savoy-Sardinia in northwest Italy to build a coalition of power between conservatives and liberals. This coalition unified aristocrats and industrialists on the common ground of protecting property against the poor. Realizing that modernization was the key to the future, Cavour analyzed the problem of Italian unification and concluded that Austria alone stood in the way.

The Italian people had rebelled numerous times prior to 1850 in an effort to achieve their national ambitions, but Austria had blocked each of these efforts.

In addition, Cavour knew that his tiny country was too weak to accomplish Italy's national goals alone. Hence, he began to look for European partners to create an Italian nation-state. He finally chose France as the best potential ally.

In 1850, a political opportunist named Louis Napoleon III, the nephew of Napoleon Bonaparte, ruled France. Louis Napoleon III had captured power in France by a coup d'etat after the failure of the French Revolution of 1848. Cavour recognized in this political adventurer the necessary personality Italy needed to construct a nation-state.

Cavour sought to seduce Louis Napoleon to the Italian enterprise by arranging reasons for the two of them to join in a common international venture. Cavour began by having his small principality aid France and Britain against Russia in the Crimean War (1853–56). Like many of Russia's and Turkey's conflicts, the Crimean War represented one of numerous struggles between the czar and sultan over who controlled Istanbul. Czar Nicholas I (reigned 1825–55) had already acquired the left bank of the Danube in a war with Turkey fought between 1828 and 1829. In 1853 he claimed to be protecting Christians from Turkish aggression within the Ottoman Empire when he prepared for his next war with the sultan. France and Britain, however, feared a too powerful Russia if Nicholas I captured Istanbul and joined forces to stop him. The British fleet blockaded the Baltic and Black seas while a combined army of British and French soldiers invaded the Crimea. Sardinia joined the British and French efforts in 1855 when Nicholas I's death that same year allowed Czar Alexander II to sue for peace. Russia gave up land along the left bank of the Danube, which became the new basis for Rumania and withdrew the Russian navy from the Black Sea; France became Christianity's protector in the Ottoman Empire.

In this conflict Cavour sent his forces to join France and Great Britain against czarist Russia, hoping all along to bring up the issue of Italian unification at the negotiations for peace that would follow. Cavour quietly reminded Louis Napoleon on numerous occasions of how his uncle had unified Italy during the fourth phase of the French Revolution (1799–1815). Cavour suggested that should the two become partners—he would give Savoy and Nice to France after he engineered a war with Austria.

Maneuvering Austria into declaring war in 1859 by mobilizing the Piedmont-Savoy-Sardinian army to protect a rebellion in a small Italian Duchy to the south, Cavour created the circumstances that would make Louis Napoleon seem like a great statesman. Louis Napoleon entered the war as an international hero to the Italians, as well as the liberal opinion of Europe, by appearing to defend a peaceful land from a foreign aggressor. But bloody engagements and threatening moves by Prussia on the Rhine shocked Louis Napoleon, who suddenly proposed a separate armistice with Austria that almost ruined Cavour's plans.

At just the right moment, however, a spontaneous revolution broke out in central Italy that drew the Austrians, Napoleon III, and Cavour into an alliance. All three decided to quiet this liberal rebellion by creating a north Italian state. This agreement included ceding Savoy and Nice to France and giving Tuscany, Parma, Modena, and Romagna to Piedmont-Sardinia. The deal forged in 1860 between France, Austria, and Piedmont-Sardinia fulfilled half of Cavour's plans to unify Italy.

With his task half done, Cavour shifted his attention to southern Italy. There a romantic revolutionary named Giuseppe Garibaldi (1807–82) had begun a guerrilla war at the suggestion of Victor Emmanuel II, Cavour's king. To everyone's surprise, Garibaldi's rebellion succeeded quite well.

Garibaldi had captured Sicily and Naples in short order, 1860–61, but now he posed a major problem for Cavour. Marching north on Rome, Garibaldi threatened to capture the Papal States. Since the French emperor had a garrison in Rome to defend the papacy, Cavour feared Garibaldi's approach might touch off a war with France. If Garibaldi attempted to take Rome, Louis Napoleon would then have to resist and Cavour's work would be undone.

Cavour met this delicate situation boldly by mobilizing the North Italian Army, marching south with his king, Victor Emmanuel II, and placing this force between Garibaldi and Rome. Having occupied most of the papal states, Cavour carefully avoided Rome, and accepted southern Italy from Garibaldi. Cavour then arranged for Garibaldi's retirement as a national hero pensioned off by Victor Emmanuel II.

Cavour had nearly completed his task. All of Italy had become one nation save for the state of Venetia and a small piece of territory set aside for the pope. These two fragments of Italy, however, joined the new nation after Cavour's death, when the Italians supported the German unification process as Prussia's ally in the Austro-Prussian War of 1866 and the Franco-Prussian War of 1870–71 (see below). Prussia's victory in both wars removed Austria from Venetia and a French army from Rome. Cavour himself died suddenly, only six months after his triumph in 1861. Evidently, the strain of his diplomacy had cost him dearly.

Yet despite Italy's success at unification, the new Italian nation-state retained two economic characters:

the north was industrial; the south was rural. The unification achieved by Cavour created a political entity that lacked the ubiquitous industrial infrastructure needed to reinforce internal coherence. The coalition of property designed by Cavour that brought aristocrats and industrialists together did not have an urban hierarchy to complete the task of making the new nation-state a social and economic reality.

Nor was the new Italy a democracy. Instead, Cavour's new government relied on tradition and authority to rule its people. An Italian could not participate in politics without sufficient wealth to qualify for the vote. These property restrictions limited the franchise to only 600,000 Italians out of a population of 20 million people. Thus, the methods used to achieve national formation, and the type of authoritarian-republic that emerged in Italy, produced only the façade of a democracy. A new era had dawned in European politics.

Cavour had accomplished what no Italian could do since Niccolo Machiavelli first proposed the idea back in 1513. And his methods revealed to Central Europeans that an alternative existed to the Western European liberal style of national formation. Indeed, Cavour had demonstrated that if conservatives joined with moderate industrialists to form a new consensus of wealth to control the poor, they could neutralize the popular vote and rule a nation-state with impunity.

Germany

The lessons of Italian unification were not lost on Otto von Bismarck (1815–98). As Chancellor of Prussia, Bismarck, however, did not have to use the same level of diplomatic finesse Cavour had employed to unify Italy. Bismarck's Prussia was a powerful principality of the Holy Roman Empire comprised of a German speaking population that had successfully joined the Great Powers of Europe after the Reformation. Prussia's continued growth and victories at war during the seventeenth, eighteenth, and nineteenth centuries offered Bismarck the military means to more than match Austrian strength alone. Yet Bismarck also understood that any war to unify Germany would have to be carefully engineered lest it mushroom into a general European conflict.

Otto von Bismarck got his chance to apply Cavour's lessons when the new Prussian king, Wilhelm I (1797–1888), pressed the *Landtag*, Prussian parliament, to enlarge the size of the army in 1862. Fearing the power that an enlarged army would grant the king, the liberal Landtag refused. Bismarck then promised to give Wilhelm I his army if the king would make him chancellor.

Once at his new post, Bismarck set out to unify Germany. In a loose interpretation of the Prussian constitution, he dissolved the Landtag, extended the budget of 1862 into a new fiscal year, and appealed to his people to pay their taxes because it was their duty. A docile and obedient population in Prussia gave Bismarck the support he needed. Yet the Prussian people also surprised Bismarck by reelecting the liberal majority in the Landtag. To seduce the Prussian people away from liberalism, Bismarck decided to link their passion for national formation with Wilhelm I's request to increase the size of the Prussian military.

Bismarck's plan was simple. He hoped to separate nationalism from personal freedom by unifying Germany through warfare. What Bismarck knew about Prussia that his liberal opponents failed to see was that nothing succeeds like success itself. In other words, the popularity and joy generated by military victory far overshadowed any ethical qualms the people might have had. Bismarck proved his theory when he linked Wilhelm I's military program to German unification. He stated bluntly that only "blood and iron" would resolve such major national and international issues like national formation.

Blood and iron indeed became Bismarck's formula for implementing his plan to unify Germany. Engineering one war after another, Bismarck created a series of partnerships with his neighbors that he used to achieve his military and diplomatic goals. First Denmark, then Austria, and finally France found themselves maneuvered into international confrontations that led to war and defeat. Each step in this process fit Bismarck's design to form a new nation-state.

In 1864, Denmark became Bismarck's first victim. Here, he exploited an old issue of who owned the northern provinces of Schleswig and Holstein, the Danes or the Germans. This issue was guaranteed to create a passion for war because Schleswig and Holstein had belonged to the Old Holy Roman Empire—the rough geographic outline used by German nationalists to define their potential nation-state. Enlisting Austria as a partner to defeat the Danes and divide the spoils, Bismarck then arranged a peace treaty designed to infuriate the Austrians. He gave Austria the northern province of Holstein and took Schleswig immediately to the south. By persuading Austria to accept Holstein, Bismarck then told his fellow Germans that his ally had helped defeat Denmark for selfish reasons rather than defending territory belonging to the Holy Roman Empire. Bismarck also used Schleswig's geographic location south of Holstein to obstruct Austria's administration of its new territory. Finally, he further suggested that Holstein's chief port, Kiel, might make a good Prussian naval base.

Simultaneously, Bismarck maneuvered to isolate Austria diplomatically. He banked on Russia's sympathy by reminding the czar of two key events. First, Prussia had suppressed a Polish revolt in 1863 that threatened to create a new nation-state comprised of Russian territory. And second, Russia's old friend and ally, Austria, had not quietly sat by during the czar's agonizing defeat in the Crimean War—in fact, Austria had mobilized and threatened to enter the war on the Turkish side because the Habsburgs coveted control of the Balkans as the czar's rival. At the same time, Bismarck knew that the British would not intervene in a Prussian-Austrian war because of Great Britain's policy of "Splendid Isolation." Finally, Bismarck hinted to Louis Napoleon III that he could expand France at the expense of Belgium, Luxembourg, and the Bavarian Palatinate, if Bismarck were given a free hand to deal with Austria. Freed from fear of foreign intervention, Bismarck challenged the now isolated Austria to war in 1866. His calculated risk paid off, as Prussia quickly defeated Bismarck's old partner the Habsburgs.

The victory over Austria gave Bismarck the opportunity to create the North German Federation. Then Bismarck promptly reneged on his implied promises of territory to France. Bismarck knew that Napoleon would be furious. He also knew that Napoleon had gravely miscalculated by allowing Bismarck to create a powerful new neighbor to France on its eastern frontier. Thus, Bismarck began to set up his next victim—Napoleon III. A revolution in Spain gave Bismarck the opportunity he needed.

The Spanish offered their crown to Wilhelm I's cousin, Prince Leopold von Hohenzollern-Sigmaringen. The possibility of surrounding France with Prussian princes drove the French to pressure Wilhelm I to remove his cousin as a royal candidate. Manipulating the way the French approached Wilhelm I, Bismarck created a media event by editing and publishing diplomatic cables. Enraged by his highhanded methods, Louis Napoleon III found himself maneuvered into a third Bismarckian war, the Franco-Prussian war of 1870–71. Victory against France again came swiftly, this time due to superior German railroads and artillery that permitted Bismarck to complete the unification process when he absorbed the southern German states.

Bismarck had unified Germany, accomplishing in six years what the Germans had failed to do since Otto I revived the Holy Roman Empire in 962. At the same time, Bismarck had given the Germans what they most wanted: a modern Germany. Unfortunately, Bismarck's success had built this new nation on a foundation of violence.

By this time, both Germany and Italy had demonstrated to Europe that the use of an amoral, Machiavellian strategy to achieve national goals worked. Each had employed whatever means necessary for success. And, each had used the knowledge they had of their opponent in a style of thought that seemed to imitate scientific dispassion. Furthermore, each had created a community that linked language, a people, and a national culture to a new political entity. Finally, each had created their nation-states by bringing a new realism to European politics.

The apparent scientific qualities of this new style of politics became popularized by the historical term *realpolitik*, the realistic politics of tangible rewards. Ironically, the dispassion of realpolitik rested on the passions of nationalism to link an amoral process with a national, cultural purpose in the best manner of politique practices. Thus, as Cavour and Bismarck addressed the problem of national formation with what appeared to be the precision of science, and gained a clear cultural goal that their peoples craved, both political leaders released a new violent and cynical standard for Europeans to follow.

Germany, however, differed from Italy in two fundamental ways. First, Germany had industry to integrate all its geographic space. And second, Bismarck had such confidence in his success that he did not fear universal male suffrage. His rapid unification of Germany had given him control of the new nation's public opinion.

Bismarck knew that the great military victories he had won carried their own political momentum. Simultaneously, the economic integration of industry and the popular vote revealed that the new Germany had obtained complete cohesion through geographic internal coherence. In contrast, Italy remained politically and economically divided with an urban north and a rural south.

Before Bismarck came to power, Prussia had laid an economic foundation for national formation through a policy of liberal education and industrial development after its defeat by Napoleon Bonaparte (1806) during the French Revolution. Developing a new, efficient central government, Prussia's monarchs encouraged reforms based on the lessons learned from the French. As a result, Prussia created a professional state bureaucracy that promoted industrialization and the urban skills of its people: literacy, the ability to calculate, and a capacity for critical thinking.

As the Prussians developed a strong educational system that reached from elementary schools through the university level, they also produced the best technically trained population in Europe. Simultaneously, the government followed a mercantilist tradition of intervening in economic planning to stimulate and integrate industrial development. Free-market principles so popular in Western Europe did not influence Prussian economic thinking.

This curious mixture of government control, modern technological and economic development, and public education placed a higher value on the principles of order than on individual freedom. With an eye to the future, Prussia maintained an equal footing with Western Europe as an act of political and economic will. Following the momentum of commercial integration as an impetus for political order, Prussia merged its market structure with its German neighbors by using a tariff union as the basic strategy.

Beginning in 1818, the Prussians encouraged many tiny German states to include Prussia in their formation of local economies. Called the *Zollverein*, this growing tariff union stimulated a pattern of market integration in the German principalities that made Prussia's Berlin a centerplace city. The result was a common railroad system that transformed local economies into a new urban hierarchy prior to the unification of Germany. Hence, Bismarck simply had added political unity to an economic reality.

Bismarck's swift victories could not have been won without the Zollverein. Austria's defeat came at the hands of a superior Prussian army whose use of industrial weapons included the so-called needle-gun, a breech-loading rifle whose name came from the needle-like firing pin that struck the rear of a cartridge to launch the bullets. Such a breech-loading weapon allowed the Prussian infantry to fire repeatedly from a prone position, while Austrian soldiers had to stand to reload their weapons. Furthermore, industrial integration gave the Prussians a rail system that allowed them to transport, supply, and deploy their military rapidly. Thus, Prussia could deliver larger and better-equipped armies to the critical battlefields quicker and more efficiently than the Austrians.

Like Austria, France soon fell victim to the industrialized German war machine. France had dominated military history on the continent ever since the Reformation (1648). Accustomed to having the best army and being at the forefront of military preparation, France expected an easy victory against Bismarck's North German Federation in 1870. Yet Prussia used a General Staff to coordinate their surprisingly more powerful military.

The General Staff exploited an effective mobilization plan, used a superior railroad system that integrated supply with troop movement, and deployed rapid-firing, breech-loading, rifled cannon. In contrast, the French relied on a smaller, more professional army and still used muzzle-loading cannon. This combination of Prussian technical advantages gave the North German Federation a numerical superiority that won crushing victories: the battles of Sedan and Metz. At Sedan the Prussians captured Louis Napoleon III and 81,000 French soldiers; at Metz the Prussians trapped, defeated, and took prisoner 137,000 Frenchmen in a single stroke. Together, these two victories neutralized two-thirds of the French Army.

Bismarck's blood-and-iron policies certainly had "blood" in the form of a general German passion for national formation. The "iron" clearly existed in the form of the Zollverein and a Prussian-centered industrial-urban complex. Bismarck merely brought to bear in European affairs a crude but equally effective form of amoral, politique diplomacy as developed by Cavour in Italy. Bismarck's success then produced its own momentum.

Bismarck's successes allowed him to create a constitution in Germany that neutralized the democratic force of the vote. The lower house of Germany's new legislature, the *Reichstag*, created a general sense of democracy by allowing universal male suffrage. Yet the nation was so constructed that ministers of state came from royal appointment and not from elected representatives. These ministers were responsible to the emperor and implemented his will.

Moreover, Germany comprised territory taken in war, with each ex-principality keeping its own laws, government, and constitution. At the same time, the princes of the new German Federation sat in the upper house of the new legislature. The emperor, for example, ruled the empire under one constitution, and Prussia under another instrument of law. In effect, the German empire ended up magnifying the power of Prussia over Germany by allowing the Prussian king to set policy, both domestic and foreign, for the rest of the new nation.

Thus, Germany appeared to be a democracy but in fact was not. In actuality, the new German empire served as an instrument to enhance Prussian foreign policy. The new Germany magnified the role of Prussia in Europe, increased the power of the Prussian army, and brought the Prussian aristocracy forward as the leading ministers of the new state as well as its officer-corps. Bismarck had, in reality, conquered Germany as he built his new nation. And like Cavour, Bismarck had demonstrated that political adventure, if carefully planned and executed, could achieve nearly any end.

Suggested Reading

The Nation-State

Bagwell, Philip, *The Transportation Revolution from 1770* (London: Batsford, 1974).

Baker, Keith Michael, *Inventing the French Revolution* (Cambridge: Cambridge University Press, 1991).

Beales, Derek, *The Risorgimento and the Unification of Italy* (London: Allen and Unwin, 1982).

Brown, Richard, *Society and Economy in Modern Britain, 1700–1850* (London: Routledge, 1991).

Chartier, Roger, *The Cultural Origins of the French Revolution,* Translated by Lydia G, Cochrane (Durham, N.C.: Duke University Press, 1991).

Foucault, Michel, *The Order of Things: An Archaeology of the Human Sciences* (New York: Vantage Books, 1970).

Furet, François and Denis Richet, *The French Revolution* (New York: Macmillan, 1970).

Hunt, Lynn, *Politics, Culture, and Class in the French Revolution* (Berkeley: University of California Press, 1984).

Morgan, Kenneth, *The Birth of Industrial Britain: Economic Change, 1750–1850* (London; New York: Longman, 1999).

Perkins, Harold, *The Origins of Modern English Society, 1780–1880* (London: Routledge and Kegan Paul, 1969).

Sheehan, James J., *German Liberalism in the Nineteenth Century* (Chicago: University of Chicago Press, 1978).

Smith, Denis Mack, *Cavour* (London: Weidenfeld and Nicolson, 1985).

Sutherland, D. M. G., *France, 1789–1815: Revolution and Counter-Revolution* (New York: Oxford University Press, 1986).

Thompson, E. P., *The Making of the Working Class* (New York: Vantage Books, 1966).

Wrigley, E. A., *Continuity, Chance, and Change* (Cambridge: Cambridge University Press, 1988).

Woloch, Isser, *The New Regime: Transformation of the French Civil Order* (New York: Norton, 1994).

XXII

THE DIFFERENTIAL
OF POWER

Between 1400 and 1750, the Commercial Revolution redefined global trade. European explorers, missionaries, and merchants had used their new transoceanic trade routes to take the initiative in intercultural contacts and travel around the world making commercial exchanges wherever possible. Supported by their kings or parliaments, these European adventurers began to assemble new mercantile empires unlike any the world had ever seen before. Ultimately, these European travelers created a new global trade network that laid the foundation for the Industrial Revolution.

At first, the appearance of these European adventurers sparked curiosity in local peoples, but hospitality soon gave way to suspicion as the underlying aggressiveness of these foreign intruders began to surface. Those traditional cultures that could, either broke off relations with these alien travelers or attempted to control European access to local markets. Those cultures that could not break off relations soon found themselves overwhelmed by the strangers.

The differential of power, the varying social, economic, political, and military resources available to different cultures, defined how Europeans related to non-European communities around the world after 1492. So long as the differential of power permitted, most traditional peoples closed their doors to, or attempted to control, European influences. For example, the Tokugawa Shogunate of Japan (1600–1867) had expelled all Europeans except the Dutch, whom they confined to Nagasaki. The Ch'ing Dynasty of China (1644–1911) had restricted exposure to European merchants by limiting trade to Macao and by evicting all Christian missionaries. The Sunni Muslims in the Ottoman Empire (1300–1918) had occupied all of the Middle East, as well as the Balkans, while competing with Europe for control over the trade routes to India. The Shiite Muslims in the Safavid Empire of Persia (1501–1722) had the strength to restrict both European and Turkish influences within their domain. And the Mogul Empire of India (1525–1857) had chosen to engage in commerce with European merchants but

managed to dictate the terms of this trade until the eighteenth century.

In contrast, the numerous corporate lineages below the Sahara Desert, as well as those along Africa's West Coast, had allowed a major new slave trade to develop despite having the good fortune of a disease barrier to restrict European penetration into the interior. Simultaneously, many peoples in the Americas and South Africa had either fallen victim to European epidemics or a superior military technology, as native cultures located there suffered colonization. Accordingly, European communities had so thoroughly displaced the native peoples of the Western Hemisphere and the African Cape that the aboriginal populations there found themselves submerged in a new cultural environment.

Outside the American or South African experience, however, the initial policies of the Japanese, Chinese, Indians, Persians, Turks, Arabs, and, to some degree, the Russians was to withdraw from, restrict, or control the activities of Europeans. Simultaneously, disease shielded sub-Saharan African civilizations from European cultural penetration with a lethal barrier of pathogens. Consequently, each of these native cultures, either deliberately, or with the accidental aid of biological agents, limited contact with Europe; in the deliberate cases, this made sense in the light of the West's appetite for controlling world trade. At the same time, since these Europeans brought with them modern attitudes that included hostility toward tradition, each of these Middle Eastern, Asian, and African civilizations had recognized that contact with the West would threaten the very essence of their sacred beliefs and practices.

Yet whenever these traditional societies decided to cut off or to control commercial interaction with Europeans, they only temporarily blocked cultural exchanges. Ironically, by restricting contact with the West, these same traditional civilizations had denied themselves access to knowledge about the process of modernization, eliminating the possibility of an equivalent political, military, economic, social, and intellectual transformation of their regions. Without such contact, the people living in these traditional societies drifted toward a future confrontation with Europe as modernization continued to augment Western economic, political, and military power after 1800.

Thus, by 1850, Europeans had at their disposal the tools they needed to enter almost any traditional culture. For example, in the 1840s the French had discovered quinine, which fights malaria, and this allowed them to overcome a major African disease barrier. In addition, dangerous foreign epidemics like cholera increasingly fell under European control as scientific investigations developed germ theory, isolated parasites, and produced vaccines. Furthermore, besides germ theory, Europeans had refined clinical techniques that allowed them to save more of their wounded after the 1860s. Finally, at the same time, Europeans had refined the use of a deadly weapon called the rifle.

In 1849, the development of a new soft, hollow, and elongated bullet by Captain Claude Étienne Minié saw the American, British, Prussian, and French armies replace the musket with the rifle. Europeans had long known the advantages of the latter over the former. The rifle had grooves that spiraled down its barrel; these grooves imparted spin to a bullet that helped it travel in a straight line—like a spiral on a football—assuring accuracy up to 1,000 yards. In contrast, a smoothbore musket had an effective firing range of only 200 yards, and it had to be fired in volleys to ensure accuracy. The musket's single advantage was that it could be charged more quickly than the rifle in the heat of battle; it took one three times as long to pound the bullet down the grooved barrel of a rifle. Captain Minié, however, had eliminated this advantage because his new soft bullet could be dropped down the barrel of a rifle as easily as a ball down a musket's bore. Suddenly, European armies had an efficient instrument of war that extended the killing range of an armed soldier by 800 yards.

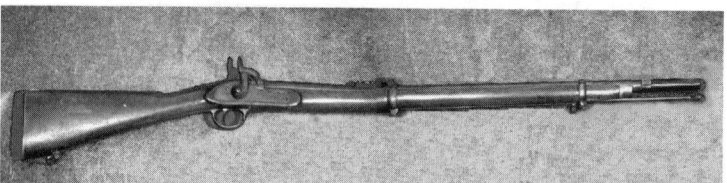

In 1849 French army captain Claude Étienne Minié invented this innovative bullet (right). The "Minié ball" was designed to spin, vastly increasing its range, velocity and accuracy. It was fired by the muzzle-loaded Minié rifle (above) and breech-loading Enfields and Springfields. The simple rifle-musket and Minié ball were the deadliest weapons of the American Civil War and the Crimean War. Rifle courtesy Civil War Preservations. Bullet courtesy Gordon Bakken.

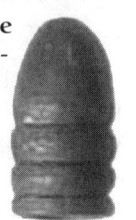

By 1866 the Prussians had rearmed their infantry with the aforementioned needle gun. This new, breech-loading rifle eliminated the necessity of a soldier standing up during combat to pound powder and shot down his barrel. Simultaneously, the needle-gun increased the rate of fire an infantryman could deliver from a prone or kneeling position. Hence, European soldiers suddenly became more deadly in three different ways: one, they could kill with greater safety; two, they could strike the enemy with greater accuracy; and three, they could fire with greater speed. As a result, the breech-loading rifle had made each European soldier a killing machine; the average man could now hit his target at such a distance that the act of war became a more impersonal, dispassionate, and mechanical exercise.

Meanwhile, the steamboat had developed rapidly after Robert Fulton had built the *Clemont* in 1807. With Fulton's success, steamboat technology was soon transferred to ocean-going vessels capable of complementing, or even replacing, the sail. By the 1860s, these ocean-going vessels were also outfitted with armor and an assortment of cannon. At the same time, the steamboat gave Europeans the ability to enter the interior of every foreign continent, for the steamship had the capacity to maneuver in a limited space and travel against the currents of rivers. Thus, the steamboat had opened up every continent on Earth to European aggression.

The combination of these tools, complemented by a host of other modern inventions, gave the West the ability to explore, invade, and subjugate any native culture that tried to resist European entry. Simultaneously, as Europeans developed all these new technologies, they also increased their ability to acquire foreign markets, which in turn allowed them to produce more efficient industries that added to their growing power. Taken all together, the productive resources of these newer and more efficient industries, and the development of modern medicines, weapons, and transportation, combined with the unique political institutions of the nation-state to create the military potency of a nation-in-arms. The nation-in-arms, in turn, augmented Europe's potential for gaining mastery over global trade and allowed the West to use its resources to reshape the world in its own image.

As Europeans started to assume the role of global leadership, they also began to acquire a new sense of cultural superiority that became part of this shift in the differential of power. Their sense of cultural superiority took its energy from the discovery of culture itself, as embedded in the philosophies of Adam Smith and Immanuel Kant. Interpreting Smith's and Kant's work, intellectuals like Georg Wihelm Friedrich Hegel, David Ricardo, and Karl Marx created a new philosophy of *teleology* (the study of ends, or goals) to explain change as a series of rational, i.e., human-imposed, events on nature leading toward a clearly defined cultural goal. The relationship between humankind and nature would never be the same.

The New Teleology

Based on the political economy created by Adam Smith, or the redefinition of objectivity developed by Immanuel Kant, nineteenth-century Europeans produced a new teleological style of thought that identified the ultimate purposes found in the relationship between natural and human processes. This new teleology revealed what Europeans believed to be the absolute truth about reality. In short, Europeans thought they had finally captured an understanding of the forces that would lead humanity to recover the link between the good, the beautiful, the true, and the real as originally described by Socrates, Plato, and Aristotle.

Hegel

Building on Kant's *Critique of Pure Reason*, Georg Wilhelm Friedrich Hegel (1770–1831) extended the consequences to knowledge. Kant had confined all human sense data to events trapped in the perceptual limits of time and space, arguing that people shaped this subjective data into knowledge by processing their impressions of the world through the rational architecture of their minds. Comprised of objective chambers, this rational architecture used the symbolic systems of logic and math to shape our sense data into human languages that, in turn, allowed people to share what they had learned.

Born in Stuttgart, educated at Tübingen, and becoming a professor of philosophy at the University of Jena in 1805, Hegel used Kant's objective mental architecture to create *The Phenomenology of Geist*. Hegel produced this new philosophy in 1807 to show how our subjective sense data, the rational categories of logic and math, and human language generated a "collective consciousness" that served civilization as the cultural energy needed to reshape the world. Hegel bundled this collective consciousness into his concept of *Geist* (spirit and mind) to demonstrate the power of the human will and intellect. Geist, in turn, produced a synthesis of existence that integrated humanity and nature into one common reality.

Geist is a German term that means both spirit and mind. Both words are necessary to capture the full meaning of Geist because each reveals how the human will (spirit) and intellect (mind) produce a hunger for knowledge. Once acquired, this knowledge then gives humanity the power to interact with nature and shape the circumstances of life. Thus, for Hegel, Geist captured the human process of acquiring knowledge and combined it with the human purpose of commanding the forces of nature.

Accordingly, Geist both produced, and was the product of, each individual's awareness of the world. Translated into rational concepts, then spoken as words, and finally assembled as collective consciousness, Geist was the result of severe mental trials based on the rational architecture of the mind and expressed in language. Geist was a collective intellectual entity that represented the sum total of all human data and wisdom produced by an ongoing rational dialogue that took place between serious-minded people. Hence, Geist became the only form of reality humans could know.

Hegel argued that Geist became reality itself through the formula, "the real is the rational and the rational is the real." What Hegel meant by "the real is the rational" is that nature (i.e., external reality governed by rational, natural laws) served as the sole source of data for our collective consciousness. What he meant by "the rational is the real" is that collective consciousness captured the rational in nature, which became human knowledge and could be used to interact with the external world to reshape reality. Thus, as humanity acquired knowledge through the data received from nature, so people could use their collective understanding of the external world to reshape the natural setting in order to meet their needs. Thus, human knowledge and nature eventually combined in a reciprocal relationship to generate a common cultural existence that Hegel called the "Absolute." This Absolute so thoroughly synthesized nature and human creativity in one cultural entity that neither could exist apart from the other. Thus the unity between the world (nature) and knowledge (culture) became the ultimate purpose, or *telos*, of human existence.

Hegel's Geist, however, was limited by the objective architecture of the mind. Reason dictated the rules of logic and math and gave shape to language. Hence, what humans knew at any one time depended on their location in the dialogue. By dialogue, Hegel meant the development of human knowledge as a "collective consciousness" engaged in a rational discourse with itself as individual participants (thinkers) pruned human understanding of error over time using the ever-vigilant powers of math and logic. This location in the dialogue led other German philosophers to coin the concepts of *Zeitgeist* and *Volkgeist*—terms derived from Hegel's *Phenomenology*.

A Zeitgeist was the collective consciousness of a specific age in human history. In contrast, a Volkgeist was the collective consciousness of a specific people living within a specific culture and using a specific language. Universal Geist combined all human knowledge in one dialogue whose logic, math, and language directed humanity toward one absolute telos or end: ultimate truth and reality united as the Absolute.

Thus, where a culture sat on the scale of time measured by absolute telos depended on a specific people's Zeitgeist or Volkgeist. And since all humans followed the same rules of reason, and everyone traveled the same intellectual path toward ultimate truth, every culture in the world could be measured by a common, rational scale defined by Geist. Along this line of thought, each culture's location on the scale of reason represented an integrated consequence of this society's thoughts and deeds as its Volkgeist interacted with the world.

Implicitly, Hegel's *Phenomenology* had created a standard that Europeans could use to define themselves and their location on the scale of Geist, which lead to the development of the concept of *progress*. Volkgeist defined the national awareness of a people represented by their language and culture. Zeitgeist explained how far a people had progressed on the scale of time that measured truth and reality by a culture's scientific achievement, or their level of industrial development. Together Volkgeist and Zeitgeist joined the Absolute, as Geist, to define a universal evolutionary path that described all of humanity's achievements by a common, objective, and rational standard.

Now, since Europeans reasoned that they had come the farthest down Geist's rational trail of truth through dialectic logic, they concluded that their new nation-states represented the pinnacle of human success. Europeans "alone" had come the greatest distance in the quest for ultimate knowledge. One could see their accomplishments in the material wealth and the intellectual artifacts of their civilization. Hence, by Hegel's scale of human consciousness, Europe represented the "zenith" of humanity's intellectual, social, political, and economic attainment.

Ricardo

A British economist of Dutch-Jewish parentage, David Ricardo made a fortune on land, securities, and commodities that allowed him to retire at the age of twenty-five and devote the rest of his life to reading, study, and writing. Disagreeing with Hegel but generating another equally binding teleology, David Ricardo chose to devote his energies to economics over philosophy. Revising Adam Smith's theory of production in three editions of his *Principles of Political Economy* (1817–21), Ricardo corrected what he thought were Smith's

fundamental errors. According to Ricardo, Smith had erred when he failed to see the role population dynamics and machinery played in the global history of production. Ricardo proposed to correct these errors in Smith's theory; these corrections, in turn, converted economics into a new teleology.

Smith had written his work in 1776, before the first factory had actually been constructed. Still, in many subsequent editions of his classic work, Smith had not developed an understanding of the industrial changes occurring around him. Like his contemporaries, Smith was only witnessing the beginning of this economic revolution and could not report fully on its consequences. This task fell to David Ricardo.

Using Thomas Robert Malthus's theory of population, also published in three editions between 1798 and 1803, Ricardo redefined Smith's relationship between rents, wages, and profits as developed in *The Wealth of Nations*. According to Malthus, human reproduction constantly outstripped agricultural productivity so that famine alone checked the number of people alive at any one time. Any advance in productivity soon led to growing human numbers, so that population dynamics inevitably neutralized all economic gains and famine reappeared.

In essence, Malthus explained why poverty would always exist. He did so to dismiss Adam Smith's economic paradox (i.e., that the laboring poor created all the wealth enjoyed by society, but experienced few of its fruits). Malthus attacked Smith's economic paradox to show that the poor were responsible for their own poverty. He made this claim to undercut the desire for rapid social and political change suggested by the new enlightened public opinion. As a gentle, kindly Christian minister turned conservative economist, Malthus felt that the liberal trends of contemporary enlightened criticism were too optimistic in the face of economic reality. Also, as the son of a comfortable English landowner, Malthus feared Smith's paradox.

Smith had argued that each advance in productivity relied on the continued division of labor, simplification of jobs, and falling wages. As the output of goods increased, so did the number of laboring poor living at subsistence levels. Consequently, the history of production created a general rise in wealth for society, while the mass of humanity sank into poverty. With poverty came drudgery, and with drudgery came occupations that reduced laborers to what Smith called "stupid cowardly brutes."

Hence, Malthus avoided the problem of Smith's paradox by turning it on its head. Malthus concluded that the huge pool of laboring poor that led miserable lives at the bottom of the social hierarchy did so because they reproduced blindly like the beasts found in nature. This blind reproductive pattern created so many offspring that the poor trapped themselves in drudgery simply trying to feed their children. Simultaneously, no amount of public education could elevate these "brutish creatures" quickly enough for them to develop the mental habits needed to check their sexual drives. Thus, all populations in nature, as well as in any given civilization, grew so fast as to ensure that misery and famine would be constant companions of life. Finally, Malthus's theory of population described poverty as natural and inevitable, not paradoxical at all.

Ricardo accepted Malthus's conclusions but developed a new explanation of production. Arguing that constant growth in human numbers forced an increase in the demand for land, Ricardo showed that human history was punctuated by the rising cost of food. As human society developed its ability to produce food more efficiently, human numbers grew to absorb the new levels of agricultural productivity. This relentless increase in human population forced farmers to occupy all the land until none was left available for sale. At that moment, the owners of land could then charge rent according to the fertility of their soil.

The best land was always measured by its superior fertility when contrasted with the worst land in cultivation. The quality of an acre's capacity to yield crops determined the degree of demand for specific fields and set the cost of rent. Thus, the rents charged matched exactly a field's fertility. Accordingly, the demand for the land defined the income of the landlord and always reflected the quality of soil available for cultivation in any society as a whole.

To these conclusions Ricardo added his "Iron Law of Wages." The Iron Law of Wages stated that an employer could not pay laborers less than the price of food because humanity would not survive on any income lower than subsistence. Consequently, the lowest wage that could be paid was the price of food. Yet, if the price of food constantly increased due to the impact of population dynamics, then the cost of labor also had to rise. Thus, population history, and its impact on rents, posed a fundamental danger to the future of humanity.

As wages rose to meet the price of food, profits had to fall. Profits came from the difference between the cost of labor, which also defined the cost of production, and the demand for an object available for sale. If wages rose with the price of food, so did the cost of production. Thus, profits had to fall as the margin between the cost of production and demand for goods decreased. At the same time, however, profits supplied the capital needed to pay for all the productive energy of society.

According to Ricardo, profits provided the basis of all capital investments through the "wage-fund" (i.e., the money used to pay labor). Thus, profits created a pool of capital that paid for every purchase involved in production. This pool of capital, in turn, organized and financed all the labor employed to generate the goods available for sale. Without high profits, the wage-fund would erode, productive labor would cease, and society would sink into abject poverty.

As a result, Ricardo argued that labor's happiness ultimately rested with high profits to sustain the vitality of a growing economy. Ricardo believed that laborers should be pleased with low wages so that they could guarantee their future through a large wage-fund. The wage-fund in turn determined the amount of money available to employers to hire labor and produce the necessities and luxuries of society. Therefore, this meant that when profits fell, the wage-fund collapsed, and all the productive classes, capitalists and laborers alike, ceased to be able to produce.

This bleak future could be forestalled, but not put off forever. The way to delay ultimate poverty was through the development of machinery. Machines were labor-saving devices. Introducing a new machine cut the cost of labor by making certain workers redundant. Redundant people, themselves, were ex-laborers that machines had replaced.

By cutting out redundant people, Ricardo argued that the cost of production fell, profits increased, and the wage-fund grew. Thus, he believed that in the long run machinery was a benefit to all of society, including the redundant population. Machines ensured higher profits that would lead to new jobs. All these redundant people had to do was to seek new employment elsewhere—even if this meant leaving Europe itself.

Ricardo's economic theory was clearly teleological. The telos, or end of human history, was the abject poverty that threatened us all. Only our genius for machinery and the reorganization of productive labor would save us. Knowledge of these fundamental economic laws had an impact on all humans, no matter what culture they came from. Ignorance of these productive laws, in fact, was a crime against humanity because failure to apply the principles of political economy permitted behavior that would ultimately destroy us all.

Since "knowledge was power," and since Ricardo had revealed the power of production as the universal, cultural force that governed the evolution of all societies, the most modern organization of the economy had to be the best solution for humanity. Economics dictated the politics that defined the hard decisions that had to be made where the whole of human happiness

Karl Marx (1818–83), the German social, political, and economic theorist, is perhaps the most influential socialist thinker of the nineteenth century. He is known particularly for his analysis of class struggles and the workforce. Marx's writings on capitalism, and political and social activism influenced many, including his close friend Friedrich Engels, with whom he coauthored their most famous work *The Communist Manifesto.* Shelfmark: C.115.h.2.(5) Copyright © The British Library.

KARL MARX

was at stake. A few people had to be sacrificed along the way for the happiness of the vast majority as we all followed the universal evolutionary path that production dictated.

At the same time, using Ricardo's theory to view the world, one could immediately identify the most "advanced" societies on the globe. These advanced civilizations had produced the greatest integration of knowledge, machinery, and productivity. These societies were industrial nation-states. They alone had come the farthest along the universal path of human economic evolution. They alone had discovered the scientific laws that governed human survival. They alone had created the highest levels of productivity using the most modern technology. They alone were clearly the most "civilized." Therefore, they alone should use their knowledge and power to organize the rest of the world to save humanity from itself.

Marx

The son of a lawyer, a student of law at the University of Bonn and Berlin, and a recipient of a Ph.D. in philosophy from the University of Jena, Karl Marx spent a lifetime (1818–83) refining modern socialism while making money as a journalist. Disagreeing with Hegel's *Phenomenology* and Ricardo's *Political Economy*, Marx generated yet another teleology as binding as the first two. Writing some twenty-seven years after Ricardo, Karl Marx responded to the revolutionary passions in Europe to create the basis for international communism. Building on David Ricardo's new social category called *class* (Ricardo's term for the social groups generated by rents, wages, and profits), Marx argued that any system of production based on private property would cause "class warfare." Rejecting Ricardo's ap-

peal to economic forces that transcended class interests, Marx focused on the social strife he believed private property created. While Ricardo claimed that society should struggle as a whole to defeat the drift toward universal poverty caused by population dynamics, Marx argued that social justice required a new organization of the community that had to destroy private property altogether. Thus Marx created a radical ideology designed to capture public opinion while applying "science" to the problems of establishing universal social happiness.

According to Marx, all social organization sprang from the mode of production, which, in turn, defined the division of labor and technology that organized society into different income groups. And each stage in the development of the mode of production determined shifts in the incomes that governed the history of status for each class. Finally, these shifts in income then gave shape to the social awareness of each class as it marched through time.

Because of private property, Marx argued that the mode of production generated the three broad social classes defined by Ricardo's *relative status* whose economic interests caused conflict between one another. The word *relative* in relative status defined all positions within society by contrasting one against the rest. Since one position relied on a specific income (rents, wages, or profits), and since the contrast required by *relative* meant that one class could not be high unless the other two were low, class interests bound up in the phrase relative status generated class conflict.

This conflict surfaced as each class created its own system of beliefs based on its interpretation of work experience, or *praxis*. Praxis shaped specific social attitudes that reflected the reality of relative status, which, in turn, represented the occupational structure of the current mode of production. Meanwhile, each class soon discovered that its material success depended on the economic subordination of the other two incomes. Thus, relative status and the mode of production, generated a persistent conflict of economic interests that defined each class's political attitudes.

Over time, each class developed its own ideology, formed a political party, and advanced its interests at the expense of the other two classes. This constant economic struggle created the social and political strife called *class warfare*, which itself drove societies through history and mirrored the evolution of the mode of production as a culture's economy changed from era to era.

According to Marx, the history of revolution itself produced the five stages of human development. The first stage occurred before agriculture and represented the beginning point of all human history. From this stage, all the rest of humanity's story followed a universal path of teleological development. No human society could vary from this path without risking failure through productive collapse. Accordingly, every civilization found itself compelled by economic necessity to develop some form of social and political organization that reflected the realities of the mode of production as it evolved along this singular path of cultural change. Yet, along the way, humanity could generate a vast range of creative variations for each stage.

All human societies, Marx held, began as hunters and gatherers in which private property did not exist. Called "primitive communism," success in this stage of history increased human numbers, made game scarce, and hunting increasingly difficult. Eventually, as human numbers reached a crisis point, gathering became more important than hunting. At that moment, agriculture began. Cultivation, however, placed an enormous value on land and created the concept of private property.

Agriculture represented the second stage of human production. Those who organized society, priests and kings, took possession of the land to create the first social revolution. Their rise to power generated inequality, caused wars to occur between cultures, and captured labor in the form of slavery. Thus, Marx called this second stage *oriental slavery*, for it had originated in what nineteenth century Europeans such as himself called the *orient* (the Ancient Near East and Egypt).

Oriental slavery created great agricultural empires like those found in Mesopotamia, Egypt, Persia, and later Rome. Continued population growth among those who were free, and expanding agricultural production based on slavery, provided the food surpluses for each succeeding empire. Yet all these empires replaced their slaves by warfare because bonded laborers were so dispirited that they could not reproduce.

By the time of the Roman Empire, however, Marx argued that oriental slavery had realized its full potential. The empire had expanded to its geographic limits, based on contemporary economic, political, and military resources, and could no longer acquire fresh slaves by warfare. Since Roman slaves failed to reproduce, the labor base began to erode. Thus, in the second half of Roman history, a social transformation began as the empire tried to replace its slaves with serfs.

According to Marx, Rome's internal design, however, caused this effort to fail, and the Roman Empire collapsed under the pressure of barbarian invasions. The German tribes that took over instituted the third stage, feudalism, based on Rome's initial efforts at replacing slavery with serfdom. These German tribes divided the Roman Empire into great political estates and bound labor to the soil through an inherited status the worker could not escape. The conditions of laborers, however, had improved to the point that serfs could reproduce their numbers, but their income level still bordered on starvation.

Yet by defining private property solely as real estate, Marx argued that feudalism omitted other forms of wealth when it equated social status and political states with the land alone. Thus, real estate ignored the value of capital and deliberately excluded this form of wealth from legal definition. Since capital accumulated in cities, those who lived by trade developed a hostility toward those who controlled the land and denied legitimacy to money as a form of property. Those who owned capital demanded social recognition and organized "corporations" with the aid of kings. Thus, capitalism developed naturally out of feudalism as this third stage fully realized its productive potential. Yet capital was alien to real estate and generated the seeds of the fourth stage in human history. As the enemy of land, capital prepared the way for the next revolution.

Marx held that the revolutions that occurred in France and Great Britain in the nineteenth century, the French and Industrial Revolutions, saw capitalism destroy feudalism as effectively as the barbarians had destroyed Rome. Capitalism itself replaced serfs with wage-earning industrial laborers. Called the *proletariat*, these wage-slaves lived at the margins of subsistence and were just as miserable as those confined to the land during the preceding two eras of agricultural development. Like serfs, however, the industrial working class generated an abundance of children and became the vast majority of humanity.

Yet unlike all other eras in the history of private property, Marx argued that proletarians acquired literacy and analytical skills because they lived and worked in cities. Awakened for the first time by these new urban skills, laborers discovered their long history of misery and mobilized into one massive revolutionary party. This massive new revolutionary party marshaled the vast majority of humanity for the final confrontation with private property. This, in turn, set the stage for the telos of human history: communism.

For Marx, communism was the fifth and final stage of socioeconomic development. Marx believed that when the communist revolution occurred, private property would cease to exist. With the demise of private ownership, Marx argued, all social warfare would also end. According to Marx, communism would eliminate class warfare.

Marx believed communism would create a new sense of justice based on the equity experienced in the new distribution of wealth using public, instead of private, ownership. Communism would make the entire pool of productive wealth based on modern industry available to everyone using the concept of distributive justice: "to each according to his need, from each according to his ability." Communism would focus humanity's attention on social harmony rather than on personal gain as prescribed by the selfish impulses of private ownership. Accordingly, Marx believed that communism would return the full value of production to its creator, the laborer, as all wealth took one form—wages—in a classless society.

Thus, Marx joined Hegel and Ricardo in offering one teleological path of development for humanity. Where a culture existed along this path determined its maturity. Europe was the most "advanced" because it had assumed the capitalist form and had traveled the furthest in its economic trek toward communism. If one left Europe and reviewed the world, Marx would argue that China was "less mature" because he would place Chinese culture in the material era called feudalism. Africans were even more "backward" still because they were in transition between hunters and gatherers and oriental slavery. Native Americans, Pacific Islanders, and the Aborigines of Australia were the "least advanced" because they were still at the initial point of economic development: primitive communism.

Marx generated communism, Ricardo became the champion for English liberalism, and Hegel produced German conservatism. Each disagreed with the other politically but all three helped to create the principal ideologies of nineteenth-century Europe. Yet, all three used historical teleology to account for "the truth," "objective knowledge," and "the scientific organization of society." At the same time, all three produced a universal evolutionary path that dictated the terms of human development.

Now Europeans—and by extension their former colonists in North America—began to believe that they had a historical duty to intervene in world affairs. As the most advanced civilization, cultural teleology compelled Europeans to venture out into the world and prepare the way for a new global reality. Conceived as "the white man's burden" for conservatives and liberals alike, Europeans believed that they held the cultural means to help "primitive" peoples rise up to a higher level of social existence. Seen as a stage in the development of the mode of production, Marxists condemned imperial adventure as evil, but also saw it as necessary to change the face of the world in preparation for communism. In all three cases, Europe's new cultural teleology suggested aggressive action on a global scale. Accordingly, all three nineteenth-century ideologies

mobilized the national will of the various peoples living within Europe to exercise their collective political, economic, and military advantages as depicted in the differential of power.

Nation-States and Industry

A nation-state combined the unity of a national community with a positive consensus produced by public opinion. The unity of the national community came from the way public opinion mobilized this positive consensus through a combination of an industrial culture, urban skills, mass transportation, and mass media. An industrial culture contributed to national unity through the role that factories played in creating an urban hierarchy that ranked all cities within the domestic economy and assigned to each an appropriate slot according to the goods it produced and the commodities it consumed. Urban skills fuelled national unity by providing such skills as literacy, critical thinking, and computation that served as the means to form public opinion. Mass transportation generated a basis for national unity by functioning as the web that held together industry's urban hierarchy through a system of supply and demand that integrated a nation's regional economies. The mass media supported national unity by exploiting such urban skills as literacy and critical thinking in order to marshal public opinion. The combination of all of the above served as the means for mobilizing a nation-in-arms.

The nation-in-arms, in turn, utilized a modern state bureaucracy to muster the political apparatus needed to assess, tax, and collect the nation's resources when preparing for war. Fuelled by industry's urban hierarchy, the people's capacity to read and think for themselves, and the popular consensus produced by public opinion, a modern state bureaucracy had access to the general will of its citizens. Such access allowed the government to tap into the total resources of the national community. With these resources in hand, the government could then exploit the internal coherence that united a nation's resolve to accomplish its specific political goals. Considering the nation-state's ability to assemble this national will, one can begin to see how much power these new cultural institutions could mobilize.

Simultaneously, while the wealth generated by industry sustained the internal design of the nation-state, these riches had also recast the role that European governments played in world trade. But in the nineteenth century, for the first time, industry had increased the total productivity of the economy of the nation-state until it suffered from an inventory crisis: too many goods for domestic consumption. New levels of efficiency had developed out of industry's capacity to concentrate labor in factories while accelerating output. This increased efficiency had generated so many commodities that the seventeenth- and eighteenth-century market system created by the Commercial Revolution could no longer consume the nation's wealth. Accordingly, industrial manufacturing had produced a motive for European nation-states to redefine the global economy.

Meanwhile, the new riches generated by industry had reinforced the concentration of power in the nation-state. Each new industrial society now had the capacity to manufacture the weapons, equipment, supply, and transport needed to capture the desired new markets. Europeans could use these resources to overwhelm native resistance to their empire building, as each new nation-state set about constructing the system of supply and demand required to relieve the inventory pressures created by industry. Thus, industry had also generated the means that allowed the nation-state to redefine its location within the global community.

Yet the wealth and power produced by an industrial nation-state had also created a major institutional paradox. On the one hand, internal coherence sustained by public opinion and an urban-industrial economy pulled a people together to form a distinct national culture. On the other, this same internal coherence pulled these people away from any other human communities to create a unique sense of political separation. This new sense of political separateness consumed a feeling of self and purpose that distinguished one people from the rest of humanity as if these new citizens belonged to a different species. Often identified by the term *race*, this new political identity mixed culture, ethnicity, and language to create a belief in one nation's superiority when compared to the rest. Combined with nineteenth-century teleology and the new political ideologies, this sense of purpose set each national community on its own historical path of self-perfection. Accordingly, this new sense of uniqueness and purpose produced by the nation-state did more to divide the world into specific human communities than had any other political system.

At the same time, the Industrial Revolution had created a need for global economic integration on a level the world had never before seen. Industry required new markets to absorb the growing levels of productivity generated by increasingly more efficient machines. And industrial production required an ever-expanding supply of raw material and cheap labor that no one nation could provide for itself from within its own boundaries. Now people around the world found themselves drawn more tightly into an emerging global economy.

The tendency for the nation-state to separate peoples from one another combined with industry's need to integrate national productivity within the new global economy. This simultaneous but contradictory tendency to separate and integrate created an institutional paradox for nation-states that proved potentially dangerous. And this danger increased as each new nation-state joined the international scene and developed a sense of racial superiority over traditional cultures that had not as yet made the transition into the modern age.

To meet the global tensions caused by this institutional paradox, European nation-states began an arms race that converted their military services into industrialized armies and navies between 1840 and 1914. In the 1840s, the French, the British, and the Prussians took the lead by abandoning well-established practices for mobilizing their states for war. These changes were hard to make because they challenged long-established rules of international conflict that had been refined over the course of several centuries, 1500 to 1800. And once a military institution had made a commitment to a particular manner of making war, it was very difficult for the officers and soldiers to change their habits and training. Still, no one could ignore the modern sources of power embedded in an industrialized nation-in-arms.

The first arena where military practices began to change was in the area of transportation. New methods of assembling, moving, and supplying an army or navy proved just as important to achieving victory as developing new weapons. Ironically, revolutionary methods in mobilizing the armed forces did not occur in the military itself; rather, these changes came from civilian innovations.

Steamboats and railroads began the process of change because they communicated a simple fact: the nation that held the current capacity to mobilize the greatest number of men might not have that advantage in the future. Both the steamboat and the railroad developed quickly after Robert Fulton and George Stephenson had produced prototypes in 1807 and 1815 respectively. Consequently, when Stephenson completed a functioning railway line connecting Liverpool and London in 1829, and Fulton's steamboat became an ocean-going vessel between 1807–37, even second-ranked European powers began to consider the possibilities of assembling modern armies.

In 1837, Macgregor Laird's paddlewheel powered *Sirius* of the British and American Steam Navigation Company in Liverpool had crossed the Atlantic in eighteen days under sustained steam, even though this ship was assisted with sails. Two years later, the crossing time had been reduced by three days and sixteen hours. In the 1840s, propellers had replaced the paddle wheel, and produced far more power to drive a ship through water. Also, steam engines increased in efficiency so that the *Sirius*'s 320 horse-powered mechanism soon gave way to the 1,600 horse-powered machine that drove the *Great Eastern* designed by Isambard K. Brunel, chief engineer of the Great Western Railway Company, and later a British ship architect. The *Great Eastern*'s massive power plant represented Brunel's discovery that the resistance of a ship's hull to motion in the water increased as the square of its physical dimensions, but that its capacity to carry cargo increased as the cube of these same dimensions.

Such rapid changes in the methods of moving ships through water suggested that steam-driven vessels had considerable military potential. At the same time, how-

Top: The North Church Tunnel of the London & Birmingham Railway. Engineered by Robert Stephenson, the L & BR was one of the first intercity railways in the world upon its opening in 1838. Today it serves as the southern section of the West Coast Main Line. "Railway Practice. A collection of working plans and practical details of construction in the public works of the most celebrated engineers" by Samuel Charles Brees. Shelfmark: 713.i.7 volume II . Copyright © The British Library.
Bottom: This 1807 woodcut shows the first steamboat of American engineer Robert Fulton, 1765–1815. Collection of Archiv f.Kunst & Geschichte. Photo: akg-images, London.

ever, the British Admiralty chose to ignore these innovations in shipbuilding. Great Britain had controlled sea power from the seventeenth to the nineteenth centuries. By 1815, all the ships of the Royal Navy were made of wood, powered by sail, and fired cannon from gun-decks along the sides of their hulls. The British also had the largest number of trained naval officers and men, all of whom were accustomed to operating these wooden sailing ships. Furthermore, possessing an empire that could supply the British navy with all the timber and ship stores needed to maintain the fleet, the Admiralty saw no reason to pay any attention to the new steamboat. The French, however, were quick to take advantage of these steam-powered vessels and began producing military prototypes.

The French reasoned that if they could revolutionize naval warfare, they could at long last neutralize Britain's numerical advantage. Accordingly, in 1822, the French General Henri J. Paixhans published a book entitled *Nouvelle force maritime*, in which he argued that iron armor-plated ships, equipped with large-caliber cannon, and powered by steam could make the entire British navy obsolete. Simultaneously, Paixhans had developed a new cannon shell that he used against a derelict wooden hull in 1824 to demonstrate the destructive potential of contemporary large-caliber weapons. The French Navy officially adopted Paixhans shells in 1837 and began redesigning steam-powered warships to carry new cannon between 1842 and 1850.

French efforts forced the Royal Navy to adjust to the changing reality of naval warfare. One year after the French adopted Paixhans shells, the Royal Navy followed suit. The latter had also realized that wooden hulls would soon be a thing of the past.

Simultaneously, in the 1850s, the French had developed two steam-powered naval prototypes, the *Napoleon* and *La Gloire*; each ship threatened Britain's naval hegemony. The *Napoleon* appeared in 1850, traveled at 13 knots, and was propelled by a 950 horse-power engine. *La Gloire* appeared in 1858, had four and one-half-inch steel armored plates, and could resist all shot fired from any cannon of its day. Both demonstrated to the British Admiralty that it could no longer ignore industrial innovations because such inventions would change the face of naval warfare.

The Crimean War (1853–56) reinforced these conclusions. This struggle highlighted the deficiencies of a government that did not pay close attention to the modern instruments of destruction that industry had to offer. The Russians, for example, did not have the rail system they needed to supply their troops at Sevastopol on the western tip of the Crimean Peninsula, and had to rely instead on 125,000 peasant-carts. In contrast, the British and the French could ship all their supplies in by sea. In addition, the Russian infantry still used muskets whose range and accuracy could not match British and French Minié rifles. Thus, after 1856, all of Europe's nation-states became aware that they had to keep up with changes occurring in industry. Prussia's needle-gun illustrates this point.

The needle-gun mentioned above revealed that small-arms manufacturing in Prussia still relied too heavily on artisan skills. This fact emerged when the machinery needed to reequip the Prussian army simply did not exist. Consequently, it took the Prussians twenty-six years (1840–66) to complete the task of making the 320,000 rifles they required. Their timing was excellent, however, because they produced the needed supply just before the Austro-Prussian War erupted, and the needle-gun proved to be decisive at the Battle of Königgrätz. Yet the Prussians had also learned that they could not afford to rely on artisans when machinery could perform the work more efficiently. Accordingly, rifle production in Prussia adjusted to the demand for small arms by 1870. Cannon, however, took longer.

The Bessemer process for manufacturing high-grade steel in 1857 solved the first problem in manufacturing high-quality cannon. Casting the barrels for artillery, however, still took another thirty-three years to produce the desired weapon (1857–90). During this period, competition between cannon designers kept changes in the field lively. Alfred Krupp was an early leader whose cannon during the Franco-Prussian War (1870–71) determined the outcome at the Battles of Metz and Sedan. Rapid changes in cannon design, however, illustrated the need to standardize the production process. Only after 1890, when scientists finally understood the chemistry of steel, did some type of stability enter the field of artillery manufacturing.

The problem of the breech-loading rifle and high-grade steel cannon illustrates a significant point: new weapons dramatically changed warfare. Yet to get the European military establishment to adapt to these modern instruments of destruction took time. Generals and admirals alike had to see the disastrous consequences of those who did not pay attention to these innovations. The Crimean War (1854–56), the Austro-Prussian War (1866), and the Franco-Prussian War (1870–71), however, provided the examples needed to sway Europe's professional soldiers.

Meanwhile, as European nations adjusted to the political and military realities of industry, so all these states tried to unify the surface of the globe to meet their specific industrial needs. Bringing weaker Middle Eastern, Asian, and African civilizations into centrally managed imperial systems, all these European nation-states tried to create separate market structures. Each of these imperial systems, in turn, allowed a European nation to export finished products in exchange for raw materials and cheap labor. This pattern of international commerce fuelled the national economies that armed and supplied the nation's army and navy. Therefore by accelerating the process of assimilating non-European societies into each nation's commercial empire, states acquired the resources needed to maintain the balance of power in Europe.

Yet the military rivalries that took place at home soon led to an equivalent global competition. The relative differences in military resources that made up the arms race in Europe soon became a Western export that Asians, Africans, Muslims, Latin Americans, and Pacific Islanders had to deal with. Decisive in this process of expansion was the differential of power.

While European rivals constantly pursued ever more destructive military systems, weaker non-European civilizations entered an era of political and cultural decay. The weakness of these native societies occurred just when European nation-states had reached the apex of their political, economic, social, and intellectual strength. Thus, when one Western nation took control of a traditional culture's territory, this same European nation denied its neighbors access to this foreign land. Accordingly, while western nations participated in an arms race at home, so they also began a contest to be the first to occupy the rest of the world.

Suggested Reading

Doyle, Michael W., *Empires* (Ithaca, N.Y.: Cornell University Press, 1986).

Headrick, Daniel R., *The Tools of Empire: Technology and European Imperialism in the Nineteenth Century* (New York: Oxford University Press, 1981).

———, *The Tentacles of Progress: Technology Transfer in the Age of Imperialism, 1850–1940* (New York: Oxford University Press, 1988).

Hobsbawm, Eric, *The Age of Empire, 1875–1914* (New York: Pantheon Press, 1987).

McNeill, William H., *The Pursuit of Power: Technology, Armed Force, and Society* (Chicago: The University of Chicago Press, 1982).

Pakenham, Thomas, *The Scramble for Africa* (New York: Random House, 1991).

Porter, Bernard, *The Lion's Share: A Short History of British Imperialism, 1850–1970* (1975).

Smith, Woodruff D., *The German Colonial Empire* (Chapel Hill: University of North Carolina Press, 1978).

Wolf, Eric R., *Peasant Wars in the Twentieth Century* (New York: Harper and Row, 1968).

XXIII

THE UNITED STATES
and Japan

The United States and Japan appear as the first two cultures outside of Europe that developed into nation-states early enough to resist falling victim to European imperial ambitions and launched expansionist programs of their own. The United States emerged in the Americas as a neo-European nation with a segregated mosaic of ethnic subcultures while the majority of U.S. citizens benefited from the Enlightenment's political principles. At the same time, the United States avoided falling victim to the massive debts that its Latin American neighbors (see Chapter Twenty-four) contracted with the European powers after achieving their independence, and thus the U.S. maintained financial autonomy. In contrast, Japan emerged as a nation-state due to a Japanese variation on modernization that occurred during the Tokugawa era (1603–1868) plus the deliberate planning of a tiny oligarchy that ruled Japan after 1868. Accordingly, Japan developed national institutions based on centralized governmental directions that allowed rapid industrialization using nationalism and institutions imported from abroad.

Because of the timely appearance of national power in both the United States and Japan, each of these new nations acquired the tools needed to protect its territories from foreign domination. Both also developed the means to imitate imperial Europe, even as the remainder of the world feared the fruits of power acquired by the West between 1800 and 1914. Hence, the concentration of military and political authority, in both the United States and Japan allowed each of these new neo-European and non-European nation-states to rival the West in its quest for empire.

The United States

The United States represents a complex case in which the basic design for national formation occurred before the French Revolution. In their first attempt to build a national community, British colonists in mainland North America successfully rebelled against Great Britain and, having secured their independence through a com-

bination of warfare and ideology, formed a federal republican government. The Americans chose the federal design because they had to integrate several regional cultures under one government.

Following this first episode, a second effort at nation-building occurred during the U.S. Civil War (1861–65), when one of these regional cultures, the North, became dominant and tried to shape the rest of the nation's political development. Given these two different stages of national formation, the United States represents a complex example of how a nation-state came into being.

In European eyes, all of the Americas belonged to different colonial empires. In North America, the Native Americans took on multiple roles as trading partners, potential military allies, or enemies, until the nineteenth century. The French in Canada worked with Amerindian tribes to facilitate a brisk fur trade. The English from New England to Georgia traded with tribes for fur and hides. The Spanish and Portuguese conquered tribes, converted souls, and enslaved thousands for work in mines or on haciendas from Florida and the Southwest to Meso and South America.

All the Europeans had germs and guns on their side in the conquest of the Western Hemisphere. Some tribes, like the Ojibway, retreated before the onslaught, but most Native American peoples suffered massive population loss due to disease and war. The bargaining power some of the tribes maintained through the early decades of contact had eroded by the early nineteenth century. Woodland tribes were most successful in maintaining a semblance of sovereignty. Their style of guerilla warfare—emphasizing rapid movement, ambush, surprise, and retreat to minimize casualties—was successful until they were overwhelmed by U.S. troops trained in marching, musket fire, unit cohesion, and a constant offensive closing with enemy ranks. The advantage of the middle ground for tribes was largely gone by the 1790s.

While addressing the military resistance of Native Americans to expanding English communities, American colonial history began when British immigrants carried to the Western Hemisphere traditional attitudes from England. Mixed with tradition, however, were the new entrepreneurial practices and religious beliefs that had emerged from the Commercial Revolution and Reformation in Europe.

In the colonial South, where the Virginia Joint-Stock Company began the British colonial enterprise in 1607, the growth of commercial agriculture developed alongside a social hierarchy both typical of European tradition and completely new. Based on large, self-sufficient farms called plantations, the southern British colonies produced an elite who sought to recreate the gentry status so cherished in traditional England. In addition, southern colonists developed familiar symbols of social obligation and deference so highly prized back in England. Yet southern colonists who enjoyed this neo-gentry status achieved their position largely by resurrecting a lost institution: slavery.

But the people that the American colonists enslaved were not from America: they were imported against their will from Africa. Consequently, these transported Africans added a new dimension to North American culture. They generated an African American experience outside the mainstream of British southern life. And although African slaves existed throughout the North American colonies in small numbers, these bondspeople became the labor base of the elite living in the South.

In the meantime, the North and the Middle Colonies followed their own socioeconomic evolution. In the North, an ethnically homogeneous migration of Puritans to New England sought a new covenant with God. They also wished to recover a lost village pattern highly prized in medieval English life. This lost village pattern had fallen victim to the socioeconomic changes that took place in England during the Reformation and Commercial Revolution. Enclosures, commercial agriculture, and the changing conditions of land tenure had undermined village life after 1500. Feeling this loss, Puritans had successfully recreated the sense of community found in their old medieval villages by transplanting them to the New World as townships.

The transfer of the traditional medieval village to New England, however, contradicted a complex and evolving modern economy that developed there. Founded by the Massachusetts Bay Company on a charter granting the Puritans the right to fish, trade, and establish profitable enterprises in North America after 1629, the colonists of New England developed several colonial communities that produced a diverse economy based on subsistence agriculture, livestock, timber, fish, commerce, and shipbuilding. As a result, the Puritans

joined the Commercial Revolution and ended up participating in two modernizing movements: they were part of the Protestant rebellion, and they were active in the Atlantic trade system.

Their original goal was to create a sacred utopia based on the medieval village design. The residents of each village were to renew their religious covenant with God. Thus, they hoped to practice their interpretation of primitive Christian values in peace in the New World. Simultaneously, they wanted to prosper as part of the Atlantic trade system. Ironically, their success in trade undercut the sanctity of the villages they hoped to preserve and introduced them to modernization, while the demand for labor brought some African slaves into an otherwise homogenous society.

To the south of New England, in the Middle Colonies, residents and new immigrants composed a socially mixed population. Comprised of captured colonial holdings like New York, or established by land grants to Quakers such as Pennsylvania, New Jersey, and Delaware, the Middle Colonies absorbed local and foreign immigrants. There, economic opportunity established what became known as "the best poor man's country." Those who settled in the Middle Colonies prospered if they worked hard and participated in commercial agriculture; many of the colonists who ventured to the Middle Colonies produced staples that they sold to urban populations in New England and in Europe.

The Middle Colonies comprised land left over after the establishment of the South and New England. The poor who took up residence in the Middle Colonies started late and took advantage of the urban markets of the North to sell their crops. As a result, their social organization reflected patterns found more commonly in the North than in the South. Thus, these similarities between the middle and northern colonies, which included some slaves, stimulated the possibility of a complex rural-urban society that integrated both regions into a common culture.

In New England, commercial opportunities slowly eroded original traditional values, as trade with Great Britain, the Caribbean, and Africa, as well as the rise in land values undercut piety and village designs. In the Middle Colonies, the growing demand for food in Europe and the North led colonists to seek profits that elevated the status of local farmers. In the South, slavery generated a bipolar culture whose caste-like top and bottom seemed alien to the North and Middle Colonies. Finally, in the Western Hemisphere in general, the desire for European goods and a higher standard of living spurred economic development everywhere.

Yet traditional values had many allies as well. Of these three colonial patterns, the South and the North represented the extreme variations in the mixture of tradition and opportunity. In the South, a market-oriented behavior gave way to a new tradition based on local cultural and geographic circumstances. Cash crops became the center of the economy, but plantation owners did not like the business of engaging in trade.

To carry out the chore of collecting local products and buying imports, these planters hired merchants who provided this economic service as outsiders. Bookkeeping smacked too much of a servant's task to be considered as appropriate labor for a gentleman farmer. Thus, planters themselves shunned the tedium of buying and selling.

At the same time, the planters also developed racial attitudes to justify their "superiority" over and ownership of African slaves. These attitudes mingled with biases the English had long held about the color black as it related to creatures marked so by nature. Most Europeans and white colonists from all regions concluded without evidence that all darker skinned peoples had to be inferior.

These emerging racial attitudes helped to foster an image that southern planters cherished. The social elite of the South saw themselves as paternal figures who benevolently ruled a childlike lineage of laborers in need of stern but loving masters. Eventually, aristocratic planters came to believe that the bondage they imposed on Africans was a form of kindness. Finally, once these attitudes crystallized into accepted convention, these planters could not abandon their social mythology, which they shared with the remainder of the British colonists in the South.

As a result, southern aristocratic planters sought a maximum return from a social structure that they had created. They enjoyed status, a sense of benevolence through *noblesse oblige* (i.e., the kindness of the well-born to the poor), growing wealth, deference, and luxury at the top of an increasingly rigid social hierarchy. And as these plantation owners grew accustomed to the leisure generated by slave labor, they increased their commitment to the racial prejudice that justified African bondage.

Thus, the southern social structure became more stable with time. The great landowner sought to imitate British standards of gentlemanly conduct and recreate in the South a traditional aristocracy. They invested in secure patterns of income: land, slaves, and regional crops such as tobacco, rice, and indigo that produced a distinct stamp to their local culture. And they dominated a social hierarchy of lesser statuses that included middle-class farms, subsistence agriculture, and a significant population of slaves. All the while they ran up debts, for they did not like the tedium of accounting books.

In contrast, the North developed economic, social, and cultural features that reflected the business opportunities of the British Empire. Acting on these opportunities, first Puritans, and then later, a more religiously tolerant and diverse community living in New England developed entrepreneurial behavior. These modernizing business values permeated the North and began to spread south into the Middle Colonies.

The typical northern merchant, however, found his trans-Atlantic business limited by political as well as local circumstances. His desire for maximum profits had to live within the realities of British Imperial rule. The laws of the British Empire, for example, restricted freedom in the marketplace due to the mercantile principles Adam Smith criticized so effectively in his *Wealth of Nations*. This lack of freedom created a low-level colonial hostility to external controls.

After the Glorious Revolution, 1688–89, the British king and parliament reorganized the colonies for the benefit of the mother country's economic development. Royal governors, their advisory councils, and the imperial bureaucracy created positions in local government that they doled out to royal appointees meaning none of the governmental positions could be won by competent colonists on the basis of their merits. Even success in business began to depend on connections, not skill. Those who rose to the top did so with the help of powerful friends. Influence within the imperial network meant access to land and military contracts and the profits they generated.

While association patterns determined economic opportunities, the crown and parliament imposed on the North American mainland colonies the Navigation Acts, which restricted shipping and trade. In addition, capital accumulation in the colonies, so important to entrepreneurial behavior, was retarded by laws that controlled banking. Furthermore, parliament restricted the development of effective colonial currencies. Finally, the British denied the formation of colonial corporations and limited any manufacturing that might compete with British goods.

The imperial government wanted to make the colonists dependent on British production. Simply stated, Great Britain wanted to control the balance of trade and have access to the cheap labor and raw materials available in the Western Hemisphere. Hence, the empire limited the entrepreneurial spirit and behavior of the New England colonists.

From these few observations about the formation of colonial culture, one can see the complexity with which tradition and opportunity mixed. The imperial government and regional culture stimulated as well as discouraged entrepreneurial behavior. Despite mercantile restrictions, however, economic opportunities in the colonies abounded, that is, if one could figure out how to overcome imperial control and local conditions.

Given the cultural complexity of the colonial environment, the addition of enlightened public opinion during the eighteenth century created a volatile mix. The enormous distance between Great Britain and the Western Hemisphere bred attitudes of autonomy in the colonies that developed out of necessity. Since the French and the Spanish also occupied portions of the Western Hemisphere, and since all colonies were considered legitimate targets of war, self-reliance and self-defense made the British colonials aware of how self-sufficient they had to be in order to survive. Long wars with France had kept the colonies in as close an association with Great Britain as mutual defense would allow. Yet, when France lost Canada in 1763 after the Seven Years' War (1756–63), the basic relationships between the thirteen North American mainland colonies and mother country changed. Twelve years later, rebellion began.

After 1763 the British tried to impose a form of political control on North America to which its European subjects had already grown accustomed. Yet given the degree of autonomy experienced by British Americans, European standards of obedience and submission were unacceptable to them. Now the colonists resented paying taxes imposed by parliamentary law to finance soldiers to occupy the thirteen colonies after a common enemy, the French and their Indian allies, were no longer a threat.

Displaying traditional British hostility toward the Royal Army as an instrument of tyranny, and harkening to John Locke's argument in favor of taxation based on legislative representation, the American colonists argued that parliament did not represent them and therefore could not tax them as it pleased. Mobilizing public opinion, colonists joined a rebellious movement that offered independence. The North and Middle Colonies argued that they could develop an unregulated commercial market system, while the South knew it could dissolve its debts to its British creditors. The struggle between Great Britain and American colonists over the extent of parliamentary authority to legislate and the king's authority to govern resulted in war. English military units marched to disarm American rebels and blood was shed at Lexington and Concord (outside Boston) in 1775.

The supporters of freedom from British rule united colonial resistance with the *Declaration of Independence* in 1776, and George Washington was able to keep a rebel militia in the field long enough to build a regular army. The *Declaration of Independence* converted John Locke's definition of property, "life, liberty, and possessions," into the natural rights of "life, liberty, and the pursuit of happiness," which made the American struggle one that opposed tyranny. Within a year of the *Declaration*, Washington's army at Valley Forge, during the winter of 1777–78, trained under an ex-Prussian officer, General von Steuben, in linear warfare and discipline. Prior to Washington's winter in Valley Forge, superior tactics and field fortifications organized by rebel generals Benedict Arnold and Horatio Gates had defeated a British army under John Burgoyne at Saratoga, and the French had entered the war in support of the Americans. Finally, in 1781 a French fleet cut off British reinforcements to yet another British army and a joint French and American blockade forced General Charles Cornwallis to surrender at Yorktown, ending the military phase of the war. American troops with training in conventional warfare supported by the French army and navy won on the battlefield. In London, the calculation was simple: the cost of maintaining these commercial colonies was too high.

The United States had won political autonomy, and had established the concept of natural rights with the *Declaration of Independence*, but had not organized an effective central government after the revolution. Instead, a confederation of states existed in the early 1780s; it failed due to a lack of the power to tax and regulate commerce. Hence, a new government based on federalism and the written *Constitution* had to emerge between 1787 and 1789. This document, plus the first ten amendments, known as the *Bill of Rights*, declared the authority of the state, separated and balanced the legislative, executive, and judicial powers, and declared the rights of the citizen body. Yet not included in the freedom of this new republic, but subject to its laws, were non-European ethnic minorities and African slaves.

Meanwhile, to secure the future economy and regional cultures of the U.S., Congress provided for the protection of inventive ideas under a patent law giving property rights to the inventors to protect their inventions from infringement. As mentioned above, the concept of federalism, so heavily debated prior to the Revolution, became part of the constitutional structure with a central government supreme within its realm while the state governments ruled within their jurisdictions. The concept of checks and balances came directly out of the revolutionary controversies because it was obvious to Americans that the balance between monarchy in the king, aristocracy in the House of Lords, and democracy in the House of Commons did not work. Rather, the writers of the United States *Constitution* of 1787 put their trust in a balance of powers among institutions such as the executive, the legislative, and the judiciary as suggested by the French philosophe Montesquieu.

Parallel to issues such as federalism and the separation and balance of powers were several key questions: the relative power of large versus small states, the issue of slavery, and a general fear of political authority that divided the delegates empowered to frame the *Constitution* as well as the American people that would have to accept the new government. The solutions to these issues included: a bicameral system that gave small states equal representation with large ones in the Senate; a second representative chamber that recognized the political significance of citizen numbers by apportioning seats in the House based on population; and a final acknowledgment that part of the southern population comprised slaves who were noncitizens, but still part of the political mix—each bondsman and woman was then counted as three-fifths a person to calculate representation in the House. Beyond the framing of the *Constitution* was the issue of ratification. Since the *Constitution* did not include any explicit sections to ensure the natural rights of the *Declaration of Independence*, the first ten amendments, mentioned above, balanced freedom with authority in a manner similar to David Hume's *Justice and Property* (see Chapter Nineteen) to create the positive consensus that supported the new government.

Furthermore, after the U.S. public accepted the new government, the concept of the rule of law as a restraint upon the legislative and executive authority gave the judiciary increased power in American society. With the doctrine of judicial review based upon a reading of a written constitution, courts had authority to control sovereign power, giving the rule of law ultimate theoretical expression. The interplay of the United States Supreme Court, the Congress, and the president over the next two hundred years gave historical substance to that authority and its limits. Americans had separated the concept of the rule of law from legislative command and entrusted stewardship to federal judges appointed for life.

The new nation-in-formation acquired western lands by the revolution, purchased lands such as Louisiana from the French, and secured control of the West with wars against Native Americans and Great Britain. The War of 1812 against Britain ended in a negotiated treaty but forged American nationalism based on Oliver Hazard Perry's naval victory on Lake Erie and Andrew Jackson's success at New Orleans over a professional English army fresh from destroying Napoleon's last bid for power at Waterloo. The symbols and slogans of American nationalism emerged from these battles.

The federal government started down a path of selling land to raise revenues and put private property in the hands of American entrepreneurs. The government gave Revolutionary War veterans land bounties in western territories. In the 1785 Land Ordinance, Congress set a pattern of surveying the land prior to sale and continued the practice with ever-smaller tracts of land at lower prices to encourage development. This process of making western lands available to younger generations of citizens and European immigrants continued the colonial practice of moving into the West, developing property, and producing products for sale to a market. The United States from its inception was a commercial nation exporting natural resources and foodstuffs to an Atlantic world eager for those products. Yet this westward expansion brought the United States into conflict with numerous American Indian tribes and Mexico.

American expansionism brought people to Mexican Texas. Initially welcomed to Texas by the Mexican government as frontier guards against the Commanches and other tribes, the American settlers held their own against these tribes, carved out ever greater territorial realms and then sought independence. The Mexicans moved under their president and General Antonio de Santa Ana to crush the Texas rebellion, wiping out the defenders of the Alamo and a smaller garrison at Goliad in 1836 only to be decisively defeated at San Jacinto by the rebel General Sam Houston. The Republic of Texas was born but a little more than a decade later annexation of Texas led to a conflict known in the United States as the War with Mexico in 1848.

Despite being outnumbered in every significant engagement except one, the U.S. Army and Marines crushed Mexico's armies in what became the southwest United States and the heart of Mexico proper. In a major infantry campaign transported to Mexico's east coast by the U.S. Navy, the U.S. Army invaded overland and captured Mexico City. The U.S. victory, despite the odds, was due to effective reconnaissance, careful massing of artillery, the American soldier's belief that he could not be defeated by a "backward" foe, and political infighting among Mexican leaders. The resulting Mexican cession to the United States of 40 percent of its territory opened all of the present-day American Southwest including all of California, Arizona, New Mexico, and Colorado to settlement by Americans.

Now the Pacific coast with numerous deep-water ports was open to American commercial expansionism. Then, the California gold rush of 1848 poured population into the territory and the completion of the transcontinental railroad in 1869 enabled further emigration and commercial activity.

The fact that Texas and California maintained the Mexican system of community property and separate ownership enabled women to become a greater part of the economic and social fabric of these states. American women had demanded equal rights in 1848 at a convention in Seneca Falls, New York, heightening awareness of the continuing gender bias in the political system and inequality of citizens. In addition to Texas and California, other states afforded women greater rights to own, manage, and retain the profits on property.

Yet, at the same time, a deeper cultural story was unfolding. As the nation expanded, the Industrial Revolution began, but instead of pulling the country together as it had in Great Britain, it actually pulled the United States apart. The Industrial Revolution sent the South in one direction and the North in another. The textile industry in Great Britain drew the South away from the North by making plantation owners economic associates of English and Scottish manufacturers. Textile factories in Great Britain needed the raw cotton fiber produced by slave labor in the South.

In short order, the American South became the world's chief producer of cotton. The demand for this plant fiber encouraged and expanded slavery in this region. At the same time, southerners became the favored customers of British manufacturers. The South favored buying goods from abroad rather than purchasing more expensive products from the North. Thus, the South preferred that the federal government maintain no or very low import tariffs despite the need for high taxes on imports to protect vulnerable northern factories.

In contrast, the North developed industry and sought high tariffs to protect the manufactured goods of their new firms. Northern factory owners and their workers naturally opposed importing British finished products into the domestic market. Simultaneously, northerners invested in the construction of an infrastructure to support increased industrialization, such as canals and railroads to expand their access to the U.S. market. In doing so, however, they chose an east-west integration pattern rather than a north-south link.

The West (territories north of the Ohio River and most of the land west of the Mississippi except for Texas) in turn developed an agricultural system much like that of the Middle Colonies. These western lands produced staples such as corn and pork that fed the North's new industrial-urban centers. Hence, the North slowly came to dominate the economy of the rapidly developing western states after 1820. Consequently, the North captured a majority of economic interests that shaped the future political attitudes of the United States.

Finally, both the North and most of the West slowly came to oppose the spread of slavery, contrary to the wishes of the South. Industry had the tendency to teach manufacturers that a free labor market was the best economic design for production. At the same time, humanitarian principles opposed enslaving people in any form. Northerners thus began to criticize southerners for spreading slavery. The South in turn complained that factory owners treated their workers worse than slaves.

But even as the North mobilized opposition to slavery, northerners themselves had perfected segregation as a legal device to keep liberated slaves from settling in free states. Furthermore, both the North and the South had agreed to keep the United States "white" by writing naturalization laws that denied citizenship to any foreigners except those from Europe. Thus, while the argument over slavery raged, the "white" north encoded a system of racial segregation.

Established in practice long before it became embedded in law, segregation provided a new approach to controlling people of a different ethnic heritage from the European majority. It denied the democratic principles that U.S. citizens cherished and excluded ethnic minorities from access to the material pursuits that made the United States a land of opportunity for the

Cotton pickers in the South. This photograph, taken c. 1899, illustrates that the work done by freedpeople after the Civil War, was about the same as that done by slaves. Library of Congress, LC-USZ62-75650.

poor. Consequently, segregation, whether an explicit legal system, or a common cultural practice, created a social, economic, and legal barrier to the concept of equality that undermined true freedom in a liberal society. Nonetheless, those practices that segregated ethnic minorities ultimately created the mosaic of social differences that prevented the true assimilation of all peoples who lived in the United States.

Yet the issue of slavery focused the North's political attitudes on the future. As stated above, northerners and southerners both had been expansionists whose desire to control all the land between the Atlantic and Pacific coasts of North America had led to the acquisition of vast territories at the expense of Native Americans and Hispanics. Adding Native American tribes and Hispanics to the minorities already within the territory controlled by the United States deepened racism, while the argument over slavery continued. Eventually, the North hardened its position and refused to allow the southern plantation system to expand west. Since the North came to control national politics as it integrated with a majority of new western states, those with northern sympathies came to dominate the federal system. By 1850, the South knew its future as part of the United States was limited when California entered the Union as a free state, giving the North an absolute majority in both houses of Congress.

The drift toward civil war continued. In the presidential election of 1860, the northern-based Republican party selected Abraham Lincoln as the most effective spokesperson against the spread of slavery and for their vision of the future. The South decided that if Lincoln won the election, the slave states would secede from the Union. When Lincoln won, the South made good on its promise. Now the North, however, was unwilling to let the South leave the Union, declaring all states that had seceded to be in rebellion. The Civil War, the second stage of nation-building in the United States, had begun.

The Civil War (1861–65) was a blood bath, taking more than 500,000 lives due to the inability of military leaders in both the North and South to fully understand the devastating effect of rifled musketry, the impact of massed artillery, and the necessity of field fortifications. Soldiers still marched in linear formations, packed tightly together, against weapons that were lethal at great range. As the war progressed, field commanders realized that entrenchment was necessary, resulting in the use of massive frontal assaults and flanking actions to break heavy field fortifications. The casualties mounted, but the North had the resources necessary to carry the war to the South and it did so, devastating its people and economy in 1864–65. With the northern victory, amendments to the *Constitution* abolished slavery, guaranteed access to property for the freed people, and assured voting rights for all men. But soon economic, social, and legal segregation neutralized these amendments.

Accordingly, while slavery disappeared, sharecropping soon replaced legal bondage as African Americans, much like feudal serfs, found themselves bound to the land through debt. Meanwhile segregation reinforced these debts by isolating African Americans in their own world of poverty and out of sight of white society. Jim Crow laws divided blacks from whites by creating separate schools, hospitals, prisons, restaurants, bars, hotels, boarding houses, theaters, toilets, railway and streetcars, and waiting rooms, just to name a few. Trapped in this new social and economic solitude, African Americans did not have equal access to wealth with whites. Hence, a new form of socioeconomic exclusion based on debt replaced slavery.

The nation in general sanctioned segregation as a solution to the issue of multiple ethnicities during the 1880s. In 1882, the Supreme Court in the case of *The United States* v. *Harris*, declared laws punishing crimes such as murder and assault to be matters decided by the states rather than the federal government despite the fact that many local crimes were racially motivated. In 1883, the Court struck down the Civil Rights Act of 1875 stating that Congress cannot be proactive in producing legislation to prevent discrimination; rather Congress must wait for a state to pass a discriminatory

In the trenches at Petersburg, Virginia, well-supplied Union soldiers are shown before General Ulysses S. Grant's spring offensive of March 1865. Grant's forces would go on to defeat Lee's army on April 2, 1865, after the nine-month siege. Hundreds of thousands died in the war, with diseases such as typhoid, malaria, tuberculosis, smallpox, and even measles, killing many more. United States National Archives & Records Administration. ARC # 524576.

law. Also, the Fourteenth Amendment that guarantees all persons born in the U.S. to be citizens, and that no state shall deprive any person of life, liberty, or property without due process of law, was in fact silent on matters of racial discrimination by private parties. In 1896, the Court held, in *Plessy* v. *Ferguson*, that the principle of "separate but equal" met the constitutional requirement to ensure equality before the law. Finally, in 1898, the Court held in *Williams* v. *Mississippi* that literacy tests to qualify for voting were nondiscriminatory and therefore legal. Thus, national integration through northern industrialization, urbanization, and mass communication made the United States into a true nation. Yet, this integration also included national segregation as a way to define race relations.

National segregation denied the principles of equality defined by opportunity for all the people living in the United States in the nineteenth century. The result was that the United States combined industry with democracy for those of European ancestry only. This meant that if a person's parents were from Europe, they might aspire to one day enjoy the full benefits of citizenship: liberty, freedom, and democracy based on public opinion. If a person's parents were non-Europeans, they experienced some degree of segregation. Such a person was then partly or wholly excluded from the equal opportunity promised in liberty, freedom, and democracy, despite growing pressure after 1900 to end these restrictions.

Thus, issues of race and ethnicity had created a mixed political story of integration and segregation that continued to plague politics in the United States into the twentieth-first century. As a result, the United States seemed to reflect national features that included both the democratic and autocratic qualities found in Europe that its dominant population of European extraction enjoyed as they made up the majority until the twentieth century. These people experienced the overall democratic flavor of life in the United States, yet they also excluded ethnic minorities as a marginal population whose life seemed similar to the poor living in central Europe.

Japan

The *Tokugawa Bakufu* (military government) laid the foundation for national formation through a process of modernization unique to the Japanese islands. Despite the fact that the Tokugawa Shogunate had closed Japan to European influences, except for one port at Nagasaki, Japan still experienced its own process of rapid internal change symptomatic of the modernization process. Consequently, when the United States forced the Japanese to open their home islands to global trade after 1853, the basis for assimilating European institutions was already in place. And since Japan had imported alien cultural features from Korea and China twice before, during the Yayoi era (250 BCE–250 CE) and the Nara period (600–900 CE), the adaptation of western practices to the modernizing foundation laid by the Tokugawa permitted a quick diffusion of national formation into the islands. Hence, a look at the Tokugawa regime is an appropriate place to start.

The Tokugawa Bakufu was a highly centralized feudal society like those found in Western Europe at the end of the Middle Ages. The Tokugawa shoguns were the rulers of all the other *daimyo* (feudal lords) and imposed on them a system of alternate attendance that kept them in line. Each daimyo had to spend alternate years in residence in Edo (present-day Tokyo), the Tokugawa capital. And when they were in their own domains, they had to leave their wives and sons in Edo as hostages. This gave the shogun physical control over the daimyo and their families, as well as depleted the financial resources of the daimyo, who had to expend huge amounts of money to maintain two residences. The shogun further called upon the daimyo to support public projects such as waterworks, roads, and fortifications, and to make loans to the Bakufu that would never be paid back. This system of extortion also served to strengthen the shogunate at the expense of the daimyo. But just as the shogun forced the daimyo to reside in the capital, so the daimyo forced their samurai to live in their castles. Consequently, castles grew into castle-towns.

The shogun also enforced a policy of freezing class lines and creating a near caste-like social system. Apart from the emperor's family, society was divided into four ranks: samurai, peasants, artisans, and merchants, in that order. The Japanese had adopted the Chinese Neo-Confucian model of social hierarchy, but had substituted the samurai for the scholar-officials. Samurai were the warrior class: only they could bear swords and hold official positions in the state bureaucracy.

Yet the Tokugawa transformed the samurai into protomodern civil servants. During the era of civil war prior to the rise of the Tokugawa, the Japanese estates system, the *Sheon*, collapsed, forcing the redefinition of land tenure. Successful daimyo began to convert the income their samurai received from land allotments to *koku* of rice (the amount of rice needed to feed an adult for one year). After the Tokugawa victory over all its rivals, this system of payment became permanent. Accordingly, by 1700, 90 percent of all the samurai took their income in koku. This style of payment meant that the samurai became an urban military force that had to

Tokugawa
Iyeyasu
(1542–1616).
A prominent
figure in
Japanese
history,
Iyeyasu was
the founder
and first of
the Tokugawa
Shoguns. The
Tokugawa-era
government,
also known as
a shogunate
or bakufu,
began shortly
after Iyeyasu's
victory of
Sekigahara in
1600 and
continued
until the Meiji
Restoration in
1868. Photo
courtesy of
Okazaki City.

In most cases, merchant families with special privileges granted by the Bakufu, or local daimyo regimes, controlled the economy of a town. Merchants also became financial agents for the daimyo and the samurai caste because each year the former sold their crops, and the latter converted their koku stipends into cash. In addition, merchants managed daimyo accounts and samurai money, while often becoming their creditors. When inflation followed prosperity, the samurai frequently found themselves trapped in debt because their fixed stipends lost value. Accordingly, the theoretical high status of samurai and the low status of merchants did not necessarily reflect social reality much as the Commercial Revolution in Europe had changed the rank and power of many new social groups. Accordingly, merchants became a wealthy and influential class.

The Tokugawa government's main source of revenue was farm taxes, but it taxed the village rather than the individual cultivator or owner of the land. Therefore, the village was left alone as long as it paid its taxes and provided labor services. This hands-off policy gave the villages a great deal of autonomy. Agricultural production increased, which in turn made a new division of labor possible. So-called big houses in villages would go into the manufacturing of sake and silk, or open pawnshops. Men from these families typically developed leadership abilities. In time, villages developed into stable economic entities.

The stability of Tokugawa Japan did not cause stagnation, rather it was a time when Japan developed a prosperous moneyed economy, a sophisticated territorial government much like Europe, and staffed its bureaucracies with educated and disciplined samurai. In addition, a productive agricultural population and the rising wealthy merchants created the basis for a strong social fabric. Hence, Tokugawa Japan had created many of the building blocks needed for a modern Japan.

Ironically, however, traditional Japanese merchants, who enjoyed many privileges under Tokugawa rule, did not develop into a revolutionary force that would strive to overthrow the Bakufu. As Japan pushed toward modernization, these traditional merchants faded from the scene. In this respect, they were very different from their European counterparts who became a major force behind modernization. The mission of leading Japan into the modern age fell to other social classes. It was the villages that provided the primitive investment necessary for Japan's initial moves toward modern state-building. Village headmen became grassroots leaders of a modern Japanese nation. Also, the warrior-turned-administrator samurai quickly became government, military, and business leaders in Japan's

maintain their martial arts skills, but were now free to become Japan's new intelligentsia. While they could not own land or switch allegiance to other lords, the samurai lived in castle-towns and used their free time to become literate. Since the Tokugawa regime maintained peace across the land, the samurai had no occasion to fight in combat, they began to study both classical Chinese philosophy and books introduced into Japan by the Dutch—the one European state the Tokugawa allowed to trade through Nagasaki. Consequently, the samurai were transformed into a salaried class of administrators who staffed the government bureaucracy.

With the peace that the Tokugawa regime brought to Japan, social and economic stability created a local Commercial Revolution, with a steady population and economic boom taking place. The alternate attendance system and the growth of castle-towns dramatically increased the demand for trade. The daimyo, who needed cash to purchase goods and services in the capital and their castle-towns, had to sell the crops from their landed estates on the open market. Osaka became the commercial center of Japan, especially in its rice trade. Many other commercial towns also emerged. In short, Japan experienced its own form of commercial capitalism.

drive toward modernization, even though their traditional status ceased to exist in the process.

Nonetheless, the process of national formation began when the United States forced Japan to open its home islands to international trade. Commodore Matthew Perry arrived in the Edo harbor in 1853 with a fleet of ships capable of destroying Japan's coastal cities. The Japanese had closed their islands to European influence in 1636 in order to eliminate the introduction of dangerous ideas and practices, but they had lost their military equality to rising western industrial nation-states. As a military society, however, the Japanese immediately recognized their weaknesses as well as their inability to respond to a potential foreign invasion. Yet the daimyo of Japan disagreed violently on what to do next; accordingly, war broke out, the shogunate fell in 1868, and the Japanese began to look to Europe and the United States for models to imitate.

The daimyo of Choshu and Satsuma formed an antishogunate alliance. They had a long history of feuding with the Tokugawa family and some limited success at building a modern military. Now they led an open military assault on the shaky Tokugawa regime under the banner of "revere the emperor; expel the foreigners." They destroyed the Tokugawa regime in 1868, restored Emperor Meiji (sixteen years old at the time) to power, and relocated the royal capital to Edo, renamed Tokyo. They issued the Charter Oath in the name of the emperor. The oath was brief and vague, but it contained important new ideas: it called for a legislature, the freeing of people from the feudal system, the acceptance of international law, and openness to foreign ideas.

This was the Meiji Restoration. The Meiji leaders were young, ambitious, well-educated samurai knowledgeable in warfare and statecraft. Their goal was to "enrich the country; strengthen the army." They knew that Japan could become powerful only through westernization, and they boldly launched Japan on a course of modernization despite the fact that they had begun their rise under an antiforeign banner. Their push for Japan's transformation imitated Machiavelli's principles (of the ends justifying the means), producing amazing results.

The Meiji leaders set about building a modern, unified, and centralized national government. They were the power behind the throne. In everything they did, they showed the greatest respect to the boy emperor, but in fact made all the major decisions among themselves. In accordance with the Charter Oath, they also provided for a legislature in the new government structure, but delayed its implementation. An oligarchy (government by the few) ruled Japan.

The Meiji leaders had to dismantle the feudal system, which was a major obstacle to building a modern nation. They had to get rid of the daimyo's domains, the privileged status of the samurai, and the restrictions on commoners. In 1870, they freed commoners from earlier occupational and residential restrictions and gave them the right to have surnames. In 1871, they abolished all the domains, organized the country into prefectures, and later retired all the daimyo with generous pensions. In 1872, they decided to build a new conscript army to replace the samurai warriors. Now anyone could be a soldier. In 1876, they prohibited samurai from wearing swords. With the abolition of feudal domains, the samurai were deprived of their sociopolitical function as well as their stipends, for which they were forced to accept government bonds in exchange.

Meanwhile, the main source of government revenue in Meiji Japan continued to be agricultural taxes, as it had been in Tokugawa times. Yet the tax-collection system was different. Under the new tax code, the government collected revenues from the owners of the land. Those who received certificates in recognition of their land ownership rights were, however, not the absentee landowners of the Tokugawa period; instead, they were the cultivators and rich villagers who actually paid the taxes.

The reforms created widespread dissatisfaction in the country. Many peasants were unhappy with the new land and tax system and compulsory military service. In protest they staged many uprisings. Traditional merchants were unhappy to lose their feudal privileges, and many big houses went bankrupt. Most problematic were the samurai. As the educated class with administrative experience in Tokugawa Japan, they entered government service as administrators, entered the military as officers, entered the business world, and became teachers and colonists. Yet a great many others failed to make a successful transition.

Meanwhile, the oligarchy's reforms had led to a split in the Meiji government between reformers and conservatives. Reformers pushed for westernization, while conservatives emphasized the restoration of the traditional samurai class and its values. In 1873, the conservatives in government decided to go to war with Korea. Their purpose was to force Korea to open up to Japanese trade and to use this military operation to restore samurai strength, values, and status. When the reformers rejected this Korean war, the conservatives left the government. This Crisis of 1873 left the reform-minded leaders in control of the government.

In 1874 the government launched an invasion of China's small island of Taiwan as a way to mollify the samurai who had favored an invasion of Korea. Defeated, China was forced to pay reparations and recognize Japanese sovereignty over Taiwan and the Ryuku Islands. Yet, disaffected samurai staged the Satsuma Rebellion in 1877, which the Meiji government put down with military force. This ended the samurai threat to Japan's modernization and permitted the Meiji revolution to continue.

The Meiji Restoration was revolutionary in many ways: it destroyed the feudal system of domain autonomy and established a centralized national government; it abolished the feudal near–caste system and allowed all people to take part in all social activities; and it opened up Japan to the outside world. It was a revolution from above, carried out by a small group of aristocratic samurai in a manner that would have made Cavour and Bismarck proud. The Meiji reformers' task was made easier, however, by the fact that they took advantage of the governmental bureaucracy created by the Tokugawa Shogunate, and they acted in the name of the long-established authority of the emperor.

The Meiji leaders adopted this strategy of using the old to justify the new because of its conservative values. They aimed for modernization but kept many old values and practices to ensure that Japan remained Japanese. In 1868, they proclaimed Japan a Shinto state and proceeded to make Shintoism Japan's only religion. Large numbers of Japanese Buddhists, however, were strongly opposed to this plan. Also, the Western powers exerted enough pressure to make the reformers lift the old ban on Christianity in 1873. Thus Japan allowed three religions to flourish in peaceful coexistence.

Meanwhile, the reform-minded Meiji oligarchs dominated the government between the war crisis of 1873 and the Sino-Japanese War of 1894. During this time, they developed a constitutional monarchy, a modernizing economy, and an army and navy that demanded international respect.

Still, they faced repeated outbursts of opposition. The opposition's central demand was a national legislature that would guarantee political rights and local interests. The protesters drew on Western political theory for support. By 1878, the government announced that the emperor would issue a constitution to take effect in 1890.

The Meiji oligarchs framed the Meiji Constitution (1889–1945) and announced it as a gift from the emperor to his subjects. It did not even have a pretense of being an instrument developed by the people to curb the power of the emperor. Based on the conservative German model, power was concentrated in the hands of the emperor. The emperor, "sacred and inviolable," was supreme. The *Diet* (legislature) was, by design, an instrument to rally public support for the implementation of the emperor's will. It consisted of two houses: the House of Peers, made up of old court nobles, ex-daimyo, and Meiji oligarchs; and the House of Representatives, made up of men elected by a constituency of taxpaying property owners (1.1 percent of the total population). The ministers of the cabinet were responsible to the emperor, not the Diet. The emperor was the final authority, but he was also above politics. Therefore his power was divided between the Privy Council, the Cabinet, the Diet, and the military general staff. The Constitution provided no mechanism for coordination between these branches, so elder statesmen of influence (the oligarchs and court nobles) decided major questions in private consultation. They, for example, decided on the selection of a prime minister, who initially would be one of them. Yet the Diet did control the purse strings. It alone had the power to approve or veto government budgets.

Then, the oligarchs called for a General Staff based on the German model. This new General Staff ran the combined military services. The Japanese army reflected the best Europe had to offer in way of design: the Prussian-German model. When it came to their navy, the Japanese followed the British example, for Great Britain's naval tradition had no equal. Finally, the Japanese General Staff shaped national budgets and sent it forward to the Diet for approval.

As in Bismarck's Germany, in Japan, if the Diet could not reach agreement on a budget, then the General Staff merely implemented last year's fiscal plan. Thus, the old budget began another year of legal existence. This money then spurred industry to equip Japan with modern, mass-produced weapons. As a result, the Meiji rulers did not intend for democracy to interfere with their plans for military equality with European nation-states.

The Meiji oligarchs saw their mission as one of conservative nation-building. They believed in a "transcendental" cabinet: one that placed the nation above any petty personal and party factions. They saw themselves as representing the good of the country in contrast to the interests of political parties who represented private concerns. Yet their power was personal, not institutional. Meanwhile, the political parties turned out to be tougher than the oligarchs had anticipated.

Speaking for political parties, Japanese intellectuals such as Fukuzawa Yukichi embraced the heritage of the European Enlightenment in which freedom, reason, and progress were the yardstick of justice. An ex-samurai, Fukuzawa (1835–1901) became a private citizen after the Meiji Restoration of 1868. Prior to the fall of the Tokugawa, however, he had studied Dutch scholarship, which made him one of best-qualified Japanese intellectuals to travel to the United States and Europe to investigate foreign ways. Once in America, and later in Europe, he carefully studied Western science and technology as it related to national wealth and international power. He returned to Japan during the civil wars that brought the Meiji oligarchs to power, becoming a powerful resource for change. Translating his knowledge of Western scientific, economic, and political thought into recommended governmental actions he developed and reported his opinions through several newspapers he helped to found and run. Early in the Meiji period Fukuzawa preached individualism, freedom, and personal autonomy; he argued it was the individual citizen that shaped national politics. Later in his career he moved firmly into the camp of patriotic nationalism at home and imperial expansion abroad. In short, he stayed ahead of the dominant political policies that shaped Japan's national formation and served as the voice that gave it direction.

Complementing Fukuzawa's change in heart toward a more aggressive view of national formation, Japan made considerable progress in building a national educational system based on conservative principles. The Iwakura Mission, a group assembled to study Amer-ica and Europe on tour, saw the strength and complexity of the modern West, and returned home to emphasize the importance of education in preparing the next generation for Japan's modernization and international competition. They realized Japan needed a workforce with basic literacy and math skills to staff factories and become business clerks, soldiers, and sailors; Japan also needed people with a higher level of education to become managers and officers. To jump-start its modern education, the government sent students to study in Western countries at government expense and hired foreign experts at high salaries to teach in Japan. Yet the government quickly cut back on the number of students in foreign schools and replaced foreign experts as soon as the Japanese had acquired enough expertise at home.

The Ministry of Education, established in 1871, adopted the French system of a highly centralized administration. Government policy determined the general direction and specific content of education, although schools were locally financed. The first Normal School (teacher-training school) was established in 1872, and Tokyo University was established in 1877. Over time, four-year and then six-year compulsory education was put in place.

The Prescript on Education, issued in 1890, was the basic statement on the purpose of education for half a century. It put a premium on Confucian values and

Fukuzawa Yukichi (1835–1901). Born into a low-ranking samurai family, Fukuzawa Yukichi became instrumental in the modernizing of Japan during the period known as the Meiji Era. His writings spoke of individual strength, government and social institutions, and western political theory to the Japanese who, just coming out of the Bakufu era, were ready to embrace change.

service to the throne and state. Japanese schools became widely known for training their students in basic skills through rote learning and indoctrinating them with radical patriotism. The goal was to ensure loyalty to the emperor.

While education supplied the urban skills required for a positive conservative consensus to support the new nation, Japan's agriculture provided the necessary capital and labor for industrialization. Agricultural production rose significantly because of the introduction of new strains of seed, new fertilizers, new methods of cultivation, and newly opened farm land. Surplus agricultural laborers migrated to cities to supply industry with workers; some even left Japan to go abroad.

The Meiji government played a significant role in modernizing Japan's economy. Japan completed its first railroad line in 1872, and Kyoto became its first city to have trolley cars in 1895. The government invested in so-called demonstration factories such as silk factories, cotton mills, and cement plants—to show private capitalists the feasibility and profitability of these industries. The government also made large investments in strategic industries such as shipyards, munitions plants, and coal mines to fortify Japan's military might.

The government decided to sell much of its enterprises at public auction in the late 1880s as its financial problems grew. Men with close ties to the government purchased these concerns at bargain prices. Over time, this small handful of well-connected businesses grew into huge financial and industrial corporations that controlled the modern sector of the Japanese economy. Called the *Zaibatsu* (treasury-rich families), these giant corporations functioned very much like the cartel system developing in Bismarck's Germany.

From the beginning, Japan's modern businesses claimed credit for building the economic foundation of this first Asian nation. To build a strong bank, trading company, shipyard, or shipping company was to offer a service to the state and the emperor. This ideology made it possible for the Zaibatsu to recruit capable and dedicated executives, especially from the samurai class, who traditionally shunned making money. In addition, this ideology transferred the traditional Japanese value of group solidarity and mutual responsibility into company loyalty. Finally, this ideology justified a national policy of a free market actually under the umbrella of strong government support and guidance. The government made strenuous efforts to preserve Japan's economic independence. The oligarchs protected Japan's domestic market, conserved foreign currency, avoided foreign loans, and held down domestic consumption.

Accordingly, government initiatives in industry dominated this field of production. Heavy industry, shipping, railroads, mining, and metallurgy each received intense governmental attention. Governmental control concentrated efforts to integrate the whole pattern of industrial development while maintaining the conservative tone that the oligarchs demanded. At the heart of such an effort lay the Ministry of Industry.

After the auction of the late 1880s, the overall policy of the Ministry of Industry kept Japan on an integrated path. Model shipyards, arsenals, and factories provided the experience needed for the Japanese to see how to spread their new economy. The national marketplace thus became a national school at the same time. Expanded technical training with a parallel development in public education permitted the government to maintain a steady pattern of economic growth.

To this setting the state added numerous public services, including a government-supported banking system, a modern postal system, and standardized commercial laws to secure property rights and contracts. Japanese society seemed to form a phalanx of national proportion that moved in a singular, integrated effort toward a common modern goal. This goal fit the design set by the oligarchs.

These early phases in Japanese industrialization took place in a nation poor in natural resources save for its human potential. Japan had to depend on Western equipment, technical skills, and capital to get started. Once in motion, however, the Japanese economy required a rapid turnover in international commerce to maintain a flow of raw materials and capital into Japan and a flow of finished products out of Japan. At the same time, all that Japan achieved had to be won while keeping Europe and the United States at arm's length.

Japan did not want to fall dependent on foreigners or lose command of its political destiny.

Exports were vital to pay for machines, raw materials, and weapons that secured Japan's future. Silk became the key product that generated a national income in the hard foreign currencies needed for international trade. Production of silk goods became Japan's principal export, and the bulk of these silk products ended up in the United States or Europe. Sweatshops and household production generated the supply of silk goods so vital to trade. Based on this fragile cottage industry in textiles, Japan managed to move through the transitional period to industrialization as an independent culture.

Low pay for labor, cottage industry, and textiles served to supply Japan's chief export that allowed the Japanese to acquire the foreign currencies needed for industrialization. This style of managed industrialization required the Japanese to combine protoindustrial production involving entrepreneurs and cottagers, such as those found in England in the seventeenth and eighteenth centuries, with large industrial factories, such as the urban-based production found in Germany in the nineteenth century. Japan achieved all this under the direction of the state; Japan succeeded, but it had gained success through a highly disciplined culture directed from above.

Hence, when reviewing the political system implemented by the oligarchs, and the problems of industrializing Japan, the model of national formation imported from Europe seemed to follow a Central European design. Strict controls from above with an eye on preventing democracy became the hallmark of Japan's first steps into the modern arena. The militancy of the effort matched Japan's traditional past, while the speed with which it achieved its goals reflected the work ethic and obedience of the Japanese people. Once again Japan had transformed itself without losing sight of its cultural identity, just as it had done during the Yayoi era and the Nara period.

Accordingly, the character of the Japanese nation-state developed sharp autocratic tendencies, with Japan entering the modern era with the same kind of aggressive energy found in Germany. This made the new Japanese nation an ambitious one. Thus, as a result of the new strength generated by national formation based on modern industry, Japan began to look upon its neighbors as potential imperial targets. In this fashion, Japan imitated Germany, for both new nations had to scramble in order to catch up with Britain and France as great powers that commanded great empires.

The Germans, the Japanese, and the Italians each felt that since they had not enjoyed the benefits of protomodern commercial development, and the accompanying empires, that the modern age would have to make room for their new imperial hunger. This hunger redefined the global arena as each nation-state sought to secure markets that all industrial nations needed. Thus, Japan, Germany, and Italy developed ambitious imperial programs designed to make all three the equals of Britain and France.

Now a curious by-product of nation building began to occur. Nations integrated by industry sought international markets and began to compete with one another. The world became a common arena for international trade and imperial ambitions in which nation-states had the advantage of modern military institutions.

Thus, Great Britain, France, Germany, Italy, the United States, and Japan all found themselves drawn into an era of imperial expansion. To each nation this felt like a natural consequence of modernization. For the rest of the world, however, modernization meant occupation, violence, and transitional change, with foreigners dictating the terms. This experience created the foundations for both the end of tradition and twentieth-century warfare.

Suggested Reading

The United States
Calloway, Colin, *One Vast Winter Count* (Lincoln: University of Nebraska Press, 2003).

Doughty, Robert A., Ira D. Gruber, Roy K. Flint, George C. Herring, John A. Lynn, Mark Grimsley, Donald D. Howard, and Williamson Murray, *American Military History and the Evolution of Warfare in the Western World* (Lexington, Mass.: D.C. Heath and Company, 1996).

Ellis, John, *Brute Force: Allied Strategy and Tactics in the Second World War* (New York: Viking, 1990).

Gaddis, John Lewis, *The Cold War: A New History* (New York: Penguin Press, 2005).

Riley, Glenda, *Inventing the American Woman*, 3rd edition (Wheeling, Ill.: Harlan Davidson, Inc., 2001).

Japan
Duus, Peter, *Feudalism in Japan* (New York: Alfred A. Knopf, 1969).

———, *The Rise of Modern Japan* (Boston: Houghton Mifflin Company, 1976).

Eisenstadt, S. N., *Japanese Civilization: A Comparative View* (Chicago: The University of Chicago Press, 1996).

Hall, John Whitney, Nagahara Keiji, and Koso Yamamura, eds., *Japan Before the Tokugawa: Political Consolidation and Growth 1500–1650* (Princeton, N.J.: Princeton University Press, 1996).

Hane Mikiso, *Japan: A Historical Survey* (Charles Scribner's Sons, 1972).

———, *Modern Japan: A Historical Survey*, Third Edition (Boulder, Colo.: Westview, 2001).

Mason, R. H. P. and Caiger, J. G., *A History of Japan*, Revised Edition (Boston: Tuttle Publishing. 1997).

Reischauer, Edwin O., *The Japanese* (Cambridge, Mass.: Harvard University Press, 1981).

———, *Japan: The Story of a Nation* (New York: Alfred A. Knopf, 1970).

Sansom, G. B., *Japan: A Short Cultural History*, Revised Edition (New York: Appleton-Century-Crofts, Inc. 1962).

XXIV

RUSSIA
and Latin America

In contrast to the United States and Japan, Russia and Latin America represent the first examples of major cultural zones outside of Europe that attempted to imitate many of the modern features of the West, but failed to produce the internal coherence of nation-states within their respective territories. Also, Russia and Latin America appear together in this chapter because both technically managed to preserve their political independence and territorial integrity during an era of rapid Western imperial expansion, but both suffered from such severe internal divisions that it weakened their capacity to deal with Western nation-states as equals. Finally these same internal divisions in both Russia and Latin America resulted from similar institutional paradoxes that they both shared: each of these major cultural zones tried to mix modern and traditional attitudes and practices that contradicted one another.

Russia

To understand Russian history, one must begin with geography, which describes the natural features of Russia and provides a context for explaining why this Eurasian culture had such a difficult time launching a civilization. Most of the Russian landscape, its topography, rivers, climate, and poor soil, discourage human occupation when contrasted with Europe or the rest of Asia. Bound by a continent exposed to the cold winds of the Arctic Circle, Russia is a relatively uninviting place that seems to deter human settlement. And given the impact of the past several Ice Ages, which had removed many of the topographic barriers to human movement, Russia became a primary migratory route for nomads during most of world history. Only at the beginning of the modern era did the circumstances for developing a stable civilization seem to favor the possibility of creating a society that could survive countless nomadic assaults. Thus, the history of an independent Russia as we know it began only after the year 1460.

The principal barriers to forming a sedentary society in Russia were an inhospitable physical and bio-logical environment. As a geographic setting, Russia is a very cold and arid place with a short growing season. This limited the production of food surpluses needed to feed the labor required to build and defend an urban culture. Hence, many attempts to establish cities in Russia failed due to nomadic pressures and Russia's inhospitable physical environment.

The majority of Russia's landscape bears the imprint of the most recent Ice Age. The European portions of what was once the Soviet Union bears the scars of a system of continental glaciers that scoured the countryside, removing most of the tall mountain ranges that once shielded Russia from the Arctic winds. Reaching as far south from the Arctic Circle as the Caucasus Mountains and the Caspian Sea, sheets of ice ground through Russia leveling much of the landscape. In Asian Russia, mountain ranges survived because the snowfall in that region was far lighter, while the landlocked conditions there produced one of the coldest places in the world. Then, as the Ice Age ended, retreating ice left northern Russia pockmarked with extensive marshlands, lakes, and great morainic dumps (the pulverized rocks left behind by melting glaciers) in its wake. This was a difficult topography for human settlement.

Simultaneously, in the southern half of European Russia, the ice sheets deposited much finer soils from the meltwater of continental glaciers as well as the dust-bearing winds from the Arctic Circle. Thus, Ukraine received very thick, fertile sediments that included a supply of fine loess that made this region the best site for agriculture in Russia. In the southern half of Asian Russia, the melted ice left a legacy of frozen soil called *permafrost* in places where the continental glaciers did not scour away the mountains. While this permafrost made agriculture impossible, it supplied the local forests with an unusually stable supply of underground moisture, which kept great forests alive in a very dry place.

While the Ice Age ground up the landscape, the nature of Russia's rivers and lakes also discouraged human occupation. Some of the broadest, longest, and least useful rivers exist in Asian Russia, the primary defect of which being that they flow from south to north and thaw first at the sources of their water rather than at their mouths. The result is a flood pattern that spreads meltwater across a cold marshy landscape while the river's exit into the sea is still frozen. Consequently, these rivers frustrate human attempts to develop them as sources of irrigation, communication, or cultivation.

In contrast, the most coherent or valuable group of rivers are those found in European Russia. Here, rivers formed a radial pattern of flow with a hub located near present-day Moscow. This pattern played a key role in explaining why Moscow became the centerplace city in modern Russian. From Moscow, Russians had access to the tributaries of the Oka and Volga rivers and were fairly close to the Dnieper and West Dvina. Low portages, and later a canal system, connected all these waterways to Moscow. However, all the rivers north of the Caucasus ice over during winter: the Dniester near Romania remains frozen for two months out of the year, while the Pechora, northeast of Moscow, remains icebound for seven. When these rivers thaw, they flood rapidly due to spring rains that make the volume of water rise dramatically. Hence, all these rivers have very irregular natural patterns that measure their high and low water levels.

The third natural factor, Russia's climate, is a product of continentality, a term that refers to the sheer mass of land that blocks Russia from access to the oceans of the world. Simultaneously, however, Russia is wide open to the Arctic Circle, which sends freezing air blowing south from the North Pole. In the south, mountain ranges such as the Sayan and Altay, the middle Asian Tien Shan, Alay, and Pamir, the Himalayan, and the Caucasus block moist, warm air from the south. The general westerly airstreams blow from the Atlantic across Europe before they reach Russia. These winds make the European half of the Russian countryside far warmer than the Asian portion, but they do not raise temperatures near the comfort level enjoyed by Europe itself. And no airstream enters Russia from the Pacific side of this continental country; consequently, the Asian half of Russia is subject to far colder and drier air than the western, European part. The result is less snowfall in Siberia, but also much colder temperatures.

Furthermore, since Russia does not have direct access to air coming in off any major warm body of water, except for the Black and the Caspian seas, the atmosphere is far dryer than it is in Europe, India, or China. Consequently, Russia receives far less rainfall than does many of its neighbors. In contrast to Russia, all parts of the British Isles receive at least twenty inches of rain per year, with some portions getting far more; one can say the same for at least half of the United States. Only a quarter of Russia, however, receives this amount of rain, while those portions that get as much as forty inches are far smaller than similar regions in Great Britain, and are only a tiny fraction of the equivalent zones in the United States.

Finally, the soils of Russia are either the rocky debris left behind by continental glaciers, permafrost, or the rich and fertile zone of Ukraine, but that, too, suffers from a very short growing season. Thus, while Europe enjoys an eight-to-nine month growing period, the best land in Russia experiences only four-to-six months of fair weather during which farmers can try to produce the food surpluses needed to feed cities.

The best land in Russia stretches from the Caucasus Mountains to Kiev. Often called the black earth district, one can divide this good land into three zones. First, the acreage located on both sides of the Caucasus and around the Crimean Peninsula enjoys temperatures and rainfall similar to southern California or the Corn Belt in the Midwest. A second region, the southern portion of Ukraine, resembles land around Iowa and Nebraska. The third agricultural section, the heartland of Ukraine around Kiev and Kharkov, which is the region that has experienced the longest history of cultivation, is much like North and South Dakota. As one can see, the best land in Russia would be considered marginal acreage when compared to the richer farming districts of the United States.

The Beginning of Russian Civilization

For centuries, wave after wave of nomadic shepherd peoples moved across Central Asia through the steppes of southern Russia as they edged toward Europe, the Middle East, or China. Along what much later became known as the Silk Road, these nomads engaged in patterns either of migration, invasion, or trade as they interacted with established sedentary cultures. Russia itself served as a pathway rather than a stopping point along these nomadic trails until sometime around the eighth century CE.

By 700, Slavic-speaking peoples had moved eastward from the Carpathian Mountains to take up residence on the best agricultural lands of Russia. Choosing sites along the Dnieper, Volkhov, and Volga rivers, these first settlers were primarily hunters and gatherers who also garnered furs, skins, and honey for trade. Later, after developing a semisedentary slash-and-burn style of agriculture, the first Russians began to live in scattered hamlets that supported well-defended permanent trading sites along the European-Russian rivers. The people were an ethnic mixture of Slavs and Scandinavians that took the name *Russians* from the *men of Rus*. Led by Rurik (d. 872), the Scandinavian portion included Norse raiders who settled in Novgorod, founded the first Russian state, and belonged to the same Viking Age that produced communities in Normandy and Great Britain. From these humble beginnings, the modern Russian state slowly started to emerge.

Settled by Oleg, son of Rurik, in 882, Kiev began as the first centerplace city in Russian history because it lay on a strategic site along a bluff overlooking the Dnieper River. Concentrating all the local political, economic, and military power of the region, Kiev became the first cradle of Russian civilization. Soon, Novgorod developed as a rival political center on the Volkhov River to the north. The trade routes between these two Russian cities, and from them to the Byzantine world of Constantinople—along with the expanding Islamic civilization in the Middle East—generated the first flush of surplus wealth enjoyed by this young Slavic culture. Kiev's well-being, however, depended on the relative strength of the various nomadic confederations that used

A medieval Russian Orthodox Church. Basilius Cathedral was built from 1555 to 1560 by Barma and Postnik under Ivan the Terrible. Moscow, Vassili-Blashenny (Basilius Cathedral) on Red Square. 1992 Photo: akg-images, London.

Russia as a thoroughfare for their herds. Destroyed but reconstructed several times, Kiev held sway as the dominant city in early Russian history until the Mongol invasion of the thirteenth century.

Commonly called Tartars, the Mongols who invaded Russia early in the thirteenth century formed the last great nomadic invasion to sweep through Central Asia (mentioned in Chapter Thirteen). Part of a complex assault pattern that began with Genghis Khan (1155–1227) and continued through the lives of his grandsons, Batu, Hulegu, and Kublai Khan, this wave of Mongols captured every major sedentary culture in Eurasia except for India and medieval Europe. Constructed due to the irresistible pressures mounted by this Mongol assault, the three great empires Genghis Khan and his grandsons built stretched from Kiev to Korea and encompassed Persia and Southeast Asia. Those Mongols who followed Batu and overran Russia slaughtered all who resisted them. The result of their onslaught was the destruction of the Kievan state.

Kiev did not recover from this final nomadic invasion, and the center of Russian culture moved north and east. During the Mongol centuries, medieval Russia generated four regional cultures. The first, Great Russia, was centered on the Volga and Oka rivers, where Moscow soon became the dominant city. Second, western Russia, was centered on Ukraine and remained under the control of a greatly diminished Kiev. The third, northern Russia, was centered on Novgorod and escaped the Mongol invasions due to its geographic isolation in the forested north and the overextended reach of Batu Khan's armies. Finally, southern Russia, was a thinly populated region from which people often fled the Mongols to live in the other three Russian sites. Thus, southern Russia lost any chance of gaining a position of cultural leadership during these Mongol years.

Meanwhile, Novgorod survived for more than two centuries after the eclipse of Kiev and was the only part of Russia to remain truly free from Mongol rule. As a commercial center, it expanded its hinterlands (commercial outposts) as far east as the Ural Mountains to provide goods for sale in late medieval Europe (1300–1450). At the same time, Novgorod expanded southward to capture Kiev and eventually reached as far as the Black Sea. As a partner to the Hanseatic League (an association of north European commercial centers), trade generated enough wealth in Novgorod for it to survive incursions mounted by the Teutonic Knights who tried to deny Russia access to the Baltic Sea. Despite Novgorod's commercial successes, however, the soils around this city could not sustain a large enough population to dominate Russia's political future. Control of that future, therefore, eventually fell to the more strategically sited Moscow.

The demise of Kiev, and increasing nomadic pressures from the south, relocated the seat of Russian culture to Moscow. To the refugees from Ukraine, Moscow must have appeared to be considerably less hospitable than the warmer, more fertile, and richer districts found in the black-earth lands they had fled. Still, safety from the Mongols took precedence, and soon these immigrants began to cultivate the thickly forested regions around Moscow. Situated in the strategic hub of the Oka and Volga rivers, these new settlers found compensation in trade opportunities for what they could not cultivate for themselves. Indeed, their new site gave them access to four seas: the White, the Baltic, the Black, and the Caspian, the ports of which made up for the loss of the rich soil of Ukraine.

In the heart of this new strategic location, Moscow developed into a major urban center four centuries after the rise of Kiev and Novgorod. Within a short period, the princes of Moscow had transformed their city into a rallying point for a new Russian state by not only making it the wealthiest urban center in the region, but also by making it the seat of authority for the Russian Orthodox Church. Meanwhile, the Mongols themselves had also contributed to the rise of Moscow by relying on this well-situated city to serve as the administrative center to collect the tribute owed them. Hence, as Mongol power began slowly to wane during the fifteenth century, Moscow rose to become a potential replacement as the cultural leader in northern Russia.

The Mongol Decline and the Rise of Moscovy

For years the great cities of Russia had paid tribute to the Golden Horde, one of three Mongol empires established by Genghis Khan's grandson Batu. From 1236 to 1552, the Mongols had ruled the core lands of Eurasia and had facilitated the movement of commerce along the Silk Road. Ironically, the Mongols had also made possible the diffusion of gunpowder from China to Europe and the Middle East. This movement of potassium nitrate, charcoal, and sulfur helped to neutralize the military advantages enjoyed by the Mongols for centuries. Gunpowder created the basis for cannon that, when concentrated, could destroy cavalry on the battlefield.

Thus, while the Mongols had encouraged trade to support their growing population, they had also caused the transfer of Chinese technology to those Eurasian cultures that eventually would put an end to the Mongol's pastoral way of life. Indeed, they had contributed a significant new weapon to Europe, the Middle East, Russia, and China, one that helped lead to the dawn of the modern age and an era of Eurasian prosperity between 1500 and 1750. Among the recipients of this new military technology was the Duchy of Moscovy.

The Grand Duke of Moscow, Ivan III (1440–1505) began the process of building a new, independent state by capturing and consolidating his hold on the cities of Novgorod, Vyatka, Tver, Yaroslavl, Rostov and the surrounding territories by 1485. Then, in 1480, he repudiated his subordination to Kazan, the capital of the Golden Horde located on the Volga River. Collecting for himself the tribute, formerly sent to the Mongols, from the lands he had taken, Ivan III next replaced the Great Khan as the overlord of the region.

Then Ivan III declared Moscow to be the "third Rome" because Constantinople, the "second Rome," had fallen to the Turks in 1453. By making Moscow the heir of Constantinople and the Roman Empire alike, Ivan III hoped to develop the concept of power behind the title of *czar*, the Russian term for Caesar. This hope he left to his sons and grandsons to promote so that they could later build the political authority he planned for his new state.

Gunpowder had made Ivan III bold enough to break the hold of the Mongols. Yet to maintain the military superiority acquired with cannon, the czars who followed Ivan III had to develop a curious relationship with Europe that marked the next four and a half centuries of Russian history. To support their expanding imperial form of monarchy, these czars had to modernize partially while trying to maintain absolute control over their growing political system.

The Czarist Paradox

Aware of their technical inferiority to European states, and yet intentionally avoiding the general cultural changes that made Europe militarily superior, the czars tried to import new tools from their western neighbors without including the political, social, and economic trappings of modernization. Thus, the czars tried to prevent any changes to the feudal elements of power that supported their expanding regime. Accordingly, the czarist domain gradually evolved into a political paradox: a society that hoped to import the modern features of Western wealth and power without transforming Russia's traditional society.

This new institutional paradox created a dysfunctional link between the European process of modernization and the czar's reliance on a revitalized feudalism. In Europe during the early Modern Era (1500–1750), several parallel revolutions had occurred that had caused a spontaneous pattern of change. Explained in the first half of this unit, this rapid process of cultural transformation included the Commercial Revolution (1492–1763), the Reformation (1517–1648), the Rise of the Territorial State (1494–1689), the Scientific Revolution (1543–1687), and the Enlightenment (1620–1789). Each of these represented a different institutional pattern of change, but all of them tended to reinforce one another as European states evolved from traditional cultures into modern societies. Hence, the wealth generated by the Commercial Revolution tended to sustain the religious warfare of the Reformation, while also supporting the successful institutionalization of sovereignty in such powers as Great Britain and France. The significance of this parallel pattern of change is that the most successful modernizing states in Europe had experienced these parallel revolutions as a process of transformation that would reintegrate their societies into modern nation-states after the French and Industrial revolutions (1789–1815 and 1750–1850 respectively).

In contrast, the czars of Russia sought to embrace certain features of the modernizing process while ignoring the rest. Thus, as Europe allowed the individual to emerge as an independent political, economic, and social agent, the czars actively sought to reduce all their people to the role of passive, obedient subjects. Furthermore, as the czars waxed in power due to modern weapons, they supported a new form of feudalism that actually pulled Russia away from the modernization process. Accordingly, just as Europe was abandoning the feudal distinctions between land and capital, separating an established church from the state, and allowing the formation of public opinion, czarist Russia was reviving the feudal principle of patrimony, spreading serfdom across the Russian landscape, and creating a Russian Orthodox theocracy.

Central to the czars' new form of feudalism was the principle of patrimony, which gave the czars control over all the land in Russia by utilizing the medieval concept of dividing title from the right of possession. Thus, while the czars retained title to all of Russia, they bestowed the possession of the land to those nobles who loyally performed services for the state. This practice allowed the czars to establish a new form of ownership where they would grant lifetime possession of property to a service nobility that they used to replace the *boyars* (the traditional Russian aristocracy who could inherit their estates). Hence, the czars wanted to elevate new men to offices of responsibility to ensure that each Russian monarch held direct control over the state while he tried to eliminate the boyars from government. And at the same time that the czars were creating this service nobility, they also were spreading serfdom as the primary form of agricultural labor in this expanding neofeudal system.

But even as the czars looked back to the concept of feudal agricultural labor, they also hoped to expand their authority by developing modern military technology. Thus, the czars tried to engage in a controlled form of diffusion from the West that would exclude any dangerous ideas that might undermine their expanding neofeudal state. So while the czars hoped to acquire the authority generated by a new royal army, they also denied the possibility of creating a truly functional society.

This odd combination of modern techniques and neofeudal institutions placed Russia on a developmental path that denied it a fully integrated culture. The czars would alter only those conditions of life that enhanced their control over the state. Simultaneously, they insisted on retaining their hold over those traditional features of power that sustained their claims to authority. In short, the czars were willing to trap their people in an oppressive autocracy even as modernization increased the monarch's ability to acquire effective weapons. The first czar to start down this path of paradoxical development was Ivan III's grandson, Ivan IV (1530–84).

Ivan the Terrible

Ivan IV, or Ivan the Terrible (i.e., the Awe-Inspiring), realized that his hold over Russia could not withstand an invasion from the West unless he expanded the structure of power in his Duchy. Beginning by reequipping his military with imported European weapons, Ivan IV turned to the problem of financing the improvements he had in mind. What he hit upon was a revolution from above.

After a period of cooperative reform during which Ivan IV consulted his great nobles (the *boyars*), formulated new laws, encouraged trade, and convened the first *zemski sobor* (the advisory assembly of 1550), he became secretive, suspicious, and vindictive. Ivan IV then turned to a policy of centralization where he seized the land of his great nobles and assigned these estates to a new service nobility loyal to him. To overcome potential palace plots against his new centralizing program, he created a separate realm (*oprichnina*) for himself that he staffed with a black-robed secret service (the *oprichniki*) to fight treason everywhere. Responsible to the ruler alone, this corp of 6,000 men instituted a reign of terror after 1565 that destroyed anyone Ivan imagined to be a threat to his personal authority. Fueled by what appeared to be paranoia, Ivan's raging temper and basic distrust of those around him caused many innocent Russians to die, including most of the people of Novgorod (1570). Although grim, this state of affairs ensured unquestioned obedience to Ivan's will.

Crowned Russia's first czar in 1547, Ivan IV immediately began a program of conquest and expansion that spread his brand of power. He took Kazan in 1552 to end Mongol rule on the steppes. Then his drive to acquire new lands pushed Russia in two directions at once: east toward the Baltic Sea, and west across Central Asia. This expansion created a standard policy of acquiring new territory throughout his reign: Astrakhan fell with Kazan in 1552; he sought to take Livonia on the Baltic Sea in 1558; and he conquered Siberia after 1558. While invading Livonia, however, Ivan came into contact with Swedish and Polish armies. Their military superiority frustrated his efforts but inspired Ivan to accelerate the development of his quasitraditional, quasimodern state.

Ivan's efforts at maintaining an equal military footing with the West focused on the lands he had taken during his reign. In these territories, he instituted a Russian style of serfdom that bound peasants to the land they worked but would never own. This servile form of agricultural labor saw the serfs working the soil to pay both the taxes and the rents that supported Ivan's new state and service nobility. This nobility in turn supported the czar and assured him the financial and human resources he needed to modernize his armies and expand his regime.

Thus, Ivan improved his access to power over his people by creating a system of labor that contradicted the process of modernization he hoped to control. Serfdom reflected a pattern of social development completely contrary to the system of labor evolving in Europe under commercial capitalism. Serfdom denied outright the freedom of choice essential to the inventiveness that made modernization possible. Accordingly, Russian society began to polarize: the relatively few number of people who enhanced the czar's power grew rich, while the rest sank into abject poverty.

Ivan had deliberately mixed modernization with feudalism in his regime. To guarantee agricultural surpluses, the czars who followed Ivan's lead would continue to confine Russian peasants to the land. They would pass laws that extended the restrictions on peasant movement while increasing the demand for the products of agricultural labor. Serfdom ensured regular revenues for the czars, but it also contradicted the social trends needed to establish a modern society. Thus, the social and economic polarization that Ivan set in motion simply grew more intense with each passing year.

When Ivan IV died in 1584, this new political system proved troublesome. The design of the Russian state that Ivan passed to his heirs placed the czar at the top, his nobles next, townspeople and merchants third, and the serfs at the bottom. Without a competent ruler at the top, however, this quasimodern, quasifeudal hierarchy did not work well.

The Time of Troubles

Upon Ivan IV's death, a regency was established to raise two of his young sons, Fredor and Dimitri. Ivan himself had killed his heir apparent (also named Ivan) in a fit of rage that left the throne in the hands of his second son, the child-king Fredor I. Acting as the sole regent, Ivan's favorite advisor, Boris Godunov, tried to seize power.

Godunov controlled the destiny of Ivan's two heirs. Then, the murder of Dimitri, followed by the natural death of Fredor, gave Godunov the chance to try to seize the title of czar for himself. But, as he was accused of Dimitri's murder, Godunov could not win the support he needed to consolidate his hold on the state. Subsequently, the appearance of a false Dimitri in 1604 ended Godunov's reign and allowed the old nobility, the boyars, to reassert their claims to power. Thus, the country quickly decentralized, the military floundered, and Russia stood on the verge of collapse.

The period that followed became known as the time of troubles. Weakness at the center of authority inspired the semisettled Central Asian nomads to rebel. They had chafed under the rule of the foreign czars and now they tried to return to their traditional lifestyle of herding and raiding. In addition, after Ivan IV's death, a surge in Polish power in the name of aggressive Catholicism during the Counter-Reformation threatened to undo Russia's expansion in the Baltic region.

Rather than one of Ivan's relatives rising to save the state, the Russian Orthodox Church became the institution that protected the floundering new regime. The Russian Orthodox Church had taken the Eastern Roman form of Christianity from the Byzantine world and had become part of Ivan III's vision of creating a third Rome in Central Asia. Now the church became a key prop to the czarist regime.

Since Russia found itself threatened in the south by *cossacks* (peasant-soldiers of several Russian provinces who held certain privileges granted by the czar for military service), and Polish armies mounted pressure from the west in the name of Catholicism, the Russian Orthodox Church saved the fledgling new state by becoming a focal point to rally resistance. Townspeople, merchants, and the clergy joined to bind the boyars, Ivan IV's new service nobility, and their serfs to a common cause. Together all six social groups combined to drive the Poles out, defeat the cossacks, reconstitute the czar's office, and defend the Russian Orthodox faith.

The Romanovs

In 1613, the zemski sobor (Ivan IV's advisory assembly) representing the different social and economic groups of Russia combined to choose a new czar. They selected the son of the Patriarch of Moscow, Michael Romanov, who also was Ivan IV's grandnephew, to rally the Russians. Michael represented a resurgence of power at the center that designated the Romanov family as the dynasty to rule Russia. He struck an agreement with his social and political allies that gave some power back to his nobility and allowed both to work together to defend Russia. At the same time, the Russian Orthodox Church joined the czar's regime to create a powerful new theocracy.

Autocracy, however, remained at the heart of the czarist monarchy. After Michael drove out the Poles and captured part of Ukraine, including Kiev, he recovered the stability needed to command the new Russian state. He continued the policy of bonding his peasants to the soil, and he left a well-organized monarchy to his heirs.

His son, Alexis Romanov (reigned 1645–76), continued the policy of creating a new theocracy by purging the church of pagan practices to create a clearly defined dogma, and spread the newly revised faith across the land as part of state policy. Alexis's efforts at purifying Russian Orthodoxy eradicated Mongol practices that had become popular among the general population. This purge required the exile of the so-called "old believers," all those who rejected these reforms, to Siberia, which helped to give that region its reputation as the czar's vast prison.

Furthermore, during the economic recession of 1625–1700 (mentioned in Chapter Seventeen), Alexis Romanov intensified the general pattern of tying peasant labor to the soil. He did so because of the rising expenses caused by his desire to increase his control over the administrative structure of Russia. The cost of these efforts raised the tax burden during the recession and ignited a major cycle of riots in his principle urban centers. To stem the tide of these riots, Alexis convened the zemski sobor in 1649, exiled Boris Morozov, who was Alexis's brother-in-law, tutor, and chief minister until 1648, and hammered out an agreement with his great nobles, the boyars. Issuing the Code of 1649 (*Sobornoye Ulozheniye*), Alexis made all agricultural laborers into serfs in Russia, subject to the absolute will of the nobility. These serfs could be bought or sold along with the land as if they were chattel. In exchange, the great nobles agreed to serve the czar's military and pledged absolute obedience to their ruler. Consequently, the Code of 1649 illustrated the extent to which individual freedom had disappeared in Rus-sia; the code also stood in sharp contrast to the tendency toward social and economic independence developing in northwest Europe. Nevertheless, what Michael and Alexis Romanov set in motion, the next Romanov czar, Alexis's son, Peter the Great, consolidated.

Peter the Great (1682–1725) represented the culmination of the czarist drive to autocracy prior to 1750. Between 1689 and 1725, Peter built the framework of this autocracy on the same paradoxical combination of modernization and neofeudalism begun by Ivan IV. Peter expanded czarist controls over his lands, new and old alike. He also made select changes in the Russian economy to enhance military power. Furthermore, he imitated Europe only in those areas that increased his personal command over technology and political authority.

Intelligent, ruthless, and imposing in his giant six-foot, eight-inch frame, Peter focused solely on those political and military improvements he hoped would make him the equal of Europe's monarchs. Peter streamlined his bureaucracy and altered his military to reflect the latest developments in Western warfare. He also separated his civil service from his military command to refine the efficiency of both while enhancing his personal control. He eliminated representative assemblies wherever they existed and substituted royal, advisory councils in their place. Now, all provincial governors received their assignments directly from St. Petersburg, Peter's new capital on the Baltic Sea, a European flavored city that became the czar's window to the West.

Peter kept the Russian Orthodox Church firmly within the control of the state by making the directory of bishops responsible to the czar. He had legal experts rewrite Russian law so that a single, common system applied evenly throughout his state. He extended the tax structure so that all peasants remained fixed to the soil, paid an increasing share of the tax burden, and responded to the demands of his new bureaucracy to finance his expanding authority. Finally, Peter tried to make certain his nobility remained equal to their European counterparts by requiring of them European dress, hairstyles, education, and state service. Nothing escaped his eye when it came to his development of centralized authority—even to the extent of ordering his nobles to shave their beards, which had been a traditional symbol of their status.

In terms of conquest, Peter concentrated on extending Russia's command over the Baltic Coast in order to expand commercial contacts with Europe. At the same time, he initiated a drive to acquire access to the Black Sea by invading Turkish territory. These two drives to control the Baltic and Black seas became the focus of his military career.

Peter the Great fought the Northern War against Sweden (1700–21), eventually capturing Karelia, Ingermanland, and Livonia. In his struggle with the Turks between 1695 and 1699 and in 1711, and with the Persians between 1721 and 1724, Peter temporarily captured holdings that increased access to both the Caspian and Black seas. Yet these territories were soon lost back to the Turks and Persians. At the same time that Peter fought these protracted wars, all his military efforts tied in closely with his reforms at home.

Russia after 1750

After 1750 Russia displaced the Uzbeks, Afghanis, Persians, Kazaks, Kalmucks, and Ajerbaijani Turks as the leading power in Central Asia. All these Muslim states either fell or retreated before an advancing czar. Such aggressive energy seemed to signal a very strong centralized government. Thus, one could easily confuse Russia with its more powerful neighbors to the west: those European territorial states that soon became nations.

Like Great Britain's acquisition of India between 1750 and 1850, Russia achieved major landmarks in its quest for territorial gains. By 1796, Russia occupied the Baltic coast between Finland and the frontier of Prussia. By 1800, Russia acquired lands to the south that reached all the way from Georgia in the west, to the Aral Sea in the middle, to the Ob River to the east. By 1849, Russia captured the land south of the Aral Sea reaching into the Amu Darya Valley. By 1855, Russia added Finland to its western possessions, reached the frontier of China, and established its borders with Afghanistan and Persia. Much of this southern thrust made Britain very nervous, as the czar's armies approached India. Thus, Persia became a buffer zone between Great Britain and Russia as both vied to control that culture.

This type of expansion, however, masked the underlying contradictions within Russian culture. The czar continued to rely on a domestic policy riddled with conflicting elements. The paradox of neofeudalism and modernization remained in place to benefit the czar's social and economic allies while the people of Russia suffered. The czar's record of expansion against weaker cultures made Russia appear far stronger than it actually was.

The most successful monarch of this post-1750 era was Catherine the Great (reigned 1762–96). As Russia's most celebrated "enlightened despot," Catherine brought to Russia a fresh European political and philosophical outlook. Born a German princess, she

Peter the Great (1672–1725) succeeded a semi-imbecilic brother and overthrew a half sister to become czar from 1682 to 1725. He implemented a policy of Westernization, expansion, and reform to modernize Russia and transform it into a major power. "Peter I" by John Smith, after Sir Godfrey Kneller, 1697–98. National Portrait Gallery, London.

married the ineffectual Peter III (reigned January to June 1762), but Catherine quickly adapted to her new home in Russia. She became a member of the Russian Orthodox Church, learned to speak Russian, and read Russian literature extensively.

Meanwhile, Catherine's husband, Peter III, quickly alienated his Russian subjects. Born the son of Charles Frederick, the dispossessed Duke of Holstein-Gottorp, and Anna Petrovna, Peter the Great's daughter, Peter III inherited the throne of Russia through his aunt, Empress Elizabeth. Completely enamored with Frederick the Great of Prussia, the enemy of Russia during the Seven Years' War (1756–63), Peter III's first act as czar was to take Russia out of this conflict. By abruptly making peace with Prussia, Peter III saved Frederick the Great from almost certain defeat, sacrificed all of the military advantages the Russian armies had won, and excluded Russia from any potential gains it might have achieved by abandoning its allies, France and Austria. Mentally unbalanced, licentious, and, perhaps a bit mentally challenged, Peter III neglected and insulted his wife with outrageous behavior that quickly provided Catherine with the means she needed to overthrow her husband.

Claiming the throne in 1762, after a palace coup and the mysterious death and disappearance of Peter III, Catherine then had to defend her crown against countless pretenders who asserted that they were either the son or daughter of Peter III's aunt, the Empress Elizabeth. The most threatening of these claims came from Emelian Pugachev, who led the great Cossack rebellion of 1773–75 that nearly succeeded in displacing Catherine. To defend herself against such threats, and to win support for her right to rule, Catherine transformed her service nobility into a hereditary class.

Accordingly, over the course of her long reign, Catherine found herself progressively drawn deeper in the debt of the nobility. Since she had acquired her crown through usurpation, she felt she had to elevate these aristocrats to new heights of power to ensure their support; this she did immediately after replacing her husband in 1762. Then she renewed her commitment to the nobility after the chaos caused by the Pugachev rebellion. Finally, she confirmed her alliance with the nobility when she issued the Charter of the Nobility in 1785.

The Charter of the Nobility empowered Russia's aristocrats in numerous ways. First, it legally granted them their rank and hereditary privileges as both inviolate and in perpetuity. Second, it ensured that a nobleman could only be judged by his peers and could not be subjected to corporeal punishment. Third, it bestowed economic benefits on the landlords, which included: buying and selling their villages, as well as the people within them; authorization to sell for a profit all agricultural and manufactured items produced by their peasants; and permission to develop and operate factories as independent economic enterprises on their estates. Finally, the charter created an "Assembly of Nobility" in each province that empowered aristocrats to initiate, debate, and legislate legal matters in local affairs. Thus, the Charter of Nobility confirmed the aristocracy's new authority and made these men of estate the chief bulwark of Catherine's regime.

While Catherine elevated the nobility to new heights of authority, she also eliminated any rights or privileges that Russia's serfs might have still possessed after the reign of Peter the Great. For example, landlords now had literally gained the power of life and death over their peasants. An aristocrat could separate his serfs from their families, order them to go wherever he wished, and even enlist them in the army for twenty-five years of military service. Furthermore, male or female serfs were routinely put up for sale or used in exchanges of property, and female serfs were sexually abused without legal recourse. Thus, while the aristocracy rejoiced at Catherine's generosity, her peasants suffered miserably.

As Catherine cast her lot with the nobility, she also hoped to use the European Enlightenment to educate the aristocracy. Just as her legislative initiatives confirmed the authority of her nobility over their serfs, she also encouraged her aristocrats to read the political and legal philosophies of Cesare Bonesara, Marchese di Beccaria (1729–81) and Charles Louis de Secondat, and Baron de la Brère et de Montesquieu (1689–1755). Catherine hoped to use the benevolent principles of these authors to soften the power she had granted the aristocrats over their peasants.

Just as Catherine hoped to educate her nobility, so she wanted to win a reputation as an enlightened despot. Accordingly, her first successful project as the new ruler of Russia was to develop a code of laws based primarily on Beccaria's *Essay on Crimes and Punishments* and Montesquieu's *L'Esprit des Lois*. The publication in 1768 of her "Instruction," as she called it, secured her reputation as one of the most farsighted monarchs in Europe. In 1766, to prove her sincerity, she called together the Great Commission, a general assembly comprised of 564 members who represented a cross-section of Russian society, except for the serfs and nomads. Catherine encouraged this legislative commission to develop a program to eliminate social, economic, and legal abuses within her realm. While assembled, this body discussed many matters but could not really effect any change because the true seat of Catherine's support, the nobility, wished to maintain the status quo. Since Catherine had to placate the nobility, the primary feature of Russian society in need of reform—the misery suffered by the serfs at the hands of the aristocracy—remained unchecked.

Simultaneously, the second most blatant abuse of power was the autocratic authority that Catherine herself wielded. Because Catherine felt that her security rested on her ability to maintain this authority, she did not intend to relinquish any portion of her command over Russian society. Consequently, every effort at reform by Russia's most enlightened despot soon became nothing more than an insincere enterprise. This was made abundantly clear near the end of her reign when the French Revolution threatened all of Europe's monarchies. Since Catherine perceived that the nature of this revolution derived from enlightened principles, she quickly abandoned pursuing even the appearance of reform based on such ideas.

Thus, over the course of the long reign of Catherine the Great, the initial promise of an enlightened despotism receded as the lust for the use of raw power continued. Catherine could not effect real change because she could not afford to alienate the nobility or surrender any of her authority. Like those of her predecessors, Catherine's rule became ever more deeply mired in the czarist paradox of modernization within a feudal context.

The Liberation of the Serfs

As is evident in Catherine's rule, Russia's underlying weaknesses came from its cumbersome autocracy and the illusion of reform that continued to create heavy taxation and crushing poverty for the vast majority of the Russian people. This general state of misery worsened with each new czar's attempts to change the internal structure of Russian culture during the nineteenth century. Hidden in the czar's policies of reform were new demands placed on the Russian people that exacerbated their misery. One such reform is a classic example: the so-called liberation of the serfs in 1861.

Although serfdom ended in 1861, the former serfs still found themselves trapped by a new set of complex obligations embedded in the reform itself. These new responsibilities were typical of Russia's paradoxical neofeudal modern society. Ironically, just as Czar Alexander II (1855–81) hoped to free his peasants in order to avoid a revolution, he also managed to intensify their misery by placing them in a new social context shrouded in the illusion of liberty.

In this case, their liberation only meant release from service to the Russian nobility. This release, however, did not improve the quality of life in Russia's villages. Peasants did not acquire ownership of the land with their freedom; rather they had to rely on a village council to distribute the number, type, and quality of fields they could use to grow food.

And since the czar did not want his nobility to suffer a loss of income due to the emancipation of agricultural labor, these ex-serfs had to purchase their liberty. But since the vast majority of Russia's peasants could not afford such an expense outright, they made yearly redemption payments. These two features of Russian agriculture after 1861, the village council and redemption payments, combined with the regular tax structure to impose a new burden on peasant life in the midst of their so-called freedom.

Considering the village first, the communal council that allocated land to peasants defined the dynamics of village politics. Typically, rich peasants who could afford to purchase and distribute the greatest supply of vodka during an election dominated these councils. Once in control of the councils, the rich peasants could then regulate village life. In time, the rich peasants came to be what the nineteenth-century social commentator, Anatole Leroy-Beaulieu, and the modern historian, Eric R. Wolf, identified as "mir-eaters," *mir* being the word for village in czarist Russia.

Through their control of the village council, the mir-eaters manipulated land assignments so that the poorest peasants received the least fertile fields. At the same time, the mir-eaters rewarded themselves and their associates by taking the best land. Since a family's yearly income was a reflection of the fertility of their soil, the richest peasants, and their village allies, soon enjoyed the best harvests. With their handsome yearly returns, they both maintained control over the council and continued to farm the best soil.

Two decades after the liberation, the mir-eaters and their associates comprised approximately 20 percent of all the households in Russia villages. This minority had captured control over daily life. With their extra capital, they purchased or rented land from the nobility and expanded their holdings outside the mirs. Next, they hired the poorer peasant families to work these privately controlled fields. Since these poorer peasants needed the extra work to supplement their income, they happily accepted these new assignments.

Between 1877 and 1905, the mir-eaters bought between 60 and 99 percent of all the lands sold by the nobility. Depending on the provinces in which they lived, and the availability of fields for sale, mir-eaters purchased everything that came on the market. At the same time, these rich peasants rented somewhere between 43 and 83 percent of all the land available for lease in these same provinces.

Control of the best fields in the mir, private ownership of the new lands that they had purchased, and cultivation of all the soil they could rent, combined to give mir-eaters sufficient income to live comfortably. They could then pay their redemption fees and meet the czar's increasing tax requirements. But, as their lives improved in terms of material comfort, so did the hardships suffered by their poorer neighbors.

Simultaneously, the tax burden itself also fell on the entire village. Jointly responsible for taxes since 1722, the mir supervised the tax performance of its members. Like the quality of soil on allocated fields, so the revenue burden had to be distributed by tax collectors responsible to the village council. Once again the mir-eaters took advantage of this council to manipulate the amount each family paid.

Poor peasants with no connections to the council received tax allotments disproportionate to the yields of their less fertile fields. What savings they might have earned after they paid their redemption payments now went to satisfy their tax obligations. As a result, the poor peasants found themselves trapped in a living standard that oscillated just above or below subsistence.

In a good year, the poor Russian peasants lived just above subsistence. In a bad year, they went into debt to the mir-eaters whose income increased with the interest on the loans. Once in debt, the poor peasants found themselves bound to the rich peasants' household through a new financial obligation called "debt-peonage" that shackled the debtor to the mir-eater in a manner as binding as the serfdom they had just escaped.

Like the plight of African American sharecroppers who found themselves trapped in debt after the Civil War in the United States, the debt-peonage of the Russian peasants, however, was only one layer among many that ensnared them. These layers included the debt, a mixture of an excessive tax burden plus poor soil allotments assigned by the mir council, the redemption payments to the nobility needed in compensation for the privilege of "liberation," and the unique social environment represented by the mir itself. The term *mir* represented the ideas of both a commune and the universe, that is, the commune was the peasants' universe—the beginning and end of the earth. In contrast, an African American sharecropper owed a debt to an individual landowner whose commitment to racial segregation added to the ex-slaves' burden. In both cases, the legal obligations of financial liability represented a common burden, but the social and political context of the mir differed sharply from the issue of racial segregation.

The mir was a complex social matrix that went beyond the boundaries of the village, the authority of the village council, or the debt the peasant owed the mir-eater. The mir was the peasants' world outside of their respective status in Russian society. The mir was also a collective entity that functioned as the conscience of the community. It not only determined the land allotments and tax responsibilities, but it also reviewed the labor history, moral conduct, and social qualities of its members.

Hence the mir-eaters had gained control of the village conscience, while the capital they accumulated went into private investments to augment the money available in Russia to expand the economy. The czar was pleased with the effects that the liberation of the serfs produced because he now had private investors to help him in his projects of modernizing Russian industry. Yet even with these new investors, the czar expanded the economy so rapidly that he had to borrow capital from France.

What the czar achieved after 1861 was corrosive to the social and economic stability of Russia. First, he increased Russia's foreign debt. Second, he expanded the general tax burden on a peasant population already overloaded. Third, his policies allowed mir-eaters to manipulate village politics to polarize wealth and status on communal farms, which in turn permitted rich peasants to become investors in his economy. Finally, his so-called liberation of the serfs transformed each mir into a microcosm of the miserable state of Russian society in general.

Industry

Even as the mir became a pressure cooker of rural discontent, rapid industrialization added a second hostile population to Russian society. Industry created a highly concentrated collection of workers who lived a marginal existence in urban squalor. The product of an evolving labor pool, these industrial workers differed from the peasantry in one significant way: they could assemble, share their complaints, and create a social network based on rage. As members of the new urban destitute, factory workers spread this rage among themselves as a social group and then joined the more dispersed pool of miserable people throughout the Russian countryside.

Industry began in Russia in the cottages of peasants much as it had in Great Britain. For cottage laborers, industry served as a source of supplemental income for those who needed extra money. More common in regions of infertile land than in the black earth districts where Russia produced most of its wheat and rye, cottage industry emerged in the seventeenth century. This cottage industry then functioned as part of the czar's plan to create a modern, but controlled future.

By the eighteenth century, the number of cottage laborers grew to become a potentially mobile workforce that depended completely on wages for survival. Somewhere between 20 and 33 percent of adult male labor in non–black earth provinces had converted to manufacturing as a means of making a living. The number of these cottagers continued to grow, but serfdom restricted their movement. Hence, factory labor had to wait until 1861 when the liberation of the serfs allowed people to leave their mirs.

Thus, the liberation of the serfs not only created the mir-eater as partners to the czar's pattern of industrial investments, but it also released laborers to move to cities. By 1860, 33 percent of the 800,000 industrial workers in Russia were serfs. Liberation, however, allowed the number of industrial laborers to grow dramatically, as ex-serfs expanded the industrial labor pool to 3 million by 1900.

In 1866 there were 644 factories in Russia employing more than 100 workers. By 1890 that number grew to 951 factories while the average number of workers within the industrial complex expanded as well. More than 40 of these 951 factories employed more than 1,000 workers to reach a total of 62,800, or an average of 1,495 per factory. A second and larger group of 99 factories employed 213,000 workers, or an average of 2,151 workers per factory. The percentage of factories employing more than 1,000 laborers had grown by 27 percent from 1866 to 1890.

Besides this full-time labor force, much of Russia's working population also included peasants who spent part of the year in urban manufacturing. In 1901 about 4.6 million peasant-workers belonged to a part-time migratory labor force. They moved back and forth between their villages and local cities depending on opportunity and the need for extra income. They also tended to work as manual laborers in the textile trades rather than in heavy industry. Finally, they represented a potential labor pool that could allow Russia to expand even faster if the czar could find new sources of capital.

Such economic growth demonstrated the heavy investment in industry made by czarist Russia during the nineteenth century. The poor distribution of wealth, however, meant that the new value created by industrial production went to meet state demand rather than satisfy consumer needs. Railroad construction, steel manufacturing, military supply, and heavy industry in general followed the ambitions of the czar rather than the needs of the Russian people. Hence, the Russian economy grew in such a way that the misery of the Russian people increased without a consumer safety valve to release pressure.

Low consumer income and no significant consumer market denied the possibility of a spontaneous balance between supply and demand to fuel industrialization in Russia. Since the government viewed any effort to organize labor unions to raise wages as a form of treason, neither workers nor peasants could take action to improve their conditions. Thus, the czar and his associates functioned just like mir-eaters themselves but on a national scale.

The Potential for Revolution

Misery and poverty on the mir and in an expanding industrial economy combined with social polarization to foment revolution, with conspiracies against the czar's life becoming commonplace between 1825 and 1917. Assassins, nihilists, professional revolutionaries, Marxists, socialists, populists, and democrats were rife. The czar had to be constantly vigilant to avoid death. His secret police had to rule with an iron hand.

Hence, czarist Russia lacked all signs of the internal coherence of a European nation-state. Although the czar attempted to keep up with Europe in terms of imperial ambitions and industrial development, the czarist paradox infused the Russian regime with a deeply fragmented social fabric. Responding with an intense distrust of his people, the czar refused to assess accurately what needed to be done to heal the fractures within his community. Hence, Russia spiraled toward a major social upheaval while the czar looked upon the subjects merely as a means to his imperial ends.

Consequently the czar reacted violently to any sign of unrest, with any protest, demonstration, or strike becoming a rebellion in his imagination. Despair was so common that spontaneous peasant revolts occurred somewhere in Russia yearly. In effect, the czar ruled a seething mass of potential revolutionaries. In the meantime, he focused all of his attention on imperial expansion, ignoring the internal weakness of his regime.

The ambition for new lands set the czar on a course of violence that ultimately meant self-destruction. A sign of this came when the Russians suffered defeat in the Russo-Japanese war of 1905. Japan's success indicated the degree of modernization this island culture had achieved in only thirty-seven years (1868–1905). Japan's victory also revealed the weaknesses deeply buried in the czar's regime. Furthermore, defeat in the war with Japan, and the massive spontaneous revolution of 1905 that swept through Russia after the conflict, indicated what might happen if the czar did not pay more attention to domestic issues rather than foreign adventure. While the Russian Revolution of 1905 foreshadowed the events of 1917, the last czar, Nicholas II (1894–1917), ignored the lessons buried in his polarized country and continued to support the Russian paradox.

Latin America

Like Russia, the culture developed by Spain in Latin America reflected the paradoxes of a neofeudal system in the modern era. Yet the context for this new colonial world differed sharply from the Russian experience. In the eyes of their European colonizers, all of the people in Latin America—from the top of society to the bottom—existed for only one purpose: to serve the interests of the mother country.

In the seventeenth and eighteenth centuries, the Spanish and Portuguese created massive bureaucracies dedicated to the extraction of wealth from their New World colonies. This treasure, measured principally in gold and silver, but also in tobacco, sugar, cacao, other agricultural products, and hides became both a fabulous resource as well as a perverse obstacle to the economic development of Spain and Portugal. As a fabulous resource, the colonies supplied Spain and Portugal with an immediate inventory of wealth in both specie (i.e., metal for coins) and primary good (i.e., commercial resources generated from the land) that lasted for nearly a century and an half. As a perverse obstacle, this virtually unlimited supply of gold and silver distracted the Spanish and Portuguese from investing their new treasure in domestic economic development and drew them both into extravagant royal display and foreign adventure.

Lavish palaces, government centers, cathedrals, and immense outlays for military adventures absorbed a great deal of the millions of pounds of gold and silver that flowed out of Mexico, Peru, and Brazil. This river of bullion distorted the domestic economies of the Iberian peninsula, encouraged monarchs to spend without regard to the future, and helped provide the ongoing stimulus to Europe's political and economic modernization. This treasure also corrupted the Habsburg administrative system in the colonies, rendering it so inefficient that its successors, the Spanish Bourbons, had to initiate a thorough reform campaign in the eighteenth century.

After the conquest of Mexico by Cortés, a new system for control of land, labor, and tribute gradually took shape in the developing Spanish Empire. Based on Spanish experience from the Caribbean, Cortés assigned his victorious subordinates grants of land and the right to use the labor of its residents in Mexico during the 1520s.

These grants, called *encomiendas* (plantations that belong to the owner only during his lifetime), conferred status and wealth on the *conquistadores*, the veterans of the Spanish conquest. Pizzaro and other captains would do the same in Peru, Chile, and other areas conquered later. The idea was to establish Spanish control over the former Indian empires, consolidate control of the natives as a workforce, and extract tribute from them in labor, precious metals, or agricultural goods. This made Cortés and his men very rich and powerful. It proved disastrous, however, for the native peoples because it exposed them to epidemic diseases and brutal labor conditions. As discussed earlier, Native American populations declined rapidly in the sixteenth century, at times reaching a 90 to 95 percent mortality rate. This alarmed and chagrined Spanish officials who were charged with protecting the king's possessions; it also led to conflict with the conquistadores and their heirs in later decades.

Nearly two centuries after Cortés conquered the Aztec Empire in 1521, European wars forced the Habsburgs to relinquish both Spain and then the Atlantic trade routes to rival powers like Great Britain (see Chapter Seventeen). While Spain controlled these trade routes, gold, silver, and a vast array of agricultural products flowed from colonial ports in Mexico and South America to the Iberian Peninsula.

The first decade of colonization exposed two basic problems for the Spanish monarchs. The first became obvious as Native American communities suffered dev-

Silver mining in New Spain. Slaves from Guinea were used to mine silver and gold for the Spanish. Illustration from "America—Part V" by Theodore de Bry after Benzoni. Shelfmark: C.115.h.2.(5). Copyright © The British Library.

astating population losses. This meant fewer workers for the developing silver mines of Mexico and Peru, as well as for the *haciendas* (plantations that the recipient's family could inherit) and workshops in the new cities. The second issue surfaced when the first colonial officials, the viceroys, or king's representatives, arrived in the Americas to take up their posts and look after the king's interests. Of paramount concern to the Spanish monarchy was "the royal fifth," or the 20 percent of all products generated in the colonies that went directly to the monarch. Conflicts quickly arose between the viceroys and the former soldiers of the conquest, such as Cortés's men in Mexico and Francisco Pizzaro's troops in Peru.

As these disputes became deadly and began to disrupt the flow of wealth to Spain, the Habsburg kings took action. In the second half of the sixteenth century, the monarchs put several new legal codes into effect. What emerged by about 1600 became a blueprint for both the Spanish and Portuguese empires in the New World until the regional revolutions of the early nineteenth century challenged, and then threw off overt European control.

As mentioned in Chapter Seventeen, Spanish possessions in the Americas were divided into administrative units known as vice-royalties. Mexico, officially named New Spain, and Peru, were the largest and most important of these units. Officials sent from Spain governed as viceroys, governors, auditors, and mining supervisors, and in hundreds of other jobs. In Portugal, officials followed the Spanish example, sending a staff of bureaucrats to Brazil to regulate the gold and diamond-mining districts discovered there in the late seventeenth century. In short, the Spanish colonies in the Americas maximized the mercantilist ideal: they supplied precious raw materials for the mother country and then became the best market for European manufactured goods.

Since the colonists needed everything from boots to muskets to iron nails, they became excellent customers. As a bonus, the colonies also became a first-rate employment market for surplus Spanish, Portuguese, French, and Dutch officials. The Netherlands, France, and later Britain obtained colonies in the Caribbean and North America to exploit the growing worldwide demand for sugar and tobacco. Before these European rivals arrived, Spanish viceroys asserted their authority over their ex-soldiers and gradually gained the upper hand. The king stopped the practice of granting encomiendas, and it died out over time. The institution of the hacienda replaced it, becoming most important in the Spanish colonies and generating fortunes in sugar, hides, tobacco, cotton and other products.

Spanish officials later developed methods to assess the effectiveness of their colonial regime, sending auditors and later judges, known as members of the *audiencia*, to their colonies. The audiencia functioned both as a court and an administrative center for accountability within the empire. Both the Portuguese and Spanish kings also retained the right to appoint officials of the Catholic Church to high positions in the colonies. In effect, this gave the king great control over church policy. In the case of a conflict, such as that between Jesuit missionaries and colonial officials over the right to enslave Native Americans for labor purposes, the king sided with his officials and ordered the Jesuits expelled from the Spanish colonies in 1767. Their thirty missions, which sheltered more than 130,000 Native Americans in the Rio de la Plata region (present-day Argentina and Uruguay), were turned over to merchant groups and other missionaries.

Thus, the Iberian colonies were governed by a system filled with redundant, sometimes overlapping, layers of authority—some of which were modern, but most feudal. There were elaborate and cumbersome checks and balances that often stifled creativity and innovation but ensured that wealth flowed back to Europe. Mirroring this economic and political control was another system that defined and regulated labor. This was an elaborate caste system, that divided Latin America and denied the possibility of internal coherence in the future. The Iberian monarchs developed a system of administration to favor the Spanish- and Portuguese-born administrators, merchants, and landowners and place them at the top of a social pyramid that dominated colonial communities.

The privileged European-born individuals from Spain and Portugal, known as *peninsulares*, controlled high offices and occupied the top of the social structure. They became the political elite. Creoles, or the children of European parents born in the Americas, looked to land ownership and commercial ventures for their successes and became the economic elite, but they were second after the peninsulares. When creoles were permitted to buy offices in the 1700s, however, they rose to positions such as viceroys and members of the audi-encias, but they still felt intense rivalry with their social superiors. Mixed-ethnic populations, or *mestizos* (Europeans and Native Americans), third in status, began appearing almost immediately—as soon as European males chose the only available females for wives, Indian women, and produced children who became laborers, artisans, shopkeepers and soldiers in the colonies. At the bottom of the social strata, in places that did not have African slaves, the Native Americans filled most of the menial labor demands during the first two centuries of colonization, both in the mines and on the great haciendas. Below the Native Americans, however, African slaves could occupy an even lower status if they had been imported in large numbers. Parallel to the slave population were *mulattoes* (of mixed European and African parentage) who held a superior status to their African mothers.

Generally, the more European blood one could claim, the higher his or her social and economic standing in the colonial community. However, many of the Native American peoples did not speak Spanish or Portuguese, the languages of power. Meanwhile, as Native Americans gradually acquired biological immunities to diseases such as smallpox—around 1650—their numbers increased and, despite the sometimes brutal labor regimes in the colonies, eventually established substantial populations, which made them more politically significant. Hence, the Americas began to fill with a complex ethnic mix of people and new social hierarchy.

This system adapted to the changing economic and political fortunes and realities throughout the colonial period. Local officials gained more power and autonomy as the Habsburg monarchy decayed and collapsed late in the seventeenth century. When the War of the Spanish Succession ended in 1713, the French Bourbons replaced the Habsburgs and moved to rebuild Spain and its colonies. But years of corruption and inefficiency under the Habsburgs had already eroded both the administration and the flow of wealth from the Americas.

In the 1760s, the third Bourbon ruler of Spain, Charles III, turned his attention to the colonies. He tightened administrative control, reduced mercantile barriers to economic success, raised taxes, and tried to improve the quality of royal officials. His results were mixed and are still debated by historians to this day. One clear result, however, was a growing sense among people in the Spanish colonies from Rio de la Plata to Mexico that Spain hindered the development of its colonies. Yet change was in the air, as democratic revolutions shook the Americas and Europe in the eighteenth century.

In 1775, the first phase of nation-formation in North America began as the thirteen British colonies rose in revolt, ultimately forcing the British to grant independence to a new United States of America by 1783 (see Chapter Twenty-three). A few years later, the French deposed, and then executed, their Bourbon king, ending, at least temporarily, royal rule in France (see Chapter Twenty-two). These two popular revolutions sparked interest throughout Latin America as news spread through books, magazines, and letters, releasing the power of public opinion among the literate colonials. Many educated creoles and mestizos now looked to the new United States as a model for self-rule and economic development.

Perhaps the single most significant event in the long process towards revolution in the Spanish colonies occurred in 1808, when Napoleon Bonaparte, seeking to close off any opening for his British opponents, invaded the Iberian Peninsula, taking control of both Spain and Portugal for the next six years. This era of French rule set off political and social repercussions throughout Latin America.

When the Spanish royal family meekly surrendered its throne, and Napoleon Bonaparte made his brother, Joseph, the new king, creole leaders in the colonies, long disenchanted with the Spanish Empire, led popular movements that demanded the removal of viceroys and other officials throughout Latin America. These movements initiated regional changes that took decades to realize. In Mexico, long-simmering resentment of the power and arrogance of royal officials and their Spanish-born allies started a mass uprising of poor mestizos and Native Americans inspired by Father Miguel Hidalgo, a creole priest. By 1810, forces of liberation also began to develop in Venezuela and Argentina. Revolutionary leaders such as Simón Bolívar ("El Libertador"), Antonio José de Sucre, José de San Martin, and Bernardo O'Higgins (the "Liberator of Chile") led creoles, mestizos and Indians in the battle against Spanish forces trying to preserve Bourbon rule in South America. As the revolutions launched their opening phases, slaves and free blacks often joined as well. The rebels received help from English authorities and experienced both dramatic victories and defeats when Spanish troops reinforced exhausted royal garrisons in 1815 and 1816 after the Bonaparte episode in Spain came to an end.

Napoleon's defeat by the British, Prussians, Austrians, and Russians restored Ferdinand VII to his Spanish throne in 1815. He could have reconciled differences with his colonies by making some concessions to creole demands, continued the Bourbon reforms, and perhaps salvaged his colonial empire for another generation. Yet he chose another path, attempting to destroy the revolutionary movements at home and abroad and impose harsh new controls on the colonies and in Spain. His heavy-handed authoritarianism, however, flew in the face of national ideals inspired by the French Revolution and resulted in 1820 in a revolt that forced him to grant more power to a constitutional government in Spain and to give up any reconquest plans in the Americas for the moment.

Encouraged by Ferdinand's problems, the American revolutionaries won impressive victories and pressed to drive the Spanish from Latin America. San

Martín liberated Argentina and helped drive the Spanish from Chile. Bolívar, after many disappointing reversals, defeated royal troops in Venezuela and Colombia, and finally, Ecuador, by 1821. The only major center of resistance was now Peru, and rebel armies waited in both the north and south, bent on victory.

San Martín struck first, invading Peru and convincing Spanish officials to abandon the capital, Lima. He entered the city to the cheers of its people and proclaimed independence. A large Spanish army, however, remained garrisoned there and threatened the forces of San Martín, who traveled north to meet Bolívar. The two generals decided that Bolívar's larger and better-equipped army could more effectively confront the Spanish, so San Martín withdrew his men and returned to Argentina in 1822. After a year of preparation, Bolívar's forces arrived in Peru and sought out Spanish forces. After several sharp engagements, the last major Spanish command fell at Ayacucho in December of 1824. The South American colonies were now largely free of Spanish authority.

The fighting in Mexico waxed and waned over the decade between 1810 and 1820. At times, peasant armies, enraged by centuries of mistreatment, followed the battle cry of Father Miguel Hidalgo, roaming through central Mexico killing, looting, and burning. Hidalgo gathered support from landless peasants, Native Americans forced to pay tribute three centuries after their conquest and some reform-minded creoles. He issued decrees abolishing slavery and tribute and began to address the issue of land reform. His army, however, lacked discipline and suffered a series of battlefield defeats and desertions. As he fled north to the United States, Hidalgo was captured, tried, and executed. Now the leadership of the revolutionary movement fell to another priest, José María Morelos, a brilliant military commander and social reformer who continued to push for the reforms sought by Hidalgo. By 1814, however, thousands of Spanish troops arrived in Mexico to combat the uprising. Skillful Spanish commanders defeated Morelos' forces and captured the priest. He, too, was tried, condemned, and executed.

After the death of Morelos, the fighting in Mexico continued between small bands of rebels and Spanish troops. This dynamic and ever-changing military situation soon led to massive losses, as haciendas, ranches, and small towns were destroyed by both sides, determined to inflict as much damage as possible. By 1820, weary royalists, military commanders, and rebel leaders sought a way to end the constant fighting. Backed by conservative political leaders, Agustín de Iturbide, a royal officer, offered peace and independence for Mexico to Vicente Guerrero, the main rebel leader. The key to this offer was the fear that the government in Spain might reduce or restrict the rights and privileges of Mexico's conservative upper class in 1820.

Guerrero was reluctant, fearing that the dream of a Mexican republic might slip away. Yet he too despaired of the violence and destruction of the last decade, so he agreed. The combined forces of Iturbide and Guerrero swept the remaining Spanish forces out of Mexico by the end of 1821. In 1822, Iturbide accepted the crown as emperor of Mexico. This regime, however, quickly failed and the country convened a constitutional convention, created a new federal constitution, and elected its first president, the former rebel general Guadalupe Victoria, in 1824. Spanish rule in Mexico had ended.

Meanwhile, the path to independence in Brazil ran much smoother. When the French armies invaded Portugal in 1808, the king, Dom João VI, fled to his American colony, thanks to the intervention of his powerful allies, the British. Eventually making his capital in Rio de Janeiro, João brought new trade, industry, construction and a sense of purpose to the lightly populated colony. Brazil had few connections with the nineteenth-century world of industry, trade, and development. British ships now flocked to Brazil, opening the colony to world trade. The Brazilians reveled in these new circumstances and embraced the Portuguese royal family and its court.

When the defeat of Napoleon cleared the way for João's return, he hesitated. He knew the Brazilians would be angry if he left Rio de Janeiro and, given the revolutionary tide sweeping the Americas, he was reluctant to offer his colony an excuse to become independent. His hand was forced in 1821 when Portuguese political leaders demanded his return.

He sailed home but left his son, Pedro, behind. When Portuguese military officials tried to force his return, Pedro defiantly proclaimed Brazil independent. Pedro had the support of Brazil's landed aristocracy, merchants, and people in the street. His most important ally, however, was the British navy, which effectively blocked Portugal's attempt in 1822 to reconquer its wayward colony. An independent Brazil offered British merchants a pristine market to exploit. Pedro approved a new constitution in 1823 that created a British-style constitutional monarchy, albeit one that conferred on Pedro extraordinary political prerogatives. Thus, Brazil became a monarchy, the only successful example of such a government in the Western Hemisphere. Brazil's constitution guided the country until it was replaced in 1889. Pedro's revolution had been largely bloodless and achieved success in just a few weeks; it stood as a dramatic counterpoint to the prolonged and destructive revolutions throughout Latin America in the years between 1790 and 1826.

In the Caribbean, the Island of Hispaniola produced two independent states, Haiti and Santa Domingo, while all the rest of Europe's holding remained with Spain, Holland, France, and Britain. The Haitian Revolution began as discontent against French rule reached a crisis point during Phase II of the French Revolution (1792–95). In 1791, an abortive attempt at independence was led by Vincent Ogé, a wealthy free mulatto. Toussaint L'Ouverture, a self-educated ex-slave, then formed a guerrilla army and led a revolt that the French could not defeat. L'Ouverture moved into the highlands of Haiti where he could not be uprooted. Meanwhile, in 1795, the Spanish ceded Santo Domingo to France as part of a process that had been set in motion prior to the French Revolution. L'Ouverture then led his forces across Hispaniola and captured the Spanish half of the Island in 1801. In 1802, the new French Regime under Napoleon Bonaparte sent a fresh French army commanded by General Charles Victor Emmanuel Leclerc to deal with L'Ouverture. Leclerc won several victories against L'Ouverture, but could not dislodge the guerrilla leader. Finally, by offering peace, Leclerc tricked L'Ouverture into a meeting where he captured and imprisoned the rebel leader. L'Ouverture died in prison, but his revolt continued, and when war in Europe forced Napoleon to withdraw most of his troops, the guerrilla army of Haiti won independence in 1804. The inability of the African population to form a stable government, however, led to the expulsion of all the Europeans, and civil war in Haiti soon followed. Meanwhile, cultural differences between the Spanish and the French half of Hispaniola led to a partition in 1821.

Yet the newly independent countries of Latin America entered the nineteenth century with significant internal divisions. The social structure imposed by the Spanish and the Portuguese still divided the people of European heritage from their mestizo, mulatto, Native American, and African neighbors. As mentioned, many of these mestizos, mulattos, Native Americans, and Africans did not speak either Spanish or Portuguese. Furthermore, the educational system imposed on Latin America by its colonial rulers had focused on the colleges and universities used to prepare an elite to rule rather than on the elementary schools needed to expose a general population to urban skills such as literacy, computation, and critical thinking, skills required to forge nation-states or participate in forming public opinion and a positive political consensus. Hence, most of the new territorial governments created by the Latin American revolutions lacked the raw human resources necessary for building a popular national consensus that could sustain stable political societies. Therefore, Latin America entered the nineteenth

century vulnerable to internal strife, continued revolutionary change, and external foreign domination. The legacy of a feudal administration, reinforced by a caste-based, ethnically divided status system, created expectations among the creole elite to dominate politics. Hence Latin America remained mired in a feudal past as it entered into the modern era.

Being trapped in this manner with obsolete institutions, the inability to shape a broad positive political consensus, and rigid social system denied Latin America one hundred years of stable government. Instead a cycle of revolutions erupted between members of the creole elite who could not agree on how fast modernization should take place, if at all. Hence, such political weakness laid a foundation for parallel economic weakness and trapped Latin America in an era of financial dependence on Europe (see Unit IV).

Hence, like czarist Russia, Latin America entered the 1800s with a significant neofeudal legacy that helped to shape events for the next one hundred years. A large rural population separated by caste-like status wherein wealth, privilege, education, ethnicity, and opportunity divided an elite from the poor masses, rendered internally polarized states. In addition, exporting primary goods in a global economy controlled by Europeans imposed a system of credit and debt on these new Latin American states that merely exacerbated the already well-established social, ethnic, and economic divisions plaguing them. Hence, instability and violence punctuated Latin America history into the twentieth century.

Suggested Reading

Russia

Alexander, John, T., *Catherine the Great: Life and Legend* (Oxford: Oxford University Press, 1989).

Anderson, M. S., *Peter the Great* (London: Thames and Hudson, 1978).

Blackwell, William, *The Industrialization of Russia*, Third Edition (Wheeling, Ill.: Harlan Davidson, Inc., 1994).

Blum, Jerome, *Lord and Peasant in Russia: From the Ninth Century to the Nineteenth* (Princeton, N.J.: Princeton University Press, 1971).

Bonnell, Victoria, ed., *The Russian Worker: Life and Labor Under the Tsarist Regime* (Berkeley: University of California Press, 1983).

Cartwright, Frederick F., in collaboration with Michael D, Biddiss, *Disease and History* (New York: Dorset Press, 1972).

Dukes, Paul, *The Making of Russian Absolutism, 1613–1801* (London: Longman, 1982).

Fennell, J. L. I., *Ivan the Great of Moscow* (New York: St. Martin's Press, 1961).

Hooson, David, *The Soviet Union: People and Regions* (Berkeley: The University of California Press, 1966).

Raeff, Marc, ed., *Russian Intellectual History* (Atlantic Highlands, N.J.: Humanities Press International, 1986).

Riasanovshy, Nicholas, *A History of Russia*, Fifth Edition (Oxford: Oxford University Press, 1992).

Wolf, Eric, *Peasant Wars in the Twentieth Century* (New York: Harper and Row, 1969).

Latin America

Bethel, Leslie, *The Cambridge History of Latin America*, Vol. IV (Cambridge: Cambridge University Press, 1986.

Graham, Richard, *Britain and the Onset of Modernization in Brazil* (Cambridge: Cambridge University Press, 1968).

Hassig, Ross, *Mexico and the Spanish Conquest* (London: Longman, 1994).

Kandell Jonathon, *La Capital: A History of Mexico City* (New York: Random House, 1988).

Leon-Portillo, Miguel, *The Broken Spears* (Boston: Beacon Press, 1972)

Restall, Matthew, *Seven Myths of the Spanish Conquest* (New York: Oxford University Press, 2004).

Stein, Stanley and Barbara Stein, *The Colonial Heritage of Latin America* (New York: Oxford University Press, 1966).

XXV

INDIA
and China

Normally, one would consider India and China in the same chapter only for the purpose of contrasting two great Asian civilizations: India produced an original Asian culture but failed to create a stable political society. In contrast, China generated arguably the most stable political tradition in world history. The absence of a political center in Indian history not only made it difficult for scholars to chronicle India's past, but it denied the civilization a common language and a coherent society. In contrast, outstanding written primary sources unify the Chinese historical narrative, while a process of Sinification created a common cultural and linguistic tradition and a largely united people who controlled an empire of 3.5 million square miles. Finally, while Indian history is punctuated by invasions in which one foreign regime after another imposed control over the Indian subcontinent, China eventually absorbed its foreign conquerors into the dominate Han community.

Nevertheless, India and China belong to the same chapter in the modern era because both cultures represented vast human numbers that suffered massive foreign intervention from 1800 to 1914 at the hands of imperial Europe. India fell victim to European pressures first because its absence of an effective central government and intense religious conflicts which left it vulnerable to colonization and economic manipulation. China fell victim soon thereafter, when the dynastic cycle that had preserved its political and territorial integrity at the beginning of the modern age began to disintegrate about halfway through the Qing Dynasty (1644–1911), just when Europe had entered its era of nation-building and had tipped the differential of power. Hence, India succumbed to European occupation even before the appearance of the first nation-states and industrialization (1756), while the Chinese lost control of their political destiny after the new European nation-states and their new mass-produced weapons had equipped them with the tools they needed to penetrate China's frontiers (1839).

India

As has been noted throughout this text, Indian history differs from that of all other Eurasian cultures in that religion and not politics dominates the storyline. This is because India did not have a central government to provide the internal coherence that organized other cultures. In the absence of a stable political authority, different, sometimes competing, religions captured the Indian imagination and provided order in the midst of political disarray. The modern era differs only slightly from this general trend in Indian history in that the intolerance by Muslims toward any faith they deemed pagan intensified the level of division in Indian society. In terms of Europe's role in Indian history, the West exploited this religious division, using it as a wedge to penetrate Indian territory.

As mentioned in Chapter Twelve, the Muslim rulers of India had produced only a semistable system of power under the Delhi Sultanate (1206–1526). The first dynasty of the Delhi Sultanate, the Slave Sultans, got their unusual name from the Turkish and Persian slave-soldiers that ran the new Muslim realm in much the same way as the Janissaries had run the Ottoman Empire and the Mamelukes had governed Egypt. As mentioned, slavery was considered the first step to conversion in many Muslim realms. These Slave rulers of India, however, did not have enough Mamelukes to command India with unquestioned authority. Therefore, they had to come to terms with local Hindu rulers and landowners who supplied the men and resources they needed to control the subcontinent.

The easygoing form of Islam practiced by the Turkish-Persian rulers of the Slave Sultans, and the remaining dynasties that made up the Delhi Sultanate, permitted a level of official tolerance by Muslim overlords that was uncommon to Islam, but necessary for political power in India. Some of the lower-caste Hindus converted to Islam because they found the equality of the souls of worshippers among Muslims attractive. But the vast majority of Indians preferred well-established tradition and Hinduism; roughly 25 percent of the people of India were Muslim, while 75 percent remained Hindu.

Meanwhile, court politics created a level of government instability that plagued the Delhi Sultanate throughout its history. Indeed, in the case of the sultans, death by natural causes seemed the exception rather than the rule, with one ruler after another suffering a violent death, often at the hands of an assassin. This feature of sultanate politics left India wide open to invasion.

Baber the Mongol exploited this weakness to win a kingdom in India in 1526. Claiming descent from Tamerlane, who had swept through India in the fourteenth century, Baber declared his right to rule the subcontinent as Tamerlane's heir. Using a relatively small army of 25,000 infantrymen and artillery, he invaded India from his base in Afghanistan. With this small force Baber began a conquest that ultimately resulted in the Mogul Empire (1526–1857). Hence, a far more effective Muslim government took root on the subcontinent.

Close proximity to the Safavid Dynasty of Persia, which practiced the Shia form of Islam, forced Baber and his son Humayun (reigned 1530–56) to be flexible in their religious loyalties. Baber and Humayun moved back and forth between the Shia and Sunni forms of Islam depending on the conditions of power in Persia, Afghanistan, and India. Both men proved to be competent rulers who then passed on to Akbar, Baber's grandson, the means to finally unify India. Akbar (reigned 1556–1605) finished the conquest of India, put the Mogul Empire on a stable footing, and began an era of religious tolerance that allowed the subcontinent to become a harmonious realm.

Satisfied to rule all of India and command only his religious community, Akbar allowed Hinduism to flourish. He also permitted Christian missionaries to visit India as part of Europe's Commercial Revolution (1492–1763). Furthermore, Akbar allowed a level of intellectual experimentation uncommon in most Muslim realms.

Yet such tolerance lasted only the length of Akbar's reign. His successors slowly accepted a stricter form of Sunni Islam that required the absolute obedience of all its subjects. Accordingly, by the time Akbar's grandson Aurangzeb (reigned 1658–1707) came to power, religious tolerance ended abruptly.

Aurangzeb oppressed both his Shiite and Hindi subjects. He injected a level of religious hostility in India that remained intense into the twentieth century. Near the end of Aurangzeb's reign, Hindus formed an underground movement that maintained a level of guerrilla warfare that severely weakened the Moguls. Thus, Aurangzeb was responsible for laying the foundations of a religious division that eventually provided imperial Europe with an opening wedge.

Meanwhile, the religious story in India became even more complex with a major revival of Hinduism in the sixteenth century. As mentioned above, Muslims composed the minority of the Mogul Empire in India, while Hindus made up the majority. Hence, the real issue of political stability focused on how well the Hindus coped with a powerful Muslim dynasty whose growing intolerance introduced antipathy into the social fabric. Since Hinduism is a religion whose disassociation of experience from reality had allowed its adherents to get along with everyone in the past, their easygoing nature did not prepare them to face the passion for purity of Islam expressed among the new Mogul rulers.

After 1565, Akbar's conquest of the subcontinent had eliminated every independent Hindu state. Now Hinduism confronted a threat to its very survival. But instead of disappearing into Islam, as had so many other so-called pagan faiths, Hinduism enjoyed a revival. In the sixteenth century, three inspired individuals, a holy man and two poets, captured the imagination of the Hindu population and prepared it for an increasingly hostile foreign rule.

The holy man was called Chaitanya (d. 1527) whose birth into the Brahman caste placed him at the apex of India's society. While growing up, Chaitanya had several intense mystical experiences that gave him an inner calm. This serenity convinced his followers he was an incarnation of the god Krishna. Offering spiritual guidance in the waning days of the Delhi Sultanate, Chaitanya launched a revival of Hinduism that prepared India for the intolerance imposed by the more powerful Mogul dynasty. Chaitanya's charismatic authority and personal holiness generated a Hindu sect in Bengal that rapidly spread outward.

Hungering for the same mystical awakening as their leader, Chaitanya's followers ignored caste distinctions. Their neglect of the caste system strengthened the appeal of Hinduism over that of Islam to lowborn Indians. Indeed, the tendency among the lower castes to convert to Islam, especially in Bengal, stopped after Chaitanya's influence spread. The warmth of holiness communicated by someone believed to be an incarnation of Krishna profoundly influenced the religious community in India. Chaitanya generated a sense of spirit deeply felt by his followers. This spirituality spread and more than matched the passion of Islam.

Supporting Chaitanya's revival of Hinduism were the poets Sur Das and Tusi Das—the former died in 1563, the latter in 1623. Both created a generation of inspired poetry that communicated stories and images from the epic poems of ancient India, the Mahabharata and the Ramayana (mentioned in Chapter Four). Both poets reconnected Hindus with their past epic poetry. As powerful in the Hindu imagination as was the spread of Protestant Bibles in Reformation Europe (1517–1648), the work of these two poets expanded the power of Hinduism and reinforced this faith throughout India.

All three men gave Hindus a new awareness of their spiritual identity, reminded Hindus who they were, and reconnected India with its ancient heritage. Focusing on Krishna or Rama gave the Indians a center of religious gravity that allowed them to intensify their worship. The vast web of other Hindu gods continued to receive their due, but the god-man connection of Krishna and Rama, generated by these manifestations of a savior incarnation of Vishnu, rejuvenated Hinduism.

Since Krishna and Rama were incarnations of Vishnu, their personal differences were inconsequential. In addition, because Vishnu and Shiva were both savior deities, their divine differences (life versus death and birth, and continuity versus discontinuity, respec-

tively) eroded through their commonality as sources of immediate salvation. Hence, the Hindus were well fortified even as the Moguls moved in, established their rule, and increasingly became more rigid in the religious purity they demanded.

At the same time that the Hindus enjoyed their religious resurgence (1500–1750), a new faith appeared in India whose worshippers were called Sikhs. The Sikhs formed a tiny but intense minority who created their new religion by combining sacred ideas that seemed similar to both Islam and Hinduism, yet the Sikhs did so in a completely original way.

Although many have argued that Islam's monotheism combined with Hinduism's monism to create the Sikh religion, so others have claimed that the new faith was purely an Indian invention. In either case, the unique quality of the Sikh worldview was its ability to unite seemingly opposite beliefs. A *monism* requires that the creator (i.e., one plain of divine existence) and the creation (i.e., another plain of divine being) subsist as one entity throughout eternity. In contrast, a *monotheism* separates the creator from the creation, making the former an omnipresent, omniscient, and omnipotent Deity, and the latter a passive, neutral, and natural medium subject to a Divine will. To have both in one religion requires a unique cosmological perspective.

Beginning in sixteenth century, the Sikhs seemed to have discovered a common ground between monotheism and monism. The founder of the new faith, Nanak (1469–1539) was an original thinker whose religious vision argued for the oneness of God, the brotherhood of humanity, and the need for social charity. He rejected the caste system, advocated the equality of all worshippers, and advanced a sacred vision of the community. Furthermore, his vision of God was multilayered. In one sense, God was ultimately unknowable, without form, and universal, as in a monism. In another

Sikh Nanak (1469–1539). Guru Nanak, the founder of the Sikh religion, is shown engaged in debate with Hindu holy men. From "Rani Jindan's book." Shelfmark: Mss.Panj.D.4. Copyright © The British Library.

sense, however, God granted salvation to humanity through revelations that He had given to chosen gurus who had discovered that He possessed the monotheistic qualities of a gracious, generous, and separate creator. Thus, God was a formless and ineffable Being who also existed as a knowable and personal Deity that made salvation available for anyone willing to open his or her eyes and see.

Those willing to share Nanak's vision of God formed a sacred society that accepted nonviolence as their ultimate moral goal, attracting as converts Hindus and Muslims alike. Yet Islam's opposition to faiths it deemed pagan rejected the possibility of a peaceful relationship with the new Sikh community. After 1658, the degree of hostility between the Muslims and the Sikhs increased exponentially. Within two centuries (1500–1700), the intolerance practiced by the Muslims towards the Sikhs caused this originally pacifist community to transform itself into a militant society. In time, Islam's drive for purity within India alienated both the Sikhs and Hindus, making both groups hostile to the Mogul Empire. Yet the Sikh's complete about-face with regard to pacifism reveals the level of religious divisiveness that had entered Indian society by the end of Aurangzeb's reign.

The Europeans

Because religious intolerance offered Europe a way into Indian society, India was the first regional culture to fall to European imperial aspirations. India seemed to be the ideal candidate for invasion given its long history of political weakness and its new degree of religious intolerance and the resultant infighting. Simultaneously, while the Moguls increased their hostility toward their Hindu and Sikh subjects, they also allowed their military forces to decay severely. As a result, both the Hindu majority and Sikh minority in India had become intensely antagonistic toward their Muslims rulers and welcomed the arrival of European traders—just at the moment Mogul power began to wane.

From the Hindu and Sikh point of view, European merchants were probably easier to get along with than were the Muslims; yet, as mentioned in Chapter Four, in the monistic worldview both Christians and Muslims belonged to Maya, the realm of experience and illusion, and neither had any real impact on the ultimate reality of Brahma (i.e., the creator and the creation). Since Hindus and Sikhs held such a monistic orientation to the world, they could just as easily ignore Christian missionaries as they had Muslim scholars, and since Europeans proved to be distant partners in trade when compared to the immediate political presence of the Moguls, Hindus, and Sikhs were willing to welcome European intervention in their lives.

At the same time, the Moguls had entered an era of profound military weakness. Neither the Moguls nor their Persian neighbors had attempted to maintain the high-quality armies needed to face a foreign foe. In addition, the Europeans had perfected a new level of military potential with their emerging nation-states. Furthermore, the Moguls did not even try to prepare their soldiers for battle as they fielded some of the most poorly equipped, poorly trained, and poorly led armies to face the Europeans after 1750. Even Europe's eighteenth century technology proved superior to what the Moguls could muster forty years before the first nation-state or industry had actually appeared. British officers using Hindu soldiers in the pay of the East India Company (1600–1858), a joint-stock enterprise chartered by Parliament for a monopoly of trade with Asia, discovered they could easily defeat Mogul forces between 1756 and 1763.

Between 1756 and 1763, Europe fought a general war that had international consequences. France, Austria, and Russia engaged Britain and Prussia in combat (mentioned in Chapter Twenty-four with reference to Catherine the Great). Called the Seven Years' War (known as the French and Indian War in U.S. history), Britain chose to focus on international commerce as their principal strategy rather than win victories on the European continent. Aware of France's commercial empire built by Louis XIV's chief Minister of Finance, Jean Baptiste Colbert (1619–1683), Britain's Prime Minister William Pitt, later Lord Chatham, used this strategy to capture Canada, drive France from India, and employ Robert Clive, a former clerk turned military adventurer in the East India Company, to begin the conquest of the Indian subcontinent.

Robert Clive used the Seven Years' War as an opportunity to focus his attention on Bengal. There, the French held a favored position with the local Muslim ruler, Suraja Dowla, who, after ordering the British to leave Calcutta, took some 146 Englishmen as prisoners, confining them in a small windowless room that later became known as "the Black Hole of Calcutta," in which most of the captives died of suffocation within twenty-four hours. Clive, who had not yet departed, cited the brutality of this act, calling it one of native "savagery," to raise the fighting passion of his private army.

Comprised of British regulars and Indian *sepoys* (native mercenaries), this private army welcomed the chance to kill Moguls. Thus, Clive easily defeated Suraja Dowla in the Battle of Plassey in 1757, took command of Bengal, and then placed a puppet ruler on the throne. Britain's control of India had begun.

While Clive captured Bengal, British sea power isolated the remainder of French holdings in India. Naval forces dispatched to India allowed Clive to focus his attention on the principal French strongholds in Madras and Calcutta to eliminate France from India altogether. Simultaneously, British ships blockaded every French commercial outpost around the world.

Britain's strategy worked well. France lost its commercial empire in the Americas and India to the British by 1763. These commercial gains helped Britain's Industrial Revolution by expanding a ready-made international market network that absorbed increased output from British factories. In addition, the defeat of France propelled the French people to expand their criticism of their own monarchy, helping to foment their national revolution.

In India, the defeat of Suraja Dowla by the powerful British demonstrated to other Muslim rulers the need for reform if they wished to continue on their respective thrones. Threatened by Hindus and Sikhs at home, challenged by warlike Afghans to the west, and viewing the newly arrived British as potential rivals, these Muslim rulers chose a policy of accommodation rather than resistance. They turned to England for protection as this emerging nation-state developed a system of indirect rule. The British government allowed actual power to pass into the hands of the East India Company, which parliament placed under the supervision of its cabinet in 1773, while Muslim rulers, now increasingly powerless, at least enjoyed the luxury of their thrones.

The British in turn supported existing states. So long as the East India Company could give advice on policy and receive information on the conditions within each Muslim realm, the British tolerated Mogul puppet rulers. Without firing a shot after 1764, the East India Company maneuvered itself into the role of official protector of India. Hence, Great Britain had created a new policy of using a private company as an arm of the state to convert India into a protectorate rather than a colony.

By 1800, Britain's hold on India increased sufficiently to allow the English to maintain a monopoly of power on the subcontinent. To defend against the threat of invasion during the French Revolution, the British expanded down the east coast of India under the leadership of Richard Colley Wellesley (ruled 1797–1805). Governor General of India, Lord Wellesley used his younger brother Arthur, later the Duke of Wellington, to defeat Tippoo Sahib, Sultan of Mysore. Taking control of the east coast, Lord Wellesley developed command over the most populous provinces in India. In effect, this policy of expansion closed the subcontinent to other European occupiers and trading partners. Af-

ter Lord Wellesley's era, the British were determined to rule in India alone.

For example, in 1818 British troops put down the last bid by the Mahrattas to achieve independence in India. The Mahrattas had risen to power in west and central India to challenge Mogul authority in the eighteenth century. Seeing them as the principal native threat, the British waged several wars against the Mahrattas. After their victory in 1818, Great Britain allowed the surviving Mahratta states, Baroda, Gwalior, and Indore, to continue to exist, but only under the rule of puppet monarchs. Thus, west and central India joined the east coast in this expanding protectorate system.

Between 1839 and 1842, a British army invaded Afghanistan to secure India's northwestern frontier. The Afghanis, however, proved to be tougher frontier neighbors than the British expected. This northwestern zone became a region of constant unrest that shifted back and forth between British and Russian interests, with each foreign power using Afghani representatives to advance their control. Consequently, Afghanistan remained a troubled zone; the East India Company, and later the British Foreign Office, concentrated much of their military resources there to protect India.

Within what remained of the Mogul Empire itself, Muslim princes continued to enjoy a life of luxury at the good graces of the British. At the same time, the Hindu majority and Sikh minority accepted British rule with an indifference typical of their detached worldviews. The combination of these three attitudes allowed the British to command Indian politics. Consequently, so long as the Indian soldiers, the sepoys, remained loyal, the East India Company held sway on the subcontinent in both a private and public capacity.

The sepoys, however, rebelled in 1857–58. They did so for a number of confusing and complex reasons. Many Indians had come to believe the British would withdraw on the centennial celebration of their victory at Plassey (1757). Also, numerous Indian princes feared continued confiscation of their lands and privileges as British rule expanded. Next, the Bengalese sepoys were Brahmans who took offense when Britain annexed the kingdom just east of Bengal called Oudh, their home province. Then, many of the sepoys came to believe that the British had devised a complex plot to convert them to Christianity, one that involved them losing their caste; this occurred whenever Indians soldiers left India through overseas service. Finally, when the British furnished their sepoys with new rifles that used paper cartridges, the Indian soldiers assumed that the cartridges were coated with fat taken from the sacred flesh of cattle to keep the gunpowder dry. This odd combination of cultural fears and insults inspired the Sepoy Rebellion, which swept through India in 1857.

The Sepoy Rebellion erupted at the city of Meerut, in northwest India, where rebel forces tried to capture the town unsuccessfully. Then the rebellion swept through north central India, gained popular support, captured Cawnpore, on the Ganges River, and Delhi, and placed Lucknow, the capital of Oudh, under siege. At Delhi, the rebels proclaimed the Mogul emperor, Bahaduh Shah, sovereign of all India when he appeared to receive their leaders. Among these leaders was Nana Sahib, the rebel who had led a massacre of the British settlement at Cawnpore.

Only the loyalty of the Sikhs, the sepoys in Madras, Bombay, and the Punjab, and the superior organization of British regulars, defeated this broad-based effort to throw off British rule. Nevertheless, defeat of the revolt required a level of brutality that exceeded the terror inspired by the rebels; the captured leaders were tied to the muzzles of cannon to be dispatched. At the same time, this ended the East India Company's tenure on the subcontinent and replaced it with the British Foreign Office as well as brought the Mogul Empire to a close. Now professional civil servants ventured to India to integrate completely the local economy with that of Great Britain in the form of a protectorate.

The Sepoy Rebellion generated numerous changes beyond the mere transfer of authority from a joint-stock company to the British Foreign Office. Mutual fear now fell over the subcontinent, as British soldiers and native Indians squared off under the professional eye of Great Britain's civil service. The British continued to maintain an army staffed by native troops, but the British increased the number of European officials and military personnel to keep a watchful eye on all the natives. As before, the army drew its pay from revenues generated by taxing the Indian population, but eventually the cost of protecting the subcontinent rose to the point where one-third of India's revenue went to the army. Such a financial burden made economic sense from the British point of view because the Indians paid to police themselves, but the native population was hard pressed to meet these expenses.

The Foreign Office also transformed the Indian economy to meet Great Britain's financial needs. British manufactured goods exchanged for India's raw materials and cheap labor set the balance of payments in favor of Great Britain. Removal of Indian tariffs against British goods ensured that cheap industrial production undercut the prices Indian artisans charged for their goods. Those Indians involved in the manufacturing crafts quickly lost their livelihood, as the subcontinent's occupational structure shifted from 24.5 percent arti-

sans in 1750 to 2 percent by 1914. Forced out of business, a multitude of redundant craftspeople joined the growing mass of the native unemployed, even as changes in land tenure also forced small farmers out of agriculture. Then, during the United States' Civil War, when the South's plantation system lost its British markets, the Foreign Office in India encouraged landowners to dedicate acreage to growing cotton instead of food production. Success in these efforts ensured India's place in the British economy but increased the local danger of famine. Then in the 1870s, with a series of droughts, starvation hit the subcontinent and forced many unemployed and starving Indians to migrate to other British colonies to survive.

Finally, the introduction of the railroad into India consolidated Great Britain's hold on the economy of the subcontinent because of the efficiency with which this low-cost, high-bulk, long-distance mode of transportation integrated geographic space. Now, despite the many local ethnic and linguistic subdivisions of Indians, the British had direct access to the entire community. Hence, given this access, and their improvements in military technology after 1860, the British were able to rule the massive and growing native population with a relatively small number of professional soldiers. As a result, India remained firmly within the British system of imperial rule.

Yet, distrust still functioned as a major undercurrent in Indian affairs. The British segregated themselves into defensible communities to ensure that the terror of another native rebellion could not occur. Equality existed as a legal principle, but was not practiced under British rule. The contradictions within the application of raw power in India, and the rise of liberalism in Great Britain's democracy at home, created a moral dilemma for the British civil service that eventually played a role in the rise of Indian opposition to British rule in the twentieth century. But during the nineteenth century, imperial aspirations dominated local affairs. Accordingly, Indians found themselves excluded from social, economic, and political power unless they worked as agents on behalf of the British government, while the European population in India held itself stiffly apart from the native majority. India had become the "jewel in imperial Great Britain's crown," meaning that the vast subcontinent had become firmly locked into the modern imperial system, helping to feed, at its own expense, the global market behind a modern nation-state.

China

In contrast to India's political weakness, China enjoyed two more eras of political unity. The Ming and Qing were China's last two dynasties. They were powerful, prosperous, and long-lasting, each enduring for roughly three centuries. Yet despite their great armies, vast territories, and great wealth, they lacked the vigor and creativity of Tang and Song China. Accordingly, China had lost much of its creative momentum from the middle years of world history.

The founder of Ming Dynasty, Ming Taizu (1328–98), had the humblest of origins. When he was a boy, his home province was devastated by flood. Orphaned and starving, he became a beggar and sought refuge in a Buddhist monastery. He later joined a peasant rebel army, the Red Turbans, and rose through the ranks to the very top. He founded the Ming Dynasty and made Nanjing his capital (his brother later moved it to Beijing).

Ming Taizu had the formidable task of reestablishing Chinese institutions and values after a century of Mongol rule. He promulgated the *Great Book of Ming Law*, which was based on Tang Law. This book strengthened China's traditional system of monarchy and set standards for government operations and social behavior. He also revived the imperial examination system. Exam topics included the interpretation of Confucian classics and solutions to current problems. Those who passed would also be tested for archery, horsemanship, math, and knowledge of the law.

Ming Taizu built a more-centralized government bureaucracy, and he was more despotic than were his predecessors. He concentrated all-important decision-making powers in the emperor's hand by abolishing the position of prime minister, thereby removing checks on the emperor's authority put in place in the Tang Dynasty. He was infamous for his paranoia and massive executions. Even those who had fought with him to found the Ming Dynasty could not escape his persecution. In order to remove potential rivals, he would frame his ministers and generals on charges of disloyalty and then put them to death. He used many of the more barbaric punishments of the Mongol Dynasty, such as caning high officials in open royal court. Other forms of punishment included public execution, death by a thousand cuts, and the execution of entire extended families. He personally controlled secret service agencies that had their own spies and informants, made secret arrests, ran their own jails, used torture, and carried out executions of officials and commoners whom they suspected of disloyalty. In short order, the power of the emperor became absolute.

During the reign of Ming Taizu, it was of vital importance to reinvigorate agriculture after years of neglect and war. He adopted policies to encourage peasants to settle on the land, including rewarding the rec-lamation of deserted farmland, exempting farmers from taxes, providing farm cattle to able-bodied peasants, and relocating powerful southern families to the north and then dividing up their land among farmers. He compiled household and land registries and organized families into the "mutual responsibility system" wherein the group was responsible for an individual's conduct, tax collection, and law enforcement.

Commerce achieved new growth during the Ming Dynasty. The Lower Changjiang River had been the granary of the country during the middle years of world history. But now peasant families increasingly turned to growing cotton, spinning yarn, and weaving cloth; or to growing mulberry trees, raising silkworms, and making silk. Started as a sideline occupation, the cotton and silk textile industries gradually became the region's major employment, with cotton cloth and silk fabric replacing rice as the main products. Both textiles sustained the prosperity that centered on Suzhou.

The producers of these cottage industries could realize an economic benefit only through selling their goods in the marketplace. They also needed to purchase their food and everyday necessities in the same marketplace. Hence, an essentially subsistence economy had now become commercialized, market-oriented and currency-based. Silver soon became the main form of money, and the government began to convert taxes, labor service, and salaries of officials into silver. Thus, instead of exporting grain, the lower Changjiang now had to import rice. In contrast, the middle Changjiang region became China's granary.

Early Ming emperors adopted a foreign policy of peace and friendship with countries to the south that led to a Chinese Age of Discovery. Led by Zheng He's voyages, the Ming emperors created potential trade routes as dramatic as Europe's after 1498. Zheng He (1371–1433) was a Muslim eunuch admiral working for the Ming who went on seven voyages over a period of twenty-eight years to display Ming's wealth, power, and good will. On his first voyage (1405), more than 27,800 people sailed in a fleet of 208 ships. His largest ship was 136 meters long, 56 meters wide, had a displacement of 14,000 tons, and a carrying capacity exceeding 7,000 tons. He set sail from Quanzhou on the southeastern coast of China and crossed the eastern Pacific Ocean, the Indian Ocean, and reached the African continent. He also visited ports of Southeast Asia (in present-day Vietnam, Indonesia, Malaysia, the Philippines, and Thailand), the South Asian subcontinent (today's India and Pakistan), Arab countries in the Middle East (Iran and Saudi Arabia), and Africa's eastern coast (Madagascar, Somalia, and Kenya). Along the way, he offered expensive gifts to local rulers, made friends, and extolled the wealth and power of China and its emperor.

Yet Zheng He's voyages came under fire in the royal court. Opponents argued that the expeditions were costly and served no practical purpose. They also made personal attacks on Zheng, arguing that a eunuch was unfit to command a naval fleet. The emperor decided to cancel further ventures. Later he issued a seclusion order: the coast would henceforth be closed to foreign contact, and Chinese people would be banned from leaving the country and foreigners banned from entering it. As a result, the Chinese under the Ming missed the chance to capture trade in the Indian Ocean before the Portuguese arrived. China had closed it doors to the outside world.

Even though the Song Dynasty had encouraged overseas trade and Zheng He's voyages had been successful, the Ming chose a conservative attitude toward global commerce: China needed nothing from the outside world, and merchants held the lowest status in the Confucian social hierarchy. Accordingly, China's efforts to reach out to the world withered on the vine. The government limited official trade with foreign countries to a minimum while altogether banning private overseas commerce. The policy of exclusion prevailed throughout Ming and Qing dynasties—for roughly six hundred years. The exchange of people, goods, and ideas between China and other countries dwindled to a trickle. Meantime, the West was going through the Commercial Revolution, the Reformation, the Scientific Revolution, the Enlightenment, and laying a foundation for the rise of the nation-state and industry.

Ironically, as the Chinese domestic economy became more commercialized, the demand for foreign trade also grew. This demand naturally collided with the official policy of exclusion. Facing unrelenting government restrictions, merchants eager for the profits from foreign trade turned to smuggling and piracy, a major problem in Ming Dynasty.

Simultaneously, a major intellectual movement began in opposition to the conservative Confucianism imposed by the Ming. A scholar holding the highest degree in the imperial examination system (*jin-shi*), and a bureaucrat in the Ming administration, Wang Yangming (1472–1529) launched a philosophical revolution with his heretical School of Li that posed a serious challenge to the government's hard line on imposing Confucian orthodoxy. Wang taught that whether an idea is true or false should be determined by one's heart and not by Confucian classics, that truth can be found through introspection, and that "knowing is acting and acting is knowing." He rejected the Confucian classics as the foundation for philosophical thinking and replaced them with a foundation of an individual's beliefs. His was an attack on the hierarchical and group-oriented values of Confucianism and offered individualism in its place.

Since it became the state ideology of the Song Dynasty, Confucianism had become stifling, oppressive, and hypocritical. Wang's "doctrine of the heart" freed people from rigid Confucian restraints. Yet it also had a negative influence. Once they had embraced it, many of Wang's followers indulged in empty talk and unchecked fantasy. Scholars prided themselves on not reading and not discussing real issues. Officials prided themselves on their ignorance of matters of state. In carrying individualism to absurd extremes, Wang's followers ignored reality.

While this intellectual debate raged on, the Ming entered the second half of the dynastic cycle. Like the major dynasties before it, the Ming Dynasty, gradually entered a stage of decline. Two major forces finally brought the Ming down: one was peasant rebellion; the other was the Manchus. Li Zicheng (1606–45) led the most important peasant force. Born in Shensi (northwestern China), and raised as a peasant, Li Zicheng worked as a *kuli* (bitter laborer) and lived as a Buddhist monk. While trying to survive, he found himself falsely sentenced to death for an imagined crime against the Ming, but he escaped capture and joined a rebel army. His leadership ability soon elevated him into the top ranks where he commanded a movement that swept through large areas of central China. Eventually, his formidable armies took the Ming capital at Beijing, and the Ming emperor hanged himself to escape capture. Meanwhile, the Manchus in the northeast arose to establish a new regime. The Manchu ruler proclaimed himself the revenuer of the Ming Dynasty, declared war on the rebel leader Li Zicheng, marched his armies across the Great Wall, and captured Beijing from Li's defeated forces.

The Manchus were a partly nomadic, partly agricultural people who originated from Manchuria northeast of China proper. Taking advantage of China's domestic turmoil, the Manchus successfully invaded China and established the Qing Dynasty. Like the Mongols, they were a non-Han people. Unlike the Mongols, they were highly Sinisized. Their rule was as Confucian as any Han (native Chinese) regime before it. The Manchus structured their government on the Ming model, but they were even more autocratic and conservative. They too lacked the creativity of the Tang or Song dynasties.

Since the Manchus made up only 2 percent of the empire's population, these farmer-nomads were very sensitive to any signs of Han nationalistic sentiment. To force the people into total submission, the Manchus massacred and imprisoned large numbers of Han on the slightest pretext. But once they had established firm control over the country, the Manchus brought the Han people into the regime as junior partners. This broadened the regime's base and partially explains how such a tiny minority could rule over such a vast empire for roughly three hundred years.

The first three emperors of the Qing Dynasty (Kangxi, Yongzheng, and Qianlong) ushered in a period of robust economic growth. Much credit for this development goes to new ways of farming, new foods from the Americas, government encouragement of agriculture, and population increase. The government adopted tax policies to reward land reclamation and larger families using a process of internal colonization. Peasants in the south widely adopted double cropping (sowing and reaping rice twice a year) and the use of new, high-yielding crops, such as potatoes and corn introduced from the Western Hemisphere. The increase in grain production, corn, and potatoes fed an ever-growing population. By around 1750, China under Manchu rule was the word's largest, richest, and most populous country.

Yet a population explosion foreshadowed a major crisis. The population more than doubled between 1650 and 1850. During the same period, per capita farmland dropped by half. Consequently, per capita food consumption decreased while food grain prices increased by five times. Whenever natural disasters struck, widespread famine followed. This in turn would lead to massive resistance to paying taxes and rents, while mobs raided granaries.

China's population explosion caused social instability. The White Lotus Society led a peasant rebellion in Central China that involved hundreds of thousands of desperate peasants. The society was a secret religious sect founded to oppose Mongol rule prior to the rise of the Ming Dynasty. Taking its beliefs from Daoism and Buddhism, the White Lotus Society claimed to be able to communicate with the spiritual world. Leaders of the White Lotus also claimed to be able to heal the sick, forecast the future, and perform miracles. Powerful among the powerless, the society attracted peasant followers and focused opposition against the government whenever times were bad. If suppressed, it often paradoxically gained strength, and the society continued to function long after the fall of the Yuan (Mongol) dynasty (1260–1368). During the Qing, it led a rebellion that lasted nine years. By the time the government forces put it down in 1804, however, the Qing had entered its stage of decline.

It is reasonable to speculate that China would have gone through the dynastic cycle of rise and fall and rise again, and the Qing Dynasty would have been replaced by another imperial line, as had happened repeatedly in previous centuries. But now a new and powerful force had shown up on the scene: Western powers had arrived in China, and they would push Chinese history into new directions.

China and the West

The earliest Westerners to go to China were merchants and missionaries. The Italian merchant Marco Polo allegedly visited China during the Yüan Dynasty. The Portuguese reached China in 1514 and received the emperor's permission to establish colonial rule over Macao in 1555. The Italian Jesuit missionary Mateo Ricci (1552–1610) arrived in China in 1582 and was allowed to live and preach in the Ming capital of Beijing in 1600. During Ming and Qing dynasties, no less than five hundred Jesuit missionaries entered China; they had a profound and lasting influence. Through them, the Chinese learned about the achievements of post-Renaissance Europe. Open-minded Chinese would soon be impressed by this foreign civilization and realize that the ancient traditions saw them falling behind other world civilizations. Over time, the Chinese would see Western powers both as aggressors and as models to emulate.

The primary purpose of the Jesuit missionaries was quite naturally the conversion of Chinese to Christianity. Yet their religion was a hard sell, for the Chinese had a highly sophisticated culture and a strong sense of cultural superiority. To make themselves more acceptable, Jesuit missionaries studied the Chinese language and culture until they became masters of Confucian classics. They exchanged their Catholic garb for the scholar's hat and long gown of the Chinese. They also tolerated certain traditional Chinese practices that were in conflict with Catholic teachings, such as ancestor worship and the veneration of Confucius.

Adopting a strategy of working from the top down, the Jesuits first approached the emperor and high officials and worked their way down to the common people. Significantly, they also put their superior command of science and technology at the emperor's service. Their mastery of mathematics, astronomy, metallurgy, calendar making, map making, and cannon casting won them respect among the Chinese elite. Only then did they have limited success in converting a small number of serious followers.

A student of the Jesuits, Xu Guangqi (or Paul Hsu, 1562–1633) was a Confucian scholar and high official in the Ming court. He studied Western science and technology with Mateo Ricci and excelled in mathematics, astronomy, and agricultural technology. He translated Euclid's *Elements* and other works into Chinese, making him China's first translator of European books. He also converted to Christianity. He was the first Chinese person in whom Chinese and Western learning met, and he became a strong proponent for introducing Western learning into China.

But Xu Guangqi was the exception. Overall, the Chinese were interested in Western science and technology but resistant to Western political and social doctrines, which became a pattern. Hence an avenue for the diffusion of modern tenets did not open for the Chinese. This response was the same whether the Western belief system was Christianity, Enlightenment principles, public opinion, communism, democracy, or human rights.

Jesuits who had established their presence in the royal court of the Ming regime were able to win the acceptance of the early Qing emperors as well. In fact, Qing Emperor Kangxi was an ardent student of Western learning. He and his sons studied with Jesuit priests until this relationship sparked internal strife in the Catholic Church in Rome. In what became known as the Rites Controversy, the Jesuits came under fire in their own church for diluting Catholic doctrine in their efforts at winning over Confucian scholar-officials through the Sinification of Catholicism.

To Confucians, the practice of attending annual rituals at the ancestral temple of the clan and at the Confucian Temple was of vital importance. These social functions provided a formal core for the clan and the social class of scholar-officials. The Jesuits accepted these Chinese rituals as a social expression of reverence to their ancestors and to the great teacher-philosopher Confucius. Yet, their rival orders, the Franciscans and Dominicans, accused the Jesuits of tolerating idolatry. The debate eventually involved both the pope and the Chinese emperor. In 1742 the pope issued a bull condemning the Jesuit practice. The emperor wrote back to defend the Jesuits in China. In time, this religious debate developed into a diplomatic and political crisis. Henceforth, the pope would only send missionaries whom he knew the emperor would reject. Accordingly, few educated Chinese would embrace Christianity at the cost of isolating themselves from their extended family and their fellow scholar-officials.

The Franciscan missionaries further damaged the Catholic Church's image with the Chinese emperor. Unlike their Jesuit brethren, the Franciscan friars had come from the Spanish colony of the Philippines, and they approached their missionary tasks by working first among the lower classes. This gave the Chinese government reason to suspect them of having ties with European colonialism and subversive intentions. Now the imperial government began to see things foreign, whether religion or trade, as a threat to imperial rule. The Qing ordered crackdowns on Catholics and restrictions on foreign trade. Catholic influence in China then began a dramatic decline.

In contrast to the missionaries, the government constructed the Guangzhou System (1760–1842) to control foreign merchants. This system funneled all foreign trade through Guangzhou, the farthest port city from Beijing. The emperor appointed an imperial commissioner to oversee foreign trade and granted a monopoly to a merchant guild that paid for the privilege. The guild, known as the Hong, was responsible for handling all trade, providing for foreign traders' needs, and controlling their conduct. Foreign merchants were restricted to living and trading in an area outside the city called the foreign factories. They were banned from entering the city, barred from having contact with local inhabitants, and forbidden to visit the commissioner. Revenues collected from foreign trade were sent directly to the manager of the imperial household.

The Guangzhou System was unsatisfactory to Europeans. For one thing, it was based on the traditional Chinese Tribute System, which assumed foreign envoys were representatives of barbarian lands come to pay homage to the emperor of the Celestial Empire and therefore required to perform the *kaotao* (kowtow) before the imperial throne by prostrating themselves in front of Qing. Trade with the Chinese was seen as a favor the emperor bestowed on the barbarians. Equality between the states and free access to China's markets were out of the question. This arrangement was personally humiliating and commercially harmful to European traders.

The Opium Trade and the Opium Wars

In a strictly commercial sense, trade with China was going badly for Europeans. European markets had a great demand for Chinese goods such as tea, silk, and porcelain. China's agricultural economy, on the other hand, was self-contained and self-sufficient, and government restrictions all but guaranteed that the Chinese market was purchasing precious little from Europe. This left European merchants with an unfavorable balance of trade and forced them to pay for their purchases in gold and silver, something no Western merchant or emerging nation-state wanted.

Then the British found a commodity that would turn the tables on China. They grew opium in India (a British protectorate by 1818) and sold it in China. Thereafter Britain's unfavorable trade balance quickly turned into a favorable one. Now American merchants also entered the opium trade, acquiring their opium from Turkey.

Opium had long been illegal in China, and its importation in large qualities did far more harm than just ruining China's balance of trade. Opium smuggling led to widespread corruption in the government, and the widespread use of opium destroyed the health of peasants, artisans, and soldiers. The outflow of Chinese silver led to higher silver prices. This in turn increased the tax burden of peasants since they had to pay for silver (China's public currency) using copper coins (China's currency for private transactions) in order to pay their taxes. All this created a national crisis.

The emperor sent a special commissioner, Lin Zexu, to Guangzhou to enforce vigorously the ban on opium and the opium trade. Lin warned local and foreign traders before he acted. When foreign traders refused to heed his warnings, he confiscated their large drug supplies, mixed them with lye, then dumped them in the Pearl River. British merchants lost the most opium, and the British government took this incident as a pretext to make war.

But Britain's war goal went far beyond the question of the right to trade in opium. Economically, the British wanted to open up the Chinese market for industrial goods as well as opium. Diplomatically, the British wanted to end its humiliating status in the tribute system; Britain wanted to free its diplomats from

the expected kaotao. Finally, the British intended to subdue the Chinese government because the British had learned, partly from three previous diplomatic missions, that the Qing Dynasty was like a sinking ship; despite China's imposing appearance, it was in decline.

The British launched a series of attacks on China's coastal cities in what became known as the First Opium War (1839–42). Backed by a nation-state, an industrializing home base, superior firearms, steam-powered ships, and sophisticated military training, the British overwhelmed the Chinese forces. Defeated in war, China was forced to sign the Treaty of Nanjing in 1842 on a British warship. In this treaty, the Chinese government agreed to open up ports such as Guangzhou and Shanghai, where British subjects could reside and engage in commerce. In addition, the British government could station diplomats in these ports. Furthermore, the Qing ceded the island of Hong Kong to Britain (later leased for ninety-nine years in 1898), paid heavy reparations, accepted restrictions on import duties, and allowed British merchants to do business with any Chinese merchant in the treaty ports. Although the treaties made no mention of opium, the opium trade became de facto legal and thrived.

The British then followed up the Treaty of Nanjing with a supplemental treaty called the Treaty of Bogue. In this second treaty, the British gained the right to "extraterritoriality," which meant that British nationals in China would not be subject to Chinese criminal law but to British domestic law, administered by the British consul. Another provision gave Britain the right to "the most favored nation status," which is that any concession China granted to another foreign nation would automatically be extended to Great Britain. After the Treaty of Bogue, all Western powers inserted the provision of the most favored nation in their treaties with China. For example, sensing Qing weakness after Britain's recent successes, both France and the United States joined forces and won two treaties of their own in 1844. Both included extraterritoriality, which the United States extended to civil law, and the most favored nation clause. Both new treaties now gave Western powers a common interest and united them at China's expense.

But the unequal treaties totally shattered China's centuries-old policy of exclusion. They reduced the once powerful and arrogant Chinese empire to semicolonial status. China, in addition to losing large expanses of territory and enormous amounts of money, lost its sovereign right to garrison its own ports, control its tariff, and exercise jurisdiction over foreign nation-

Opium Trade Ships. This illustrates the flourishing trade of "Bengal Opium" at its peak in the late nineteenth century. Bengal farms occupied 500 miles of prime land across the Ganges. "Opium fleet descending the Ganges on the way to Calcutta," produced in London, June 24, 1882. Shelfmark: Colindale. Copyright © The British Library

OPIUM FLEET DESCENDING THE GANGES ON THE WAY TO CALCUTTA

als in China. Foreign goods, troops, diplomats, missionaries, educators, and medical doctors would begin to enter China in ever-greater numbers.

Britain and France soon became dissatisfied at China's treaty implementation and joined forces to make war again. In the Second Opium War (1858–60), Anglo-French troops occupied Beijing, killing, burning, looting, and raping. In an act of pure vandalism, they also razed Yuan-ming Yuan, the summer palace in Beijing, to the ground. A few broken walls and cracked pillars now stand at the site of what was once China's "garden of gardens."

Foreign trade increased soon after the end of the Second Opium War and continued growing until the worldwide Great Depression of the 1930s. Tea and silk remained China's main exports; its main import remained opium until 1870, when cotton, textiles, kerosene, and various manufactured goods overtook it.

The intrusion of Western merchants, missionaries, diplomats, and troops shook the foundations of the power structure of traditional China. Overbearing Westerners undermined the authority of the imperial Chinese government. Christianity cast doubt on the orthodoxy of Confucianism. Cheaper and better-made industrial goods destroyed China's traditional self-sufficient agricultural economy. A balanced albeit stagnant society had been thrown into turmoil.

When conflict broke out between Chinese subjects and Westerners and their followers, Western governments would put pressure on the Chinese government to make decisions favoring the latter. The Chinese government would punish local officials for losing control of the situation and order crackdowns on the inhabitants for making trouble. Not surprisingly, most Chinese resented Westerners and their Chinese followers. This sentiment would sometimes erupt into mob action.

The local Chinese gentry would often encourage mob violence because the Chinese followers of Westerners had challenged traditional Chinese authority. In 1870 at Tianjin, just south of Beijing, a mob attacked a French Catholic church, killing ten nuns and eleven other foreigners. Using the Tianjin Incident as an excuse, the French extracted heavy indemnities and more privileges from China. In 1883, the French made war on China when the Qing sent troops into Vietnam, a Chinese protectorate, in a futile attempt to stop the French from creating Indochina (which lasted into the 1950s). During the war, the French attacked China's coastal city of Fuzhou, destroying part of its Western-style dockyards and navy, which, ironically, had been built with French assistance. China was again defeated in this conflict, which became known as the Sino-French War.

China's problems continued to mount as many forces came into play. There would be a declining imperial Manchu government, peasant uprisings and rebellions, and the constant presence of Western powers in China. While the administrators of the Manchu government proved incapable of defending the country against foreign encroachment, other people began to take matters into their own hands.

The Taiping Rebellion

In 1843 a man named Hong Xiou-quan (1814–64) organized the Worship God Society and founded the Heavenly Kingdom (i.e., Taiping), becoming its king in 1851 when he led a successful uprising against the Qing from southern China. Hong Xiou-quan had started out as an impoverished scholar from China's backwaters who had failed in three imperial examinations. Between his second and third attempts, he picked up a Christian tract distributed by Western missionaries. After failing his last examination, he suffered a state of delirium. Waking from it, he claimed he was the brother of Jesus Christ, had met with God in Heaven, and had received orders to return to earth to destroy the Devil and establish heavenly peace in China. In his vision, the Manchu government was the Devil. Later, he threw Western powers into the same category. When he raised the standard of rebellion in 1851, millions of destitute people rallied to his ranks. They were mostly peasants and transport and handicraft workers who had lost their livelihood. He led this loosely organized mass with irresistible force as they roamed the country south of the Changjiang River. He defeated government troops in battle after battle until he eventually arrived at Nanjing and made it his capital. His regime lasted fourteen years.

The religious and political doctrines of the Taiping Movement was a peculiar mix of traditional Chinese peasant utopian ideals and fragments of Christian Old Testament teachings. They included such concepts as common ownership of property and equality, including equality between the sexes and all peoples, even foreigners. When he launched his rebellion, Hong Xiou-quan ordered his followers to sell their property and pool the proceeds in a public coffer. When they were crisscrossing South China in unending combat, they looted government storehouses and dispossessed the rich of their wealth, which they distributed among their followers. As Heavenly Emperor, Hong Xiou-quan also issued a document for the redistribution of land to peasants, but it remained a paper project that was never implemented. After they established themselves in Nanjing, the regime deteriorated into a hierarchic bureaucracy whose upper echelons became totally corrupt.

The Taipings had a peculiar relationship with Western powers, at first seeing them as brethren in Christ. Yet, Western powers took a hostile stance toward the Taipings. The West had a vested interest in the unequal treaties with the Manchu government and had no intention of embracing a rebel force that advocated equality among nations. Instead, the West financed, armed, and organized troops to bolster the teetering Manchu regime and fight the Taipings. But despite Western support, the imperial court was no match for the rebel forces. Three centuries of privilege had destroyed them as a ruling class and a fighting force. Having lost most of South China to the rebels, the Qing realized that they had to enlist the support of the landed gentry of Han ethnicity.

Han landlords had fought valiantly against Manchu conquest at the beginning of Qing Dynasty. But since that time, the majority of the Han had gradually accepted the rule of the totally Sinizised Manchus. Now faced with the choice between the Manchu conquerors and Taiping peasant rebels, the Han realized that they had more in common with the former. The Taiping advocacy of Christianity rather than Confucianism, of land redistribution to peasants, and of equality of all people struck at the foundations of the Han's economic interests and value system. So the Han sided with the Manchu government in the great struggle for survival against the Taiping rebels.

The Han landed gentry were represented by Zeng Guofan (1811–72) and Zuo Zongtang (1812–85), later joined by Li Hongzhang (1823–1901), all prominent officials in the Manchu government. Zeng was the first to organize a militia force in his home province to fight Taiping rebels. This militia was locally based and financed. Zeng's troops, from top generals to lowly foot soldiers, were all connected through family and clan ties. Other Han officials followed his example. They had the backing of the imperial government, received support from Western powers, had some modern weaponry, and enjoyed broad support from the Han population. They became the main force in the war against the Taipings and tipped the balance of power against them.

The Taiping Movement began to lose momentum after establishing its capital in Nanjing. Its leaders indulged in seizing personal wealth and power, internal bickering and intrigue, and killing each other in bloody feuds. Weakened, the Taipings suffered one military defeat after another. Zeng Guofan's troops laid a long siege to the capital and eventually captured it. Hong Xiou-quan died, and the regime ended. Pockets of resistance continued, but they too were eventually wiped out by government troops.

The Taiping Movement was a peasant response to the hardships that descended on them during a time of imperial decline and Western intrusion. The Taipings saw the imperial government as representative of everything the peasants opposed and had made it their primary target of attack. Since Western powers were in collaboration with the Manchu government, the Taipings attacked them as well. Western Christianity influenced the Taipings, but that did not hide the fact that their beliefs and interests were at odds with those of Western powers.

Although defeated, the Taiping Movement had shaken the Manchu regime to its foundations. The imperial government had lost much of its control of the country, not only to foreign powers but also to provincial Han scholar-generals. Han officials, now with their own military and economic bases, would play an increasing role in shaping China's future.

The Self-strengthening Movement, 1860s–1890s

The Self-strengthening Movement was China's first institutional effort at modernization and Westernization. China's ambition was the age-old goal of "enrich the country; strengthen the army." Yet its approach had a unique twist. China would adopt Western arms and technology to bolster traditional values and institutions (i.e., Confucian philosophy, the imperial political system, and the existing system of land ownership). This guiding principle was defined as "Chinese values; Western means."

Led by Han scholar-official-generals such as Zeng Guofan, the Self-strengtheners built arsenals and shipyards with limited success during the Taiping upheaval. After successfully putting down the rebellion, they joined forces with reform-minded Manchu nobles at the imperial court to expand the scope of their reforms. As they continued their efforts at using Western methods to manufacture arms, train troops, and even build a navy, the Self-strengtheners began to branch out into mining, steel smelting, shipping, and building telephone and telegraph offices, railroads, and textile plants. This expansion was necessary partly because industry needed a vast support structure in order to succeed, and partly because there were profits to be gained in commercial manufacturing.

The government policy for running these enterprises was "government supervision; merchant operation." This public-private mix gave the companies the benefit of government investment and business. Yet it also made them vulnerable to government interference and exploitation. The China Merchant Steam Navigation Company, established in 1872, was partly funded by the government and enjoyed a monopoly on the shipment of tax rice. Yet it was also required to provide free transportation for government troops and accept political appointments. Government officials would also frequently withdraw funds from the company. In the end, these enterprises faired poorly because company business needs clashed with the arbitrary decisionmaking of government bureaucrats.

The Self-strengtheners also introduced reform in government. They established a Foreign Office to handle foreign affairs, an imperial customs agency to collect import duties, and schools to teach foreign languages and translate Western books. They even sent Chinese teenagers to the United States to receive an American education. All these reforms, however, were thwarted or defeated because of strong conservative opposition in government.

Japan, China, and New Spheres of Influence

While the Self-strengtheners failed to define modernization in terms acceptable to a conservative but faltering dynasty, the first Sino-Japanese War (1894–95) broke out over Korea, a Chinese protectorate. When Japan sent troops to Korea, China went to war with Japan, but was again defeated. China's armies were forced out of Korea, and its new navy was decimated. In the following peace settlement China turned the island of Taiwan over to Japan (1895). By 1896 Japan had acquired all the privileges Western powers had wrested from China. China's defeat in war and the terms of settlement for peace demonstrated the failure of the Self-strengthening Movement.

Now began a scramble to stake out "spheres of influence" in China. Taking their cue from Japan, foreign powers rushed in to seize concessions where they had railroad rights, reduced tariffs, large leaseholds, control of local jurisdiction, police forces, militia, and stationed troops. Russia acquired Liaodong Peninsula in addition to vast territories to the far north; Germany acquired Shangdong Peninsula; and Britain expanded its control around Hong Kong and Shanghai. The United States was emerging from the Spanish-American War of 1898 and consolidating its position in the Philippines at the time. Unable to project a strong presence in China, the United States declared an open-door policy, proposing equal commercial opportunity for all foreign powers in China. This was a strategy to get something for nothing, for the United States had no sphere of influence to open up to other powers in exchange for such a privilege.

China faced the danger of total disintegration. An alarm sounded throughout the country. Leading Chinese had come to realize that "Chinese values; Western means" was no longer a viable option. In order to survive, China had to begin modernization in fundamental ways. Yet modernization meant some kind of Westernization. Adopting institution from barbarians would be a process fraught with complexity, difficulty, and perils of immense magnitude. Such an assimilation of foreign ideas and practices would be a struggle against China's own traditions, a struggle to choose between competing Western models—most notably the Anglo-American model of capitalism and democracy versus the new Marxist model—and a struggle to decide how far to go. China would be moving through a series of reform and revolutionary movements in the next century. As one movement failed, China would move on to another.

The Imperial Hundred-Day Reform, 1898

One such reform movement began with a talented young scholar named Kang Youwei (1858–1927). Educated in traditional Chinese learning and armed with a smattering of knowledge about the West, he argued that the only way to save China from being carved up by foreign powers was to introduce Western-style reforms. His inspiration was not traditional Chinese models but foreign rulers such as Russia's Czar Peter the Great and Japan's Emperor Meiji. His goal was to set up representative bodies to allow popular participation in government while transforming China's imperial system into a constitutional monarchy.

On the occasion of an imperial examination in Beijing in 1885, Kang Youwei rallied 1,300 candidates to write an open letter to the emperor pleading for reform. Although this letter never reached the emperor, subsequent ones did. A sympathetic Emperor Guangxu (1871–1908) decided to adopt Kang's proposals. In a series of edicts the emperor ordered sweeping reforms. They included eliminating the eight-legged essay in imperial examinations, establishing Western-style schools, banks, railroads, and postal service, encouraging modern enterprises, proposals on matters of state, the writing of new books and the translation of Western texts, and allowing private newspapers and associations. Noticeably absent from his reforms was any mention of a congress or constitution. Yet he could not implement his edicts, for he was only a figurehead. Real power rested in the hands of Empress Dowager Cixi (1835–1908). She engineered a coup d'état, put the emperor under house arrest, and publicly decapitated six high officials who had supported the reforms; Kang Youwei fled the country.

Although this reform movement was short-lived, its impact was significant. Unlike the Self-strengthening Movement, which clung to traditional Chinese values and institutions, the emperor's Hundred Day Reform aimed at systemic modernization. Leading reformers had come to see that Western military might, nation-formation, and mass production were the products of Europe's modern political and economic systems. They also saw that China could not recover the differential of power unless it changed its political, economic, and educational systems. In a flurry of publications, printing houses turned out large numbers of books and periodicals not only on Western science and technology but also on Western political and educational thinking.

The Boxer Rebellion and Foreign Intervention

While reform from the top down had failed, rebellion was percolating from the bottom up, which erupted in the peasant-driven Boxer Rebellion. The name came from the fact that the participants believed that their martial arts had the magic power of protecting them from swords and bullets. Their original goal was to overthrow the Manchu regime and expel the "foreign devils." The Boxers enjoyed widespread popular sympathy because of decades of pent-up resentment against foreign encroachment. The opportunist Empress Dowager Cixi managed to win them over to her side. The Boxers abandoned their earlier goal of overthrowing the Manchu regime and focused on expelling the foreign devils. The Empress Dowager allowed them to enter the city of Beijing, where Chinese imperial forces joined the rebels, declared war on the treaty powers, and laid siege to the legation quarters. Alarmed, eight foreign powers mustered an expeditionary force that captured the capital, lifted the two-month siege, and rescued the foreign nationals. Meanwhile, the Empress Dowager fled her capital.

The failure of the Boxer Rebellion forced the empress to sign the Protocol of 1900 to satisfy the foreign powers. In it, China agreed to huge reparations and the right of foreign powers to maintain permanent military forces in the capital. Although the Boxer Rebellion had produced disastrous consequences, it apparently did stop foreign powers from dismembering China. The Chinese had proven themselves too numerous, too angry, too homogeneous, and too militant to be conquered and occupied like the Indians.

By now, even conservative Chinese leaders were convinced of the need for reform. Empress Dowager

Cixi, under foreign and domestic pressure, now agreed to a series of modern changes. Educational reform began in 1901 with the opening of new Western-style schools that taught new subjects—physics, chemistry, mathematics, and a new, nationalistic version of Chinese history. The new Chinese history would be a vehicle for anti-Western imperialist sentiment. The imperial examination system ended in 1905.

Henceforth, officials would be drawn from "new school" graduates and students returning from overseas. The royal court appointed Yuan Shikai (1859–1916) to organize a New Army based on the Japanese and Western models. Provincial assemblies were formed in 1909 and a consultative assembly at the national level was formed in Beijing in 1910. "Preparations for a constitution" began. Yet, instead of rallying support for the dynasty as intended, these reforms attracted forces opposed to the Manchu Dynasty and foreign powers and became a means to develop revolutionary action.

Cixi's reforms went far beyond the Hundred Day Reforms, but they were too little, too late. In the first decade of the twentieth century, the Manchu regime was rapidly losing its grip on power. Confucianism had become irrelevant to one's career in government after the abolition of the exam system. The most powerful local governors were now Han, not Manchu. The stron-

Empress Dowager Cixi. After the death of Emporer Xianfeng, Cixi, his major concubine, became the powerful and charismatic ruler of the Manchu Qing Dynasty from 1861 until her death in 1908. Cixi / Painting by Hubert Vos, 1905. Photo: akg-images, London.

gest fighting force in the military (the New Army) took command from Han generals and became a hotbed for new thinking. And the political forces in the assemblies had little in common with the Manchu rulers and their foreign supporters. The time was ripe for the total collapse of the Manchu Dynasty and the emergence of a new order.

Accordingly, revolution and not reform would determine China's future. Traditional values had collapsed in the face of European pressures and the desire for the modern tools needed to expel the foreign devils. The West's control over the differential of power had taken its toll on the oldest continuous political system in world history. Hence, even though China faired better than India by not becoming a European protectorate, or being completely dismembered into colonies, the ancient pattern of life that had shaped the Han, Tang, Song, Yuan, Ming, and Qing dynasties had exhausted its capacity to guide the Chinese people. Now modern nation-formation, European technology, and a new national loyalty would have to take an acceptable Chinese form to restore China to the Han people. Now began an era of revolution and world war.

Suggested Reading

India

Bayly, C. A., *Indian Society and the Making of the British Empire* (Cambridge: Cambridge University Press, 1988).

Bearce, G. D., *British Attitudes Towards India, 1784–1858* (Oxford: Oxford University Press, 1961).

Chandra, Bipan, *Nationalism and Colonialism in Modern India* (New Delhi: Orient Longman, 1989).

———, et al., *India's Struggle for Independence 1857–1947* (New Delhi: Penguin Press, 1989).

Ludden, D., *Peasant History in South India* (Princeton, N.J.: Princeton University Press, 1985).

Mason, P., *The Men Who Ruled India*, Revised Edition (New York: Norton, 1985).

Moon, Penderel, *The British Conquest and Dominion of India* (London: Duckworth, 1989).

Moorhouse, Geoffrey, *India Britannica* (London: Harvill, 1983).

Pemble, John, *The Raj, The Indian Mutiny and the Kingdom of Oudh, 1801–59* (Cranbury, N.J.: Associated University Press, 1977).

Raychaudhuri, T., and Ifran Habib, eds., *The Cambridge Economic History of India, Volume One, 1200–1650* (Cambridge: Cambridge University Press, 1982).

Richards, John F., *The Mughal Empire* (Cambridge: Cambridge University Press, 1993).

Rothermund, D., *The Economic History of India* (London: Crown Helm, 1988).

Spears, P., *Twilight of the Mughals* (Cambridge: Cambridge University Press, 1951).

Wolpert, Stanley, *A New History of India* (New York: Oxford University Press, 1982).

China

De Bary, William Theodore, *The Trouble with Confucianism* (Cambridge: Harvard University Press, 1991).

———, William Theodore, Chan Wing-tsit, and Burton Watson, *Sources of Chinese Tradition* (New York: Columbia University Press, 1964).

Elvin, Mark, *The Pattern of the Chinese Past* (Stanford, Calif.: Stanford University Press, 1973).

Gernet, Jacques, *A History of Chinese Civilization*, Second Edition (Cambridge: Cambridge University Press, Reprinted 1999).

Hucker, Charles O., *China's Imperial Past: An Introduction to Chinese History and Culture* (Stanford, Calif: Stanford University Press, 1975).

Lao Tzu, *Tao Te Ching: The Chinese Book of Integrity and the Way,* translated by Victor Mair (New York: Bantam Books, 1990).

Loewe, Michael, *The Pride That Was China* (New York: St. Martin's Press, 1990).

Reichauer, Edwin O., and John K. Fairbanks, *China: Tradition and Transformation,* Revised Edition (Boston: Houghton Mifflin Company, 1989).

Twitchett, Denis, and Michael Loewe, eds., *The Cambridge History of China, Volume One: The Ch'in and Han Empire,* (New York: Cambridge University Press, 1986).

Wei-mung Tu, *Confucian Thought: Selfhood as Creative Transformation* (New York: SUNY Press, 1985).

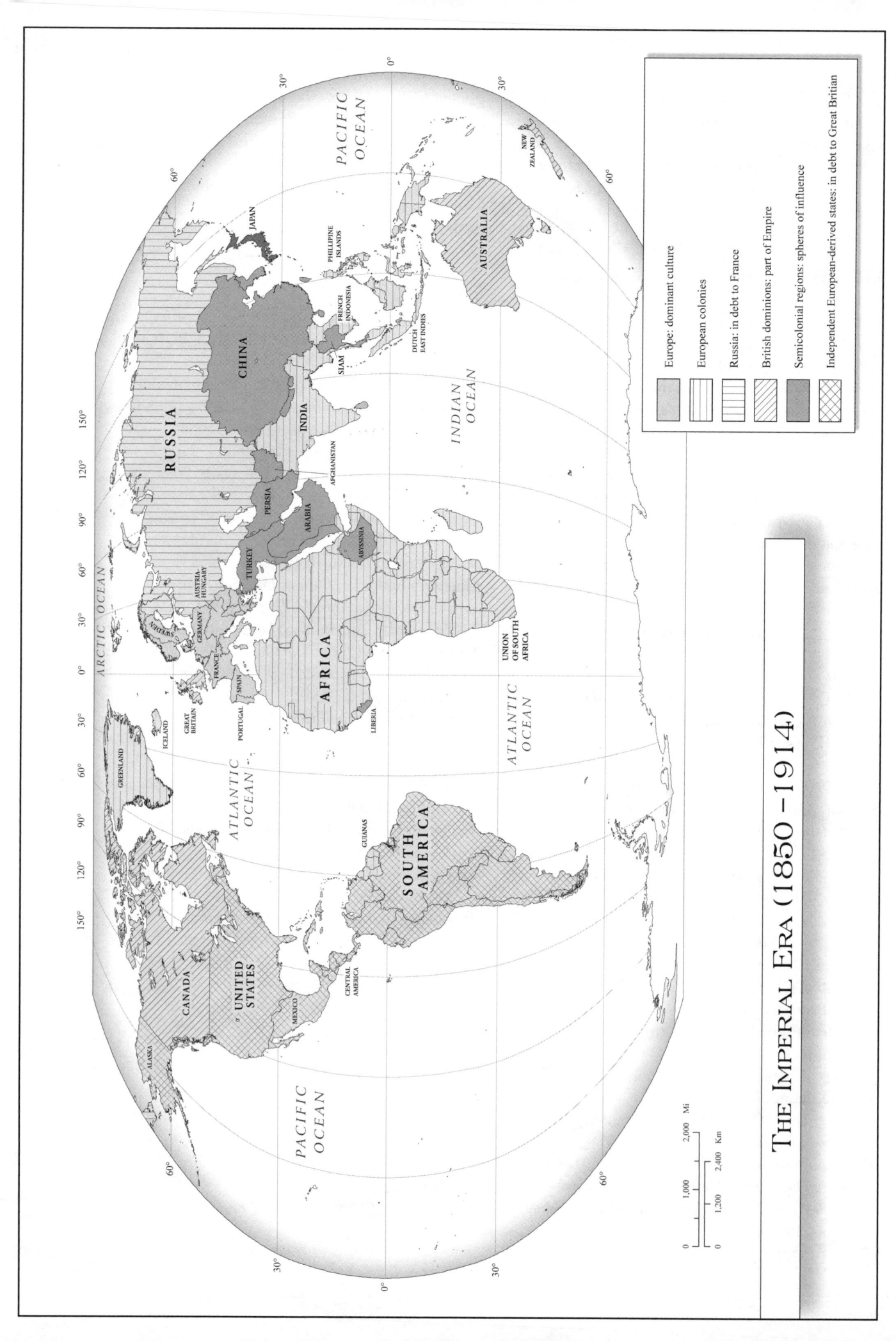

THE IMPERIAL ERA (1850–1914)

Europe: dominant culture

European colonies

Russia: in debt to France

British dominions: part of Empire

Semicolonial regions: spheres of influence

Independent European-derived states: in debt to Great Britian

XXVI

AFRICA
and the Middle East

Africa and the Middle East are discussed here in the same chapter for several reasons. First, these two cultural zones overlap geographically in North Africa because this region belongs to the African continent physically, but to the Middle East culturally. Second, Islam dominated most of the local history of Africa, and the entire history of the Middle East, where the quest for religious and communal purity played a major role. Finally, both cultural zones fell victim to European imperialism for largely the same reasons: Europe held an irresistible command over the differential of power; the continued development and spread of industrial technology in Europe fuelled a quest for new global markets; and the rise of several industrial nation-states, both inside and outside Europe, fed a growing rivalry over who would take the greatest share of the world.

Yet both Africa and the Middle East produced unique local histories that reflected their different reactions to European imperial pressures. The African story entails several unique cultural responses in West-Central Africa, North Africa, East Africa, and South Africa. Each local history combined contradictory impulses; the first, the native answer to the slave trade combined with the second, a new European desire to keep labor within Africa to exploit local resources while honoring new humanitarian ideas generated by the Enlightenment. Also, each of these local histories varied according to new Islamic pressures to purify all regional communities. Furthermore, local events varied according to the degree and length of time African societies had been exposed to a European presence. Finally, each varied according to local living conditions based on food production, commercial agriculture, mining, the potential for famine, disease history, population pressures, migrations, and the rise of new military institutions.

Africa

Africa began to change internally as two new and alien socioeconomic and political forces collided there: the arrival of Europeans from newly formed nation-states and a resurgence of Islamic power. The West waxed stronger than the Muslims in the nineteenth century due to the differential of power, yet Islam provided a revival of intense local resistance to European influences that did not disappear. Meanwhile, Western nation-states combined industrialization with Enlightenment principles to end the slave trade to the Americas. The development of industry and free enterprise argued for an unregulated marketplace where capitalists believed that labor should have the liberty needed to acquire the best working conditions possible. Also Enlightenment thinkers claimed that rational social organization required respect for each human being as a thinking cultural agent. Simultaneously, the resurgence of Islamic power presented a more complex face to the world: Muslim commercial elites still supported the Oriental and internal slave trade, while a renewed drive to create pure Islamic societies generated stubborn opposition to European influences. Suddenly there arose several new contenders for command over the African continent, which created various complex local cultural environments.

European reform movements spread after 1800, as European industry sought cheap labor and raw materials that shifted the focus of commerce from the slave trade to agricultural products. Great Britain led the way, but others eventually followed, because the industrial nation-states saw that a greater supply of wealth could be extracted from Africa if a sufficient number of laborers remained on the continent. Hence, the industrial revolution created an economic hostility to the slave trade among its participants, while Enlightenment ideals provided antislavery sentiments that the rest of a nation's population could support.

Accordingly, political-religious institutions in Africa that had supported the slave trade weakened as two new types of competing elites began to square off concerning the future of slavery. On the one hand, a Europeanized African urban commercial elite joined with Europeans themselves, and returning slaves, to apply revolutionary Enlightenment ideas of liberty, equality, and fraternity to resist the deplorable institution of the slave trade. On the other hand, a new Muslim urban merchant elite proved less amenable to Enlightenment ideas and supported slavery. In fact, this last group became more determined than ever to maintain slaving advantages through a buildup of military and territorial expansion in such kingdoms as the Futa state of Jalon and Yorubaland, where human sacrifice was used perhaps to terrorize male slaves.

West Central Africa

Meanwhile, opposition to merchant elites, whether Western-oriented or Muslim, prompted the rise of Islamic religious leaders in West Central Africa who united peasants and pastoral nomads against their commercial overlords with the new Islamic doctrine called "Islamism." Islamism was critical of both Western and animist African practices—dancing, smoking, ornate dress, and ostentatious living—and united passionate Muslim groups that found solace in a blend of traditional local ancestor worship and rekindled ideas of Islamic justice. As always, the balance of these two broad forces varied from place to place, but their interplay propelled sub-Saharan Africans into new experiments with political organization underpinned by religious fervor.

Islamism triumphed in West Central Africa. One form of Islamic organization was a new state based on jihad (Arabic for struggle at three levels: personal purity, communal harmony, and a true global religion). The most celebrated of these states was the creation of Usuman dan Fodio (1754–1817). In his jihad of 1804 in Hausaland (modern Nigeria), his passion for religious purity swept the countryside to eliminate Western and animist opponents. A Muslim fundamentalist scholar turned political leader, dan Fodio, envisioned a renewal of Islam's medieval caliphate and the recovery of a theocracy in which imams enforced religious simplicity and purity. He counseled that the foundation of government should include five principles: the lack of ambition and the use of consultation, clemency, justice, and good works. Dan Fodio's teachings inspired a jihad that took Hausa territory and founded his first capital city of Sokoto for a modernized caliphate. In its heyday, the Sokoto Caliphate later moved its great capitol to Kano, a city of some 50,000 persons protected by a red mud wall thirty to sixty feet high. Dan Fodio's title was Sultan of the Muslims. Emirs headed the substates, and slaves often staffed the highly centralized bureaucracy and army.

Highly prosperous through trans-Saharan trade of salt, slaves, cattle, and especially the prized glistening indigo fabric (*yan kura*), the Sokoto Caliphate provided the model for several other Muslim reform states. One was the Tokolor Empire that emerged in the mid-nineteenth century near Timbuktu in present-day Mali. A second example occurred south of the Sokoto Caliphate; there the old indigenous slave elite centralized its rule from the Ashanti Kingdom (modern Ghana). The once fragmented gold and slave trades became state monopolies; state bureaucracy replaced the rule of hereditary subchiefs; and a centralized army replaced a force composed of conscripts. With very few exceptions, however, internal dissent, factional squabbling, regressive taxation, and brutal slave raids tore most of these Muslim reform states apart.

North Africa

Given its proximity to Europe, the coast of North Africa was more amenable to modernizing attempts by the West. From the sixteenth through eighteenth centuries, the Ottoman Turks had tried with great difficulty to pull the myriad tribes, clans, associations, guilds, and groups of Africa north of the Sahara into their empire ruled from Istanbul. Constant fighting hindered prosperity and political stability, but it also had the effect of weakening Ottoman control in all the North African states, making them susceptible to Western reformist ideas. The three big Ottoman states of the Barbary Coast—Tunisia, Algeria, and Libya—enjoyed partly autonomous leadership. Morocco had preserved its own Filali Dynasty since 1631. These countries employed the notorious pirates of the Barbary Coast to coax "protection" revenues from Europe and even from the United States of America, which paid Algeria $25,000 annually as "tribute" in exchange for not attacking its merchant vessels.

By the nineteenth century, the proximity of North Africa to the European powers was making the former more vulnerable to foreign interference. In Morocco, Algeria, and Tunisia several African rulers began modernization programs with the financial aid and advice of European experts and companies. These programs resulted in an enormous monetary debt to Western nations, but they also sparked opposition from other Europeans who thought that a weak North Africa would offer greater potential profits. Furthermore, these efforts at modernization brought criticism from the North African local elites who resented foreign European influence. Europe retaliated to native opposition in a sometimes amusing fashion as, for instance, France's concoction of a pretext to invade and occupy Algeria: the Ottoman ruler of Algeria had ignored protocol and hit the French consul with a fly whisk. In the 1870s and 1880s, the French gained indirect hold of Tunisia, and by 1912, Morocco through similar ruses.

Egypt was the one exception to this pattern and a beacon of potential modern change in the region. Ruled by the Ottomans since 1517, patriotic fervor soared under the tutelage of the great Ottoman mercenary commander Mohammed Ali (1805–48). Arriving in Egypt as a *pasha* (representative) of the Ottoman sultan, Mohammed Ali nevertheless harbored dynastic ambitions for himself. He defeated Egypt's local military rulers, the Mamelukes, and enlarged Egypt's borders north to Syria and south into the Sudan.

The army was the backbone of Ali's power, and he sought to modernize and strengthen his forces through reform of all the institutions that supported it. The core of his reformed army was made up of peasant conscripts inducted for life. So horrendous was this service, it was said that families of young men would intentionally maim their boys to keep them out of the military. Over half the state budget went to the army, prompting an overhaul of agriculture.

Mohammed Ali introduced perennial irrigation, ending thousands of years of reliance on the annual flood-basin irrigation. He built up weapons industries and replaced rice and sugar with cotton on Egyptian government–regulated textile plantations, worked by thousands of Sudanese slaves. He cut tax privileges for the military, nobility, and even the peasantry. He expanded schools whose curriculum was limited to state needs, especially the military and industrial requirements. His improved health services lowered death rates, and the population grew.

Ultimately, however, Egypt's modernization came to a halt through pressure from Great Britain, which wanted Egypt to import more British goods and reduce its military investments. Furthermore, the British and the French opposed Mohammed Ali's political ambitions because his military campaigns in the Sudan, the Levant, Arabia, and Greece revealed his desire to make Egypt a leading power in the Eastern Mediterranean.

His military actions both for and against the sultan exposed Mohammed Ali's long-range goals and alerted Europe to his military strength. Fighting for the sultan against Greek rebels in their war of liberation (1822–28), Mohammed Ali's successes prompted a combined British, French, and Russian naval action at Navarino (1827) that destroyed the Egyptian navy. Furthermore, Mohammed Ali's invasion of Syria (1831–33), and his defeat of the sultan at Nizip (1839), incited a British and French intervention to cut his entire military program short. Neither Britain nor France wanted a strong ruler in the eastern Mediterranean because that would complicate their imperial ambitions in both Africa and the Middle East. Thus, by 1850, Great Britain undercut Mohammed Ali's military ambitions and created economic stagnation in Egypt that forced Egyptians to resort to exporting mainly raw materials like most other African states. This fit Europe's industrial needs best, and ensured that Egypt's future weakness would allow Great Britain to occupy that country.

East Africa

In East Africa, after the abolition of the Occidental slave trade, a power vacuum, a new cast of players, and new products emerged in a changing economy. The European middle class's demand for luxury items like ivory for piano keys, chess pieces, and billiard balls made big-game hunting highly profitable. Lubricants required for European industrialization encouraged exploitation of palm groves. Simultaneously, reactionary slave states intensified their efforts to find new human supplies and new customers for their slave trade.

The East African interior was a cauldron of seething conflict among various groups. Regional warlords like Tippu Tip or Mirambo, empowered by newly acquired European firearms, competed for dominance. With armies of slave-soldiers and young mercenaries who grew up playing games of "traders and slaves," merchant-states like Shaba became mired in tribal warfare. Others, such as Rwanda, the most populous area, were caught up in an endless cycle of attack and revenge. The pastoral nomad Tutsi King, Kigeri Rwabugiri (reigned 1860–95), exploited disunity due to population pressure and competition for land among the Hutus, and attacked with Tutsi armies, forcing the Hutus to pay tribute, while the Masai fought both the Tutsis and the Hutus in the Rift Valley. Devout Muslims, usually Fulani, pastoralists of Northern Hausa, followed the example of the jihad reform movements and in particular the Sokoto Caliphate to set up uncompromising theocracies to try to keep the peace. Echoes of this strife are seen in modern-day East Africa, such as in Eritrea, Rwanda, Somalia, and Sudan. On the other hand, Ethiopian leaders like Menelik II around 1850 managed to establish viable and progressive states with Western aid and advice.

On the east African coasts, the great trade towns such as Kilwa and Mombasa were beehives of activity—ivory and slaves arrived via human porters from the desert and rain forests, and immigrants and merchants from India and Arabia exchanged cloth and firearms. A distinctive Swahili (African and Arab coastal) culture remained very strong. The nearby island of Zanzibar provided the world with cloves, and the resultant prosperity led Arab Sultan Sayyid Said of Oman

Shaka Zulu. This is the only known drawing of King Shaka, the dominant and driven Zulu leader, shown standing with a long throwing assegai, which contrasted with his famous short stabbing weapon, and heavy shield in 1824. It is possibly the most accurate likeness of the chieftain.

to move to the island about 1830 to dominate better its emergent commercial empire.

South Africa

In South Africa, a long history of European colonization plus expanding African military societies created a volatile mix. The great trading empires headed by Islamic elites in west and central Africa had not reached so far south. Most of the European population had been Dutch cattlemen and ranchers (Boers), descendents of the Dutch colony that had taken over from the Portuguese in 1652. Right after 1800 British commercial traders began to swarm into Cape Colony, which became a British possession in 1841, as much to protect the sealanes past the tip of Africa as to exploit wine and wool production. The British brought with them eighteenth-century liberal ideas ("Cape Liberalism") such as abolition of slavery and began enforcing them, though halfheartedly at first. Instead of leading to a more just society, these innovations first caused confusion and conflict. For one thing, the Dutch Boers (Afrikaners) resented emancipation, needing slaves to run their sprawling ranches. To escape British interference, the Boers took their wagons on their Great Trek inland, eventually claiming and lightly settling two regions they called the Transvaal and the Orange Free State. Meanwhile, in the two British areas of Cape Colony and Natal, a minority of whites were trying to accommodate the newly freed and enfranchised black and Indian population, who otherwise were uneducated, unskilled, and impoverished.

While this British-Dutch struggle ensued, the inland ranges towards which the Dutch were heading were rife with embattled Zulu tribes. The period itself is designated the *mfecane* (crushing/scattering) era. Zululand, comprising well-watered grazing areas between Drakensburg and the sea, had supported a growing pastoral population for three hundred years. Now the Zulu population, facing droughts and the Dutch, erupted into major tribal warfare frequently led by Shaka Zulu.

The son of a minor chief, Shaka Zulu (1786–1828) rose to power based on a combination of personal charisma and brutality that made him legendary. Alert to the influential ideas of his time, Shaka was intent on unifying all the Zulu tribes into a militant state. Glorying in his reputation as an exceptionally disciplined, rigorous, and violent man, Shaka was not unlike his more ruthless European contemporaries, Napoleon of France or Bismarck of Prussia. One of the world's great military leaders, innovative in strategy (such as the renowned tactic of the "bulls' horns"), and weaponry (the short stabbing spear) and merciless towards the defeated, Shaka Zulu organized half a million Zulus into the Sparta of Africa. After his death at the hands of a brother, his vision of a regimented military state continued to inspire neighboring African leaders.

Shaka's martial response to intra-African-European competition was not the only possible one. An admirable king, Moshoeshoe (1786–1870) of Zululand in the Sotho-Tswana tribal area created the Lesotho mountain kingdom. Moshoeshoe followed the "big man" model of rule, building clientage through marriage, redistribution, lending of goods, and personal relationships. He was described as pleasant and intelligent, noble and assured, with "a smile of great good will." Broad-minded, diplomatic, and embracing, Moshoeshoe was a man of peace.

As the nineteenth century progressed, Europeans in South Africa got richer through the progressive monopolization of the most prosperous businesses in Africa, while independent black entrepreneurs sank into servant status. Segregation in hospitals, churches, and schools grew, justified by articulate white racists like the British entrepreneur Cecil Rhodes, who dreamed of an Africa "all British from Cape to Cairo." Two events associated with Cecil Rhodes, which accelerated all the trends of taking African land, were the discovery of diamonds in 1867 and the discovery of gold in 1886 in South Africa. Africans and Europeans of all classes poured into the newly opened diamond fields for the first few years. Yet, led by the British, Europeans forced out most native owners, who ended as a low-paid and highly constrained labor forces. In diamond mining, whites earned five times as much as blacks. By the late 1880s, Rhodes-Barney-Barnato had maneuvered to control 90 percent of the diamond mines through the De Beers Company. The gold mines were similarly monopolized, to the anger of native Africans as well as the Dutch Afrikaners. Toward the end of the century, the British fought the Afrikaners with a ruthless disregard for human rights. Ironically, though, it was Englishmen and their Boer counterparts whose arguments and armaments made and kept relative "peace" in South Africa.

European Ambitions

Changes in the differential of power made Europe's presence in Africa irresistible after 1880. New medicines and germ theory eliminated Africa's age-old disease barrier against foreign immigration. The steamboat defeated the currents of Africa's rivers and opened the interior. The rifle, machine-gun, and cannon destroyed concentrated resistance from native populations, such as those offered by the new states founded on Islamism. Nationalism, race, and a nation-in-arms mobilized European countries with a desire to carve up African real estate, while competing with one another for new colonies. And the quest for new markets to absorb growing European inventories of mass-produced manufactured items in exchange for raw materials and cheap labor provided the economic incentives needed to mobilize these medical and military resources of each new nation-state to take as much of the African continent as possible for itself.

By the 1870s, however, most of Africa still remained in the hands of Africans—West and Central African Islamic reform or jihad states, North African heirs of the waning Ottoman Empire, East African Swahili trade states, and southern African military states. Despite their attempted influence, foreigners controlled only about 10 percent of the continent: Ottoman representatives in North Africa, the French in Algeria, the Sultan of Oman on the Island of Zanzibar, Dutch Afrikaners and British in the south, and a scattering of traders, missionaries, and soldiers of fortune everywhere. Europeans, in particular, wanted more and were ready to grab it.

Imperialist motives were mixed, partly unconscious, and dynamic. European nationalism and liberalism had fostered a new can-do attitude, an arrogant sense of racial superiority and destiny in an unknown world of mystery and promise. Africa was not that attractive to Europeans at first because of the forbidding Sahara Desert and claustrophobic rain forests. Yet Africa's resources—gold, ivory, palm oil, rubber, diamonds, and cheap labor—as well as its markets, beckoned. Christian and humanitarian activists saw unparalleled opportunities for "improving the world" by saving souls. Technophiles envisioned trains, roads, and bridges linking imposing new cities. Explorers wondered exactly where the Nile River began, just how high Mt. Kilimanjaro was, and where the legendary city of Timbuktu might be located. Hunters and zookeepers eyed the teeming wildlife. Political strategists and military leaders targeted potential ports and military posts.

The European scramble for Africa intensified in the 1880s, with powerful nation-states beginning to move inland from coastal Africa and coming into conflict with each other. King Leopold II of Belgium, in cooperation with the British explorer Henry Stanley,

The Kimberley Diamond Mine, South Africa. Known as "Big Hole" the De Beers mine owned by Cecil Rhodes is the largest man-made mine of the nineteenth century, dug only with picks and shovels. Long ropes reach down to hundreds of separate claims, hauling up rawhide buckets of diamond-laden soil to the surface. This photo was taken during the height of the diamond rush, around 1872–73. De Beers Images.

moved towards the Kongo River rubber forests. France began to recolonize West African lands. And Bismarck's Germany viewed Africa as a potential means to compensate for centuries without a global empire. Before tensions could worsen, Germany's Otto von Bismarck called the Berlin Conference in 1884 to draw up a "gentlemen's agreement" for a balance-of-power division of Africa among the Europeans. In his view, the future map of Africa lay in Europe.

Bismarck had inaugurated a race for colonization. France and Great Britain led the way, having established footholds in the nineteenth century in northern and southern Africa, and having gained the industrial lead among European nations. Still, other European powers were not far behind. Germany grabbed Tanzania and Namibia; Italy took Libya and Somaliland; Portugal entered Mozambique; and Belgium claimed the Kongo. Western nations resorted to every means imaginable to gain land. If they could conclude just and equal treaties with African chiefs, well and good, but conniving, treacherous treaties concluded after gin parties or bribes were also acceptable. Finally, there was outright invasion and occupation. By 1914, Europe had gained nominal or actual control of 90 percent of Africa. Only Ethiopia, Liberia, and parts of the Sahara Desert escaped domination.

Once territory was claimed and marked, the first objective was to maintain order so that economic activity could commence. To this end, the Western powers and their African allies chose either direct or indirect rule. Direct rule established urban centers for foreign colonial administrators, lawyers, educators, doctors, and all the support personnel for a European state within an African state. Indirect rule left government ostensibly in the hands of the Africans, but a European envoy, advisor, or representative was always nearby to guide policy and offer financial and military aid in favor of the colonial power. In both types of rule, cheap, efficient, swift, and often ruthless implementation was the goal. It was a form of protectorate.

French colonialism as well as Belgian and Portuguese, was generally direct rule. From Algeria and Morocco, down through West Africa, and to Madagascar, the French imposed a type of Napoleonic centralization and Gaelic conceit in which they treated their colonies as inferior French provinces. Only French staffed and administered important offices, and they mandated for everyone an immersion in French language, history, and culture. They did not hesitate to enforce this foreign occupation by harsh law and military power.

Great Britain leaned towards indirect rule. Its crown colonies in southern Africa (South Africa and Rhodesia), East Africa (Uganda and Kenya), and West Africa (Nigeria and Ghana) shared power or used traditional British-type institutions to govern "correctly." When traditional authorities were lacking, such as elders of the tribe, the British invented them according to their own preconceptions of African history. Furthermore, in order to save money, as few British authorities as possible were dispatched to Africa; in Nigeria, for example, there was one officer for 70,000 inhabitants.

In the special case of Egypt, rulers like Khedive Ismail, who succeeded Mohammed Ali in the second half of the nineteenth century, were committed both to Islam and to Enlightenment ideals and Western modernization and welcomed European advisors and material aid. A celebrated spokesperson for his fusion of Egyptian and European ideas was Mohammed Abduh of Al Azhar University. In his Modernist Movement he joined early Islamic rationalism with Western science and technology.

Hand in hand, the Egyptian and European elites bought up the best land, promoted extravagant development projects, and linked Nile cities by railroad. Egypt ended up overextended, deeply in debt to the West, and confused about its traditions and its future. A case in point is the Suez Canal. From 1854–69 the Frenchman Ferdinand de Lessups supervised the construction of this waterway linking the Mediterranean Sea to the Red Sea, touted as Egypt's most economically promising venture. When the Suez Canal opened in 1869 to a gala international soiree highlighted by the opera *Aida*, Egypt was so bankrupt that it was forced to sell its shares in the venture and thus its control of the canal to Great Britain. A British-French led commission took over management of Egypt's finances. Then, during the 1880s, Britain and France effectively governed Egypt, appointing the harsh and vindictive Lord Cromer to reorganize Egypt's finances. By 1900, British General Gordon had taken control of the Sudan as well.

With a colonial government in place, the second imperialist goal was to collect heavy taxes from profitable economic enterprises. Each African country was to specialize in a few commodities highly valued in the European cash economy, for instance, cotton from Egypt, tropical fruit from West Africa, cocoa and gold from the Gold Coast, diamonds from South Africa, phosphates from Tunisia, and copper from Kongo.

The European colonial powers employed various methods to develop these productive enterprises, which could be benign and nondisruptive if the specialized product had long been in the world market, such as Egyptian cotton. However, if the product was to be newly exported, brutal and wrenching changes often occurred. One example is the exportation of rubber from Kongo: the Belgian Kongo under Belgian King Leopold II is broadly seen as the most unprincipled form of colonialism. In that protectorate, the African population fell from 20 or 30 million to 8 million. Any man who put up resistance to Belgian rule lost his hands and sexual organs.

Far milder than the brutality practiced in the Kongo between 1890 and 1910, private Western companies were allowed to exploit local African resources with the use of cheap labor. An example is the American Firestone Rubber Company in Liberia or the De Beers Diamond Mines in South Africa, each of which supplemented their special status with tax exemptions and low overhead costs.

African-owned companies could develop as well, and Africans could own their own land to grow cash crops to export for modest profit. This put pressure on Africans to monopolize the best land for constant cropping, which in turn led to soil exhaustion and deprived women of their former valued position in agriculture and the marketing of agricultural products.

Former slaves entered the new economy as migrant workers, with huge numbers of them clustering in the grimy mines, cash-crop plantations, and urban skid rows to earn meager pay, some of which they had to relinquish as a head tax. Afterwards, they traveled long distances back to their families to pay for their loved ones' subsistence. Overcrowding in the cities and absences from rural homelands led to the deterioration of both these areas.

To transport workers and new white settlers, and to carry goods to internal markets, railroad construction was introduced into northern and southern Africa in the 1880s, the lines built with unpaid, forced state labor. A typical peasant might owe the state five months of labor a year. Understandably, raw force was necessary to assemble and maintain these labor gangs. Automobiles and trucks followed the railroad. Though facilitating growth of the new economy, European imperialism destroyed the centuries-old caravan and porter networks and with them all the auxiliary activities.

A third European goal was the manipulation of the legal system, since law was a less expensive form of political and social control than military action. Legal codes also provided a logical rationale for white supremacy and a means to manipulate the African public. But if the law failed and a military response was necessary, the European nations ultimately had at their disposal a cutting-edge arsenal, including the repeating breech-loading rifle, the Maxim machine gun, and the gunboat.

Given the formidable array of high-tech weapons on the European side, it is no wonder that native rebellions against colonialism usually failed. However, a lack of firepower was not the only reason Africans succumbed to European rule. Europeans played on Africa's centuries-old historic differences and rivalries; intra-tribal competition among chiefs could reveal useful allies. In addition, many Africans genuinely believed in European modernization philosophies and benefited personally. Finally, there were the recurrent climatic and medical disasters—drought, famine, cholera, plague, sleeping sickness, and influenza—that weakened any resistance movement and exacerbated tensions.

Most native revolts against colonial rule combined widely varying groups who shared a common hostility toward their foreign masters. These included small farmers, herders, and urban workers who shared a common tradition, or religious heritage, and who rejected European controls as profane. Poorly educated, inadequately armed, and trained mostly in customary methods of warfare, these popular movements nonetheless could mobilize huge numbers despite their lack of any internal coherence or well-established institutional organization.

For instance, in 1880s Sudan, a Muslim holy man named Mohammed Ahmed (1848–85) revealed that he was the *Mahdi* (guided one) sent to free his people from oppression. As Mahdi, Mohammed Ahmed became the man "who would arise at the end of the world" to lead the faithful in a war of liberation from the European infidels. His followers viewed him as a savior and dedicated themselves to his cause with reckless abandon. Attacking Khartoum, the Anglo-Egyptian capital of Sudan, in 1884–85, and killing Lord Gordon, the rebels ultimately floundered with the death of the Mahdi in the year of his triumph (1885). Shortly thereafter, the slaughter of his men at the battle of Omdurman (1898) marked the end of this spontaneous, holy rebellion.

At Omdurman, Lord Kitchener, the commander-in-chief of Anglo-Egyptian forces, used artillery, Maxim machine-guns, and rifles to kill 16,000 Muslim horsemen in a single afternoon. Subsequently Britain imposed its control over what now had become "Anglo-Egyptian" Sudan.

In German East Africa (Tanzania) in 1905 the Muslim prophet Kinji Kitile attracted followers by giving them a supposed magical *maji* (potion) to protect them against bullets. The potion seems to have worked for two years before the "maji maji" rebellion was savagely repressed. Women sometimes played a leading role in these types of revolts. In 1899, the Queen Mother and military chiefs of the fearsome war-state of Asante went into combat against the British in Ghana for half

Lord Kitchener (1850–1916). Portrayed here as a British soldier and statesman, 1st Earl and war hero Kitchener acted as chief of staff of the South African Field Force. Major-General Lord Horatio Herbert Kitchener of Khartoum and of Broome. Shelfmark: 1766.a.3. Copyright © The British Library.

a year, finally surrendering. In 1929, women rose en masse in Nigeria.

Other rebels tried to beat the Europeans at their own game by pitting their best military technology and traditions against the foreigners. In 1880s Egypt, Colonel Urabi was only one of several military figures heading popular and army revolts against Westerners using modern techniques, but he was still unable to defeat the British. One African country, however, successfully ousted Westerners by turning their technology against them. In the 1890s Ethiopia's Emperor Menelik II accepted Italian help in modernizing his land with railroad and communications lines. When the relationship between the two nations soured in 1896 and the Italians brought in their troops, Menelik surprised them with a huge army five times the size of the Italian forces. With the latest in organization and equipment and his best efforts, Menelik routed the Italians and forced them to accept Ethiopia's autonomy.

The imperial era, from 1880 to 1918, was a watershed in African history. Western ways and ideas had penetrated African societies to varying degrees with uncertain results. Ironically, raw imperial power and humanitarianism had mixed with the European pres-

ence. Since European culture itself was heavily committed to the ideals of the Enlightenment, its impact on Africa had to be balanced against the brutality of naked force. As mentioned in Chapter Nineteen, the Enlightenment advocated reason, equality, and freedom as the principles that should shape human society. Yet the application of these ideals obviously brought mixed results to the Africans and other peoples of the world, when set in a context of rival imperial ambitions among competing European nation-states.

Perhaps the coastal areas of Africa harvested the most enlightened benefits from Europeans, for these areas became more integrated into the global economy with the formation of cities possessing modern, urban, technological, and scientific infrastructures. In law and politics, Europeans often introduced modern governmental efficiency. Medicine, health facilities, and modern sanitation dramatically reduced the incidence of epidemics although nutrition and pediatrics were not much changed. Another legacy, albeit only recently recognized, was an emerging multiculturalism awakened by the imperial powers.

Complementing enlightened ideals and modern inventions, European settlers also brought Catholic and Protestant Christianity to Africa. Protestant clerics arrived in the mid-1800s, and Catholic churchmen after World War I, to establish missions and churches that helped slaves, refugees, the displaced, and the dispossessed, many of whom were women. Missionaries were welcomed for their efforts in opposing slavery and providing literacy, medical care, and a humanistic perspective. They attracted the young with the promise of literacy, modernity, and self-realization. However, when they failed to live up to their own Christian doctrine, these missionaries were condemned as agents of the government or European companies to enforce European rule or make a profit.

Islam, however, was generally far more attractive to Africans then Christianity due to the Muslim's respect for traditional African culture. Islam's long history in Africa and its noncolonial, nonwhite character made it far more attractive as a form of monotheism to African societies. Muslim communities acknowledged all humans as equals in the eyes of God, and rejected the theories of race that animated many of their Christian counterparts. Thus, by World War II half of Africa's population submitted to Allah.

Schools of all types were among the most beneficial European institutions for Africans. At first schools served only the elites, such as those in Dutch and British sections of South Africa, but eventually schools were opened to others, facilitating entry into low-to-mid-level jobs. Higher education was slower in coming. A few universities began to appear in Cairo in 1909, but it was not until after World War II that West and Central Africa introduced them. Education was increasingly seen as bringing, at least to males, a secure job, money, and white-collar ease.

Yet the negative consequences of colonialism far outweighed the few benefits of the Enlightenment or the spread of Christianity. In addition to the destruction of age-old societies and traditions, especially in rural Africa, colonialism saw the loss of natural resources and control of local wealth and commerce. Oppression, rootlessness, dependency, and a weakening of local African economic development in such industries as textiles, iron smelting, and the luxury trades followed on the heels of the command over wealth. African entrepreneurs were hindered and discouraged; consequently a stable native middle class did not emerge. European firms grew disproportionately large compared to native establishments, often through dominating transportation in trucking and railroads.

Like other great cultural hearths around the world, Africa had temporarily lost command over its local social, economic, and political autonomy. And European controls would stay in place there as long as the differential of power rested with Europe. Yet the strong Muslim resurgence, and the success of Islam among African converts, revealed that a hidden resistance to foreign rule existed. All that remained was time: time to see if the thirst for colonies and the pursuit of power would drive rival European nation-states to the brink of war.

The Middle East

At the beginning of the modern era, the dynamic energy of expanding cultures filled the Islamic world. Three gunpowder empires emerged to redefine jihad for Muslims throughout their heartland. Among the Sunni Muslims, the Ottoman Turks rose from obscurity as a political-military adventurer named Osman or Othman (1290–1326) developed a small principality in what today is northwestern Turkey. To the east, the Shiites mobilized later under the Safavids and began the formation of a new Persian Empire in 1501. Finally, as covered in Chapter Twenty-five, a Mongol-Turkish adventurer named Baber invaded the weak Muslim Delhi Sultanate of India to found the Mogul Empire in 1526.

As a result, Islam did not lose any of its vitality in the Middle East, Persia, or India. Muslims witnessed their religion generate a new political design to rule the geographic regions that had fallen under Mohammed's vision. The Ottoman Empire began first, but had an uneven early history. Osman and his heirs had a difficult time pressing their military goals against the Byzantine Empire and Christian Europe. Yet, their growth nearly ended permanently when their ruler, Bajaret I (1347–1403) fell captive to Tamerlane after the battle of Ankara in 1402. Luckily for the Ottoman Turks, Tamerlane focused more on raids than building a permanent state, and he withdrew from Anatolia with his eye set on China.

Surviving Tamerlane's brief invasion, Mohammed I (1339–1427) replaced his father, Bajaret I, in 1403 and continued the Turkish drive for conquest. Learning the secrets of gunpowder from the Chinese through trade with the Mongols, Mohammed I's grandson, Mohammed II (1429–81) used this new source of military power in taking Constantinople. Impregnable to assault prior to cannon due to the combination of land-based fortifications and supply by sea, Constantinople had survived, as mentioned, numerous Muslim assaults. The cannon, however, ended this success when Constantinople fell in 1453 to Sultan Mohammed II, who led a combined land-sea attack. After only three months of siege, cannon fire breached Constantinople's walls and the last bastion of the Eastern Roman Empire collapsed. With this dynamic urban site as the centerplace of his growing domain, Mohammed II was poised for rapid expansion.

Now the Ottoman sultan developed a military state based on Islam. Dedicated to the theory that Allah had assigned the Turks the divine task of expanding the realm of the faithful, the Ottoman ruler conquered pagans and Christians alike in a holy war. At first, growth for the Turks focused solely on Christendom, where rich infidels could be found. Even though Christians were what the Prophet had called "People of the Book," the Turks had witnessed the Crusades, had captured Greek Orthodox territory, and had conquered the Christian-held Balkans (a peninsula in southeast Europe framed by the Black, Aegean, Mediterranean, and Adriatic seas). In the process of converting ex-Christians to Islam, the Turks discovered a new source of fanatical warrior by kidnapping and raising Christian children as slave-soldiers called *Janissaries*.

Since slavery was not a demeaning status in Muslim states, Janissaries could and did become personal bodyguards and administrators of the sultan. He had discovered that captured Christian children could be molded into obedient political tools. Raised in special palace schools, the young slaves learned whatever skills the sultan deemed necessary for their future careers. Talent became the standard for advancement since the sultan had reshaped the identities of these children after taking them from their parents.

Upward mobility, wealth, and power knew no limit in the expanding world of the Ottoman Turks. Avenues of social mobility made these slaves extremely loyal to their Muslim master. Hence, the sultan had molded an ideal human resource for his purposes when he developed the practice of kidnapping children from crude farming villages and raising them in a palace of luxury and potential power.

Once he had educated them, the sultan then sent these slave-soldiers back to rule their parents and the rest of their generation. This parent-child authority reversal created deep scars in the cultural development of the Balkans. On one level, the young Christians had lost their parents, their heritage, and their freedom; on another, these same children ended up as masters over their parents, their ex-neighbors, and all other subjects in the sultan's realm. This shift in roles, however, created great rage among the Christian parents who had lost their sons to Islam.

As rulers, the slave-soldier-administrator was tireless and obedient to his master's will. As a result, the Janissaries enhanced the sultan's power. Yet, at the same time, these talented slave-rulers created the seeds of anger that even today continues to divide the Balkans into a region filled with a bloodlust based on the desire to redress ancient grievances. This anger brewed just beneath the surface during in the sixteenth century to make this region a hotbed of potential rebellion.

To suppress any possible uprising, the sultan's slave soldiers developed a rigorous practice of periodically impaling (executing by piercing a victim's body with a sharp stake) unruly subjects. Since the sultan selected Serbian children most frequently to become Janissaries, these slave-soldiers sometimes ended up impaling their own parents and neighbors. This practice created a three-way pattern of rage: Serbs learned to hate Muslims, while Croats hated Janissaries, whom they identified with their Serbian neighbors.

But even as the sultan planted this rage in the Balkans, the Turks enjoyed their greatest military successes against their fellow Muslims, the Shiites. Having carved out an impressive realm at the expense of Christians, the Ottoman Empire did not reach its fullest dimensions until the Safavids emerged as potential Shiite rivals to the east. Hence, the explanation of the next step in Ottoman expansion involves a mixed story of two opposing gunpowder Muslim empires, one Sunni, the other Shiite.

In 1501, Ismail Safavi claimed to be the descendent of the Seventh Imam and therefore the true leader of the Muslim world. As a descendent of an Imam, Ismail immediately captured the leadership of the Shiites, for Imams came from the familial line of Ali, Mohammed's son-in-law, as the rightful heirs of the Caliphate. As the legitimate leader of the Shiites, Ismail

posed a threat to any Sunni ruler. Hence, any success enjoyed by Ismail would eventually lead to a challenge of ultimate authority with the Ottoman Turks.

The Safavid sect had existed for many years as a secret society that used an underground system of propaganda to arouse Persian opposition to Arab and Turkish rule. Using Turkish adventurer-soldiers of his own in his rise to power, Ismail organized an effective Shiite army based on a tribal design similar to the one developed by Mohammed back in the 600s. The passion of Shia now had a political leader that could release centuries of pent-up rage in order to right what the Shiites felt was a basic injustice: the Sunni form of Islam created by the Omayyad Caliphs, who had begun their reign with the murder of Ali's son, Husain, and all his family in 680.

Ismail won a rapid series of victories when he began his campaign to reestablish the caliphate under Ali's line. In 1502 he took Tabriz in present-day Iran, crowned himself Shah, and turned to the west to recover the holy lands of Islam. By 1508 he had captured Baghdad, the old capital of the Abbasids, took control of Mesopotamia, and turned north on the Uzbeks. By 1510 he had defeated the Uzbeks and advanced on Anatolia where the Ottoman Turks had begun their rise to power. At this point, the sultan, Selim I (1467–1520), realized that the future of the Ottoman Empire depended on stopping Ismail.

Selim I mobilized all his imperial forces and fell upon the Shiite threat. With the advantage of superior cannon, Selim crushed Ismail's thrust into present-day Turkey. He then began the task of eradicating Shiites wherever his Turkish armies found them. Yet the grim determination of Selim I's efforts to recover lost lands could not capture the heart of Shiite power in Persia. The Shah's passionate troops successfully defended the Persian homelands as a stalemate began to set in.

Realizing that he could not eliminate the heart of Shiite power, Selim then decided on the next best course: to capture all possible lands in the Middle East to prevent the spread of Shia. Again with grim determination, Selim I swept through Syria, Palestine-Israel, Egypt, and parts of Arabia. His goal was simple: to restrict Persia's chances of expansion. The single-mindedness of Selim's expansion resulted in two major consequences: the rapid growth of Ottoman power in the Middle East, and the change of Selim's name to "Selim the Grim."

Two great gunpowder empires now had emerged out of the Safavid-Ottoman contest. The Safavids settled down to rule Persia and what is now Afghanistan, while the Ottomans, under their new ruler Suleiman the Magnificent (reigned 1520–66), prepared to expand Turkish power to its maximum extent. Suleiman conquered all the lands from the rich coast of North Africa to the gates of Vienna in Europe.

Religious Passions

Meanwhile, religious passion throughout the Middle East and Persia proved both to be the strength and a weakness of Islam. Islamic passion led to conquest but also made Muslim rule unstable. The issue of religious purity still divided Islam internally along Sunni and Shiite lines. This division made Muslim rulers oppressive to those whose loyalty belonged to an opposing line of caliphate descendents. Such an emphasis on religious purity also made Islamic rulers intolerant of their non-Muslim subjects. These religious disagreements serve as the basis for the remainder of the Islamic story during the era 1500–1700.

The Sunni Muslims of the Ottoman Empire represented the majority of the faithful. Their reaction to the Shiite challenge crystallized under Suleiman the Magnificent. He created an intellectual environment within his empire that ensured that the power and influence of Shia would not win converts.

Called the "lawgiver" by his own people, Suleiman focused the intellectual energy of his massive empire on Sunni orthodoxy. Schools and universities generated experts in Sunni law who created a carefully designed hierarchy of religious offices. Every Ottoman city or town had a Sunni official who ensured that a common religious and political message disseminated among the Turks and Arabs of the Ottoman Empire. Suleiman tolerated unorthodox *dervish* communities (i.e., Islamic beggar friars who emphasized mysticism in their religious practices). Yet Suleiman allowed such communities to exist only in remote areas where their form of Islam could not stir up uncontrollable religious passion.

Suleiman's strategy of creating a highly legalized, well-organized, and broadly distributed orthodoxy worked well. Shia ceased to be a rebellious threat in the empire, for once again, the Shiites went underground to create secret but silent societies. Shia continued to exist, but now it faced a far better organized Sunni orthodoxy. Sunni influence blended politics and religion into a seamless bond of authority. As Sunni traditions reached their apex, they created a stable, traditional base that held the Ottoman Empire in place while Europe modernized.

The Shiites managed to survive behind the scenes, yet they were poorly organized when compared to Suleiman's Sunni orthodoxy. The religious passion released by Ismail Safavi's rise to power faded rapidly after his movement failed to sweep the entire Islamic world. Confined to Persia, Ismail's heirs soon found themselves in a quarrel with experts on Shiite law that drove a wedge between religious and political authority.

These religious scholars, the ayatollahs, denied the shah's claim to authority over religious matters. They argued instead that only they, the ayatollahs, had the knowledge and religious purity to understand Allah's Will. As a result, the shah and ayatollahs argued among themselves about who held jurisdiction over religious matters. Nevertheless, both agreed only Shia could be tolerated as the correct form of Islam.

Shia became the only form of Islam practiced in Persia, as the shahs and the ayatollahs pressed for the elimination of Sunnis within their realm. The doctrine of faith that became the standard for Persia was called the "Twelvers," named after the twelve known caliphs in hiding from Ali's line whose underground authority reflected the legitimate path of succession until this line disappeared. The Twelvers, however, represented the ayatollahs' success in separating political and religious authority.

The Twelvers became the official form of Shia in Persia despite the fact that other Shiites recognized different paths of descendents. For example, the Shah Ismail Safavi claimed to come from the Seventh Imam, which the ayatollahs now rejected. Hence, no tolerance for any deviation from the Twelvers was acceptable in Persia despite the fact that this undermined Safavid royal power. Thus, Persian culture developed an intensity of intolerance whose passion exceeded Suleiman's orthodoxy but weakened their country. In addition, this stubbornness froze Persian society in a singular pattern of beliefs.

As Sunnis and Shiites divided their world to create a religious barrier between them more intense than the Catholic and Protestant divisions in Europe, Islamic intolerance spread to non-Muslim subjects as well. Successful at creating massive empires, Muslims nonetheless had a hard time dealing with the people they came to master. This quality of intolerance created a built-in weakness that foreigners would eventually exploit.

In much of the Muslim world outside the core of the Middle East, the faithful comprised the minority in foreign populations; they were the rulers and great landowners who found themselves surrounded by a hostile people. The vast majority of non-Muslim subjects in these foreign lands, the peasants, generated the food that fed their Islamic rulers. Also, most artisans in towns belonged to the non-Muslim laboring poor. Hence, the laborers in the lands outside the Middle East felt little love for or loyalty to their Muslim overlords.

True more for the Ottoman Empire and India than for Persia, this weakness in social design created a religious division that outsiders could exploit. For the Ottoman Turks, the zone where they had the greatest number of non-Muslims was in the Balkan states of Europe, where the practice of taking Christian children to create Janissaries ceased after 1638. Thereafter, administrators and soldiers came from already existing slave-soldier households.

This break in the pattern of kidnapping future generations of Janissaries had the positive effect of reducing the immediate rage felt by Christian parents, the subject peoples. Yet this basic shift in Ottoman policy also led to several negative drawbacks to the sultan's power. First, the practice of converting Christian children into Muslim Janissaries had proven to be a way to control these angry parents. Once the practice of kidnapping ceased, the immediate cause of anger diminished, but the deeply embedded rage over past injuries remained. In other words, kidnapping Christian children had both caused and solved the problem of rebellion.

Second, when this practice ended the sultan lost an important feature of power. The practice of kidnapping each generation of Janissaries had established talent and loyalty as the two criteria used to determine upward social mobility among these slave-soldiers. Now, since the sultan came to rely on established Janissary families to fill future administrative jobs, this shift in policy replaced talent and loyalty with birth as the sole standard for social status. As a result, this pattern of inheritance made Janissaries an obstacle to the Sultan's power.

Since these slave-soldiers formed the sultan's bodyguard, they gained control over his person. Commanding the life and death of a sultan allowed the Janissaries to form a sociopolitical block that grew to manipulate the state. Once, they understood their power, the Janissaries began to extort privileges from the sultan.

Third, still angry from past kidnappings, Christians in the Balkans felt the full brunt of Muslim intolerance during this era of orthodoxy. Now Janissary officials came only from Muslim families. With Suleiman's policy of creating a strong Sunni orthodoxy, Muslims in the Ottoman Empire became increasingly less tolerant. This proved especially true among the Janissaries as their sense of power grew with each succeeding generation.

Since the Janissaries no longer came from remote villages and ceased to understand life as Christian peasants, Muslim officials became distant and oppressive. The texture of rage shifted from familial pain to religious hostility. Resources that could have been used to enhance Muslim power instead were wasted on controlling Balkan rage.

Finally, the European Commercial Revolution (1492–1763) had rerouted the basic patterns of global trade away from the Middle East. This deprived the Ottoman Empire of the middle position in Eurasian-African commerce that Muslims had enjoyed for centuries. Cut off from the prized central role on the Silk Road and to the Indian Ocean, the Turks saw wealth and revenues slip away to Europe, as the British, the French, the Dutch, the Spanish, and the Portuguese slowly redirected world commerce away from the Middle East.

Ottoman power visibly decayed with this major realignment of global commerce. Such a shift in trade took centuries to develop, yet the ultimate influence on the differential of power was unmistakable.

European Imperialism

The decay of Muslim dynasties throughout the Middle East offered Europe a final region for imperial expansion. Political events in the Ottoman Empire, among the Safavids of Persia, and the Moguls of India seemed to belie the promise of Allah's favor. The Middle East had entered the post-1750 era of contact with Europe when the differential of power had given the European Infidels the military as well as the economic initiative.

Traditional Muslim power faded, just as traditional solutions had failed in Japan, Russia, India, China, and Africa. The military advantage of the gunpowder empires gave way to superior European technology. Early in the transitional era, when Europeans gained the differential of power, the Ottoman Turks suffered their first reversals. Austria took Hungary in 1699, an indication that the sultan was about to begin a long retreat.

Of the three great gunpowder empires of the Ottoman, Safavid, and Mogul, the Ottoman Turks showed the greatest promise of survival. Leader of the Sunni Muslims, the sultan made serious efforts to revive the Ottoman Dynasty and maintain control of his lands. He had to rely, however, on his Janissaries. As mentioned above, the Ottoman Turks had lost their military edge when the practice of kidnapping Christian boys ceased in 1638. Now the sons of Janissary families inherited the office of their fathers. Since the Janissaries served as the personal bodyguards of the sultan, they could hold their ruler hostage within his own palace if he pressed too hard for reform. Thus, by 1700, any effort to reorganize the empire would have to begin with a massacre of the Janissaries.

To the north of the Ottoman Empire, czarist Russia began to press on Turkish holdings in the Balkans. Joining them, the Austrians also expanded against the Turks. The sultan seemed to be in no position to stop either assault.

Russia, for example, invaded the Ottoman Empire while the rest of Europe recovered from the Seven Years' War (1756–63). Crushing the Janissaries in battle, the Russians dictated the Treaty of Kuchuk Kainarji in 1774. This treaty gave Catherine the Great the northern shores of the Black Sea and rights of passage through the Bosphorus, the Sea of Marmora, and the Dardanelles. By 1800, Russia was easily capable of overwhelming the Turks, but pressure from Europe kept the Czar in check.

Now, Europeans simply took bits and pieces of the Ottoman Empire as the opportunities arose. The Austrians, for example, joined the Russians and began their drive into the Balkans. Invading Turkish territory, the Habsburgs acquired Hungary and Transylvania. Austria's success, however, alarmed Russia, and the two became rivals over who would take control of the Balkans.

The sultan had internal problems as well. As mentioned in the African section of this chapter, one of his most valuable provinces, Egypt, won its independence in 1809. Now the sultan watched helplessly as his own governor, Pasha Mohammed Ali, broke away to create a new Egyptian Dynasty and threaten the very existence of the Ottoman Empire. Only European intervention saved the sultan when such actions served the interests of Western nation-states.

In the meantime, Serbia became autonomous in 1815 as a result of a successful revolt begun in 1804. Greece won its independence from the sultan in 1830 after raising the standard of rebellion in 1822. Rumania achieved statehood as a byproduct of the Crimean War (1853–55) when Moldavia and Wallachia elected Alexander John Cuza prince in 1859 and formed an union in 1861. Finally, Algeria fell to French annexation in 1830. The sultan survived until 1918 because of internal reforms that required first the destruction of the Janissaries in 1828 and the modernization of the Turkish army.

These efforts arrested the collapse of the Ottoman Empire, but the sultan could not keep up with the rate of change occurring in Europe. Hence, a resurgent Ottoman military only postponed the final collapse of the Ottoman Empire, which occurred as part of the process known as World War I.

Like the Ottoman Turks, the Safavids of Persia also began a long retreat. Early in the eighteenth century, a Sunni revolt in Afghanistan resulted in the capture of the eastern provinces of the Persian Empire and siege at Isfahan, the shah's capital. In 1722, while surrounded by Afghanis, the last impotent Safavid ruler allowed 80,000 people in his capital to perish from starvation and disease before the city fell. Then, these Sunni rebels established an aggressive state to the east that threatened the survival of Shia in Persia.

Yet a Persian named Nadir (1688–1747) restored Persian independence in the 1730s and overran the Sunnis of Afghanistan. At first, he used an infant son of the last Safavid shah as a puppet monarch while Nadir ruled as regent. Once this child died, however, Nadir took the title of shah for himself and became Nadir Shah. Then Nadir Shah gathered enough power to expand into Afghanistan and even compel the Moguls of India to pay a ransom to keep him from invading Indian territory. Yet, his military projects quickly outstripped the resources of Persia, so that when he died in 1747 his new regime rapidly decayed.

Afghanistan soon produced its own great liberator, Ahmed Shah (1723–73). Ahmed Shah won back Afghani independence and created the modern frontiers of this new state. Because of Ahmed Shah's drive for sovereignty, the victories he enjoyed against the Persians and the Moguls laid the foundation for present-day Iran, Afghanistan, and Pakistan. Simultaneously, these setbacks to Persian power forced this Shiite realm to turn inward as an outcast state surrounded by hostile Sunni neighbors to the east and the west.

Meanwhile, the rulers of Persia from 1794 to 1925 were Qajar shahs. Unlike the Safavids, the Qajars made no claim of descent from the Shiite imams. Under Qajar rule, the religious authority of Shia became less and less connected with the political structure of Persia. This separation of church and state, however, weakened Persian resistance to European imperial pressures because the ayatollahs and the mujtahid (those qualified as scholarly Islamic guides) mobilized popular Shia support against the Qajars for failing to keep out Western influences.

A kind of religious, commercial, and popular opposition to the Qajars grew during the nineteenth century as the British penetrated Persia from the south and the Russians moved in from the north. The ayatollahs and the mujtahid and their secular commercial partners had developed a hard-line opposition to the shahs for their weakness. In particular, the ayatollahs, the mujtahid, and Persian merchants turned a critical eye toward any effort on the part of the Qajars to allow Western ideas and modern technology into Persia. As a result, the shahs found themselves in an impossible double bind: if they resisted European influences by using traditional Islamic tactics to win support from the religious and local leadership, the Qajars did not have the modern means to expel the foreigners; on the other hand, if the shahs modernized to acquire these necessary means, the Qajars would lose the popular support of the Shiite community who resisted these changes. In the latter case, the ayatollahs, the mujtahid, and Persia's commercial interests would have grouped the Qajars with the British and the Russians and struggled to throw all three out of Persia. The Qajars never found a way out of this dilemma and sank into political impotence.

All the while that the shahs and the religious and commercial leaders squared off against one another, British and Russian interests put pressure on Persia as the crossroads to India and the Persian Gulf. Internally, the ayatollahs, the mujtahid, and Persia's merchants pressed their criticism of the shah's weakness to undermine further this Muslim kingdom. In addition, the warrior tradition of the Ghazi princes that led the shah's armies bridled under the inability of their ruler to march against Shia's enemies. Consequently, internal divisions functioned like an open invitation to foreign interests as the British and Russians became rivals to control Persia. None of Persia's efforts seemed to matter as the Europeans simply grew more powerful with each passing year.

Accordingly, early in the nineteenth century, the Qajars failed to deal effectively with the Russians and the British. Britain wanted to control Persian affairs to protect the trade routes to India, while the Russians wanted access to the Persian Gulf. Russia moved first by defeating the Qajars in two wars that forced Persia to sign the Treaties of Gulistan (1812) and Turkmanchay (1828): Persia lost all its territories in the Caucasus, which included very rich oil fields. Then, in the second half of the nineteenth century, Russia compelled Persia to surrender all its claims to lands in Central Asia. Meanwhile, the British used troops twice to press the Qajar to give up all claims to Herat, a city located in northwest Afghanistan; the purpose of this military pressure was to secure access to India's frontiers. The Treaty of Paris (1857) ensured Britain's hold on Herat and helped to complete the definition of Afghanistan.

Russia and Britain also competed to control Persian commerce and internal affairs. Given the differential of power, neither could be resisted by the Persians because of vastly superior cannon, machine-guns, and rifles wielded by the British nation-in-arms and the Russian neofeudal, quasimodern, and multinational empire. Simultaneously, internal divisions within Persia allowed both Britain and Russia to shape Persian affairs.

An example of these internal problems occurred during the reign of Naser ad Din (1848–96). When Naser ascended the throne, his Prime Minister, Mirza Taqi Khan Amir Kabir, tried to improve the shah's command over the court, the bureaucracy, the army, and the tax system, while reducing corruption. He proposed modern reforms in education, importing Western science and encouraging the learning of foreign languages. His successes, however, inspired opposition within the bureaucracy and eroded the shah's trust. Accordingly, Naser dismissed his prime minister and had him executed in 1851.

A second reform effort in 1871 guided by Prime Minister Mirza Husain Khan Moshir of Dowleh led to a European-style administrative cabinet that could have integrated governmental functions at top levels. Yet when Mirza granted a railroad concession and economic access to Persia's interior to a British financier, Baron Julius de Reuter, this touched off opposition. The ayatollahs, the mujtahid, Persia's commercial interests, and members of the bureaucracy forced the shah to dismiss his prime minister and cancel the concession. Nevertheless, internal demand for reform continued to grow.

Then, when Naser turned to Britain for protection from the Russians, the British put pressure on the shah to open his country to foreign trade and modernize his government. In 1888, Naser attempted to implement British suggestions; the shah opened the Karun River in Khuzestan to foreign ships and gave Baron de Reuter a banking concession. Furthermore, in 1890 the shah gave the British a monopoly on the country's tobacco market. The tobacco concession immediately mobilized the religous leaders and commercial interests in opposition. The clerics in particular issued a religious ruling against foreign tobacco that led to a boycott, and the shah once again had to retreat. This last defeat caused the Qajar ruler to pay heavy penalties that his treasury could little afford.

Near the end of his life, Naser virtually gave up trying to address the need for reform to protect his realm. As a result, bureaucratic corruption increased, and rural taxes fell more heavily on Persian peasants; meanwhile, the ayatollahs, the mujtahid, and Persia's commercial interests continued their opposition to the shah, and those wanting modern reforms grew frustrated. Paralyzed from within, even while facing mounting pressures from the outside, the Qajar regime responded with indifference. Finally, with the encouragement of the clerics, an assassin killed the shah, and Persia continued to drift without effective leadership.

While the Qajars floundered, imperial pressures continued to mount against Persia until the French, Russians, and British struck a deal between themselves in 1907 that resolved Iran's future in Europe's favor. Russia received the northern third of Persia, Britain got the southern third, a demilitarized zone lay in the middle, and France gained an alliance linking Russia and Britain together with the French to confront Germany. Simultaneously, Persian modernists joined forces with the religious leaders and commercial interests to force the Qajars to accept a constitution that lasted from 1906 to 1911. Yet this alliance did not bridge the doctrinal differences between the conservative religious leaders, their commercial partners, and the newly acquired modernist friends. Accordingly, Persia continued to flounder under Western pressures well after World War I.

Like the Ottoman and Mogul empires, the Qajar Regime of Persia proved helpless against European nation-states. Hence, the Middle East joined with Africa, China, and India to experience a long retreat from autonomy. The differential of power, the nation-in-arms, and modern industry had simply proven too powerful for their original cultural hearths to resist.

Yet as these European nation-states scrambled to carve up the world into massive global empires, they sowed the seeds of change that would redefine world history in the twentieth century. The reliance on superior firepower and violence that had developed during the imperial era (1800–1914), the pursuit of power that had armed European states so thoroughly, and the emerging theory of race, linked with language, national identity, and cultural teleology that had bestowed so much power on European nations also had created national rivalries that would not rest. Bismarck's Germany had instilled in France a desire for revenge that had in turn inspired a new type of diplomacy, which divided Europe into armed camps. At the same time, new non-European nations like the United States and Japan wanted their fair share of global trade, while neofeudal/quasimodern powers like Russia and Austria-Hungary worried about their place on the world scale of military and political power. The quest for wealth and the means to acquire it had made European modernization potentially very dangerous, the full extent of which will become clear in Unit Four of this text.

Suggested Reading

Africa

Boahen, Adu, *African Perspectives on Colonialism* (Baltimore: Johns Hopkins University Press, 1987).

Davidson, B., *Africa in History: Themes and Outlines,* Revised Edition (London: Cox & Wyman, Ltd., 1991).

Illiffe, John, *The African Poor* (Cambridge: Cambridge University Press, 1983).

Marah, J., *The African People in the Global Village: An Introduction to Pan-African Studies* (Lanharm, Md.: University Press of America, 1998).

Mazrui, A. and M. Tidy, *Nationalism and New States in Africa* (London: Heinemann, 1984).

Oliver, R., *The African Experience* (New York: Praeger, 1992).

Shillington, K., *History of Africa* (New York: Macmillian Education, 1989).

Tordoff, William, *Government and Politics in Africa,* Third Edition (Bloomington: Indiana University Press, 1997).

The Middle East

Armajani, Y., *Iran* (Englewood Cliffs, N.J.: Prentice Hall, 1972).

Cook, M. A., *A History of the Ottoman Empire to 1730* (Cambridge: Cambridge University Press, 1980).

Hodgson, Marshall, G. S., *The Gunpowder Empires and Modern Times,* Three Volumes (Chicago: Chicago Univesity Press, 1974).

Hourani, A., *Arabic Thought in the Liberal Age, 1789–1939* (Cambridge: Cambridge University Press, 1967).

Inalcik, Halil, *The Ottoman Empire: the Classical Age 1300–1600* (London: Weidenfeld and Nicolson, 1973).

Keddie, N. R., *Iran and the Muslim World: Resistance and Revolution* (New York: New York University Press, 1995).

Kinross, Patrick Balfour, *The Ottoman Centuries: The Rise and Fall of the Turkish Empire* (New York: Morrow, 1977).

Lewis, Raphaela, *Everyday Life in Ottoman Turkey* (New York: Putnam, 1971).

Savory, R. M., *Iran Under the Safavids* (Cambridge: Cambridge University Press, 1980).

Sevket, Pamuk, *The Ottoman Empire and European Capitalism, 1820–1913: Trade, Investment, and Production* (Cambridge: Cambridge University Press, 1987).

Shaw, Sranford J., and Ezel Kuran Shaw, *History of the Ottoman Empire and Modern Turkey,* Two Volumes (Cambridge University Press, 1977).

Global Violence
and the Postmodern Era

As mentioned in the introduction to Unit Three, the modern age ended and the postmodern era began with World War I (1914–18). Although conventional historical wisdom states that the postmodern era started with the end of World War II, this text contends that changes wrought by the Great War irrevocably altered the differential of power worldwide and thus the general state of global affairs. The destruction of World War I caused the European states to lose their primacy as the world's economic, political, and military powers, setting in motion the postmodern era. The shock of the Great War so completely upset the Europeans' sense of self that they questioned things taken for granted since 1492: that they were superior in might, intellect, and energy compared to other peoples of the world. Europeans had used this sense of superiority to justify their actions against traditional ("uncivilized") cultures in an effort to shape the direction of the world based on their own notions of reason and progress. Infected with similar ideas of superiority, several non-European nations, such as the United States and Japan, had joined the European states as imperial adventurers. Each of these nation-states hoped to "civilize" the rest of the world by changing peoples they considered backward for the supposed benefit of all.

Meanwhile, the rest of the world had begun to learn enough from Europe to start building the means to resist the Western imperial powers during the post–World War I era (1918–39). Hence, by 1918 the world had changed sufficiently for a process of decolonization to begin. Europeans had broken their own hold on the world when they threw their resources into the suicidal conflict of 1914–18 and then completed the process of self-destruction with World War II (1939–45). Both global wars sapped Europe's military, financial, and intellectual capacity to command the world. Simultaneously, the non-European regional cultures of Russia, China, the Indian subcontinent, the Middle East, sub-Saharan Africa, and Latin America were ready to redefine themselves using such European cultural creations as the nation-state, industrialization, and the values embedded in modernization. The timing of their efforts coincided with the decades between World War I and World War II as well as the years immediately following World War II. The entire world would then experience a major transformation.

To understand this transformation, one must begin by considering the factors that sparked global warfare in the twentieth century. Then one must consider World War I carefully to ascertain the new forces it released and how the so-called Great War all but paralyzed the European imagination. These new forces included the rise of the United States, Japan, and the Soviet Union to a level of power equal to that of Europe's great nation-states before 1914, while modern revolutions began to unfold in China, India, and in portions of the Middle East, Africa, and Latin America. At the same time, demoralization in Europe undermined the will of the victorious allies, which curtailed their capacity to respond to native liberation movements, while also creating a form of political impotence that allowed radical conservative regimes to appear in Italy and Germany. Of these latter two, the German experiment with fascism set the tone for the next European conflict, which laid a foundation for World War II when Nazi Germany joined with Japan to usher in one last major effort at nineteenth-century-style empire-building.

In the meantime, the national revolutions, or liberation movements, that occurred in China, India, Mexico, Cuba, Nicaragua, Algeria, and Vietnam, to name but a few, spoke to a twentieth-century rage felt by peasant societies that marked a growing resistance to modernization at the hands of foreigners. Indeed, these peasant uprisings spoke to the intense anger created by the imperial controls imposed on them from the outside when the industrial nation-states from Europe, the United States, and Japan built their empires. This widespread discontent also encouraged agents of the Soviet Union, after the Russian Revolution of 1917–21, to experiment with an international communist movement for world revolution. Soviet leadership applied the lessons the communists had learned from guiding a rural, peasant society through the modernization process with a totalitarian regime and a planned economy. Eventually, Marxism itself experienced a revision that transformed a radical philosophy designed for an urban-industrial society into an ideology of liberation for peasants.

The communist revolutions that erupted in twentieth-century peasant societies occurred under circumstances that Marx himself would have questioned. As a radical European who criticized his own industrial-urban culture in an effort to cause revolutionary change, Marx had created Marxism; yet Marx himself harbored a deep distrust of all peasants. He saw them as a conservative, illiterate, and counterrevolutionary force easily exploited by landlords for aristocratic purposes. Nonetheless, Marxist ideology in the hands of Soviet political leaders such as Vladimir Lenin and Josef Stalin reshaped world history and served to mobilize such men as the Chinese revolutionary Mao Zedong. Mao, in turn, received the intellectual tools needed from this revised form of Marxism to repel foreign influences in China while fighting off Nationalist rivals at home. Then, what had helped to reshape Chinese politics in the years between the world wars took on a completely new dimension after World War II.

Since World War II finally broke Europe's hold over its various empires, decolonization became complete, as two new superpowers—the United States and the Soviet Union—squared off to fill the power vacuum left by a retreating European civilization and entered a Cold War that would last until the collapse of the Soviet Union in 1991. The lessons of World War I and II reveal that with the advance of military technology, the death rate due to open conflict would increase exponentially with each new global engagement. The defensive weapons of World War I claimed the lives of 10 million people with a collateral death rate of more than 20 million due to the ensuing flu epidemic. The offensive weapons of World War II killed 55 million people, with a collateral casualty rate approaching 45 million, making the total 100 million. (Collateral death rates refer to people who die indirectly from warfare due to famine, disease, etc.) A World War III therefore would have the potential to eliminate the entire human species.

This horrific conclusion became a real possibility with the introduction during World War II of the atomic and hydrogen bombs. The atomic bomb created a fission explosion that, while less forceful than a hydrogen bomb's, released enough nuclear energy to destroy an entire city. The hydrogen bomb, which created a more powerful fusion explosion, seemingly could bring the energy of the Sun to the surface of the Earth, exposing humans to an estimated 55 million degrees Fahrenheit and saturating the ground with radioactive material with a half-life of 25,000 years. Such numbers excluded the possibility of total war after World War II because both the United States and the Soviet Union had nuclear arsenals after 1949. Accordingly, unrestrained total conflict would have converted both cold war combatants, their allies, and all neutral cultures into ashes.

Simultaneously, the ideological differences between the United States and the Soviet Union locked both of the superpowers in a diplomatic struggle in which words were as effective as weapons: the U.S. advocated the values of private property and free enterprise, while the U.S.S.R. espoused the virtues of public ownership and communal responsibility. In addition, the organization of both superpowers were exactly the opposite. The Soviet Union used vertical articulation to run a vast nation based on a single-party state with no legal restraint on its political conduct, while retaining absolute control over the media and right of assembly and offering the world a vision of society built on the principle of equality. In contrast, the United States used horizontal articulation to build a political-party system under the scrutiny of privately owned newspapers, radio stations, and broadcast networks to generate a national consensus based on the principle of individual freedom. Accordingly, the Soviet Union successfully criticized the United States for ignoring the value of equality within its social fabric, while the United States successfully charged the Soviet Union with ignoring personal liberty and human rights.

Given these philosophical and structural differences, the United States and the Soviet Union began a struggle nearly as intense as a total war, but without the ability to engage one another with their modern nuclear arsenals. The entire world then became their arena of conflict. Asian, African and Latin American and Caribbean cultures, ethnic groups, and peoples seeking independence from the last vestiges of empire listened to appeals made by the United States and the Soviet Union to choose their best course toward autonomy. Sometimes, these cultures, ethnic groups, and peoples joined one camp or the other, or they simply played one side against the other. But, in any case, this process became part of the final phase of decolonization and included brushfire local wars, guerrilla engagements, and extremely intense diplomatic confrontations. Like a total war, the demands of the struggle known generally as the Cold War stretched the United States and the Soviet Union to their limits until the latter collapsed under the strain. This occurred in 1991 when the Soviet Union broke up into many individual nation-states, each with its own composition of ethnicities.

After 1991, the almost century-long era of violence released by the fallout of World War I shifted ground when human beings, as a species, entered the twenty-first century. The last sections of this unit will assess the contemporary world to determine how we humans (*Homo sapien sapiens*) will deal with globalization, the byproduct of modernization. The goal of the unit will be to determine what remains of the modernization process as all the cultural zones of the world enter a phase of existence without a clear economic, social, political, or intellectual center. Meanwhile, nation-formation still seems to have captured most peoples' vision of the future.

To date, most nation-states have survived the violence of the twentieth century. At the same time, however, the phenomenon known loosely as globalization, based on the integration of a world economy, has made us all aware that every nation of the world is now interdependent on the others. Consequently, several fundamental questions emerge as to how we will address common problems in the twenty-first century. The first ponders how well we will integrate our national identities with the reality of a global economy. The second addresses the levels of rage that still exist in the non-European world based on the residual effects of the imperial era. The third considers to what degree the divisiveness of race, ethnicity, and nationality will continue to impede our capacity to develop the intercultural communication skills needed to achieve common international goals. Finally, we must contemplate what level of intolerance still exists in terms of the ethnic and religious differences that even now separate us as peoples.

Responses to these questions take place in the short global study of the contemporary world that concludes this text. Here we will look at global integration, status, freedom, and equality, as well as population dynamics in the context of the development of national identities, as each cultural hearth struggles to define the role it plays in the world economy. Therefore, the last portion of this book should help us establish a meaningful sense of the present, that is, our contemporary moment in world history. One hopes this will help us as citizens of our various nations and of the world, decide what are the basic issues that we all must face. This, in turn, should bring some closure to the text and reveal the power of history as a means to understand the present and plan for the future.

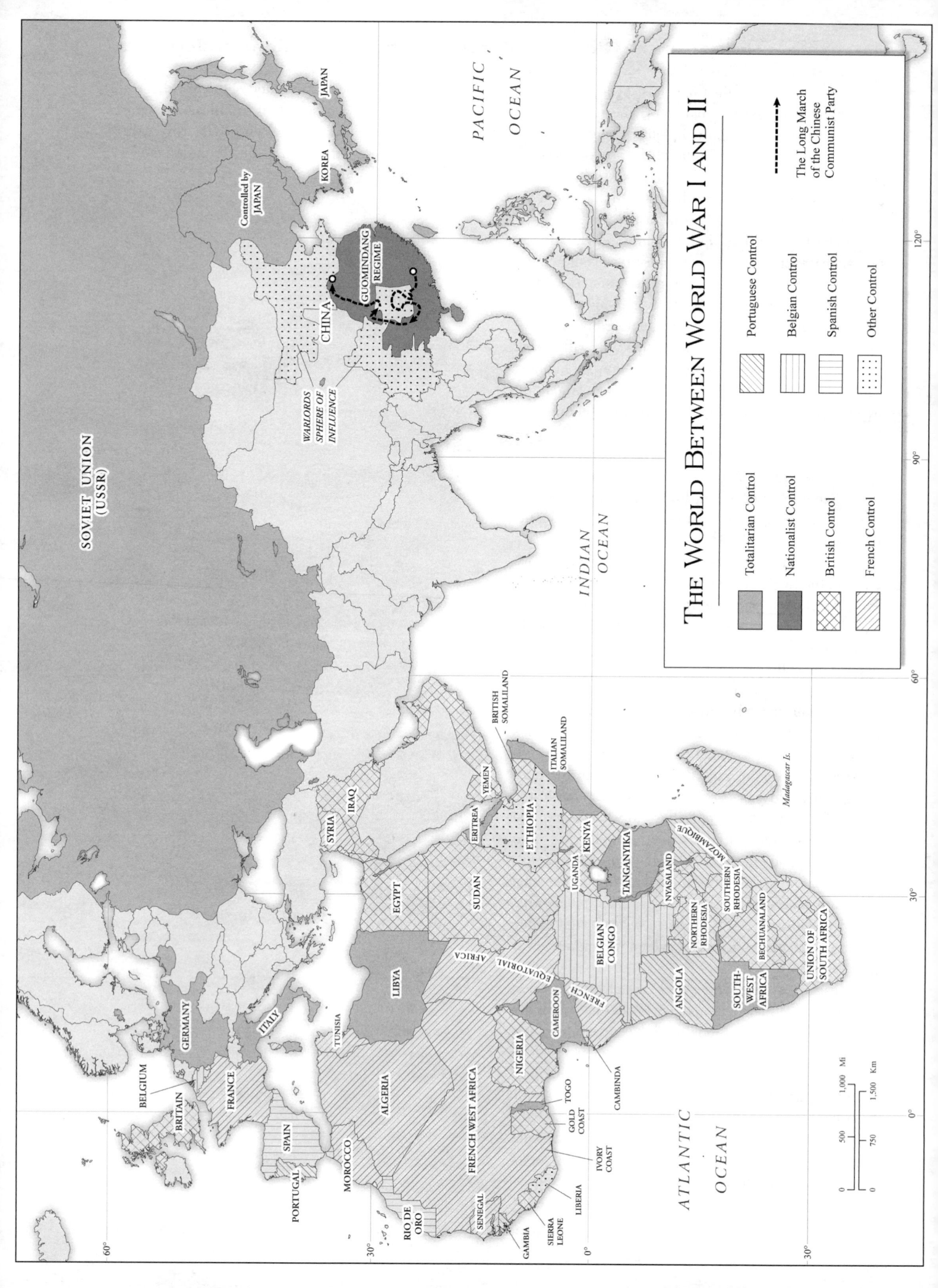

The World Between World War I and II

The Long March of the Chinese Communist Party

Totalitarian Control	Portuguese Control
Nationalist Control	Belgian Control
British Control	Spanish Control
French Control	Other Control

SOVIET UNION (USSR)

PACIFIC OCEAN

JAPAN

JAPAN

KOREA

Controlled by JAPAN

CHINA

GUOMINDANG REGIME

WARLORDS SPHERE OF INFLUENCE

INDIAN OCEAN

SYRIA

IRAQ

YEMEN

BRITISH SOMALILAND

ITALIAN SOMALILAND

ERITREA

ETHIOPIA

EGYPT

SUDAN

UGANDA

KENYA

TANGANYIKA

BELGIAN CONGO

NYASALAND

MOZAMBIQUE

NORTHERN RHODESIA

SOUTHERN RHODESIA

ANGOLA

BECHUANALAND

SOUTH-WEST AFRICA

UNION OF SOUTH AFRICA

Madagascar Is.

LIBYA

FRENCH EQUATORIAL AFRICA

CAMEROON

CABINDA

NIGERIA

TOGO

GOLD COAST

IVORY COAST

LIBERIA

SIERRA LEONE

GAMBIA

SENEGAL

RIO DE ORO

FRENCH WEST AFRICA

ALGERIA

TUNISIA

MOROCCO

SPAIN

PORTUGAL

FRANCE

BRITAIN

BELGIUM

GERMANY

ITALY

ATLANTIC OCEAN

0	500	1,000 Mi
0	750	1,500 Km

60°

30°

0°

30°

0°

30°

60°

90°

120°

WORLD WAR:
The Consequences of Power

Between 1800 and 1914, European nation-states became so intoxicated with their control of the differential of power that they found themselves competing with one another for command over global imperial holdings. Also, modernization had linked science, industry, and nation-building in Western and Central Europe to a faith in progress that converted Sir Francis Bacon's assertion that "knowledge is power" into a justification for assimilating the rest of the world into different national empires. Finally so much power had concentrated in European hands that Western nation-states easily confused what they knew with how they should act.

As parallel areas of progress, science, industry, and nation-formation had convinced Europeans that their command over progress had elevated their culture to the telos (the ultimate end) of civilization. As the telos of cultural development, Europeans forgot that science, industry, and nation-formation were merely the products of knowledge and not the definition of reality (the culmination of human creativity). Thus, Western public opinion had fallen into the conceptual trap of confusing the processes of power with the purposes of cultural existence.

The public whose opinion had created the internal coherence of nation-states had come to believe that culture itself constituted the basis of ultimate reality: its processes (productivity/ creativity) and its purposes (human existence). The teleology of philosophers like Hegel, Ricardo, and Marx (mentioned in Chapter Twenty-two) had recovered a lost sense of purpose that science had eliminated when knowledge of God ceased to be the ultimate cause in natural events during the Scientific Revolution (1543–1687). As a result, teleology linked civilization to a unilinear model of evolution that placed Europe at the pinnacle of human success. Simultaneously, teleology had demoted every other culture in the world to a backward status.

Connected to this elevated sense of self and reality, however, was the routine use of violence that clouded the judgment of the European nation-states. These habits suggested another teleology to Western nation-states. This second teleology linked the formula, "the ends justify the means," to a new political ethic based on the differential of power, one which suggested that their power ought to be the principal means to achieve any end European culture desired. Thus, command over the sources of power mixed Europe's definition of progress with empire to blend this ethical teleology with the ultimate end of cultural development.

The Illusion of Progress

Indeed, Europeans could take pride in statistics as they hailed their progress. The death rate in England, France, and Sweden, for example, had fallen from 25 per 1,000 before 1850 to 19 per 1,000 by 1914. The same example in what Europeans called backward cultures revealed a death rate of 40 per 1,000 for the same period. These figures helped convinced Westerners they were on the right cultural path.

At the same time, the rate of infant mortality after 1870 in all nations using modern medical techniques dropped dramatically to less than 5 per 1,000. Now, women whose pregnancies came to full term could choose to have fewer children since their offspring were likely to survive. In addition, these same women could afford to take more time in between pregnancies, allowing their bodies sufficient time to recover before attempting to conceive again. This period of rest helped ensure healthy mothers and children, so the women could feel relatively safe in knowing that they had given birth to the heirs of their families.

European life expectancy grew from an average of 40 years of age in England in 1840 to 59 years by 1933. In contrast, in India the average life span was only 27 years in 1931. To the English, this extended life expectancy meant that their modern command over nature was far superior to India's traditional approach, which the British believed was rife with "superstition and folly."

Literacy rates approached 90 percent in industrial, urban nations, for life in cities demanded skills that required nation-states to provide public education systems. Children of European parents now acquired the means to breach some of the status barriers that traditional societies used to ensure people remained in the occupations of their families. Thus, in traditional cultures the average literacy rate fell somewhere between 0 and 20 percent, while one's life typically began and ended in the same social and geographic location.

Yet Europeans failed to consider that perhaps the rise in their life expectancy, or the fall in their death rate, might somehow be connected to the poor statistics they used to condemn cultures they deemed as backward. Citing India as an example, while the British might have prided themselves on an average life span of 59 years in 1933, and criticized India for offering only 27 years in 1931, Great Britain had derived much of the wealth it had used to generate its high standard of living from India and other cultures it had exploited—the cultures that made up the British Empire.

Indeed, one can see the role that non-European cultures played in the British standard of living through the balance of payments the United Kingdom achieved in international trade. As an importing nation, Great Britain held most of the world's debt in its control by 1914. Yet the British took into their ports the value of ten times as many foreign goods at the beginning of the twentieth century than they had imported during the nineteenth century, while Britain's exports had grown only eightfold in value despite the United Kingdom's industrial production. Thus, British imports exceeded exports by 200 percent without the nation having fallen into debt. This imbalance in value between imports and exports reflected the wealth the British had accumulated by their command of global economic services that included shipping, insurance, and loans. Like invisible exports, these services more than compensated for the monetary imbalance between imports and exports.

This extra income allowed Great Britain to lend $20 billion in gold to other cultures around the world. The income generated by the interest on these loans was enormous. Non-European cultures paid anywhere from 10 to 14 percent interest due to their demand for hard currency, while the British paid only 6 percent because of the concentration of gold and silver in Europe. Combined with deflation (the falling price of goods) caused by the gold standard, Britain controlled the lion's share of the world's income generated by loans.

Since the gold standard limited the global money supply to the global supply of gold, and industrial production increased the supply of goods at an extremely rapid rate over the course of the nineteenth century, the value of each product for sale fell precipitously. Accordingly, any traditional society that went into debt during this same era, and then tried to pay off its loans by increasing its supply of goods, only made matters worse. Each time the supply of goods increased, while the supply of currency remained the same, deflation also increased.

This economic fact struck at the heart of cultures that produced primary goods because their commodities had the lowest value in the global market. Primary goods, such as food, fuel, and raw materials fed industry, which added more value to the manufactured product, or secondary goods. The major services like shipping, insurance, and loans, added more value still and became the tertiary level of the global economy. Consequently, cultures like Mexico, Russia, or India that exported primary goods to industrial nation-states like Great Britain, and received manufactured goods in exchange, carried by British shipping and insured by British companies such as Lloyds of London, found themselves hopelessly mired in debt. Debt led to loans, and then more loans during an era of deflation, which only extended the amount of money owed. Thus, Britain's command of shipping, insurance, and credit compared favorably to India's export of primary goods like cotton. In contrast, France held $8.7 billion in global loans and Germany $6 billion.

Keeping in mind that one-quarter of all the wealth owned by the inhabitants of Great Britain consisted of holdings outside their country, the British could afford to buy foreign goods at a spectacular rate of exchange. With this wealth, the British imported goods from any number of sources. Their wheat came from the American Midwest and Odessa, while their lumber came from Canada and the Baltic. Their wool came from Australia, gold from Nigeria and South Africa, and silver from Peru. Their tea came from China, coffee from East Indian plantations and Latin America, and rubber from Southeast Asia. After the American Civil War (1861–65), their cotton came from Egypt and India.

Goods, services, money, capital, and people moved back and forth in a new world economy that allowed Britain to manipulate the finances of Latin America, the United States, the Far East, Africa, and India. Britain's control of $20 billion of the world's debt indicated that most of the money circulating under the gold standard concentrated in British banks. There, in the United Kingdom, one could expect to see the highest standard of living.

Using textiles as an example of how the empire served the economic interests of the United Kingdom, the British removed Indian tariffs on English clothing in 1879 and forbade India from restricting such imports. Textiles represented only one item in Britain's broad-spectrum assault on India's manufacturing occupations. By opening the Indian market to competition with British industry, Great Britain basically destroyed India's manufacturing crafts.

As mentioned in Chapter Twenty-five, those Indians who had made their living as artisans in 1750 fell from 24.5 percent of the occupational structure to a mere 2 percent by 1914. British policy had in effect reduced India's economy from a complex division of labor to a simple producer of primary goods. Such a primary economic structure complemented Great Britain's industry and met its people's needs. Britain wanted to exploit cheap labor and import raw materials while exporting finished products.

Hence, as the standard of living improved in Great Britain, the material wealth of India declined per capita. Furthermore, while the British condemned India for such poor material statistics, the United Kingdom's high standard of living masked the contributions of India's economy to Britain's well-being. The irony here is that while Westerners believed they were best suited for mastery over the world, they were creating a global economy that sustained only the illusion of progress.

This illusion bolstered Europe's pride in itself and its civilization. Imitating the Europeans, citizens of the United States and Japan developed the same sense of pride. To maintain this pride, however, required control over the affairs of traditional societies, but this control carried with it a very heavy price: violence.

The Quest for Empire and the Habits of Violence

Between 1800 and 1914 the world underwent a level of tension and division that it had never before seen. As more and more territories fell to one European nation or another, less remained for other would-be empire builders. When the United States and Japan entered the race to acquire foreign lands, so-called open spaces (non-European territory) decreased even further. This declining amount of open global space paralleled a growing appetite for empire that increased the competition for what was left. Tellingly, all the imperial nations forgot that what they called open territory had long been occupied by native peoples.

Also, every participant in the scramble to acquire new territories had to develop the military means to consolidate their hold on an expanding empire. Ignoring the natives while divvying up the world, competitor nation-states began to look upon one another as the only other groups of humans about whom they had to worry. Therefore, in order to settle disputes among themselves, Western nations would simply give away parts of someone else's land.

For example, in the new age of empire France and Britain seemingly forgot centuries of international rivalry through a division of territory involving other peoples' land. These two nation-states settled their differences and cemented their *Entente Cordial* of 1904 by France recognizing Britain's hold on Egypt and Britain recognizing France's hold on Morocco. In 1907, France and Great Britain expanded their Entente by including Russia in another deal that saw Russia and Britain dividing Persia to ease tensions over Russia's access to India as described in Chapter Twenty-six.

Great Britain, France, and Russia put together their Triple Entente after Germany, Austria-Hungary, and Italy assembled their Triple Alliance. Established in 1882, the Triple Alliance served to assure Germany that France would not seek revenge for defeat in the Franco-Prussian War (1870–71). Yet when the Entente confronted the Alliance in 1907, Europe suddenly found itself divided into two armed and hostile camps. France, Britain, and Germany were each nation-states, while Italy came close to national status and Austria and Russia represented multiethnic empires that mixed industry with neofeudalism.

Simultaneously, rapid imperial gains in Africa and Asia in the closing years of the nineteenth century had created the illusion that carefully planned and executed violence solved complex problems. Thus, competition for empire and the formation of hostile alliances had combined in the first decade of the twentieth century to create a high level of international tension. The typical response to these tensions was a pursuit of power in Europe that led each nation-state to develop ever more effective instruments of destruction, as described in Chapter Twenty-two.

For example, the Maxim machine-gun appeared in 1884, revealing how efficient the Europeans had become at killing. Using this weapon, a machine-gunner could fire 660 rounds of ammunition in one minute with deadly accuracy from a range of 300 meters. First used against the followers of the Mahdi, Mohammed Ahmed (1848–85) as mentioned in Chapter Twenty-six, Maxim machine-guns proved to be devastating weapons. In the final battle at Omdurman (1898), Mohammed Ahmed's successor Khalifa Abdallahi and his cavalry fell to this modern level of concentrated fire. The commander-in-chief of Anglo-Egyptian forces, General Horatio Herbert Kitchener (1850–1916), systematically slaughtered an estimated 16,000 horsemen in a single afternoon. Such a death rate in war was entirely new in world history. Yet Europeans never imag-

Top: William Randolph Hearst (1863–1951), the only son of a self-made multimillionaire, accumulated his own wealth as magnate of the world's largest publishing empire which included newspapers (notably the *New York Journal*), magazines, news services, radio stations and film studios. His sensationalist style of journalism was known as "yellow journalism" which he successfully used to create competition and increase sales. Hearst was not only a visible figure in publishing but in politics and art as well. Credit: Library of Congress, Washington, D.C. LC-USZ62-68945.

Bottom: Hungarian-born Joseph Pulitzer (1847–1911), alongside his chief rival W. R. Hearst, helped form a style of modern newspaper by combining exposés of political corruption and investigative reporting with publicity stunts, self-promotion, and yellow jounalism. In his will he established the Pulitzer Prizes "for the encouragement of public service, public morals, American literature and the advancement of education." Pulitzer and cover of *The World*. Credit: Library of Congress, Washington, D.C. LC-USZ62-49254.

ined that such slaughter might befall their own people someday.

To the habits of violence developed by Western nation-states, one must add that Europeans had lost touch with the sources of power they commanded. By 1914, no one fully understood the deadly power national armies produced. The political and physical unity of the nation-state had created a military base of such magnitude that Europeans and non-Europeans alike no longer grasped what they would have to do to one another in order to win a general war.

Victories achieved against native armies had lulled Europeans into a sense of invincibility. The danger signs of how destructive war had become were present but ignored. European generals preferred to point out that most of the recent international military disputes had been resolved quickly. They also liked to dwell on the tactics of those modern nation-states that had won these short and relatively painless wars.

Danger Signs in the Short-War Phenomenon

European generals cited the Spanish-American War (1898), the Boer War (1899–1902), and the Russo-Japanese War (1905–06) as examples of how military conflicts had become short engagements. Yet the speed with which each of these conflicts ended masked very important signals for the future.

The Spanish-American War, a conflict between Spain and the United States over Cuba, began when the free press in the United States created one of the first media events (i.e., creating the news rather than reporting it) in world history. The free press told citizens of the United States such an unbalanced account of the struggle for independence in Cuba (a Spanish colony) that these newspapers virtually manufactured "the truth." Thus, the principal function of newspapers in a democracy, keeping the public informed, had been compromised.

The leading American newspapermen of the day, William Randolph Hearst and Joseph Pulitzer, engaged in a circulation war to sell newspapers. In their competition with one another, they distorted the events in

Cuba so badly that they had created a "jingoistic" fever for war in the United States. These distortions trapped the nation's leadership in hostility focused on Spain. Thus, these two newspaper magnates had actually undermined the function of a free press in a democracy by creating public opinion rather than keeping the general population fully informed with accurate information. In effect, Hearst and Pulitzer had taken control of political decisions for U.S. citizens so that the United States had fallen victim to propaganda, very much like the manipulation of the news found in an autocracy.

As a result of the manipulated public opinion, the United States engaged in a war with Spain that utilized naval forces to decide the outcome. The Spanish could not supply or reinforce their colonies in both the Caribbean and Pacific due to superior, modern ships that the U.S. Navy had recently built. Accordingly, the Spanish lost the remainder of their old commercial empire to the United States through several naval engagements that were supported by a minimum of land forces.

In contrast to the Spanish-American War, the Boer War involved two very dangerous levels of conflict: conventional and guerrilla warfare. By focusing on the ability of Afrikaner riflemen on horseback to strike at will in cavalry campaigns against the British infantry, European generals placed too much value on the horse as an effective weapon in conventional war. These generals still believed that mounted troops in Western armies could be decisive in war long after such military formations had outlived their usefulness against modern, mass-produced ordnance. Also what the generals missed was the way the Boers mustered unexpected resistance. Like the Confederates in the American Civil War, the Boers were farmers who proved to be a stubborn and innovative foe.

The Boers in effect fought two wars: first with conventional tactics, the other, with hit-and-run guerrilla tactics. In the conventional phase, the Boers proved very effective marksmen with their breech-loading, magazine-fed Mauser rifles, using them to kill at a long distances. Then, with the development of smokeless gunpowder, the Boers could fire without giving away their positions. Thus, these weapons made the standard infantry assaults the British employed very costly, because attacking a concealed marksman using a magazine-fed, smokeless weapon ensured a high casualty rate long before visual contact with the enemy could be made.

Then, the bitter struggle took a harsh, acute turn. The Boers eventually lost the conventional conflict due to the superior numbers and resources of Great Britain; the United Kingdom simply overwhelmed the Boers. Yet, no one, not even Lord Kitchener, expected the Boers to wage the unconventional war that followed. Using guerilla tactics, the Boers took the nation-in-arms developed during the French Revolution one step further when they committed every man, woman, and child to resisting Lord Kitchener's regulars. At first the astounded British could not defeat this second effort, because the Boers would attack British regulars and then disappear into the civilian population or countryside. Indeed, it was only after Lord Kitchener realized the British were fighting an entire population and adopted the same form of ruthlessness used by his opponents that the British regained the upper hand and secured victory.

Britain's victory over the Boers came only after Lord Kitchener developed a system of blockhouses and barbed-wired stations he called "concentration camps." He used these prison stations to confine Boer women and children while his soldiers burned every farm and farmhouse in the countryside. The unsanitary facilities and inadequate medical supplies in the camps caused many of the confined women and children to die of diseases, even as the resistant Boer partisans starved in the field. Hence, the British had discovered that in order to win a guerrilla war, a nation had to perfect a new level of *total war*: one that destroyed an entire population's will to resist.

A final example of the turn-of-the-century short wars, the Russo-Japanese War (1905–06), saw two significant industrializing powers fighting one another from afar. Supplied only by one railroad, the trans-Siberian railway that connected the European and Asian halves of Russia, the czar had a difficult time massing troops a continent away. Yet, despite this distance, trench warfare developed in the zones of combat.

Trench warfare offered infantry protection from the deadly fire generated by modern weapons. Using parallel lines of fortified ditches, reinforced with barbed-wire and communication trenches, this style of combat compensated for the failure of offensive ordnance keeping pace with defensive weapons. The magazine-fed rifle, the machine gun, and the breech-loading rifled cannon killed more efficiently from concealed stationary positions than on the move. Hence entrenched soldiers outlived anyone on the attack.

Both the Japanese and the Russians had modern rifles. The Japanese could match the Russians on every level of modern technology because Japan had prepared for this struggle. Both had the new Hotchkiss machine-gun (a gas-operated, rapid firing, automatic weapon) and eleven-inch howitzers before they engaged in warfare. The entrenched positions around Port

Arthur, on the Liaodung Peninsula, opposite Beijing, where the combat took place looked very much like Flanders between 1914–18 when British troops faced Germans soldiers in trenches during World War I.

Yet the Japanese developed small assault teams that could penetrate the Russian front lines. Japan's military traditions based on the samurai practice of fighting to the last man while giving a 100 percent effort to succeed had been used by the Japanese to develop such intense infantry attacks that they could cross a no-man's land despite the trenches and withering defensive fire. Aiding the Japanese efforts were the great distances (over 5,000 miles) between the combatants. This distance from European Russia, where the czar concentrated his military strength, and Port Arthur in China, reduced the ability of the Russians to respond effectively.

In addition, Russia's potential for domestic unrest led to the massive Revolution of 1905. Collapse on the home front undermined the czar's ability to focus on the war. This collapse was a signal of how victory would come in the great war that followed. If the czar had heeded this lesson, that commitment to foreign wars might lead to revolution at home, the future of Russia might have been very different.

But it was naval power that ultimately decided the outcome of the Russo-Japanese War. Russia lost two fleets to the effective tactics of able Japanese admirals. The Japanese opened the war with a surprise attack on the Russian fleet at Port Arthur, and then the czar lost his Baltic fleet after it had sailed half way around the world only to suffer destruction in the Tsushima Straits off the coast of Japan. With no other means to effect a victory, the Russians had to sue for peace.

Each of these short wars, the Spanish-American, the Boer, and the Russo-Japanese, forecasted features of World War I. The use of the mass media in the United States to manipulate public opinion, the appearance of concentration camps and the revelation that victory required defeat of an entire enemy population, as well as the appearance of trench warfare combined with the Revolution of 1905 all provided unmistakable signs for the future. Yet none of these signals convinced European generals how dangerous the next war might be, for they continued to believe that modern conflicts would necessarily be short ones. They also believed that both sides would remain rational and seek peace through negotiations if the war lasted longer than a few months.

Misunderstanding the Short-War Phenomenon

The lessons European generals missed, however, were significant. They miscalculated the passions that war released, and they did not understand that a nation committed to victory would not surrender until unconditionally defeated. Yet to cause the unconditional defeat of an enemy nation required the total disintegration of a culture's internal coherence, which had proved to be the basis of national strength. The expense of such a victory, however, would reduce the conquering nation to nearly the same level of collapse as the vanquished state. Ironically, this combination of lessons was not lost on a Russian economist named Ivan S. Bloch.

Bloch wrote a six-volume work published in St. Petersburg in 1897–98 that nearly anticipated every feature of World War I. Bloch's work declared that a great war in Europe would inevitably lead to stalemate. He argued that the combination of political and economic forces supplying armies with modern weapons would hold both sides in a grinding, stagnant struggle. Belligerent nations would be trapped along static fronts until attrition and starvation finally decided the outcome. Civilian populations would be drawn into the struggle on a level never before experienced. And, finally, when the war was over, the victors would have suffered nearly as much loss and devastation as the losers.

Military leaders, however, gave little credence to Bloch's warnings and rejected his judgment across Europe, believing he lacked the training needed to make such declarations. Besides, were they to accept Bloch's conclusions, what would become of their profession? Their reading of warfare was entirely different. They still believed in a war of movement in which such traditional styles of combat as cavalry charges were effective. They believed that the best use of Bloch's work was to intensify the means of warfare to forego Bloch's conclusions. Therefore, they applied Bloch's lessons about the economics of war to increase the nation's ability to resist. Hence, not only did they completely ignore Bloch's warning, but they integrated his knowledge into the tragedy about to unfold.

Partly because Europe had divided itself into two defensive alliances, the Triple Entente (France, Great Britain, and Russia) versus the Triple Alliance (Germany, Austria-Hungary, and Italy), and partly due to both sides anticipating that the next war would be a short but decisive conflict, the assassination of one man launched World War I. A nineteen-year-old Serbian nationalist named Gavril Princep killed the visiting heir to the Austrian throne, Archduke Ferdinand, in a Serbian protest over Austria-Hungary's acquisition of Bosnia-Herzegovina in 1908. What should have been a tragic but minor international incident, however, mushroomed into a major diplomatic confrontation. Russia backed Serbia while Austria-Hungary, with the support of Germany, issued an ultimatum that would have eliminated Serbian sovereignty. When Serbia failed to adhere to Austria's ultimatum, a chain-reaction followed: one nation after another declared war.

Austria-Hungary began first by declaring war on Serbia. Russia responded by mobilizing its forces and declaring war on Austria-Hungary. Germany came to the support of Austria, and France came to the support of Russia as both entered the war. Announcing its decision to go to war with France on August 3, Germany immediately marched through neutral Belgium to attack French forces. Due to its defense pact with Belgium, Great Britain declared war on Germany on August 4. A number of other declarations of war followed.

World War I lasted from 1914 until November 1918, when the armistice ending the conflict was signed. At the start of the war, the major Allied powers were Britain, France, and Russia, soon joined by Japan and later by Italy. Among the other Allies were Belgium, Greece, Montenegro, Portugal, Romania, Serbia, and members of the British Empire—Australia, Canada, India, South Africa, and New Zealand. Opposing them were the Central powers of Germany and Austria-Hungary, with Turkey (the Ottoman Empire) and Bulgaria added later. After a period of neutrality, the United States entered the conflict on the Allied side in 1917.

World War I:
Total War, the Geographic Arena of Combat, Victory, and Defeat

During the Great War of the twentieth century, a style of combat emerged that forever changed the structure of global wealth and power. World War I was the product of three elements: nationalism, the nation-in-arms, and industrial technology. Nationalism concentrated the loyalty of a people on the enterprise of war until either they or their opponent collapsed, either physically or economically, or both. The nation-in-arms mustered the strength of the nation-state to the task of combat as an integration of all its various institutions with a single purpose in mind: victory. Finally, industrial technology determined the geographic space of warfare by defining the "killing zone," which became the physical parameters of combat.

In short, World War I laid the foundations for understanding the twentieth century. Simply put, World War I locked Great Britain, France, Germany, Austria-Hungary, Italy, and Russia, to name a few states, in a confined space of combat defined by the modern weapons of the day. The participating nation-states armed more than 65 million men to fight this war. Each participant sustained its portion of the struggle by mobilizing its public and economy to perpetrate violence.

Each nation-state fought until the stalemate and mutual devastation that Ivan S. Bloch had forecasted became a reality: both sides found themselves locked in a grinding, stagnant war of attrition.

The effort itself was "total" in the sense that all the combatants continued until a power ceased to be able to maintain its integration as a nation-state; thus, "disintegration" of the state defined defeat, and redefined the physical boundaries of the states as well as the defeated peoples' sense of nationalism.

What governed a nation-state's specific military efforts during World War I was the quality of its weapons and leadership. The new weapons locked the combatants together in clearly defined fronts while opposing generals could not devise a method to break the stalemate. Each front held a nation-state in place until its resistance slowly eroded through attrition as the various generals launched attack after failed attack. Each nation's will to fight eroded as troops faced the physical and psychological horrors of World War I. Thus, the weapons of this first global conflict, plus the inability of military commanders to effect a conclusion to war, characterized both the geographic space and the emotional consequences of total war.

The national armies that confronted one another between 1914 and 1918 used weapons that had been developed over the course of the nineteenth century. The most common weapon, the breech-loading rifle, fired a bullet that traveled at 2,000 feet per second and could hit any target a soldier could see. Fed by a magazine of five to eight rounds, the projectiles of the rifle followed a specific line-of-flight at a rate of speed faster than sound. Capable of covering several miles in a few seconds, the bullet could strike a lethal blow against any advancing soldier as the human target approached the concealed rifleman.

To aim the rifle effectively, the marksman had to be stationary. From his hidden position, a soldier could kill an enemy combatant at a range of approximately 300 meters. As a soldier advanced toward an enemy, he could not effectively return fire while in motion. Hence, moving soldiers presented excellent targets and could not fire their rifles as accurately. The use of these types of rifles made soldiers on the defensive (entrenched), far more effective than those in an attacking (advancing) formation.

Complementing the defensive function of the breech-loading rifle, the machine-gun fired 660 rounds per minute, using a rifled barrel. Given this rate of fire, the friction of the bullets flying through a machine gun's barrel created enormous heat. To cool the weapon, and keep it operational, machine guns came equipped with metal-jacketed casings that held water to bathe the heated barrel. But because water weighs eight pounds

The carnage of World War I. Top: A British soldier lies dead, stuck in the barbed wire, November 1918. Courtesy Library of Congress.
Bottom: A Chief Petty Officer demonstrates the operation of a Maxim 1-pounder machine gun, ca. 1898. The Maxim was the world's first automatic machine gun, increasing the slaughter of battle. USS Hist (1898–1911). Photo #: 19-N-14187. Photograph from the Bureau of Ships Collection in the U.S. National Archives.

per gallon, and since the metal-jacketed casings were quite large, machine guns were originally very heavy. Thus, this weapon too became stationary.

A third weapon used in World War I, the rifled-cannon, fired various shells at a range of 18 miles. Rapid-firing, breech-loaded cannon varied in size from a standard 75-millimeter barrel, or 3 inches in diameter, to 280 millimeters, or 11 inches in diameter. Firing shells that carried high explosives, shrapnel, or gas, cannon laid down a field of fire called a barrage. Designed to fill a space the shape of a box with continuous explosions as long as ammunition held out, these weapons could maintain bombardments for days. Since they too had to be stationary to function, cannon joined machine guns and rifles to create a defensive perimeter.

Thus, the three most common weapons of World War I caused soldiers from belligerent nations to assume defensive positions on the battlefield. Movement

stopped when one belligerent nation-state confronted another after their first attempts to win a quick victory had failed. Frontal assaults against entrenched positions proved to be very costly. Thus, each side went through a series of flanking actions that spread expanding trench-networks along a common front. These networks eventually crisscrossed the countryside.

In short order, two complex sets of trench systems appeared on the Western and Eastern Fronts. In the West, these trenches stretched 485 miles from the North Sea to Switzerland's frontier. On the Eastern Front, the length of the trench system progressively increased as Russia retreated until it tripled the area of combat on the Western Front to more than 1,500 miles.

Since Germany fought France and Britain on the Western Front, the high level of industrial power concentrated there allowed each side to develop "defense in depth." As a result, both sides dug a series of parallel trenches, strong points, and enforced bunkers called pill boxes that supported the front lines and offered 50 miles of defensive perimeter. This entrenchment created a front so wide that even cannon fire could not cut through it.

To attack a position on the Western Front required several days of bombardment. Concentrated artillery fire was supposed to cut as much of the enemy trench network as possible. Yet when an assault began, so many attacking soldiers had to be amassed for a drive through the remaining trenches that they marched like an ancient Greek phalanx into a well-prepared defensive front. Charging into machine-gun fire, creeping barrages of high explosives, and stationary riflemen, the attacking force typically lost thousands of men and gained little in exchange. The death toll in these trench-warfare clashes exceeded anything ever previously imagined.

On the Eastern Front, the length of the trenches precluded the possibility of defense in depth. With a front of over 1,500 miles, the Russians could not concentrate as many troops in support fortifications and reinforced bunkers behind their front lines. Despite the enormous manpower available to the czar, a combined assault by German and Austrian troops slowly drove the Russians back and weakened their army. There, movement was possible, but the rate of advance was very slow.

In this way, three years of combat took place before the czarist regime in Russia began to show signs of collapse. To keep the pressure on the czar, the Germans hit upon an effective strategy that almost gave them victory: use offensive tactics on the Eastern Front, and assume the defensive on the Western Front.

To relieve pressure on the czar, the British and the French attempted attack after attack on the Germans on the Western Front. Consequently, a slow, grinding war of attrition developed in the West, forcing both sides to acquire the techniques of indirect warfare, such as the use of magnetic mines (underwater explosives) and U-boats (submarines).

Indeed, the navies of the belligerent states ignored surface warfare after just one battle, off Jutland in 1916. The German grand fleet left port only to be turned back, but both sides suffered heavy losses: eleven major German ships to fourteen British ships. Rifled cannon fire had proved too accurate to give either side a decisive victory, and the German surface fleet never left port again. Instead, confrontation at sea now involved war zones in which any ship traveling to a belligerent nation lay vulnerable to surprise attack from a magnetic mine or a submarine. Such attacks killed civilians from neutral nations as efficiently as they killed enemy combatants. Neither mines nor submarines conformed to the existing rules of war, yet both sides used them freely.

Britain violated international law first when it laid mines in the North Sea, declaring the whole area off-limits to shipping. Germany followed suit by developing a war zone around Great Britain using unlimited submarine warfare to starve the island nation into submission. Both techniques violated the law because a blockade required surface vessels to halt all ships approaching an enemy port to safeguard the noncombatants and neutral personnel traveling by sea. Hence both Britain and Germany should have offended the United States equally. But President Woodrow Wilson's strong sense of respect for Great Britain created a bias in the United States in favor of the Allies.

President Wilson spearheaded a diplomatic assault on Germany, trying to force that power to restrict its use of submarines. At the same time, Wilson put very little pressure on the British to change their naval tactics or use of magnetic mines. The result was that the United States drifted toward war with Germany. The timing of American hostility proved critical because the United States entered the war just as British and French strength waned on the Western Front. Prior to that entry, however, a foundation for conflict between the U.S. and Germany had already been laid.

On May 7, 1915, the German submarine, *U-20*, had hit the British passenger ship, the *Lusitania*, with two torpedoes. Carrying ammunition and other war contraband purchased in the United States, the *Lusitania* exploded and sank rapidly off the coast of Ireland, killing over 1,000 people, 128 of them U.S. citizens. The German assault on the luxury liner sparked an international incident that almost led to a break in diplomatic relations between Germany and the United States. Yet vigorous protests by Washington, and Germany's willingness to limit submarine warfare in the second year of the war prevented an open breach between the U.S. and the Kaiser. By 1917, however, the military situation had changed: Russia was near collapse, and the possibility of war on one front encouraged the Germans to resume unlimited submarine warfare. This change in policy pushed the U.S. to the brink of war.

By maintaining pressure on Russia, Germany succeeded in sparking a major revolution in March of 1917. Anticipating this potential collapse, the Germans had resumed unlimited submarine warfare in January. Calculating that war would eventually occur between the U.S. and Germany, and knowing that Wilson had won reelection in 1916 by boasting that he had kept the United States out of World War I, the Germans hoped to complete Russia's defeat, and launched an offensive on the Western Front, prior to a U.S. mobilization for war. Yet the Russian Revolution of March 1917 had briefly changed that autocratic state into a democracy.

Given the fact that all the major forces fighting Germany in April 1917 (Russia, Britain, and France) now appeared to be democratic in form, Wilson decided to declare war on the Germans. He did so as the first step in a crusade to make "the world safe for democracy." This decision created a delicate balance of power on the Western Front that Germany ultimately lost.

Even as the United States mobilized for war, the Russian Revolution shifted phases when the Germans aided Vladimir Ilyich Lenin (1870–1924) to return to his native land to lead the *Bolsheviks* (Lenin's Communist Party). The Bolshevik phase of the Russian Revolution ended the war on the Eastern Front with a Germany victory (the Treaty of Brest Litovsk, 1918). Yet this military success did not come in time for Germany, for by then, the United States had mobilized an army of 4.5 million. By the summer of 1918, 1 million of these soldiers had arrived in France to help stop the German offensive of March 1918.

The German generals then squandered 1 million of their reserve soldiers without breaking American, French, and British resistance. More fresh American troops then joined Allied forces now confronting an exhausted German army, reversing conditions on the Western Front, and slowly driving the Germans back. Pressed to its limits, the German nation-state collapsed. As in Russia, food riots at home and a defeated army in the field forced the General Staff to report to the Kaiser that the war had been lost. Austria then fell as well.

Defeat was total. The losers underwent profound change. Czarist Russia saw the beginnings of the first communist experiment under Bolshevik rule. Austria-Hungary lost 85 percent of its territory through the creation of Poland, Yugoslavia, Hungary, Czechoslovakia, and an enlarged Romania. Germany struggled through two political experiments: the Weimar Republic and the rise of the dictator Adolf Hitler. All three political upheavals completely transformed each nation as well as Europe's role in the world.

At the same time, the European victors of the Great War ceased to be the richest creditor nations of the world. Both Britain and France had gone into debt to the United States to raise the funds to defeat Germany. In addition, both Great Britain and France had sacrificed the best and the brightest of their youth on the Western Front. Exhausted from war, demoralized from the irrational manner in which they had won their victory, and no longer convinced that Europe was the apex of human civilization, these two Western European states lost their sense of purpose. Unfortunately, they had managed to fulfill Ivan S. Bloch's prediction completely: they were the victors, but they had suffered nearly the same degree of loss as the vanquished.

World War I had cost Europe its hold on the differential of power. Weakened to the point of collapse, the victors now depended on the United States for financial strength, while Russia had begun transforming itself into the Soviet Union. Germany and Austria floundered through attempts at redefinition that ended with a form of political insanity under Adolf Hitler that galvanized both states onto a new war footing. And non-European cultures saw an opportunity to apply the lessons that Europe had taught about power and nation-formation to redefine their role in the world. The international scene had now completely mutated.

Suggested Reading

Albertini, Luigi, *The Origins of the War of 1914,* Three Volumes. Translated by Isabella M. Massey (London: Oxford University Press, 1952–57).

Eckstein, Modris, *Rites of Spring: The Great War and the Birth of the Modern Age* (Boston/New York: First Mariner Books, 2000).

Fieldhouse, D. K., *Colonialism (1870–1945)* (New York: St. Martin, 1981).

Gilbert, Felix, *The End of the European Era, 1890 to the Present* (New York: Norton, 1979).

Gilbert, Martin, *The First World War* (New York: Henry Holt and Company, 1994).

Hale, Oron J., *The Great Illusion, 1900–1914* (New York: Harper and Row Publishers, 1971).

Joll, James, *The Origins of the First World War,* Second Edition (New York: Longman, 1991).

Keegan, John, *The Face of Battle* (New York: Penguin Books, Reprinted Edition, 1995).

Keegan, John, *The First World War* (New York: Alfred A. Knopf, 1999).

Liddell-Hart, Basil H., *History of the First World War* (London: Pan Books, 1970).

Preston, Richard A., Sydney F. Wise, and Herman O. Werner, *Men in Arms: A History of Warfare,* Revised Edition (New York: Praeger, 1965).

Mommsen, W. J., *Theories of Imperialism.* Translated by P. S. Falla (New York: Random House, 1980).

XXVIII

TOTALITARIANISM:
The Soviet Union and Nazi Germany

After World War I, Russia and Germany began a political experiment that ensured the twentieth century would be one of the most violent in world history. As the two most potentially powerful vanquished states of the Great War, Russia and Germany entered a new age of autocracy using lessons learned from World War I. Russia became the Soviet Union and Germany fell under the control of the dictator Adolf Hitler.

Both states now had totalitarian regimes that produced a new political reality through the sheer willpower of a people transfixed by dictatorship. Both were hostile to the external world, which they hailed as threatening enough to require maintaining a despotic central government. Both mobilized national politics along military lines based on lessons learned from the war, and each distrusted the other enough to desire its destruction.

At the same time, the victors of World War I had lost faith in themselves as well as in their definition of civilization. Since Europeans measured reality through human creativity expressed in culture, how could any so-called rational, modern, and advanced civilization claim to be the pinnacle of human achievement and yet engage in four years of war where the only species that prospered were trench rats? Since these rats thrived on both fronts by eating the flesh of the dead and dying, what type of animal species were the "civilized" humans who had created these battlefields?

How could European nation-states continue to condemn the rest of the world as backward when Western society had used science and technology to kill 10 million young men and had made 20 million vulnerable to the flu? How could the nations of Europe hold their heads high knowing that the deaths of these people had eliminated the very best generation their culture had to offer the world? Where was the reason that Europeans claimed to have whenever they engaged in political action if they allowed such a war to continue despite the unimaginable destruction it produced? Un-

able to answer these questions, European demoralization set in.

The demoralization that followed was profound. For the victors, it took the form of international weakness. Britain, France, and the United States had lost faith in their moral codes, while the British and French had suffered a devastating human and material loss. Yet nowhere was demoralization more profoundly felt than among the people of the defeated powers. Their degree of demoralization would have to be very high to allow someone like Adolf Hitler to come to power.

The world was now in transition, as the location of power began to shift away from Europe. New powers including the United States, the Soviet Union, and Japan emerged to take Europe's place.

European empires everywhere began to show signs of erosion. Europe had not only paid heavily in human life, but it had squandered the wealth its nation-states had accumulated over the course of the nineteenth century. Britain and France had liquidated their combined $28.7 billion in loans and gone into debt to the United States for some $10 billion in gold. Germany had lost its $6 billion entirely, lost its empire, and was forced, by the terms of the peace treaty the Allies drafted in Versailles, to submit to a penalty, a war indemnity of $35 billion. While the United States and Japan had become creditor nations, the financial structure of the world was in disarray.

Totalitarianism

The vast demoralization suffered by the defeated powers of World War I led to a new model of political authority—*totalitarianism*—which changed the face of world history. Extending autocratic power to its logical conclusion, totalitarianism transformed the principle of authoritarian rule into its most intense and modern design. Totalitarianism concentrated the instruments of national politics in the hands of a single dictator who sought a self-proclaimed historical destiny based on the unrestrained application of Machiavelli's notion that "the end justifies the means."

Combining a common formal design with a set of personal political objectives, totalitarian states differed in content but not in design. The formal features of totalitarianism linked the lessons of total war with the complete mobilization of a nation's will during times of peace. The actual features of totalitarian power depended on the specific cultural circumstances of the nation utilizing it. In one state, the features might reflect the philosophy of Karl Marx adjusted to local cultural needs. In another, it might reflect the racist intuitions of a national Fascist leader whose rise to power combined defeat in World War I with postwar demoralization and economic dire straits. In either case, both the form and structure of the totalitarian state blended together to generate the most intense concentration of authoritarian rule to date.

In the aftermath of World War I, the Soviet Union, Italy, and Germany/Austria each became fully developed totalitarian states. They were the first to establish the political forms needed for total command over their societies. To achieve this control, they integrated four key features of power: first, each developed a single-party state; then, each introduced absolute control over mass communications; next, each extended this control to any social, economic, or political form of assembly; and finally, each refused to allow any legal restraints on the will of their leader.

All four of these features of totalitarianism revealed that the new autocratic state had taken on a war footing using revolutionary authority as its justification. But whether these despotic governments were radical or conservative, they all used the total war model for mobilizing the home front.

The Soviet Union

The style of totalitarianism in the Soviet Union was an expression of its unique revolution under an all-powerful leader, Vladimir Lenin. Lenin required absolute control over all socioeconomic conditions in what was once czarist Russia in order to create a Marxist society in a country not yet ready for communism. Given the steps he took to win the Russian Revolution (see below for details), and to shape the future society he desired, Lenin found himself forced to create the first totalitarian regime.

The first step in achieving his Marxist goals, however, had occurred long before the Russian Revolution, when Lenin defined the revolutionary function of a political party in 1903. During a meeting of the Russian Social Democratic Party held in London, Lenin

set the standards of political conduct needed to establish totalitarian rule.

During this Party Congress, Lenin demanded a strongly centralized party; he wanted to concentrate absolute authority at the top of the party structure. From this position, he wished to create a "party-line" for all other members to obey. Issuing from a central revolutionary committee at the top, the party-line would then pass down the ranks to the base of his political organization. Through this vertical power scheme, Lenin hoped to create one professional, revolutionary will that would shape all political action.

Lenin's new design for this political party reflected the conditions facing him as a Marxist hoping to create a communist society in a culture that had not yet achieved the capitalist phase of history. Lenin wanted to avoid what Karl Marx condemned as voluntarism, which involved launching a revolution prematurely, before a state's industrial economic base was fully developed. Such an effort not only would fail but would also cause Lenin to produce capitalism—the very thing that he hoped to destroy.

Russian Marxists knew that capitalism and the industrial revolution were necessary to create the vast working class needed for communism. An industrial revolution transformed society by relocating the majority of people in cities where they could acquire literacy, the ability to calculate, and the capacity to engage in critical thinking that would make them politically active. The industrial proletariat was essential to Marxism because the working class alone had the correct social experiences and mental skills needed to understand the "scientific" truths of communism.

Proletarians could read, write, add, subtract, and engage in the political thinking needed to mobilize the masses of oppressed labor whose energy (according to Marx) had created all the wealth of the world, but who were historically mired in poverty. They alone could generate the numbers needed for a swift victory in a Marxist revolution, a brief dictatorship of the proletariat, and the necessary transition period to a stateless and classless society as described by the Marxist vision. Yet, not enough of these precious industrial workers existed in Russia to achieve the reality that Marx had predicted. Like all other Russian Marxists, Lenin found himself forced to develop a political strategy that would allow him to avoid voluntarism, complete the evolution of capitalism without becoming a capitalist himself, and establish a Marxist reality.

Given the small proletariat available in Russia in 1900, this country seemed the least likely place for a communist revolution to occur. Only 7.5 percent of the total population had become proletarians. Also, 64 percent of Russia's population remained peasants. The likelihood of Marxism taking root in this social environment would be very remote. Marx himself despised peasants for their lack of literacy and critical thinking skills, which made them subject to superstitious beliefs (religion) and political manipulation.

Marx had described peasants as politically untrustworthy. Their *praxis*, or work experience, derived from both rural and traditional sources. As a result, peasants were illiterate, bound by tradition, and dependent on religion. Consequently, peasants represented a major threat to any true radical movement, especially a communist revolution, even though they might happily participate in spontaneous revolts against their immediate circumstances.

Peasants were dangerous because they were fundamentally conservative and had been used as counterrevolutionaries in nineteenth-century Europe. Peasants had fought the Radical Republicans in the Second Phase of the French Revolution (1792–95) and had aided in the defeat of spontaneous revolutions in Europe during the 1820s, 1830s, and 1848. Any political leader who appealed to the peasant's appetite for bread and land could easily manipulate them. Lenin, therefore, saw them as a revolutionary tool, but, clearly could not trust a Marxist future to the free will of peasants.

Since any Russian communist thoroughly trained in Marx's political theory believed that the only acceptable socioeconomic system was communism, he could not tolerate having to fight a revolution to establish capitalism first. Yet, if he did not, then he would be surrounded by peasants, not the proletariat. Only a capitalist experience could convert peasants into working-class people while focusing their political rage on the owners of stock.

Without this necessary step of social transformation, the Marxist revolutionary would become a voluntarist and as such the source of capitalist change and the target of peasant rage. Ironically, such a Marxist would then himself be overthrown by other Marxists who had waited until the right moment to rebel.

As a careful reader of Karl Marx, Lenin had discovered that his political mentor spoke with two voices. The first advocated pure theory to criticize private property. The second analyzed society from the socioeconomic perspective. The first voice spoke of class struggle, while the second tended to dissolve class as a social entity. Each voice functioned in a different way and did not share a common intellectual space.

As an advocate of pure theory, Marx argued that class created a cohesive social group that divided society into hostile camps whose work-experience defined collective consciousness. As a historical commentator, Marx demonstrated that class was not actually as cohesive as his theory suggested. His analysis of the French Revolution, the Sepoy Rebellion, and the Revolutions of 1848 identified individuals whose moral consciousness might elevate them above their personal socioeconomic experiences and allow them to escape their class consciousness. Marx's historical commentaries revealed that within class specific individuals might function like chance personalities (i.e., individuals capable of free thought independent of social existence) in human history. These people Marx called "the educators."

Noting that all revolutions in modern history had been instigated by the educators, not the oppressed, Marx argued that these so-called chance personalities were essential to his vision of history. Marx himself fit into this category. He came from the professional class that composed the heart of the *bourgeoisie* (the capitalist middle class). His moral detachment from the bourgeoisie, however, allowed him to attempt to educate the proletariat.

Marx's father was a lawyer. Marx himself was a historian and newspaper reporter. Yet Karl Marx chose to abandon his bourgeois roots and take up leadership of the proletariat because he had a unique personality and a strong sense of indignation at what he called, "humanity's long history of exploitation."

Like Marx, Vladimir Lenin also came from the bourgeoisie. His father was an inspector of education for the czar and a member of Russia's upper–middle class with a bureaucratic rank equal to that of a major general in the military. Like Marx, Lenin rejected his social upbringing and abandoned capitalist values. He accepted Marxism as the one true social science.

Vladimir Lenin (1870–1924), Bolshevik leader and founder of the Communist Party in Russia, leads the Russian Revolution in Moscow, 1917. Austrian National Library, ÖNB/Wien #1556181–Pf 7521 C(18).

Lenin joined the cause of the proletariat after the execution of his older brother in 1887 for plotting against the czar. A student demonstrator and resident of the czar's prison system in Siberia, Lenin converted to Marxism in his youth. As a passionate ideologue, Lenin built his political agenda on Marx's concept of the educator. He proposed the idea of creating a professional revolutionary party within Russia that could function as a corps of educators to oversee and direct the revolution. Functioning as the vanguard to this Marxist revolution, the educators would convert Russian peasants to Marxism and prepare them for revolutionary change. Made up of a tiny minority of radicals in the international Marxist movement, Lenin's party, the Bolsheviks (the majority)—so-called because they had won the majority vote of the Party Congress in 1903—accepted the discipline of a professional revolutionary cadre.

Lenin developed his party of educators into a corps of 6,000 professionals by 1917. Using these people as skilled agitators, Lenin built a revolution on the ashes of the czarist regime after World War I. With this tiny coterie of leaders, Lenin hoped to transform the destiny of Europe after capturing power in Russia.

In the midst of World War I, with an exhausted Europe seemingly on the verge of collapse, Lenin saw the Russian Revolution begin in March 1917 and hoped it would become a potential political tool for global change. Viewing World War I as a capitalist exercise in profit-seeking, Lenin called total war the final phase of capitalism, in an ultimately flawed system that could only end in class and international warfare. His political goal was to gain control of the revolutionary process in Russia and then export it to Europe. Once in power in Europe, Lenin hoped to use the human resources of the industrialized West—the vast pool of angry proletarians—to succeed.

Joined by Leon Trotsky (1879–1940), a Menshevik (one of those who voted against Lenin in 1903), Lenin produced the idea of "Minority Revolution" to capture leadership in the unfolding revolutionary drama occurring in Russia. Linking with Trotsky's theory of Permanent Revolution (1905), Lenin argued that once the proletariat struggle began, it had to continue without regard for national boundaries and spread from Russia into Europe. Since Marxism had declared that the state was the instrument of oppression used by the ruling class, all nation-states had to be destroyed. Thus a Marxist revolution in any location on Earth was, in fact, an international movement dedicated to liberating the entire world from the evils of private property.

Consistent with Lenin's vision of exporting revolution, Trotsky's concept of a continuous Marxist insurrection matched Lenin's ideas in November 1917. Adapting Permanent Revolution to Minority Revolutionary Theory allowed Lenin and Trotsky to capture leadership of the revolutionary process and convert Russia into a political platform for world change. Thus, they both saw the Russian Revolution as only the first step in a general European/global struggle that would meet the needs of Marxist theory.

Lenin initiated his first phase of the Russian Revolution in November 1917. He captured power and began War Communism (i.e., class warfare in Euro-Russia). Declaring peace with Germany in 1918, Lenin gave away most of European Russia to the Germans, believing he would recover these losses later when he captured all of Europe.

Having a mere 6,000 original Bolsheviks to work with, Lenin faced an enormous task. He had to recruit Mensheviks, socialists, anarchists, and other radicals to carry out his political plans. He also needed this growing political party to implement an expanding revolutionary process. Yet each new recruit to his party came from an undisciplined, untrustworthy source he generally considered to be outsiders.

Growing rapidly from 6,000 to 200,000 and filled with these unreliable people charged with the function of political education, Lenin's party tried to control the historical destiny of 170 million Russians. Forced to exclude from the political dialogue all other opinions except Bolshevism, Lenin had to ensure that only his original 6,000 had a legitimate political voice. He therefore had to police his own party, divide the inner circle from the new recruits, and see to it that party discipline was rigidly enforced everywhere.

Lenin imposed a military discipline to his vastly expanded party's internal organization. Commands came from the central revolutionary committee at the top. Freedom of speech existed only in this central committee, while everyone else had to obey. Even still, Lenin saw the need to develop a secret police force to watch the conduct of each party member as well as that of the general population.

As the revolutionary struggle unfolded, War Communism created pure class conflict in Russia: Lenin had begun Marx's Dictatorship of the Proletariat. According to Marx, such a dictatorship was necessary because only the working class had the correct social consciousness needed to make the correct social decisions and be trusted to obey Marxist policy. All other classes were suspect and had to be eventually eradicated.

Yet if the proletariat did not constitute the vast majority of the people, this stage of dictatorship could go on indefinitely. Would not the dictatorship then become a state, function as the instrument of a new class, and thus violate Marx's vision of a classless and stateless society? These were Lenin's problems.

Promising the peasants "Land, Peace, and Bread" to win their loyalty, Lenin gave 64 percent of his population what they craved: their own farms, carved out of the vast supply of land captured in the revolution. Ruling by expediency to meet immediate needs, Lenin controlled sufficient popular support to retain power while World War I played out in Europe. Organizing the *Cheka* as a secret police to suppress any political opposition within or outside his party, Lenin's revolution moved toward the day when it could be exported to Europe. Yet, just when that day seemed to dawn, the general European revolution failed to materialize. Now Lenin found his movement trapped within Russia and surrounded by peasants.

European Marxists like Rosa Luxemburg, Karl Leibknecht, and Bela Kun had launched Marxist revolutions that complemented Lenin's efforts in Russia. Luxemburg and Leibknecht had organized the Spartacist Movement in Germany between November 1918 and January 1919. In January 1919 they attempted to overthrow the new Social Democratic government of Germany. Yet the German army, members of the radical right, and the new Weimar Republic (1919–33) joined forces to destroy the Spartacists. Their revolutionary failure led to their summary execution in January as communism lost two of its brightest stars.

Bela Kun led a Bolshevik-style revolt in Hungary. Captured on the Russian Front during World War I, Kun had joined the Bolsheviks during Lenin's revolution. Kun was then sent back to Hungary in March 1919 to persuade the Hungarian communists and Social Democrats to form a coalition government. Under his dictatorship, Kun set out to spread the revolution throughout Europe. He managed to overrun Slovakia and influence affairs in Bavaria, but his regime collapsed after his defeat by a Romanian army of intervention. Bela Kun himself then fled to Russia, where he met his death during the great purges of the 1930s.

Even though he was absorbed with his own revolution, Lenin hoped to give all possible aid to the leftist-socialist movements in Europe. As part of the overall design of world revolution, the Bolsheviks sent large sums of money to Germany, Sweden, and Italy. These investments, however, accomplished nothing given the ideological hostility of the victorious Allies to Bolshevism, coupled with the determination of anticommunist elites who took political control of the new states created in Central and Eastern Europe out of territories taken from Austria and Russia. While Lenin contemplated supporting Bela Kun with a military expedition, he had to abandon the idea as strategically infeasible as the success of conservative opposition to the Bolsheviks became firmly established in Finland, Estonia, Latvia, Lithuania, Poland, Czechoslovakia, Hungary, Yugoslavia, and an expanded Romania.

Meanwhile, the majority of European socialists seemed to reject Lenin's movement and watched as Bolshevik efforts failed wherever they sprang up in Europe. No collapse of capitalism followed World War I as Lenin and Trotsky anticipated. Even when the Red Army tried to invade Poland to spark revolution in 1920, the Poles defeated this Bolshevik drive.

Late in 1920 the political crisis of revolutionary isolation began as Lenin was confined in a country that he did not admire or trust. Now he had to revise his plans to transform Russia into a communist society. Simultaneously, Lenin faced a hostile population of peasants caught up in the midst of a famine.

Russia's growing social rage rested on the chaos caused by war and revolution. Industrial production had fallen to 13 percent of its output in 1914. The new Soviet Union was in complete disarray after seven years of conflict (1914–21). Some 20 million people suffered near-starvation. Meanwhile, an internationally distrusted Russia began 1921 with no prospect of foreign aid.

To retain power, Lenin had to rethink his principal political goals. His new objective was to transform Russia into a suitable Marxist society. At the same time, he wanted to maintain an international revolutionary movement. Finally, to accomplish both goals he had to avoid becoming the capitalist Marx had forecasted for those who began a communist revolution too soon. All these concerns combined to place a heavy burden upon Lenin.

Abandoning War Communism, Lenin launched the second phase of his revolution, the New Economic Policy. Tolerating private property in agriculture, Lenin allowed the peasants to keep their land, produce food, and sell excess grain for a profit. He hoped to tax the surplus as a source of revenue to revive industry and supply a growing industrial working class. He also allowed private management to appear in small firms of twenty or less workers. Yet the state would retain control of heavy industry, transportation, finance, and international commerce.

Simultaneously, Lenin redefined Soviet foreign policy. He proposed a dual form of international rela-

Leon Trotsky, the Marxist and Bolshevik revolutionary is shown addressing the Red Guard, which consisted of armed workers as well as defectors, mutineers, or decommissioned soldiers. The purpose of the militia was to instigate, support, or defend communist revolutions. Trotsky, the People's Commissar for War from 1918 to 1924, is often credited with its founding at the time of the Revolution. Credit: Library of Congress, Washington, D.C. LC-DIG-ggbain-3302.

trajectory that required, paradoxically, a state designed to end all states.

Thus, in the midst of the New Economic Policy, Lenin set up the first totalitarian regime. The Bolshevik party was to be the heart of this new state. Its membership provided the educators Lenin needed to train the different ethnic groups in the Soviet Union to accept a Marxist reality. These educators required access to all the people, so they had to control all forms of the mass media and assembly.

Their message had to speak with one voice. Hence, the party design had to be vertically articulated, and its members had to obey the central leadership without question. Free speech existed only in one location: the *Politburo* (the committee at the apex of political power), in which all political decisions would be made. Since the Politburo could not err due to its role as the brain trust of Marxism, abrupt shifts in policy required the use of terror as an instrument of revolution. Terror transferred responsibility for errors in judgment from the Politburo to Soviet society so that the Bolsheviks could continue to claim omniscience in the revolutionary process. Thus no legal restraint on how the party imposed its will on Soviet society could be used to limit the Politburo as it struggled to design the correct revolutionary path to follow. The law itself became a political fiction created by the state for its arbitrary use. Lenin still believed, however, that the Bolshevik state would continue to exist only as long as revolutionary action was necessary.

Lenin completed each of these steps just before he suffered a series of stokes that ended his life. Having survived revolution and having restructured Russia into a Union of Soviet Socialist Republics, Lenin died at exactly the wrong moment. He left an instrument of power that needed his command of theory to achieve his revolutionary goals. Into his place stepped Josef Vissarionovich Stalin (1879–1953).

Stalin rose to power because his colleagues misjudged his appetite for command and his tactical skills at party politics. They had allowed Stalin to take the post of Secretary General of the Communist Party because they felt that this administrative office was appropriate for someone without a significant intellectual Marxist reputation. Misjudging Stalin as a dullard, his colleagues allowed him control of the Bolshevik party's

tions that offered two conflicting styles of diplomacy. While maintaining a Communist International Committee for World Revolution, the Comintern, Russia also entered an era of "peaceful coexistence" with Europe. Lenin developed this double diplomacy to create normal relations with powerful European nation-states he wished to exploit as a source of foreign aid while pursuing his hidden goal of world revolution.

Such a mixture of peaceful and revolutionary goals required absolute political control. This control had to descend from the top based on the Bolshevik variation of Marxist theory. Also, such control would help Russia avoid "neo-capitalism" as a alternative form of the fourth productive stage in human history that Marx had defined in his unilinear teleological model of social evolution. Each step in creating this new level of control had to be seamless in design.

The goal of world revolution was essential, but it would have to go underground. Until the day when communism actually materialized, a new state apparatus of awesome power had to be constructed in Russia. This state would have to impose the Dictatorship of the Proletariat upon the emerging Soviet Union until private property collapsed everywhere else in the world. Consequently, Lenin had to launch a revolution of infinite administration because they viewed him as a workhorse. They had no idea that he harbored secret ambitions of his own.

Stalin began his rise to ultimate power by staffing key posts in the vertically articulated party hierarchy with men loyal to him. Gaining control over the party structure in this manner allowed him to swing key votes. In the debate between his colleagues as to the next appropriate policy move, Stalin isolated his rivals and excluded or expelled them from the Bolshevik party for failing to follow the party-line. As each went, so did his legitimate voice in shaping the vision that would guide the Soviet Union.

Playing one against another, Stalin eliminated Leon Trotsky, Gregori Yevseyevich Zinoviev, Lev Borisovih Kamenev, Nikolai Ivanovich Bukharin, and others between 1924 and 1928. Each fell by fighting one another, while Stalin used the party apparatus to back one side or the other and exclude all their voices. At the same time, he eliminated the right for anyone to have a legitimate political opinion other than his own. By 1936 he felt strong enough to purge the party structure. He executed all his old colleagues who had remained in Russia and had recanted. Finally, in 1940, he killed Trotsky, the only original revolutionary and rival who had left the Soviet Union in 1929 to oppose Stalin from abroad (for more on Stalin's purges, see page 468).

At the end of this process, Stalin alone commanded the future of the Soviet Union. Yet his vision was blurred in the sense that his understanding of Marxism reflected the expediency with which he rose to power. Having no firm anchor in Marxist theory, Stalin's political voice shifted with domestic and international circumstances. His goal was to make the Soviet Union a world-class power. Russia as a platform for worldwide revolutionary change would come second, if at all.

For Stalin, success simply meant survival. As international circumstances shifted around him, he adjusted his domestic politics. At the core, his sole claim to an intellectual reputation revealed what he wanted to achieve. In 1924 he wrote a pamphlet to proclaim *Socialism in One Country* and adhered to its dictates throughout his life.

Hence, world revolution gave way to communism in Russia, as Stalin set about creating a state capable of defending itself against all external challenges. Yet the absence of a clear international strategy for world Marxism threatened to make the state designed to end all states a permanent political reality. Should such a state actually come into existence, then the Russian revolution would have failed to achieve its Marxist goals. A state,

any state, was the instrument of an oppressing class. Paradoxically, Lenin had created the monster he tried to destroy. Simultaneously, the language of revolution that justified the Bolshevik state required an international revolution. Accordingly, the Soviet Union between World War I and World War II found itself caught in a political contradiction it would never resolve.

Nazi Germany

While Stalin fought to consolidate his hold on the Soviet Union, a second defeated power of World War I also adopted the totalitarian form of governance. Germany, however, fell to a revolution from the right rather than from the left. Prior to this fall, a crestfallen and demoralized German people had struggled for fourteen years to maintain a democracy, the so-called Weimar Republic (1919–33).

Democracy, however, did not sit well with an autocratic nation-state like Germany. Shocked by their defeat, certain that they should have won, and eager for revenge, the Germans could not accept the outcome of World War I. Forced to accept the Weimar Republic by the Allies, the Kaiser's Second Reich (the state created by Bismarck) and the people of that state, had little patience with liberalism and admired only strong, cunning men like Frederick the Great, Bismarck himself, and General Field Marshal Count Helmuth von Moltke, the military architect of 1864, 1866, and 1870–71. These were men who had maintained that Germany's political destiny required "blood and iron." Such men mocked the liberal tradition of Germany that had won nothing but failure in the past, such as all of the liberal revolutions of the 1820s, the 1830s, and 1848.

Coupled with the collapse brought on by defeat in the Great War, most Germans could not understand why Germany had to surrender in November 1918 while their army still held enemy territory. They did not know that Wilhelm II had been persuaded to abdicate by his generals, Hindenburg and Ludendorff, for the good of the nation, because his armies would not and could not continue to fight. Instead, the Germans watched a new democratic regime take the Kaiser's place and accept the humiliation of surrender under terms dictated by the Allies. Then, they saw this same Weimar government sign the Versailles Treaty, in which the Allies forced Germany to accept an impossibly high war indemnity, blame for the disastrous war itself, and a reduction of German military power to utter impotence (see insert below). In the German mind, this "stab in the back" caused by the democratic forces of Germany appeared consistent with the weakness and disaster that democrats had always imposed on Germany in the past.

The Versailles Treaty

The Versailles Treaty coupled the desire for revenge and national security after four years of total war suffered by France and Britain, with the territorial ambitions of Italy (who had joined the Allies in 1915 for material gain) and the idealistic goals of the United States. Expressed by President Woodrow Wilson in a speech concerning his fourteen points, which he presented to the world in January of 1918, U.S. idealism comprised such principles as: 1) the end to all secret treaties and diplomatic agreements; 2) freedom of the high seas both in wartime and during peace; 3) the removal of barriers and inequities to international trade (a global opendoor policy); 4) the worldwide reduction of armaments by all powers; 5) colonial readjustments to meet the needs of subject peoples; 6) evacuation of all enemyheld territories; 7) the self-determination of ethnic groups in Central and Eastern Europe seeking national identity; and 8) the creation of an international organization to prevent future global wars, the League of Nations. The contradictory nature of these Allied goals, revenge, security, material gain, and idealism, denied the possibility of the victorious powers producing a coherent and effective document in 1919.

Delegates from 27 nations and traditional cultures assembled in Paris in January 1919, but both Russia and Germany had been excluded from the negotiations. Trying to achieve a treaty that Wilson had described as "an open covenant openly arrived at," soon became impossible given the cross-purposes of everyone present. Instead a more secretive process began where conferences held by the United States, Great Britain, France, and Italy, the Big Four, set the tone for the agreement. In these conferences, Wilson's stern and stubborn idealism ran headlong into British Prime Minister David Lloyd George's fiery and quixotic nature, French Premier George Clemenceau's determined patriotic cynicism, and Italy's Premier Vittorio Orlando's obstinate insistence that the Italians receive territorial concessions to compensate for the cost of the war. What emerged was a document that no one truly liked.

With regard to European security, the Allies designed the treaty to provide protection against any future German aggression. On this subject, Clemenceau refused to yield. He hoped to reduce Germany to a size smaller than France, eliminate the German capacity to initiate conflict, and impose the cost of the war on this vanquished nation. Partially successful, Clemenceau gained control of Germany's Saar coal mines for fifteen years, established a demilitarized zone in the Rhineland (German territory west of the Rhine), recovered Alsace-Lorraine (lost to Bismarck in the Franco-Prussian War), and was to receive 70 percent of some 19 billion gold marks to compensate France for war damages. Also to protect France's future, Clemenceau received the promise of defensive alliances with Britain and the United States against any further German military resurgence.

For the Germans, they lost all their colonial holdings, which were turned over to the League of Nations for administration as mandate lands. The Germans also lost their fleet; the treaty reduced their army to 100,000 professional soldiers; and Germany could not have any military aircraft. Furthermore, the treaty explicitly prevented the Germans from manufacturing heavy artillery, building future capital ships, refining any form of aviation, or developing a submarine fleet. Hence Wilson's universal disarmament had been applied to one country only—a vanquished Germany—while the rest of the world continued to pursue military power. For the specific purpose of imposing an unspecified amount of money on Germany to pay for all war damages (an amount later determined by an indemnity commission to be 132 billion gold marks or 35 billion dollars), the German people had to accept full responsibility for causing the war. This clause of the Versailles Treaty explicitly imposed "guilt" for World War I on the Germans so that they would be held liable. Hence, Germany lost all its gold reserves, control of its natural resources, and had to surrender its merchant marine as partial payment for the war.

In Eastern Europe, the Allies set up a buffer zone against Bolshevism in Russia. Like Germany, Russia had not been invited to Versailles to participate in the peace process. The new regime in the old czarist territories was a pariah state that the Allies wanted to quarantine. A new series of nations run by conservative elites and supported by the Allies, formed what the French called a "cordon sanitaire" (sanitary belt) to prevent the westward spread of the communist infection. Finland, Estonia, Latvia, Lithuania, Poland, Czechoslovakia, and Yugoslavia made up the new nations in this buffer zone. Romania doubled in size at the expense of Austria-Hungary. Austria and Hungary separated into two new states. The Ottoman Empire disappeared to create an enlarged Greece, the new state of Turkey, and numerous mandated territories that would eventually lead to a redefinition of the Middle East.

Outside of Europe, Wilson's promise of colonial adjustments to meet the needs of subject peoples opened up a discussion on the topic of empires and their consequences. The complexity of this issue, plus the principle of self-determination offered to the ethnic groups in Europe as a justification to form new nations, proved too much for the delegates at Versailles to resolve. The ambitions of peoples trapped in colonies, protectorates, and spheres of influence to seek independence from European imperial controls proved too complex for the treaty process, or the League of Nations after 1920. Hence decolonization and nationformation began outside of Europe, and the decisions made at Versailles, that revealed the diverse forces released by World War I.

As for the United States, Congress never ratified the Treaty of Versailles. A wave of isolationism and nostalgia for the days before the war swept through the country. Also Wilson's personal negotiations of the treaty without a bipartisan support team made the document suspect to Republicans back home. The numerous compromises Wilson had to make in Europe made him unbinding in his approach to ratification. To further complicate matters, as pressure mounted due to the political process of ratification, Wilson was incapacitated by a stroke. This gave the Senate a free hand to repudiate his work. Hence the United States did not join the League of Nations or honor Wilson's promise of a defensive alliance with France against a resurgent Germany. Thus, the League was nearly stillborn without U.S. or Soviet participation while the Versailles Treaty had promised solutions to far more problems then it was capable of addressing. As a result, the Allies won the war but lost the peace.

Palmer, R. R. and Joel Colton, *A History of the Modern World*, **Fifth Edition (New York: Alfred A. Knopf, 1978), 681–89.**

Next the Germans experienced a sequence of economic catastrophes tied to the problems caused by the Versailles Treaty and the peace terms dictated by the Allies. The German mark plunged from 4 per U.S. dollar in 1914 to 4 billion per dollar in 1923; runaway inflation, caused by the war indemnity imposed by the Versailles Treaty wiped out the savings of the German middle class. Recovery required Weimar Germany to tie its financial future to the United States through two lending programs called the Dawes (1924) and Young (1929) plans. The stock market collapse of October 1929 (see Chapter Thirty for details) brought economic chaos to Germany as the Great Depression gripped the world economy. From the German point of view, once again the democrats of the Weimar, working in conjunction with the democrats of the United States, had exposed Germany to fiscal crisis.

Finally, from the moment it assumed power, the Weimar Republic faced nothing but political conflict at home. The radical left under Rosa Luxembourg and Karl Liebknecht staged the abortive Spartacist Revolution of 1919–20 (mentioned above), and paid with their lives by being murdered in captivity. Then two failed right-wing efforts to overthrow the government followed: a local military revolt called the *Kapp Putsch* (a Putsch is an armed uprising) of 1920, and Adolf Hitler's "Beer Hall" Putsch of 1923. Yet, unlike Luxembourg or Liebknecht, neither the leaders of the Kapp Putsch nor Hitler died in custody. In fact, Hitler only received a five-year sentence, serving less than a year, and enjoyed enough freedom to be able to write *Mein Kampf* (*My Struggle*), a convoluted mix of racism, nationalism, personal intuitions, and distorted theories of history designed to serve as the intellectual basis of his new ideology.

Following Hitler's jail term, the Weimar enjoyed a brief period of calm, but the Great Depression soon accelerated radical activities and paralyzed the German government. Thus, within fourteen years, 1919–33, demoralization, indemnity payments, and a general hostility toward democracy in Germany had brought the Weimar Republic to its knees. Germans in general blamed the Weimar for virtually all the ills that Germany faced after World War I: signing the Versailles Treaty; accepting guilt for the Great War; the runaway inflation of 1923 due to the burden of indemnity payments, and the loans brokered with the United States between 1924–29 that tied Germany's financial future to American prosperity—a prosperity that suddenly collapsed. With no friends at home or abroad, the Weimar Republic also collapsed. With its demise, Germany fell under the political spell of Adolf Hitler (1889–1945).

Hitler quickly developed a political apparatus like the one in the Soviet Union, creating a single-party state based on vertically articulated power, absolute control over the media and assembly, and no legal restraint on national leadership. Yet in Germany, Hitler's single-party state implemented a political vision that sprang solely from his personal intuitions. Although Hitler concentrated political power in the same fashion as found in the Soviet Union, Germany's future emerged from the convoluted imagination of *Der Führer* (the leader).

Building on the rage that followed from near victory in 1918, Hitler used German hostility to democracy, the myth of "the stab in the back" (see below), the military impotence imposed by the Versailles Treaty, the financial chaos of inflation and depression, and the demoralization that followed the Great War to develop his program. First, he constructed an elaborate conspiracy theory to explain Germany's defeat. Then he posited the thesis that the Germans should assign the guilt for their failure on a vague, shadowy domestic figure: the Jewish-democratic-liberal-Marxist who spoke of peace and freedom but really wanted to rob the powerful races of the world of their birthright, a global empire. Never concerned with contradictions, Hitler pressed this theory on the Germans until their frustrations through the 1920s and 1930s culminated in their raising him to power. Once in power, he redesigned Germany.

Hitler's thesis developed a view of war that defined it as a natural condition for humanity. Believing that race represented a subdivision of the human species, each race of humans made war on the others as part of the evolutionary process. In this way, superior races eliminated the inferior ones and refined the entire human species. In his racist teleology, Hitler extrapolated his vision of war from Charles Darwin's Theory of Natural Selection (1859).

Hitler built his thesis on the misuse of the scientific theory of natural selection, mutated into a perverse sociological idea called Social Darwinism. In fact, Hitler's entire worldview derived from his transformation of Social Darwinism into his unique vision. To understand this worldview, and to see how it shaped Germany's political future, one has to return to the nineteenth century to see how Social Darwinism completely misrepresented Darwin's principles of evolution.

Social Darwinism

As mentioned in Chapter One, natural selection pairs success in the struggle for existence with the frequency of reproduction, for only those individuals who survive to reach sexual maturity and reproduce, pass their genes on to the next generation. The frequency of reproduction defines successful individuals in a population and determines the direction of speciation. Since no one could predict the frequency with which each individual would reproduce, natural selection created a nonteleological explanation of evolution. Social Darwinists of the nineteenth century, however, tried to link the general teleology of that era to natural selection by misrepresenting Darwin.

Social Darwinists dropped the key concept of reproductive success from Darwin's theory to focus solely on the struggle for existence. They borrowed an expression from Herbert Spencer, who coined the phrase "survival of the fittest," and converted Darwin's theory into a *tautology* (a logical fallacy called a circular argument). Social Darwinists argued that in the case of human beings as well as other animals, the fit survive because they are the fittest, and since they are the fittest, they naturally outlive their inferior competitors. Hence, the fittest survive due to their fitness, and their survival defines them as the fittest. Social Darwinists furthermore applied this tautology to the marketplace, arguing that the fittest were the richest individuals and the richest nation-states.

The degree to which they erred can be seen by the fact that Darwin's theory always pointed to the number

Adolf Hitler gives a speech at the Grazer Waggonfabrik, a railway car manufacturer, in the city of Graz in Styria, Austria, on April 3, 1938. Austrian National Library, ÖNB/Wien #1138533–S 60/34.

of offspring produced by survivors as a measure of their fitness. If any of the survivors had no offspring, these individuals ceased to play a part in natural selection. In this case, even so-called winners were as unfit as those individuals who died before reaching sexual maturity for they left behind no genetic trace of their existence.

Ironically, in the economic world of the marketplace where Social Darwinists named the rich as the fittest, these individuals followed David Ricardo's and Thomas Robert Malthus's theories of economics. Both had argued against reproduction and for deliberately reducing the number of offspring produced by the rich to ensure their continued wealth. In addition, both theorists had condemned the poor for creating their own poverty, through producing too many babies. But according to Darwin, the reproductive status of the poor would help them determine humanity's biological future as a species through natural selection. Hence, by Darwin's standards, the Social Darwinists were completely wrong when they named the rich and childless as fittest and the poor with numerous offspring as unfit.

This gap in logic, however, did not stop Social Darwinists from pressing forward their misunderstanding of natural selection. And this glaring error was evidently too subtle for Adolf Hitler to grasp. He merely adapted Social Darwinism to his brand of racism to explain why war was the natural state of human and international affairs.

Hitler's Racism

Hitler's variation of Social Darwinism compressed individuals into races that populated nation-states. According to Hitler, humanity divided itself into nations on the basis of race, with the qualities of each ethnicity creating a unique culture, volkgeist (spirit of the people), and language. Hitler then assumed that these races would naturally mobilize their ethnic and cultural resources as nation-states to fight one another. Of all the human races, Hitler argued the Germans were the fittest; they comprised the highest form of human raw material needed to forge a new social order that would lead the world.

According to Hitler, the success of a race depended on how much land it owned as well as its potential for future conquest. Great Britain, he posited, was a German nation comprised of Angles, Saxons, Danes, and Norsemen whose conquest of the United Kingdom and the British Empire proved their superior qualities. In contrast, Germany was the greatest industrial power of Europe, with pure Germanic racial qualities that made this nation Great Britain's continental cousin, destined to expand east to eradicate the Slavs (an inferior race).

Yet, according to Hitler, both Britain and Germany faced a conspiracy of inferior people whose survival depended on peace. These people had no land and could only survive as parasites among superior peoples. These inferior peoples attempted to frustrate the natural struggle for survival between races, tried to mix their inferiority with superior people through intermarriage, and sought to erode a superior race's potential for the future. These inferior people had to be unmasked and eliminated.

With this vision in mind, Hitler turned his attention to the Versailles Treaty that ended World War I in 1919. For Hitler, Germany's defeat could not have been due to its weakness. Instead, Germany had to have been "stabbed in the back."

While the German army was still on foreign soil, the General Staff informed the Kaiser that defeat was at hand, and the General Staff deliberately kept its decision secret so that the German public never learned of the impending military collapse. This coupled with the food riots at home spurred an internal disintegration that convinced many Germans that a conspiracy led by civilians had betrayed Germany. Yet who were these civilians? What was their motive? How could Germany's defeat profit anybody living within the Reich's borders?

These questions led many Germans to agree with Hitler that the war had been lost due to a domestic conspiracy rather than military failure. They listened to Hitler when he argued that the victors were democratic states—the United States, Britain, France, and Italy—that had imposed a peace treaty on Germany designed to ensure its perpetual weakness.

Hitler held that democracy itself resided at the heart of an international conspiracy against the German race. He believed that inferior races had created

Mussolini's Italy

Although Hitler created a true totalitarian regime on the fascist model, Italy succumbed to radical conservatism ten years before the Nazis came to power. Italy had entered World War I cynically on the side of the Allies to acquire territorial spoils at its victorious conclusion. During the war, however, Italy had suffered dramatic setbacks, lost territory, and suffered 600,000 casualties, which weakened the Italian claim to spoils at Versailles. After the war, a postwar depression and unemployment created political unrest while territorial gains at the expense of Yugoslavia did nothing to compensate Italy for its material frustrations. Exploiting these weaknesses, a political adventurer named Benito Mussolini created Europe's first experiment with fascism.

Seizing power in October 1922 in a march on Rome, Mussolini used a general fear of a Bolshevik-style revolution to come down hard on the side of law, order, and property, which won him financial support from the wealthy and a growing popular following. Able to capture power as Premier because the liberal-democratic coalition that ran Italy's legislature had resigned in frustration when they could not get the king, Victor Emmanuel III (reigned 1900–46), to confront Mussolini's "Blackshirts" or support their effort to impose marshal law during his 1922 coup. Hence Mussolini was given one year to create political stability. Before the year had expired, he forced a law through Italy's legislature that allowed any party receiving a majority of votes to gain two-thirds of the seats in the Italian Parliament. In the election of 1924, Mussolini's fascists won 60 percent of the vote against seven opposition parties and came to dominate Italian politics.

Never completely successful, nonetheless, Mussolini did impose a high level of censorship on the press, destroyed Italy's labor unions, deprived workers of the right to strike, abolished all other political parties, and occasionally assassinated effective political
opponents. He also developed a secret police force, reduced universal suffrage (the vote), and established tribunals to eliminate those who might oppose him. Finally, Mussolini introduced his theory of political organization: organicism.

According to organicism, the state was a living entity that comprised institutional limbs and organs that carried out the vital functions of the body politic. National solidarity, political leadership, state-managed agriculture and industry, and all levels of productive labor worked together to achieve common goals. The survival and prosperity of one equaled the survival and prosperity of all as each individual fit within the body politic as a cell within a living being. Hence, everyone had to pull together to achieve a common goal.

Yet, despite this political vision, Mussolini was never able to master Italian affairs. As a nation incapable of autarky (national economic self-sufficiency), Italy found itself subject to global fluctuations in the world economy. Although the head of an organic state, Mussolini could not solve problems posed by the Great Depression. Hence, even though he could mobilize a national effort to address specific issues, he found himself drawn into foreign adventure to try to distract Italian attention from his failed domestic programs. Wars in Ethiopia and Spain, however, eroded Italy's capacity to solve economic problems at home due to high costs without equal compensation in spoils. Also Mussolini eventually joined Hitler in World War II, which proved disastrous for his regime. Accordingly, even though he captured power at home in 1924, he was never really the master of Italian affairs both foreign and domestic. Hence, he was subject to the whims of his age rather than the leader of Italy's destiny.

Weiss, John, *The Fascist Tradition: Radical Right-Wing Extremism in Modern Europe* **(New York: Harper and Row, 1967), 31–45, 92–94, and 101–05.**

democracy to spread peace around the world in order to ensure their own survival. In Hitler's eyes democracy was inherently destructive to the German people, which, in turn, made it destructive to humanity as well.

The mixtures of races allowed by democracy through the maintenance of peace confirmed Hitler's suspicions. From his perspective, democracy could only be the brainchild of those races that could not survive any other way but through acts of miscegenation (interbreeding). Hitler placed the Jews at the heart of this democratic conspiracy.

Hitler's hatred of Jews ran very deep, and he blamed them for personal as well as international misfortunes. He saw them as the authors of both democracy and socialism, placed them at the forefront of international capitalism, and even made them the creators of communism. This all-pervasive anti-Semitism shaped Hitler's conspiracy theory into a massive racial plot hatched by inferior peoples to bring down all the superior ones. Hitler believed that Jews had succeeded, thus far, because no one had unmasked their sinister plans.

In Hitler's vision, the Jews made up the leading capitalists of the world. Yet Karl Marx, half Jewish by birth, was the creator of Marxism and the inspiration behind the Soviet Union. Also, Jews had led Europe as proponents of peace and freedom through the intellectual traditions that had fostered great works of art, music, literature, philosophy, and science, which in turn supported democratic principles. According to Hitler, Jews had carefully masked their "malignant plot" against superior races behind the trappings of universal peace and humanitarian language that fostered the democratic state.

Hitler believed that as capitalists, Jews managed world finance. At the same time, as communists Hitler believed that Jews led the revolution against private property and capitalism. He claimed that as leaders of both movements, Jews had to take responsibility for most international conflict.

He also believed that Jews had devised this state of international warfare in order to get superior peoples to fight among themselves—he never bothered to explain how a supposedly inferior people could consistently fool superior people. Thus, despite their inferiority, Hitler claimed that Jews had successfully conspired to pit the superior mass of humanity in a constant struggle that only weakened those races with the greatest potential. Only in this way, Hitler felt, could the Jewish people, without a homeland of their own, have found space to live in the territory of other races.

In Hitler's mind, the terms laid down by the Allies in the Versailles Treaty proved the existence of this plot.

Called the *Diktat* because the victors had excluded German diplomats from the peace process, the Versailles Treaty became a symbol of the international betrayal of Germany. In Germany's view, the victors had broken a sacred trust by denying a defeated power the right to participate in shaping the future peace for the first time in European diplomatic history. Furthermore, the Ver-sailles Treaty transformed Germany, a once great nation, into a weak one.

Building on the rage generated by the Diktat, Hitler developed his political program. According to Hitler, the Versailles Treaty symbolized the way the Jewish-democratic conspiracy worked. His logic held that the treaty sprang from "a stab in the back" by suspicious civilians in Germany working for the democratic victors. Then, the treaty imposed a financial burden on Germany that only international bankers could have devised. Next, the treaty reduced the German army to a mere 100,000 men, eliminated German aviation, and confined the German navy to a fleet of tiny surface vessels. The treaty required that Germany work for international peace and forced it to accept a new democracy that would enforce the restrictions of the Diktat on the German people.

Hitler reasoned that Germany had to break the Versailles Treaty, recover its military spirit, and conquer those inferior races that had tried to deny the Germans their rightful living space (*Lebensraum*). Rousing nationalist passions among those Germans who wanted to right the wrong of 1918, Hitler hammered away at their domestic rage. He repeated endlessly the same simple message that Germany had suffered betrayal by inferior peoples living within its own borders. A combination of the Great Depression, national demoralization, and domestic rage fueled Hitler's political career, bringing him to power in 1933.

Hitler's solution to the international conspiracy against Germany was to start a war that would reflect his vision of race and guide the superior peoples of the world to their destiny, thereby respecting the "natural" process of survival of the fittest as expressed in his understanding of Social Darwinism. Integral to his vision was the eradication of the Jewish people.

Hitler's war on Jews would exterminate them, seize their property, and destroy every vestige of their memory. He would then conquer those who had fallen most deeply under their spell. These second-tier victims would comprise races that had no German traits in their language, culture, or heritage. Such races, which would pose the greatest threat to a world led by the Germans, were an inferior people known as the Slavs. (For more on the Holocaust, see page 469).

Devising a foreign and domestic policy designed to implement his distorted vision, Hitler set out to reassemble the German people into one nation, one he planned to place on an equal footing with Great Britain, the "other Germany." He planned to violate the Versailles Treaty progressively, reversing its restrictions one by one at a pace that allowed Germany to regain its strength before launching an attack. He sensed correctly that the victors of the West—themselves exhausted from World War I and having retreated into semi-isolationism—would permit him the time he needed to prepare. First he recovered the military forces and territories taken from Germany in the war, except for Alsace-Lorraine held by France. Then he threw off the financial burdens of the Treaty, rearmed the German nation, and prepared for his projected invasion of the east.

In October 1933, he withdrew Germany from the League of Nations. In June 1934, he eliminated potential rivals in his own party while eradicating democracy in Germany. Throughout 1935, Hitler rearmed his new regime, which he deemed the Third Reich, with weapons designed to allow a successful attack in the east. In March 1936, he reoccupied and rearmed the Rhineland despite strict prohibitions against such action by the Versailles Treaty. In March 1938, he effected the *Anschluss* (union) of Germany and Austria to create the Greater Germany that nineteenth century German nationalists had dreamed about before Bismarck's Second Reich. In October 1938, Hitler persuaded Britain and France to accept his acquisition of the Sudetenland: the mountainous frontier between Germany and the newly minted nation of Czechoslovakia. In March of 1939, he took the remainder of Czechoslovakia despite his promise to the British Prime Minister, Neville Chamberlain, in October 1938 that he would not. This forced Chamberlain to broadcast on radio a promise of war if Hitler took any further territories. Meanwhile, Stalin, hoping to stop Hitler's drive east, saw an opportunity in March 1939 to turn the Führer back west; Stalin and Hitler agreed to a Non-Aggression Pact in August to free Hitler from having to fight a war on two fronts. Then, on September 1, 1939, Hitler attacked Poland to recover the Danzig Corridor that separated East Prussia from Germany. Chamberlain then made good on his promise of war: World War II had started in Europe.

Poised to go east, however, Hitler was shocked by the reaction of the Allies to his failure to keep his promises. His desire to recover a wedge of land between East Prussia and Germany called the Polish Corridor led to an invasion of Poland that sparked World War II in Europe. Ironically, Hitler had to make peace with Stalin first to launch his attack on the Polish nation. Thus, Hitler formed an alliance with an enemy he was sworn to destroy to secure his eastern flank. Hitler then went west against a people he believed to be part or all German. He had to do this before he could turn his attention to the living space he coveted, currently occupied by the Slavs whom he intended to eliminate as he created his new German nation. World War II began in Europe by Hitler going in the wrong direction.

Such a misdirection of warfare was symptomatic of Hitler's military planning. His war goals were never really clear because his thinking was intuitive rather than rational. Hence, war began in the wrong sector of Europe, the Germanic or semi-Germanic west rather than the Slavic east, and his army stumbled along from one German success to another because the German military was better prepared to fight the Second World War than were the Allies. Ironically, German victories made Hitler look like a genius to his people, when in fact he had unleashed a war he never fully understood. Nevertheless, once trapped in Hitler's racial vision of the future, the German people had no choice but to follow him until the end.

Suggested Reading

Bullock, Alan, *Hitler: A Study in Tyranny*, Completely Rev. Ed. (New York: Harper and Row, 1964).

Fitzpatrick, Sheila, *The Russian Revolution, 1917–1932*, Second Edition (New York: Oxford University Press, 1984).

Hingley, Ronald, *Russia: A Concise History*, Revised and Updated Edition (London: Thames and Hudson, Ltd., 1991).

Kershaw, Ian, *The Nazi Dictatorship: Problems and Perspectives*, Second Edition (New York: Oxford University Press, 1989).

Lafore, Laurence, *The End of Glory: An Interpretation of the Origins of World War II* (New York/Philadelphia: J. B. Lippincott Company, 1970).

Lincoln, W. Bruce, *Red Victory: A History of the Russian Civil War* (New York: Da Capo Press, Inc., 1989).

Malia, M., *The Soviet Tragedy: A History of Socialism in Russia, 1917–1991* (New York: The Free Press, 1994).

Mazower, Mark, *Dark Continent: Europe's Twentieth Century* (New York: Vintage Books, 1991).

Pipes, Richard, *The Russian Revolution 1899–1919*, Second Edition (London: Harvill Press, 1997).

Rauch, Georg von, *A History of the Soviet Union,*
     Fifth Edition (New York: Praeger Publishers,
     1971).

Ulam, A. B., *The Bolsheviks* (New York: The
     Macmillan Company, 1965).

Toland, John, *Adolf Hitler* (New York: Ballantine
     Books, 1976).

Weiss, John, *The Fascist Tradition: Radical Right-
     Wing Extremism in Modern Europe* (New York:
     Harper and Row, 1967).

Wolf, Eric R., *Peasant Wars in the Twentieth Century*
     (New York: Harper and Row, 1968).

XXIX

THE UNITED STATES
and Japan

The two other great powers to emerge from World War I, nations that would shape the circumstances of combat in World War II, were the United States and Japan. Both powers had sided with the Allies in the Great War, but each had their own reasons for supporting the victors. The United States had become a direct participant (Chapter Twenty-eight) on the Western Front and helped Great Britain and France win the Great War. Japan had been an ally of Britain since 1902 and had hoped to exploit the war as an opportunity to cement its wealth and power in China. With Europe distracted, and the United States ever more slowly committed to an Allied victory, the Japanese government hoped for a free hand in Chinese affairs.

But the failure of the Versailles Treaty, the demoralization that had followed the Great War, and the absence of a true center of global politics placed more power in the hands of the United States and Japan than either expected. After an exhausted Europe could no longer guide the world politically or economically, the United States and Japan had found themselves thrust onto the center stage of global affairs. In order to understand how they played their new roles requires a quick review of their history before World War I, as well as an analysis of their response to the peace that followed.

The United States

The American Civil War had solidified the United States as a nation-state, but it had cost the American people dearly. Nonetheless, the years immediately after the Civil War saw the industrial revolution proceed uninterrupted, for the demands of the war itself had pushed the United States to expand its key industries as well as its agricultural output, making it an economic power. One such industry essential to the Union's prosecution of the war, the arms industry, expanded and prospered, becoming well known internationally for its innovations. So too, did steel, produced for domestic use as well as for the world market. The Besse-

mer hot-blast furnace fostered the rise of the steel industry, resulting in a forty-fold increase in output between 1869 and 1880. In the 1890s, the new open-hearth process produced specialty and high-quality steels strong enough to use in the construction of bridges and high-rise buildings in America's growing cities. The steel industry, originally centered in Pennsylvania, moved progressively west during the nineteenth century, finally settling in Chicago with the building in 1908 of a United States Steel Corporation facility, the largest in the world. Specialized manufacturing remained in the East, producing small arms, hardware, knives, sewing machines, typewriters, and machine tools that demanded specialty steels. These eastern industrial concerns also sold to a world market, and by 1900 the United States fabricated fully one-third of the world's industrial products, more than England, France, and Germany combined.

To spur agriculture and help settle the West (and push out the American Indians), Congress passed the Homestead Act of 1862, giving American citizens free grants of land in the public domain in exchange for making the land productive. Men and women in the thousands took up this land and paid their fees to take title. The Civil War Congress also passed the Morrill Land Grant Act, which created the land-grant colleges dedicated to advancing scientific knowledge in the fields of engineering and agriculture. At the University of Wisconsin, the invention of the Babcock butterfat test revolutionized the dairy industry and enabled increased productivity and quality in its products.

The dynamic of easily acquired land continued, and American farms pursued profits by producing for growing urban markets. Foreign commercial outlets, however, were subject to restrictive regulations and taxation when foreign governments observed robust American competition with locally produced goods. While American diplomats worked diligently to erode these trade barriers, they refused to reciprocate, and American import tariffs remained high even as American manufactures and agricultural goods flooded the world market. In addition to diplomatic efforts to maintain favorable trade relationships, the United States launched an ambitious naval-building program in the 1880s to create a modern level of sea power. This new ocean-going navy engaged the Spanish fleet in 1898 in the Spanish American War and destroyed it, which allowed the United States to take the Philippines and Puerto Rico while gaining control of Cuban foreign affairs, and helped to fuel the "short-war" myth prior to World War I.

To further enhance American economic advantage and bind the industrial North to the agrarian West, the transcontinental railroad, funded largely by federal land grants and bonds, forged a national link in 1869. Although the new railroad stretched from St. Louis to San Francisco, the promise of moving massive amounts of goods from American farms to the growing U.S. cities took a quarter century to become a fact. Also, as the transcontinental rail link expanded to include the Great Northern, Northern Pacific, Atchison, Topeka, and Santa Fe, and Southern Pacific, U.S. access to Asian markets was not realized until the 1890s. This is when the U.S. industrial base and railroad system had integrated to the point that a single market structure had been built, a national scheme of productivity had become a reality, and contact through global exchanges had been achieved.

While the economic and diplomatic interests of the United States advanced noticably in the years between the end of the Civil War and the turn of the twentieth century, the forces for equality at home made few gains. Not only were Native Americans not granted U.S. citizenship until 1924, but in the last quarter of the nineteenth century the U.S. Government made and broke treaty after treaty with the remaining Indian tribes. The U.S. Army killed many thousands of Indians as it drove them off the plains onto reservation lands of little or no agricultural value. For their part, African Americans, especially those in the South, fared little better after their emancipation than they had under slavery. Many southern blacks were forced into agrarian peonage as sharecroppers, while any black thought to be idle by white authorities could be arrested and made to work on a chain gang. Meanwhile the violent lynching of African Americans by whites for all manner of real and imagined offenses was commonplace well into the twentieth century. In the North and South, racial segregation prevailed, with separate facilities for whites and blacks in most public places. Although some states granted women the right to vote—Wyoming Territory was the first to do so in 1869—not until 1920 would all American women have voting rights; by no means, however, did this signal an equality of the sexes. Finally,

Americans of Mexican descent, many of whom hailed from families that had been living in the states of the Southwest well before they became American territory, were relegated to rural *colonias* and urban *barrios*, where they largely kept to themselves and maintained their Mexican culture. To make a living, many Mexican Americans ventured out of their ethnic enclaves to perform what jobs whites would give them, often low-paying, strenuous work such as picking crops and working in factories.

Parallel to the issue of equality at home, the United States tried to absorb and assimilate a vast new pool of immigrants between 1870 and 1914. During those thirty-four years, some 22 million people crossed the Atlantic from Southern and Eastern Europe to escape the collapse of peasant agriculture in their home countries due to global trade in such staples as wheat, or because of religious and ethnic persecution from national majorities that had little tolerance for cultural minorities. These new arrivals, who settled mostly in industrial cities, differed sharply from the original European immigrants who had made up the U.S. population prior to the Civil War, having immigrated from northern and western Europe. The new immigrants comprised an enormous number of unskilled laborers who moved into twenty-one major industrial cities and mining centers and made up 66 percent of the workforce. In major U.S. cities, they formed ethnic neighborhoods where they joined African, Native, and Mexican Americans to add to the subcultural mosaic composing the U.S. population profile.

Meanwhile, America had emerged as a world power, based more on its economic might than military performance. By 1900, a corn belt stretching from central Ohio to central Nebraska had emerged, as had a spring wheat belt in the Dakotas and a winter wheat belt in Kansas and western Oklahoma. The use of gasoline-powered Caterpillar tractors and combine engines in California wheat fields demonstrated the potential of advanced mechanization in farming. Dairy farms dominated the landscapes of New York, Michigan, Wisconsin, and Minnesota, producing more cheese than Americans could consume. Clearly, American manufacturers and farmers wanted even more access to world markets.

Growing U.S. productivity, the integration of agricultural and industrial output, and the development of the United States' role in global trade made America a great power at the beginning of the twentieth century. By World War I, the U.S. was a force to consider as the Allies fought the Central Powers. When the United States finally entered the Great War in April of 1917, with the slogan of "making the world safe for democracy," the addition of the U.S. Army and Marine Corps turned the tide of battle by applying mass aggressive assault pressure.

While America's contribution to victory did not in fact save the world for democracy, it did bring more profits for American exports. As mentioned in Chapter Twenty-eight, President Woodrow Wilson personally attended the peace talks at Versailles, where he pushed hard for the formation of a League of Nations, a world authority to prevent another war. But the U.S. Senate failed to approve America's entry into the league as the United States, like its European allies, settled into a mood of isolationism that did little to stem the rise of totalitarian regimes in the Soviet Union or Germany.

Then, with involvement in European wars seemingly behind it, the United States exhibited a split cultural identity that pitted an urban hedonism against a rural fundamentalism. Indeed the extraordinary cultural dichotomy that occurred in the "Roaring '20s" created a type of nostalgia in the rural populations of the United States that made them long for the past while urbanites hungered for the pleasures of the present. Neither the rural nor the urban sectors of the United States, however, seemed to have had much of a vision for the future. Accordingly, the 1920s saw race riots, a new form of *xenophobia* (fear of foreigners) that virtually closed the United States to future immigrants for a time, and a return to very conservative national politics, with the nation becoming largely divided, unfocused, and demoralized. At the time, the United States had difficulty helping itself, much less the rest of the world.

The United States seemed to be as lost as the nations of Europe in determining what direction to take next. Ironically, even though Woodrow Wilson had proposed the League of Nations to help restructure the world after the war, he found that he could not lead his own nation into the future he hoped to develop.

At the same time that the world floundered as it tried to adjust to the new power vacuum in international politics and finance, the United States had taken control of international loans. As a creditor nation after World War I, the United States held the debts of the victors who in turn commanded the finances of the vanquished in Central Europe. Yet, here too the United States provided weak leadership. Governed by Republicans who restored a conservative vision of economics, the United States returned to the unfocused financial policy of laissez-faire and high import tariffs.

Allowing its own economy to grow without significant fiscal regulations, the United States entered a consumer era using credit-spending in its domestic market. Also, the United States built an inventory of consumer goods so large that it eventually exceeded both domestic and foreign demand. Furthermore, the United States maintained a balance of payments that did not allow debtor-nations to earn enough U.S. currency to repay their loans. As a result, American banks developed an international financial system built on weak foreign economies and took on a series of increasingly risky loans.

Rather than realigning the world's financial structure in a manner similar to Great Britain's strategy during its era of financial leadership, the United States failed to import more than it exported. If the United States had done so, foreign powers could have earned enough U.S. currency to pay back their loans. Instead, debtor-nations had to ask for more and more loans to refinance their debts, creating a fragile international credit system.

The global credit structure built by the United States was a house of cards. Simultaneously, the domestic economy in the United States was increasingly unstable. Generating more goods than Americans could consume, the U.S. shifted from a producer to a consumer economy. By 1920, the United States had built its industrial base. Now American citizens had to replace American producers as the U.S. economy's chief customer. To keep customers buying, however, producers had to pay laborers sufficient wages to maintain a growing domestic demand. But since higher wages meant reduced profits, producers chose to sell goods on credit instead.

Credit-spending at home, however, absorbed the consumer's future income just when U.S. producers had adopted the assembly line and the managerial techniques of time-space studies by efficiency experts. These productive innovations expanded domestic inventories while credit-spending tied up future domestic demand. This combination of absorbing future incomes with increasing debts and expanding domestic production created an inventory crisis by 1929. Unfortunately this caused the U.S. economy to slow just when speculation on the stock market was the most active in the nation's history.

Credit-spending had infected the stock exchange, just as it had every other sector of the U.S. economy, with many private investors having purchased stocks on speculation, i.e., credit, in anticipation of constant growth in the U.S. economy. The inventory crisis of 1929, however, caught these investors short of funds. Consequently, all of them had to sell their stocks at once to pay their debts. But since every speculator tried to sell at the same time, with no one else in a buying mood, the mass selling triggered the great U.S. stock market crash of 1929. With this plummet, the financial structure of the United States, and then the global one, began to unravel.

American banks were among the speculators who lost their fortunes. As their assets disappeared, they called in their loans, domestic as well as foreign, spreading the crisis abroad. At the same time, depositors flocked to their banks to withdraw funds to pay their debts, but so many people withdrew their funds at the same time that they caused runs on the banks. Soon hundreds and thousands of American banks closed their doors.

Compounding the problems facing the banks, the Federal Reserve System created artificial deflation by instituting a hard-money policy that restricted the money supply at the worst possible time, in October 1931. Wanting to ensure the best conditions for a business recovery, the Federal Reserve Board reacted cautiously and significantly increased the prime interest rate, the rate at which member banks loaned money to one another. The effect of this decision was to restrict the money supply just when more currency was needed to meet depositor demands, increase consumer confidence, and reduce growing inventories. The result was accelerated deflation, increased debt burden, reduced profits, elimination of consumer demand, rising inventories, increased layoffs, and an expanding credit crisis.

The Great Depression. In the absence of substantial government relief programs, free food was distributed with private funds in some urban centers to large numbers of the unemployed. Here, the unemployed men are queued outside a depression soup kitchen opened in Chicago by Al Capone, February 1931. United States National Archives & Records Admninistration, ARC # 541927.

Finally, since domestic production and international loans were now linked to the health of the U.S. economy, the financial crisis on the New York stock exchange and in the American banking system spread throughout the world. Now the global economy simply unraveled. Debtor-nations could not pay their loans to the United States, a tariff war began, international production fell by 33 percent, and international trade fell by 66 percent. This began what became known as the Great Depression.

No social safety net was in place as the depression deepened. As a result, the Republican Party, the party of big business, laissez-faire (hands-off) business policies, large veteran's pensions, and social stability lost the 1932 Presidential election to Democrat Franklin D. Roosevelt. Leading a Democratic Party willing to put most of the ideas espoused decades earlier by the Socialist and the Populist parties into law, FDR started a network of government agencies and policies known generally as the New Deal, which resulted in the birth of Social Security, unemployment insurance, and public works among other well-known programs. This New Deal of Franklin Roosevelt's Democratic Party also brought regulation to American farms.

Before 1930, corn belt farmers in particular had been reluctant to invest in tractors, despite the obvious advantages of this form of mechanization. In the 1920s, farmers lived in a deepening depression with an investment climate that discouraged the expenditure of the large sums demanded for tractors and other farm machines. The New Deal regulations stabilized prices, provided easy credit, and encouraged machinery manufacturers and private bankers to rethink their strategies. Farmers responded and reaped the benefits of the productivity dividends that tractors and combines brought to agribusiness. This productivity positioned farmers to profit handsomely if demand should increase.

In the meantime, the United States spent the remainder of the 1930s attempting to recover its economic balance in the face of a collapsed global market. Far better off than any other nation-state or culture at that time, the United States limped through the 1930s without truly rebounding from the Great Depression. At its worst, the Great Depression had left 13 million industrial workers without jobs (one in four unemployed) while the gross national product had fallen 50 percent, and agricultural production of staples went down by 63 percent. Millions stayed alive by lining up for free soup, scavenging in city dumps, or waiting for garbage trucks. Starvation became a national illness, and victims of disease associated with malnutrition grew in number. Roosevelt's New Deals, both in their first and second forms, practiced sufficient deficit-spending to recover consumer confidence partially, but not enough to reintegrate supply with demand. Pure free enterprise became a thing of the past, as the idea that "the government that does the least is the best" gave way to the concept of federal interventions in every segment of the economy that needed help.

Hence, the economic crisis of the 1930s undermined the ideal of freedom sufficiently to change the face of American democracy to the point that U.S. citizens became accustomed to federal intervention and regulations. Ironically, the United States had taken a step toward cultures with a planned economy as the American people faced the worse economic crisis of their history. Indeed, crisis politics had become the norm, which had also greatly enhanced the power of the presidency, as the American people placed their hopes in the hands of their first four-term chief executive, FDR. The social, economic, and political influence of this era changed the American mind profoundly.

Japan

While the United States grew into a world economic leader despite itself, Japan's rapid modernization had changed the balance of power in the Far East. With Japan having quickly surpassed China in military potential during the second half of the nineteenth century, the oligarchy that ruled the island nation wanted to test its modern army and navy. Korea presented an appetizing target.

Korea had been a tributary state to China for centuries, while Japan had often eyed the Korean Peninsula as a potential zone of expansion. During the Yayoi era (250 BCE–250 CE), the Japanese had held an enclave at the tip of the peninsula called Mimana, which the Tang Dynasty of China had helped the Kingdom of Sulla destroy. Then, from 1592 to 1598, Japan's reigning military dictator, Toyotomi Hideyoshi, had sent several hundred thousand samurai to Korea to capture the peninsula. Once again the Japanese failed due to China's support of the Korean resistance. Thus, during its Meiji restoration (1868–1912), Japan finally felt strong enough to retest its arms against the Chinese for command of the Korean Peninsula.

Now, conflicting interests between China and Japan over Korea set all three cultures on a collision course. In 1876, the Japanese succeeded in forcing Korea to establish diplomatic relations with Japan and open up three treaty ports (the same types of concessions Europe had won from China). Rioting in 1893 and a rebellion in 1894 brought Chinese troops into Korea. Discontent among the Korean people over foreign (especially Japanese) intervention had led to the formation of the Tong Hak Society, a conservative religious cult that combined Shamanism, Daoism, Buddhism, and Confucianism to save Korea from outsiders. In 1894, the Tong Hak Society staged uprisings in southern Korea that attracted widespread support from peasants venting their frustration over high taxes. As China responded to a Korean governmental request for aid in putting down the rebellion, Japanese troops marched into Seoul where they broke into the royal palace and kidnapped the king. Thanks to their modern weapons, these Japanese troops prevailed in the ensuing war between them and the Chinese forces sent to stop them. Now the Japanese marched northward through Korea, crossed the Yalu River, and captured Dalian, on the tip of Liaodong Peninsula. Meanwhile the Japanese navy made quick work of China's fleet of warships. In short, Japan had quickly and efficiently defeated China both on land and at sea in what became known as the Sino-Japanese War of 1894–95.

In the 1895 peace settlement, the Treaty of Shimonoseki, China agreed to heavy war reparations, the recognition of Korea's independence, the cession of Taiwan and the Penghu Islands (also called the Pescadores), the opening of additional treaty ports, and the extension of most-favored-nation status to Japan. Japan had also received the Liaodong Peninsula in the settlement, but Russia, Germany, and France saw this as a threat to their interests and jointly intervened to force Japan to disgorge the peninsula. The Triple Intervention of those Western powers in a patently Eastern affair became fuel for a strong anti-Western nationalist sentiment in Japan.

Nevertheless, Japan's victory in the Sino-Japanese War marked the beginning of the Japanese Empire. In emulation of Western powers, Japan had not only achieved some degree of industrialization but also acquired colonies. As the only non-Western nation-state, Japan had joined the club of imperialist powers as a junior member.

Meiji leaders put a premium on national security and international equality. They insisted that Japan must not only defend its "line of sovereignty" but also its "line of interest." Both lines ran through Korea and into China. At the same time, the army seemed satisfied with the acquisition of Korea, while the navy believed that Japan needed to dominate the surrounding seas and was pleased with the acquisition of Taiwan. Both were unhappy, however, at giving up the Liaodong Peninsula to German, French, and Russian pressure. Yet when Russia moved into Manchuria, took the Liaodong Peninsula, and set its eye on Korea, the Japanese saw the czar as their next military victim.

Czarist Russia was determined to be a major player in East Asia. The czar built the Trans-Siberian Railway (1891–1903) to connect European Russia and the Pacific coast. Then Russia acquired a foothold in China by running the railroad through the northeastern province of Manchuria. Russia's lease of Dalian from the Chinese also gave it a much-needed warm-water port (a long-standing czarist goal given that the rest of Russia's coast was frozen at least part of the year). Russian expansion, however, not only threatened Japan, but earned the notice of the British. Now Japan and Great Britain signed a treaty in 1902 that committed them to mutual support in the event of war. This new alliance strengthened Japan's hand and enhanced its status.

The imperial ambitions of Russia and Japan soon clashed over China and led to the aforementioned Russo-Japanese War of 1904–05 (Chapter Twenty-seven). After launching a surprise attack on Russian troops in Dalian, the Japanese defeated Russia on land and virtually wiped out its navy at sea. Japan's swift victory surprised the European powers and triggered the 1905 Russian Revolution. At the same time, Japan quickly expanded its colonial control from Korea into Manchuria. Like Western colonial powers, Japan ruled its newly taken colonies—Korea, Manchuria, and Tai-

Russo-Japanese War, 1904–05. Japanese officers (foreground) and soldiers awaiting an attack from Russian cavalry. This image was captured near Tehling, Manchuria. LC-USZ62-79125.

wan—in order to benefit itself, not its subject peoples.

This was the first time an Asian nation had defeated a state seen by many as Western. Prominent individuals in many modern nations hailed Japan's victory as a sign of the power of progress in a non-Western sector of the world. The American president, Theodore Roosevelt, hailed it as the victory of a "progressive" Japan over a "backward" Russia. In traditional cultures such as China and India, where modern nationalists were beginning to appear, they hailed it as proof that an Asian nation could defeat a Western power.

The wars against China and then Russia, as well as the spoils of war, boosted economic growth in Japan, where heavy industry, steel, munitions, and shipbuilding grew rapidly. Japan built ships that equaled any in Europe and the United States in quality and quantity. Light industry also flourished. Japan's export of silk outstripped that of China. Japan's import of raw materials and export of manufactured goods indicated a change in the nature of its national economy.

By 1912, the industrial sector accounted for 36 percent of Japan's Gross National Product (GNP). The *Zaibatsu* (Japanese business cartels) with close ties to the government were the biggest beneficiary of this economic growth. Meanwhile, responding to a widening gap in the standard of living between the city and countryside, the *Diet* (Japan's legislature) sponsored a program to establish agricultural cooperatives in 1899. These politicians hoped to avert the kind of class or income conflicts that plagued Western nations.

Despite this growth, however, conditions for those employed in industry were still harsh. Sixty percent of the workforce was female in the 1910s, but laws to protect women and child laborers were weak and late in coming. In 1916 one such weak law passed to limit the workday of women and children to eleven hours, while the general, unbearable employment conditions for all laborers led to violent strikes, such as the copper miners' strike of 1909 and the Tokyo streetcar workers' strike of 1911. In response to labor unrest, government repression was heavy handed. In 1900 the Diet passed a law banning strikes; it not only dispatched troops against striking workers but also framed and executed labor leaders as radical, antigovernment elements.

Emperor Meiji, the oligarchs, the drive for modernization, and the prosecution of quick wars had held Japan's body politic together for more than four decades. Then Emperor Meiji died in 1912 and was succeeded by the mentally ill Emperor Taishō (reigned 1912–26). By this time, most of the oligarchs were also either dead or very old. And all the wars had been won. Consequently, solidarity was breaking down at the highest levels of power.

In the meantime, while the Meiji oligarchs and their protégés continued to dominate political decision-making, their influence was on the decline as three new political factions began their rise. The first were new men entering the bureaucracy through civil service examinations after 1885. These highly educated and ambitious young men began to replace those who had received their jobs by patronage, making the bureaucracy increasingly less beholden to its elder statesmen.

Next, the power of the military was on the rise. Imperial ordinances issued in 1889 and 1907 placed supreme command of the military completely beyond the control of the Japanese legislature. On matters concerning military authority, the chief of the general staff reported directly to the emperor, totally bypassing the cabinet. Also the military had the power to interfere in political matters when the imperial ordinance of 1900 stipulated that only the top two ranking officers on active duty in the army and the navy could be ministers for their respective armed forces in the cabinet. This ministerial requirement in effect gave the army and the navy the power to veto any cabinet decision; their resignation effectively dissolved the government.

The Seiyukai party of 1900 (the liberal, constitutional party of Japan) had strong support in the bureaucracy and business community; with Zaibatsu ties this political party grew stronger. In addition, the Seiyukai Party hoped to reshape Japanese politics along more democratic lines. The interplay between these three forces determined government policy. Decision-making became a subtle and complicated process.

Meanwhile, economic conditions in 1912 mandated cutbacks in government spending. This brought tensions between the three new factions to a head. The Seiyukai party insisted on increased domestic spending, while the army insisted on increased military spending. In this clash, the army ordered the Minister of the Army to resign, which forced the rest of the cabinet to follow suit. Politicians, journalists, and businessmen then organized massive demonstrations to "protect constitutional government." Emperor Taishō called his prime minister, Katsura Taro, to form a new cabinet, but the Seiyukai party defied an imperial order to support him and brought down his cabinet. For the first time in Japanese history, a political party, one supported by public opinion and the press, had brought down a cabinet. This incident became known as the Taishō Political Crisis of 1912–13. Yet, of the next three men who held office as prime pinister, two of them were still generals.

The political coalition that Prime Minister Katsura eventually put together survived and became the Min-

saito party (the equivalent of the conservatives). Together, the Minsaito and the Seiyukai parties ushered in a two-party system that continued until 1931, when militarism took over.

When World War I erupted among the European powers, Japan took the opportunity to expand its own influence in East Asia and Russia. In 1914, the Japanese government declared war on Germany and seized German-held Shandong Peninsula in China and German islands in the Pacific. In 1915, the Japanese presented China with the Twenty-One Demands. These moves extended Japanese influence at the cost of creating strong nationalism and anti-Japanese sentiment in China and led directly to the May Fourth Movement of 1919—China's first major riot based on national identity, which revealed that nationalism had replaced family in the hierarchy of Chinese values. When the Russian Revolution broke out, the Allies and Japan sent troops in support of the czar after the Bolshevik "October Revolution" of November 1917 (Russia still used the Julian calendar, which placed the Russians nearly a month behind the rest of the world). Japan sent 75,000 men, three times more than those sent by the Allies (the United States, Great Britain, France, and Canada). Finally, in opposition to Bolshevism, Japan had taken control of Eastern Siberia in addition to Manchuria and Korea in 1918.

World War I was another big boost to Japan's economy. European preoccupation with war withheld Western competition from Asia and crēated a great demand for Japanese manufactured goods. Production and export rose dramatically. Now Japan joined the United States by changing from a debtor to a creditor nation. Yet all was not well. Inflation, especially in the price of rice, created hardship for city-dwellers, chiefly for factory workers and people in traditional occupations whose wages had not kept pace. A rash of "rice riots" broke out across Japan. Considered the most violent and widespread riots in Japanese history, these protests had several major effects: 1) they brought down the current government; 2) they inspired a growing demand for reforms; 3) they caused the existing political cliques to enlarge the franchise; 4) and they gave a boost to democracy.

Elder statesmen met amid these raging rice riots and settled on Hara Kei, leader of the Seiyukai party, naming him as the next prime minister, the first party leader to take that office (1918–21). During his tenure, however, Hara Kei focused on conservative goals and let the mood for reform slip through his fingers. His policies included educational reform, expansion of mass transportation and communication, national defense, and industrial growth. These were the same goals of

Hara Kei (1856–1921). This influential leader of the Seiyukai (Friends of Constitutional Government Party) was elected to the House of Representatives where he would serve eight consecutive terms. He then served as the third president of the Rikken-Seiyukai and in 1918 became prime minister, assembling the first official political party cabinet. Image from NDL Website, used with permission of the National Diet Library, Japan.

the Meiji oligarchs during the previous generation. In the end, Hara proved unresponsive to the demand for reform.

Hara's foreign policy revolved around cooperation with Western powers. At Versailles, it was he who successfully persuaded the Big Four powers (Britain, France, the United States, and Italy) to recognize Japan's claims to China's Shandong Peninsula and some Pacific islands formerly controlled by Germany, but he failed to get them to make a declaration of racial equality. He signed the Washington Treaties in the early 1920s, in which he accepted the 5:5:3 ratio between the U.S., Britain, and Japan for the construction of large warships, and acceded to America's open-door policy in China. He also agreed to Japanese withdrawal from Siberia in 1922.

Hara Kei's approach toward China was conciliatory. Japan's investment in that country had accelerated after 1914, and by 1931 composed 80 percent of Japan's foreign holdings. Given Japan's economic commitment to the Chinese market, Hara wanted to avoid costly boycotts, the antiforeign strategy of protest that subject peoples used to frustrate their imperial masters. During Hara's tenure, anti-Japanese sentiment was already running high in China.

After Hara Kei was struck down by a young assassin with his own political agenda, a string of short-lived prime ministerships followed. Noteworthy among them, Prime Minister Kato Komei (1924 and 1926) pushed through the Universal Suffrage Act, which gave voting rights to all males twenty-five years of age and older. He balanced this step toward democracy with the conservative Peace Preservation Act, which outlawed "dangerous thought," that is, public advocacy of revolutionary changes in the national political system and the abolition of private property. Yet he was also successful in introducing moderate social reforms: legalizing labor unions, setting standards for factory conditions, establishing mediation procedures for labor disputes, and providing insurance for workers. His legacy represented the main accomplishments of the period of party government.

Succeeding Kato as prime minister was Tanaka Giichi (1927–29). Tanaka was a general who had entered politics and was elected president of the Seiyukai party. The selection of a military man as party leader indicated the continued prestige of the military, and the fact that a general would accept the position of party leader indicated the rise of party influence. But the political parties remained weak, and the voters were not politically independent. Japanese politics was still mainly the business of the traditional elite.

Tanaka departed from Kato's foreign policy of conciliation. Prime minister when the Nationalist party in China launched the Northern Expedition (1926–27), Tanaka sent Japanese troops to the edge of the Japanese sphere of influence on the Shandong Peninsula. This led to clashes between Japanese and Chinese troops. In 1928, a group of Japanese officers assassinated Zhang Zuolin, the Chinese warlord who controlled Manchuria and collaborated with the Japanese. They had hoped that this would lead to a war with China in which Japan would seize all of Manchuria. Instead, it led Zhang's son to join the Nationalists and take Manchuria with him. Since most foreign powers came to recognize the Nationalist Chinese government in Nanjing, Tanaka was forced to do so too. The Tanaka government collapsed when the prime minister incurred the displeasure of Emperor Showa (reign 1925–89) by Tanaka's failure to punish the murderers of Zhang Zuolin. This was an important event. First, it was one of the rare occasions when the emperor intervened in a political decision. Second, the assassination foreshadowed unilateral army action in the future despite the government's will.

The Hamaguchi government that followed (1929–31) returned to Kato's foreign policy of cooperation with Great Britain and the United States and conciliation with China. He signed the London Naval Treaty of 1930, which provided for a 10:10:7 ratio for all classes of ships smaller than battleships. This enraged the military and ultrapatriotic societies in Japan; then a young fanatic belonging to one of these groups shot Hamaguchi in an assassination attempt in November 1930, which led to his death in April 1931. His successor, Inukai Tsuyoshi, then lost control of the military almost as soon as he came to office in 1931. Hence, from 1931 on, the military began to act independent of the cabinet by presenting the prime minister with a *fait accompli* (done deed) without consulting the civilian leadership (an example would be the conquest of Manchuria—see below).

Prior to the 1930s, however, party politics gave the impression that Japan was becoming democratic, but this in fact was not true. Party government in Japan was the result of shifting alliances between elite groups: court nobles, military leaders, bureaucrats, and business leaders. Since party politics was not based on mass participation, it did not take root in the populace in general. Its factionalism, corruption, ties with business, brazen manipulations, pork-barrel politics, and appeals to self-interest made it suspect to many.

Meanwhile, economic problems as well as ultra-nationalistic sentiment were pulling Japan away from party politics. The period from 1920 to 1931 was a time when Japan was experiencing the throes of transition from a traditional agricultural economy into a modern industrial one. The process was made more painful by the return of competition for Asian markets from Western nations after World War I and the resurgence of nationalism in China. Not surprisingly, the Zaibatsu were reaping the greatest benefits of modernization. Small businesses and manufacturers were suffering. Meanwhile, the farmers' real income declined by a third between 1925 and 1930; the poorest of the farmers had to eat tree bark, grass roots, and wild weeds, and sell off their children in order to survive. By the end of the 1930s, the global Great Depression brought all these tensions to a head.

The Great Depression sparked a sharp rise in Japanese militarism. The Japanese army saw itself as an independent agent of the imperial will and saw party government as an usurpation of imperial prerogative. The army therefore hoped to achieve a "Showa Restoration," a second imperial restoration modeled on Meiji.

Military extremists embraced Kita Ikki's ideas. Kita Ikki (1883–1937) was a radical nationalist who argued for an organic vision of the state where every individual served the emperor who was the heart of the body politic. Kita believed that each Japanese person had to take direct responsibility for his actions in an effort to obey and protect the emperor. Such personal action included intimidation of pacifists, assassination of the unpatriotic, and launching unauthorized acts of war. These beliefs inspired the leaders of Japan's military to target Manchuria, for that province of China had rich potential as an economic and military base for imperial expansion. They began a war policy that once again placed Japan and China on a collision course.

In 1931, Japanese army officers stationed in Manchuria started a war, nominally over disputed water rights and the murder of two Japanese agents, seized Manchuria, set up a puppet government, renamed the province Manzhouguo (home of the Manchu), and made China's last emperor, Pu Yi, its puppet emperor. When the League of Nations condemned Japan's occupation of Manchuria, Japan simply quit the international body. Japanese marines then launched an attack near Shanghai in 1932. Chinese troops there put up a stubborn fight, but the invaders prevailed. The party government in Tokyo was not officially in favor of the above actions, but neither did it firmly oppose them; the government merely accepted the outcome.

After the Manchurian and Shanghai Incidents, extremist politics by assassination replaced party politics. Right-wing radicals in the army attacked and killed prominent party, business, and liberal leaders. Coups and mutinies followed. Army assassins and mutineers became martyrs in the eyes of much of the public. Yet the emperor intervened and the navy, considered more enlightened and moderate than the army, responded by cracking down on the politics of social disorder and personal attack.

The cabinets formed between 1932 and 1936 still included party men, but they were headed by prime ministers from the navy. Although a semblance of order was restored, tensions remained high between the various centers of power. The general trend was a power shift away from the political parties to the army, navy, and civilian bureaucrats in the government. Both the military and government bureaucrats saw overseas expansion as Japan's only way out of the Great Depression. Together, they were strong enough to change the direction of the nation.

Ultranationalism gripped Japan, as a totalitarian atmosphere formed without the rise of a single-party state. Japan's leaders anticipated Hitler's moves to war and laid the foundation for total conflict in the Far East. In rapid succession, the Japanese government withdrew, as mentioned, from the League of Nations in 1933 to protest its condemnation of Japanese aggression in China, and then withdrew from the naval limitation agreements, substantially increasing its military budget. Next, the government stepped up censorship, persecuted liberal authors, and banned their books, even as they intensified domestic propaganda and indoctrination, filling the media with ultranationalistic sentiment and war hysteria. The Japanese army planned an expansion northward and war with the Soviet Union, while the navy contemplated southern expansion into resource-rich Southeast Asia. Finally, in response to the prospect of war with its old allies in World War I—Britain, France and communist Russia—Japan entered an alliance with Germany in 1936 that was expanded in 1940 into the Tripartite Pact between Imperial Japan, Nazi Germany, and Fascist Italy. Clearly, Japan's solution to the Great Depression, like Hitler's, was economic self-sufficiency at the expense of its neighbors.

Now Japan stood poised for war just when Hitler was setting his sights on living space in Slavic lands. Unlike the Germans, however, the Japanese did not need to construct a totalitarian regime in order to impose the will of the military through the symbolic authority of the emperor. Instead, the military traditions of the samurai combined with an independent-minded Japanese army, ultranationalism, a national education system that taught loyalty to the nation above all else, and an appetite for empire that focused the nation on conquest. Yet the Japanese military goals in China would awaken two sleeping giants: the Chinese people and those of the United States, neither of which was willing to allow the Japanese to create economic self-sufficiency in an Asian marketplace that they both intended for themselves.

Suggested Reading

The United States

Calloway, Colin, *One Vast Winter Count* (Lincoln: University of Nebraska Press, 2003).

Doughty, Robert A., Ira D. Gruber, Roy K. Flint, George C. Herring, John A. Lynn, Mark Grimsley, Donald D. Howard, and Williamson Murray, *American Military History and the Evolution of Warfare in the Western World* (Lexington, Mass.: D.C. Heath and Company, 1996).

Ellis, John, *Brute Force: Allied Strategy and Tactics in the Second World War* (New York: Viking, 1990).

Gaddis, John Lewis, *The Cold War: A New History* (New York: Penguin Press, 2005).

Riley, Glenda, *Inventing the American Woman*, 3rd ed. (Wheeling, Ill.: Harlan Davidson, Inc., 2001).

Japan

Beasley, W. G., *Japanese Imperialism, 1894–1945* (New York: Oxford University Press, 1987).

Duus, Peter, *The Abacus and the Sword: The Japanese Penetration of Korea, 1895–1910* (Berkeley: The University of California Press, 1995).

———, Ramon H. Myers, and Mark R. Peattie, eds., *The Japanese Informal Empire in China, 1895–1937* (Princeton, N.J.: Princeton University Press, 1989).

———, *The Rise of Modern Japan* (Boston: Houghton Mifflin Company, 1976).

Eisenstadt, S. N., *Japanese Civilization: A Comparative View* (Chicago: The University of Chicago Press, 1996).

Goodman, Grant, ed., *Imperial Japan and Asia* (New York: Columbia University Press, 1967).

Hane Mikiso, *Modern Japan: A Historical Survey*, Third Edition (Boulder, Colo.: Westview, 2001).

Mason, R. H. P., and Caiger, J. G., *A History of Japan*, Revised Edition (Boston: Tuttle Publishing, 1997).

Reischauer, Edwin O., *The Japanese* (Cambridge, Mass.: Harvard University Press, 1981,

———, *Japan: The Story of a Nation* (New York: Alfred A, Knopf, 1970).

Sansom, G. B., *Japan: A Short Cultural History*, Revised Edition (New York: Applton-Century-Crofts, Inc, 1962).

XXX

DECOLONIZATION: Phase One

In the aftermath of World War I, the differential of power began to shift away from Europe. Even though the Western empires retained their hold on their subject peoples, opposition to imperial rule was already underway. The degree to which each subject culture had thrown off the yoke of imperialism depended on how successfully they had been dominated in the first place.

The vast territory of China, for example, had never truly been subjugated. Rather, every major nation-state involved in Chinese affairs either had carved out a sphere of influence, as in the case of the European powers and Japan, or had attempted to create a free market for all, as with the United States' open-door policy. In contrast, India had been reduced to a protectorate under the authority of one nation, Great Britain, and had a longer wait to achieve independence from foreign rule than did China. The Middle East, an even more complex case, comprised a diverse cultural and geographic region where multiple stories of resistance to European occupation unfolded. Finally, the people of Latin America found themselves bound to British debt during the nineteenth century, and caught up in the throes of revolution while developing a new, uncomfortable relationship with the United States during the twentieth century. This shift from European control to potential U.S. domination of Latin America made Marxism attractive to a number of local revolutionaries (see Chapter Thirty-one). The only other cultural/geographic zone, Africa, remained firmly in European hands even though Germany had lost its holdings there after World War I. Perhaps Europe's grip was still so firm because many Europeans viewed the African colonies as the ones most in need of "white" leadership.

All the national stories of decolonization, except that of Africa, reflect a major shift in the differential of power. The order in which these separate accounts appear in this text, however, reflects the degree of cultural unity or diversity that these regional social systems presented to the world as well as Europe at the time the process of decolonization began. Hence, China's story comes first because of its long history of political continuity and of the partnership that developed between the Chinese Communist Party and the Soviet Union after 1945.

The Chinese Revolution

The Chinese had never really fallen under the domination of any one imperial power. In addition, the Han people had a long tradition of political autonomy and cultural unity that included the expectation of independence. The fact that their style of decolonization began with revolution is not surprising. Their sense of self as a potential nation-state was simply too strong to ignore.

Guiding the revolutionary process was Sun Yatsen (1860–1925), the leader of the Republican Revolution of 1911 that ended China's two-thousand-year-old imperial system. Born in Quangzhou (Canton) into a poor peasant family, Sun Yatsen went to school first in China and then in the United States and England, eventually graduating from medical school in Hong Kong. Yet his passion was politics.

To mobilize for revolution, Sun developed the "Three Principles of the People." His first principle was to produce nationalism by expelling the Manchus and all foreign powers. He knew that the Chinese had to replace filial piety as their first loyalty with the love of the nation if they were to unify sufficiently to create a nation-state. Once nationalism had taken root, he then wanted to develop his second principle, democracy, based on the model found in the United States. Sun felt that the United States had managed to integrate a large geographic space into a single nation because of its pragmatism, as seen in the philosophy of John Dewey, which Sun studied. Finally, Sun wanted to provide his people with a livelihood, his third principle, by giving Chinese peasants their own land to till so that they might form individual, autonomous households in preparation for citizenship. Once this agricultural reform had taken hold, Sun envisioned a modernization and Westernization process to complete the nation-formation of China.

In 1905 from Tokyo, Sun formed the Revolutionary Alliance, a loosely organized body of reformers and revolutionaries who accepted his doctrine to varying degrees. His most active supporters were urban intellectuals and students. He also worked closely with traditional peasant secret societies, soldiers in the New Army, homeless and floating populations, and even bandits. Early in the twentieth century, he organized many ill-fated uprisings, the last of which drove him north from Canton to Wuhan in central China where his supporters infiltrated the newly established battalions of the Manchu's reform army (part of a general modernization program).

Then on October 10, 1911, revolutionary soldiers and officers in this reform army rose up in arms when the Manchu government seized their ammunition dump and captured a list of names of radical officers. Rising to forestall arrests, these soldiers and officers inspired a spontaneous revolution the swept throughout China as other parts of the country rallied to the rebellion. The Manchu regime quickly collapsed, and the Republic of China was founded in 1912, with Sun as its elected president. His supporters, the Revolutionary Alliance, became the Guomindang, or "People, Country Party"—the Nationalists.

But Sun and his revolutionary followers had little or no experience in government, and even fewer contacts at the Chinese ruling-class level. The success of the 1911 revolution gave observers the impression that Sun and his followers were the true organizers of the modern insurgency, but the fact was that military governors and provincial leaders held the reins of local power and hoped to curb any revolutionary action as soon as possible for fear of a general peasant uprising. Exploiting this desire for order at the ruling class level, Yuan Shikai derailed Sun's attempts to capture control of the 1911 revolution.

A court official, ex-governor, military reformer, and commander of the Beiyang Army (the strongest military force in China, which was stationed in the north), Yuan Shikai was in a position of considerable strength based on his contacts in the imperial army and the provinces. He took advantage of his command of the Beiyang army to force the abdication of Emperor Pu Yi (1906–67). Then Yuan engineered the resignation of Sun Yatsen as president, put down several revolts by Sun supporters, and made himself the dictator of the Republic of China. He kept the title of president, and formed a National Congress for window dressing, while he actually used the army, bribes, and the occasional assassination to suppress political opposition. Meanwhile, in 1913, Sun was forced into exile, he escaped to Japan, and his new party, the Guomindang was expelled from the National Congress.

To bolster international support, "President" Yuan accepted Japan's "Twenty-One Demands," which was a program to take control of the Chinese government and turn China into a Japanese colony. Then in December 1915, Yuan proclaimed himself emperor. His attempt to turn back the hands of the clock met with implacable opposition throughout the country. He died a broken man three months later, but he had had successfully derailed Dr. Sun's plans for nation-building.

Yuan's death left a power vacuum in China in 1916. No one was strong enough to replace him and hold the country together. A nominal central government continued to sit in Beijing, but government power became decentralized. Regional military strongmen seized control of local governments and collaborated with foreign powers that dominated their region. Without long-term goals and strategies, the warlords ran thoroughly corrupt and repressive regional governments. They also engaged in endlessly shifting alliances and bloody battles over territory. To satisfy their greed and their need of money to wage war, they levied taxes decades and even centuries in advance.

From 1916 to 1926, China then witnessed significant economic growth and intellectual ferment. World War I had shifted the focus of European nations away from China, which gave struggling Chinese merchants and industrialists a chance to build up their own enterprises. Meanwhile, none of the competing Chinese warlords was strong enough to exercise traditional control over intellectual discourse. Educated people now had a chance to discuss Western ideas and ways to apply them to China.

A period of intellectual blossoming began, one that paralleled the "Hundred Flowers" during the Era of the Warring States (403–221 BCE) that spawned Confucianism and Daoism. To this era of intellectual activity, both the Nationalist party and the future Communist party could trace their roots. Ironically, neither of them would allow intellectual freedom under their own regimes.

From this intellectual fermentation the May 4th Movement of 1919 emerged. This represented a major turning point in China's drive to independence because it showed that for the first time in Chinese history national pride could focus public opinion. The May 4th Movement began with a student demonstration that touched off riots protesting the terms of the Peace of Paris, reached in Versailles. Specifically, public opinion exploded when word reached China that the Big Four had decided to turn Germany's sphere of influence in the Shandong Peninsula over to Japan as part of the peace settlement after World War I. This was especially humiliating since China had entered World War I on the side of the victorious Allies.

The students of Peking (Beijing) University took to the streets to condemn Japan and the warlord Beijing government. They advocated a powerful nationalism that quickly spread across China, especially to cities in the South. Similar protests broke out in Shanghai, Guangzhou, and Wuhan. The ranks of protesters also broadened to include industrial workers as well as intellectuals.

In addition to nationalism, the May 4th Movement generated a consensus on the need to create a new culture. Its central target was Confucianism, the essence of traditional China: its most powerful slogan was: "Smash Confucianism!" It also opposed *wenyanwen* (classical Chinese). The "New Culture" would be that of the common people. It would make education accessible to the common people, adopt *baihuawen* (plain, colloquial Chinese) for writing, and promote the acceptance of science and democracy.

At Peking University, Professor Hu Shi (1891–1962), who had returned from Columbia University in New York City, was the most successful advocate of baihuawen. Modern China's greatest writer, Lu Xun (1881–1936), began to write in baihuawen. His novelette, *A Mad Man's Diary*, portrayed Confucian China as a place where "people eat people." The journal *New Youth* became the major forum for New Culture advocates.

The New Culture Movement, however, split over politics. Although its members all agreed that China should be transformed after a Western model, not everyone could agree on which Western nation to emulate. Those on the right preferred the Anglo-American model of liberal democracy while those on the left favored the communist model, especially after Russia's Communist Revolution of 1917. The latter began to spread Marxism-Leninism and to organize communist cells in China.

Chen Duxiu (1879–1942) and Li Dazhao (1889–1927), both Peking University professors, were not only in the vanguard of the New Culture Movement, but they were also leading figures in China's early communist movement. Chen adopted Marxism in 1920. With Comintern assistance, he founded the Chinese Communist Party (CCP) in Shanghai in 1921. Mao Zedong (1894–1976) formed a communist study group in Changsha in 1919, while Zho Enlai (1898–1976) formed one in Paris, France, in 1921.

Meanwhile, Sun Yatsen, who had fled to Japan during Yuan's rule, returned to Guangzhou after Yuan's death. Sun sought to reunify China. He enjoyed personal popularity as a political leader, but his Nationalist party was weak, and he had no armies at its command. The warlords remained entrenched in their regional power struggles, and the foreign powers—still recovering from World War I and growing isolationist—refused to help him.

From this position of weakness, Sun failed to make any headway. In 1923 he decided to accept advice and aid from the Soviet Union because it was the only major power that had no privileges in China and had reached out to him. Now things began to change. He reinterpreted his "Three Principles of the People" to include ideas to "unite with Russia and (the Chinese) communists" and "support industrial workers and peasants." He reorganized the Nationalist party along the lines of the Russian Communist party, allowed CCP members to join, and established the Huangpu Military Academy. This was the First United Front of the Nationalist party and the CCP. Then Dr. Sun died in 1925 and was succeeded by Jiang Jieshi (Chiang Kaishek, 1887–1975), Sun's lieutenant and the commandant of the Huangpu academy.

By 1926 the reorganized Nationalist party had 200,000 members, the Huangpu had graduated several thousand officers, and the party-controlled army numbered about 100,000 troops. Based in a regional government in Guangdong province in south China, the Nationalist party and Jiang had become a major force in China. Now Jiang decided to launch the Northern Expedition to unify China, and in July 1926 his troops began their march northward. By April 1927 Nationalist forces had captured Shanghai.

The Russian and Chinese communist influence in the Nationalist Party had strengthened it, but it also divided it between the right wing, headed by Jiang, and the left wing under strong communist influence. Jiang was suspicious of growing communist influence and maneuvered to whittle it down, but initially he was careful to avoid an open split. Soon after he had captured Shanghai with their support, however, Jiang sprang a bloody coup on the communists in his forces, outlawed the CCP, and wiped out the Shanghai Worker's Militia (dominated by the CCP). Now the CCP went underground, and the left-wing Nationalists accepted Jiang's unchallenged leadership. The First United Front had come to a bloody end.

In 1928, Jiang established the Republic of China with its capital in Nanjing; thus began the "Nanjing Decade, 1928–37." He continued the Northern Expedition until he captured the city of Beijing. By now he had defeated most warlords in the south and gained at least the nominal submission of most warlords in the rest of China. He became the embodiment of Chinese nationalism, and most foreign powers accepted his government as the legitimate federal body of China.

Jiang's power base lay in coastal China and along the Lower and Middle Changjiang River. His support came mainly from treaty-port Chinese businesspeople, landowners, and local representatives of the foreign powers. The reach of his government, however, was limited. Large areas of China were still under the de facto control of warlords, and local authority still lay in the hands of large landowners. Finally, foreign powers still enjoyed many of the privileges they had seized from the Manchu regime through unequal treaties.

China's most pressing problem remained the plight of the peasantry, who composed 90 percent of its population. These peasants demanded some form of redistribution of land, but Jiang could not carry out any kind of land reform for fear of alienating his landlord supporters; for the same reason, he could not assert his influence in warlord-controlled areas or eradicate the privileges of foreign powers. Thus the democratic features of Sun Yatsen's revolution began to wither on the vine.

Jiang was painfully aware that the revolution was losing momentum. Even though he remained a staunch nationalist, he believed that the only way to save China was to establish a dictatorship. Dr. Sun's "Three Principles of the People" ceased being the Guomindang's real goals: nationalism remained intact, democracy had become a casualty of political necessity, and livelihood now meant lowering rents rather than redistributing the land to the peasants so that they could own farms. In the place of a popular government, Jiang built a power structure that rested on his control of the Nationalist party and the party-controlled army and government bureaucracy. Then he strengthened his ties with Nazi Germany and began to indoctrinate his party with the Nazi principle of one state, one leader, one party, one army.

With help from German military advisors, he reorganized and expanded his army into a modernized force of 300,000. He established a secret service, significantly called the Blue Shirts after Mussolini's Black Shirts and Hitler's Brown Shirts. Jiang used the Blue Shirts to attack underground communists and anyone who was critical of his government. The Huangpu clique, loyal to Jiang personally, dominated the army and the secret service. He launched the New Life Movement to revive Confucian values and introduce some Western ideas such as personal health and hygiene. In short, he established a dictatorship.

Nevertheless, Jiang's Nanjing regime faced two constant threats. After the Shanghai bloodbath of 1927, Mao Zedong had fled to a mountainous region in Central China where he established a revolutionary base he called the "Jiangxi Soviet." Zhu De (1886–1976) joined him with his surviving troops after a failed military uprising in Wuchang on August 1, 1927. For the next decade, those two men would lead their followers in a civil war against Jiang.

Top: This badge (c. 1960s) portrays Mao Zedong, Chairman of the Chinese Communist Party. Although Mao badges were first made in 1937, they reached their height during the Cultural Revolution (1966–76). Mao badges were made by most factories and institutions and worn by almost all Chinese people. © The Trustees of the British Museum.
Right: Jiang Jieshi (1887–1975), shown here with President Eisenhower, became the leader of the Republic of China in 1928. He later relocated his government to Taiwan, serving as the President of the ROC after a failed attempt at removing Chinese Communists during the Chinese Civil War. Collection of Paul J. Gaio.

Jiang launched five "elimination campaigns" to try to wipe out the communists. Only in the fifth, devised by his German military advisors, did he manage to dislodge them from their mountain base and force them into a retreat, but only to see them reestablish themselves at Yan'an in North China.

The communists' long zigzag trek from Central China to North China became world-famous as the Long March (1934–35). Coming after a disastrous military defeat, it was also a great feat of human aspiration, endurance, and sacrifice. Traveling on foot and fighting continuous battles and skirmishes, the communists covered six thousand miles in little more than one year. Only 10 percent of the 100,000 people who set out on the Long March survived the ordeal, yet those who did arrive at Yan'an were filled with a sense of purpose, confidence, and solidarity. These toughened men and women became the core of the CCP. As a tight-knit group, they would be the CCP leaders for the next three decades in the continued civil war against Jiang, the approaching war against Japan, and the reconstruction of China.

Japan posed the other threat to Jiang's rule. After having turned Korea into its colony as a result of the Sino-Japanese War of 1894–95, Japan took control of the Chinese province of Manchuria after the Russo-Japanese War of 1904–05. When the Northern Expedition and Chinese nationalism threatened Japanese interests in China, Japan's Guangdong Army engineered a military coup in Manchuria in 1931 and installed a puppet government, Manzhouguo, mentioned in Chapter Twenty-nine. As the Japanese army moved ever farther south in the following years, Chinese nationalism demanded resistance to Japanese aggression. Yet Jiang insisted on focusing his attention on the suppression of the communists.

Consistently maintaining that "suppression of domestic bandits must take precedence over expulsion of foreign aggressors," Jiang sent his best troops to lay siege on the new communist base in Yan'an. But when he visited the front lines in 1936, his respective commanding generals took him hostage. They demanded a Second United Front of the Nationalists and Communists against Japanese aggression, releasing him only after he made a public statement to that effect.

Hence, Jiang and Mao agreed to face a common enemy before settling their differences. This agreement did not survive World War II, but it did function as a (second) united front against the Japanese when war broke out. Accordingly, China had only begun to establish its independence before World War II finished Europe's command of the differential of power. As a result, China had to postpone its redefinition of itself within the context of modernization as World War II commanded the attention of the entire global community.

India

As mentioned on numerous occasions, India suffered from significant internal divisions that included language, ethnicity, and religion, while no common political tradition existed on the subcontinent as it had in China. The British, however, served as a common enemy that could mobilize effective resistance. Hence, despite internal disunity, so long as the British Raj controlled Indian politics, the diverse population there could develop at least one common focus.

Political activism took many forms before it could present a united face to the British. One thing each of the original movements had in common, however, was the image of an independent Indian nation-state based on modernization; these early resistance factions understood that methods and political ideals from the West had to be imported and placed in an Indian context before Britain could be successfully expelled. Thus, by 1885, modernist movements began to form.

The first of these early initiatives was the Indian National Congress, a Hindu-dominated representative body that sought gradual reform and progress towards an independent state based on democratic principles. To represent those who followed Islam, however, the Moslem League developed as a separate representative body to make sure that India's vast Hindu majority did not overlook the needs of those faithful to the will of Allah. The Moslem League ultimately succeeded in creating groundwork for an independent Muslim state: Pakistan. Yet, the fact that this significant religious division had created two separate representative bodies so early in India's drive for independence ensured bloodshed would follow once Britain, the common enemy, had been removed.

As the drive for national formation began, issues of pace and determination became a problem. The *swaraj*, the National Congress's gradual program for reform and progress toward a new nation-state, suggested that a degree of cooperation with the British Raj was necessary. Helping the British make up their minds to leave required passive yet determined opposition to their presence. Chief among those who used this passive approach was Mohandas K. Ghandi (1869–1948), called the *Mahatma* (great soul).

A member of the National Congress, but also a leader who often dragged the Congress along behind him, Mahatma Ghandi developed a method of *Satyagraha* (passive resistance) that forced the British to face the contradictions within their position as "rulers" of the subcontinent. How could a nation like Great Britain that advocated democracy, liberalism, and humanitarianism also command an empire that required the use of raw power to oppress a subject people? To persuade the British of the moral bankruptcy of their position within India, Ghandi forced them to explore their conscience. His position was that no one could force him or his followers to do anything against their will or their moral sense of duty. They were willing to take the blows of an oppressive regime to maintain the purity of their souls. They also would force those who delivered the blows to consider their own actions in the light of their stated beliefs. Furthermore, since this form of passive resistance did not violate any British laws, the use of force undermined the moral position of legal officials who tried to impose the rule of law on those who resisted. Such a program worked well after World War I because of the demoralization that had followed the Great War, which enhanced Ghandi's position and added considerable force to his approach.

During the 1920s, Ghandi led several Satyagraha actions against British imports, especially cotton goods, but he had to discontinue his efforts when his followers failed to adhere to his wishes and perpetrated violence. In 1930, he led a boycott against the British salt monopoly, extracted salt from the sea, and found himself imprisoned for his efforts. But he ultimately broke the British salt monopoly. In 1931, the British released Ghandi so that he could attend the London Round Table Conference on India as the only delegate from the Indian National Congress. While he did not persuade the British to leave India yet, his moral stature had reached its apex. Eventually, his national prestige rose to the point that he could single-handedly sway public opinion, and effect policy changes, simply by threatening to "fast unto death." This threat and his subsequent fasting worked both against the British and the more violent of his followers.

Unlike Ghandi, the militant Hindu Bal Gangadhar Tilak (1856–1920) advocated a Hindu version of nationalism that quickly alienated the Muslims of the subcontinent. Tilak believed that Hinduism defined the faith of the vast majority of the Indian people; accordingly, Indians should rest nationalism on Hindu principles. As a result, Tilak worked to restore what he thought were ancient Hindu traditions: caste as the basis of social division; opposition to female education; encouraging early marriages, even for the very young; and turning religious festivals into national demonstrations against the British. Tilak advocated boycotts against British goods long before Ghandi made them a cornerstone in his nonviolent protest campaigns. Tilak demanded full independence, without delay, and threatened open rebellion if India did not achieve political autonomy quickly.

Tilak's persuasive speaking abilities at mass rallies and his religious appeal made him the first major Indian politician to shape public opinion. Yet his strong views also alienated moderates and liberals because his brand of Hinduism included intense reactionary concepts that ran contrary to modernization. Simultaneously, Tilak's version of Hinduism also antagonized the Muslim and Sikh populations of the subcontinent, for neither one had a place in the India he planned to construct. Given the success he enjoyed among the more radical members of India's population, the British grew fearful of his potential to cause revolution and arrested him. When Tilak was sentenced to a six-year prison term for his radical demands and mass appeal, his followers rioted. Now the British suppressed his movement, and Tilak's wife died during his incarceration. While the death of his wife broke his spirit, the power of Tilak's ideas survived his death in 1920 and continue to play a major role in Indian politics today.

A third and final force directed against the British Raj came from Mohammed Ali Jinnah (1876–1948). A British-trained lawyer like Ghandi, Jinnah became a fervent supporter of the Indian National Congress and an advocate of Hindu-Muslim unity early in his political career. He served as a member of the legislative council from 1910 to 1919, but he bridled under the majority voice of the Hindus. In 1916, while still a member of the National Congress, he was elected to the presidency of the Moslem League. He finally resigned from the National Congress in 1930 and spent the rest of his life working to create an independent Muslim state.

While Jinnah had the capacity to shape public opinion as effectively as Tilak or Ghandi, his willingness to use violence placed him more in the same camp with Tilak than Ghandi. Nevertheless, Jinnah's determination to create an independent Muslim state ensured that religion would divide the subcontinent as effectively as Tilak's emphasis on Hinduism. Hence, by the 1930s, the opposition to Britain's presence in India had achieved significant momentum, but buried within it was a powerful religious division that would become a political reality after World War II.

The Middle East

Turkey

The response of the Middle East to the West proved far more complex than that of China or India. Given the ethnic and religious diversity of the region, a variety of resistance and independence movements emerged that reflected local social goals. Chief among these was the nationalism that drove the creation of modern-day Turkey.

The "Young Turk" movement of 1908 that had forced reforms on the aging sultanate near the end of the Ottoman reign had paved the way for a new state after World War I. Infused with a radical nationalism that wanted to emulate Europe in order to avoid becoming part of a European empire, the Young Turks were in a position of power that allowed them to generate a new government in the 1920s. Ironically, equally eager ethnic groups—the Kurds, the Armenians, and the Greeks—with a long history of hostility to the Turks, hoped to create nations of their own. They surrounded this emerging new Turkish state.

The creation of modern Turkey emerged from the debris of a collapsing Ottoman Empire, which provided yet another example of totalitarianism in operation. Called the Turkish Republic, this new state was the brainchild of one of the "Young Turks," Mustafa Kemal (1880–1938). Kemal took the title *Atatürk*, (father of the Turks), much like Hitler hailed himself as *Der Führer* and Mussolini as *Il Duce*, so that this new Turkish leader could impose his will upon his people. He immediately set about redesigning the nation. He imposed a European-style national code of laws, abolished the caliphate, eliminated Arabic script, the Sufi mystical sects, and Arabic prayer; and he completely separated church and political authority.

The history of this new political creation followed the events of World War I. In May 1919, Kemal organized the Turkish Nationalist Party and began to form a national army to protect the Turkish state from the Allies and the sultan's subject peoples. He also set up a national congress in July, which was immediately outlawed by the last reigning sultan, Mohammed VI. Meanwhile, the Allies had forced Mohammed VI to sign the Treaty of Sèvres, which completely destroyed the Ottoman Empire and Turkey as a potential nation-state. Kemal ignored this treaty and, with support from the Soviet Union, retook Kars and Ardahan from Armenia in 1920. Then, in 1921–22, he expelled the Greeks from Anatolia and recovered a significant but small piece of land in Europe (Eastern Thrace) to protect Istanbul from future assaults. Given his military successes, Kemal then asked the Allies for a new treaty, which he received at the Lausanne Conference of 1922–23. At Lausanne, Turkey recovered full sovereign rights as well as confirmation of its holdings in Armenia, Eastern Thrace, and northern Syria.

Even as Kemal won these concessions from the victors of World War I, he felt the time was right to eliminate the sultanate, so he exiled Mohammed VI and his family in November 1922. Kemal then became the president of the new Turkish Republic in 1923, and won reelection in 1927, 1931, and 1935—all three times by a unanimous vote from his parliament.

Like Hitler and Mussolini, Kemal tolerated no opposition. He created a single-party state based on vertical articulation and he used the army to break all religious opposition to his fifteen-year rule. He implemented a style of ruthlessness that would have made his fascist brethren proud, but he also laid the foundation for a modern nation-state, one that would endure; hence, from his point of view, the end justified the means. In terms of international relations, he developed a pragmatic foreign policy of friendship and neutrality with everyone—especially the new Soviet Union, which secured for him the Balkan Entente that freed Turkey from foreign rule. Consequently, in his mind, he had earned his title: "father of the Turks."

Persia/Iran

In contrast to Turkey, Persia retained the concept of monarchy while attempting partial modernization. The central figure in the Persian story was Reza Khan Pahlevi (1877–1944). A military officer of courage and charismatic leadership, Reza Khan won fame by expelling the Russians from Persia after World War I. Using this celebrity to engineer a coup d'état against the Qajars, Reza Khan seized power in 1921, took sole control of the government in 1923, and proclaimed himself shah in 1925.

Beginning the Pahlevi Dynasty, Reza Khan started a modernization program designed to enhance his power. He reformed the army, administration, and financing of the state to produce the means to create an independent Iranian nation-state (recall from Unit Two that *Iran* is a variation of *Aryan* and is a name Persians use for themselves). He abolished the special privileges of foreigners and took command of domestic affairs without any significant response from Great Britain. He then engaged in social and economic reforms that included building the Trans-Iranian Railroad, introducing industry to Persia, and founding the University of Teheran. He made Persia a significant power in the Middle East, but he did not survive World War II. Too friendly with the Germans in 1941, Reza Khan forced the British and Soviets to reassert foreign authority in Iran. They persuaded him to abdicate in favor of his son, Mohammed Khan.

The Pahlevi Dynasty survived its founder, but it now existed in a country whose resistance to modernization remained very strong. The ayatollahs and the mujtahid, and their secular commercial partners, who had plagued Qajar rule with objections to Western influences and modern change, remained a very power-

Reza Shah Pahlevi (1878–1944). Referred to as Reza the Great, Reza Shah Pahlevi of Iran was the first monarch of the Pahlavi dynasty. A proponent of industry and technology, he is credited with greatly modernizing his nation, using dictatorial powers.

ful source of opposition. The dictatorial authority that Reza Khan established, and his son inherited, wrenched Iran into the twentieth century too quickly for many of the local people and stimulated a growing Islamic resistance to the shah's rule. Hence, even though the Pahlevi Dynasty survived World War II, Iran's isolation, internal division, and lack of a solid social base to continue the modernization process spelled trouble for the existing regime. Nonetheless, Persia had won its independence from foreign rule.

Saudi Arabia

One other major dynasty established its rule at the beginning of the twentieth century: the Ibn-Sauds. Abdul Aziz ibn Saud (1880–1953) created Saudi Arabia out of the ashes of World War I. A leader of the Wahabi movement, the ultraorthodox Muslim faction established by Mohammed ibn-Abd al-Wahabi (1703–92) who wished to restore Islamic purity to the Muslim community, Abdul ibn Saud united the Arab tribes of northern and central Arabia and drove out the remnants of Ottoman rule. Beginning as an exile in Kuwait because his family's leadership in the Wahabi movement had disrupted local politics in Riyadh (the capital of present-day Saudi Arabia), Abdul planned to recover the Ibn-Saud seat of power there. Using a small band of relatives and servants,

Abdul successfully captured Riyadh by a surprise attack in 1900. By 1912, he had completed the conquest of north and central Arabia and was in a position to begin building a strong army based on local tribes dedicated to his vision of reestablishing a pure Islamic state.

During World War I, however, the British ignored Abdul's leadership and backed a rival, Hussein ibn Ali of Nejaz (central Arabia). With Britain's aid, Hussein supported the Arab revolt led by Lawrence of Arabia. Colonel T. E. Lawrence was the British officer who successfully organized Arabic resistance for Hussein, captured Aqaba (a strategic port in southern Jordan), disrupted Turkish communication in Arabia, and supported General Edmund Henry Allenby, the Commander-in-Chief of the Egyptian Expeditionary Force, on his final march against the Ottoman Turks. Meanwhile, Abdul prepared for the postwar struggle.

While Hussein ended up the titular head of a successful revolt, and proclaimed himself king of the Arabs, his having to work with the British after the war, during the peace process, undermined his popularity with the Arabian tribes on the Peninsula. Abdul, on the other hand, had a spotless reputation as a charismatic and devout Islamic leader. Accordingly he could and did lead a successful assault on Hussein's capital, Mecca, and captured control of north and central Arabia in 1924. With command of Islam's most sacred shrines, Abdul then declared himself king of the Arabs in 1925. Steadily thereafter, he built up his power base and by 1932 created a successful absolute monarchy in Saudi Arabia.

Abdul ibn Saud instituted modern reforms that forced many of the Bedouin tribes living on the Arabian Peninsula to take up sedentary agriculture. He established a legal system that eliminated tribal warfare and vendettas as well as suppressing robbery and extortion of pilgrims performing the *Hajj* (the sacred journey to Mecca). An absolute monarch with very conservative inclinations, Abdul ibn Saud held on to his throne, built a national economy based on Arabia's vast supply of oil, and successfully navigated the treacherous political seas of the Great Depression, World War II, and the Cold War. Hence, he created a very important independent state.

Other States

The remainder of the Ottoman Empire broke apart into mandate territories under the control of the League of Nations. Turned over to the victors of World War I, France and Great Britain, future countries like Egypt, Syria, Lebanon, Palestine-Israel, and Iraq still had to contend with a foreign presence. Egypt, Iraq, Syria, and Lebanon officially obtained independence before World War II, but they had to wait until after the end of that conflict before they were truly free from foreign entanglements. Hence, their political fate depended on the influence of World War II on the global differential of power.

Less successful in terms of creating new states, but important nonetheless, were four Muslim intellectuals—politicians who saw the necessity of linking modernization to the religious force of Islam to shape the politics of the Middle East. These four men included Jamal al-Din al-Afghani (1839–97), Mohammed Abdul (1845–1905), Mohammed Rashid Rida (1865–1935), and Mohammed Iqbal (1873–1938). Each man, in his own way, advanced the power of religious faith in the context of the modern world.

Jamal al-Din al Afghani promoted the concept of unity of all Muslims against a European presence, and British rule in particular. His influence reached from Egypt to Turkey to Iran. Yet he was expelled from several government posts that he held over the course of his career in Afghanistan, Turkey, and Egypt because he raised the ire of the local religious opposition as well as the British, who grew to fear him.

His vision was one of Islamic utopianism. He wanted to create a hierarchical society that embraced the entire Islamic world and functioned on the moral principles of shame, trustworthiness, and truthfulness seasoned with the ideals of intelligence, pride, and justice. By intelligence, Jamal meant a new capacity to learn the modern means needed to advance civilization. By pride, Jamal meant the ability to compete on an international scale with other cultures successfully. And by justice, Jamal meant creating an international condition of global peace based on equality and harmony among nations.

In the 1870s, Jamal joined with Mohammed Abdul to create an Arabic journal entitled *Urwat al Wuthqa (The Indissoluble Bond)* that stated his Pan-Islamic vision most clearly. This journal published articles on numerous topics, but a general political vision began to emerge: a populist, constitutional approach to politics. Jamal, however, proved to be a man ahead of his times. He had to rely on Islamic rulers in the Ottoman Empire and Persia for political patronage, but these were men whose sources of power belonged to a traditional past. Hence, much of what Jamal had to say was lost on rulers and ministers incapable of applying his ideas. Nonetheless, his influence was not lost on the Islamic world, for his ideas were picked up and developed by his chief disciple, Mohammed Abdul.

Abdul carried on where Jamal left off. As coauthor with Jamal on the *Urwat al Wuthqa* journal, Abdul preached Islamic solidarity against European imperial rule. Like Jamal, Abdul believed that Muslims everywhere had to cooperate with each other to reverse the trend of disintegration suffered by the Islamic community under European pressures. Like Jamal, Abdul called for a return to the true spirit of Islam, a reinterpretation of the Qur'an in the context of the modern age, and the discovery of ways to make science and religion compatible.

Eventually, Abdul differed with Jamal over the use of political protest. Abdul came to believe that protest in itself was futile unless accompanied with modernization and reform from within. Hence, he abandoned Jamal's strict anti-British platform and began arguing in favor of limited cooperation. This alienated Abdul from those who hoped for immediate resistance to British rule, such as Mustafa Kamel's nationalists. But even Abdul's death in 1905 did not quiet his voice.

Abdul's chief disciple, Mohammed Rashid Rida, was the next to pick up this evolving Islamic message. Rida's magazine *al Manar* spoke for the *Salafiyya* movement (those who sought inspiration from virtuous early Muslim leaders who were the innovators of their day). Just like these *salaf*, (Islamic ancestors), Risa felt that the Muslim world needed to learn enough from the West to resist European rule. But, continued British presence in the Middle East, in Egypt in particular, forced Rida to become more and more anti-Western in outlook. Hence, Rida drifted back to Jamal's original position and became a primary influence on Hasan al Banna (1906–49) and his Moslem Brotherhood.

The Moslem Brotherhood itself was an organization founded in 1928 by al Banna based on Rida's Pan-Islamism but established in Egypt. It sought a general Muslim revival in the modern world. The Moslem Brotherhood was also willing to use political assassination to achieve its goals; ironically, an assassin took the life of al Banna in 1949.

In contrast to Jamal, Abdul, Risa, and al Banna, Mohammed Iqbal was an Indian Muslim thinker of the twentieth century and a gifted poet. He worked with Mohammed Jinnah in the creation of modern-day Pakistan. He argued for an essential bond between religion and national formation, which was explicitly linked to the message of the Qur'an. Since the Prophet Mohammed's principle achievement was the creation of the Muslim community, and since this creation had derived from a revelation, then the idea of generating an Islamic political revival anywhere (and especially in India) without considering Islam, was to deny the truth of the Prophecy and its fundamental purpose: the construction of a national polity. Accordingly, the truth of Islam was not that it merely created a church, but that it also generated a state as well. Hence, Islam and politics were inseparable.

Consequently, for Iqbal the creation of a Muslim state within the Indian subcontinent was a religious necessity. This is why he and Jinnah complemented one another in the formation of modern Pakistan. Accordingly, Iqbal belonged to a revival of Islam within the context of modern nationalism and national formation. Thus his reasoning and the power of his message were not lost on the Middle East because Pakistan joined this cultural zone after 1947.

A third type of reaction to European imperialism was the revival of the Islamic world as a pure community. Known as "Islamism," as discussed in Chapter Twenty-six, or Islamic Fundamentalism, as seen in Persian history, this third resistance movement wanted to exclude the West and tap into the original energy of Mohammed's Prophecy. Embedded in a conservative spirit that includes a revivalist mentality, this quest for purity within the Muslim community held that all the answers needed for an Islamic resurgence already existed in the words and deeds of the Prophet and the wisdom of the *Ulama* (the body of Muslim scholars). Relying on Islamic law, the Qur'an, the *Hadith* (Mohammed's other sayings and actions), and the prophetic example, this movement functioned as a powerful anchor to give Muslims a common focus when confronting Western power. This conservative impulse, however, held within its political agenda a basic weakness: the exclusion of the West denied access to the modern tools needed to expel Europe from the Middle East. Hence, the Western world would not appreciate fully this style of Muslim resistance until after World War II, when Europe had completed its process of self-destruction, and the Cold War offered several choices to the Islamic fundamentalists in the methods they used to oppose outside imperialist influences.

Latin America

Unlike the other regional cultures covered in this chapter, Latin America had experienced the beginnings of decolonization nearly a century before World War I. Yet the independence won in the revolutionary struggles of 1810–26 proved illusory. Indeed, for the remainder of the nineteenth century, internal divisions and global economics trapped emerging Hispanic nation-states in an era of subordination to Europe similar to that experienced by emerging nations in the Middle East, Africa, and Asia.

Although independent in name, most countries in Latin America struggled throughout the contentious nineteenth century to achieve true autonomy. In the decades after 1826, newly independent nations struggled with the demands of economic development, political infighting and foreign interventions. This century after independence conveniently breaks into two eras, the first extending from the 1820s to the middle of the 1870s, and the other from that point to roughly the start of World War I. Both eras have similarities and saw the dogged persistence of colonial attitudes and structures. Yet by 1910, countries such as Brazil and Argentina, for example, began to experience some success in building national economies, as well as developing a true political sovereignty.

In analyzing the causes for the persistent troubles that Latin American countries experienced, it is important to remember that most newly independent states experience such problems. In the Americas, both the United States and Canada, despite successful transitions from colonial status, faced and overcame numerous crises after independence. In the case of Latin America, a number of important factors perpetuated unstable conditions.

First, the former Spanish and Portuguese colonies had had little preparation for independent political activity. There were few of the political training grounds, such as the locally elected legislatures or town councils found in the United States and Canada, to prepare potential citizens for the responsibilities of nation building. Furthermore, the habit of deference to those of higher social and economic status remained very strong. Although the Iberian rulers had been vanquished, the caste system retained its hold into the next century. Additionally, local elites quickly developed rigid political ideologies, either liberal or conservative, and refused to compromise their positions. This often resulted in political stalemates, a failure to resolve issues for the national welfare, and, distressingly often, a resort to violence to break any impasse. Thus arose, in country after country of political strongmen, the *caudillos*, whose hold on power was based on the use of force. Caudillos in Chile, Argentina, Venezuela, and Mexico retarded the development of responsible political parties, reliable legal systems, and effective national economies. In general, little respect developed for institutions and traditions that could create a true national sovereignty based on shared values and traditions.

Second, throughout the era, Latin American nations-in-formation experienced constant interference, interventions, and outright invasions by powerful neighbors and would-be conquerors. Imperialism became a very real threat to national sovereignty. The Spanish sent military expeditions to intimidate Latin American nations in the 1820s and 1830s. France used debt obligations and diplomatic squabbles to send its military to Argentina and, most notably, Mexico. French troops invaded and occupied Mexican soil in the 1830s and 1860s. During the last incursion, they supported an

Austrian prince, Maximillian, as the ruler of Mexico as it recovered from a civil war between rival political factions. The French government removed its troops only when the United States threatened to enforce the 1823 Monroe Doctrine, and invade Mexico after 1865.

Mexico

The most serious example of this foreign influence saw the Mexicans drawn into a conflict with the United States in 1846 over disputed territorial borders in Texas. The resulting war cost Mexico more than 500,000 square miles of its national territory, as it gave up California and the present-day southwestern United States in the 1848 Treaty of Guadalupe Hidalgo. American politicians, eager to settle western North America, brazenly exploited the political and military weaknesses of their southern neighbor to annex this territory. The discovery of gold in California in 1848 had added a bitter denouement to this disaster for Mexico.

Third, since political leaders in these countries did little to resolve their differences, they must share some of the blame for continuing to struggle with rivals, plotting the downfall of governments they disagreed with, and making deals with foreign powers that undercut their own national interests. This led to a dramatic growth of foreign influence in many Latin American countries after 1826. Great Britain quickly became the dominant European power in the region, a position it held until World War I. British merchants flooded Latin America with cheap textiles, shoes, machinery, and, most notably, credit. Banking houses helped finance railroads, mining enterprises, and the expansion of exports. Coffee and cotton from Brazil, beef and hides from Argentina, copper from Chile, and sugar, tobacco and henequen (agave fiber) from Mexico flowed to Great Britain and from there throughout the world as Latin America became a prime supplier of raw materials for the rapidly industrializing nineteenth-century global economy.

Unfortunately, little of the great wealth generated by Latin American exports found its way back to the Indians, mestizos, mulattos, and slaves who produced it. The social caste system stayed largely intact, with the great landowners and powerful merchants controlling both the economic and political systems in their respective countries. Mexico and Brazil are good examples of how some of these issues played out.

Mexico elected its first president in 1824, but within a few years liberals and conservatives began to disagree over national policy. This political infighting led to open conflict and the eventual rise of a military strongman, Antonio Lopez de Santa Anna, to power. Santa Anna became a classic nineteenth-century cau-

dillo, learning to play one faction or party off against another. He managed to keep himself at the forefront of Mexican politics until the 1850s, not only by damaging the rule of law and self-government in the country, but also by leading Mexico into disastrous conflicts with Spain, France, and the United States. Successful opposition to Santa Anna finally came from a new generation of Mexican leaders who emerged in the 1840s, led by the Liberals Benito Juarez and Melchor Ocampo. They drove Santa Anna from power and introduced a period of reform in Mexico, which included the drafting of a new constitution in 1857.

Conservatives, fearing a loss of power and privilege in the new system, turned to war to stop the Liberals. However, the Three Years' War they initiated went badly for the Conservatives, and they faced a grim future by 1861. Determined to stop Juarez's and Ocampo's plans for a liberal and progressive Mexico, they turned to foreigners for help. At this point, England, Spain, and France decided to recover Mexico's debts owed to their bankers and invaded and seized control of Veracruz, Mexico's chief port, in 1862. After the other

General D. Antonio López De Santa Anna, President of the Republic of Mexico (1794–1876). Santa Anna is most famous (and infamous) for his politics during such events as the Texan revolt (1836) and the Mexican War (1846–48). Credit: Library of Congress, Washington, D.C. LC-USZ62-21276.

GENERAL D. ANTONIO LOPEZ DE SANTA-ANNA,
PRESIDENT OF THE REPUBLIC OF MEXICO.
By A. Hoffy, from an original likeness taken from life at Vera-Cruz.

Europeans withdrew, the French Emperor Napoleon III sent to Mexico a large military force that extended French control over most of the nation. When Napoleon installed an Austrian Habsburg as emperor of Mexico, Juarez and his fellow Liberals fled to Texas, where they organized an opposition. Maximillian's short-lived reign concluded when Napoleon III withdrew his troops following military reversals in Europe and pressure from the United States at the conclusion of its Civil War. Back in Mexico City, his Austrian pawn was captured, tried, and executed by Juarez in 1867.

After a decade of civil war and foreign intervention, Mexico lay in ruins in the late 1860s. Juarez and his successors, notably Porfirio Díaz, remade the nation during the 1870s and 1880s. Using foreign loans and technology to reorganize the productive export sectors, they modernized Mexico to meet the demands of the international economic order. The process of modernization, however, often meant giving preference to British or American companies and allowing them to exploit oil and mining resources at discounted rates. When newspapers criticized these actions, the government responded by closing down the offending daily. Indeed, as time progressed, Díaz became more dictatorial, aggressively shutting down all forms of opposition to his rule in Mexico by a combination of co-optation and ruthless violence. In the 1890s, to modernize agriculture, the Mexican government authorized

the seizure of lands belonging to Indian communities. When these now landless peasants protested, Díaz sent his national police force to suppress them. Order and progress became the standards of the day, as authoritarian regimes from Mexico to Argentina to Chile guaranteed a docile domestic environment that supported the export sector's drive to satisfy the world's need for raw materials.

By 1910 Mexico had rebuilt, extended electric service in its major cities, created adequate water supplies, and paved its principal roadways. The Díaz regime seemed secure and poised to move forward. Yet in Mexico and throughout Latin America, true sovereignty rested with foreign bankers, industrialists, and governments. Mexico's ability to make its own decisions remained compromised by its heavy indebtedness to outsiders. Historians refer to these realities as a state of dependent development, in which ultimate decisionmaking power on important issues lay elsewhere. The reaction to this state of dependency, as well as other long-simmering problems, erupted into revolution in Mexico in 1910, ending the Díaz regime. The promise of modernization, progress and true nation-building would have to wait another three decades due to revolution and economic crisis. Hence, before World War I, the Mexican Revolution marked the beginning of a major Third World push to eliminate external controls on a non-European nation-in-formation. As the Mexican Revolution ran its bloody course from 1910 to 1917, Mexico only had to fear intervention from the United States that might halt this effort at self-liberation and self-determination because Europe had become entangled in the killing fields of World War I.

Porfirio Díaz (1830–1915), war hero and president, became known as a dictator during his thirty-five-year rule over Mexico. He was called the "Iron Man of Mexico" by many. Credit: Library of Congress, Washington, D.C., DIG-ggbain-05876.

Brazil

The progress made by Brazil in the nineteenth century provides another example of the difficult journey from colony to nation in Latin America. Unlike most of Spanish America, which chose presidents and attempted to create republics, the Portuguese dominated as Brazil transitioned from colony to monarchy. When King João VI returned to Portugal in 1821, his son Pedro remained behind and led the Brazilians into independence. As Dom Pedro I, he ruled Brazil as emperor for nearly a decade. Despite his early enthusiasm for Brazil as an independent country and the support of the people, he developed into a selfish and lazy monarch, one more concerned with his own comforts and prerogatives than the national interest. He subsequently led Brazil into a disastrous war with Argentina in 1825, bankrupted the treasury, and alienated his once-loyal subjects. When presented with the opportunity to return to Portugal and

663. Gen. Porfirio Diaz   President of Mexico   Waite Photo

assume the throne there after his father's death in 1831, he did so, leaving behind in Brazil his young son, also known as Pedro, to one day become emperor.

After a ten-year regency during which the country nearly disintegrated in a series of regional revolts, young Pedro became emperor in 1841. He immediately made a commitment to the idea of modernizing his giant nation-in-formation. Called Pedro II, the young emperor did everything in his power to transform Brazil into a modern state. As Latin America's youngest ruler in the 1840s and 1850s, Pedro II encouraged the development of an export economy, industrialization, and a close relationship with British bankers and manufacturers. He also firmly consolidated national power within his administration, using Brazil's two largest political parties, the Liberals and Conservatives, to buttress his reign. Brazilian coffee, cotton, cacao (chocolate) and natural rubber generated profits and the hard currency needed to pay for the construction of railroads, and heavy machinery and luxury goods from Europe and North America.

One of the main stumbling blocks in Pedro II's reign proved to be slavery, an odd carryover from the colonial past. Most Latin governments had abolished the institution after the 1790s. Only Cuba, which remained a Spanish colony until 1898, the United States, and Brazil permitted slavery by 1860. Both Cuba and the United States abandoned slavery within the next decade, but not Brazil, where on the northeastern sugar and cacao plantations political supporters of Pedro II relied on slaves to generate their income. As southern Brazil became more urban and industrial, and even coffee planters there began to turn to immigrant European wage laborers in the 1870s, Pedro II resisted any general abolition movement. This led to opposition from important groups.

Army officers, members of the new Brazilian Republican Party, and officials of the nation's Roman Catholic hierarchy began to see Pedro II as an obstacle to progress for Brazil. Ironically, scholars of this period of Brazilian history, such as Robert M. Levine, find it difficult to understand Pedro II's resistance to ending slavery given his commitment to modernization. Eventually, national opposition to his rule, in addition to his own failing health, forced him to give way and accept exile in Europe when Army officers confronted him in November 1889. True to Brazilian traditions, only sporadic violence accompanied Pedro II's exit from the nation. The Bragança monarchy ended almost as calmly as it began, nearly seven decades earlier.

After the departure of Pedro II, the army imposed a half-decade of military rule before allowing a transition to electoral politics. In the 1890s, Brazil's three most prosperous and progressive states, Rio de Janeiro, Sao Paulo, and Minas Gerais, all in the center-south region of the country, captured control of political power. Over the next three decades, they rotated the presidency between them, dominated politics, and ensured that Brazil's export sector flourished. World War I presented an opportunity to expand local industrial production, and Brazilian elites began to think in national, not purely regional, terms and tentatively moved towards the beginning of political, cultural, and administrative integration. Ironically, the international economic crisis in the 1930s aided this process of national integration in Brazil. Hence, unlike Mexico, Brazil did not need violent revolution to redefine its political destiny in the twentieth century.

Nations in Formation

While Brazil's transition to nation-formation suggested a far more peaceful path than that trod by Mexico, other Latin American nations in formation emerging from colonization tended to have more in common with the Mexican experience. Differing only in detail, foreign influence, coming predominantly from Great Britain as a commercial partner, the surge in exports after the 1820s, the crisis of political development, the role of caudillos, and desire to modernize their countries appear in the history of most Latin American states after independence. Among the missing national attributes, however, were popular political participation by the masses, democratic institutions, the rule of law, and national economic integration. These, and other critical benchmarks of true nationhood, awaited the advent of the twentieth century. Hence, during the nineteenth century, Latin America enjoyed independence from Spain and Portugal in name only.

Great Britain's role in retarding nation-building in Latin America reflected the power of international trade in shaping a global market. As mentioned in Chapter Twenty-seven, Great Britain imported raw materials from the rest of the world, and Latin America in particular, in exchange for manufactured products, while providing all the loans, shipping, and insurance needed to secure a reliable system of trade. Latin America's balance of payments in this inequitable system of trade soon led to a debt burden that no state could escape. Also mentioned in Chapter Twenty-seven, international commerce used the gold standard to measure the value of all currencies, which created a general condition of deflation that struck the global marketplace. Since *deflation* means "supply exceeds demand," to pay off a debt, the debtor-state had to increase its own inventory of goods (supply), which, in turn, reduced the value of its commodities relative to the available gold-backed money supply (currency used to purchase or create demand). At the same time, the gold standard itself kept the supply of money fixed to the supply of gold, which was limited. Hence, the falling value of commodities relative to money reduced the debtor-state's income, while the value of money rose. Since the increase in the value of money represented the value of the debt itself, the debtor-state had caused its debt-burden to grow even as it had tried to increase production. Consequently, the harder a debtor-state worked to increase their income by increasing their exports (supply), the faster it reduced the value of its goods and increased the weight of its debt burden (the value of money as part of demand).

At the same time, the rural economies of Latin American states preserved the caste-like social and economic distinctions imposed by the Spanish and Portuguese colonial systems. The creoles had replaced the peninsulares as the political elite given the former's command over commercial agriculture and mining in Latin America as well as their access to higher education. Mestizos and mulattos came second because they could at least claim a partial Hispanic heritage. Indians and Africans came last, for they often did not speak either Spanish or Portuguese and belonged to an "alien" race. On top of these ethnic, social, economic, and educational distinctions, the absence of an elementary school system beyond the rudimentary level offered by the Catholic Church denied the development of the literacy, computation, and critical-thinking skills needed to generate public opinion. Hence, the political elite, those most likely to become caudillos, felt no general political, social, or economic bond with those they deemed their inferiors, while the mestizos, mulattos, Native Americans, and Africans lacked the intellectual skills needed to defend themselves or make their wishes known. The revolutions of the twentieth century would finally address these problems.

Suggested Reading

China
Clubb, Edmund O., *Twentieth Century China*, Third Edition (New York: Columbia University Press, 1978).

Gasster, Michael, *Chinese Intellectuals and the Revolution of 1911: The Birth of Modern Chinese Radicalism* (Seattle, Wash.: University of Washington Press, 1969).

Guillermaz, Jacques, *A History of the Chinese Communist Party*, translated by Anne Destenay (New York: Random House, 1972).

Price, Don C., *Russia and the Roots of the Chinese Revolution, 1896–1911* (Cambridge, Mass.: Harvard University Press, 1974).

Schiffrin, Harold Z., *Sun Yat-sen and the Origins of the Chinese Revolution* (Berkeley: University of California Press, 1968).

Wibur, Martin, *The Nationalist Revolution in China, 1923–1937* (Cambridge: Cambridge University Press, 1984).

Wright, Mary Clabaugh, ed., *China in Revolution : The First Phase: 1900–1913* (New Haven, Conn., Yale University Press, 1968).

Wong, Young-tsu, *The Search for Modern Nationalism: Zhang Binglin and Revolutionary China* (Oxford: Oxford University Press, 1989).

Young, Ernest, *The Presidency of Yuan Shih-k'ai: Liberalism and Dictatorship in Early Republican China* (Ann Arbor: University of Michigan Press, 1977).

India
Bayly, C. A., *Indian Society and the Making of the British Empire* (Cambridge: Cambridge University Press, 1988).

Brown, Judith, *Gandhi and Civil Disobedience* (Cambridge: Cambridge University Press, 1977).

Brown, Judith, *Gandhi's Rise to Power* (Cambridge: Cambridge University Press, 1972).

Chaurasia, Radhey Shyam, *History of Modern India* (New Delhi: Akansha Publishing House, 2000).

Fischer, Louis, *Gandhi* (New York: Vintage Books, 1963).

Mehta, V., *Mahatma Gandhi and his Apostles* (New Haven, Conn.: Yale University Press, 1993).

Srinivas, Mysore, N., *Social Change in Modern India* (New Delhi: Allied Publishing, 1966).

Wolpert, S, A)., *New History of India*, Seventh Edition (New York: Oxford University Press, 2000).

The Middle East
Antonius, George, *The Arab Awakening: The Story of the Arab National Movement* (New York: G. P. Putnam's Sons, 1946).

Balfour, Baron J. P., *Atatürk: The Rebirth of a Nation* (London: Weidenfeld and Nicolson, 1964).

Donohue, J. J., and J. L. Esposito, eds., *Islam in Transition: Muslim Perspectives* (Oxford: Oxford University Press, 1982).

Hourani, A., *Arabic Thought in the Liberal Age, 1798–1939* (Cambridge: Cambridge University Press, 1967).

Keddie, N. R., *An Islamic Response to Imperialism: Political and Religious Writings of Sayyid Jamal al-Din "al-Afghani"* (Berkeley: University of California Press, 1968).

Sachar, H. M., *The Emergence of the Middle East 1914–1924* (New York: Alfred A. Knopf, 1969).

Smith, W. C., *Islam in Modern History* (Princeton, N.J.: Princeton University Press, 1957).

Upton, J. M., *The History of Modern Iran* (Cambridge Mass.: Harvard University Press, 1960).

Vatikiotis, P. J., *The History of Egypt* (Baltimore: John Hopkins University Press, 1985).

Latin America

Burns, E. B., *The Poverty of Progress: Latin America in the Nineteenth Century* (Berkeley: University of California Press, 1980)

Bulmer-Thomas, Victor, *United States and Latin America* (Cambridge, Mass.: Harvard University Press, 1999)

Bushnell, Thomas, and Neill Macaulay, *The Emergence of Latin America in the Nineteenth Century* (New York: Oxford University Press, 1988)

Haber, Stephen, *How Latin America Fell Behind* (Stanford: Stanford University Press, 1997)

Levine, Robert M., *Vale of Tears* (Berkeley: University of California Press, 1992)

XXXI

WORLD WAR II
and the Start of the Cold War

World War II completed the process begun with World War I of removing Europe as the center of world power. The scale of devastation released by World War II quintupled the direct casualty rate caused by warfare in World War I, while dislocating or destroying the lives of a far greater number of people and completely realigning global politics.

Out of the ashes of this second global conflict emerged two new superpowers: the United States and the Soviet Union. No longer did the world have one dominant political or economic core that could attempt to direct global affairs. Now, two new states of continental proportions attempted to replace Europe and guide international politics. Each superpower claimed to have the best interests of humanity at heart, but neither one could dominate global events.

At the same time, the destructive power of modern mass-produced weapons had eliminated the possibility of open conflict, that is, of the style fought in World Wars I and II. Instead, these weapons of mass destruction had generated a new diplomatic concept called *infinite deterrence* (the fear that a possible World War III would destroy both superpowers and maybe even the human race) and had created a new level of international competition for a balance of power in the so-called Third World, developing, non-European cultures. This new level of international competition offered these non-European developing states a chance to complete decolonization. Hence, World War II, and the beginning of the Cold War redefined global politics and set the stage for a multicentered, multicultural global history.

World War II

World War II resurrected all the features of total war experienced in World War I, but a new military technology produced the principal difference between the two wars. These new tools of mass destruction redefined the geographic space of combat, the targets of war, and the casualty lists. The end goal of combat, however, remained the same: the destruction of an enemy nation.

Once again, nationalism, a nation-in-arms, and industrial weapons defined the geography of combat. Yet the differences in strategy and tactics of this second global conflict resulted from a new mobility offered by offensive weapons. Furthermore, World War II relocated the center of conflict by introducing modern Japan, Nationalist China, and the Soviet Union, as three new major participants in total war, redefining the role of the United States in the Allied effort to achieve victory. Thus, World War II involved far more geographic space and human numbers than did World War I.

When the Great Depression caused international financial chaos (mentioned in Chapter Twenty-nine), world production fell by 33 percent while world trade declined by 66 percent. Nations like Japan with few natural resources had come to rely on international exchange to sustain a modern economy. Japan required a rapid turnover of imports and exports in order to feed a large urban population and maintain a delicately balanced standard of living. As a result, the Japanese had to realign themselves to a newly collapsed global economy or endure famine on a scale never before experienced.

Within pre–World War II Japanese society, military traditions from the feudal era began to reemerge to define Japan's future. As we have seen, extremist politics-by-assassination replaced party politics after 1931. Right-wing radicals attacked and killed prominent party, business, and liberal leaders. Coups and mutinies followed. Army assassins and mutineers became martyrs in the eyes of much of the public. Only the intervention of the emperor and the navy could temporarily contain the violence.

This militant ultranationalism in Japan created the same level of national passion found in Nazi Germany. Hence, the Japanese achieved a form of political intensity similar to totalitarianism without having instituted the vertical articulation required by such a government. Consequently, ultranationalists set Japan's sights on freeing the Japanese from any weaknesses of parliamentary rule.

Parallel to Japan's drift toward a military society, its interest in China had also increased. Yet, as mentioned in Chapter Thirty, the Chinese were locked in their own struggle to define a new political destiny for themselves after the fall of the Qing Dynasty in 1911. In this fight to achieve national formation, Chinese leaders like Sun Yatsen had originally expressed interest in democracy. This interest in creating a democratic nation-state reflected Sun's loose association with the United States as the least aggressive nation whose open-door policy had seemed to promise a guarantee of China's continued independence.

Yet disappointment at the failure of President Woodrow Wilson's Fourteen Points (mentioned in Chapter Twenty-nine) to direct the treaty process at Versailles had shifted China's attention to another potential ally: the Soviet Union. Upset with the United States because Wilson had not been able to keep his promise in point number five, which declared a free, open-minded, and absolutely impartial adjustment of all colonial claims, Sun decided to redefine China's political agenda. Wilson had created an expectation in China that France and Britain had to reject to preserve their empires. Failure to keep this promise by turning over what had been the German sphere of influence in China to the Japanese had led to the first major surge of nationalism and antiforeign rage in Chinese history (mentioned in Chapter Thirty).

Called the May 4th Movement, this nationalist surge reflected the passion of the Chinese people to support a major drive to recover Chinese sovereignty, expel foreigners, and redefine China as a nation-state. Since the United States had bitterly disappointed Sun, he had turned instead to the Soviet Union. Agents from Comintern visited China in 1922 to create a so-called United Front between the Nationalists and the Chinese Communists. The Chinese Communist party had also formed a revolutionary movement in the midst of this political turmoil.

Together, the Chinese Nationalists and Communists launched a major drive to establish China's national independence in 1926. Unfortunately this drive occurred just after Sun's death in 1925. Soon, as we have seen, disagreement over revolutionary goals developed between the new leaders of the Nationalists and Communists. These disagreements led to a violent split in 1927.

The Nationalists, now led by Jiang Jieshi (Chiang Kai-shek), chose political assassination as the means to dissolve their partnership with the Chinese Communist party. In March and April of 1927, Jiang assigned the task of systematic murder to his army and several criminal organizations he associated with in Shanghai. His failure to kill all the Communists, however, exposed China to internal division which occurred just before the beginning of renewed Japanese aggression against China in the 1930s.

Thus both Japan and China were in the midst of redefinition after World War I when international political and financial chaos drove them back into war with one another. In short, Japan needed resources that China had, making the Middle Kingdom a primary Japanese target for territorial expansion. The world that European imperialism had united in the Far East had fallen apart in the absence of Western domination.

World War II, therefore, did not begin in Europe. Rather, two key participants, Japan and China, had become entangled in conflict several years before the European war erupted, revealing that World War II would have an entirely different geographic character than that of World War I.

And as we have seen, Japan and China had drifted toward war through a series of episodes beginning with Japan's capture of Manchuria in 1931, which proved to be only the first step in its aggressive drive for new territory. In 1932, the Japanese assaulted Shanghai briefly, then pressed China to demilitarize its northern frontier with Manchuria, and finally invaded China in 1937. Two years before Hitler moved in Europe, Japan had advanced toward war with China with the same diplomatic momentum as Der Führer.

Because it erupted in different locations at different times, World War II drew most of the globe into conflict in a seemingly spastic manner. First one continent, then another joined the war: Japan engaged China in 1937; Germany drew Britain and France into the conflict in 1939 with an attack on Poland; numerous neutral nations became the victims of Germany and Japan's offensives in 1940 and '41; and the Soviet Union and the United States joined the combat after surprise assaults by Germany and Japan respectively in 1941. Meanwhile, the new offensive military technology restored movement to combat.

Tanks, mechanized infantry (troops transported by vehicles to combat zones), strategic bombers, and amphibious assault ships allowed attacking forces to cut through trenches and defensive positions, even well-fortified bunkers. Armored columns made zones of combat so fluid that no clear lines of battle existed. Entire *theaters*, instead of *fronts*, commanded strategic attention as whole continents became embroiled in the war. The European, Russian, North Atlantic, North African, Chinese, Southeast Asian, and Pacific theaters named the key arenas of struggle.

When the war first began, Japan and Germany were better prepared for the new circumstances of combat than were their opponents. Japan had the most modern army in Asia, and Germany had learned how to fight a new style of warfare after rethinking its defeat in World War I. Each of these two aggressive nations had already developed tactics of speed capable of bypassing the main defenses of their opponents to attack the enemy civilian population directly. Commanding the most highly concentrated military mass in the opening phases of the war, both won stunning victories.

By 1940, Japan occupied 33 percent of China's territory and controlled more than two-thirds of the Chinese population. Japan's initial successes on several fronts had quickly broken the strength of the conventional forces of the Nationalists. Like the Boers in the Boer War, after the Chinese lost the conventional struggle, they turned to guerrilla tactics instead. Spearheading this guerrilla war, however, were the survivors of the Chinese Communist party, and their success against the Japanese revived Chinese Marxism in the face of the Nationalists' failure.

Like Japan in China, Germany invaded Poland and crushed it in a twenty-six-day campaign that began in September of 1939. Germany's attack on Poland brought a stunned Britain and France into the war. Hitler had made an alliance of convenience with the Soviet Union to surround Poland completely and ensure the rapid destruction of that emerging nation-state. Thus, a quick victory in the east and friendship with Stalin freed Hitler to turn his attention to the west. Yet, as we have seen, this thrust to the west ran contrary to Hitler's racial vision for the future.

Therefore, after a winter of Phony War (neither side attacking), Germany invaded Norway, Denmark, Holland, Belgium, and France in the spring of 1940. The main contest took place in France where the Germans bypassed the French forces that had been amassed since World War I on the Maginot Line, what France hoped would be a defensive perimeter on its border with Germany. Hitler's mechanized infantry and armored divisions cut through the Ardennes Forest between British and French defenses and placed an entire army corps behind enemy lines. Thus, Hitler's tanks turned the southern flank of the British Expeditionary Force (BEF) and the northern flank of France's defenses simultaneously, which then sent this block of German *panzers* (tanks) and mechanized infantry thrusting through the French countryside. This primary German attack through the poorly defended Allied center cut the lines of communication between the main Allied forces and their supply.

The combined British and the French resistance in northeastern France quickly collapsed, the British falling back in disarray. Now the Allied position in France became a strategic nightmare. The BEF fled to the French coast, abandoned its heavy equipment, and barely escaped through Dunkirk while the French surrendered to the Germans.

Having knocked France out of the war in a few short months, Hitler turned his attention to Great Britain. Yet, because he viewed the British as "German," at this time Hitler had made no preparations for a possible invasion of the British Isles. As a result, Hitler now found himself confronted with an enemy his land forces could not reach. Developing what became know as Operation Sea Lion, the German navy proposed an assault by barges across the British Channel while using air cover to neutralize the British navy. This assault from the air, however, asked too much of the German *Luftwaffe* (air force). The Germans had developed their military aircraft as a part of the army, not as an independent military service. Hence, German airplanes functioned as an extension of land operations.

Focusing entirely on strategic command of the air over southeast England, the Luftwaffe was asked to accomplish something neither Hitler nor the German General Staff had envisioned when they accepted aircraft designs for their future military operations: the strategic bombardment of Great Britain. The German aircraft were designed to function as extended artillery rather than carry out independent campaigns. The Luftwaffe did not have a significant number of long-range heavy bombers or fighter escorts. Instead, their planes were short-range, light, and designed to strike targets just in front of an advancing army.

Expecting to go east in his war of conquest to create the living space for his new Reich, Hitler never imagined a war against his fellow "Germans," the British. Now confronted with an invasion of the British Isles, the Germans hoped to use their limited-range aircraft in their assault on Great Britain. Although Germany had three times as many airplanes as did the British Royal Airforce (RAF), the Germans could only engage in brief air assaults over British territory. Any extended combat caused the German fighters to run out of fuel.

Nevertheless an invasion of Britain required a confrontation between the Luftwaffe and the RAF. The fact that combat would occur over the British Isles, however, neutralized Germany's superior numbers. Each German plane had to fly to and from the combat zone expending precious fuel—something short-range fighters and medium-range bombers could ill afford. Therefore, engagements had to be brief. Any German plane

German U-Boats. Left: Ex-German submarine U-3008 off the Portsmouth Naval Shipyard, Kittery, Maine, August 30, 1946. Photograph from the Bureau of Ships Collection in the U.S. National Archives. Photo #19-N-95866. Right: German Submarine U-3008 at Wilhelmshaven, Germany, June 1945. From "Naval Technical Mission in Europe Technical Report Number 403-45: The Influence of High Submerged Speed on German Submarine Hulls." Photo # NH 96270, Official U.S. Navy Photograph, from the collections of the Naval Historical Center.

shot down over England represented a pilot lost, either killed or captured, while the English could rescue any airman who survived. Finally, because of the limited conditions of the combat, a war of attrition began that the Germans might have won if Hitler had not intervened.

Hitler shifted the focus of the Luftwaffe's attack from the RAF to London in the second week of September 1940. This decision gave the RAF a badly needed respite that saved Britain's Fighter Command. Hitler's decision allowed the RAF to recover its initial losses and defend its capital. The RAF survived, and the German invasion never materialized. Consequently, Britain remained in the war.

During 1940, Hitler's successes in Western Europe drew Italy and Japan to his side. Both powers joined the struggle as they signed the Tripartite Agreement. Japan needed Hitler to declare war on the United States, whose opposition to Japan's role in China would soon lead to conflict. Hitler planned to achieve his ultimate military goals when he invaded the Soviet Union, and he hoped the Japanese would simultaneously attack that massive country from across the Chinese frontier. Italy had joined Hitler when his victory in France prompted Mussolini to attempt building a second Roman Empire in the Mediterranean world.

From 1940 to 1941, Hitler's General Staff had concluded that the best way to defeat Great Britain was to take its perimeter empire. This strategy saw Hitler's forces enter the Balkans and North Africa in a drive to capture the principal routes to India and the oil-rich

Middle East. Again winning easy victories against a much weakened British military, Hitler swept through each targeted area with apparent ease.

Yet Hitler's early victories, and his dramatically extended control over Europe's geographic space, severely alarmed Franklin Delano Roosevelt (1882–1945), president of the United States. Now Roosevelt sent U.S. forces to occupy Iceland and Greenland while expanding strategic U.S. naval patrols of the North Atlantic. Roosevelt's loose interpretation of the Monroe Doctrine that allowed him to ease Britain's war in the North Atlantic by seeking out and reporting the location of German U-Boats so that the British navy could avoid deadly waters excused these potentially hostile actions toward Germany as protecting neutral rights on the high seas. Roosevelt also saw what was happening in Europe and Asia and was eager for the United States to enter the war, but Congress still hesitated, with many powerful legislators maintaining that, after having helped Europe in World War I, the nation should stay out of "foreign wars."

By 1941, Germany and Japan had laid the foundation for their key shift in World War II and still held the military initiative. Given their advantages of mass and movement, they could strike wherever they wanted. Yet both powers made major strategic blunders when they chose to attack the Soviet Union and the United States.

Hitler chose to strike at his partner Stalin and capture the living space he craved in the Soviet Union. Japan decided to take Southeast Asia, attack the United States, and create a fortified perimeter so intensely

Stalin's Purges and Labor Camps

Although Hitler's invasion of the Soviet Union proved to be a military blunder in the long run, initially, Stalin nearly handed victory to the Germans due to his use of terror prior to World War II. Stalin's purges of the 1930s not only eliminated most of the Soviet Union's most talented generals, it also undermined the willingness of Bolshevik leaders to take the initiative in terms of governing because anything politically creative during the 1930s might bring down the wrath of the Soviet leader.

Beginning in 1934, when a disgruntled nonentity assassinated Sergey Kirov, a rising star in the Bolshevik Party, Stalin exploited the opportunity to kill his rivals. Assumed to be Stalin's heir apparent, Kirov was a member of the Politburo and the First Party Secretary of Leningrad. Popular and charismatic, Kirov, however, posed a potential threat to Stalin's absolute rule, so that Kirov's death not only removed a possible future rival, but also gave Stalin the excuse he needed to clean house. Reputed to be the victim of Stalin's assassination squads by Nikita Khrushchev, Stalin's actual successor after his death in 1953, this timely political murder allowed Stalin to assume the mantle of a martyr to the revolution who had to watch his close friends and associates die for the cause.

What followed was an orgy of reprisals. Kirov's murder allowed Stalin to eliminate thousands of Leningrad leaders as well as all his old colleagues among the original Bolshevik party. Among the most prominent to be purged were G. Zinoviev and L. B. Kamenev, once the leaders of the Comintern, and N. I. Bukarin, the author of the New Economic Policy, and his ally A. I. Rykov. Using a combination of physical and psychological torture, reinforced by their interrogators' use of the Marxist vision of history, where the individual proved to be only a pawn in the flow of materially determined events, each of these once powerful men confessed to extraordinary charges—wholesale sabotage of the Soviet economy, espionage for the Germans, British, and Japanese, and plotting to restore capitalism in Russia. Once having acknowledged their "guilt" for the good of the party, Stalin then executed each of his past colleagues.

He followed up this exercise in political power by purging the Soviet military services as well as the educated and managerial segment of the party. In a murderous campaign began in July 1937, Stalin eliminated his top ranking generals, removed tens of thousands of officers from the army, navy, and air corps, and imprisoned a majority of those men with the rank of colonel or above. Thus the Soviet capacity to face a major mechanized enemy like Hitler's war machine was severely damaged by Stalin's political machinations.

Since all senior personnel, both military and civilian, belonged to the party, Stalin's use of terror to ensure his mastery of domestic politics crippled the Bolshevik organ-ization. To give some idea of how many people were involved, Stalin charged an estim-ated 60 percent of the Seventh Party Congress of Victors (1934) with counterrevolutionary crimes; and to be charged meant being found guilty. He also executed 71 percent of the Central Committee elected by the same Congress in 1937–38. Comparable numbers among his officer corps revealed an equal wrath leveled against the military. To purge one's own power base so thoroughly prior to a major war is to undermine a nation's capacity to resist. Hence Stalin's actions prior to World War II laid a foundation for Hitler's early successes and almost handed victory to the Nazis.

Yet to achieve a full appreciation of the power that Stalin wielded over his countrymen's lives, one has to consider these purges in the context of the labor camps known as "the Gulag Archipelago." In 1931–32, the Gulag had approximately 200,000 prisoners; that number grew to 800,000 by 1935 with another 300,000 situated in Siberian colonies that also used forced labor. Stalin's purges of 1937 set the stage for a sudden increase of these prisoners: 1,300,000 in the camps and 350,000 in the colonies by 1939.

Given the desperate struggle that the Soviet Union faced during World War II, however, the number of political prisoners in the camps suddenly dropped. Hundreds of thousands of inmates found themselves conscripted into penal battalions sent into the worst part of the fighting; there the majority died in combat. But as the Soviet armies turned the tide against the Germans, Stalin's willingness to release prisoners to fight the war gave way to his fear of treason. Hence, after World War II, the number of inmates in the labor camps and colonies reached approximately 2.5 million. Most of these new political convicts were repatriated prisoners of war from Eastern Bloc countries, people deemed unreliable, and inmates taken from Soviet nationalities that Stalin considered untrustworthy: all of whom he accused of treason and "cooperating with the enemy."

To estimate the number of deaths caused by Stalin's use of terror seems like an exercise in futility. The fact that he executed over 1 million people for "political offenses" belies the long-range effects of Stalin's policies. Approximately 20 million people died, which includes an estimated 14.5 million who pointlessly starved to death during the economic dislo-cations of Stalin's collectivization and industrial-ization pro-grams, and another 5 million who died while in his camps. Additionally, 9.5 million people served out their prison terms, but survived. Some scholars include all those killed in combat at the beginning of World War II due to Stalin's purges of 1937. Unlike Hitler who kept an accurate accounting of the people his regime exterminated, Stalin's death toll rests more on the collateral consequences of his actions rather than on direct executions. Hence, the state of terror that existed in the Soviet Union produced an indirect method of destroying human lives when compared to Nazi Germany; nonetheless, the consequences were equally deadly.

Hingley, Ronald, *Russia: A Concise History,* **Revised and Updated Edition (London: Thames and Hudson Ltd., 1991), 176–81.**

Rauch, Georg von, *A History of the Soviet Union,* **Fifth Edition (New York: Praeger Publishers, 1971), 238–54.**

Hitler's Final Solution

According to Hitler, Europe was not a geographic region, it was a complex racial zone. While Woodrow Wilson tried to empower national ethnic groups through self-determination using the authority of the law as instituted in the League of Nations, Hitler hoped to uproot the "inferior" minorities of Europe and replace them with the most "superior" of all the races: the Germans. In pursuit of this goal, Hitler believed certain existing nations had to be destroyed, millions of undesirable people had to be moved, and even more "sub-human" races had to be exterminated. In effect the map of Eurasia had to be completely redrawn.

This new state policy of mass murder and cultural obliteration became known as "genocide," a word coined in 1944 by a Polish-Jewish lawyer named Raphael Lemkin to describe what everyone had learned about the Nazi racial program at the Nuremberg trials after World War II. Among the victims of this program were the Jews, but Hitler's "final solution" to the Jewish problem, as he called it, was really only part of a far greater scheme to change the ethnic composition of Eurasia.

The overall scheme was a plan to repress racially undesirable peoples and safeguard the future for the Volksgemeinschaft (the new order). This new order involved measures to eradicate the Jews, Gypsies, and various Slavic peoples in an order based on their historical capacity to claim and hold land. In Hitler's view, since the Jews and Gypsies held no national territories, they proved to be most inferior of the humanoids as well as the most parasitic because they had to find ways to live off the wealth generated by other superior peoples. The Slavs, on the other hand, had staked a claim to national boundaries and had held these states against various invasions in the past; this made them superior to the Jews and Gypsies, but since these Slavs lacked any Germanic blood, their right to exist depended on their ability to face a future racial war that would settle the issue. Hitler counted on German superiority to determine the result of this racial conflict; only victory or death would determine the outcome.

Once World War II began, Hitler's racial vision had to adjust to the realities presented by the unfolding events. Conquest of Poland, then continental Western Europe, and a final surge into the Soviet Union presented the Nazi regime with countless millions of people to eliminate. Transportation or extermination hung in the balance as methods of eliminating through forced emigration, or killing and disposing of the bodies of so many "inferior" cultures, had to be considered. Death camps did not exist in 1939; by 1942 the Nazis had killed "only" 1 million people using machine guns and mass graves. The only way Hitler's vision for the future could be implemented required an industrialization of the process of mass murder.

The key to the problem of the "final solution" came with the construction of special extermination camps. Here the energy of the Third Reich could be focused through its vanguard, the SS, to collect, concentrate, and eliminate mass numbers of people classified as inferior. Chief among these, the Jews, suffered the most because they stood out as the first to be disposed of, were collected the earliest, and used as guinea pigs to discover the cheapest and most efficient methods of annihilation. By the war's end some-where between 5 to 6 million Jews had been killed while a total of 11 million people had received special "treatment" in these racial centers. Nowhere in history has any other attempt at "ethnic cleansing," or genocide, approached such efficiency. As a result of this efficiency, twenty-two Nazi leaders were tried at Nuremberg after the war for crimes against humanity and world peace. All but a few were exe-cuted as the evidence of their deeds was both massive and incontrovertible. Hence the German example stands out as the most extraordinary for its use of a rational, industrial, and thoroughly modern consideration of how the change the racial face of a continent.

Mazower, Mark, *The Dark Continent: Europe's Twentieth Century* (New York: Vintage Books, 1998), 157–74.

Below: Slave laborers in the Buchenwald concentration camp near Jena, April 16, 1945. United States National Archives & Records Admninistration, ARC # 535561.

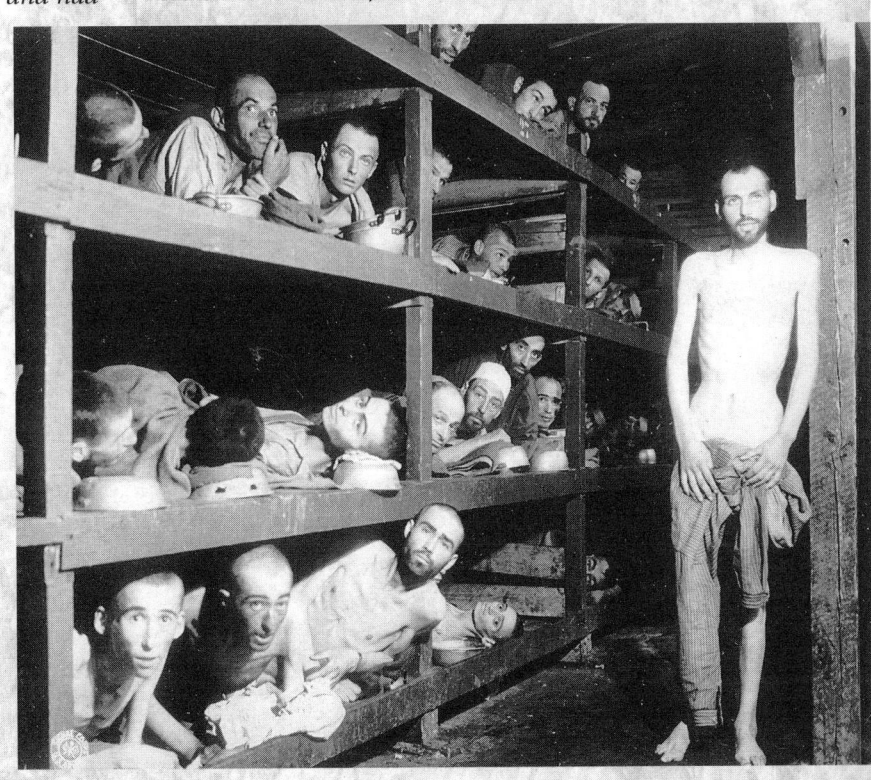

defended that U.S. troops would not attempt to retake this new empire. These two decisions shifted the conditions of victory away from Germany and Japan to the Allied forces. Both the Soviet Union and the United States had potential military power that the Japanese and the Germans had not properly evaluated.

After Hitler launched the invasion east, German forces cut deeply into Soviet territory and destroyed much of the Red Army, but they failed to knock Stalin out of the war in a single campaign. Meanwhile, Japan captured the defensive perimeter it sought within six months and spread its forces throughout the Pacific. Now Japan chose to defend a region that stretched from the tip of the Aleutian Islands in the North Pacific to the edge of Midway Island in the Central Pacific, which included all of Southeast Asia, the Dutch East Indies, and a portion of New Guinea. As part of this effort, the Japa-

nese tried to destroy the U.S. Pacific Fleet by launching a strategic surprise attack on it as it lay docked in Pearl Harbor, Hawaii. This assault, however, mobilized the United States to add its industrial potential to that of the Soviet Union in the struggle that followed.

Japan's failure to win the victory it hoped for was due primarily to economic reasons. Japan entered the war with superior naval equipment and aircraft when contrasted with the military technology of the United States. Japanese aircraft carrier–based airplanes, torpedoes, and its Pacific fleet outperformed that of the United States. Also, at the beginning of the war, the fact that Japan could concentrate its navy in the Pacific, while the United States had to divide its fleet between two oceans gave the Japanese a numerical advantage. Tactically, the Japanese had a superior force, but strategically Japan was not equal to the task of winning a total war. Put simply, Japan could not maintain the concentration of military power needed for victory.

Up to 1944, Japan had lost 275 combat ships, excluding escort vessels and had managed to replace 162 of them. During the same period, the United States—

Destruction of Hiroshima by the atomic bomb in World War II. Top: Pre-attack mosaic view of Hiroshima, Japan, April 13, 1945. United States National Archives & Records Administration. ARC # 540225.
Bottom: Post-attack mosaic view of Hiroshima Japan, August 11, 1945. United States National Archives & Records Administration. ARC # 540226.

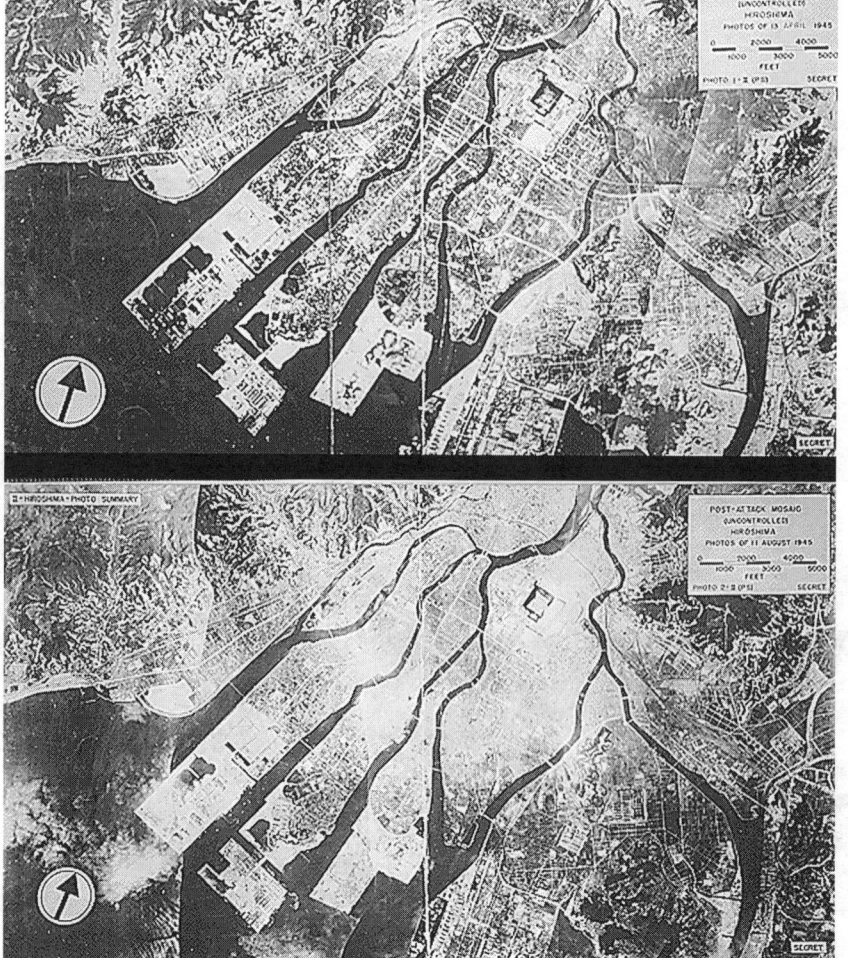

which had redesigned its economy to put the nation on a war footing—lost 128 combat vessels, and it replaced them with 1,005 more. Japan's industrial output depended on supply from overseas, but U.S. submarine warfare strangled Japan's overseas trade. Japan lost 5 million tons of merchant shipping, its harbors were mined, its industrial cities reduced to rubble, and its remaining military resources drained from a protracted struggle in China and Southeast Asia. Japan simply did not have the industrial strength to match the military mass produced by the United States.

This same kind of productive capacity supplied the Soviet Union, which in turn gave the lives of 22 million of its people (soldiers and civilians) in defense of their country against Germany. As an example of the Soviet contribution, Stalin's victory over Germany at the Battle of Stalingrad cost him 400,000 soldiers so that he could destroy the German Sixth Army of some 338,000 men. This willingness on Stalin's and Russia's part to overwhelm the Germans with superior human numbers (both regular army and partisans) combined with the productive potential of the United States to create a military mass the Germans could not resist.

One example of the stunning level of U.S. productivity during the war was the nation's manufacture of the most important offensive weapon in the European theater: the tank. The Germans produced 24,000 tanks per year, in which time the United States generated 80,000. In addition, the United States developed a re-supply system in Europe that allowed destroyed tanks to be recycled as tank parts for every new tank introduced into combat. Hence, the critical years of 1942 and 1943 saw the German military spread too thin to defend the geographic space they had won. Accordingly, the momentum of the war shifted in the favor of the Allies and away from Germany and Japan.

To the men fighting on the ground, however, the war had to go through three more long years of combat. To each soldier on the battlefield, the outcome always seemed uncertain. Yet, the issue of mass proved to be ultimately decisive.

The United States and the Soviet Union simply overwhelmed Germany and Japan in a series of campaigns that recovered territory taken by the Nazis and the Japanese when they had held the tactical advantages. So-called island hopping by the U.S. marines and army in the Pacific theater brought American ground forces to the shores of the Japanese mainland, while the U.S. navy and airforce reduced Japan's surface vessels and domestic economy to impotence. In Europe, as the Soviet Union went on the offensive after Stalingrad in 1942, the United States and Great Britain launched a series of successful land campaigns. First, the U.S. and United Kingdom mounted a two-pronged attack in North Africa that eventually trapped Rommel's famous *Afrika Korps* in Tunisia in 1942. Then, in 1943, the U.S. and Britain launched a combined attack on Sicily and Italy that drove Mussolini from the war until Hitler shored up the Italian fascist regime and fought a rearguard action up the peninsula. Finally the United States and Great Britain invaded Normandy on June 6, 1944, opened up a second front on the European continent, and assisted the Soviets in destroying the Third Reich. Up to 1944, the U.S.S.R. had faced 66 percent of the German army within Soviet territory alone; after 1944, the combined mass of the Allied forces could finally be used to crush the Germans.

In the end, World War II took on a character bordering on madness. On the one hand, Hitler fought a war based on his racial theory of global politics (see insert above). This theory included the extermination of millions of people. On the other hand, the United States introduced a new weapon in the Pacific war that finally persuaded the Japanese to accept unconditional surrender—the Atomic Bomb. This weapon obliterated two cities, Hiroshima and Nagasaki, with one airplane carrying one explosive device to each target. Hence, at the close of the conflict, the world saw the degree of polarization that had taken place between the two sides as well as discovering the lengths to which nation-states felt they had to go to achieve victory in a total war.

World War II finished what World War I had begun. Western and Central Europe lay in shambles. The sheer physical destruction caused by warfare had completely disrupted the infrastructure of a cultural zone that had once commanded the global differential of power.

Displaced persons on the European continent seemed to outnumber those who still had homes. For at least two years after the Allied victory in May 1945, people wondered if Europe could ever recover. Simultaneously, postwar European weakness meant the people of some of the remaining non-European subject states were now free to choose their own political destiny either by negotiations with their imperial masters or through armed resistance. What could be said about Europe could be also said of Japan.

Also World War II had greatly increased the death toll of total global warfare. While 10 million young men had died in the trenches of World War I, civilian populations had joined military personnel as victims of World War II. Some conservative estimates place the total death rate at 18.5 million soldiers killed in combat. Yet this figure does not accurately reflect the lives taken in air raids, in extermination camps, by the disruption of food production, or by disease as an indirect consequence of war.

Remembering that twice the number of people had died from the flu epidemics that followed World War I when compared to those actually killed in the war itself, the number of civilian deaths caused by World War II had to exceed the official count of those killed in action; most scholars place the death toll at 40.5 million civilians, including the number of people killed through indiscriminate combat, genocide, strategic bombing, and the massive social and economic dislocations caused by the destructiveness of total global war. Combined with combat deaths, 59 million people lost their lives in World War II. In all cases, the lessons were clear. Given the way technology had elevated the efficiency of killing people, a Third World War would finish humanity.

Hence, the possibility of World War III loomed as a nightmare at the end of World War II that everyone hoped to avoid. Yet the two superpowers that emerged as the victors of World War II, the Soviet Union and the United States, almost immediately disagreed over the conditions of the peace that was to follow. This disagreement set up the future global conflict. Accordingly, just as one major total war had ended, the world now faced the constant threat of possible annihilation: the Cold War had begun.

The Cold War: Redefining World Power after 1945

What had been a global power vacuum after World War I, as European strength eroded and demoralization took hold, became a political void after World War II. Colonies, protectorates, and spheres of influence outside of Europe that had witnessed Europeans killing one another, and in many cases had been recruited by European forces to do the same, proved far more restless after World War II. Dislodged from global leadership after 1945, Europeans everywhere found they could not return to their former imperial holdings without facing powerful native resistance.

As mentioned, the location of the differential of power had shifted from Europe to the Soviet Union and the United States. Between these two new superpowers a different kind of struggle, the so-called Cold War, began. Each developed a level of military technology that made a total war against one another infeasible, as it might well end human life on Earth. Both nations created a whole new way to clash based on ideologies and local, limited wars that appealed to cultures seeking liberation from colonial status. In the Soviet Union, Marxism had become the official ideology of the Bolshevik Regime. In the United States, a variation of British liberalism had made a home for itself. The antagonisms between the two belief systems were the basis of the Cold War.

As mentioned in Chapter Twenty-eight, Lenin and Stalin had used Marxist ideology to organize a totalitarian state, imposing the "Dictatorship of the Proletariat" on the Russian peoples in order to prepare them to create the first "communist society." Yet instead of producing a brief episode of autocracy as a necessary transitional stage from industrial capitalism to the stateless, classless society that Marx had envisioned, Lenin and Stalin had planted their authoritarian institution in a country made up mostly of peasants. They ended up creating a revolution of infinite trajectory by failing to heed one of Marx's greatest warnings: do not start a revolution before its time, or you will become the monster you are trying to destroy.

Lenin and Stalin had produced a regime that was compelled to control modernization in order to create the correct social mix at home, export revolution abroad, and simultaneously avoid falling into voluntarism, which occurred when a revolutionary tried to skip Marx's required stage of economic development. At the same time,

the correct social mix at home involved creating capitalism without becoming capitalist. Such a complex social, economic, and political program required an authoritarian system that imposed absolute power concentrated in the hands of a single party. This vertically articulated political authority gave commands from the top down and received information from the bottom up. Personal freedom disappeared, while equality became the norm.

In contrast, the United States' variation of British liberalism had generated a democracy based on horizontal integration, in which political communication developed within local political parties that generated regional agreements. Each regional consensus then combined with others through horizontal communication to form a political platform at national party conventions. Such a system allowed for wide variation in opinions, but it integrated those heterogeneous regional differences into an acceptable national, political program.

As mentioned in Chapter Twenty-three, the United States had made a commitment to Natural Rights Theory during the American Revolution (1775–83) and had advanced the principle of individual freedom. Yet the founding fathers had only offered this freedom to those of European ancestry. Over the course of American history, this principle of individual freedom stood in direct contradiction to slavery and then legal racial segregation. This was obviously at odds with with the concept of equality in America's democracy. Hence, the issue of equality became a central issue in the Cold War.

While challenging the Soviet Union over its failure to make freedom available to its citizenry, but still claiming to be a democracy, the United States had to confront its own understanding of Natural Rights Theory as it applied to the problem of equality for the entire population living in the U.S. despite their ethnic origins. Still occupied today in the effort of redefining equality in relation to segregation, the United States confronted the Soviet Union in a long and involved contest that included a complex set of diplomatic and military engagements around the world.

Both the United States and the Soviet Union wanted to serve as a model for modernization to non-European nations-in-formation. The primary socioeconomic value of the United States, freedom, underlay a political system in which a popular consensus served as the foundation of politics. To generate this consensus, the United States had formed political parties that functioned best in local politics. There, consensus formed at the social base rather than in a political party's national committee.

Legally organized by each state in the federal union, the United States' political party system literally generated fifty Democratic and fifty Republican parties.

Strongest at the county, precinct, or ward level, both of the major parties identified and advanced local candidates to represent local opinions. These candidates vied for political office and if elected, were free to vote their conscience.

As individual representatives, each elected official had to accept the political consequences of their actions in government. In this fashion, a consensus emerged from representatives who reflected local concerns through debate to identify the major issues in the political arena. Politics in the United States did not produce ideology, for a general acceptance of the way this system worked supported the political design of the nation as a whole.

In contrast, the Soviet Union had created a single-party state. Accepting Marx's view of history as essentially correct, the leaders of the Soviet Union had one enemy to defeat: private property. According to Marx, as mentioned in Chapter Twenty-two, private property divided people by income: rents, profits, and wages. These three incomes, in turn, created three broad social classes based on praxis, or work experience, that shaped the worldview of each class.

As Marx had argued, each class soon discovered that their income improved only when that of the other two suffered. Thus, when one class enjoyed high status and political power, the other two endured subordination. Therefore, status itself gave rise to class warfare, since the social domination of one income group required the oppression of the others. The state itself became the principal institution used to enforce this oppression. Consequently, private property generated socioeconomic classes, which in turn, produced political parties to advance their own economic interests. Unfortunately, Marx argued, these interests could only succeed when one class influenced the state to subjugate the rest of society.

This vision of political parties and class warfare served to justify public ownership of the nation's the means of production since that form of possession created a common and universal praxis. Marx argued that public ownership created a common socioeconomic existence that, in turn, generated a uniform social value called equality. This value became the standard used by the Soviet Union to justify its organization. Equality by Soviet standards, however, could only exist through one political belief system: Marxism.

Hence, the two contrasting systems of the Soviet Union and the United States ended up pitting equality against freedom, with each one justifying its struggle by the other's existence. Each appealed to the world to choose between the two, an appeal that generated alliance systems formed on the basis of the confrontation.

Remnants of the Berlin Wall, a series of walls, barbed wire, and other obstructions which divided communist-held East Berlin from free West Berlin during the Cold War. Courtesy of Paul Waibel.

Complicating this intense struggle was the new military technology that had developed over the course of two total wars. This technology had generated such a high death rate by 1945 that victory became too costly if unlimited combat served as the means used to settle disputes. Under such conditions, the victor and the vanquished would look too much alike after the struggle had ended. Furthermore, science had unleashed new levels of destruction that made both *victory* and *defeat* meaningless terms.

Shortly after the United States and then the Soviet Union acquired the atomic bomb, both superpowers produced a newer, more powerful, and even more deadly hydrogen bomb. The hydrogen bomb replaced the atomic bomb's fission with a fusion reaction to release the energy of the Sun on Earth. Capable of generating temperatures of 55 million degrees Fahrenheit and destroying a region of approximately seventy-five square miles, the hydrogen bomb represented the potential for universal devastation, a real life doomsday.

To augment the power offered by nuclear energy, both the United States and Soviet Union went on to develop systems of intercontinental guided missiles that could deliver multiple hydrogen explosions. To these weapons they added radio-controlled delivery systems, proximity fuses, and an arsenal of biological weapons. Science had created unlimited destructive power while the competing states struggled to develop the good judgment to regulate it.

Even before World War II ended, quarrels between the Soviet Union and the United States began to surface that set the tone of the Cold War. The three Allied powers that had defeated Germany and Japan could not agree on what common strategy should be used to ensure world peace in the wake of the most destructive war in world history. In their last few conferences, at Yalta (February 1945), Potsdam (July 1945), and San Francisco (1946), the Allies created the United Nations as an instrument for a new world order, but open hostility had already erupted between the superpowers because the Soviet Union announced that wherever Stalin's armies had gone to liberate Europe they would stay. This extended the control of the U.S.S.R. into Eastern Europe, including half of Germany, the Balkans, and part of Asia. Hence, the Soviets began setting up a series of satellite communist states that the Allies found unacceptable.

In February 1946, Stalin had spoken of the Western democracies as the new enemy, while Winston Churchill, a month later, delivered his famous "Iron Curtain" speech. Churchill had warned against a new communist conspiracy that would divide Europe and set the stage for a potential new global conflict. Also, early in 1946, George F. Kennan, a U.S. Foreign Service Officer, wrote a detailed telegram which reached President Truman, in which he outlined how the Soviet Union had become a prisoner of its own ideology. Kennan argued that Stalin saw the world divided into communist and capitalist camps with irreconcilable differences. The Western powers could only *contain* Soviet aggression while waiting for a profound change in Soviet leadership that might finally ease global tensions.

By 1947, trouble in Greece set the stage for the development of the United States policy of containment. In February 1947, the British warned President Truman that they could no longer defend Greece against a communist-backed civil war led by local Marxist guerrilla forces and supported by Moscow. On March 12, 1947, Truman went before a joint session of Congress and declared what became known as the Truman Doctrine: if Greece or Turkey fell to communism, all the Middle East might be lost; hence, communism had to be stopped. As a result, Truman stated that it had become the policy of the United States to "support all free people" wherever communist subjugation might occur.

The United States followed up on the Truman doctrine with the so-called Marshall Plan, a program that offered broad economic aid to all European states on the condition that they work together for their mutual benefit. The goal of the Marshall Plan was twofold: produce economic recovery on a war-ravaged continent, and prevent the use of financial insecurity as a means for any totalitarian regime to rise to power—especially one sponsored by the Soviet Union. In announcing the plan, Secretary of State George C. Marshall had recalled

how Adolf Hitler had used runaway inflation and the Great Depression to rise to power. The United States was determined to deny the same opportunities to Stalin.

The United States invited the Soviet Union and all its satellite states in Eastern Europe to join in as recipients of this aid. While Finland, Czechoslovakia, Poland, and Hungary showed signs of interest, Stalin flatly rejected the U.S. offer and spoke for all of Eastern Europe. He did not want any U.S. involvement in Eastern Europe, and he especially did not want wealth from the United States to encourage defection from the security he planned for his eastern frontier.

Therefore, in 1947 Stalin called on representatives from communist nations from around the world to assemble in Warsaw. There they were to create a new bureau to share information concerning Western actions and reconstitute the Communist International Committee for World Revolution (Comintern): which Stalin had suspended during World War II to please his Allied partners. Then, in 1948, Stalin expelled all democratic leaders from Czechoslovakia's coalition government and arranged for the murder of Jan Masaryk, the son of the founder of that nation after World War I and its current foreign minister. The Soviet actions in Czechoslovakia now brought the question of Germany into focus.

At the end of World War II, the Allies had divided Germany, and its capital, Berlin, into occupied zones. Stalin had been given East Germany, which he stripped of all its industrial equipment to help rebuild the war-torn Soviet Union. Since the Marshall Plan had set reconstruction in motion in the Western portions of Germany, the stark contrast between the Western sections of the nation and the dismantled Soviet zone placed Stalin's policy in a bad light. As a result, he decided to isolate his section of Germany and close Berlin: a city shared between the United States, Britain, France, and the Soviet Union. The Allied portions of Berlin had become the beneficiary of democratic generosity from the West, while the vengeful avarice of Stalin created an abject contrast.

In the summer of 1948, Stalin ordered Berlin closed to Western access. The Soviets declared that all land routes to Berlin that ran through Soviet territory suddenly needed (fictitious) repair. Only the air route remained open. Accordingly, the United States and its allies began the Berlin Airlift, which supplied the city as the United States and the Soviet Union reached their most intense postwar crisis. Given U.S. experiences with supplying Nationalist China by air during World War II, the Berlin Airlift worked and the people of Berlin escaped starvation; by May 1949, Stalin had to admit defeat. By September, Germany became a divided country and a hotbed for Cold War politics.

By 1949, the Marshall Plan bore strategic fruit. In March 1948, Belgium, Luxembourg, France, and Great Britain had signed the Treaty of Brussels, which provided for their mutual defense. In April 1949, Italy, Denmark, Norway, Portugal, Iceland, the United States, and Canada joined the new alliance to create the North Atlantic Treaty Organization (NATO). NATO produced a defensive parameter in Western Europe to secure that continent from further Soviet aggression. In that same year, Stalin reciprocated with formation of the Council of Mutual Assistance (COMECON). By May of 1955, COMECON became known as the Warsaw Pact, which included the Soviet Union as the hegemon (leader) of Albania, Bulgaria, Czechoslovakia, East Germany, Hungary, Poland, and Romania. The division of Europe into armed camps was complete.

Stalin had carved out a sphere of influence in Eastern Europe to ensure his nation would never suffer a direct invasion from the West again. The United States had matched Stalin's sphere with a Western, Central, and Northern European alliance to block Soviet influence in Europe. Germany, once the most aggressive nation in Europe, had become a zone of confrontation divided between the Western Allies and the Soviet Union.

Thus, the Cold War had begun. Now the two great superpowers squared off in a bipolar contest, each accusing the other of ignoring the democratic principles it advocated and requesting the rest of the world to judge its system as superior.

The rest of the world, in turn, completed the process of decolonization in the context of this contest. Some cultures borrowed Marxism as an ideology of liberation, while others chose Natural Rights Theory. In between, a third group played one side against the other, exploiting the Cold War between the United States and the Soviet Union as a source of foreign aid. The result was the creation of a multicultural global system. Understanding such a system is the goal of the remainder of this text.

Suggested Reading

Boyle, J. H., *China and Japan at War, 1937–1945* (Stanford, Calif.: Stanford University Press, 1972).

Bullock, Alan, *Hitler: A Study in Tyranny,* Revised Edition (New York: Harper Torchbooks, 1964).

Dower, J., *War Without Mercy* (New York: Pantheon Books, 1986).

Dziewanowski, M. K., *War at Any Price: World War II in Europe, 1939–1945* (Englewood Cliffs, N.J.: Prentice Hall, Inc., 1991).

Feis, Herbert, *From Trust to Terror: The Onset of the Cold War, 1945–1950* (New York: Norton, 1970).

Hildebrand, Klaus, *The Foreign Policy of the Third Reich* (Berkeley: University of California Press, 1973).

Hingley, Ronald, *Russia: A Concise History,* Revised and Updated Edition (London: Thames and Hudson Ltd., 1991).

Keegan, John, *The Second World War* (New York: Viking Penguin, 1990).

Kolko, Joyce and Gabriel, *The Limits of Power: The World and the United States Foreign Policy, 1945–1954* (New York: Vintage Books, 1970).

LaFeber, Walter, *America in the Cold War: Twenty Years of Revolution and Responses, 1947–1967* (New York: John Wiley and Sons, 1969).

Mazower, Mark, *The Dark Continent: Europe's Twentieth Century* (New York: Vintage Books, 1998), 157–174.

Rauch, Georg von, *A History of the Soviet Union,* Fifth Edition (New York: Praeger Publishers, 1971).

Sherwin, M. J. A., *A World Destroyed: Hiroshima and the Origins of the Arms Race* (New York: Viking Books, 1987).

Toland, John, *Adolf Hitler* (New York: Ballantine Books, 1976).

Ulam, Adam, B., *The Bolsheviks* (New York: The Macmillan Company, 1965).

———, *The Rivals: America and Russia since World War II* (New York: Penguin Books, 1977).

Wint, G., Calvocoressi, P., and Pritchard, J., *Total War* (New York: Random House, 1991).

XXXII

GLOBAL DECOLONIZATION:
Phase Two

In the wake of World War II, the Cold War fostered the second phase of decolonization. Decolonization now represented the aspirations of "self-determination," as suggested in Woodrow Wilson's Fourteen Points, the notion that every ethnic group, culture, or people could decide its own political destiny. The Cold War, in turn, saw the two superpowers vying to aid and advise developing nation-states around the world as long as they adopted an ideology sympathetic to one side or the other. Consequently, the Cold War provided the nations of the third world opportunities to exploit one or both superpowers as they sought to redefine themselves in the context of a new global differential of power.

No longer trapped by European military, political, and economic superiority, the peoples of the old imperial regimes of the Middle East, Africa, and Asia asserted their will in an effort to shape their own future. Free to import weapons and advisors from the United States or the Soviet Union, well-equipped native armies stood capable of defending themselves, their soldiers willing to die in an effort to realize self-determination.

The path that each people took during the process of decolonization, liberation, and nation-formation depended on local circumstances. Determining factors included what form of opposition to imperialism had grown up in each of these Third World countries, whether they favored one side or the other in the Cold War; and how had these native opponents to imperialism managed to exploit the superpowers successfully.

The most effective way to tell the history of post-1945 decolonization is to consider the process regionally, beginning first in Asia and then moving on to Africa and the Middle East. Finally, the Latin American story, that is out of pace with the others, will complete the chapter. Remember, Latin America had achieved independence from Spain in the nineteenth century but had fallen into debt to Europe and the United States (as mentioned in Chapter Thirty). This makes the Latin American story unique but still part of the process of decolonization, liberation, and national formation.

China

After the Japanese surrender in 1945, U.S. president Harry Truman made a halfhearted effort to avert a major civil war brewing in China between Jiang Jieshi's Nationalists and Mao Zedong's Chinese Communists. The United States tried to act as a neutral mediator between the two, even though it clearly favored the Nationalists as its ideological partner. Jiang and Mao humored the United States by paying lip service to peace and a coalition government even as each leader vigorously prepared his forces for the eventual conflict. When the all-out struggle finally began, the U.S. government—loathe to support the spread of communism anywhere—stood solidly behind Jiang. Hence the Chinese civil war became a part of the broader struggle between what the United States hailed as "the Free World" versus "the Soviet Bloc."

Mao's forces defeated Jiang's armies despite American aid—some 2 billion dollars between 1945 and 1949. In general, Mao had diagnosed China's needs far more accurately than had Jiang. Mao knew that China had to expel all foreigners, establish true sovereignty as a nation-state, and meet the needs of China's massive peasant population. Jiang, on the other hand, relied too heavily on foreign aid from the West, ignored the issue of peasant poverty, and depended completely on an isolated, but wealthy, urban landlord population. Out of step with his own nation, Jiang and his Nationalist regime fell. He along with his supporters and the remainder of his armies then fled to the tiny island of Taiwan. There they established the Republic of China, which still exists today. Triumphant Mao, in turn, announced the founding of the People's Republic of China on the massive Chinese mainland.

Thus, a new communist regime was born in 1949. At the ceremonial rally held on October 1 to mark the founding of the People's Republic of China, Mao declared to the world, "The Chinese people have stood up!" Ironically, his words resonated with the patriotic-nationalism of the majority of the Chinese population, while Marx himself would have condemned all nationalist movements as manifestations of capitalism. Simultaneously, Mao's party aspired to launch a new beginning after two centuries of war, corrupt and incompetent governments, and bullying at the hands of foreign powers. While Mao's political coffers were overflowing with this ideological capital, he would quickly squander his mandate by implementing costly and impractical programs.

While China could once again boast of unification and independence, Mao and his comrades-in-arms were not traditional empire-builders; instead they were communists in a peasant society about to attempt radical changes that Marx himself would have questioned. They would strive not only to restore China's past glory, but they would also attempt to create a communist paradise one stage before its time according to Marx's historiography.

Combining traditional Chinese autocratic methods of an imperial ruler and certain features of Soviet totalitarianism, Mao's Chinese Communist Party (CCP) held a stronger control over the "nation" than any previous Chinese state, traditional or otherwise. Yet, the concept of the nation itself, was, in this case, a political tool first developed by the Soviet Union, and then used by Mao to transform peasants into the proletariat needed to create a communist state. Supported by a Soviet-style single-party state and a party-controlled army, the CCP developed an autocratic regime. Both the CCP and its army were highly disciplined and battle-hardened after decades of war with both the Nationalists and the Japanese.

The CCP had a membership of 4.5 million in 1949. Its cadres were in leadership positions at all levels of the government and the military, at factories and stores, schools and universities, villages, and even in neighborhood committees. In a vertically articulated command system, Mao issued orders that the CCP put into practice throughout the country. Over the decades, Mao had developed what he called the "mass line" as an effective method of implementing his policies. Whether it was to carry out land reform, fight the Japanese aggressors, or force the indoctrination of intellectuals, he always mobilized the masses to execute his goals. He would continue to launch mass campaigns for the next three decades.

Mao's immediate plans to rebuild China, however, were interrupted by the Korean War (1950–53). Shortly before the end of World War II, the Soviet army entered northern Korea and the armed forces of the United States entered southern Korea. The Soviets supported a communist regime north of the 38th parallel under Kim Il Sung, and the U.S. backed a longtime Korean Nationalist, Syngman Rhee, to the south. The two leaders and their respective regimes—henceforth known as North Korea and South Korea—divided the troubled peninsula.

In 1950 North Korea launched an all-out offensive across the 38th parallel to unify the Korean peninsula. North Korea was backed by the Soviet Union and China from behind the scenes. Harry Truman, as president of the United States, decided to stop this act of communist aggression. Suffering politically for the "loss" of China, Truman had discontinued aid to Jiang in August 1949, after Jiang refused to implement democratic reforms. Truman felt he had to take a hard line against North Korea. Accordingly, he got the United Nations to declare North Korea an aggressor state and to send a UN force to protect South Korea.

Although fourteen nations contributed soldiers to the international army, U.S. troops composed the bulk of the UN forces, all of which were under the command of the decorated American general Douglas MacArthur. The UN troops successfully beat back the North Koreans, but when they drew close to the Chinese border, a worried Mao sent Chinese troops to fight on the side of North Korea. While both sides gained and lost ground, the conflict eventually stalemated at the 38th parallel, where 45 percent of the 33,686 Americans killed in action during this war died between July 1951 and July 1953.

The Korean War. An F-51 "Mustang" releases two napalm fire bombs over North Korea targeting a Communist industrial military post. A sister plane at far left, of the same 18th Fighter Bomber Wing, will follow up with the same type of destructive missles, ca. 08/1951. United States National Archives & Records Admnistration. ARC # 542243.

When North Korea and South Korea signed a ceasefire in 1953, the forces of the two sides were positioned roughly where they had been when the war started but had lost a combined 2.3 million civilians and military personnel. The Korean War demonstrated the assertiveness of the new American global policy known as containment; yet it cost $50 billion and made defense-spending a priority in U.S. budgets thereafter. It also established China as a major power in the communist bloc despite the loss of between 145,000 men (Chinese figures) or 500,000 to 1 million by Western estimates. Finally, this bloody conflict created a deep animosity between Red China and United States that would take a long time to overcome.

The Korean War did not distract Mao from his visionary goals. Rather, it radicalized the measures he would take to transform China. The CCP's primary concern after the founding of the People's Republic of China (PRC) was the consolidation of the new regime; that completed, a communist paradise was their long-range, if idealistic, objective.

According to Mao's vision, private businesses were contrary to Marxism and therefore had to be transformed into state-and-private joint enterprises. For all practical purposes, the state became the owners of the businesses, while their expropriated private owners received token compensation for running them. With control over the urban economy, the CCP now had a tighter grip on the least reliable portion of the Chinese population, the old, wealthy stronghold of the Nationalists.

Meanwhile, shoring up peasant support for the PRC was also essential. For decades land reform had been a proven way of mobilizing peasant support. Depending on circumstances, land redistribution sometimes took the extremist form of stripping landlords of all their property and turning it over to peasants, or the more moderate form of mandating reduced rent and interest rates. From 1949–56, the CCP launched a campaign of radical land reform across the nation.

Yet making peasants small-property owners was not an orthodox communist goal; it was only a tactical expedient. The success of these agrarian tactics, however, raised Mao's popularity to its zenith. Feeling confident about his own political capital, and worried about the bureaucratic nature of his party structure, Mao decided to launch a new intellectual campaign. This, however, would prove to be a very risky affair.

Between 1949 and 1956 the CCP had already introduced a new ideology they called "Mao Zedong Thought," a Chinese version of Marxism-Leninism. This ideology was quite alien to China's educated people, since they largely came from displaced business- and landowning families and were educated in Confucian or Western-style schools. Now the CCP decided the time had come to indoctrinate these "untrustworthy" intellectuals with "Mao Thought." They isolated China's well-educated persons in *danwei* (communist work units) and put group pressure on them to take the party line. Through these drastic measures, the CCP succeeded in remolding the thinking of some of them and silencing the rest.

By 1956 Mao apparently was so confident of his economic and ideological successes that he called on China's "reeducated" intelligentsia to offer constructive criticism of his regime. He hoped to use this useful appraisal to prevent the bureaucratic stodginess he observed among the Bolsheviks who had held power too long in the Soviet Union without achieving a communist paradise. Accordingly, Mao called this the "Hundred Flower" policy, an allusion to the intellectual blossoming in the late Zhou period in ancient China. Yet once the intellectuals were allowed to offer real criticism of the PRC, negative commentaries flowed out in torrents.

Clearly, the majority of China's intellectuals had not accepted Mao Thought and were not satisfied with communist rule. Shocked, Mao responded by launching the Anti-Rightist Campaign (1957–58) to crackdown on those who had criticized him—despite the fact that they had done so at his request. As punishment, Mao sent millions of educated people to work in factories and on farms. Once again, Mao had silenced the cream of China's educated populace.

Having squelched China's intelligentsia, Mao next turned on China's farming masses. In 1958, he declared the "Great Leap Forward" to complete China's primary economic tasks: creating a "classless society" and surpassing Great Britain in industrial production. He began by creating massive farming cooperatives called "people's communes" in which peasants no longer had private property rights and their income was based on their labor only. By pooling land that the peasants had only recently gained through Mao's land reforms, Chinese food production was supposed to return to a barter economy, farmers were supposed to eat in vast new dining halls, and a new rural-urban link was supposed to feed the growing mass of anticipated industrial workers. But the reality of the people's communes, in stark contrast to Mao's vision, was a disaster.

The abolition of privately owned farms, and the leveling of income, destroyed the peasant's incentive to work. Weeds soon filled in fields that once grew crops. Unrealistically high output targets were set, and taxes based on those fantastic targets gave the government a legitimate excuse to rob peasants of grain that they needed for food and seed. Thus, between 1959 and 1961 famine followed the "Great Leap Forward," as an estimated 25–30 million people died of starvation.

Within the CCP, there was widespread concern over the disastrous consequences of the establishment of the people's communes. Mao's longtime comrade-in-arms and favorite general, Peng Dehui, became an open critic. Mao framed him on charges of conspiracy and treason and had him removed from power and imprisoned in 1966 until he died in 1974. Mao then followed up with a campaign to purge other critics within his party. Hence, criticism within the CCP stopped cold.

Having rid himself of critics both within and outside of his party, Mao pressed ahead to transform the remainder of China's economy. As part of the Great Leap Forward, Mao believed that modern economic development was mainly a matter of increased production of steel. Falling back on experience, he launched a mass operation to make this metal. Factory workers and peasants, students and teachers, in short, people from all walks of life were mobilized to build furnaces and make steel. Yet, they produced only large quantities of useless metal, primarily due to its brittleness because of a low-carbon content. In the meantime, they wasted enormous amounts of human and natural resources.

Finally, nervous leaders within the CCP realized that the economy could not survive Mao's meddling. As both industrial and agricultural output plummeted, party leaders forced Mao to back off; he retired to the "second line of command" in the early 1960s, leaving day-to-day management of matters of state and party to Liu Shaoqi (1898–1969), Zhou Enlai (1898–1976), and Deng Xiaoping (1904–97).

Liu, Deng, and Zhou now had the daunting task of restoring order and reviving the economy. They dismantled the people's communes, allowed the operation of small, privately owned businesses, and gave intellectuals a little more freedom. Their policies smacked of neocapitalism but worked remarkably well.

Yet, Mao was unrepentant. He believed Liu, Deng, and Zhou had taken advantage of his setbacks to push him aside. He eyed their employment of neocapitalistic policies with contempt and disapproval. To settle the scores, he launched the "Cultural Revolution" in 1966. After years of secret preparation, he had put Field Marshall Lin Biao (1907–71) in charge of the military and his wife Jiang Qing (1914–91), known as Madame Mao, in charge of the media. With them in place, he launched his attack on his rivals. Since Liu, Deng, and Zhou all held high office, in order to bring them down, Mao had to effect an all-out assault on the party and government bureaucracies. This was a bizarre situation in which Mao set out to destroy the party and government apparatus that he had worked so long and hard to build.

Taking advantage of his undisputed reputation as the leader of the Chinese Revolution, Mao denounced Liu and Deng as revisionists of Marxism, "capitalist-roaders," and traitors of the Chinese Revolution. He called on the nation to attack them and their followers. His targets included the majority of the party leaders, the government, and the military. Anyone with any social standing also came under attack. University and secondary-school students were the first to respond to Mao's call. Then, factory workers in cities joined in, and finally some peasants became part of what became known as the "Cultural Revolution." The mobs stormed established institutions and effectively subjected Mao's rivals to vigilante rule, abandoning all legal and humanitarian criteria. Social order broke down, and civil war broke out in many parts of the country.

Students fell easy prey to Mao's revolutionary rhetoric. Young, idealistic, and inexperienced, they plunged their energies into what they believed was a truly revolutionary crusade. As Mao's first wave of attack cadres they suspended all classes and organized themselves into units of the Red Guards, terrorizing the nation. Yet their unchecked power in an anarchist environment corrupted them, and the Red Guard soon deteriorated into warring bands of destructive power-seekers. Then, once his rivals had fallen, Mao had no further use for the student cadres. He put schools under martial law and sent the students to the countryside for "reeducation" (as peasants), leaving them there to rot. The Red Guard Movement had come to a dismal end. A generation of young people grew up uneducated, disillusioned, and cynical; their future was bleak.

Now Mao began rebuilding the party and government apparatus under his trusted followers. Yet Mao soon discovered that his most trusted lieutenant, Field Marshal Lin Biao, was involved in a plot against him. Mao acted quickly. Lin was killed when his airplane crashed in 1971. While both Mao's reputation and his ability to control the situation suffered from the "Lin Biao Incident," he still managed to surprise the world by pulling off a major diplomatic feat.

When Mao founded the PRC, he put his regime firmly in the communist bloc under the domination of Stalin, signing a treaty with the Soviet Union and adopting a foreign policy he called "leaning to one side"— that of the Soviet Union. The Korean War further solidified his reputation as a communist leader and a sworn enemy of the United States. Yet Mao's fanatical Great Leap Forward had alienated him from the Soviet Union. Now, instead of yielding to Soviet criticism, Mao decided to go his own way. He even challenged Soviet ruler Nikita Khrushchev's position as the leader of the communist bloc after Stalin's death in 1953.

Mao condemned Khrushchev as a "revisionist," one who had betrayed Marxism-Leninism and given up the pursuit of a communist new world order out of fear of war with the United States. Khrushchev, however, had no intention of handing over his leadership role to Mao. A polemic broke out between the two men and the two parties. Domestically, this provided the backdrop for the Cultural Revolution in China. Internationally, it developed into armed border clashes between China and the Soviet Union in 1969. Faced with two powerful enemies, China found itself in total international isolation.

At this point, U.S. president Richard M. Nixon entered the dispute. Nixon had a new strategic view of the world. He modified his earlier fervent anticommunist stand, through which he had furthered his own political career in the 1950s and 1960s, and rejected a bipolar world; now he saw the world as multipolar. Accordingly, he embraced a global strategy of the balance of power among the major nations of the world. He hoped to establish a new balance of power between the United States, China, and the Soviet Union that would allow him to extract the United States from the war in Vietnam (see Chapter Thirty-three) and de-escalate the nuclear arms race then raging between the United States and the Soviet Union. This was a time, Nixon realized, when China and the United States needed each other.

On October 25, 1971, the United States supported the PRC's takeover of the Republic of China's (Taiwan's) seat on the security council. After Nixon made a highly publicized and ceremonial visit to mainland China in 1972, China stepped down its aid to North Vietnam, making it easier for Nixon to withdraw American combat troops from that embattled nation. The United States extended diplomatic recognition to the PRC in 1979. China had broken out of its diplomatic isolation.

His health deteriorating, Mao coasted along for a few more years. When he died in 1976, so did his artificial revolution. The Old Guard wasted no time in arresting Madame Mao and her supporters, the so-called Gang of Four. The Old Guard rallied around Deng Xiaoping, who quickly steered China onto a new and irreversible course: capitalism within a communist context. Such a course mocked Marxism, the very ideology that had spawned the PRC, because two antagonistic stages of economic development based on the means of production had now become one.

Hence, Marxism never fit well in China. In the hands of Mao, it had functioned more like a visionary ideology that promised a vast political potential, but, out of necessity, had to be coupled to simple revolutionary expediency. On the one hand, Mao set out to create a Marxist paradise in a culture even less pre-pared than the Soviet Union's to enter the communist stage that Karl Marx had envisioned in the nineteenth century. On the other hand, Mao had effectively used Marxism to mobilize the revolutionary passion needed to drive out all foreign influences in China, including that of the Soviet Union, and free the Chinese people from imperial rule. Hence, Mao's combination of visionary politics and the pragmatic application of power had created internal contradictions within the PRC. Therefore, Mao had managed to solve China's problems with European and American imperialism, but he could never successfully impose a revolution of infinite trajectory on a peasant society ill-prepared for the industrialization needed to create true communism.

Hence, like the Marxist leaders of Russia, Mao had launched a revolution with no end, a direct contradiction to Marx's dictum that economics defined politics rather than politics shaping the mode of production. Ironically, Mao had inverted the Marxist edifice. The superstructure (the political world) gave shape to the foundation (the mode of production) in a manner precisely the opposite of that which Marx had prescribed.

As a result, Mao floundered in a surreal world of his own creation. Only his pragmatic political sense allowed him to retain power throughout his life and die "the great liberator of China." After Mao left the political scene, he turned over the future of the PRC to men who could apply capitalist principles within a communist context. Hence, the PRC, like the Soviet Union, appeared to have become "the monster" Marx warned against in his concept of voluntarism: they were in fact neocapitalists.

Japan

Unlike China, Japan did not have to expel foreigners to create a nation-state. Yet after their surrender to the Allies in World War II, the Japanese were, for the first time in their history, under foreign military occupation. The war had destroyed Japan's cities, economy, confidence, and even its psyche. When U.S. forces moved in to occupy Japan after the war, the Japanese expected a vindictive rule, but their American occupiers surprised them.

Helping the United States' wish to rebuild Japan were the postwar hostilities between the U.S. and the U.S.S.R. The Cold War created a need for allies in every corner of the globe, and the United States could ill afford to alienate the Japanese people. Furthermore, as seen in Chapter Thirty-one, the United States had hit upon a successful antifascist, antitotalitarian campaign in Europe with the implementation of the Marshall Plan. Using a similar program in Japan, the Americans helped the Japanese economy make a rapid recovery. All together, these factors combined to enhance Japan's receptivity to change and encouraged its cooperation with U.S. efforts to remake the Japanese government in the image of American democracy. Hence, Japan became a success story for the "Free World."

The United States went into Japan with a set of occupation policies. The U.S. government had determined that it needed to reconstruct what it saw as Japan's militaristic tradition and feudalistic mindset. The United States had also decided to work toward the goal of reconstruction with the support of the emperor and through the Japanese bureaucracy.

General Douglas MacArthur (1880–1964) headed the American Occupation under the direction of the U.S. government. Despite his reputation as the "blue-eyed shogun," he did not rule like a monarch. Rather, his occupation policies were worked out between him, Washington, and the occupation bureaucracy, with active Japanese participation.

First on the list of issues was the fact that Japan faced an economic catastrophe. The protracted war had exhausted the resources of the nation, leaving it like a squeezed orange. Japan's cities, industrial installations, roads, and railroads all lay in ruins. Its farms were starved of fertilizers, its financial institutions were shattered, and its currency was worthless. The best and the brightest members of its population had died in war. The most frequently cited figures on Japanese casualties from World War II are 1.74 million killed in com-

bat and 240,000 killed in conventional air raids, with another 300,000 dead, missing, or injured from the Hiroshima and Nagasaki attacks alone. Added to this chaos was a mass of demobilized troops and repatriated civilians without any jobs. Famine was imminent, but the occupation authorities averted the worst by bringing in food and medical supplies.

The basic long-term policy of the American Occupation was the demilitarization and democratization of Japan. In the short run, this goal demanded the immediate dismantling of the military, political, and economic establishment responsible for the war. Hence, Japan's World War II leaders had to face the same charges of war crimes that had led to the execution or imprisonment of Nazi leadership.

The international war crimes tribunal (1946–48) tried twenty-eight leaders charged with responsibility for the war, seven of whom were condemned to die. Tojo Hideki, prime minister during the war, was hanged. In the end, roughly 200,000 officers, officials, businessmen, and teachers were implicated, with about half of them members of the military. Most of these people, however, were reinstated, and some of them went on to hold very important positions. Since the occupation, officials had decided to keep the Japanese bureaucracy intact; a large degree of continuity was preserved in government.

Although the occupation leaders decided to preserve the institution of the emperor, they also decided to put it through a process of demystification. In 1946, the emperor openly denied his divinity in a public address, and under the new constitution he became the symbolic head of the nation.

Inside MacArthur's headquarters, U.S. officials wrote Japan's new constitution, which the Diet adopted in 1947. This document replaced the Meiji Constitution and changed Japanese polity, establishing a British-style parliamentary government wherein the leader of the majority party becomes prime minister and forms the cabinet. This new legislative system ensured freedom of the press and freedom of assembly. It also contained a no-war clause, which renounced war as a sovereign right and committed Japan to never again maintaining armed forces for aggressive purposes.

Traditional values changed slowly, but the legal changes encouraged social change. In education, the occupation abolished old ethics courses and purged textbooks of militarism and ultranationalism. The constitution ensured women's right to vote and equality in marriage. The occupation saw economic reform as the foundation of social and political change, but was most successful in its land reform policy. It banned absentee landlordism and set a cap on the amount of land a

The U.S. occupation of Japan. General of the Unites States Army Douglas MacArthur (center) talks with Allied and Japanese newsmen after his arrival at Atsugi airfield, Japan, on August 30, 1945. Standing behind General MacArthur, at right, is General Robert L. Eichelberger. Photo #: NH 84346, U.S. Naval Historical Center Photograph.

single landowner could hold. Excess land had to be sold to the government, who then had to resell it to former tenants. This policy created a nation filled with small farms. It also saw the agricultural sector become the first to recover.

Japan's political parties were reinvigorated under the American Occupation. These new parties studied the politics of the premilitarist decades. The prewar conservative parties, Seiyukai and Minseito, reemerged as the Democratic and Liberal parties. The prewar Socialist Mass party became the Japanese Socialist party.

The occupation saw concentrated economic power in prewar Japan as a major culprit of the rise of Japanese authoritarianism and militarism. Initially, therefore, the U.S. had little interest in reviving Japan's industry. In fact, the occupation set about to decentralize the economy, breaking up the old holding companies and banning Zaibatsu families from occupying leadership positions in the economy. The occupation also decided to foster labor unions by giving them the right to organize and engage in collective bargaining. A vigorous labor movement sprang up, but it turned out to be politically oriented, working in collaboration with the socialist and communist parties, and bringing Cold War fears to a head.

A rising fear of global communism, plus the development of a new labor movement in Japan encouraged General MacArthur to press for a treaty with the Japanese and end the occupation. Since the international situation was rapidly producing a Cold War, a firm treaty with Japan became a diplomatic goal to ensure a new ally in the Far East. Hence, John Foster Dulles received the task of preparing the treaty in 1950, and by September 1951, it was complete. All the major powers of World War II signed it, except for the Soviet Union and China, and Japan's occupation came to an end in August 1952 when it ratified the treaty.

Meanwhile the Cold War came to dominate international attention. As seen in Chapter Thirty-one, by 1947 the Cold War was well underway and, as mentioned above, by 1949 a communist regime had taken power in China. The United States was also having second thoughts about many of its earlier Japan policies encouraging unions and withholding investments in Japan's industrial future, because a weak economy might invite a communist takeover.

As Cold War economic and strategic considerations came to prevail, the United States decided to make Japan an ally and a beachhead against communist expansion in Far East Asia. Now the occupation officials suspended measures to break up the Zaibatsu, assisted in rebuilding Japanese industry, and made generous loans available. The United States then opened U.S. markets to Japanese exports, purged communists from Japanese labor unions, and allowed the old World War II "enemies" that had been excluded from public life earlier to reenter national affairs.

Yoshida Shigeru (1878–1967), head of the Liberal Party, was prime minister between 1946 and 1954. A probusiness, antiunion, and anticommunist leader, his main goal was Japan's economic recovery and growth; his main fear was to have Japan drawn into burdensome military spending. In foreign policy, he staunchly sided with the United States in the Cold War in exchange for the security and economic benefits that his nation could not afford on its own. He refused to build up more than a skeleton military for the purpose of securing domestic peace. In general, his goals for Japan paralleled those of the United States.

The Korean War (1950–53) brought the United States' "reverse course" toward Japanese industry and unions into full swing. American war procurement led to a surge in Japanese manufacturing. In 1947, Japanese production was 37 percent of prewar levels, but by 1955 it had fully regained prewar levels. With American encouragement, Japan created a self-defense force in 1950. As mentioned above, in 1951, America signed a peace treaty with Japan that provided for U.S. bases in Japan and a Mutual Security Treaty that committed the United States to Japan's defense. The security treaty would remain the cornerstone of Japan's minimalist defense policy into the twenty-first century.

Japan continued the Yoshida policies throughout the 1960s, 1970s, and 1980s, with the Japanese taking advantage of the international situation of the Cold War to advance its own goals of security and economic growth. By the 1980s, its economy had become the world's second-most powerful. The Liberal Democratic Party (LDP), which held power throughout this period, was formed through a merger of the Conservative Liberal and Democratic parties in 1955. It comprised many factions, each with its own leader and members, and it built strong ties with business and the bureaucracy, which worked closely with the United States.

What opposition existed was composed of a range of small, fragmented parties. The three leftist parties, the Socialist party, the Democratic Socialist party, and the Communist party stood opposed to the recreation of a military establishment and did what they could to delay the expansion of the Self Defense Forces. They also opposed the government's consistently pro-U.S. foreign policy and protested against American military bases and nuclear weapons on Japanese territory.

In the 1960s, political confrontation between the LDP and the opposition parties reached its greatest intensity over the issue of the renewal of the Security Treaty with the United States. Many Japanese felt that the treaty threatened to involve Japan in any war the Americans might enter. The specter of nuclear war was particularly terrifying to a people who had experienced the horrors of Hiroshima and Nagasaki. Yet Prime Minister Nobusuke Kishi was able to ram the treaty through the Diet in a way that many thought undemocratic. The fact that Kishi had been a member of the World War II Tojo cabinet suggested to them the extent to which the old establishment had survived.

The focus on economic growth in the 1970s and 1980s, however, directed Japanese politics away from tumultuous confrontation and ushered in a more peaceful era. Japan's single-minded drive for economic growth produced an economic miracle. Shipbuilding, steel, heavy chemicals, automobiles, machine tools, consumer electronics, and optics led the way. By the 1970s, names like Sony, Toyota, and Canon had become household words across the world. In 1955, Japan had a Gross National Product (GNP) of $24 billion and a per capita product of $268; by 1989 the figures were $2,830 billion and $23,000.

The spectacular economic growth Japan managed to achieve was the result of favorable domestic and international conditions as well as the nation's ability to take advantage of them in the context of the Cold War. Oil was cheap, Japan had a well-educated, highly skilled, highly disciplined, and relatively inexpensive workforce. Japan had revived the manufacturing, marketing, and banking systems developed before the war. Free trade in the U.S. global sphere of influence gave Japan easy access to sources of raw materials and markets—especially the American market. Meanwhile, Japan made more and better educational opportunities available to the population. By the early 1980s, Japanese universities were turning out more engineers than their American counterparts. Labor unions were weak. Under a system of state-protected free enterprise, the government continued to provide aid and guidance to help businesses grow and compete overseas. The United States sponsored Japan's entry into international trade and financial organizations, and the American security umbrella enabled Japan to maintain a smaller military budget than any other developed nation. This in turn helped to keep taxes low.

The rate of economic growth, however, slowed down as the economy matured. An earlier double-digit growth rate was replaced by a 4 percent growth rate in 1973. While an open world market and low defense spending continued to favor Japan, other factors were changing. Labor became more expensive. Oil became more expensive with the formation of OPEC (see below). Government expenditure increased as new welfare and environmental policies were implemented. Competition in the manufacture of electronics and automobiles began to come from South Korea, Taiwan, and Hong Kong, who now enjoyed even cheaper labor. The composition of Japan's economy shifted to more capital-, research-, and technology-intense products and service industries. Nonetheless, Japan's export economy continued to thrive because of product quality and protectionist government policies, with Japan enjoying a huge trade surplus, especially with the United States. By 1989 the Tokyo Dow, a national stock exchange and real estate values index, had almost tripled in four years. Japanese living standards had risen to match European levels.

Japan's rapid economic growth led other Asian nations to look to Japan for the secret of successful economic modernization, while still others feared the specter of an economic Japanese empire. Scholars began speaking of an "Asian model of development," one which included a market economy combined with strong government involvement, an emphasis on education, high technology, group-oriented moral values, and authoritarian politics rather than true liberal democracy. A new nationalism was taking shape, one that incorporated a sense of dissatisfaction at being a junior partner to the United States.

As the Japanese economy changed, so did the structure of its society. At the end of World War II, nearly half the Japanese population lived in the countryside, but by 1989 most lived in cities and worked in modern industries where they enjoyed higher pay, shorter hours, and better benefits. With a higher income and at least a high school education, most of them thought of themselves as middle class. They took affluence for granted and expected small pleasures in life.

At the same time, the Japanese vision of the family and standard of living changed. The ideal in the 1960s was to have two children, but by 2000 the average family had one child or no children. Residential housing became cramped as the cost of land and dwellings soared. Finally, consumerism caught on, as the Japanese began coveting the same material goods they had been exporting for decades. A typical apartment was full of electronic equipment: television and stereo sets, rice-cookers, washers and dryers, and computers.

The condition and status of women improved. They had gained the right to vote and to receive an education, even at the best universities. Most women worked for a time after graduation and before marriage. The sexes mixed more freely, the rate of arranged marriages declined, and love marriages became the norm. Yet the feminist movement was still weak, as indicated by the very small number of women in high places in politics, industry, and business today.

Minority groups in Japan still tended to suffer varying degrees of social and occupational discrimination. The Koreans, most of whom were born and educated in Japan, are a case in point. They belonged to a subordinate people under the pre–World War II Japanese empire. Hence, they were viewed with a suspicion that did not erode after World War II. Keeping in mind that Japan's geographic isolation as an island nation produced a nearly homogeneous population, Koreans found themselves in the unenviable position of being one of the few postwar minorities. Hence, prejudice against them endured well after 1945.

Nonetheless, Japan's postwar history is one of economic success and political recovery. Under the umbrella of a Cold War–partnership with the United States, Japan became a counterpoint to Mao's China. Yet the emergence of Japan as an economic superpower in the Pacific Rim in the 1970s and 1980s set the stage for its liberation from subservience to U.S. leadership. Still, friendlier relations between the United States and Japan, compared to Mao's posture toward the Soviet Union in the 1960s, speaks to a more successful long-term alliance between the two nations.

India

India won independence as a result of World War II, yet the subcontinent once ruled as one vast British protectorate did not remain united. Four nations emerged out of British India: India, Pakistan, Bangladesh, and Sri Lanka. Tangentially connected to the Indian story are the histories of Burma (Myanmar) and Malaysia—all of which had formed a nearly singular unit within the British empire. After 1945, they all became nations-in-formation.

Despite the complex histories of these various holdings, the heart of the story remained India and Pakistan, both of which gained their independence in 1947; India became a Hindu state, Pakistan, a Muslim one. Each derived its existence from a mutual antipathy that had developed between the two groups during India's long exposure to Islam in the middle years of world history. Hence between 1945 and 1947, the Hindus and Muslims first won their freedom and then discovered they could not live with one another.

During World War II, the British had committed the subcontinent to war without consulting the Muslims or the Hindus. Mohammed Ali Jinnah, leader of the Moslem League, resigned from the National Congress and immediately demanded the creation of an independent Muslim state. Mahatma Gandhi led a new

nonviolent demonstration asking the British to leave India. To slow the protests, the British promised dominion status after the war. Hence, World War II had begun by laying a foundation for domestic autonomy and, perhaps, independence for India after the global conflict.

At the conclusion of World War II, the British sent a three-man commission to India to make recommendations. They returned home with a proposal that promised India autonomy, but only so long as it retained its membership within the empire. Both Muslim and Hindu leaders greeted these suggestions with doubt, but soon religious riots broke out that accelerated the political discussion. Direct intervention was needed to phase out the imperial system and create a new government as quickly as possible. Hence, the British sent a member of the royal family to the subcontinent, Lord Louis Mountbatten (1900–79), who concluded that Britain needed to withdraw entirely from India. The date was set for August 15, 1947.

Independence, however, did not reduce the hostility between Muslims and Hindus. Riots escalated until it became obvious that the two communities could not occupy the same nation at the same time. Partition of the country followed: the Muslims acquired East and West Pakistan as one stated separated by 2,000 miles, while the Hindus got the heartland of India in between. An orgy of bloodshed followed as minority populations caught in both states scrambled to migrate to a religious zone where followers of their faith would com-

Mahatma Gandhi. Courtesy of the Indian Embassy, Washington, DC.

pose the majority. During this great upheaval 8 million people were displaced and 1 million lost their lives. On January 30, 1948, a militant Hindu assassinated Mahatma Gandhi, forever silencing the one voice for unity and peace between the two communities.

Gandhi's death pushed Jawaharlal Nehru (1889–1964) forward to become the first President of India. A colleague of Gandhi in the National Congress, Nehru had become an advocate of Indian independence immediately after the Amritsar Massacre of 1919. On April 13, 1919, British Brigadier-General Reginald Dyer had stationed pickets throughout the city of Amritsar and banned all demonstrations or meetings for India's independence. Yet several thousand Indians used the open-air market in Amritsar to celebrate their spring festival on April 13. Dyer confused this celebration with an assembly of Gandhi's followers, marched in his troops, and ordered them to open fire. Dyer's men had occupied the only entry or exit into the market, offered no warning, and only withdrew after they exhausted their ammunition. Such brutality persuaded Nehru that the British had to leave.

Working with Gandhi, Nehru soon built himself a national reputation based on his charm, intelligence, and speaking ability. Arrested numerous times for organizing nonviolent demonstrations during the 1930s, nonetheless, Nehru was elected president to the National Congress four times prior to independence. The only difference between Nehru's and Gandhi's vision of India's future was that Nehru had studied Marx, accepted his vision of an industrial society, and therefore rejected Gandhi's advocacy of an ideal agrarian nation. Yet Nehru was not a Marxist; rather, he believed that a workable socialism could evolve out of a nonviolent political process.

Indian independence changed the National Congress into the Congress party, moved it from an opposition posture into the representative source of power, and authorized it to build a nation out of 400 million people, most of whom were poor and illiterate. Nehru became the Congress party's first prime minister and began a process of constructing a blend of socialism and nationalism into a nation-state built on India's numerous languages and ethnic groups. Under Nehru's leadership, India adopted the British model of government, with the presidency replacing the crown as a figurehead, representation in a legislature through multiple political parties, and national policy developed by a parliamentary cabinet.

Nehru patterned his economic policies after the British Labour Party with the state taking a commanding role in building the national economy as well as creating a social net for India's population. The state took over the development of heavy industry, raw materials and fuels, and transportation and the utilities, while the private sector supplied most consumer goods. Agriculture remained in the hands of the people, while the government encouraged the farmers to form voluntary rural cooperatives that could compete with private enterprises. This rural program, however, was only partially successful.

In terms of domestic politics, Nehru believed in the benefits of Western materialism. As stated above, he differed from Gandhi over the role of industry in India's future. Gandhi had opposed Western materialism as a source of spiritual corruption and advocated that India should rely instead on the productive potential of India's agrarian villages. Nehru argued for creating a wealthy industrial nation to provide for the comforts of its people by integrating the urban and rural sectors of the economy through an urban hierarchy. Accordingly, Nehru proposed to build a democratic society mixing voluntary cooperatives and privately owned enterprises with state-sponsored assistance in order to generate a condition of general prosperity. Additionally, Nehru refused foreign investment as much as possible because he believed that India's independence depended on self-reliance.

In the context of the Cold War, Nehru proposed a neutral position that placed India outside both the Soviet bloc and what the West called the Free World. Under his guidance, Nehru wanted to make India a leader among all nations in the Third World, one that did not want any part of the bipolar confrontation that the United States and the Soviet Union were constructing. The primary themes of Indian foreign policy were simple: anticolonialism and antiracism. Such a foreign policy had powerful appeal to nations-in-formation in Asia, Africa, and Latin America.

Yet Nehru's neutrality confused the United States, for India was a democracy with socialist tendencies that encouraged a free and open political process, but still did not actively oppose the Soviet Union. The United States wanted to mobilize all free and open societies into one camp to reject totalitarianism and communism, especially in the 1950s, when U.S. foreign policymakers spent millions of dollars on confronting international Marxism. India's insistence on self-reliance and independence raised concerns in Washington, as did Nehru's willingness to be on friendly terms with the People's Republic of China.

Meanwhile, Nehru's acceptance of Western materialism tempered his foreign policy with a significant quotient of national self-interest. India's relations with Pakistan entered an era of difficulty near the end of Nehru's life over disputed territory in Kashmir—a northern state in India that borders on Pakistan. Conquered in the late fourteenth century by Muslims, made part of the Mogul Empire in 1586, and populated by Islam's faithful, Kashmir became a disputed zone after 1947. Although Kashmir belonged to India, Pakistan, never surrendered its claim to this state.

Tensions between India and Pakistan increased over Kashmir during the early 1960s. One year after Nehru's death in 1964, war broke out between the two countries. India won a quick victory and retained the disputed territory, but Pakistan refused to relinquish its claims to it. Hence, Kashmir remains a hot spot in international affairs today and continues to exacerbate foreign relations between India and its western Muslim neighbor. Then, in 1971, anti-Pakistani riots erupted in East Pakistan, where a minority of Hindus lived. This led to a war in December 1971 that culminated in the creation of Bangladesh as an independent country, which reduced Pakistan's power to threaten India on two potential fronts. Hence, although India advocated a highly moral anticolonial, antiracist foreign policy, the Indians knew how to apply realpolitik (i.e., the end justifies the means) at home.

The loss of Nehru, a charismatic national leader, in 1964 raised some anxiety internationally. Yet Indira Gandhi (1917–84), Nehru's daughter, stepped into the political void left by Nehru. Although she shared her last name with Mahatma Gandhi, the two were not related. With the same qualities of charm, intelligence, and public oratory that had made her father famous, Indira Gandhi soon became the new leader of India.

A very strong-willed woman whose determination allowed her to dominate the politics of India in what many believed was a man's world, Indira Gandhi's style of leadership resembled that of her father's in some ways but surpassed it in others. Like her father, she embraced democratic socialism and neutrality in foreign affairs. Unlike her father, she was more willing to intervene in domestic affairs. She introduced national campaigns to reduce rural poverty by nationalizing banks, providing low-interest loans to peasants, and helping to finance cheap housing. She launched a land-redistribution program to give the propertyless a stake in society. And she reformed the electoral laws to give the vote to the poor. Finally, she introduced a birth-control program that reduced poverty by both limiting the number of children parents had to raise and decreasing the cost of the national social safety net.

During Indira's tenure in office, India did not deviate from its neutral foreign-policy stance. Hence, the country remained independent and detached throughout the Cold War and offered the world a third option with regard to issues concerning liberation from Western imperialism. India proved that a nation-in-formation did not have to fall into an alliance with either the United States or the Soviet Union to achieve freedom. Instead, a developing country could join the Third World seeking to cut a separate course through the anticolonial, antiracist waters of the post-1945 era.

Despite the fact that Indira Gandhi still faced massive problems, and that she, as well as her son, Rajiv Gandhi, died violent deaths at the hands of assassins, the Indian model of international conduct and domestic politics was not lost on the world. Hence, while Indian history followed its own separate course as militant Sikhs in the Punjab fought for an independent state, the island of Ceylon (now known as Sri Lanka) became a war-torn country between the Buddhists and Tamils, and radical Hindus gained political ground at home, India still stood for a third clear option in the Cold War: neutrality and independence.

Africa

Following World War II, the future looked uncertain for African nationalists. In their postwar conferences the victorious Allies seemed determined to hold onto some colonies as well as to gain new ones. France stood firm against decolonization, Great Britain somewhat less so. All the Allies continued to discuss their respective spheres of global influence while giving lip service to self-determination and independence. Meanwhile, the new United Nations was formed to serve as a secular, moral force in international relations.

India's independence from Britain in 1947 provided a model for Africa. In addition, Europe's postwar prosperity created liberal sentiments toward decolonization. Finally, the Cold War drew European attention away from Africa.

From 1945 to the early 1970s, popular enthusiasm for liberation from colonial governments unified the African people: *Uhuru* (Swahili for *freedom*) became a battle cry. Thus it happened that the 1950s and 1960s witnessed one African colony after another throwing off its colonial regime and struggling to create a modern nation-state. Some followed the republican model of Western countries, while others veered towards socialism or communism.

From four independent states in 1945, to more than forty by 1994, the African political landscape changed profoundly. Once in power, however, the new nationalist governments faced a perplexing combination of challenges. Fortunes have varied in the dozens of new nations. Close to the coast, the West African democracies have invested heavily in urban centers. Meanwhile, much of the interior of Africa remained mired in poverty.

The millennia-old African tendency towards localism, provincialism, and corporate lineage (sometimes called tribalism) generated one of the insoluble problems for the postwar nationalists. The European form of nationalism had relied on clear ethnic groups with a common language, religion, history, culture, and territory that could produce agreed-upon political boundaries and governments. In Europe, the most viable nations had been those in which these conditions flourished. In colonial Africa, however, no such homogeneous ethnicity, language, culture, history, or territory existed. Hence, no postcolonial African nation-in-formation had a sound political base from which to start.

Traditional African communities defined themselves through corporate kinship patterns, largely ignoring political borders. Consequently, ethnic factionalism and tribalism prevailed, retarding the formation of centralized governments to conduct political affairs. Many towns housed different kinship groups with a local history of antipathy. Special-interest groups such as military veterans, rural migrants, unskilled laborers, Westernized civil servants, Muslim devotees, and the wealthy elites had become politically active as rivals in the process of forming new states. Hence, these groups coexisted uneasily within the new African nations-in-formation.

In addition to having to try to overcome this intense localism/tribalism, the new rulers of the African states were unevenly trained in democratic government, and some of them lacked the skills to oversee representative institutions. Having inherited bloated bureaucracies from the Western imperial era, these new rulers tended to turn their new state administrative structures into systems of personal patronage, with relatives and cronies admitted to the new civil service regardless of talent. Often, these well-connected job seekers received employment as a payoff, or as the result of marriage relationships, and adopted a high-spending lifestyle without performing much work. Eventually, these new political bureaucracies developed into the highly centralized interest groups who used their positions of power to disenfranchise the bulk of the people who composed the national community.

Accordingly, during the entire postwar period, liberation movements and nationalist forces in the African urban centers and towns clashed repeatedly, sending shock waves into the countryside to generate continuing civil wars. Rebel opposition did not hesitate to use traditional animosities to mobilize African and colonial military forces. By the mid-1970s, half of the governments in Africa had come to power through coups d'état. From 1952 to 1985, fifty-four military coups were conducted in independent states. So even though the various new governments superficially followed the Cold War rivals down a "democratic," "parliamentary," or "socialist/communist" path, in practice, they tended to end up with simple, straightforward authoritarian rule.

An analysis of emerging nations in Africa requires a regional study. Beginning with North Africa, factionalism and violence underlay the liberation of Morocco, Algeria, Tunisia, Libya, and Egypt. From the time Napoleon set foot in North Africa, French immigrants had made an excellent living in the Mahgreb, in what would become the states of Morocco, Algeria, and Tunisia. Composing only 10 percent of the total population, their political and economic dominance alienated Arab and Berber natives who organized against them for the first time after World War II. The struggle was relatively nonviolent in Morocco and Tunisia, but in Algeria the Algerian National Liberation Front, in which women played significant roles, confronted 500,000 determined French troops in 1958. The battle of Algiers witnessed atrocities on both sides and did not end until France bestowed emergency powers on General Charles de Gaulle, the leader of the Free French during World War II, to arrange peace terms in 1962. De Gaulle promptly divested France of Algeria as well as other French colonial claims in Africa.

In contrast to Algeria, Egypt's fortunes as a nation seemed more promising because World War I had already broken the Ottoman Empire into several states, and Egypt had won technical independence from Great Britain in 1936. Yet Egypt remained a British ally in military affairs and foreign trade; therefore, Egypt tolerated Britain's control of its Suez Canal and its great Mediterranean port city of Suez.

At the time, two-thirds of the oil consumed by Europe passed through Suez, and Britain's hold on the waterway was vital. In 1952, a military coup forced out the last Egyptian monarch, the corrupt King Farouk, and installed President Gamal Abdul Nassar in power. In 1956, Nassar promulgated a single-party constitution and invited both the United States and the Soviet Union to compete for favor in Egyptian affairs. In that same year, Nassar nationalized the Suez Canal and then instituted his own form of socialism. This action sparked the 1956 Suez War, in which Britain, France, and Israel tried to seize the Canal Zone, and depose Nassar. But U.S. intervention on Egypt's behalf halted this effort and saved Nassar's regime.

On the domestic front, Nassar redistributed Egyptian land more equitably among peasants, opened up a national education system, federalized the most productive parts of the economy, and built the Aswan High Dam near the Nile's first cataract (rapids) to assure year-round irrigation and hydroelectric power. Even though he was an Egyptian nationalist with socialist tendencies, Nassar was a leading advocate for a pan-Arab state, which encouraged him to enlist Soviet aid and advisors in developing Egypt's economy and foreign policy. But Islamic socialism differed from both Western and Indian mixed economies (capitalism and socialism), or the more totalitarian Soviet style of communism, which allowed Nassar to impose his own stamp on Egypt. He died in office in 1967, shortly after the shock of defeat over the loss of the Canal Zone in the war that same year with Israel.

Under the leadership of Anwar Sadat, Egypt's president from 1970 to 1981, Egypt turned more to the West for investment, aid, and advice. In 1972, Sadat expelled Nassar's Soviet advisors not trusting their intervention in Egyptian affairs. Meanwhile, his capitalist measures removed the social net that Nassar had used to ease poverty and generated local discontent and a resurgence of Islamism after 1972. But his recovery of the Canal Zone during the Yom Kippur War with Israel (1973) temporarily assuaged these concerns and made Sadat a national hero. Yet, in 1977, when Sadat traveled to Israel and recognized its right to exist, he released a new shock wave of radical Islamism. A peace treaty between Egypt and Israel in 1979 proved too much to bear for fundamentalist Muslims, who now sought to create a reformist Islamic state under Muslim law. On October 6, 1981, Sadat died at the hands of Islamist fundamentalist assassins.

The North African country of Libya was a former colony of Italy that had fallen under French and British control after World War II until the UN granted it independence under a monarchy in 1951. Then Colonel Muammar al-Qadhafi overthrew Libya's king, Idris I, in a 1969 coup and instituted an Islamic socialist form of government with a commitment to Arab nationalism and opposition to Western programs. One of his first acts as ruler of Libya was to nationalize the majority of foreign petroleum assets, close British and U.S. military bases, and seize Italian and Jewish properties. For decades thereafter, Qadhafi used the proceeds of Libyan oil fields to finance that country's support of the Palestine Liberation Organization (PLO), interventions in the African countries of Chad, Sudan, and Uganda, and modernization at home. But since Libya's oil revenues have declined since the 1980s, due to the increasing global supplies and declining prices, so has Qadhafi's ability to support his revolutionary causes. Hence, he has toned down his support of alleged international terrorist actions and sought to improve Libya's image in the West.

Algeria has also found prosperity through oil and natural gas from the time of its liberation from France in 1962 until the downturn in oil prices in the 1980s. But economic slowdown and the rise of Islamic funda-

Egyptian President Anwar Sadat shakes hands with President Jimmy Carter and Israeli Prime Minister Menachem Begin at the signing of the Egyptian-Israeli Peace Treaty on the grounds of the White House. March 26, 1979. Library of Congress, Washington, D.C. LC-U9-37435-13.

mentalism brought the Islamic Salvation Front (FIS), a dissident popular political organization, to victory in municipal elections in 1990. Then the FIS won political recognition on a national level by routing the National Liberation Front (FLN), the party that had won independence from France in 1962. Yet the military nullified these elections, and a political struggle erupted between the FIS and FLN that led to violence, with numerous atrocities on both sides, that continues to this day.

As in North Africa, factional fighting also characterized independence movements in West Africa, but it was checked initially by a charismatic, passionately nationalist, and Western-educated group of leaders. Combining the ideal of self-determination with a new appreciation of precolonial history and institutions, these leaders emphasized the virtues of national formation based on "negritude," or the claim that Africans have occupied a unique place in humanity's past. These leaders believed that Africans had valued the people far more than the land and therefore had a far better understanding of true democracy than their European counterparts. Paradoxically, however, while these same leaders appealed for support from all classes, wherever they succeeded, they largely ignored a major segment of West Africans—the vast pool of urban poor and unskilled laborers.

Urban civil servants, businesspeople, doctors, and lawyers in West Africa had been well trained in administration and management. These people wanted to put their skills to use for all their fellow citizens. The Gold Coast (later Ghana) provided the model and inspiration for liberation struggles against Great Britain. Guided by the thoughtful and legal-minded prime minister Kwame Nkrumah during the decade following 1947, Ghana nurtured a large and involved middle class that served as its base. Through grass-roots organization and media participation, Ghana finally won independence in 1957, with Nkrumah as president. The rest of Great Britain's African colonies, Nigeria, Sierra Leone, and Gambia, followed Ghana's example and were independent by 1965.

The French colonies of West Africa did not find the liberation process as smooth as did the English colonies. Several parties vied for power, the *Reassemblement Démocratique* and the *Démocratique Sénégalais*, while wealthy Africans feared the political aspirations of the poor. As public opinion expanded and strengthened the African electorate, the wealthy sided with the French who hoped to retain control of their holdings in Africa. Yet the alliance between the rich and the French proved to be ephemeral due to their contest to ultimately control the wealth of West and Equatorial Africa. Hence the rich among French colonial Africans came to terms with local democratic parties and their combined leadership persuaded France's President, De Gaulle, to grant independence to Senegal, Guinea, Benin, Togo, the Ivory Coast, and Cameroon by 1960.

In Central Africa, some 120 political parties in 1960, experienced the most violent factionalism. In the Belgian Congo (Kongo or Zaire), powerful African strong-men warred for dominance. They seized the opportunity to achieve self-rule in the 1960s when the Belgian colonial administration, having witnessed prolonged, expensive, and vicious struggles in Algeria, announced Congolese independence. The problem was that the Belgians had not taken the necessary steps to prepare the population through education and training to make them effective rulers. Native contenders to head the new state were Patrice Lumumba, who had Soviet support, Moise Tshombe, the darling of wealthy Belgian copper companies, and General Joseph Mobutu, head of the military and mercenary forces. Ultimately, Mobutu took power.

Since 1970, under native leadership, West and Central Africa did not create stable governments. Instead the populous has suffered through numerous military-civilian conflicts, and most of the countries have had more than their share of harsh dictators or autocratic generals. Even as the great capitals in Senegal and in the Ivory and Gold Coast states prospered through the intake of international investment and foreign aid, countries of the interior languished through neglect and mismanagement. Factions within the countries continued to fight over control of natural resources and argue over Cold War ideologies and Islamism. Famine and epidemics such as AIDS have only added to the misery. Ghana and Nigeria were two cases in point.

Nkrumah had accepted the presidency of Ghana in 1957 to great acclaim and optimism, but he allowed the country to deteriorate into a corrupt military autocracy. From the mid-1960s until today, one military coup has followed another, with the victors executing their predecessors by public firing squads. Similarly, the promising future of heavily middle-class, well-educated Nigeria vanished in the mid-1960s as military officers engineered a coup, leading to the temporary secession of the Republic of Biafra with tragic consequences. Since the 1980s, the country has undergone several more military coups.

As in West and Central Africa, in postwar East African liberation movements were generally victorious, but only after some struggle. They were epitomized in the late 1950s by Kenya's Mau Mau (Land Freedom Army) secret society, which attacked British colonists, a large number of whom had long monopolized the fertile highlands and adamantly opposed land redistribution programs. British-educated Kikiyu leader, Dr. Jomo Kenyatta, tried to implement land reforms while working to achieve independence. Nevertheless, displeased radicals of his tribe turned to terrorism. Somewhat exaggerated in media accounts, violence perpetrated by the Mau Mau led to a British crackdown and imprisonment of many Kikiyu, including Kenyatta. By 1963, however, Great Britain was ready to give Kenya independence and recognize Kenyatta as its first president.

About the same time, in British Tanganyika (present-day Tanzania) Julius Nyerere rose from a Catholic socialist group to gain independence for his

A UN soldier walks through the site of a Tutsi army operation. Over 400 Hutus were killed when the army opened fire on the 10,000 refugees. Thousands were crushed in the panic; many more were shot or macheted by the RPA. The 1994 genocide in Rwanda claimed over 800,000 lives, creating a refugee crisis that affected over 3 million. Photo by Paul Lowe/Panos Pictures.

AIDS

AIDS is an explosively dangerous disease that appears to have evolved from a virus that had long used wild African monkeys as a host. A sexually transmitted disease that may have jumped from monkeys to humans through a mosquito bite, AIDS creates a state of declining immunity to all other infections. Called Acquired Immune Deficiency Syndrome, AIDS exposes its victims to assaults by wide varieties of other pathogens that seek out hosts without sufficient resistance to fend off an infection. Human hosts infected with AIDS usually die from these secondary infections.

Among the most flexible of infecting agents, the AIDS virus has developed the capacity to adapt to its host's defenses. The way the AIDS virus does this is by manufacturing antigens (proteins or carbohydrates that stimulate the production of antibodies), which AIDS uses to neutralize the host's immune system. Also these AIDS antigens evolve as the host's body mobilizes its defenses and progressively overwhelms the host's capacity to fend off the erosion of its resistance.

The most recent in a long line of diseases to infect agricultural communities due to their abundant supply of readily available humans living in a sedentary setting, the AIDS virus first appeared in 1959 to take advantage of the people cultivating the soil in West Central Africa. Trans-mitted originally through sexual intercourse, AIDS has adapted in its travels from host to host through exchanges of bodily fluids other then semen or vaginal secretions. One example would be blood: AIDS has entered the medical blood supply and has traveled via blood transfusions as well as from mother to fetus during pregnancy. Now AIDS has left the African continent and sought out hosts worldwide.

Recognized as a new disease in the United States in 1981, this African infection revealed a new wrinkle in its history. Isolated initially as an infection experienced by the homosexual population of the U.S., little government funding went into AIDS research and treatment. Critics of the U.S. govern-ment charged that a general hostility to the "gay" community allowed the disease to spread and take root in a large number of hosts. Then when the AIDS virus entered the medical blood supply and crossed the lines of sexual preference through bisexual inter-course, heterosexual couples found themselves infected. Finally, in 1991, with the death of such prominent figures as Rock Hudson, a gay movie star, and the infection of basketball star, Earvin "Magic" Johnson, the U.S. government took the disease seriously.

To date, in the United States, more people have died from AIDS than the Korean and Vietnam Wars combined. What is true about the United States is also true about the world. AIDS has made an appear-ance in Europe, Asia, the Middle East, and Latin America. Like the United States, many of these cultural zones were slow to recognize the threat and the disease spread. Since then, however, new treat-ment strategies, combinations of drugs, and knowl-edge of the way the disease travels has sharply reduced the number of infections and deaths. But African countries that cannot afford expensive treatments have not been able to retard the spread of AIDS. Hence the number of people suffering from this virus has continued to grow.

Diamond, Jared, *Guns, Germs, and Steel: the Fate of Human Societies* (New York: W. W. Nor-ton and Company, 1999), 197, 199, 201, 205, 208. Henretta, James A., David Brody, and Lynn Dumeril, *America: A Concise History*, Third Edition (New York: Bedford and St. Martin Press, 2006), 966–67.

country. In contrast, anticolonial forces in neighboring Uganda never succeeded in identifying a common en-emy and remained politically fragmented after World War II. Meanwhile, an independent Ethiopia cheered the return of Emperor Haile Selassie during the war, but the people grew disappointed in his failure to re-distribute wealth or liberalize his autocratic rule. He lost touch with the economic and social problems of his country and was finally deposed in 1974 by a com-mittee of left-wing army officers.

Since 1970, the history of the independent coun-tries of East Africa has been particularly heartbreak-ing, with all of them experiencing economic and politi-cal difficulties through the devastation of drought, famine, or civil war. During the same time, the region underwent a resurgence of militant Islamism. Recur-ring drought in Sudan and Sahel since the 1960s has prompted vast population upheavals and relocation across borders and into refugee camps. Food provision and distribution has been inadequate despite interna-tional aid, and diseases have ravished the area. War-lords fought over the meager spoils, visiting horrific reprisals on anyone standing in their way. The new mili-tary leaders of Ethiopia experimented with socialist pro-grams, but the collapse of their Soviet ally in 1991 weak-ened their hold on the country, and the province of Eritrea successfully seceded in 1993. In Somalia the same combination of drought, famine, and clan war-fare caused such widespread starvation that the United Nations intervened in 1992 to mediate solutions. The UN forces were quickly withdrawn within three years, this after Somali warlords shot, mutilated, and publicly displayed the bodies of UN peacekeepers.

Meanwhile, Rwanda experienced the upsurge of a violent ethnic rivalry between the native Hutus and the Tutsis stemming from the nineteenth century, when the Tutsis, who dominated the colonial government, op-pressed the Hutu majority. With independence, Hutus gained power in 1973 and began persecuting Tutsis in retaliation. In the spring and summer of 1994, the Hutus decided to "cleanse" Rwanda of Tutsis and killed one half million. Yet when the Tutsi controlled Patriotic Front prepared to retaliate, 1.7 million Hutus fled to neighboring Zaire. There they stayed to starve in refugee camps while the United Nations struggled to resolve the problem through repatriation. Yet none of these Hutu refugees feel safe in returning home.

Similar civil wars continue in Sudan, Chad, the Congo, Angola, Mozambique, and Kenya and Tanzania. The central problem is that in the 1990s tribalism based on precolonial kinship networks that cut across national boundaries had regained political strength after the withdrawal of European authority. While Europeans were happy to impose borders on their holdings, they ignored the fact that many of their territorial claims had overlooked the corporate lineage systems the Africans had used to create their earlier states. Hence the boundaries of various colonies cut across many kinship groups and isolated them from one another. Also, coupled with single-party governments implemented by autocratic elites who captured control of the newly liberated African colonies, these divided ancient lineages were easy to exploit as they sought the restoration of their traditional command over the land. Hence, dictators and strongmen could take advantage of the fact that European nationalism linked culture, language, and self-determination with national boundaries, while African lineages sought to redress ancient injuries at the hands of their ethnic enemies.

Finally, in Southern Africa, white colonial governments—Dutch Afrikaner, and to a lesser extent, English and Portuguese—fought African nationalism most fiercely in the 1950s. In the Republic of South Africa, the Afrikaner and British ruling minority instituted a policy of racial *apartheid* (apartness) in which different racial and ethnic groups were physically separated into their own communities. Of course, the fundamental division was between whites and nonwhites (Bantu-speaking blacks like the Zulus and Southeast Asian and Indian "coloured"), which left nonwhites with the poorest housing, schools, health facilities, and jobs. Under this enforced segregation, interracial marriages were forbidden, and nonwhites had no voice in government. Over the years Western countries ignored this racial op-pression and continued in partnership with the South African economy and state, affording that country enormous prosperity and influence through which it suppressed guerilla opposition from within and protests from abroad.

Three decades of internal conflict in South Africa followed. In the 1960s, peaceful demonstrations and strikes against the cruelest of the apartheid laws provoked massive reprisals from the Afrikaner government—massacres of civilians, torture, detention without trial, assassination, and the infamous imprisonment of Nelson Mandela, the leader of the African National Congress, a moderate organization founded to promote the interests of the disenfranchised. Mandela languished in jail for a quarter century, while the Afrikaner ruling government banned the African National Congress (ANC), forcing its members underground.

During the 1970s, the violence escalated on both sides, with popular black leaders like Steven Biko dying suspiciously while in police custody in. Finally, the world community began to respond. Regionally, Angola and Mozambique sided with the guerillas, while one after another, the leading nations of the world divested themselves from the South African economy, leaving only the United States offering trade, aid, and investment to its government.

By the late 1980s, the world community soundly condemned apartheid, and the South African economy and government lay in crisis. In a bold move that won the Nobel Peace Prize, the new president of South Africa, a white man named F. W. de Klerk, released Mandela from prison, reinstated the ANC, and began to dismantle apartheid.

Free elections in 1994 placed Mandela in the presidency and De Klerk in the vice-presidency. As a unity president, Mandela and his current successor have started reforms in every sector, economic, political, and social, but they are hampered by the same problems facing every state in Africa, in addition to the deeply entrenched legacy of apartheid. Violence continues against both black and white residents of the Republic of South Africa.

In Southern Rhodesia (what is now Zimbabwe) in the mid-1970s, the small white elite in power broke with Great Britain in refusing to allow the black majority its rights. Racial guerilla warfare involving Rhodesia's mostly African neighbors (Mozambique, Malawi, and Zambia) persisted until Robert Mugabwe, the leader of the Sona liberation movement (a central African lineage) with British help, was elected President of the newly named country of Zimbabwe in 1980. Since then, his government has followed a mixed capitalist and socialist economic program that has left Zimbabwe plagued by attacks on white farmers to oust them from the best land.

Portugal's former colonies in Angola, Mozambique, and Guinea Bissau came out from under dictatorial colonial rule in the mid-1970s after a decade of insurgencies and in the wake of a Portuguese military coup against the Portuguese government itself. Conflict among capitalist, socialist, and communist sympathizers have kept these countries unsettled since that time.

Hence, Africa has undergone massive transition since World War II. The new nationalist governments once in power have faced a perplexing combination of challenges. Factionalism, tribalism, local colonial interest groups, massive poverty, illiteracy, the rise of militant Islamism, and perhaps most devastating, the spread of AIDS have denied the positive general consensus that nations need to achieve stability. Accordingly, every region in Africa has struggled to define itself based on local conditions. Unfortunately, only one thing is clear: the African people have been liberated from colonial rule.

The Middle East

As mentioned previously, the history of the Middle East and Africa overlap in North Africa where North Africans both belong to Africa geographically but to the Middle East culturally. Hence Middle Eastern history includes North Africa where basic cultural trends have often led to instability. For example, while a majority of Muslims accepted a commitment to the common goals of decolonization, modernization, and nation-formation, others preferred the purity of faith as originally proposed by the prophet Mohammed. At the same time, three other major events dominated this cultural region's imagination. The first was the appearance of Israel in territory sacred to Jews, Christians, and Muslims alike. The second was the increased importance of oil in the global economy. The third was the revival of Islamism as a primary political, social, and religious movement in this cultural zone.

As mentioned above, as well as in Chapter Thirty, France and Great Britain had granted Saudi Arabia, Egypt, Syria, Lebanon, and Iraq independence after World War I. Yet military obligations to both France and Britain had denied true autonomy in these Middle Eastern countries until political, military, and economic exhaustion from World War II completed the liberation process. Thereafter, France and Britain progressively withdrew allowing a series of states to claim the status of nations.

These states appeared in the following order: Saudi Arabia, Egypt, Iraq, Syria, and Lebanon (prior to 1945), Jordan (1946), Libya (1951), Morocco and Tunisia (1956), Algeria (1962), and Yemen, Oman, the United Arab Emirates, Qatar, Bahrain, and Kuwait (after 1971). But they were not true nation-states as yet since they lacked the internal coherence offered by an urban hierarchy, still comprised a predominantly rural or nomadic population, and had not developed a positive political consensus supporting national loyalty based on widespread urban skills (literacy, computation, and critical thinking). One thing they did share, however, was an intense antipathy for the new Jewish state of Israel.

From the Muslim point of view, the state of Israel represented a continued intrusion of European imperialism into land sacred to Islam. Founded in 1948, Israel ultimately emerged from a nineteenth-century effort by European Jews to find a homeland to escape increased anti-Semitism and racism in Europe. Called "International Zionism," the movement to form a modern Jewish homeland began with Theodore Herzl in 1897. He tried to create a new state by buying land in Palestine and facilitating immigration there of European Jews. Generating a small but significant population before World War I, these Jews won recognition from Great Britain in 1917 when the latter issued the Balfour Declaration promising the creation of a Jewish homeland. Yet, the vast majority of Palestinian Muslims in the area also wanted their own homeland, which forced the British to support a split Arab-Jewish mandate state under the authority of the League of Nations but occupied by the British during the 1920s and '30s.

In the years between the two world wars, more Jews continued to migrate to Palestine while the British failed to settle growing political and religious tensions in the area. In the mean time, Hitler's genocide against the Jews during World War II changed the situation in Palestine dramatically. International sympathy for the plight of Europe's Jews between 1939 and 1945 combined with a mass exodus of the survivors of the Holocaust caused millions of new refugees to immigrate to Palestine after 1945. British attempts to stop this process of Jewish immigration combined with a growing Palestinian fear that they were about to be displaced in their own homeland turned these territories into a zone of violence and terror. Continued conflict between the Jewish and Palestinian settlements persuaded the Zionist leaders that they needed to form a secret army—the *Haganah*. While the Haganah protected the growing Jewish population, the protracted confrontation between Palestinians and these European refugees convinced the British that they could not solve the problem. Hence they turned the whole matter over to the United Nations.

The UN's solution to the problem was to create two new states: Israel and Palestine in 1948. Meanwhile, all the new Arab countries in the Middle East refused to accept the UN resolution to create the Jewish state, which triggered the first Arab-Israel War in 1948–49. All of Israel's neighbors, Syria, Lebanon, Jordan, Egypt, and Saudi Arabia joined with the Palestinians to try to expunge this Jewish state from the region. But a determined Haganah managed to secure Israel's frontiers and drive off every attack. At the same time, the Haganah managed to expel most of the Palestinians from their adjacent territories, which enlarged the Jewish state but created a massive new problem that accompanied the exacerbated Muslim antipathy to the existence of Israel—a large population of displaced Palestinians in the region.

While many of these displaced—and outraged—Palestinians ended up in neighboring Arab states, they had no future there. Accordingly, they eventually formed the Palestine Liberation Organization (PLO) to try to recover their homeland. Hence, Israel won the battle, but had created a multilayered international struggle. First, no Arab country recognized Israel's right to exist. Second, the creation and expansion of the Jewish state had displaced millions of Palestinians who needed their own homeland. Third, a growing sense of nationalism and internationalism among Arab states had suffered a severe wound to its pride due to military defeat by a vastly outnumbered people. And fourth, the land on which Israel sat was sacred to three monotheisms—Judaism, Christianity, and Islam—all of which claimed rights of access.

From 1949–90, an uneasy and armed ceasefire existed in the area, one punctuated by wars in 1956, 1967, 1973, 1978, and 1982. Each time, Israel either gained more territory, successfully fought off attempts to recover lost ground, or occupied the soil of neighboring Arab countries. Only Anwar Sadat's recovery of the Canal Zone in the Yom Kippur War of 1973 revealed that Israel might lose ground on the battlefield.

Besides armed conflict, however, the Palestinian problem remains unsolved. A deep rage felt by these people has led to a long-standing guerrilla war against Israel that has only worsened whenever the Jewish state took more land through military action. Led by the PLO, with the support of radical splinter groups, militant Palestinians have repeatedly turned to violence, lashing out at the Israeli military and civilian populations alike. At the same time, occasional outbursts of civil disobedience on a massive scale, like the *intifada* (armed resistance) of 1987, have disrupted Israel's capacity to rule either its own territory or the occupied lands. Hence, the embattled state of Israel has found itself in the unenviable position of having to use the same oppressive, brutal techniques against the Palestinians that drove the Jews to create their homeland in the first place. This irony has not been lost on the Israelis.

While Israel has functioned as a center of ethnic and religious animosity in the Middle East, the Jewish state has also played a key role in the Cold War; Israel's existence has shaped the strategy of both superpowers. The Soviet Union chose to support the Arab position, which exacerbated the oppression of Jews throughout this multinational empire. The Soviet thinking was simple: the value of oil in the international economy outweighed both the value of Israel and the Jews at home; this led the Kremlin to form repressive, anti-Semitic domestic policies. At the same time, persecuting a Soviet religious community like the Jews, or any religious community for that matter, was consistent with a general antipathy felt by a Marxist state toward all people who might profess their first loyalty to God rather than to their country.

In contrast, the United States tried to support both sides: Arab and Israeli. This created an ambivalent strategic position for the U.S. in its Middle Eastern foreign policy. On the one hand, it was clear that the value of oil had increased the importance of the Arab states in the global economy. On the other hand, the strong ties between the Jewish community in the United States and Israel had produced a major commitment to the new Jewish state that became known as the Jewish lobby in Congress. This lobby was able to funnel billions of dollars in military and economic aid to Israel that ensured the survival of this new nation.

In the meantime, the role that oil played in the global economy changed the strategic value of the Middle East. By World War II, petroleum had become one of the most valuable global commodities. Used in the production of everything from synthetics to fertilizers, the demand for the by-products of oil is equaled only by the demand for high-octane fuels. Given the vast pools of oil available in and around the Persian Gulf, the global demand for petroleum-based-products has elevated the Middle East into a major economic powerhouse. Hence, oil-rich countries have gained a major diplomatic tool—the threat of cutting off the world's oil supply—to shape global politics.

Given this new diplomatic tool, the oil-rich states of the Middle East joined other oil-producing countries in the Third World to form a cartel named the Organization of Petroleum Exporting Countries (OPEC) in 1960. The idea was to regulate the global price of oil since Saudi Arabia, Kuwait, Iran, Iraq, and Venezuela alone generated 80 percent of the world's supply. Although foreign oil companies did not recognize OPEC at first, a subordinate branch of this organization, the Organization of Arab Petroleum Exporting Countries (OAPEC) made its presence felt in the 1973 Yom Kippur War. In order to force the United States and its Western Allies to take them seriously, OAPEC reduced the output of oil, which caused an economic shock wave in the global economy: the price on exported crude oil suddenly shot up. This created serious economic problems in the United States, Europe, Japan, and in the Third World. Hence, no one ignores OPEC or OAPEC any more.

Iran's role in the oil industry is a case in point as to how petroleum affected international politics. The Shah of Iran, Mohammed Reza Pahlevi (1919–80), replaced his father, Reza Khan, in 1941 under pressure from the British when Reza Khan's pro-Nazi tendencies proved too much for Great Britain. Mohammed Reza, however, satisfied Allied concerns during World War II, and the Pahlevi Dynasty survived into the postwar era. Under Mohammed Reza's rule, Iran then became one of the richest oil-exporting nations in the world.

For the most part a loyal ally of the United States, Mohammed Reza used oil to carry forward his plans for social and economic change within Persia. From 1945 to 1979, per capita income increased dramatically, a modern infrastructure laced Iran together, educational reform introduced Western ideas into Persian society, and the literacy rate brought Iran up to pre-industrial European standards. Yet, the oppressive nature of Mohammed Reza's regime, designed to impose his will on a country still under the influence of the ayatollahs (religious experts) and the mujtahid (Islamic guides) alienated Persia's poor. In addition, the influx of money generated by oil exports caused severe inflation, which further separated the poor of Iran from the middle class and the wealthy, who benefited from the shah's modernization program.

Among the discontented were a growing number of Muslims whose loyalty to the ayatollahs and the mujtahid would spell disaster for the shah's regime. Their religious resistance to the shah's program polarized the country and set up the overthrow of Mohammed Reza's government in an Islamic Revolution, which forecasted the power of the third major trend in Middle Eastern post-1945 history: Islamism. The new ruler of Iran, the Ayatollah Ruholla Khomeini (1900–89), redefined politics in Iran and its relationship with the United States.

The revolution led by the Ayatollah Khomeini represented a return to the religious fervor of pure Islam as envisioned by the prophet Mohammed. The emphasis on religious purity demanded by the ayatollah's fundamentalist Shiite worldview ran contrary to the very nature of modernization and the political ambitions of the shah and Iran's Sunni neighbors. The ayatollah's society would be guided by the divine inspiration of its leaders, who would mobilize the Shiites of Iran for a return to the original Islamic faith. As such, Iran would then spearhead a drive against agents of Western im-perialism, especially the "Great Satan," the United States, that would free the Muslim world from any taint of foreign influence. In fact, one of the first acts of the Khomeini regime was to attack the U.S. embassy in Tehran on November 4, 1979, take fifty-one members of its staff hostage, and demand the return of the shah, who had come to the United States for political asylum and treatment of his incurable cancer. Khomeini's militant followers held these hostages for the next fourteen months of President Jimmy Carter's presidency, laid a foundation for the election of Ronald Reagan, and awakened the United States to a new awareness of radical Islamism.

Trying to build a lasting state based on pure Shiite precepts, however, had to occur within the context of the modern world, as well as the situation of living next to Sunni neighbors. At first, the Ayatollah Khomeini found that his revolution required the destruction of the modern contaminants within his own state. He introduced new laws to restore Islamic values, set up a reign of terror to punish those who ignored his legislation, and executed people who had been loyal to the shah. Then he had to expand through warfare to restore religious purity among his misguided Muslim neighbors. If success followed the ayatollah's efforts, his revolution would have had the potential of sweeping the globe. Eventually, however, so much opposition developed against such a militant approach that the mounting number of opponents to Khomeini's regime frustrated his efforts.

The war with Iraq, for example, consumed the revolutionary energy of the ayatollah's movement. Lasting nearly a decade, 1979–88, the Iran-Iraq war trapped the ayatollah in a struggle he could not escape. Determined to destroy Saddam Hussein, ruler of Iraq, for impeding the divine purpose of the ayatollah's revolution, Khomeini refused to make peace. Squandering his nation's young men and resources, the ayatollah fought on with a blind faith in his mission.

Iran exhausted its reserves of modern equipment, while its revolution against modernization eliminated the possibility of rebuilding this Shiite state with external aid—especially from the United States. Simultaneously, as the war with Iraq dragged on, Iran's soldiers went into battle with fewer and fewer modern arms against a determined foe. Hundreds of thousands of ill-equipped Iranians died before the aging Ayatollah Khomeini finally agreed to a humiliating peace in 1988. As a result, the force of his revolution was broken, the ayatollah himself was near death, and an oil-rich Iran suffered shortages of food, fuel, and basic equipment.

These conditions naturally led the Iranians to reassess their situation. They realized they had to make

Poster of Ayatollah Ruhollah Khomeini (1900–89). After being exiled to Iraq in 1964 and France in 1978, the outspoken Shi'ite leader returned to Iran and declared an Islamic Republic in 1979 exercising ultimate authority. His conservative ideology opposed Western practices, and he developed a strong religious and political following over the years. The Ayatollah's rule was punctuateded by the hostage crisis in Iran and the Iran-Iraq War.

some adjustment to the modern world if Iran were to function as a nation-state in a global economy. Like the Soviet Union between 1921 and 1939, and the People's Republic of China between 1960 and 1972, Iran found itself trapped within its own ideological (in this case religious) boundaries. It had to create a form of peaceful coexistence while still maintaining its revolutionary vigilance. Only in this manner could Iran fit within the political structure of the twentieth century while retaining all three levels of jihad as the source of its internal coherence.

Although the Ayatollah Khomeini did not succeed in fulfilling the goals of his Islamic Revolution, the version of Islamism that it represented still proved to be a powerful force in the Middle East. In the spirit of earlier Muslim resurgence movements, many people throughout the Middle East want to return to the premodern, pure Islamic life that had motivated the prophet in the seventh century. This type of longing for purity within the faith is one of the most vital and powerful features of Islam, and it has animated reform movements periodically throughout Middle Eastern history.

Hence, the Ayatollah Khomeini's version of this resurgence, and its apparent lack of success, did not undermine the original impulse for religious reform. Khomeini's successors in Iran have not been tainted by politics; they still shape events in that country by trying to find the right mix between Islam and teleol-

ogy in a modern context. To the east and north of Iran, Islamism has found another fertile ground for development. In the former Soviet Union, some 40 million Muslims chafed under Marxist repression as did 30 million followers of Islam in The People's Republic of China. In these two communist states, persecution of all religions, including Islam, grew under the power of totalitarian reform imposed by Marxist governments that viewed religion as the "opiate of the masses." Hence Central Asia joined Iran as a fertile ground for radical Islamism.

Also, prior to its fall in 1991, the Soviet Union exacerbated radical Muslim feelings with an invasion and occupation of Afghanistan, timed to exploit the chaos that Khomeini's revolution had caused in Iran. Some scholars have argued that the Soviet Union wanted to extend its control over the oil fields to the south. Instead, the U.S.S.R. inspired an organized resistance that managed to receive aid and advanced weapons from the United States despite its radical Islamic tendency to agree with Khomeini that the U.S. was indeed "the Great Satan." Accordingly, a guerrilla-style war unfolded that dominated the landscape for nine years (1979–88). Tied to the end of the Cold War (see the next chapter), the failure of Soviet arms in Afghanistan left chaos in its wake. The victors launched a new Islamic reform movement based in Afghanistan that attracted discontented Muslims from all parts of the Middle East. Hence, Afghanistan became the headquarters for exporting a resurgent Islamic guerrilla army throughout the world. This army occupied the full attention of international observers as the target of their next attack remained unknown.

Latin America

Once again, Latin America experienced the second state of decolon-ization along a different time line than the rest of the Third World, as many new nations-in-formation sought to win and strengthen their autonomy. While the era 1945 to the present witnessed the completion of the process of decolonization for the rest of the Third World, Latin America had begun its drive for true independence in 1914. Freed from Spanish and Portuguese rule by 1826, except for Cuba and Puerto Rico (1898), the Latin American countries did not achieve full sovereignty until well after World War I. Consequently, the beginning of the twentieth century set the stage for emerging nation-states in the Hispanic regions of the Americas.

As the twentieth century unfolded, the developing states of Latin America continued to struggle with how to wrest control over their own natural resources—such as mineral and agricultural wealth—from domination by Europe and North America. Latin American states wanted to assert their own national authority, even as they tried to emulate the industrial giants of Europe and North America by acquiring modern technology. Since most of the capital and expertise for industrial advancement remained with European or U.S. banks and companies, this task proved difficult for the elites in Mexico, Brazil, and Chile as they sought modernization after 1900. Ironically—and tragically—world events during the next half century created opportunities for economic and political development in these countries that were almost unimaginable just a few decades earlier.

Both world wars and the ensuing Cold War created a diplomatic space that allowed Latin American states to develop more national spirit as well as some control over the pace and direction of their domestic economies. Yet the single greatest influence on Latin America after 1900 was the rise of the United States as both a world superpower and the dominant power in the Western Hemisphere. In addition to the patterns already mentioned, a demand by the Latin American people for more direct participation in their political life also arose. This demand sometimes appeared as a call for reform, and other times as a call for revolutionary change in places as diverse as Cuba, Nicaragua, and Chile.

The era roughly from World War I to the end of World War II saw a significant rise in local manufacturing in countries such as Argentina, Brazil, and Mexico. The world wars disrupted the flow of industrial goods from Europe, which encouraged local capitalists to start factories to supply the domestic markets with shoes, clothing, tools, and processed foodstuffs. Latin American cities such as Rio de Janeiro in Brazil, Mexico City, and Buenos Aires, the capital of Argentina, became centers of industrial manufacturing by the 1920s. The collapse of commodity prices during the Great Depression (1929–39) also fueled this trend, as exports such as coffee, sugar, beef, tobacco, and copper fell drastically, both in quantities and in prices. In some cases, these exports did not recover until World War II began. By the late 1920s, industrialists in Brazil began demanding national policies that supported manufacturing. Under the regime of Getulio Vargas (1930–45), the Brazilian government responded with laws that encouraged manufacturing as well as regulated working conditions for the country's emerging urban working class.

Population growth in national capitals and other industrial hubs accompanied these changes, as workers left the haciendas and ranchos of the countryside and poured into cities. One can trace this process back to the late nineteenth century in Mexico and Argentina, but it certainly accelerated in both countries in the decades after 1900. These new urban workers, encouraged by recent immigrants from Italy, Germany, and Spain who brought a European trade union tradition to their new countries, began demanding higher wages and decent working conditions. As the number of laborers grew and factories began to assume more economic importance, this urban industrial working class also became a potent new political force, one to be reckoned with in later decades.

In addition to popular movements, revolutions, and urbanization, the twentieth century saw the region's relations with global economic forces, especially the United States, intensify. A brief look at the relationship between the United States and Latin America over time will reveal the recent history of this multifaceted region within the larger context of world developments.

In the 1890s, U.S. interest in Latin America grew dramatically, as companies sought new markets for their ever-growing industrial production. Companies from the United States began aggressively to compete with, and then supplant, British influence in Latin American countries that had looked to Europe for guidance for a century. World War I intensified this process, as did the worldwide depression. Both Germany and Great Britain retained considerable influence in Latin America, however, until World War II completely shattered European economies for an extended period. In the 1940s, American companies consolidated their dominance, as American-made products flooded into the region without any real competition. This tide held for a generation or so, until global economic changes provoked by the oil crises of the 1970s began to shift investment capital, and American companies began to experience formidable foreign competition. Interestingly, these challenges came not only from Europe, but also from new leaders of the global economy such as Japan and South Korea. Similarly, Asian investments, as well as new products, have flowed into Latin America increasingly over the last three decades.

The key event that thrust the United States into Latin American affairs was the Spanish-American War (1898–99). This odd conflict developed when Cuban patriots tried at long last to shake off Spanish control. Long a declining European power, Spain desperately tried to hold on to its last major New World colony by brutally suppressing the Cuban independence movement. Drawn by large U.S. investments in Cuban sugar and tobacco plantations and encouraged by sensational newspaper coverage of the war, which put the Spanish in the worst possible light, citizens of the United States demanded that their government come to the aid of the beleaguered Cuban revolutionaries. When an American warship, the USS *Maine*, exploded in the harbor at Havana, killing hundreds of sailors, the United States moved toward war. Only much later did investigations reveal that the ship sank because of an internal explosion, most probably a terrible accident in the boiler room. Nevertheless, the war became a convincing demonstration of U.S. naval and military power, as U.S. fleets destroyed the Spanish navy, invaded Cuba and the Philippine Islands, and decisively ended the war within months. The Spanish-American War thrust the United States onto the world stage, and it created an instant empire. In the Caribbean, President Theodore Roosevelt then solved the age-old problem of oceanic travel around Latin America by encouraging the Panamanians to form a new government, and then negotiating the right to build a canal across the new country. Completed in 1914, the Panama Canal assured U.S. control of shipping, both military and merchant marine, which determined what nations had access to the region for the next half century.

At virtually the same moment as these military adventures, the United States began to compete with the British for markets and raw materials in Latin America. Additionally, several countries experienced internal political problems that encouraged aggressive U.S. presidents, such as Theodore Roosevelt (1901–09) and Woodrow Wilson (1913–21), to intervene in Latin American affairs. The Caribbean especially suffered from poorly run local governments which badly mismanaged their affairs, and U.S. officials saw an opportunity to expand their influence. Roosevelt grandly proclaimed the Caribbean as "an American lake," and warned European nations that the United States would police the region, permitting no interference from them. Needing U.S. support in 1914, the British backed off from posing any challenge to what became known as the Roosevelt Corollary to the Monroe Doctrine, which had long ago warned European nations to stay out of the Western Hemisphere. U.S. presidents dispatched military forces to occupy Latin American nations on dozens of occasions from 1902 to the 1930s to enforce what critics called Teddy Roosevelt's "Big Stick" policy. These interventions, while resulting in some positive actions, caused many in Latin America to regard the United States as a threat to local autonomy.

Relations improved when Teddy Roosevelt's cousin, President Franklin D. Roosevelt (1933–45), tried a new approach to countries to the south with the "Good Neighbor" policy in the 1930s and 1940s. FDR promised to curtail interventions, help with economic development, and recall U.S. military units stationed in states such as Nicaragua. Roosevelt not only wanted better relations with Latin American governments, but he also saw the need for potential allies as another war loomed in Europe. His thinking bore fruit as almost all the governments in Latin America supported the Allied cause in World War II. For example, Brazilian soldiers fought in Italy with American units against the Nazis, and Mexican pilots flew combat missions in the Pacific against the Japanese.

The Cold War ushered in a new phase in U.S.–Latin American relations. Determined to check the spread of Soviet influence, U.S. policy supported any ally, and virtually any government, that rejected the Soviets. This put the United States in the uncomfortable position of supporting dictatorial and corrupt regimes that suppressed political participation, imprisoned and murdered political opponents, and generally embarrassed the United States in the court of world opinion. When popular rebellions against such repressive government broke out, the U.S. usually supported the tyrants, as long as they continued to give lip service to supporting democracy over socialism.

Additionally, agents of the U.S. Central Intelligence Agency (CIA) acted to help such dictatorial clients maintain their control with advice, funds, and training. Thus, in 1954, the CIA helped the Guatemalan army overthrow a democratically elected president who supposedly became a threat when he invited Eastern European technicians to help develop Guatemala. U.S. intervention in Latin America was, of course, an outcropping of the global conflict between the two superpowers in the decades after World War II, for the Soviets followed much the same policies in Asia and Africa. Yet Latin Americans tended to see such Cold War actions as old-fashioned imperialism by the U.S. Even well-intentioned U.S. initiatives, such as the Alliance for Progress and the Peace Corps, initiated by President John F. Kennedy in the 1960s, did little to change Latin American public opinion of the United States. As the Cold War thawed, and then concluded in the 1980s and 1990s, U.S. policy towards Latin America became erratic at best. In the 1980s, President Ronald Reagan revived the old interventionist policy by sending covert military and economic aid to those trying to overthrow governments in Central America. Since then, the attention of successive U.S. presidents has been drawn away from Latin America by global crises in Africa and Eurasia.

Mexico and Brazil perhaps offer the best case studies of the successes and failures in twentieth-century Latin America. These two important countries contain the three largest cities in the region (Mexico City, São Paulo, and Rio de Janeiro), the largest urban working classes and political parties, and the strongest domestic economies. They also have had the closest and most contentious relations with the United States. While events in countries such as Argentina, Peru, Chile, and Cuba also carried great significance over the last century, Mexico and Brazil provide the broadest patterns for regional interpretation.

The tensions and problems discussed earlier finally exploded in Mexico in 1910–11. President Porfirio Díaz delivered on his promises to make great economic progress, modernize the country, and rebuild the capital, but few of the country's impoverished peasants or disenfranchised urban factory workers experienced better living conditions. Indeed, during his increasingly dictatorial rule, the opposite occurred. Rural people had their land taken by government decree; great landowners consolidated their power, then slashed wages and did nothing when drought and crop failure drove up basic food prices. In the cities, Díaz's police ruthlessly suppressed labor organizations, harassed and arrested even moderate reformers, censored newspapers, and offered cut-rate prices to foreign companies wishing to exploit Mexico's mineral and petroleum wealth. In his seventies, Díaz proposed running for another six-year term as president, but a broad coalition of middle-class reformers, labor unionists, socialists, land reformers, and those simply unable to bear more of Díaz's autocratic heavy-handedness rose in a series of loosely coordinated and chaotic revolts across the country.

Led in name by Francisco Madero, the revolts had some early success, managing to frighten the old dictator into fleeing the country in 1911. Madero returned from exile in Texas triumphantly and tried to create a reform-minded government in 1912. Undermined by friends and foes alike—including severe meddling by foreign ambassadors in Mexico—he failed. Madero was murdered by the elements of the Mexican army and replaced by General Victoriano Huerta. With the support of the United States and Great Britain, Huerta tried to reimpose a Díaz-style dictatorship, which triggered an all-out revolution that roared to life in 1913. Tragically, Mexico experienced almost a decade of fighting that ruined the country economically and resulted in the deaths of a million people.

The survivors of this great revolt formed new administrations in the 1920s and 1930s, ones dedicated to rebuilding the country and creating reforms that would empower Mexicans to take control of their own economic and political destinies. Successive national leaders such as Alvaro Obregón, Plutarco Calles, and especially Lazaro Cárdenas from 1934 to 1940, passed new legislation and issued decrees to redistribute land to landless peasants, restructure labor codes, and assert Mexico's independence from the control and influence of foreign companies and governments. The most dramatic example of this occurred in 1938 when President Cárdenas seized oil properties controlled by foreign companies in the midst of a serious labor dispute. When the companies refused to accept an arbitration settlement, Cárdenas acted decisively.

The Mexican government reformed the seized oil properties into a new state-run corporation, PEMEX, which dominated the exploration, refining, and sale of petroleum products in Mexico for the next half-century. Mexico enjoyed an oil-led economic boom based on escalating oil prices in those decades. More important, the president and political leaders had successfully defended Mexican workers against exploitation by foreign companies. Mexico and the companies eventually reached a settlement on claims for the seized properties.

In the 1920s, Mexican political leaders worried about political stability and how best to prepare the next generation of national figures to guide the country. These concerns led to the formation of a national political party in 1929 to unify Mexico, impose political conformity and provide for the orderly succession of power, especially at the presidential level. This new national party went through several evolutions and name changes over the next fifteen years, emerging as the *Partido Revolucionario Institucional* (PRI) by 1946. The party created the so-called revolutionary family in Mexico, and attempted to bring all sectors of the country into its family. The PRI certainly was inclusive and nationalistic, and it managed to keep control of local and national politics until 2000.

The PRI championed dynamic industrialization and job growth, as well as land and educational reform in the early years. After Lazaro Cárdenas left office in 1940, successive administrations focused more on economic development, leaving reform of all varieties simmering on the back burner of Mexican national politics. Since the demand for oil grew exponentially during these decades, Mexico generated new industries, jobs, and increased social welfare. Yet large segments of the population, most notably rural workers and those with marginal occupations in the big cities, survived on bare subsistence incomes, particularly susceptible to downturns in the economy and other disasters that stalk all nations.

The PRI-controlled congresses and presidents managed to keep prices of basic commodities low in the decades after World War II through various subsidy programs, but when the price of oil fell drastically in the late 1970s, prices for corn and cooking oil, as well as subway and bus fares soared. Nature then dealt Mexico a serious blow when a massive earthquake struck the center of the country, killing thousands and paralyzing public life in 1985. Faced with demands for change, the PRI responded with electoral fraud to keep itself in power in 1988 and 1994, and the party tried to intimidate its opponents with violence or co-optation. Riddled with defections and internal power struggles, the PRI finally fell from power with the loss of the presidential election of 2000.

The victor in that momentous contest, President Vicente Fox, the candidate of the National Action Party (PAN) was quick to initiate some serious reforms, but has been stymied by a congress still largely controlled by the PRI. The PAN's inexperience in promoting a cohesive and inclusive national vision for change also hurt the Fox administration. For its part, the PRI is far from finished, and most observers expect it to play a significant role in Mexico for years to come. Another important—and positive—point is the fact that Mexico has avoided the crisis of civil war and intervention since the end of the revolutionary period in the 1920s.

An interesting counterpoint to Mexico's struggles during the last several decades was the attempt by the leaders of the nations of North America to create a common market-type organization uniting Mexico, the United States, and Canada. The North American Free Trade Agreement (NAFTA) became a reality in 1994 and has produced some dramatic changes in all three countries. While it is too early to judge its overall effect, some striking patterns have emerged, signaling, perhaps, the future of interregional trade. Large companies in the United States have begun shifting high-paying jobs to Mexican factories, displacing workers at home but creating industrial jobs, albeit with lower pay rates, in Mexico. At the same time, American agricultural companies have flooded the Mexican market with high quality and lower priced grain and food products, severely damaging those sectors of the Mexican economy. With the inclusion of Chile, and perhaps other Latin American countries in the near future, NAFTA could very well reshape markets and industries throughout the Americas.

Tellingly, Brazil and its southern neighbors, Argentina, Paraguay, and Uruguay, are negotiating to create another such market organization, MERCOSUR. Central American countries have formed a similar organization called CAFTA. Where this will lead the interregional, even global, economy in the decades to come remains open to speculation.

Meanwhile, Brazil experienced many of the same issues as Mexico during the twentieth century, but unlike Mexico did not have to deal with a powerful neighbor on its border that could easily intervene militarily or affect its national economy. Occasionally tensions did arise between Brazil and Argentina, but relations there have stabilized, if not become exactly friendly, through most of the century. Brazil's main issues revolved around expanding its export sector, acquiring industrial technology to build a manufacturing base in the country, and finding the right political balance to ensure tranquility and popular participation in politics. The key moments for these changes occurred between the 1930s and 1960s, as Brazil made the leap into full-scale industrialization, while retaining its position in export markets for goods such as coffee, cotton, soybeans, and orange-juice concentrate.

Getulio Vargas and Juscelino Kubitschek stand out as the key figures in this progression. Vargas came to power after the chaotic election of 1930, which he and his party should have won. The tainted victory instead went to a combination of powerful coffee-producing states that had formed a coalition to practice election fraud out of fear that Vargas might not protect their interests. But the powerful Brazilian military, urged Vargas on, voided the dubious electoral outcome, and installed Vargas as provisional president. He then won a presidential term in 1934 and controlled power into the 1940s, despite the fact that he had violated constitutionally determined term limits. To retain power, therefore, Vargas had to suspend the democratic process.

Nevertheless, while in power, Vargas proved to be a resourceful and imaginative leader. In his push for change and modernization, he vigorously put forward educational reforms, new labor codes, the adoption of new technologies, and critical infrastructure developments throughout the country. He put the unemployed to work building dams, bridges, roadways, and airports. He spoke to his fellow citizens regularly on a new national radio network he had created. When World War II broke out, he acted with caution, unsure of an eventual Allied victory. When the United States approached him for support in 1942, he brokered a deal in which American companies supplied Brazil with expensive technology in return for Brazilian participation on the Allied side. One division of Brazilian soldiers fought alongside Allied forces in Italy, helping to defeat fascism there, and returning home as heroes.

If Vargas had followed constitutional limits and stepped down in 1938 when his term ended, his legacy would be undeniable. But, intoxicated with power, he felt that only he could continue the pace of change and reform. Given the opportunity by a failed Soviet-inspired revolt in the northeastern part of the country, he closed congress, censored the press, and canceled national elections. Proclaiming the New State, a local variant on the then-popular European fascism of the 1930s, Vargas continued his administration until returning Brazilian officers, some of them wounded in the defense of freedom in Italy, challenged his quasi-fascist regime. Although Vargas achieved great successes, he failed to support the constitution and governmental system he had helped create. After he was forced out of office in 1945, he returned to a call for open elections. The Brazilian people retained a fondness for him and, incredibly, gave him a stunning electoral victory in 1950. His health declined soon thereafter and, mired in political problems and personal depression, he took his own life in 1954. Nonetheless, Vargas put Brazil on the path to modernization, opened political participation in the country, and helped to create a sense of national identity for his fellow citizens.

Vargas's successors, notably Juscelino Kubitschek (1955–60), continued the country's economic development. Kubitschek envisioned a new capital for Brazil on the high western plains, a thousand miles from oceanfront cities such as Rio de Janeiro. Brasilia, with its imaginative architecture, modernistic housing, and sweeping vistas, captured the attention of the world press and its own citizens. A sense of optimism, creativity, and joy swept the country over the next decade. Yet economic problems and political paralysis among squabbling political parties plunged Brazil into crisis in 1964.

The Brazilian military, fearing the spread of Cuban and Soviet influence in the call for land reform and increased political participation, overthrew President João Goulart, established a military dictatorship, and ruled the country through a series of appointed generals for the next twenty years. The generals encouraged international investment, borrowed against the country's future, and enjoyed some successes, yet none of them demonstrated any special aptitude for governing. As the Cold War wound down in the 1980s, the need for a military government passed as a new generation of Brazilian politicians emerged. In 1985, elections produced a civilian president and an independent congress.

Over the last two decades, Brazilians have struggled with many of the same problems afflicting other Latin American countries. Despite some efforts to control birth rates, Brazil, with almost 180 million people, and Mexico, with nearly 100 million, have led a re-gional population surge since 1945. Obviously, more people require more jobs, houses, schools and clean water. Throughout the Americas, including the United States, these issues provoke concern and fear. The good news is that at the end of the twentieth century, many countries had democratic governments and had developed political parties and new constitutions. Yet many of these governments inherited massive debts, run up by military regimes in the 1960s and 1970s, and must use a large portion of their annual budgets for debt repayment, mostly to European and U.S. banks. Regional free-trade agreements may be of some help, but NAFTA's early results are mixed. Still, the prevailing mood in most areas is one of cautious hope, and there is a sense that whatever issues they face, Latin American nations are now truly nations, able to chart their own destinies.

In contrast to the histories of Mexico and Brazil stands that of the Caribbean island of Cuba, where Marxism served as an ideology of liberation and fostered the rise of a Soviet-style government under the direction of a strong-willed dictator. Like those in Russia and China before it, the Marxist regime that built a foundation in Cuba did so in an environment contrary to Karl Marx's urban-industrial vision. Yet unlike the cases of Russia and China, Cuba's Marxist revolution took place in an extremely young and relatively unformed ethnic and cultural community.

Cuba began its existence as part of the Spanish empire after the Columbian Exchange had eliminated the original native culture, comprised of Arawak Indians, through a series of epidemics. Consequently, the social structure that emerged on the island was one imported from abroad. Consisting of a relatively sparse Spanish, African, mestizo, and mulatto population, this new Cuban social structure reflected the use of the island as a strategic naval outpost to secure the flow of silver to Cadiz, the central port of the Habsburg Dynasty in southern Spain during the sixteenth and seventeenth centuries. Then, as the flow of precious metals slowed, Cuba developed an agricultural economy based largely on ranching and small-scale commercial farms. Next, sugar cane began to change the local economy, but it did not come to dominate the island's exports until the late nineteenth and early twentieth centuries. Between 1792 and 1821, the African population in Cuba grew from 60,000 to 250,000, as the French colonies on Haiti and Santo Domingo fell to a slave rebellion initiated by François Dominique Tous-saint L'Ouverture and ceased to be a major exporter of sugar to Europe (see Chapter Twenty-four). Finally, sugar became the single most important crop in the Cuban economy in the twenti-

Fidel Castro (1926–) and Nikita Khrushchev (1894–1971) at the United Nations, 1960. Part of: *New York World-Telegram* and the *Sun Newspaper.* Photograph Collection, credit: Library of Congress, Washington, D.C. LC-USZ62-127229.

eth century when the United States became the island's primary market.

The United States came to dominate the Cuban economy as a result of the Spanish-American War of 1898. Mentioned briefly above, the Spanish-American War ushered in an era during which the United States replaced Great Britain as the chief economic partner of Latin American regimes. Yet nowhere is the role of the United States' domination of a new state more obvious than in Cuba. Unlike other Latin American countries, however, Cuba was still a colony of Spain when the Spanish-American War broke out.

A war of independence had begun in Cuba in 1895. The intervention of the United States on the side of the Cuban rebels in 1898 liberated the island from Spain, but it also captured the Cuban market for the United States. The so-called Platt Amendment of the Cuban 1901 Constitution illustrates this point. Spawned in the United States, the Platt Amendment first stipulated that Cuba could not make any treaty with a foreign power that might impair Cuban sovereignty. Second, it specified that Cuba could not contract any loans with a foreign state without the interest rate being repayable by local revenues. Third, it granted the United States the right to intervene in Cuban affairs to secure life, liberty, and property as part of the Cuban government's duty to ensure domestic tranquility. Fourth, and finally, it allowed the United States the right to lease land to establish coaling stations for the U.S. navy.

Following the ratification of the Platt Amendment, and the 1901 Constitution, the United States created a tariff pact with the new Cuban government that gave sugar from the island preference in the U.S. market

and ensured Cuban consumption of U.S. manufactured goods. This new economic arrangement transformed Cuban agriculture by placing a heavy economic advantage on highly centralized Cuban sugar plantations that soon replaced smaller local farms and ranches. The result was the development of an island economy heavily dependent on U.S. prosperity. The growth of these large-scale, highly centralized sugar-producing farms concentrated economic power in the hands of fewer and fewer landowners. The number of sugar mills declined from 1,190 in 1877 to 207 in 1899, and then again to 161 in 1956. Of these 161 centralized mills in 1956, investors from the United States controlled 90 percent. In addition, by 1959, 28 of the largest sugar cane producers owned 3,458,000 acres and rented an additional 1,523,990 acres, or 20 percent of all of the arable land in Cuba. As a result, 40 percent of the sugar crops, and 54 percent of the refining capacity of Cuba's sugar mills fell directly under U.S. control, and another 85 percent of the small sugar farms in Cuba had to use the U.S. grinding capacity of these highly centralized mills to sell their sugar.

After World War II, many local Cuban intellectuals came to believe that to achieve true sovereignty as a nation-state, Cuba somehow had to break the hold of the United States on Cuba's market system. The first regime that tried specifically to achieve this feat belonged to Fidel Castro. Doing so, however, placed Castro squarely in the camp of the Soviet Union and made Cuba a pawn in the Cold War.

In the first half of the twentieth century, there was considerable political unrest in Cuba. Among the student protestors active in the 1940s was a young man named Fidel Castro Ruz (b. 1926). On July 26, 1953, he led an unsuccessful raid against a government military barracks, during which he was captured, imprisoned, and exiled to Mexico. In exile, he assembled a small revolutionary movement that returned to Cuba in 1956. Met with sharp resistance, most of the original force that landed with Castro died in combat, but several dozen of his guerillas took up hiding in the Sierra Maestra Mountains in close proximity to discontented local farmers. Following a strategy call "Blanquist" by Marxists, Castro developed a small, resolute, well-organized cadre of men who never exceeded two thousand, but who managed to survive, exploit local successes, and firmly plant themselves in the countryside. Castro's goal was to capture power and free Cuba from the shadow of the United States.

Building on repeated successes achieved by small bands of hit-and-run forces, Castro convinced these local farmers to support his movement, which grew into a serious threat to the regime of General Fulgencio

Batista, one solidly backed by the United States, which, in the interest of the Cold War, turned a blind eye to Batista's human rights violations. Within two years, Castro gained control of the Cuban countryside and had become strong enough to attack Batista's forces openly in the major cities. By 1959, Batista's regime collapsed, and Castro took the reins of power.

Once in power, Castro began a major restructuring of the Cuban economy. He rejected any form of democratic process, imposed a totalitarian regime, and imported advisors from the Soviet Union to help him repel U.S. influence. His goal was to create an independent Cuban state free from U.S. domination, but to do so, he had to subordinate Cuban foreign policy to Soviet ambitions. Accordingly, to defeat one superpower during the Cold War, Castro found himself trapped in the shadow of the other.

As a result, the Cuban Revolution of 1956–59 achieved a sharp break with the U.S. economy, but at the same time, Cuba became tied to the future successes and failures of the Soviet Union. Hence, Cuba became an outpost for a Soviet presence in the Caribbean—only ninety miles from the Florida coast—which led to numerous confrontations with the United States; it also led the formation of a Cuban exile population in Florida. In 1961, the United States supported an exile Cuban force that planned to invade Cuba and overthrow Castro and establish a democratic government. The invasion force landed at the Bay of Pigs, but promised air and naval support from U.S. forces never materialized and the would-be liberators were slaughtered by Castro's men. Then, in 1962, the United States and the Soviet Union went to the brink of nuclear war after U.S. spyplanes revealed that the Soviet Union had stationed more than forty nuclear missiles in Cuba, threatening the U.S. Ultimately, the Soviet Union agreed to remove the nuclear weapons from Cuba in exchange for a U.S. pledge not to invade Cuba. Thereafter, open hostility between the United States and Cuba cooled, and as the Soviet Union waned in power, hints of potential talks between the American government and the Castro regime occurred periodically in the 1970s and 1980s despite several earlier attempts by the CIA to assassinate Castro. Finally, the collapse of the Soviet Union in 1991 made Castro's regime the only surviving member of the Soviet bloc in Latin America.

While the leadership of the eighty-year-old Castro remains intact, the future of his regime is open to question because there is no clear successor available to replace him. Furthermore, with the loss of foreign aid from the Soviet Union, the Cuban economy is in severe need of reform. How Cuba will fit into the Latin America marketplace while maintaining its aloofness from the United States, poses a major question. Although the survival of the existing regime is problematic, Castro nonetheless did achieve his goal: he broke the U.S. hold on the Cuban economy.

Recently, U.S. policy has largely ignored Latin America except when confronted by financial crises, such as Mexican and Argentine economic woes in the 1990s. On such occasions, the U.S. tried to secure political stability through arranging international loans. American policymakers have shifted their focus to events in Asia and the Middle East, much to the dismay of leaders throughout Latin America. Hence, the so-called war on terrorism has driven Latin America to the back burner of U.S. foreign affairs. Accordingly, the end of the Cold War has probably made the United States a good, if disinterested, neighbor in Latin America after all.

Suggested Reading

China

Brugger, Bill and David Kelly, *Chinese Marxism in the Post-Mao Era* (Palo Alto, Calif.: Stanford University Press, 1990).

Clubb, Edmund O., *Twentieth Century China,* Third Edition (New York: Columbia University Press, 1978).

Dittmer, Lowell, *China's Continuous Revolution: The Post-Liberation Epoch, 1949–1981* (Berkeley, California: The University of California Press, 1987).

Guillermaz, Jacques, *A History of the Chinese Communist Party,* translated by Anne Destenay (New York: Random House, 1972).

Schram, Stuart R., *The Thought of Mao Tze-tung* (Cambridge: Cambridge University Press, 1989).

Tien, Hung-mao, *The Great Transition: Political and Social Change in the Republic of China* (Palo Alto, Calif.: Stanford University Press, 1989).

Japan

Brines, Russell, *MacArthur's Japan* (Philadelphia: Lippincott, 1948).

Buckley, Roger, *Occupation Diplomacy: Britain, The United States, and Japan, 1945–1952* (Cambridge: Cambridge University Press, 1982).

Cohen, Theodore, *Remaking Japan* (New York: Free Press, 1987).

Dower, John, *Embracing Defeat: Japan in the sake of World War II* (New York: Norton, 1999).

Gordon, Andrew, ed., *Postwar Japan as History* (Berkeley: University of California Press, 1993).

Hane, Mikiso, *Eastern Phoenix: Japan Since 1945* (Boulder, Colo.: Westview Press, 1995).

Irokawa, Daikichi, *The Age of Hirohito: In Search of Modern Japan,* Translated by Mikiso Hane and John K, Urda (New York: Free Press, 1995).

Nakamura, Takafusa, *A History of Showa Japan, 1926–1989* (Berkeley: University of California Press, 1998).

Takeda, Kyoto, *The Dual Image of the Japanese Emperor* (New York: New York University Press, 1989).

Tsurumi, Shunsuke, *A Cultural History of Postwar Japan, 1945–1980* (New York: Columbia University Press, 1994).

India

Akbar, M. J., *Nehru: The Making of India* (New York: Penguin Books, 1989).

Brown, Judith, *Modern India: The Origins of an Asian Democracy* (New York: Oxford University Press, 1994).

Embree, A., *Utopias in Conflict: Religion and Nationalism in Modern India* (Berkeley: University of California Press, 1990).

Jayakar, P., *Indira Gandhi* (New York: Vintage Books, 1993).

King, R. D., *Nehru and the Language Politica of India* (Oxford: Oxford University Press, 1997).

Misra, B. B., *The Unification and Division of India* (Oxford: Oxford University Press, 1991).

Tomlinson, B. R., *The Economy of Modern India* (Cambridge: Cambridge University Press, 1993).

Vanderveer, P., *Religious Nationalism: Hindus and Muslims in India* (Berkeley: University of California Press, 1994).

Wolpert, S., *Gandhi's Passion* (Oxford: Oxford University Press, 2001).

The Middle East

Bakhash, S., *The Reign of the Ayatollahs* (New York: Basic Books, 1984).

Burki, S. J., *Pakistan* (Boulder, Colo.: Westview Press, 1997).

Donohue, J. J., and J. L. Esposito, eds., *Islam in Transition: Muslim Perspectives* (Oxford: Oxford University Press, 1982).

Emadi, Hafizullah, *State, Revolution, and Superpowers in Afghanistan* (New York: Praeger, 1990).

Goldschmidt, Arthur, Jr., *A Concise History of the Middle East* (Boulder, Colo.: Westview Press, 1991).

Keddie, Nikki, R., *Roots of Revolution: An Interpretive History of Modern Iran* (New Haven, Conn.: Yale University Press, 1988).

Luciani, G., *The Oil Companies and the Arab World* (New York: St. Martin's Press, 1984).

Munson, H., Jr., *Islam and Revolution in the Middle East* (New Haven, Conn.: Yale University Press, 1988).

O'Brien, Conor Cruise, *The Siege: The Saga of Israel and Zionism* (New York: Weidenfeld & Nicolson, 1986).

Odell, P., *Oil and World Power* (New York: Penguin Books, 1986).

Reich, B., *Israel: Land of Tradition and Conflict* (Boulder, Colo.: Westview Press, 1985).

Smith, W. C., *Islam in Modern History* (Princeton, N.J.: Princeton University Press, 1957).

Latin America

Bethel, Leslie, *Latin America: Economy and Society Since 1930* (Cambridge: Cambridge University Press, 1998).

Burns, E. B., The Poverty of Progress (Berkeley: University of California Press, 1980).

Bulmer-Thomas, Victor, *United States and Latin America* (Cambridge: Harvard University Press, 1999).

Perez, Louis, *Cuba* (New York: Oxford University Press, 1988).

Scheper-Hughes, Nancy, *Death Without Weeping* (Berkeley: University of California Press, 1992.

Scobie, James, *Argentina* (New York: Oxford University Press, 1988).

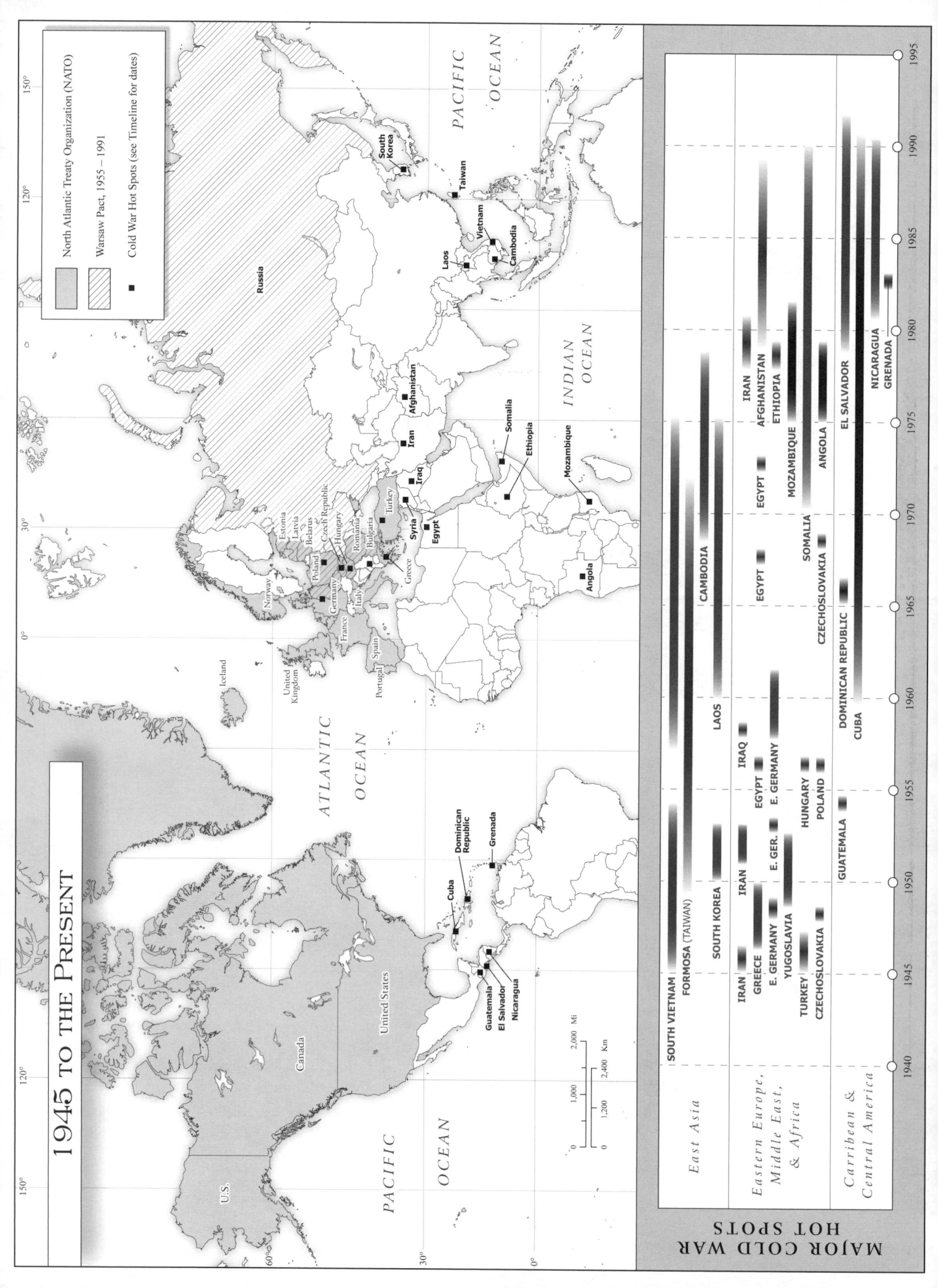

1945 TO THE PRESENT

North Atlantic Treaty Organization (NATO)

Warsaw Pact, 1955 – 1991

■ **Cold War Hot Spots** (see Timeline for dates)

MAJOR COLD WAR HOT SPOTS

East Asia

	1940	1945	1950	1955	1960	1965	1970	1975	1980	1985	1990	1995
SOUTH VIETNAM												
FORMOSA (TAIWAN)												
SOUTH KOREA												
LAOS												
CAMBODIA												

Eastern Europe, Middle East, & Africa

IRAN	IRAN					IRAN
GREECE		IRAQ			EGYPT	AFGHANISTAN
E. GERMANY	EGYPT					ETHIOPIA
YUGOSLAVIA	E. GER.					
TURKEY	HUNGARY				MOZAMBIQUE	
CZECHOSLOVAKIA	POLAND			CZECHOSLOVAKIA	SOMALIA	
						ANGOLA

Caribbean & Central America

GUATEMALA			DOMINICAN REPUBLIC	EL SALVADOR	
		CUBA		NICARAGUA	
				GRENADA	

XXXIII

THE END OF THE COLD WAR
and the Contemporary World

The End of the Cold War

In 1953, Stalin died, an armistice had been reached in the Korea, and the United States seemed willing to reconsider world politics. In 1955, Austria agreed to become a neutral state, and Soviet occupying forces withdrew from it. In 1956, the new Soviet leader Nikita Khushchev delivered a secret speech to the Central Committee of the Communist Party that was later leaked to the press, condemning Stalin's totalitarian excesses mentioned in Chapter Thirty-one. This speech seemed to foretell a loosening of party controls on Soviet society. Yet other events of that same year indicated that the conflict between the Soviet Union and the United States was very much alive.

The Suez crisis (mentioned in Chapter Thirty-two) erupted as Nassar nationalized the Canal Zone in Egypt. The Suez War followed, wherein Great Britain, France, and Israel acting together occupied the Suez Canal, but their attack occurred at the same time the Soviet Union had invaded and seized Hungary (see below). The United States condemnation of the U.S.S.R. for repression of the Hungarian revolt did not win support from its allies. Hence the U.S. in turn refused to support the British-French-Israeli action, and the Soviet Union protested so aggressively that these three powers abandoned their occupation of the Suez Canal. At the same time, the failure of the United States to back Britain, France, and Israel indicated that a crack had formed in the Western alliance protecting Europe from communism. Also, when the U.S. acted on behalf of Egypt to protest the aggression perpetrated by Britain, France, and Israel, this signaled to the world that nineteenth century–style imperial operations were off limits in the Cold War.

Simultaneously, in 1956, protests against Soviet-style regimes imposed in Poland and Hungary had produced major signs that Eastern Europe might want change. When Poland did not replace its prime minister with the choice indicated by the Soviet Union, tensions flared, but a compromise solution was made that satisfied both the Poles and their Soviet masters. In Hungary, a more serious rebellion unfolded.

Originally, Hungarians staged demonstrations in support of the Polish protest. Once started, these demonstrations led to street fighting. Next, a new ministry led by Imre Nagy (1896–1958) emerged and demanded a more independent role for Hungary within the Soviet bloc. Then Nagy made direct appeals to noncommunist groups within Hungary and called for the withdrawal of Soviet troops from his country. This greatly irritated leaders in the Kremlin, but when Nagy went further, and called for the Hungarian withdrawal from the Warsaw Pact, the Soviet Union responded with force. In November 1956, 250,000 Soviet troops and 5,000 tanks moved in and inaugurated a reign of terror. Nagy's regime collapsed, the Soviets installed a puppet government, and the U.S.S.R. reaffirmed its hold on a compliant Eastern Europe.

The combination of the Suez Canal, Polish, and Hungarian actions in 1956 indicated that the Cold War would survive the death of Stalin. In fact, under Nikita Khrushchev's leadership, the Soviet Union became even more adventuresome. Stalin had a conservative foreign policy that expanded Soviet influence through lands adjacent to his country. Nikita Khrushchev ventured out into the world and tried to make any insurgent group a potential friend of the Soviet Union and an enemy of the United States.

From 1958 to 1963, numerous incidents in the Cold War revealed that the temperature of the struggle had remained nearly at the boiling point. In 1958, Eisenhower proposed his "Eisenhower Doctrine," which promised to extend economic and military aid to any nation in need. Using this new doctrine, Eisenhower sent 15,000 troops into Lebanon from July to October to bolster a pro-Western regime at the Lebanese president, Camille Chamoun's, request. In the same year, Nassar created the short-lived United Arab Republic by forming a political union with Syria. He followed up this temporary success with support for a leftist coup in Iraq that threw out a pro-Western government. In the Far East, China renewed its military threat against the Nationalists by bombarding the strategic islands of Quemoy and Matsu just off Taiwan's coast. The U.S. Seventh Fleet had to escort Nationalist ships through the waters off these two islands. Finally, Berlin became an area of confrontation once again. In November of 1958, Khrushchev threatened to transfer the Soviet administration of Berlin into the hands of the East Germans, which would have led to another blockade. Happily, Khrushchev never made good on this threat because it might have launched a new arms race that he thought he could ill afford.

The year 1959 saw the beginning of Castro's regime in Cuba (see Chapter Thirty-two), which hailed a Soviet presence in the Western Hemisphere. While Cuba became a thorn in President Eisenhower's diplomatic side, the U-2 incident caused no end of embarrassment. On May 1, 1960, near Sverdlovsk, in the U.S.S.R., a Soviet missile brought down a U.S. spy plane. The U.S. had flown regular spy missions over Soviet territory for approximately three years prior to Naval Pilot Gary Power's fateful flight. Khrushchev used the U-2 spy plane to entrap Eisenhower by first claiming that an American plane had been shot down; the State Department responded that the incident was an accident. But the Soviets had captured Gary Powers, put him on display, and maneuvered Eisenhower into taking personal responsibility for authorizing a spy mission. This was an unprecedented event that allowed Khrushchev to cancel a summit meeting between the United States and Soviet Union to underline Eisenhower's embarrassment.

Two events then set the tone for the Kennedy Administration that took over from Eisenhower. The first was the Bay of Pigs fiasco: an invasion attempt supervised by the CIA of 1,500 anti-Castro Cubans. The Joint Chiefs of Staff assured Kennedy that the plan could succeed, but 1,200 of the 1,500 men sent into combat were captured and the rest killed while coming ashore. Castro's success derived from good Soviet intelligence that anticipated the location and strength of the assault. The Cuban Missile Crisis then followed almost immediately upon the Bay of Pigs. This time, in October 1962, U.S. intelligence discovered the presence of medium-range nuclear missiles being installed in Cuba by Soviet technicians (prior to becoming operational). President Kennedy imposed a naval blockade on the island, threatened to search Soviet ships, and brought the

U.S. to the brink of war. Yet Khrushchev wavered and the crisis passed with the Soviets withdrawing their weapons in exchange for the U.S. removal of obsolete missiles from Turkish bases—an action Kennedy had already planned. Hence Kennedy redeemed his earlier diplomatic and military failure of the Bay of Pigs.

After 1963, an easing of tensions slowly began, but the United States soon became mired in the Vietnam War, while Czechoslovakia attempted self-rule as had Hungary and suffered a Soviet invasion in 1968. For a brief moment during the first half of the year— known as the "Prague Spring"—the Czechs under Alexander Dubček experimented with liberalism and democracy. Yet this attempt at autonomy led to a Soviet invasion in August and an end to the Czech flirtation with freedom. In contrast to the tragic episode, the war in Vietnam proved far more compelling as a global issue. The war in Vietnam functioned for the United States very much like the later conflict between the Soviet Union and Afghanistan. The United States, however, inherited the Vietnamese conflict rather than initiating it as had the Soviets by invading Afghanistan in 1979.

The Vietnam War began when the French—determined to reestablish colonial control over Vietnam, Laos, and Cambodia (know then as French Indochina)—returned to the Far East after World War II. When they faced a strong independence movement led by nationalist-communist Ho Chi Minh (1890–1969), the French decided to use military force. They received substantial aid from the United States, who was op-

The Vietnam War. A Viet Cong base camp under attack by the American Ninth Infantry Division, 1968. Courtesy of the National Archives, ARC 530621.

The Legacy of Vietnam

Spanning thirty years, the Vietnam War trapped the attention of six United States presidents: Truman, Eisenhower, Kennedy, Johnson, Nixon, and Ford. Major U.S. military participation in the Vietnam War covered twelve years, 1961 to 1973, and involved over a half million troops at its high point in 1968. In human terms, the war claimed just under 58,000 American lives, and wounded 300,000 more, while 1.5 million Vietnamese died in the struggle, and the country was devastated by air raids that exceeded the intensity of that experienced by Germany in World War II. Yet the Vietnam War did not limit itself to battlefields located solely in Vietnam itself. The war spread out into Laos and Cambodia.

Neighboring Laos and Cambodia became ensnared in the war when the Viet Cong and North Vietnamese Regular Army used these neighboring states as part of their supply lines. Hence the war spilled over into these adjacent territories with disastrous consequences. While Laos suffered the occasional bombing and incursion, Cambodia fell under the authority of the Khmer Rouge. Between 1975 and 1979, the Khmer Rouge established what became known as the "killing fields." In relocation camps that isolated the educated among Cambodia's population, the Khmer Rouge planned to make a complete break with the past by executing anyone contaminated with foreign beliefs. The result was mass graves, the systematic shooting of 2 million people, and the reduction of the total Cambodian population by 25 percent.

To these figures must be added the displaced people and the tangled politics that followed in the wake of the war. All told, the war generated nearly 10 million refugees. Many of them had to immigrate to the United States seeking political asylum. In terms of politics, within the United States, the Vietnam War caused a political realignment that replaced the Democratic party's majority with a growing Republican surge that not only survived the Nixon debacle known as Watergate, but also ushered in the Reagan revolution and a new conservative trend. In the communist bloc, the Vietnam War caused no end of troubles. When the United States opened diplomatic relations with the Peoples' Republic of China (mentioned in Chapter Thirty-two), the goal was to provide mutual aid: the Chinese

helped the U.S. in Vietnam, and the United States participated in the global rehabilitation of China. What emerged was a widening split in the communist bloc: Vietnam aligned itself with the Soviet Union and the Khmer Rouge chose the People's Republic of China. The fallout was a growing tension in what had once been French Indochina. Communist China protested the treatment of Chinese nationals in Vietnam, and Vietnam prepared for the invasion of Cambodia.

The purpose of the Vietnamese invasion of Cambodia was the overthrow of the Khmer Rouge and the establishment of a puppet regime under Phnom Phet. The invasion achieved its goals in short order, and the new regime took over Cambodia once the assault began in December 1978. But the Vietnamese bid for regional hegemony caused a confrontation with Beijing that almost led to war. China met a massive Vietnamese troop build-up, coupled with a potential missile attack targeting SS-20 medium-range weapons on Chinese cities, by mobilizing its Red Army. China in fact "invaded" Vietnam in February 1979 to teach the Vietnamese a lesson and then withdrew. The United States aided the Chinese in their efforts and sent supplies to the Khmer Rouge even with mounting evidence that genocide had been practiced by this ousted Cambodian regime.

Hence, instead of the domino effect of one country after another falling to communism, the war in Indochina drove a wedge between Marxist states. The monolith of communism that confronted the West during the Cold War proved to be an illusion while the conservatives in the United States enjoyed a resurgence of political power. Accordingly what should have been enemies in the confrontation between the Free World and Marxism became an alliance of convenience, that is, the most adamant of "cold warriors"—the Republicans and the Red Chinese—seemed to become fast friends.

Henretta, James A., David Brody, and Lynn Dumeril. *America: A Concise History*, **Third Edition (New York: Bedford and St. Martin's Press, 2006), 911.**

Keylor, William R., *The Twentieth Century World: An International History*, **Fourth Edition (New York: Oxford University Press, 2001), 445–46.**

posed to colonial rule on principle but—mired in a Cold War mentality—feared that a communist takeover of Vietnam would have a "domino effect" throughout South and Southeast Asia.

By 1954, Ho Chi Minh's strength had grown steadily and his troops, the Viet Cong, outwitted and defeated the French after surrounding them in their outpost at Dien Bien Phu. At the Geneva Conference of 1954, the French decided to withdraw from Indochina, conceding that nationalism was the strongest force in the twentieth century. Accordingly, Western and communist powers decided that three Indochinese countries, Viet-

nam, Cambodia, and Laos, should become independent states, that Vietnam be temporarily divided, with a northern government headed by Ho Chi Minh and a southern government headed by the new prime minister, Ngo Dinh Diem, who replaced the discredited Emperor Bao Dai—the monarch the French had used to created a puppet government in 1950. The new regime also mandated that an election be held in Vietnam in two years to establish a coalition government to reunify the country.

The election never took place. Instead, North and South Vietnam engaged in a bitter and protracted civil war with major international involvement: the North had the support of the Soviet Union and Communist China, while the United States replaced France to back the South. In other words, the civil war in Vietnam developed into a major battlefield of the Cold War between the will and forces of the Free World and the communist bloc. Finally, in 1975, after public opinion in the United States turned against American participation in the Vietnam War and the U.S. government had pulled out all but a handful of its troops, the forces of the North Vietnamese army overran the South, leaving the Republic of Vietnam—which 57,939 U.S. troops had given their lives to support—defenseless. Communist repression and massacres followed, a phenomenon that swept across the border into Cambodia. Yet the communist victory in the unification of Vietnam did not produce the "domino effect" that the United States had feared. Indeed, it turned out that communist Vietnam was highly vigilant of any attempt at occupation on the part of Communist China. The split between the People's Republic of China and the Soviet Union further complicated local affairs in Vietnam, Cambodia, and Laos. Vietnam sided with the Soviet Union, and Cambodia's Khmer Rouge sided with China. Finally, Vietnam adopted domestic policies similar to post-Mao Chinese reforms that allow private property ownership and a somewhat freer market economy within a communist context.

While the war in Vietnam led to defeat for the United States, U.S.-Soviet relations actually improved. Under the presidency of Richard Nixon, a process of *détente* (a lessening of international confrontation) began. As mentioned in Chapter Thirty-two, Nixon visited China in 1972 in the hope of breaking down the bipolar nature of the Cold War. He also extended the policy of détente to the Soviet Union by reducing nuclear tensions in the Cold War; in 1969 the United States and the Soviet Union signed the Nuclear Nonproliferation Treaty, and a year later they initiated the Strategic Arms Limitations Talks (SALT). SALT eventually generated a significant arms-control agreement in May of 1972 (the SALT I Treaty), while a year earlier the Soviet Union agreed to Nixon's position on the status of Berlin. While the illegal activities of President Nixon and his aides, known as the Watergate crisis, ended Nixon's presidency, the scandal did not halt détente.

In 1975, U.S. president Gerald Ford attended a conference in Helsinki, Finland, in which he formally recognized the Soviet sphere of influence in Eastern Europe in exchange for guarantees from the Soviet Union of respect for human rights within all of its territories. President Jimmy Carter continued to take a stand on human rights by using the Olympic Games of 1980 as a political tool—forbidding the U.S. team from attending the Summer Games in Moscow that year—to protest the Soviet Union's invasion of Afghanistan in 1979. Nonetheless, President Carter did sign the SALT II Treaty, which reduced the number of nuclear weapons in the arsenals of both superpowers. President Ronald Reagan increased the heat of the debate with the Soviet Union during his eight years in office, backed off from détente, and managed to continue arms negotiations despite his push for the development of a controversial nuclear missile defense system for the United States, the Strategic Arms Defense Initiative (known informally as Star Wars). Spending on national defense during the Reagan years quadrupled the U.S. budget deficit, but it also bankrupted the Soviet Union, which could no longer keep pace in the arms race. This ushered in the reformer Mikhail S. Gorbachev (b. 1931) to power in the Soviet Union.

President Richard Nixon toasts Premier Zhou En-Lai during his historic 1972 visit to the Peoples' Republic of China. The first U.S. president to visit China, Nixon implemented a new political relationship after decades of mutual estrangement.

Upon assuming leadership in 1985, Gorbachev inherited a massive economic problem. The Soviet Union had developed into an equal of the United States militarily, but the U.S.S.R.'s domestic economy lay in shambles. In addition, the Soviet invasion of Afghanistan had compounded the problems faced by Gorbachev because this war—reminiscent of the sinkhole in money and servicepeople that the U.S. had experienced in Vietnam—had trapped the Soviet Union in a costly and seemingly endless conflict. Ironically, the Afghanistan invasion had mired the Soviet Union in a "People's War" fighting against a foe that the U.S.S.R. usually supported (Muslim guerrillas) against the West. Hence, the Soviet Union had taken on the mantle of an imperial power while trying to convince the world that it was the champion of all anti-imperialist efforts. Furthermore, the Muslim fundamentalists who opposed the Soviet occupation in Afghanistan had close ties with people of the same faith living within the U.S.S.R. and its satellite states. Finally, the bureaucratic nature of the Bolshevik party apparatus had calcified so completely over the sixty-eight years between 1917 and 1985 that the central government was too weak to provide workable solutions to the problems Gorbachev and the nation faced. Paradoxically, these problem-solving capabilities are supposed to be a hallmark of a totalitarian regime.

Regardless of these problems, Mikhail S. Gorbachev's accession to power brought major reforms, but these changes, in turn, ended the Cold War. Gorbachev was willing to rethink the Soviet position in light of global affairs. For one thing, he wanted to cut the cost of confrontation, and he knew that the United States had gone from a creditor to a debtor nation due to the expense of maintaining its nuclear arsenal. At home, Gorbachev introduced *perestroika* (the restructuring of the domestic market) in an effort to end the cost of a "revolution of infinite trajectory." To perestroika, Gorbachev added *glasnost'* (openness) as a means to discuss Soviet strengths and weaknesses in an effort to change the bonds of bureaucracy that had grown up within a single-party state. Soon, unprecedented reports of governmental corruption, sloppy factory management, wasteful economic planning, and the true expense of the Cold War began to appear in *Pravda*, the official Soviet newspaper. A major overhaul of the Soviet system was underway.

Between 1985 and 1990, many of the reasons for confrontation between the United States and the Soviet Union also disappeared. The spirit of perestroika and glasnost' had crossed the borders into Eastern Europe, and the Soviet bloc began to crumble. Gorbachev's reforms at home had reduced the Soviet military presence in Eastern Europe, and local rebellions began to emerge in Hungary and Czechoslovakia, reminiscent of the respective demonstrations of 1956 and 1968. This time, however, the Soviet Union was unwilling to intervene, which opened the door to the collapse of the Soviet bloc's Eastern European regimes. In fact, the momentum of Gorbachev's perestroika and glasnost' swept the entire Soviet state system from power in 1991, which eliminated one of the two sides in the Cold War. With the collapse of the Soviet Union in 1991, and the creation of the Commonwealth of Independent States (CIS), the basis of global confrontation also came to an end; hence, the world no longer faced the immediate possibility of a World War III. Now, however, a much more complex global system confronted people living at the end of the twentieth century: the contemporary world.

The Contemporary World

The contemporary world is a legacy of the modern era, the twentieth century, and the Cold War. Its hallmark is globalization. Globalization itself refers to the process of global integration that emerged from modern world trade, modern world industry, and the population dynamics associated with both. Global integration is the by-product of a mutual human dependency that developed out of globalization and modernization from 1492 to the present. Hence, global integration is the primary focal point of the contemporary world.

Global integration was clearly underway before the advent of the twentieth century, and, as we have seen, Europe had played the central role in this process. Yet Europe's fall from power after 1945 opened up the question of who would replace the Europeans as the integrating center of the world. The answer to this question remains open today.

Clearly underway in the 1920s, but culminating in 1945, Europe's decline as the economic center of the world created an enormous power vacuum. European empires had dominated the world so completely and for so long that no one society could return to its traditional methods of organizing its regional culture—even though attempts have been made. What Europe had created during the nineteenth and early twentieth centuries was a global economic structure that produced a mutual interdependency, one the world's peoples could not dissolve.

Just as symbiosis had trapped ancient humanity in a new cultural context called civilization, wherein no one culture could give up agriculture or urban life without starvation, so the global economy had trapped the world in a binding economic setting. Industrial integration in Europe, and its diffusion to the United States, the Soviet Union, and Japan, had redefined the circumstances of global trade. After the period 1800–1914, the world's population had grown beyond the means of traditional agriculture to sustain life. Now a world market integrated a global exchange system that maintained more than 6 billion human beings, some 50 percent of whom live in an urban setting.

This new level of urbanization reveals how interdependent the global economy has become. Since much of the world is still nonindustrial, the twentieth-century urban phenomenon reflected the power of a contemporary world market, modern agricultural production, and mass global communication. No longer is scarcity the problem; instead, getting food to the world's hungry people is the issue.

The world market assembled by nineteenth-century European empires had created a contradictory mix of mutual dependence, competition, and insecurity that every participant had to live with. From 1800 to 1914 the world's population lived in one loose, but binding, economic system. Regional specialization through geographic differentiation maintained global trade. At the same time, regional specialization generated wealth on a level never before seen. But a relatively small number of countries would enjoy a standard of living equal to that of a European nation-state.

Europe's achievement, or the worldwide trap it had created for the twentieth century, integrated goods, services, money, capital, migration, and nation-states into one broad but eclectic system. Directed from several national capitals in Europe, and challenged by new nations like the United States, Japan, and czarist Russia, this world market linked the countries of the world in a common pattern of reciprocal relationships directed principally from London, Paris, and Berlin before 1914.

Articles bought and sold, and services made available, all fit within one general scale of value that survived the collapse of the gold standard in the Great Depression of the 1930s. Basic commodities that had once enjoyed local monopolies now found themselves thrust into international competition. After the creation of a worldwide scale of value, all countries' economies began to wax and wane as a singular financial system.

For example, wheat produced in the United States, Argentina, or East Prussia between 1865 and 1920 competed with wheat produced by peasant agriculture in Southern and Eastern Europe to generate the collapse of small farms in the latter. This collapse set in motion major migrations between 1870 and 1929, with many of those peasant farmers ruined by international trade finding themselves pushed by necessity to relocate—more than 30 million of them ending up in the Americas.

As a result, peasants ruined by the falling price of wheat left Europe through a step-stage migration pattern similar to the way English people moved to London first and then to North America between 1600 and 1750. From 1846 to 1932, 60 million people left Europe, transferring their culture throughout the world. Approximately 35 million of these Europeans migrated to the United States, where they supplied the labor needed for that nation's industrial revolution. Another 25 million Europeans took up residence elsewhere in the world to function as agents of modernization in traditional cultures.

After the classic voyages of Vasco da Gama and Christopher Columbus at the end of the fifteenth century, no one state or international institution was in charge of the global economy. The use of empire generated one type of design that organized world markets. Empire, however, created greater hostility among subordinate societies than global integration itself could overcome. Simultaneously, major fluctuations in the world economy, like disastrous events such as the Great Depression, revealed just how vulnerable and interdependent every person on Earth had become.

Ever since Europe lost preeminence as the international financial center of the world between 1914 and 1945, an economic realignment has been underway. But, any nation that sought to replace Europe as the hub of financial leadership also has became the focus of international hostility.

International trade following the European model created tiers of wealth on a global scale that placed the industrial nations above all the rest. Nations that engaged in world trade based solely on primary goods soon contracted heavy debts to industrialized societies. These debts in turn led to outside intervention whenever foreign investors moved in to call their loans or protect their holdings. For those cultures in debt, cheap labor and raw materials seemed all they had available to sell to meet their financial obligations. Thus, only a few societies could win the bulk of the profits, control the shipping, insurance, and international loans, and hold the economic initiative.

Nation-states that could fill Europe's old economic role then became the targets of international anger in much the same way Europeans nations had once been. Those countries trapped in poverty through global trade felt the presence of foreign influence as a cultural invasion; their natural response was to resist.

If the culture involved had a tradition of internal coherence based on religion like Islam, then an alien nation-state seeking economic domination became a foreign infidel to be resisted with the intensity of a jihad.

If a culture's worldview developed a monism like Hinduism, then religion once again organized the basis of a nation in formation, but it also focused that nation's anger on old injuries suffered at the hands of other faiths like Islam. If a culture had a tradition that defined society by lineage—like those of sub-Saharan Africa—then the boundary-lines of nation-states themselves became obstacles to political redefinition. Thus, traditional cultures around the world found that their ancient customs and the internal coherence required for a nation in formation combined to make a dangerous mix in a contemporary global context. Each had to restructure itself from the ground up because of, or despite, its traditions.

In the case of sub-Saharan Africa, for example, where lineages defined local societies, the frontiers used to describe modern African nations required a redefinition of traditional political space. As mentioned in Chapter Thirty-two, given the arbitrary way that Europeans had partitioned Africa—they often divided sub-Saharan lineages or put two or more hostile ones together into one political society—when these colonies emerged as nations-in-formation after 1945, some of them sought to reassert their political identity by exterminating their neighbors.

Frequently, divided lineages tried to reunite into one national society by disrupting the political stability of several nations marked by old colonial borders. In other cases, hostile lineages forced to live within the boundaries of a new African nation would begin to fight one another in bloody civil wars. In both cases, the process of a nation in formation ran contrary to the traditional social organization of sub-Saharan Africa.

At the same time, the complex African example is only one instance of this contemporary issue. Wherever tradition and modernization clashed in a regional cultural context, specific local conflicts arose. Each non-European cultural hearth had to struggle with redefinition by adapting its traditions to the forces of modernization.

Beyond the problems caused by the clash of tradition and modernization, the Cold War itself exacerbated global instability. Command over modern weapon systems, first developed by Europeans between 1500 and 1914, had shifted to the United States and the Soviet Union after 1945. These modern weapons had made the relations of these two nation-states as volatile as those of European countries prior to World War I. From the United States and the Soviet Union, some of these weapons had also made their way into the hands of the non-European world as a consequence of the alliance systems both superpowers had sought to establish. In

some cases, several of these non-European cultures had even developed nuclear arsenals, making the proliferation of such weapons a global nightmare.

Using the conventional version of these modern weapons, non-European cultures discovered that they could defeat modern industrial powers by using a new strategy called a "People's War," conflicts that utilized guerrilla tactics and terrorism, instead of formal armies and combat methods. This style of warfare greatly neutralized national armies engaged in combat, elevating nonindustrial countries into serious military rivals that could, at the very least, frustrate industrial powers seeking economic mastery. The guerrilla strategy and terror of a People's War robbed industrial nations of the full leverage of their technological superiority.

One feature of Europe's decline between 1918 and 1945 was the return in part to regional dominance by various cultures. Such cultures as Brazil and India have come to dominate their local settings. Each had engaged in a partial importation of European economic, political, and military institutions that gave them a regional advantage in defining local affairs. Consequently, each of these countries put together a local economic system that made both of them the financial leaders of their respective regions.

Simultaneously, portions of the Middle East have struggled to create modern industrial societies, while other parts of the Middle East have generated fundamentalist Islamic revolutions to recover a religious purity muted by modernization. These contradictory attempts to solve regional problems in the Muslim world have driven various Islamic cultures into hostile camps —some of which fought local wars (such as Iran and Iraq), while others supported international terrorism against the state of Israel and its allies. Yet every player in this new regional volatility has sought to enhance its specific position by achieving nation-formation. Thus, the one thing that all such responses to modernization had in common, whether in Brazil, India, or the Middle East, is the drive to create nation-states.

The number of new nation-states created since 1945 indicates the ability of regional cultures to determine their own political destiny. The original fifty nations that founded the UN have seen their membership nearly quadruple, bringing the total to 196 states in 2004. The index of these new nations reveals the absence of a global center such as Europe once was. Yet each of these new nation-states have struggled with the issue that has plagued all modernizing, political cultures: how will public opinion be expressed?

Equally important is the question of what model of government a culture should adopt. Would a liberal-democratic model suit it, or should it take an autocratic approach? And variations of the national design in the form of republicanism, democracy, socialism, fascism, totalitarianism, or Marxism offer alternative approaches to any culture seeking the power offered in nation-formation. Selecting one of these national forms orients a nation to the world in such a way as to obstruct or enhance international peace.

At the same time that European influence decayed around the world, Europe's old command over intercultural contacts also gave way. Europe's ability to initiate and control communications between peoples that went back to the Age of Discovery (1492–1763) collapsed betwen 1914 and 1945. As a result of this collapse, non-European cultures achieved a level of independence in transportation and international exchange that kept in step with their recovery of sovereignty.

After World War I, several non-European cultures began to establish their own diplomatic and commercial links with societies hostile to Europe. These new links transformed regional politics. For example, China's alliance with the Soviet Union in the 1920s revealed how such contacts could be made. In fact, the Communist International Committee for World Revolution was eager for such contacts to occur.

Yet even as these contacts became more frequent, several cultures tried to pull back from interactions with the world in general during the twentieth century. The Soviet Union, for example, made such an effort between World War I and World War II, despite the Comintern. This Soviet effort developed out of Stalin's failures at foreign policy during the 1920s particularly in China. There, as mentioned in Chapter Thirty, the Chinese Communist party fell victim to Jiang Jieshi's sudden cycle of political assassination in 1927.

Stalin's inability to grasp the complexities of foreign affairs led him to retreat from international politics, and focus instead on building an industrial base after 1928, so that he could approach the world on his own terms. In a similar fashion, the United States pulled back from the world during an era of isolationism after World War I. Even China underwent such an episode, for Mao Zedong attempted isolationism after China's alliance with the Soviet Union broke down between 1956 and 1960.

Each of these efforts at isolation, however, did not work for long. No country in the twentieth century had the means to achieve economic self-sufficiency. Every culture came to realize that it needed contact with the others in order to gain access to the abundance of resources found in the global economy. No longer was life simple and local; now people had to interact with their neighbors—across town, the country, and the globe—to survive.

Thus, the dominant trend of the twentieth century was for emerging nation-states to initiate their own contacts. In this effort, new technology in communications and transportation generated the impression that the world was shrinking. Innovations in communication since 1945 have made intercultural contact seem instantaneous.

Today satellites and computers make world awareness commonplace. The development and regular use of international flights makes trips to destinations halfway around the world feasible and even commonplace in less than twenty-four hours. Such contacts allow for regional systems of trade to develop independently of any one economic center.

Simultaneously, international contacts created a structural paradox in twentieth-century world history. On one hand, such contacts have increased the mutual dependency of different cultures on one another as world trade integrated into new systems of economic alignment. On the other, these contacts have increased the possibility of international violence.

Just as increased contact expands intercultural exchanges, so does it greatly complicate alliances and diplomacy. The two World Wars not only broke Europe's hold over the global system, but they illustrated that new levels of international contact were necessary for any culture to survive.

With so many non-European societies seeking national formation, any number of regional centers might have emerged. The number of new nation-states joining international institutions like the United Nations transformed the non-European world into a majority block of political and economic power. In each global region, local powers became potential leaders to redefine world politics. Thus, the post-1945 world offered an extremely complex diplomatic environment.

An example of this complexity comes from the Cold War. Mao Zedong's victory over the Goumindang (the Nationalist Party) in 1949 should have locked Communist China in the arms of the Soviet Union. Regionally, two Marxist states with the common revolutionary goals of eliminating private property and class warfare should have been able to create an enduring alliance. Since in Marx's vision of the world, states themselves were oppressive instruments of a ruling class who used their power to control their rivals' classes, both communist countries should have banded together to achieve their common socioeconomic goals and end the existence of their respective states. But the alliance between the Soviet Union and Mao's China did not last long at all, nor did they strive arm-in-arm to achieve a Marxist future.

Instead, Marxism in both the Soviet Union and China created the very pitfall Marx had warned against, voluntarism. Both revolutions had occurred in cultures that were not ready for the final communist struggle against private property. Both of these cultures were peasant societies, not industrial, capitalist nation-states.

Ironically, Marxism in the twentieth century had become a tool for mobilizing revolutionary passion among peasants who wanted to throw off the power of foreign regimes, an ideology of liberation. Once these grassroots movements achieved independence, however, they used a Marxist vocabulary to maintain the internal coherence of a nation-state rather than to try to achieve pure global communism. Hence, peasant societies using Marxism returned to regional, cultural ambitions after they won their liberation.

As seen in Chapter Thirty-two and above, not long after friendly relations between the People's Republic of China (PRC) and the Soviet Union collapsed in 1960, China turned to the United States as a potential partner to defeat Soviet ambitions in the Far East. The irony of this reversal became even more pronounced when the cozy terms of this new partnership linked Chinese communists with Republican cold warriors in the United States. Forged during the presidency of Richard Nixon, this alliance between the PRC and the United States united ideological opponents.

Nixon had built a political career in the United States as a champion of the Cold War. Yet to maintain his presidency, he used this diplomatic initiative with China to recover political ground that he had lost due to his hard-line policy of expanding the aerial bombardment in Vietnam and invading Cambodia. Ironically, this new friendship between China and the United States ended a condition of diplomatic isolation initiated by Chairman Mao. Furthermore, this new friendship helped to shape an unofficial alliance constructed by the United States and China against the reputedly "communist" regimes in Vietnam and Cambodia (see insert above).

Through this diplomatic initiative, China reentered the world community. In so doing, the Chinese communists had to redefine their vision of Marxism. Using pragmatism to capture the essence of their political perspective, Deng Xiaoping, China's new leader after Mao's death, described Marxism as a means of making China rich and strong. Deng went one step further, evoking the poetic traditions of China through a metaphor he used to define China's new economy, one "that was free to fly like a bird in a very large cage."

While the diplomatic face of the contemporary world took on a flexibility seemingly denied during the Cold War, the increased number of nation-states indicated that the modernization initiated by Europeans had reshaped world politics—for the regimes that existed before 1945 as well as those that had come into

being by 1990. The monarchies and puppet rulers that Europeans had used as their imperial instruments to control their empires collapsed, replaced by attempts at democracies, totalitarian regimes, or authoritarian states.

The internal stability of a new nation-state depended on how well its leaders managed public opinion. Each new state also had to create and run a local economy while its national rulers attempted to build industry. What seems striking in this story is that non-European societies universally chose the nation-state as the model for political expression.

Status, Freedom, and Equality

The formation of new nations has set in motion a parallel shift in the definitions of social equality worldwide. The rigid inequality associated with the scarcity of food surpluses that accompanied life in a traditional, agricultural society has eased during the twentieth century in many locations. Given the ancient and medieval problem of so few food surpluses produced by traditional agricultural methods, scarcity had for centuries created solid barriers to social and geographic mobility. Accordingly, approximately 80 to 90 percent of humans found themselves confined to farms during the ancient and middle ages.

Ancient- and middle-era social barriers became firmly defined by a caste-like status system in each traditional agricultural community. While the rigidity of caste varied from culture to culture, certain features were common to all conventional societies. One's status at birth determined a lifetime's socioeconomic existence. Modernization, however, eroded the harshness of such social barriers by reducing scarcity and opening up the possibility of improving one's status and occupation in an urban setting. Then, modernization eased geographic barriers to global migration that reinforced caste by restricting human mobility to specific locations on the Earth. Furthermore, Western Enlightenment ideas that included freedom and equality as a social experience spread around the world. Finally, generated by public opinion, freedom and equality became the backbone of national identity wherever people tried to form nation-states.

Hence, major social movements worldwide have caused a reevaluation of how humanity defines itself. The end of the Atlantic slave trade in the nineteenth century was an early sign of this change. The failure of a racist Nazi regime during World War II, and the erosion of racism in general, have forced questions about social equality to surface as well. Finally, even the Cold War forced a democracy like the United States to reevaluate how it should define status and equality within in the context of its Natural Rights theory.

African American leaders. The great civil rights leaders Martin Luther King, Jr. (1929–68) and Malcolm X (1925–65) are shown here waiting for a press conference, March 26, 1964. Credit: Library of Congress, Washington, D.C. LC-USZ6-1847.

American society, asking questions about segregation that European Americans could not answer.

As his fame and movement grew, Martin Luther King, Jr., adopted the nonviolent protest tactics developed by Mahatma Gandhi to open the eyes of American citizens to social injustice and racism in their own nation. Building on a general trend toward social equality launched before he declared his dream, King rode the crest of a social wave that brought the plight of African Americans into focus one hundred years after the Civil War.

President Harry S. Truman's desegregation of the Armed Forces had led the way toward a national civil-rights policy. Thurgood Marshall followed Truman's lead with a victory for integration in the Supreme Court case of *Brown* v. *Board of Education of Topeka* (1954) where the National Association for the Advancement of Colored People (NAACP) challenged segregation in the schools. This victory for integration initiated a confrontation between a reluctant President Dwight D. Eisenhower and Governor Orval Faubus of Arkansas, who defended white parents in their protest over the integration of public schools in Little Rock in 1957. At the same time, the battle over segregation moved into the streets when Rosa Parks, an African American, tired after a long day of work, refused to surrender her seat on a bus to a white passenger in Montgomery, Alabama, in 1955.

Shortly thereafter, Martin Luther King, Jr., led the boycott against the city bus company that drew national media coverage. From Alabama, King's movement spread throughout the United States. King organized the Southern Christian Leadership Conference (SCLC), which energized African Americans nationwide after 1960 and spawned parallel organizations. By 1963, King led a march on Washington D.C. that comprised 200,000 supporters who awakened President John F.

The issue of segregation that has haunted democracy in the United States came into sharp focus as a result of its conflict with Adolf Hitler and then the Cold War, when African Americans, even those in the armed forces, were treated like second-class citizens or worse, even as the U.S. fought a racist regime and struggled against Marxism's emphasis on equality. This forced citizens of the United States to reassess their definition of "life, liberty, and the pursuit of happiness."

In the United States, equality has been defined by opportunity. Yet, historically, segregation denied opportunity to all Americans equally. This contradiction surfaced during the 1960s, when a young Baptist minister named Martin Luther King, Jr., and a radical Black Muslim named Malcolm X publicly questioned the democratic principles of United States.

Malcolm X followed Elijah Mohammed, founder of the Nation of Islam, and spoke with a voice alien to the dominant culture in the United States. Malcolm X's criticism of prejudice cut to the heart of American politics by revealing how *black* implied inferiority to most citizens of European ancestry. He remained loyal to Elijah Mohammed until the mid-1960s, when he became an orthodox Muslim over issues of corruption in the Nation of Islam.

Martin Luther King, Jr., carried the message of equality further than the Nation of Islam with his dream of the United States living up to the fullness of its promise. Martin Luther King spoke to the mainstream of

Kennedy, and the nation, to consider civil rights for minorities as a national issue.

Although Kennedy had already acted to ensure that the black student James Meredith could attend the University of Mississippi four month prior to King's march on the capitol, King's powerful "I Have a Dream" speech led the young president to choose to support civil rights over the backing of the Southern Democrats of his own party. A national political commitment to civil rights then led to federal legislation by 1964 when congress passed the Civil Rights Act spearheaded by President Lyndon B. Johnson, who had assumed the presidency after Kennedy was assassinated in Dallas, Texas, in 1963. The act outlawed racial segregation in schools and public buildings and created the Fair Employment Commission (FEC) to address issues of equal opportunity. The 1964 legislation was soon followed by the Voting Rights Act of 1965, which ensured that African Americans now held the unencumbered power to cast their votes as they pleased.

Now King's movement had eroded much of the legal barriers to equality as previously defined by de facto segregation. Yet while King was well on his way to shattering the public paradox of segregation in the U.S. democracy, the problem of privately held racist attitudes still exists as a target for change.

King paid a heavy price for his success. Early in his career, his house was bombed, and many of his followers had been beaten and jailed in states across the South. He himself had to face radical discontent among young African Americans who wanted to accelerate the achievements of his movement and realize full equality immediately. Finally, in April 1968, King was shot and killed by an angry white man. Nonetheless, the impact of King's movement and his dream could not be ignored. His vision spread beyond the African American community to mobilize Hispanics, Asians, and women.

Malcolm X paid an equally heavy price for his popularity. Fulfilling the fifth pillar of his new faith, the Hajj, he traveled to Mecca to discover the force of integration at the heart of Islam. In Mecca he saw a world free of racial prejudice united in a common bond through the worship of Allah. Stunned by this vision, he returned to the United States hoping to awaken a nation. But divisions within his own movement resulted in his assassination in February 1965.

Social unrest in the United States continued in the 1960s as inherent racism still sustained segregation on local levels. Racial conflict in the United States continued to spawn violence especially in the form of urban riots, as many ethnic minorities, finding themselves confined to inner-urban communities with decaying social services and few chances of escape vented their frustration.

Following the example of Martin Luther King and Malcolm X, the New Feminism of the 1970s came into its own. Spawning hundreds of organizations, the New Feminism demanded radical changes that caused a revolution in women's status under the laws in the United States. Condemning the proscribed role of women between 1940 and 1960 in her famous book, *The Feminine Mystique*, Betty Friedan described the silent scream millions of American females felt while trapped in suburban domesticity. Friedan's book sold 3 million copies, appeared in excerpts in numerous magazines, and spoke to a wide female audience that had experienced a mounting sense of isolation caused by the limited occupational choices available to high school– and college-educated women in terms of employment, promotions, and wages. Friedan coupled these observations with the social pressures placed on young females to marry, have children, and remain at home. This combination of restricted employment opportunities and inculcated domesticity addressed issues that concerned a growing number of white, well-educated, middle-class American women and gen-

Betty Friedan (third from left) leading a small march to present 894 resolutions to the U.N. International Women's Year conference, Mexico City, 1975. The women were barred at the door. Photo courtesy of Jacqui Ceballos.

erated a vocabulary of rebellion. From this rebellion emerged the National Organization for Women (NOW) in 1966, as the New Feminism set out to transform the American understanding of womanhood.

Despite the hundreds of feminist groups that took energy from the New Feminism, the postmodern women's organizations had one thing in common: the belief that women were barred from, and unequally treated in, a male-dominated economic and political arena. New Feminists challenged traditional stereotypes of what constitutes being a woman. They argued for changes in perception that reached back to religious definitions of being female, the meaning of being a wife and a mother, and the possibility of a woman having a career without losing her gender identity. The process of reassessing the traditional definition of womanhood was called "consciousness raising."

In general, the New Feminism became a major social effort at defining women's roles in society rather than a political movement or a cause. The goal was to lift female aspirations to a level of real equality with that of males. To succeed required changes in employment and promotion practices, access to professional opportunities, and a redefinition of women's rights under the law.

For the most part, the New Feminism succeeded, as it produced sweeping changes in the law. In 1972, congress passed Title IX of the Education Amendment Act, banning sex discrimination in education. Title IX covered athletics as well as admission, hiring, and student services. In 1974, congress outlawed discrimination against women seeking bank loans, and in 1978 this protection was extended to pregnant women with regard to their jobs. Congress further opened military academies to female students.

In terms of reproductive freedom, the Supreme Court legalized abortion. *Roe v. Wade* (1973) upheld the rights of women to have, and their physicians to perform, legal abortions of unwanted pregnancies. The court also forbade the states from prohibiting abortions during the early months of pregnancy. Hence, women finally had won control over their own reproductive systems, but *Roe v. Wade* launched one of the major ethical debates in contemporary U.S. history: when does life begin?

The courts also struck down laws that treated men and women differently when it came to Social Security and welfare benefits, worker's compensation, and access to military programs. Furthermore, the courts formally struck down laws that discriminated against women in defining adulthood, forming juries, and determining alimony. Women had almost achieved the same civil rights as won by those fighting against racial discrimination.

Finally, the New Feminism generated its own backlash. While a majority of the American people supported the drive for gender equality, conservative women in the United States formed a countermovement that challenged some of legal gains won by the New Feminism; chief among these were abortion rights. The conservatives also charged that feminists had undercut what they called "family values." Hence, as a conservative backlash picked up steam, the New Feminists lost their most important battle, when two-thirds of the states failed to ratify the Equal Rights Amendment (ERA) to the U.S. Constitution, both in 1978, and again in 1982, when congress had extended the deadline for ratification. Though the ERA would have locked many of the legal gains of the feminist movement into the U.S. Constitution, nonetheless, the definition of women had undergone a profound change in the United States.

Elsewhere in the world, equality made headway against caste and aristocracy as well. Generally, traditional social categories seemed to decay. Societies turned to new efforts at obtaining equality as a common social experience. Equality of opportunity, equal rights, and equal access to the vote made headway throughout the world. Yet countercurrents against equality such as questions of minority rights and gender issues continue to be by-products of nation-formation in emerging cultures.

An extreme example, one that runs contrary to gender equality as a global trend, was the emergence of a fundamentalist Islamist movement in Afghanistan. There, the governing Taliban restored its vision of traditional gender barriers in a Muslim culture to try to achieve religious purity.

The Taliban seized the opportunity to impose its repressive version of Islam on Afghanistan at the conclusion of a long civil war initiated by the Soviet invasion of 1979. The Soviet army had occupied Afghanistan from 1979–89, set up a puppet government, inspired a major People's War against an imperial power, and finally withdrew in defeat. The U.S. opposed this episode of Soviet aggression and supplied the Afghani rebels with aid and sophisticated weapons, but ceased its support as soon as the U.S.S.R. left Afghanistan. Then Moscow and Washington's indifference to the plight of Afghanis after 1989 left the country in chaos as numerous guerrilla factions vied for power while Pakistan, Iran, and Uzbekistan patronized rival forces. Finally, in 1996, an Afghani faction of extreme Sunni Muslims called the Taliban seized the city of Kabul, subjected the country to radical Islamism, and began to eradicate Western "decadence." Hence Afghanistan became a haven for Islamic fundamentalism—part of which was the systematic removal of women from public life.

In short order, women's rights ceased to exist in Afghanistan. Women's access to any participation in social, economic, cultural, and political life was summarily denied. Under the Taliban, women did not have access to education since their schools were closed. Also, the Taliban ordered women to quit their jobs and stay home; anyone foolish enough to hire a female employee did so at extreme personal risk. A woman could not travel without a male chaperone from her immediate family to supervise her conduct. A female's command over her health ceased; women could not see a male doctor, engage in family planning, or undergo any medical procedure that might include a male as a member of the medical team. A woman's word in court carried only half the weight of a man's, and no woman could directly petition the court for any legal ruling without the aid of a male relative. Finally, women had no access to recreation, could not show their faces in public, could not travel in private vehicles with male passengers, could not raise their voice in protest, could not laugh aloud, could not wear brightly colored clothing, and could not adorn themselves with makeup or jewelry. A woman could only appear outside the home wearing the *burqa*: a garment that covered a woman's body from head to toe, with a heavy gauze patch across the eyes to veil her completely from the view of strangers.

Punishment for any infraction of these rules was severe. Beating a woman for disciplinary reasons was immediate and swift—especially for minor infractions. One woman lost her thumb because she wore nail polish on it. Public executions, including the use of stoning for adultery, were considered valuable lessons for other women to witness. Sexual crimes against women became commonplace. Rape, murder for unrequited love, abduction of young females, and extortion for sexual purposes also became common.

All of these physical and legal assaults against women paled in contrast to a more deadly challenge to the world: the Taliban was willing to use Afghanistan as the home to international terrorist organizations. The one that has made the most powerful impression on the world at the beginning of the twenty-first century is Al Qaeda, a militant Islamic sect led by Osama bin Laden and supported by the Taliban.

The stunning assault by Al Qaeda on the twin towers of New York's World Trade Center (and other targets) on September 11, 2001, not only shaped U.S. foreign policy for President George W. Bush's administration, it also revealed a deeply embedded animosity toward the United States shared by Bin Laden, the

Afghani Woman. The Taliban ruled most of Afghanistan from 1996 until 2001. They inflicted many oppressive laws upon Afghanis, women in particular. Under the Taliban women were strictly limited, unable to work in public places or seek education and were required to cover themselves entirely in burqas. Failure to do so could attract a public beating or acid being thrown in the face of an unveiled woman by the Taliban's religious police. Photo by Babasteve.

Taliban, and the already mentioned Ayatollah Khomeini. The United States is called the Great Satan for its involvement in Middle Eastern affairs, and its "assault" on the traditional purity of Islam. From the radical Muslim's point of view, the United States is the chief exporter of Western culture to the world; within Western culture is "Western decadence" such as feminism, materialism, and modernization. Coupled with U.S. foreign policy from 1980 to 2004, the United States has become the major foreign power most active in the Middle East and easiest to single out as the leading exporter of "corrupt" beliefs and practices.

The U.S. has pursued two key goals since the end of the Cold War that has made Americans both direct and indirect targets for radical Islamic hostility. First, the U.S. is the chief protector of Israeli security through foreign aid and diplomacy. Second, the United States has systematically pursued a policy to ensure global access to low-cost oil to fuel its materialist values. Both of these objectives have made U.S. interventions in the Middle East frequent, violent, and the cause of a sharp militant Islamic backlash.

Ranging from accidents and incidents of terror to outright invasions, the United States military has made its presence known in the Middle East. The use of peacekeeping forces in Lebanon in 1983 led to the suicide bombing of the U.S. embassy in Beirut. Partly out of frustration at the continued practice of hostage-taking and acts of terrorism, the United States sent air strikes against Libyan leader Muammar al-Qadhafi in 1986 because his regime was known for its support of international terrorism. Out of fear of potential air raids against U.S. warships in the Persian Gulf (sent there to protect the flow of oil), the U.S. navy accidentally shot down an Iranian airliner in 1988 killing all aboard. This unfortunate event was followed by a major U.S. military operation in 1991 to liberate Kuwait from an Iraqi invasion. Called "Desert Storm," the operation involved more than a half million U.S. soldiers. In 1994, the United States brokered the beginning of the peace process between Israel and the Palestinians that is still underway today—much to the dismay of radical Muslims. Finally, in response to the attacks on September 11, President Bush launched an invasion of Afghanistan to eliminate the Taliban and capture Bin Laden and initiated a second war against Iraq to topple Saddam Hussein from power and establish a democracy there. While the Taliban have lost their hold on Afghanistan, they have gone underground along with Bin Laden, and, in Iraq, a growing insurgency against the United States has developed whose longevity and popular support cannot as yet be accurately gauged.

Hence the Bush administration has not achieved its foreign goals in the Middle East and a protracted war on terror has begun. Also a deepening hatred by radical Muslims directed at the United States is underway that has been exacerbated by recent U.S foreign policy. Finally, while radical Islamic fundamentalism has had a major negative impact on the status of women and the export of Western cultural values, a confrontation with fundamentalist Muslims has also opened the world to an indefinite period of conflict between the West and what appears to be an escalating use of international terrorism.

The Islamism of the Taliban had imposed a heavy ban against gender equality, Western values, and U.S. domestic security. Though not as severe, this same principle of gender inequality and hostility to Western culture seemed to be present wherever other Islamic fundamentalists had gained access to power. Contrary to the trends of modernization, and in fact hostile to modern values themselves and their sponsors, Islamism tended to draw heavily on a radical interpretation of the prophet's vision for the Muslim community. As a result, Islamist reform movements based on a resurgence of religious purity tended to run contrary to the features of modernization and the internal coherence common to the nation-state: that is, a public emphasis on equality, freedom, and access to equal opportunity.

While radical Islamism speaks of a desire to return to a premodern world, other cultures still struggle with the problems of national formation. New nations must learn the lessons of equality and freedom that older nations have not completely resolved. New nations have to travel a common path of placing their heritage in a modern context. Central to this integration of tradition and modernization are the ideals of freedom, status, and equality that reside at the heart of public opinion and internal coherence. Public opinion and internal coherence, in turn, reside at the heart of the political stability achieved by a nation-state.

Population Dynamics

Equally profound as freedom, status, and equality, but quite different in terms of world consequences, is the trend toward accelerated population growth. Human numbers have increased apace since 1750. Before 1945, the development of a modern global economy sustained these increases. Central to this accelerated population growth after 1945, however, is the role that modern medicine has played through global institutions such as the World Health Organization (WHO).

Established in 1948, the WHO is a self-governing agency of the UN headquartered in Geneva, Switzerland. Founded by the fifty countries that organized the United Nations, the WHO has a stated purpose of bringing the highest level of health to all peoples of the world. Governed by an executive board of thirty-two nations, elected by the World Health Assembly, which is composed of all sovereign states and associated territories regardless of their membership in the UN, the WHO attacks key global infections to eradicate their existence. The WHO also has a secretariat consisting of a director-general and a technical and administrative staff that guides regional agencies established in Southeast Asia, the eastern Mediterranean area, Europe, Africa, the Americas, and the western Pacific area. Despite its peaceful goals, however, the WHO was unable to escape the impact of the Cold War; in 1949 the U.S.S.R. and its client states of Ukraine and Belarus withdrew from the WHO on the so-called grounds of its being ineffectual. This break lasted until the collapse of the Soviet Union. Nonetheless, the WHO has had a global impact on world diseases.

The WHO has launched a global campaign against the ancient problem of epidemics. Between 1948 and the present, the WHO has made remarkable progress in combating diseases such as polio, smallpox, yellow fever, malaria, cholera, measles, diphtheria, whooping cough, tetanus, polio, AIDS, and tuberculosis. The fall in the death rate due to eradicating some of these killers has, however, created a sudden recurrence of an equally old problem: famine. Since human numbers tend to double in a very short period, the decline in the death rate due to modern medicine has caused food shortages to once again become a major global issue.

In 1950, the number of human beings grew to 2.5 billion; in 1985, this number had reached 5 billion or a doubling rate of thirty-five years. In short, what occurred since 1948 was a new balance between symbiosis and parasitism. Hence, solving the problem of disease has recast the issue of human survival on food production and distribution.

To support the growing number of human beings, agriculture around the world has changed. Before 1945, food production kept pace with human numbers worldwide. Starvation, however, still occurs. Agonizing local famines surface periodically throughout the world. As mentioned, the problem lies not in food production, but, instead, in food distribution.

Increased food production has taken place nearly everywhere. This transformation of agriculture, however, has come at the expense of tradition. Thus, as a solution to food shortages became available, yet another problem emerged through peasant reactions to modernization.

The reaction of peasants to the loss of their traditional lifestyles has provided the manpower for numerous rebellions throughout the twentieth century. The violence of these outbursts has remained local and intense, and in large measure explains why Marxist revolutions occurred in the wrong cultural settings. Thus, violence in Mexico, Russia, China, Korea, Laos, Vietnam, Cambodia, India, Pakistan, Afghanistan, Ethiopia, Somalia, Cuba, El Salvador, Nicaragua, Chile, Argentina, and Algeria, to name a few, has linked national formation with massive rural discontent to create intense local wars or revolutions. Yet the numbers of people killed in these struggles has not stopped the continued growth of the human population. In fact, these examples actually reflect the tensions created by population pressures as well as the desire for status, freedom, and equality as native peoples were liberated from colonialism and began to undergo national formation.

Generally, humans have managed to deal with the vast increases in their numbers. International mass transportation and famine relief organizations have often succeeded in providing essentials wherever a food crisis has occurred. Although many millions of people have died from starvation, population continues to grow. How long this equilibrium between food production, distribution, and population can continue remains open to question.

Since human numbers have grown dramatically after World War II, the total supply of food worldwide has had to keep pace. Geographers have called the dramatic changes in agriculture the "Green Revolution," wherein the use of modern fertilizers, plant genetics, and international transportation methods transfer domesticated species of plants and animals everywhere they can grow. Consequently, the symbiosis between humans, plants, and animals has become a global process.

Agriculture in the twentieth century has also seen the export of scientific cultivation from the modern nation-states to non-European countries. Plant selection and breeding, new fertilizers produced by the petrochemical industry, widespread modern irrigation, and the general application of contemporary farm technology has been nicely adapted to the needs of agricultural nations to generate abundances of food. The spread of such techniques throughout Asia, Africa, and Latin America has created a new food base to keep up with the results of modern medicine. Thus, the world's population growth rate itself would not have been possible unless food production had kept pace.

Despite the world community's success at feeding people so far, however, the concern for the future is that the current balance between parasitism and symbiosis may break down. The immediate problem is maintaining the existing balance while trying to slow the high rate of human reproduction. Just how many people the Earth can support is unknown; yet we do know that there is a limit to what the Earth can abide. If the doubling population rate continues unabated, human numbers will eventually exceed what the Earth can sustain. At that moment, famine will once again become general.

To address this issue, the industrial nations in Europe, Japan, and the United States, as well as some of those independent nations that have emerged from the former Soviet Union, have all developed birth-control programs. Although these same industrial nations have tried to export their modern contraception methods to nonindustrial cultures, these urban societies have had only marginal success. Still, the birth rate has slowed somewhat worldwide, but so many fertile people now exist that human numbers continue to increase at an alarming rate. Consequently, population growth remains the foremost global problem looming on the horizon.

What has happened to those people who cannot make a living in their native culture so far is that they have found jobs outside their place of birth. Their ability to do so reflects the differences in birth rates between industrial and nonindustrial cultures. Nonindustrial migrants move to industrial societies to fill vacancies in the occupational structure left behind by a socially mobile urban population.

As industrial nations slowed their birth rate, their general population's average age increases, so that the majority soon becomes older than thirty years. Rural cultures, whose birth and death rates remain comparatively high, generate on the average younger populations, whose numbers typically seek opportunities outside their country of birth.

As local, traditional economies become too crowded to absorb any more young people, these potential migrants begin their own step-stage movements. This migration eventually leads them to industrial nations. For example, Turks have gone to Germany, Algerians have found a home in France, Pakistanis have ventured to Great Britain, Muslims from Central Asia have moved into Russian urban centers, and finally, the United States has absorbed numerous people from the Caribbean, South America, and Mesoamerica. This solution, however, has built-in problems.

Many of the recent immigrants have taken jobs that citizens in industrial nations no longer want to do (such as manual labor), which places these relocated young people at the bottom of the industrial social scale. Industrial nations have absorbed the first generation of people desperate enough to leave their native lands. As these people form families, produce a second generation, and acculturate, their children develop expectations of joining their adopted country as equals. In addition, in most cases, these immigrants who travel to industrial nations send enormous sums of money back to their homeland to create an economic basis for continued population growth. This, in turn, feeds the demand for the right to migrate as well as a greater demand for a larger share of the world's wealth.

Therefore, this new foreign population creates considerable social unrest, which in turn stimulates residual racism found in well-established populations trying to adjust to new immigrant peoples. Thus, a mosaic of ethnicity becomes a social problem that industrial societies have to address. The United States functions as a model of how difficult solving this problem can be.

At the same time, those young people who do return to their native cultures take back with them modern attitudes. These attitudes generate questions that many traditional cultures are still ill-equipped to answer. Hence, the social unrest these returning people generate has a tendency to surface as the desire for change in their traditional societies. What will happen as a result of this continued trend of migration, diffusion, and unrest is not entirely clear.

What is clear is that global stability depends on international cooperation. Globalization, a by-product of modernization, has created an interdependency that transcends ethnicity, nationality, and social status.

Global integration demands successful intercultural communication, which requires that local social organizations develop a high level of mutual respect for one another. The basis of this respect is a sharp reduction of international intolerance, racism, and ethnocentrism, which, in turn, is a major undertaking given the power of resurgent traditional solutions to the world's problems and the general adoption of the nation-state as the preferred political form. Nonetheless, as nations build up local internal coherence, they need do so with an understanding that they somehow have to fit within the world in general.

No longer can one people prosper at the expense of others. We as a species all share a common destiny, which will be shaped by our actions. The success of our civilizations now present us with a major task: meeting the needs and rising expectations of growing human numbers. Such a problem can only be managed by international cooperation, which requires mutual cultural respect and intercultural communications. In the words of Mahatma Gandhi, "An eye for an eye will leave the whole world blind."

Suggested Reading

Bell, Daniel, *The Coming of the Post-Industrial Age* (New York: Basic Books, 1974).

Bialer, Seweryn, *The Soviet Paradox: External Expansion, Internal Decline* (New York: Vintage Books, 1986).

Chamberlain, Neil W., *Beyond Malthus: Population and Power* (New York: Basic Books, 1970).

Crummey, Robert O., ed., *Reform in Russia and the USSR* (Urbana: University of Illinois Press, 1991).

Evans, Sara, *Personal Politics: The Roots of Women's Liberation in the Civil Rights Movement and the New Left* (New York: Vintage Books, 1980).

Feagin, Joe R., and Harlan Hahn, *Ghetto Revolts: The Politics of Violence in American Cities* (New York: Macmillan Publishing Company, 1973).

Freeman, Jo, *The Politics of Women's Liberation* (New York: Longman, Inc., 1979).

Garrow, David J., *Protest at Selma: Martin Luther King, Jr., and the Voting Rights Act* (New Haven, Conn.: Yale University Press, 1978).

Goldman, Minton F., *The Soviet Union and Eastern Europe*, Ninth Edition (New York: McGraw Hill Companies, 2002).

Haq, Mahbub ul, *The Poverty Curtain: Choices for the Third World* (New York: Columbia University Press, 1976).

Henretta, James A., David Brody, and Lynn Dumenil, *America: A Concise History,* Third Edition (New York: Bedford and St. Martin's Press, 2006).

Hornby, William and Melvin Jones, *An Introduction to Population Geography* (Cambridge: Cambridge University Press, 1980).

Jervis, Robert and Seweryn Bialer, eds., *Soviet-American Relations After the Cold War* (Durham, N.C.: Duke University Press, 1991).

Keylor, William R., *The Twentieth Century World: An International History,* Fourth Edition (New York: Oxford University Press, 2001).

Laue, Theodore von, *The World Revolution of Westernization* (New York: Oxford University Press, 1989).

Nove, Alex, *An Economic History of the U.S.S.R., 1917–1991,* Third Edition (Cambridge: Cambridge University Press, 1992).

Overbeek, Johannes, *Population* (New York: Harcourt Brace Jovanovich, 1982).

Rashid, A., *Taliban* (New Haven, Conn.: Yale University Press, 2000).

Solomon, L., *Multinational Corporations and the Emerging World Order* (New York: Kenniket Press, 1978).

Stavrianos, L., *The Promise of the Coming Dark Age* (San Francisco: W. H. Freeman, 1976).

INDEX